1 9 NOV 2011

AutoCAD LT® 2009 All-in-One Desk Reference For Dummies®

Cheat Sheet

Wiley, the Wiley Publishing logo, For Dummies, the Dummies Man logo, the For Dummies Bestselling Book Series logo and all related trade dress are trademarks or registered trademarks of John Wiley & Sons, Inc. and/or its affiliates. All other trademarks are property of their respective owners. Copyright © 2008 Wiley Publishing, Inc. All rights reserved. Item 4378-7. For more information about Wiley Publishing, call 1-800-762-2974.

Commonly Used 2D and 3D AutoCAD Commands

2D Command	Purpose	3D Command	Purpose
LINE	Draws a line	BOX	Draws a 3D solid box
CIRCLE	Draws a circle	UNION	Combines two or more 3D solids together
INSERT	Inserts a block or drawing file	3DORBIT	Rotates the camera of the current view around a drawing
ERASE	Removes selected objects	3DMOVE	Moves objects in 3D space
MOVE	Moves objects	3DROTATE	Rotates objects in 3D space
COPY	Copies objects from one place to another	CAMERA	Creates a camera object in the model
ROTATE	Rotates objects	LIGHTS	Adds user-defined lights
PAN	Pans a drawing	MATERIALS	Displays the Materials palette
ZOOM	Zooms in and out in a drawing	RENDER	Renders the current view of a drawing

Commonly Used AutoCAD Keyboard Shortcuts

Keyboard Shortcut	Command	Purpose
Ctrl+N	NEW	Creates a new drawing
Ctrl+S	QSAVE	Displays the Save Drawing As dialog box
Ctrl+P	PLOT	Displays the Plot dialog box
F2	TEXTSCR	Toggles the AutoCAD Text Window on and off
F3	OSNAP	Toggles the running object snap mode on and off
F6	DYNMODE	Toggles dynamic input on and off
F8	ORTHO	Toggles ortho mode on and off
F10	POLAR	Toggles polar mode on and off

For Dumm... ...s for Beginners

AutoCAD® 2009 & AutoCAD LT® 2009 All-in-One Desk Reference For Dummies®

Cheat Sheet

Drawing Scale and Limits Chart: Feet and Inches

Drawing Scale	81/2" x 11"	11" x 17"	24" x 36"	30" x 42"	36" x 48"
1/16" = 1'–0"	136' x 176'	176' x 272'	384' x 576'	480' x 672'	576' x 768'
1/8" = 1'–0"	68' x 88'	88' x 136'	192' x 288'	240' x 336'	288' x 384'
1/4" = 1'–0"	34' x 44'	44' x 68'	96' x 144'	120' x 168'	144' x 192'
1/2" = 1'–0"	17' x 22'	22' x 34'	48' x 72'	60' x 84'	72' x 96'
3/4" = 1'–0"	11'–4" x 14'–8"	14'–8" x 22'–8"	32' x 48'	40' x 56'	48' x 64'
1" = 1'–0"	8'–6" x 11'	11' x 17'	24' x 36'	30' x 42'	36' x 48'

Drawing Scale and Limits Chart: Millimeters

Drawing Scale	210 x 297 mm	297 x 420 mm	420 x 594 mm	594 x 841 mm	841 x 1,189 mm
1:200	42,000 x 59,400 mm	59,400 x 84,000 mm	84,000 x 118,800 mm	118,800 x 168,200 mm	168,200 x 237,800 mm
1:100	21,000 x 29,700 mm	29,700 x 42,000 mm	42,000 x 59,400 mm	59,400 x 84,100 mm	84,100 x 118,900 mm
1:50	10,500 x 14,850 mm	14,850 x 21,000 mm	21,000 x 29,700 mm	29,700 x 42,050 mm	42,050 x 59,450 mm
1:20	4,200 x 5,940 mm	5,940 x 8,400 mm	8,400 x 11,880 mm	11,880 x 16,820 mm	16,820 x 23,780 mm
1:10	2,100 x 2,970 mm	2,970 x 4,200 mm	4,200 x 5,940 mm	5,940 x 8,410 mm	8,410 x 11,890 mm
1:5	1,050 x 1,485 mm	1,485 x 2,100 mm	2,100 x 2,970 mm	2,970 x 4,205 mm	4,205 x 5,945 mm

Drawing Scale and Text Height Chart: Feet and Inches

Drawing Scale	Drawing Scale Factor	1/8" Text Height	3/32" Text Height
1/16" = 1'–0"	192	24"	18"
1/8" = 1'–0"	96	12"	9"
1/4" = 1'–0"	48	6"	4 ½"
1/2" = 1'–0"	24	3"	2 ¼"
3/4" = 1'–0"	16	2"	1 ½"
1" = 1'–0"	12	1 ½"	1 ⅛"

Drawing Scale and Text Height Chart: Millimeters

Drawing Scale	Drawing Scale Factor	3 mm Text Height	2.5 mm Text Height
1:200	200	600 mm	500 mm
1:100	100	300 mm	250 mm
1:50	50	150 mm	125 mm
1:20	20	60 mm	50 mm
1:10	10	30 mm	25 mm
1:5	5	15 mm	12.5 mm

AutoCAD® 2009 & AutoCAD LT® 2009

ALL-IN-ONE DESK REFERENCE

FOR

DUMMIES®

AutoCAD® 2009 & AutoCAD LT® 2009
ALL-IN-ONE DESK REFERENCE
FOR DUMMIES®

by Lee Ambrosius

WILEY

Wiley Publishing, Inc.

AutoCAD® 2009 & AutoCAD LT® 2009 All-in-One Desk Reference For Dummies®
Published by
Wiley Publishing, Inc.
111 River Street
Hoboken, NJ 07030-5774

www.wiley.com

WILEY

About the Author

Lee Ambrosius works for Autodesk as a technical writer for the Platform Solutions and Emerging Business (PSEB) division and is based out of his home office. Before that, he worked as an independent consultant for more than three years, and before that he was a resident of a cubicle farm for about eight years, where he worked as a systems analyst creating custom applications. Even though Lee doesn't work for himself anymore, he still runs his Web site, www.hyperpics.com, and his blog, hyperpics.blogs.com. He has been using AutoCAD since 1994, when he was first exposed to Release 12 for DOS, and has been customizing and programming AutoCAD since 1996. Lee was an AutoCAD consultant and trainer for more than ten years, and has been teaching at Autodesk University since 2004.

For over a decade, Lee has authored a variety of works that include articles for CAD magazines and white papers for Autodesk and has been a contributing author on a few occasions for AutoCAD books. He has been a technical editor for the recent editions of AutoCAD For Dummies and AutoCAD and AutoCAD LT Bible. The first version of this book, AutoCAD and AutoCAD LT All-in-One Desk Reference For Dummies, was his first venture into being a co-author for a book before going off and authoring the book *AutoCAD 2008 3D Modeling Workbook For Dummies*.

Dedication

To my grandmother, Theresa Severa (Grams, GG and all the other names you go by), for always being there. I also can't forget the influence you have on my family and of course all the perks of having such a loving person in our family.

Author's Acknowledgments

I have to give a special thanks to the great folks at Wiley for being supportive through this entire project. There is always that one shining star on a project that keeps things moving like a well-oiled machine, and that individual was my project and copy editor for this edition, Susan Pink. A special thanks also goes out to my technical editor, Mark Douglas, for agreeing to work with me on this edition of the book.

Thanks to all the folks at Autodesk, who are all dedicated to the work they do. An extra thanks to Shaan Hurley and Bud Schroeder. Before joining Autodesk, they were always willing to take time out of their busy days to answer my questions during this project.

Publisher's Acknowledgments

We're proud of this book; please send us your comments through our online registration form located at www.dummies.com/register/.

Some of the people who helped bring this book to market include the following:

Acquisitions, Editorial, and Media Development

Project Editor: Susan Pink

Acquisitions Editors: Tiffany Ma, Kyle Looper

Technical Editor: Mark Douglas

Editorial Manager: Jodi Jensen

Media Development Manager:
Laura VanWinkle

Editorial Assistant: Amanda Foxworth

Sr. Editorial Assistant: Cherie Case

Cartoons: Rich Tennant
(www.the5thwave.com)

Composition Services

Project Coordinator: Erin Smith

Layout and Graphics: Claudia Bell,
Stacie Brooks, Reuben W. Davis,
Melissa K. Jester, Julie Trippetti,
Christine Williams

Proofreaders: David Faust, Bonnie Mikkelson

Indexer: Potomac Indexing, LLC

Publishing and Editorial for Technology Dummies

    Richard Swadley, Vice President and Executive Group Publisher

    Andy Cummings, Vice President and Publisher

    Mary Bednarek, Executive Acquisitions Director

    Mary C. Corder, Editorial Director

Publishing for Consumer Dummies

    Diane Graves Steele, Vice President and Publisher

    Joyce Pepple, Acquisitions Director

Composition Services

    Gerry Fahey, Vice President of Production Services

    Debbie Stailey, Director of Composition Services

Contents at a Glance

Introduction 1

Book 1: AutoCAD Basics 11
Chapter 1: One-on-One Time with AutoCAD 13
Chapter 2: Drawing on and in AutoCAD 31
Chapter 3: Navigating the AutoCAD Interface 37
Chapter 4: All about Files 65
Chapter 5: Basic Tools 85
Chapter 6: Setting Up Drawings 97
Chapter 7: Precision Tools 125

Book 11: 2D Drafting 155
Chapter 1: Drawing Objects 157
Chapter 2: Modifying Objects 185
Chapter 3: Managing Views 215

Book 111: Annotating Drawings 235
Chapter 1: Text: When Pictures Just Won't Do 237
Chapter 2: Dimensioning 267
Chapter 3: Hatching Your Drawings 303
Chapter 4: Scaling Mt. Annotation 313

Book 1V: LT Differences 321
Chapter 1: The LT Difference 323
Chapter 2: Extending AutoCAD LT 331
Chapter 3: Mixed Environments 339

Book V: 3D Modeling 347
Chapter 1: Introducing the Third Dimension 349
Chapter 2: Using the 3D Environment 357
Chapter 3: Viewing in 3D 369
Chapter 4: Moving from 2D to 3D 381
Chapter 5: Working with Solids 393
Chapter 6: Rendering: Lights, Camera, AutoCAD! 403

Book VI: Advanced Drafting 415
Chapter 1: Playing with Blocks 417
Chapter 2: Dynamic Blocks 433
Chapter 3: External References 449
Chapter 4: Organizing Your Drawings 479

Book VII: Publishing Drawings 491
Chapter 1: Page Setup...493
Chapter 2: Sheet Sets without Regret 515
Chapter 3: Print, Plot, Publish 543

Book VIII: Collaboration 565
Chapter 1: CAD Management: The Necessary Evil.................567
Chapter 2: CAD Standards...579
Chapter 3: Working with Drawing Files...............................597
Chapter 4: Sharing Electronic Files 617

Book IX: Customizing AutoCAD...........................637
Chapter 1: The Basics of Customizing AutoCAD 639
Chapter 2: Customizing the Interface 657
Chapter 3: Customizing the Tools 675
Chapter 4: Delving Deeper into Customization 705
Chapter 5: Recording Your Actions....................................717

Bonus Chapters ....On the Web
Bonus Chapter 1: Working with Surfaces BC1
Bonus Chapter 2: The AutoCAD Programming Interfaces BC13
Bonus Chapter 3: Using Custom Programs BC23
Bonus Chapter 4: Introducing AutoLISP BC41
Bonus Chapter 5: Visual Basic for AutoCAD BC79
Bonus Chapter 6: AutoCAD Utilities...................................BC101
Bonus Chapter 7: Creating Custom Linetypes, Shapes, and Hatch Patterns.....BC115

Index 727

Table of Contents

Introduction 1

   About This Book...2
   Foolish Assumptions 2
   Conventions Used in This Book 2
      Menu browser access 2
      Ribbon access 3
      Toolbar access 5
      Menu bar ("classic menu") access 5
   How This Book Is Organized..6
      Book I: AutoCAD Basics 6
      Book II: 2D Drafting 7
      Book III: Annotating Drawings 7
      Book IV: LT Differences 7
      Book V: 3D Modeling...7
      Book VI: Advanced Drafting 7
      Book VII: Publishing Drawings 8
      Book VIII: Collaboration..8
      Book IX: Customizing AutoCAD 8
      Bonus Content 8
   Icons Used in This Book..8

Book 1: AutoCAD Basics... 11

Chapter 1: One-on-One Time with AutoCAD 13

   Starting AutoCAD or AutoCAD LT 14
      Accessing the right tools for the right job 14
      Creating a new drawing 15
      What is created should be saved 16
   Drawing Setup..16
      Getting snappy and griddy..16
      Establishing the limits 17
      Organizing objects with layers 18
   Drawing and Editing Objects 20
      Walking the straight and curved 20
      Modifying objects 25
   Annotating with Text and Dimensions 27
      Expressing yourself through text 27
      Entering the drafting dimension.....................................28
   Fast Track to Plotting 29

Chapter 2: Drawing on and in AutoCAD **31**

Understanding AutoCAD Files and Formats 32
Seeing the LT 33
Using AutoCAD's Latest-and-Greatest Feature Set 34

Chapter 3: Navigating the AutoCAD Interface **37**

Starting the Application 37
Creating Start menu shortcuts 38
Using desktop shortcuts 39
Accessing files from Windows Explorer 40
Touring the AutoCAD Interface 41
Title bars 41
AutoCAD menus and menu browser..42
AutoCAD toolbars 44
Quick Access toolbar 46
Palettes 46
Drawing area 49
Crosshairs 50
The floating command window 51
The status bar 51
Communicating with Your Software 56
The command line...56
Dynamic input...57
Dialog boxes 58
Running AutoCAD Commands 58
Grasping the AutoCAD difference 58
Repeating a command 58
Canceling a running command 59
Invoking transparent commands 59
Reaching for AutoCAD Help..60
Using built-in Help...60
Tooltips 61
InfoCenter..62
Finding online resources 63

Chapter 4: All about Files **65**

File Types in AutoCAD..65
Starting a New Drawing 68
Starting from scratch 70
Using a wizard...70
Using a drawing template..72
Saving a Drawing 73
Save 74
Save As...74
QSAVE 76

Opening an Existing Drawing...76
    Open command 76
    Recent drawings 78
    Using Windows Explorer 79
The Multiple-Drawing Environment.....................................80
Closing Windows 81
File Management for AutoCAD 82
    Naming drawing files..82
    Storing your files 83
Backing Up Is Hard to Do 83

Chapter 5: Basic Tools **85**
Drawing Lines 85
Creating Circles 88
Taking a Closer Look...91
    Checking out realtime zoom 91
    Using realtime pan...91
Modifying Objects 93
Erasing and Unerasing Stuff...94
    Using the digital eraser...94
    Unerasing objects 95
Ready . . . Undo, Undo, Redo 96

Chapter 6: Setting Up Drawings **97**
Choosing Units of Measurement 97
    AutoCAD units 99
    Imperial or metric 100
    System variables...100
    Setting units in your drawing.......................................101
Setting Limits for Your Drawings 102
Understanding Drawing Scale..104
    Scaling on the drawing board 104
    Scaling in AutoCAD 105
    Scale factors..105
    Using scale factors to establish drawing settings.........106
Lost in Space: Model or Paper?...107
A Layered Approach 108
    Creating layers 109
    Defining layer properties...110
    Setting layer modes..112
    Modifying layer settings 113
    The Layer Control drop-down list 118
    Layer tools...119
Object Properties 120
    Using AutoCAD's color systems 122
    Using linetypes 122
Setting Up Standards 123

Chapter 7: Precision Tools **125**

Understanding Accuracy and Precision 125
Understanding Coordinate Systems 126
    The world coordinate system 128
    Entering coordinates 129
    Direct distance entry 135
    Dynamic input and coordinate entry 137
Setting Grid and Snap 141
Understanding Ortho and Polar Tracking 143
    Using ortho mode 144
    Using polar tracking 144
Working with Object Snaps 147
Using Point Filters 151
Working with Object Snap Tracking Mode 153

Book II: 2D Drafting *155*

Chapter 1: Drawing Objects **157**

Locating and Using the Drawing Tools 157
Let's Get Primitive 161
    Keeping to the straight and narrow 161
    Going around in circles 163
    Arcs of triumph 164
    The point of the exercise 165
Creating Construction Geometry 166
    Xlines for X-men 167
    A little ray of sunshine 168
Without a Trace 169
A Bit Sketchy 170
Drawing Parallel Lines 171
Complex Curves 174
    Lucy, you have some splining to do! 174
    Solar ellipses 176
Complex Objects and Shapes 178
    2D solids 178
    Rectang, Polygon, Donut 179
    Polylines 180
    Ahhhh . . . Wipeout 182

Chapter 2: Modifying Objects **185**

Setting Selection Options 185
Selecting Objects 187
    Selecting multiple objects 187
    Object selection modes 189
    Selection preview 191
    Object groups 192

AutoCAD's Editing Commands 193
    Removing stuff 197
    Relocating and replicating...197
    Rotating and resizing 205
    Breaking, mending, and blowing up real good 207
    Double-barrel commands 208
    Specialized commands 210
    Changing properties..211
    Changing your mind 213
Coming to Grips with Grips 213

Chapter 3: Managing Views **215**
A Zoom of One's Own 219
    Wheeling through your drawing....................................222
    Realtime zooming 222
Pan in a Flash..224
Get a Grip on the Wheel and Hang On..226
Name That View 228
    Creating views...229
    Other view options 231
Having AutoCAD Put on a Show..232
To Regen or to Redraw . . . That Is the Question 234

Book III: Annotating Drawings 235

Chapter 1: Text: When Pictures Just Won't Do **237**
Text in AutoCAD...237
    Getting familiar with text terminology 238
    Will that be one line or two? 239
    Justification..240
    Where should text go? 242
Fonts 244
    Types used by AutoCAD 245
    Using fonts in drawings 245
Working with Text Styles...245
Creating Single Line Text..249
Working with Multiline Text..252
Creating Multiline Text 253
    Formatting options..254
    Numbered and bulleted lists...255
    Controlling the flow of text 256
    Fields, masks, and other multiline text delights..........257
Editing Text 258
    Editing single-line text 258
    Editing multiline text...259

Turning the Tables 259
    Setting the table with styles..260
    Creating and editing tables 261
    Link me up Scotty..263
Finding Text and Spell Checking 264

Chapter 2: Dimensioning **267**
Understanding What a Dimension Is Made Of.........................267
Types of Dimensions..269
    Associative dimensions...269
    Nonassociative dimensions 269
    Exploded dimensions..270
Creating New Dimensions as Associative 270
Using and Creating Dimension Styles...................................271
    Working with Dimension Style Manager............................271
    Creating a dimension style..272
    Stylizing dimensions 273
    Defining the scale for dimensions 277
    Dimension variables...279
    Setting a dimension style current 280
    Modifying a dimension style 280
    Renaming a dimension style 282
    Deleting a dimension style 282
    Comparing dimension styles 283
    Importing a dimension style 283
Creating Dimensions...283
    Linear and aligned dimensions..287
    Baseline and continued dimensions 288
    Angular dimensions 289
    Arc length dimensions 290
    Radius, diameter, and jogged dimensions.........................290
    Ordinate dimensions..292
    The Quick Dimension command 292
    Trans-spatial dimensions 293
Editing Dimensions 293
    Adding overrides to a dimension 293
    Editing the dimension text 294
    Using grips to edit dimensions 294
    Associating dimensions..294
    Breaking and spacing dimensions....................................295
    Inspecting dimensions..295
Leaders...296
    Make way for multiple leaders...297
    Legacy leaders 300
Working with Geometric Tolerances 301

Chapter 3: Hatching Your Drawings 303
  Adding Hatch Patterns and Fills 304
    Adding hatch to a drawing 305
    Hatching and tool palettes 307
    Hatching and DesignCenter 307
    Advanced settings for additional control 307
  Working with Hatch Patterns and Solid Fills 309
    Predefined patterns 309
    User-defined patterns 309
    Custom hatch patterns 310
  Using Gradient Fills 310
  Editing Hatch Patterns and Fills 311

Chapter 4: Scaling Mt. Annotation 313
  The What, With, and Why of Annotation Scaling 313
  Making Styles and Objects Annotative 314
    Annotative styles and block definitions 315
    Annotative objects 316
  Adding and Removing Annotation Scales 317
  Controlling the Annotation Scale for Output 319

Book IV: LT Differences 321

Chapter 1: The LT Difference 323
  Understanding the Boundaries and Limitations of AutoCAD LT 323
  Determining Whether AutoCAD or AutoCAD LT Is Best for You 329

Chapter 2: Extending AutoCAD LT 331
  Customizing AutoCAD LT 331
    It's all in the script 331
    Linetype and hatch patterns 332
    Blocks and DesignCenter 332
    Tool palettes 333
    Changing the user interface with the CUI Editor 333
    Diesel 333
    Command aliases 334
    Desktop icons 334
  Object Enabler Technology 334
  Additional Utilities Available from Autodesk 335
    DWG TrueView 2009 335
    Viewers 335
  Companion Products from Autodesk 336
    Autodesk Symbols 2000 336
    Autodesk VIZ 2008 336
    Autodesk Impression 336

Third-Party Custom Solutions 337
  Block utilities/libraries 337
  Viewers 338

Chapter 3: Mixed Environments 339

Using AutoCAD LT and AutoCAD in the Same Office..............339
  Budgeting 339
  Training...340
  Communication 340
  Environment..340
  Customization 341
  Installation and deployment 341
Making the Trip from AutoCAD to AutoCAD LT 341
  2D drafting...342
  3D modeling 342
  Annotation...343
  Viewing 344
  Visualization...344
  CAD Standards 344
  Collaboration and sharing...345

Book V: 3D Modeling 347

Chapter 1: Introducing the Third Dimension 349

Understanding the Different Types of 3D Models....................350
Entering Coordinates above the x,y Plane.............................351
  Manually inputting coordinates 352
  Point filters...354
  Object snaps 354
  Object snap tracking and moving orthogonally..............355
  Elevation . . . going up...355

Chapter 2: Using the 3D Environment 357

Setting Up AutoCAD for 3D 357
  Orienting yourself in the drawing window....................358
  Customizing crosshairs and dynamic input 359
  Using workspaces to switch between 2D and 3D drafting...........360
  Introducing toolbars and ribbon tabs for 3D................360
  Accelerating your hardware.......................................361
Understanding What the UCS Icon Is Telling You 362
  Orientating yourself with the UCS icon 362
  Controlling the display of the UCS icon......................364
Using the Coordinate System for 3D Drawing 365
  Understanding the coordinate system 365
  Adjusting the UCS...366

Chapter 3: Viewing in 3D **369**

Expressing Your Point of View...369
    Using preset views 369
    Finding your way with the compass and tripod..........................371
    Cameras 371
    Perspective versus parallel...373
Orbiting around a 3D Model 373
Navigating a 3D Model..375
Hugging the Corners with the SteeringWheels.................................376
Cube with a View...377
Adding Color and Style to a 3D Model...378
    Visual styles in AutoCAD 379
    Shademode in AutoCAD LT 380

Chapter 4: Moving from 2D to 3D **381**

Working with Regions..381
    Creating regions...382
    Modifying regions...382
    Getting more information about regions 383
3D Polylines and Helixes...384
    3D polyline 384
    Helix 384
Creating 3D Objects from 2D Objects..385
    Thickness 385
    Extrude 385
    Loft 386
    Sweep 387
    Revolve 387
Creating 2D Objects from 3D Objects..388
    Flatshot 388
    Section Plane 388
    Solid Draw, Solid View, and Solid Profile 389
3D Modify Commands 390
    3D Move..390
    3D Rotate...391
    Align 391
    3D Align..391
    3D Mirror 392
    3D Array 392

Chapter 5: Working with Solids **393**

Creating Solid Primitives...393
    Polysolid 394
    Box...395
    Wedge..396
    Cone 396

Sphere 397
Cylinder 397
Torus 398
Pyramid 398
Editing Solids 399
Solid editing 399
Using grips to edit 3D solids 400
Complex solids 401
Filleting and chamfering 401
Slice 402

Chapter 6: Rendering: Lights, Camera, AutoCAD! **403**

Lighting a Scene 403
Default lights 404
User lights 404
Sunlight 407
Getting the Right Look with Materials 409
Setting Up a Backdrop 410
Rendering the Final Scene 411

Book VI: Advanced Drafting **415**

Chapter 1: Playing with Blocks **417**

Working with Reusable Content 417
Creating Blocks 418
Accessing the Block Definition dialog box 419
Exploring some advanced options 421
Inserting Blocks 422
Managing Blocks 424
Renaming a block definition 424
Redefining a block definition 425
Purging a block definition 425
Exporting a block definition 426
Enhancing Blocks with Attributes 427
Adding an attribute to a block definition 428
Inserting a block with attributes 430
Editing an attribute's value in a block 431
Managing attributes in blocks 431
Extracting attribute data from blocks 432

Chapter 2: Dynamic Blocks **433**

What Makes a Block Dynamic? 433
Block Editor Environment 434
Components of the Block Editor 435
Editing a block definition 437

Going Dynamic 439
    Adding parameters...440
    Adding actions 442
    Using parameter sets 443
    Visibility states 443
Using Dynamic Blocks 446
    Inserting a dynamic block...446
    Modifying a dynamic block 447
Dynamic Blocks in Older Releases................................448

Chapter 3: External References **449**
Blocks versus External References.................................449
Working with External References 450
    Path to success with xrefs..451
    Attaching an xref 452
    External reference notification 454
    Editing an xref 455
    Clipping an xref...458
    Increasing the performance of xrefs 460
    Binding an xref 460
Raster Images 462
    Attaching a raster image 462
    Clipping a raster image..464
    Controlling the appearance of a raster image 465
DWF and DWFx Underlays 466
    Attaching a DWF underlay..467
    Clipping a DWF underlay..469
    Controlling the appearance of DWF underlay 470
DGN Underlays 470
    Attaching a DGN underlay..471
    Clipping a DGN underlay..473
    Controlling the appearance of a DGN underlay.........474
Draw Order 475
Object Linking and Embedding (OLE)..............................475
Managing External References Outside AutoCAD..........476

Chapter 4: Organizing Your Drawings **479**
Why Bother to Organize Drawings?................................479
Using the Windows Clipboard 480
    Copying objects from a drawing.................................480
    Cutting objects from a drawing 481
    Pasting objects into a drawing 481
AutoCAD DesignCenter 482
    Locating resources in drawings.................................483
    Adding resources to drawings 485
    Inserting hatches and loading linetypes 486

Using the Tool Palettes Window 486
    Blocks, xrefs, images, tables, and hatches...............................487
    Command and flyouts tools 488
    Modifying tools on a tool palette 488
    Customizing and organizing tool palettes................................489

Book VII: Publishing Drawings 491

Chapter 1: Page Setup 493

Preparing for Output with Page Setups..494
    Options of a page setup 494
    Working with page setups 496
Organizing a Drawing with Layouts 500
    Working with layouts 501
Looking at a Model through Viewports..506
    Defining a viewport's shape 506
    Controlling scale..510
    Controlling the display within a viewport...............................511
    Modifying a viewport 513

Chapter 2: Sheet Sets without Regret .515

Overview of a Sheet Set...515
Sheet Set Manager..517
Creating a Sheet Set 517
    Starting from scratch 518
    Starting from an existing sheet set..522
Managing Drawings with a Sheet Set 522
    Opening a sheet set..523
    Importing existing drawings as sheets 523
    Organizing with subsets 525
    Setting up a sheet set and subset for adding new sheets 526
    Adding a new sheet 529
    Opening a sheet 530
    Removing, renaming, and renumbering a sheet.......................530
    Sheet set and sheet properties...531
    Setting up callouts and label blocks 534
    Adding resource drawings 537
    Adding model views to a sheet...538
Publishing, eTransmitting, and Archiving a Sheet Set 541

Chapter 3: Print, Plot, Publish 543

You Say Printing, I Say Plotting, They Say Publishing 543
    Working with drivers...544
    Configuring a printer or plotter...545
    Putting style in your plots...550

Output Made Easy...555
    Plotting the Model tab 555
    Plotting a paper space layout 558
    Scaling your drawing 559
    More plotting options 559
Publishing Drawings 561

Book VIII: Collaboration *565*

Chapter 1: CAD Management: The Necessary Evil 567

Getting a Handle on the Basics of CAD Management 568
Managing the Drafting Environment....................................570
Creating a Good Foundation...571
    Creating a drawing template file.................................573
    Using a drawing template file 574
    Specifying a drawing template file for use with QNEW 575
    Specifying the location of drawing template files 576

Chapter 2: CAD Standards 579

CAD Standards Overview...579
Using AutoCAD's CAD Standards Tools.................................581
    Drawing standards (DWS) files....................................581
    Managing standards..582
    Translating layers...588
    Batch checking drawings 591

Chapter 3: Working with Drawing Files 597

It's All in the Name: File-Naming Conventions.....................597
Part of a Drawing Can Be a Good Thing: Working with Partial Open 598
Controlling What Happens during a Save 601
    Getting a handle on drawing file formats 602
    Indexing the contents of a drawing............................603
Protecting Your Drawings 604
    Password-protecting 604
    Digital signatures..608

Chapter 4: Sharing Electronic Files 617

Sharing Drawings with Non-AutoCAD-based Products 617
Taking Drawings to the Internet..618
    Using an FTP site...619
    Publishing drawings to the Web..................................622
    Using Web-based project sites....................................626
Emulating Paper Digitally..628
    Design Web Format (DWF and DWFx) 629
    Portable Document File (PDF) 630
    Head-to-head comparison..630

Working with DWF and DWFx Files 631
    Creating a DWF or DWFx file 632
    Viewing a DWF or DWFx file 633
    Electronically marking up a DWF or DWFx file 634

Book IX: Customizing AutoCAD 637

Chapter 1: The Basics of Customizing AutoCAD 639
Why Customize AutoCAD? 639
Customizing the AutoCAD Startup Process 641
    Startup options 641
    Using command line switches 642
Changing Options and Working with User Profiles 647
    Launching the Options dialog box 648
    Overview of AutoCAD options 648
    Working with user profiles 649
Creating and Managing Command Aliases 652
    Editing the PGP file 652
    Working with the AutoCAD Alias Editor 654

Chapter 2: Customizing the Interface 657
Influencing Your Status (Bar) 657
    Displaying the drawing status bar 658
    Toggling the display of a control on the status bars 659
    Powering the status bar with DIESEL 660
Training Your Toolbars, Panels, and Dockable Windows to Stay ...662
    Locking toolbars, panels, and dockable windows 662
    Locking and unlocking toolbars, panels,
        and dockable windows 663
Controlling the Appearance of AutoCAD and the Drawing Window 664
    Window elements 664
    Layout elements 666
    Size of the crosshairs 667
    Other settings 667
Organizing Your Space 668
    Using the Workspaces toolbar 668
    Using the Customize User Interface Editor 670
    Maximizing the drawing space 674

Chapter 3: Customizing the Tools 675
How Customizing the User Interface Has Changed 675
Getting to Know the Customize User Interface Editor 676
    The Customizations In pane 677
    The Command List pane 678
    The Dynamic pane 679
    Launching the CUI Editor 680
    Commands in the CUI Editor 680

Customizing Toolbars, Pull-Down and
   Shortcut Menus, and the Ribbon..684
      Quick Access toolbar 685
      Toolbars..685
      Menus..688
      Shortcut menus 690
      The Ribbon..692
      Separator bars 696
   Creating a New Shortcut Key...696
   Customizing Double-Click Actions..697
   Customizing the Quick Properties Panel and Rollover Tooltips............698
   Migrating and Transferring Customization.............................700
   Working with Partial and Enterprise Customization Files 702
      Loading an enterprise customization file........................702
      Loading a partial customization file 703

Chapter 4: Delving Deeper into Customization **705**
   Working from a Script...705
      What's in a script?..705
      Creating a script file 708
      Loading and running a script file 708
      Running a script file at startup 709
   Getting Familiar with Shapes...709
   Working with Express Tools 710
      Installing Express Tools..710
      Block tools..711
      Text tools..712
      Layout tools..712
      Dimension tools..713
      Selection tools..713
      Modify tools..713
      Draw tools...714
      File tools..714
      Web tools...714
      Tools...714
      Command line only tools...715

Chapter 5: Recording Your Actions **717**
   Actions and Action Recorder 717
   Recording and Managing Action Macros 718
      Recording actions..718
      Managing and editing action macro files........................722
      Managing the location of action macro files 722
   Editing Actions and Recorded Values.....................................723
   Just Press Play..724

Bonus Chapters ....On the Web

Bonus Chapter 1: Working with Surfaces BC1
Creating Primitive Surfaces...BC1
    3D face...BC3
    3D mesh..BC3
    Planar surface BC4
    Box...BC5
    Wedge...BC5
    Cone BC6
    Sphere BC6
    Dish and dome BC7
    Torus BC7
    Pyramid..BC8
Creating Complex Surfaces BC8
    Tabulated Mesh BC8
    Revolved Mesh...BC9
    Ruled Mesh BC10
    Edge Mesh BC10
Editing Surfaces BC11
    Controlling the visibility of edges BC11
    Using grips to edit surfaces..BC12
    Working with convert to surface BC12
    Thicken BC12

Bonus Chapter 2: The AutoCAD Programming Interfaces BC13
Discovering What You Can Do by Programming AutoCAD................BC14
    The advantages of using APIs BC14
    The other side of the story BC15
Getting to Know the Available Programming Interfaces BC15
    AutoLISP BC16
    ActiveX automation..BC17
    VBA..BC17
    ObjectARX and ObjectDBX BC18
    .NET BC19
Comparing Strengths and Weaknesses
    of the Programming Interfaces BC19
Deciding Which Programming Interface Is Best for You BC21

Bonus Chapter 3: Using Custom Programs BC23
Identifying Application Files BC23
Loading and Unloading Applications..BC24
    The Load/Unload Applications dialog box.................BC25
    Loading an AutoLISP file...BC28
    Loading and unloading a VBA project file.................BC29
    Loading and unloading an ObjectARX file.................BC31
Automatically Loading Application Files BC34
    Using the Startup Suite BC34
    Getting AutoCAD to do some of the work BC36
Running a Program in an Application File................................BC38

Bonus Chapter 4: Introducing AutoLISP **BC41**

Accessing the AutoLISP Development Environment BC41
  Launching the Visual LISP Editor BC42
  Loading an existing AutoLISP application file BC42
Using the VLIDE BC43
  Controlling color-coding in the text window BC45
  Controlling text size and font style for the text window BC46
  Navigating the text window BC47
Creating a Basic Program BC48
  Creating a new AutoLISP file BC48
  Anatomy of an AutoLISP expression BC49
  Adding comments BC50
  To command or just to function BC51
  Creating your first AutoLISP program BC52
More Than Just the Essentials of AutoLISP BC54
  Supported data types BC54
  Math functions BC55
  String functions BC55
  List functions BC56
  Data conversion functions BC57
  Saving and accessing values for later BC58
  Exchanging information with AutoCAD BC58
Getting Information to and from the User BC60
  Giving feedback to the user BC61
  Other functions to note BC61
Using the Debug Tools in the Visual LISP Editor BC63
  Breakpoints BC64
  Watch what is happening BC64
  Setting up breakpoints and using watch BC65
  AutoLISP error messages BC66
Going GUI with DCL BC68
  Basics of DCL BC68
  Adding comments BC69
  Using DCL to add interaction to AutoLISP BC70
Using ActiveX Automation with AutoLISP BC73
  Referencing the AutoCAD application BC73
  Using methods of an object BC74
  Setting and retrieving a property of an object BC74
  Revising the BCIRC command BC75

Bonus Chapter 5: Visual Basic for AutoCAD **BC79**

AutoCAD Commands for VBA BC80
  VBAIDE BC80
  VBALOAD BC80
  VBAUNLOAD BC83
  VBARUN BC83
  VBAMAN BC84
  Other commands BC85

Working with the IDE BC86
   Exploring the IDE..BC86
   Project Explorer BC86
   Properties window BC87
   Editor windows BC88
   Object Browser BC88
Parts of a VBA Project BC90
   Standard code module..BC91
   Class code module BC91
   Procedure (subroutine and function).....................................BC91
   Declaring variables..BC91
   Data types..BC92
   Assigning a value to a variable BC93
   The basics of working with objects BC93
   Adding comments BC94
Introducing the AutoCAD Object Model BC94
   Creating a basic VBA project BC95
   Working with the new VBA project in the editor.....................BC96
   Adding a new procedure to a code module BC98
   Running the new procedure..BC100

Bonus Chapter 6: AutoCAD Utilities **BC101**
Filtering Objects during Selection...BC101
   Quick Select...BC102
   Filter BC104
AutoCAD Calculator BC106
   Using QuickCalc with the Properties palette.......................BC108
   Using QuickCalc with a command..BC109
Purging Named Objects BC110
Auditing and Recovering Drawings...BC111
   Auditing a drawing BC112
   Recovering a drawing BC113
   Using Drawing Recovery Manager BC113

Bonus Chapter 7: Creating Custom Linetypes,
Shapes, and Hatch Patterns **BC115**
It's All in the Linetype..BC115
   Simple linetypes BC116
   Complex linetypes BC119
Getting Familiar with Shapes BC120
Creating Custom Patterns BC120
   The structure of a hatch pattern BC121
   Creating a hatch pattern..BC124
   Using a custom hatch pattern file BC125

Index **727**

Introduction

For many reasons, AutoCAD is much different from most applications that you will ever use. The main reason goes back some 20 years to when AutoCAD was introduced as a low-cost CAD solution on microcomputers. (CAD stands for *Computer-Aided Drafting* or *Computer-Aided Design,* depending on who you ask.) Most CAD applications back then ran on very large and expensive mainframe computers, not something that you could take on-site with you.

With the introduction of AutoCAD, CAD wasn't as foreign of a topic as it once was, but it still had an uphill climb against the wide use and adoption of drafting boards. A drafting board, you might be asking yourself? Yes, before computers and CAD, all designs were done with pencil and paper; if you were really good, you used ink and paper. Today, paper still plays a role in distributing designs, but most designs are now done in a CAD application that allows you to do much more complex things that were not possible with board drafting.

As times and drafting practices changed, AutoCAD has led in setting the pace for change or has forced change. Some of these changes have helped to usher in the era of improved design collaboration across the Internet and better electronic file sharing with non-CAD users. Because all objects in a drawing are electronic, AutoCAD allows you to quickly manipulate and manage them without the need to break out the eraser shield and eraser as you would on a board. You can also use design information downstream in other processes, such as ordering parts and developing a quote to complete a project. Autodesk continues to improve the way you can visualize designs and concepts through improvements in collaboration, 3D modeling, and other features.

AutoCAD 2009 gives you the tools you need to create accurate 2D and 3D designs, but it isn't easy to just pick up and become productive right away like you might with a word processor program. This book helps guide you through the different areas of AutoCAD 2009 and AutoCAD LT 2009 so you get up to speed faster and become productive as soon as possible. The different areas of drafting that I discuss include 2D drafting, 3D modeling, annotation, creating and using reusable content, printing and plotting, collaboration, and customizing and programming.

About This Book

AutoCAD 2009 & AutoCAD LT 2009 All-in-One Desk Reference For Dummies gives you an understanding of all the main features that you need to know to be productive with AutoCAD and AutoCAD LT. The *All-in-One Desk References For Dummies* are different from other *For Dummies* books that you may have read; as much information as possible is crammed between the covers (and some has even overflowed to the Web), and the content takes you deep into the depths of AutoCAD and AutoCAD LT. This book is laid out to focus on individual topics and allows you the freedom of moving around between its minibooks. If you're not familiar (or only somewhat familiar) with AutoCAD or AutoCAD LT, I recommend that you read through Books I and II before moving on to the other minibooks. Also, make sure that you go Book I, Chapter 1, which walks you through creating a basic drawing.

After you read this book, don't let it wander too far from your desk — you'll find it helpful as a reference.

Foolish Assumptions

I expect that you know how to use the Windows operating system and understand the basics of navigating folders and starting applications. To take advantage of everything that AutoCAD offers and what is contained in this book, I assume that you have at least an Internet connection — dialup at least, but a high-speed cable or DSL connection would be best. As long as you have AutoCAD or AutoCAD LT installed on the computer in front of you and a connection to the Internet, you're ready to get started.

Conventions Used in This Book

Text you type in the command line window or in a text box appears in a **bold typeface.** Examples of AutoCAD prompts appear in a `special typeface`. When you see something like "click File menu⇨Save As," the arrow (⇨) indicates that you click the File menu and then click the Save As command.

AutoCAD offers a number of user interface elements to access commands. The following sections explain the different command access methods and the notation that you encounter throughout this book. I discuss all of these and other user interfaces in Chapter 2 of Book II.

Menu browser access

Access to and using the *menu browser* is designated as, for example, "On the menu browser, click Draw menu⇨Circle⇨Center, Radius." In plain old English, the notation means to do the following to use the menu browser:

1. **Click the Menu Browser button, which is the large red *A*, in the upper-left corner.**

2. **On the menu browser, hover the cursor over the Draw menu.**

3. **Click the Circle submenu.**

   Submenus are denoted by the arrow next to the item on the right.

4. **Click Center, Radius.**

Figure I-1 shows the menu browser with the Draw menu and Circle submenus expanded, and the Center, Radius command highlighted.

Figure I-1:
Access to
the menu
browser . . .
granted.

Ribbon access

The *ribbon* is very different from other user interfaces in AutoCAD because it has areas of commands that are normally hidden. These hidden areas are called *slideouts.* Access to and using commands on the ribbon is designated as, for example, "On the ribbon, click Home tab⇨Draw panel⇨Line."

1. **On the ribbon, click the Home tab.**

2. **On the Draw panel, click the Line button.**

Figure I-2 shows accessing a command on a panel of the ribbon.

Figure I-2:
The ribbon organizes commands with tabs and panels.

If a command is on a *flyout,* which is a single button that can contain multiple commands, the access to a command on a flyout is designated as "On the ribbon, click Home tab⇨Draw panel⇨Circle button's flyout⇨Center Radius."

1. **On the ribbon, click the Home tab.**

2. **Click the Draw panel and then click the black arrow adjacent to the Circle's button.**

3. **On the pop-up menu, click Center, Radius.**

Figure I-3 shows accessing a command on a flyout — notice the indication of a flyout by the black downward arrow — on a ribbon panel:

Figure I-3:
Accessing commands from a flyout on a ribbon panel.

Access to a command on a slideout panel is designated as, for example, "On the ribbon, click Home tab⇨Draw panel's title bar⇨Donut button."

1. **On the ribbon, click the Home tab.**

2. **Click the Draw panel's title bar, located along the bottom of the ribbon panel.**

3. **On the expanded Draw panel, click the Donut button.**

Figure I-4 shows accessing a command on a slideout panel of a ribbon. Slideout panels are indicated by the black arrow in the lower-right corner of the ribbon panel.

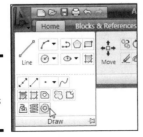

Figure I-4:
Commands on slideouts exposed.

Toolbar access

Access to toolbars is similar to how you work with the menu browser, except with fewer clicks. Access to and using commands from a toolbar is designated as "On the Draw toolbar, click the Polygon button."

Toolbars also support the use of flyouts. A flyout is a nested toolbar that is represented by a single button with a black arrow in its lower-right corner. You access a button on a flyout by clicking and holding down the mouse button, and then dragging the cursor to the button on the flyout you want to use, and then releasing the mouse button. Flyout access on toolbars is designated as "On the Draw toolbar, click Insert flyout button⇨DWF Underlay." Figure I-5 shows the Insert flyout on the Draw toolbar; the flyout on the toolbar is designated by the black arrow in the lower-right corner of the button on the toolbar.

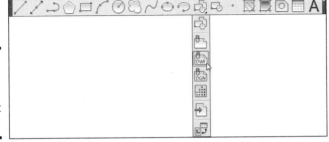

Figure I-5:
Accessing commands from a flyout on a toolbar.

Menu bar ("classic menu") access

Access to and using the menu bar (or "classic menus") is designated as, for example, "On the menu bar, click Draw menu⇨Circle⇨Center, Radius."

1. **On the menu bar, click the Draw menu.**

2. **Click the Circle submenu.**

Submenus are denoted by the black arrow to the right of the item.

3. **Click Center, Radius.**

Figure I-6 shows the menu bar with the Draw menu and Circle submenus expanded, and with the Center, Radius command highlighted.

Figure I-6:
The menu bar is the no-frills approach to accessing commands.

How This Book Is Organized

The following sections describe the minibooks that make up this book.

Book 1: AutoCAD Basics

Chapter 1 of Book I gets you heading down the path to success with using AutoCAD or AutoCAD LT. From there you dive into AutoCAD's interface and the basics of working with drawing files. This book provides some background on AutoCAD and AutoCAD LT, and lists which versions are compatible with each other. How to start the application is explained and you are sent on a tour of the interface. You also see how to interact with commands by using dialog boxes and the command line, and how to get help when you need it most from the application. You also get a brief rundown on creating and modifying some of the basic 2D objects, and using a few of the viewing commands. The last two chapters of the minibook show how to use some of the general object properties and settings, as well as the different drafting aids that help you create accurate 2D and 3D drawings.

Book II: 2D Drafting

Book II covers many of the commands that are used for creating and working with 2D drawings. The first part of the minibook focuses on creating 2D objects that range from lines, circles, and arcs to more complex objects, such as ellipses. Then you see how to select and modify objects that have been created in a drawing. Modifying objects is one of the main tasks that you perform in AutoCAD, next to viewing and creating new objects in a drawing.

Book III: Annotating Drawings

Book III covers how to create annotation in a drawing that explains a feature or shows the measurement of an object. Annotation in AutoCAD includes text, tables, dimensions, leaders, and hatch. For example, you see how to create single and multiline text objects and tables. The chapter also includes formatting specific characteristics of text and tables, performing spell checking, and doing a find-and-replace on text strings. Last but definitely not least is a chapter that covers how to work with annotation scaling.

Book IV: LT Differences

Book IV focuses on AutoCAD LT and how it is different from AutoCAD, along with using it in the same environment as AutoCAD and expanding AutoCAD LT through customization and other means. This minibook also explains what to watch out for when you use both AutoCAD and AutoCAD LT in the same office.

Book V: 3D Modeling

Book V covers how to create, edit, view, and visualize 3D objects. You get the basics of working in 3D, and see how to specify coordinates and adjust the coordinate system to make it easier for you to create and modify objects above the x,y plane. This minibook also covers how to navigate and view a 3D model in AutoCAD and AutoCAD LT.

Book VI: Advanced Drafting

Book VI covers the advanced drafting features that go beyond 2D drafting, which include working with blocks, external references, and raster images. You also find out how to reuse content that you create in multiple drawings with DesignCenter and tool palettes.

Book VII: Publishing Drawings

Book VII covers generating a hard copy (paper copy) or an electronic version of a drawing that can be viewed without AutoCAD or AutoCAD LT. You see how to use page setups to define how part of a drawing should be printed, and how to create floating viewports and layouts to help output a drawing. You also discover how you can use sheet sets to manage and organize sets of drawings. Sheet sets provide ways to open drawings, keep data in sync through the use of fields and views, and output a number of drawings. This minibook also shows how to create plot configurations and plot styles, and how to plot and publish a drawing layout or layouts to create hard copies or electronic versions of drawings.

Book VIII: Collaboration

Book VIII covers some advanced topics that include CAD standards and file sharing, as well as how to use electronic files for project collaboration. You gain an understanding of the concepts behind CAD standards, as well as how to use the available CAD standards tools to help maintain and enforce CAD standards.

Book IX: Customizing AutoCAD

Book IX covers techniques that are used to customize AutoCAD and AutoCAD LT, which allows you to reduce the number of repetitive tasks and steps that you might have to do to complete a design.

Bonus Content

The bonus chapters cover additional topics that just can't fit between the covers of this book. Bonus Chapter 1 covers working with 3D surfaces. Bonus Chapters 2 through 5 cover extending AutoCAD through some of the different programming languages that it supports. Programming AutoCAD is different from customizing it, but the goal of reducing repetitive tasks and steps that you have to do to complete a design are the same. Bonus Chapter 6 covers working with object selection filters, AutoCAD's calculator, purging unused named objects, and auditing and recovering drawings. Bonus Chapter 7 describes creating your own shapes, linetypes, and hatch patterns.

Icons Used in This Book

This book uses the following icons to denote paragraphs that may be of special interest:

This icon helps those who are using AutoCAD LT know what features are missing from AutoCAD LT that are in AutoCAD or in some cases where AutoCAD LT is slightly different from AutoCAD. At times, you may not know the differences between the two programs, and these paragraphs can help you determine whether you should be using AutoCAD instead of AutoCAD LT.

This icon highlights what's new in AutoCAD 2009 or AutoCAD LT 2009 or both.

This icon indicates a reference to additional content that is available in one of the Bonus Chapters, which can be downloaded from www.wiley.com/go/autocad2009aio.

This icon gives the gray matter an extra nudge here and there for things that I talk about earlier in the book. AutoCAD is a large program, and it takes a bit of time to put all the pieces together, so I give you some friendly reminders along the way.

These paragraphs give insight into the inner workings of AutoCAD or something that you won't typically need to know to use the program, but may find interesting. As you read through the book the first time, you might want to think of the Technical Stuff paragraphs as bonus material and not as required reading, so feel free to skip them.

This icon indicates information that may save you some time or help you to not fall too far from the path to success. For the most part, Tip paragraphs are designed to help guide you through some of the overwhelming parts of AutoCAD and give you what might not always be the most obvious way to get to the desired result faster.

This icon helps you stay away from the deep end of AutoCAD and out of trouble. Failure to adhere to the message may result in an undesired side effect to your design.

Book I

AutoCAD Basics

The 5th Wave   By Rich Tennant

"You know kids – you can't buy them just <u>any</u> multi-dimensional drafting software."

Contents at a Glance

Chapter 1: One-on-One Time with AutoCAD **13**

Starting AutoCAD or AutoCAD LT 14
Drawing Setup...16
Drawing and Editing Objects 20
Annotating with Text and Dimensions 27
Fast Track to Plotting 29

Chapter 2: Drawing on and in AutoCAD **31**

Understanding AutoCAD Files and Formats 32
Seeing the LT..33
Using AutoCAD's Latest-and-Greatest Feature Set...................................34

Chapter 3: Navigating the AutoCAD Interface **37**

Starting the Application 37
Touring the AutoCAD Interface 41
Communicating with Your Software 56
Running AutoCAD Commands 58
Reaching for AutoCAD Help...60

Chapter 4: All about Files **65**

File Types in AutoCAD..65
Starting a New Drawing 68
Saving a Drawing 73
Opening an Existing Drawing...76
The Multiple-Drawing Environment..80
Closing Windows...81
File Management for AutoCAD 82
Backing Up Is Hard to Do 83

Chapter 5: Basic Tools **85**

Drawing Lines 85
Creating Circles 88
Taking a Closer Look...91
Modifying Objects 93
Erasing and Unerasing Stuff...94
Ready . . . Undo, Undo, Redo 96

Chapter 6: Setting Up Drawings **97**

Choosing Units of Measurement 97
Setting Limits for Your Drawings 102
Understanding Drawing Scale 104
Lost in Space: Model or Paper? 107
A Layered Approach 108
Object Properties 120
Setting Up Standards 123

Chapter 7: Precision Tools **125**

Understanding Accuracy and Precision..125
Understanding Coordinate Systems 126
Setting Grid and Snap 141
Understanding Ortho and Polar Tracking...143
Working with Object Snaps 147
Using Point Filters 151
Working with Object Snap Tracking Mode..153

Chapter 1: One-on-One Time with AutoCAD

In This Chapter

✔ Setting up a drawing

✔ Drawing and editing objects

✔ Understanding the basics of plotting

*W*elcome to *AutoCAD 2009 & AutoCAD LT 2009 All-in-One Desk Reference For Dummies,* your one-stop shop for AutoCAD users of every skill level. You've read this far, so I assume you know a thing or two about the world's most popular computer-aided drafting program — enough, at least, to know that computer-aided drafting usually goes by the much friendlier acronym of CAD.

AutoCAD 2009 & AutoCAD LT 2009 All-in-One Desk Reference For Dummies is aimed at AutoCAD users in every discipline — architecture, mechanical design, mapping and GIS, product design, survey and civil engineering, diagramming . . . whatever your field, you find useful information here. I cover the entire CAD workflow process, not forgetting that 90 percent of the time, what you need to produce at the far end of the workflow is a clear and well laid-out paper drawing.

Reading about AutoCAD or AutoCAD LT is great, but without a good foundation you'll find it harder to understand other features. So roll up your sleeves because it's time to get your hands dirty — okay, get your mouse moving and keys pressing.

This chapter helps you with the basics of using AutoCAD by explaining how to set up a basic drawing, draw and edit objects, add text and dimensions, which are useful to communicate the design to others, and then print your first drawing, which will be suitable for hanging on your refrigerator. Figure 1-1 shows the cabinet that you'll create in this chapter.

Minibooks I and II will fill in many of the gaps that might leave you craving for more about the basics of AutoCAD and AutoCAD LT. This is not uncommon, because after you start AutoCAD or AutoCAD LT you'll see a lot of different things. Don't worry — I cover most of what you see on the screen. As you move through the lessons, I point you to the chapters in the book that will help you continue to expand your knowledge in that area of drafting in AutoCAD or AutoCAD LT.

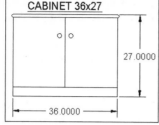

Starting AutoCAD or AutoCAD LT

Congratulations on braving into the world of CAD, but before partying like a CADstar you need to start AutoCAD or AutoCAD LT. Chances are pretty good that you're running Microsoft's Windows operating system, and how you start AutoCAD or AutoCAD LT varies slightly based on the configuration of your computer.

To start AutoCAD or AutoCAD LT, do one of the following:

✦ **Windows Desktop:** Locate on your desktop the AutoCAD 2009 or AutoCAD LT 2009 shortcut, and then double-click the icon.

✦ **Windows Start Menu:** Click the Start button➪(All) Programs➪Autodesk➪AutoCAD 2009 (or AutoCAD LT 2009)➪ AutoCAD 2009 (or AutoCAD LT 2009).

AutoCAD or AutoCAD LT starts and, like most applications, sits there and waits for you to do something. For more on starting AutoCAD, see Chapter 3 of this minibook.

The first thing you encounter is the New Features Workshop, which tells you what has been changed in the latest release and back two other releases. So you can find out what changed in AutoCAD 2007 and AutoCAD 2008 (or AutoCAD LT 2007 and AutoCAD LT 2008). For now, select the Maybe Later option on the left and click OK. The New Features Workshop dialog box will appear the next time you start AutoCAD or AutoCAD LT. In addition to the New Features Workshop, you can get an overview of some of the latest features in Chapter 2 of this minibook.

Accessing the right tools for the right job

AutoCAD and AutoCAD LT have been around for a number of years, so they offer a large variety of different commands and different user interface elements. The drawing you'll be working with in this chapter is 2D only, and most of the commands that you will use can be found on the ribbon along with a few other user interface elements in AutoCAD. The display of the ribbon and other 2D-related drafting tools is controlled through the 2D Drafting & Annotation workspace. To set the 2D Drafting & Annotation workspace current, follow these steps:

1. On the status bar, click the Workspace Switching icon.

2. Choose 2D Drafting & Annotation.

The menu browser, Quick Access toolbar, and ribbon are displayed at the top of AutoCAD or AutoCAD LT, along with the command line window and application status bar at the bottom.

To find out more about the different features of the user interface, see Chapter 3 of this minibook. You can also find out more about workspaces in Chapter 2 of Book IX.

Creating a new drawing

AutoCAD and AutoCAD LT create a blank drawing upon startup, but it's a good idea to select the drawing template that you want to use at startup and not rely on the one that AutoCAD or AutoCAD LT creates for you. To create a new drawing, follow these steps:

1. Click the Menu Browser button.

The Menu Browser button is located in the upper-left corner of AutoCAD or AutoCAD LT. The menu browser opens.

2. On the menu browser, click File menu⇨New.

The Select Template dialog box is displayed (see Figure 1-2).

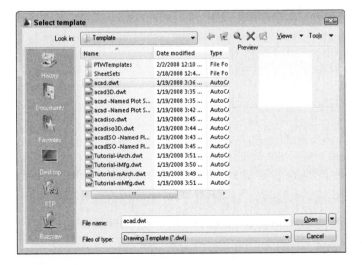

Figure 1-2: Choosing your drawing template.

3. Select the acad.dwt drawing template (or acadlt.dwt if you're using AutoCAD LT) and click Open.

A new drawing is created for you based on the drawing template selected.

What is created should be saved

When you create a new drawing it's always a good idea to save it right away, and then to save frequently as you create or modify objects in the drawing. To save a drawing, follow these steps:

1. On the Quick Access toolbar, click Save.

The Save Drawing As dialog box is displayed.

2. Browse to the (My) Documents folder by clicking the (My) Documents link along the left side of the dialog box.

The (My) Documents folder opens.

3. In the File Name text box, enter Cabinet **and click Save.**

For more on creating, opening, and saving drawing files, see Chapter 4 of this minibook.

Drawing Setup

Let's see now: You have started AutoCAD or AutoCAD LT, displayed the 2D drafting tools by setting the 2D Drafting & Annotation workspace current, and created a new drawing. Sounds like a fair amount of work, but there's plenty more to do, so grab that cup of coffee so you're ready for the rest of the chapter because this is where it starts getting good.

You have to do a few things before you start drawing objects; after all, these are technical drawings that you're creating, so they need to be accurate. Setting up your drawing and applying proper CAD standards are important.

Getting snappy and griddy

In this section, you do some initial drawing setup that allows you to draw accurately and organize the objects you'll be drawing. The following steps explain how to set up snap and grid so that you can draw in specific increments, similar to using a sheet of graph paper to plot coordinate values:

1. On the status bar, right-click the Snap Mode button.

2. On the menu that's displayed, choose Settings.

The Drafting Settings dialog box (see Figure 1-3) appears.

3. Select the Snap On (F9) and Grid On (F7) options.

4. **In the Snap Spacing area, select Equal X and Y Spacing if it's not
selected.**

5. **In the Snap Spacing area, double-click the Snap X Spacing text box,
and then type 1 and press Tab.**

Because you selected the Equal X and Y Spacing option, the value in the
Snap Y Spacing text box was updated to match the value entered in
the Snap X Spacing text box.

6. **In the Grid Spacing area, double-click the Grid X Spacing text box,
and then type 1 and press Tab.**

The value in the Grid Y Spacing text box is updated to match the value
in the Grid X Spacing text box.

7. **In the Snap Type area, select Grid Snap and then select Rectangular
Snap if they are not already selected.**

8. **Click OK.**

The Drafting Settings dialog box closes and you return to the drawing
window.

Figure 1-3:
Configuring
snap and
grid with the
Drafting
Settings
dialog box.

To find out more about other drafting settings and precision tools, see
Chapter 7 of this minibook.

Establishing the limits

The next set of steps explains how to control the size of the grid that should
be displayed. By default, the grid is 12 x 9 units in size, but the cabinet that
you will be drawing is 36 units wide x 27 units high. So in the following steps

you set the drawing limits — which control the size of the grid — to a more appropriate size for the drawing you'll be creating:

1. **On the menu browser, click Format menu⊅Drawing Limits.**

The LIMITS command starts and displays the following prompt:

```
Specify lower left corner or [ON/OFF] <0.0000,0.0000>:
```

2. **At the prompt, press Enter to accept the default value, which is displayed between the <> (angle brackets).**

The following prompt is displayed:

```
Specify upper right corner <12.0000,9.0000>:
```

3. **At the prompt, type 48,36 and press Enter.**

The drawing limits are now set to 48x36, which gives you plenty of room to draw the cabinet.

4. **Chances are you can't see the entire grid. On the status bar, click Zoom. Type A and press Enter.**

The drawing is zoomed to the extent of the drawing limits, so now you can see the entire grid.

Organizing objects with layers

Just one more series of steps and then you'll be on your way to drawing and modifying objects. You need to create some layers that will be used to organize the objects you'll be drawing. The following steps explain how to create a layer. After you go through these steps, you need to run through some of the steps a few more times to create some additional layers for the drawing:

1. **On the ribbon, click Home tab⊅Layers panel⊅Layer Properties.**

Layer Properties Manager (see Figure 1-4) is displayed.

New layer   Set current

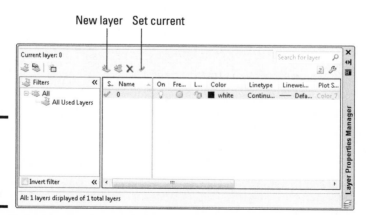

Figure 1-4:
Managing
layers and
their
properties.

2. **Click the New Layer button.**

A new layer named Layer1 is added to the list.

3. **With the name of the new layer highlighted, type** Cabinet.

4. **In the row for the Cabinet layer, click the color swatch in the Color column.**

The Select Color dialog box (see Figure 1-5) is displayed.

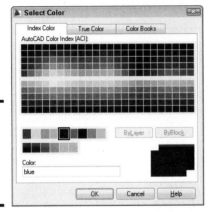

Figure 1-5:
Adding a
touch of
color one
swatch at a
time.

5. **Click the Index Color tab, select color 5 (blue), and then click OK.**

6. **With the Cabinet layer still highlighted, click Set Current.**

The Cabinet layer is now current and any objects that you draw will be placed on this layer.

7. **Repeat Steps 2 through 5 to create the following layers:**

a. **Dimensions and set its color to 4 (cyan)**

b. **Handles and set its color to 7 (white)**

c. **Hatch and set its color to 9**

d. **Text and set its color to 1 (red)**

e. **Top and set its color to 6 (magenta)**

When you're finished, five additional layers are added to the drawing.

To find out more about layers, see Chapter 6 of this minibook.

Drawing and Editing Objects

Now that a good foundation has been laid down with layers, setting up some of the precision drafting aids, and limits, it's time to find out how to draw and modify objects. For more on creating and modifying drawing objects, see Chapter 5 of this minibook, and Chapters 1 and 2 of Book II.

Walking the straight and curved

You use different drawing commands to create objects that will be used to communicate the design to the client for signoff or the shop floor so that the part can be manufactured. Drawing objects can be simple lines, circles, or more complex objects such as ellipses and splines. In this section you draw rectangles, lines, arcs, circles, and polylines to create the front elevation of the cabinet.

Don't be a square

Rectangles in AutoCAD are four-sided objects with opposite sides parallel and the same length. In this set of steps, you draw a rectangle to represent the base of the cabinet:

1. **On the ribbon, click Home tab⇨Draw panel⇨Rectangle.**

The RECTANGLE command starts and the following prompt is displayed:

```
Specify first corner point or [Chamfer/Elevation/
    Fillet/Thickness/Width]:
```

2. **At the prompt, move the crosshairs in the drawing to the coordinate point 6,6 and click (see Figure 1-6).**

As you move the crosshairs in the drawing window, notice that the crosshairs jump in increments of 1 unit; this is because snap is enabled.

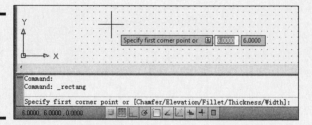

Figure 1-6: Using snap and grid to locate coordinate points.

The following prompt is displayed:

```
Specify other corner point or
    [Area/Dimensions/Rotation]:
```

3. **At the command prompt, type @36,3 and press Enter.**

    A rectangle that is 36 units wide and 3 units high is created.

Multiply segments, one object

 Polylines are objects that can contain multiple straight and curved segments. In the following steps you draw the outer edges of the doors for the cabinet:

1. **At the command prompt, type PL and press Enter.**

    The PLINE command starts and displays this prompt:

    ```
    Specify start point:
    ```

2. **At the prompt, type 6,9 and press Enter.**

    The following prompt is displayed:

    ```
    Specify next point or [Arc/Halfwidth/Length/
        Undo/Width]:
    ```

3. **On the status bar, click the Ortho Mode button until you see <Ortho on> displayed in the command line window.**

    Ortho mode is enabled and the PLINE command continues.

4. **Drag the crosshairs up, and then type 23 and press Enter.**

    A vertical line segment of 23 units is drawn.

5. **Drag the crosshairs to the right, and then type 36 and press Enter.**

6. **Drag the crosshairs down, and then type 23 and press Enter twice.**

    A polyline with three segments is created and the PLINE command ends. The object in the drawing should now look like Figure 1-7.

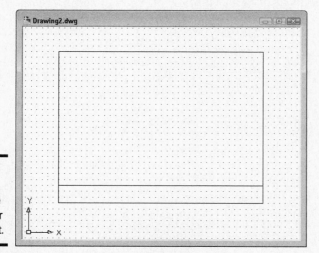

Figure 1-7:
The base
and outline
of doors for
the cabinet.

Going straight from point A to point B

Lines are straight objects that are defined between two points. In the following procedure you draw a line from the middle of the second segment of the polyline that you created in the preceding procedure to the middle of the top line of the rectangle that you drew in the first procedure in this section. The line that you draw will represent the gap between the left and right doors of the cabinet.

1. **On the status bar, right-click the Snap Mode button and choose Off from the shortcut menu.**

The crosshairs can now freely move around the drawing window.

2. **On the status bar, right-click the Grid Display button and choose Enabled from the shortcut menu.**

The dots used to represent the grid in the drawing window disappear.

3. **On the menu browser, click Draw menu⇨Line.**

The LINE command starts and the following prompt is displayed:

```
Specify first point:
```

4. **At the prompt, hold down the Shift key and right-click.**

The Object Snap menu is displayed.

5. **On the Object Snap menu, choose Midpoint.**

The menu closes and you return to the LINE command.

6. **Position the cursor near the middle of the top line of the rectangle that you drew earlier.**

An orangish triangle appears at the middle of the line and a tooltip with the text *Midpoint* is displayed near the crosshairs (see Figure 1-8).

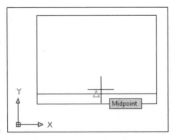

Figure 1-8:
Snapping to the midpoint of the line segment.

7. **With the marker for the Midpoint active, click to pick the midpoint of the line segment.**

The following prompt is displayed:

```
Specify next point or [Undo]:
```

8. **Right-click the drawing window and choose Snap Overrides⇨Midpoint. Move the cursor up and pick the midpoint of the polyline segment directly above the previous point you picked.**

The line is drawn between the two midpoints you just picked.

9. **Press Enter to end the LINE command.**

Just a circle thing

 Not all objects that you can create in AutoCAD or AutoCAD LT have straight edges; after all, the world hasn't been since 1492. In the next set of steps you draw a circle that represents one of the handles for the doors on the cabinet:

 1. **On the ribbon, click Home tab⇨Layers panel⇨down arrow on the Layers drop-down list⇨Handles.**

The Handles layer is set current.

2. **On the ribbon, click Home tab⇨Draw panel⇨Center, Radius.**

The CIRCLE command starts and displays this prompt:

```
Specify center point for circle or [3P/2P/Ttr (tan tan
    radius)]:
```

3. **At the prompt, type 26,26 and press Enter.**

The following prompt is displayed:

```
Specify radius of circle or [Diameter]:
```

4. **At the prompt, type D and press Enter to use the Diameter option.**

The following prompt is displayed:

```
Specify diameter of circle:
```

5. **At the prompt, type 1.5 and press Enter.**

A circle with a diameter of 1.5 is drawn. Figure 1-9 shows what your cabinet should currently look like.

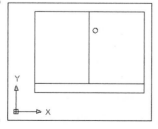

Figure 1-9:
The cabinet is starting to take shape — with circles and lines.

Going around the arc

Arcs are portions of a circle, which you can create in many ways. You use arcs to represent fillets, rounds, and even transitions between objects. In the following steps you draw an arc that will represent the right edge of the top of the cabinet:

1. **On the ribbon, click Home tab⇨Layers panel⇨down arrow on the Layers drop-down list⇨Top.**

2. **Right-click the Quick Access toolbar (located along the top of AutoCAD to the right of the Menu Browser button) and choose Toolbars⇨AutoCAD⇨Draw.**

   The Draw toolbar is displayed along the left side of AutoCAD.

3. **On the Draw toolbar, click the Arc button.**

   The ARC command starts and the following prompt is displayed:

   ```
   Specify start point of arc or [Center]:
   ```

4. **At the prompt, hold down the Shift key and right-click.**

5. **On the Object Snap menu, choose Endpoint.**

6. **Position the cursor near the upper-right corner of the polyline that you drew.**

   An orangish square appears at the endpoint of the line segment and a tooltip with the text *Endpoint* is displayed near the crosshairs (see Figure 1-10).

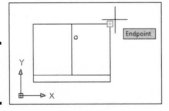

Figure 1-10: Nothing but endpoint.

7. **With the marker for the Endpoint active, click to pick the endpoint of the line segment.**

   The following prompt is displayed:

   ```
   Specify second point of arc or [Center/End]:
   ```

8. **At the prompt, right-click the drawing window and choose End from the shortcut menu to use the End point option.**

   The following prompt is displayed:

   ```
   Specify end point of arc:
   ```

9. **At the prompt, drag the crosshairs up. Then type 1 and press Enter.**

The following prompt is displayed:

```
Specify center point of arc or [Angle/Direction/Radius]:
```

10. **At the prompt, type D and press Enter to use the Direction option.**

The following prompt is displayed:

```
Specify tangent direction for the start point of the arc:
```

11. **At the prompt, type 0 and press Enter.**

The arc is drawn and the ARC command ends.

Modifying objects

Next to drawing objects, editing objects is one of the most common tasks in AutoCAD and AutoCAD LT. You might even find yourself modifying objects to create new objects instead of creating new objects from scratch. In this section you find out how to copy and mirror objects to complete the elevation of the cabinet.

Duplicating objects

AutoCAD and AutoCAD LT offer the ability to duplicate objects by using the COPY command. (What were you expecting me to say, the ZEROX command?) In this set of steps, you copy the lone circle to create a second one to represent the other handle on the left door of the cabinet:

1. **On the ribbon, click Home tab⇨Modify panel⇨Copy.**

The COPY command starts and the following prompt is displayed:

```
Select objects:
```

2. **At the prompt, position the pickbox (that square that was once the crosshairs) over the circle and click. Press Enter to end object selection.**

The following prompt is displayed:

```
Specify base point or [Displacement/mOde] <Displacement>:
```

3. **At the prompt, press Enter to use the displacement option.**

The following prompt is displayed:

```
Specify displacement <0.0000, 0.0000, 0.0000>:
```

4. **At the prompt, type @-4,0 and press Enter.**

A copy of the selected circle is created 4 units to the left, and the COPY command ends.

Here's looking at you

 Creating symmetrical objects is not uncommon in mechanical or even architectural designs. You can create mirror images of selected drawings to create a
symmetrical design or to invert the direction in which objects are created. In
these steps you mirror the existing arc to create the opposite side of the top:

1. **On the menu browser, click Modify menu⇨Mirror.**

The MIRROR command starts and the following prompt is displayed:

```
Select objects:
```

2. **At the prompt, position the cursor over the arc you drew earlier and
   click. Press Enter to end the object selection.**

The following prompt is displayed:

```
Specify first point of mirror line:
```

3. **At the prompt, hold down the Shift key and right-click.**

4. **On the Object Snap menu, choose Endpoint.**

 5. **Position the cursor near the end of the line that runs down the center
   of the cabinet and click when the Endpoint marker appears.**

The following prompt is displayed:

```
Specify second point of mirror line:
```

6. **Drag the crosshairs up and click.**

The arc is mirrored across to the other side of the cabinet and this
prompt is displayed:

```
Erase source objects? [Yes/No] <N>:
```

7. **Press Enter to keep the original arc that was drawn.**

The MIRROR command ends.

8. **Draw a line between the top endpoints of the two arcs to complete the
   top of the cabinet.**

The cabinet should look like Figure 1-11.

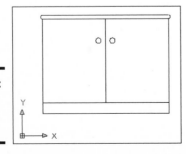

Figure 1-11:
The
completed
cabinet.

Annotating with Text and Dimensions

Annotation is used to explain features of your drawing to the shop floor so they know how to manufacture a part, or to include which materials or parts are purchased so the proper papers can be bought and put into inventory. You can place annotation in the form of text, dimensions, and leaders in your drawing. To find out more about annotation, see Book III.

Expressing yourself through text

AutoCAD and AutoCAD LT allow you to create text objects for placing titles in a drawing, populating revision blocks, or placing general notes about the design in the drawing. This set of steps explains how to create a single-line text object that will hold a basic title for the drawing of the cabinet:

1. **On the ribbon, click Home tab⇨Layers panel⇨down arrow on the Layers drop-down list⇨Text.**

2. **On the ribbon, click Annotate tab⇨Text panel⇨Single Line Text.**

The DTEXT command starts and the following prompt is displayed:

```
Specify start point of text or [Justify/Style]:
```

3. **At the prompt, right-click and choose Justify from the shortcut menu to specify a different justification for the text.**

The following prompt is displayed:

```
Enter an option [Align/Fit/Center/Middle/Right/TL/TC/
    TR/ML/MC/MR/BL/BC/BR]:
```

4. **At the prompt, right-click and choose MC from the shortcut menu to use the middle center justification.**

The following prompt is displayed:

```
Specify middle point of text:
```

5. **At the prompt, pick a point above the cabinet.**

The following prompt is displayed:

```
Specify height <0.2000>:
```

6. **At the prompt, type 2.5 and press Enter.**

The following prompt is displayed:

```
Specify rotation angle of text <0>:
```

7. **At the prompt, press Enter to accept the default rotation of 0.**

The in-place text editor is displayed.

8. **In the in-place text editor that appears in the drawing window at the point you picked in Step 5, enter** %%uCABINET 36x27 **and press Enter twice.**

The text string CABINET 36x27 is underlined and added to the text object.

Entering the drafting dimension

Rectangles in AutoCAD are four-sided objects with opposite sides parallel and the same length. In this set of steps you place two linear dimensions along the bottom and side of the cabinet:

1. **On the ribbon, click Home tab⇨Layers panel⇨down arrow on the Layers drop-down list⇨Dimension.**

2. **At the command prompt, type** DIMSCALE **and press Enter.**

The DIMSCALE system variable controls the size that dimensions are displayed in a drawing. The following prompt is displayed:

```
Enter new value for DIMSCALE <1.0000>:
```

3. **At the prompt, type** 12 **and press Enter.**

4. **On the ribbon, click Annotate tab⇨Dimensions panel⇨Linear.**

The DIMLINEAR command starts and the following prompt is displayed:

```
Specify first extension line origin or <select object>:
```

5. **At the prompt, press Enter to use the select object option.**

The following prompt is displayed:

```
Select object to dimension:
```

6. **At the prompt, select the bottommost line, which is part of the rectangle.**

The following prompt is displayed:

```
Specify dimension line location or [Mtext/Text/Angle/
    Horizontal/Vertical/Rotated]:
```

7. **At the prompt, drag the crosshairs down and pick a point below the cabinet.**

The linear dimension is created and the DIMLINEAR command ends.

8. **Press Enter to repeat the DIMLINEAR command.**

9. **At the prompt, hold down the Shift key and right-click.**

10. **On the Object Snap menu, choose Endpoint.**

11. **Position the cursor near the lower-right corner of the rectangle and click when the Endpoint marker appears.**

The following prompt is displayed:

```
Specify second extension line origin:
```

12. **At the prompt, type end and press Enter.**

13. **Position the cursor near the top endpoint of the arc on the right side of the cabinet and click when the Endpoint marker appears.**

The following prompt is displayed:

```
Specify dimension line location or [Mtext/Text/Angle/
     Horizontal/Vertical/Rotated]:
```

14. **At the prompt, drag the crosshairs to the right and pick a point to place the dimension.**

The drawing should look like the one shown in Figure 1-12.

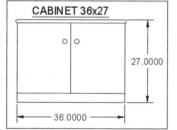

Figure 1-12:
Annotation
applied —
ready to
plot.

Fast Track to Plotting

After you've spent time creating and perfecting your design, it's time to share it with others. Typically, you'll produce a hard copy (paper copy) of the drawing or an electronic version that can be sent through e-mail and viewed by non-AutoCAD or AutoCAD LT users. To plot your drawing on an 8½-by-11-inch sheet of paper, follow these steps:

1. **On the Quick Access toolbar, click Plot.**

The Plot dialog box (see Figure 1-13) is displayed.

2. **In the Printer/Plotter area, click the down arrow on the drop-down list and select Default Windows System Printer.pc3.**

3. **In the Paper Size area, select Letter from the drop-down list.**

4. **In the Plot Area area, select Extents from the drop-down list.**

5. **In the Plot Offset area, select Center the Plot if it's not already selected.**

6. **In the Plot Scale area, select Fit to Paper if it's not already selected.**

7. **Click Preview.**

   A preview of the drawing is displayed on-screen (see Figure 1-14).

8. **Right-click the preview and choose Plot.**

   Congratulations! You've plotted your first project.

To find out more about plotting and outputting your drawings, see Book VII.

Figure 1-13: Preparing to output the drawing.

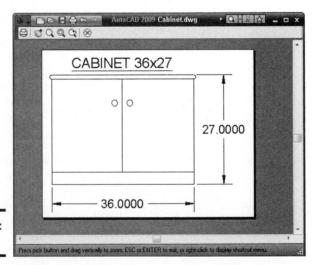

Figure 1-14: Success!

Chapter 2: Drawing on and in AutoCAD

In This Chapter

✔ Understanding the origins of AutoCAD

✔ Getting to know AutoCAD file formats

✔ Familiarizing yourself with AutoCAD LT

✔ Getting the lowdown on the newest of the new features

*P*ersonal computers revolutionized the drafting trade in the 1980s. Before that, some drafting was computerized, but the computers were mainframes or minicomputers (equivalent to the Stanley Steamers and Baker Electrics of the early days of motoring), well beyond the price range of most small architectural or engineering firms.

As a result, even as recently as 30 years ago, virtually all drafting was done by grizzled veterans wearing green eyeshades in smoke-filled back rooms. And not on computers!

In the old days, apprentice drafters (who were called draftsmen — or even draughtsmen — for it was a male profession) started their careers on the boards as tracers. Hard to believe, but there was a time before mechanical reproduction when every copy of an engineering drawing had to be traced, by hand, from an original. If you're being forced to master AutoCAD, you may grumble, but you should be thankful you do not have to go through a procedure like that!

Today, drafting is much easier because of AutoCAD. Maybe your boss is making you use AutoCAD, or you have to pass a course. But there are other reasons to use it — some of which may help you pass that course or get home from the office a little earlier. Here are some advantages to using CAD:

✦ **Precision:** AutoCAD is capable of precision to 14 significant digits (ask your math prof or your counselor why one digit should be more significant than another). That's way more precise than the best manual drafter could ever be.

✦ **Appearance:** AutoCAD-produced drawings are cleaner, easier to read when reduced, and more consistent than manually drafted drawings.

✦ **Reuse:** It's easy to copy and paste parts of drawings into other drawings for use on new projects.

✦ **Scalability:** You draw things full size in AutoCAD on an infinitely large drawing sheet. This not only eliminates the possibility of scaling errors as you draw, it also lets you print your drawings at any scale.

✦ **Sharing work:** Drawing files can be shared with consultants and contractors, who can add their own information without having to redraft the entire drawing.

✦ **Distributing work:** No more running dozens of prints and having them sent by courier to clients — using AutoCAD, you can electronically transmit drawings through e-mail or upload them to a shared Web space.

✦ **3D benefits:** You're not limited to 2D space; AutoCAD's drawing space is three dimensional, so you can create models of your projects and generate drawings from them.

Understanding AutoCAD Files and Formats

Like every other computer program under the sun, AutoCAD has its own digital file format. Unlike a Paint program, where the image is created by series of dots, CAD programs store the locations of objects in a database format. Every object in a drawing file — every line, arc, circle, dimension, and so on — is located in the 2D or 3D drawing space by using a Cartesian coordinate system. For more on coordinate systems in AutoCAD, see Chapter 7 later in this minibook.

AutoCAD is a *backward-compatible program.* This does not mean that you can open drawings backward or upside down. It simply means that files created in any release of AutoCAD can be opened in a same or newer release of AutoCAD. For example, if you have AutoCAD 2009, you can open a file created in any release of AutoCAD since the very first one. If you're working with an older release — say, AutoCAD 2002 — you can open files created in that release and older, but you can't open files created in AutoCAD 2004 or newer.

Unless indicated otherwise (for example, with an AutoCAD LT icon), when I mention AutoCAD 2009, I include AutoCAD LT 2009 as well. There are some differences between the two programs, but there are more similarities. In the next section, "Seeing the LT," I take a closer look at those differences.

Table 2-1 lists AutoCAD and AutoCAD LT releases and their file formats.

Table 2-1	AutoCAD & AutoCAD LT Releases and File Formats		
AutoCAD Release	*AutoCAD LT Release*	*Release Year*	*DWG File Format*
AutoCAD 2009	AutoCAD LT 2009	2008	AutoCAD 2007
AutoCAD 2008	AutoCAD LT 2008	2007	AutoCAD 2007
AutoCAD 2007	AutoCAD LT 2007	2006	AutoCAD 2007
AutoCAD 2006	AutoCAD LT 2006	2005	AutoCAD 2004
AutoCAD 2005	AutoCAD LT 2005	2004	AutoCAD 2004
AutoCAD 2004	AutoCAD LT 2004	2003	AutoCAD 2004
AutoCAD 2002	AutoCAD LT 2002	2001	AutoCAD 2000
AutoCAD 2000i	AutoCAD LT 2000i	2000	AutoCAD 2000
AutoCAD 2000	AutoCAD LT 2000	1999	AutoCAD 2000
AutoCAD Release 14	AutoCAD LT 98 and LT 97	1997	AutoCAD R14
AutoCAD Release 13	AutoCAD LT 95	1994	AutoCAD R13
AutoCAD Release 12	AutoCAD LT Release 2	1992	AutoCAD R12

Remember, newer releases can open older files, but older releases generally can't open newer files. However, all recent releases of AutoCAD give you the option of saving a drawing to four file formats. For example, in AutoCAD 2009's File menu, you can use the Save As command to save a drawing file back to the AutoCAD 2004 file format (which includes AutoCAD 2005 and AutoCAD 2006) or AutoCAD 2000 file format (which includes AutoCAD 2000i and AutoCAD 2002) so that anyone with those releases can open your drawing.

If you're using AutoCAD 2009, you can save drawing files so they can be opened with AutoCAD Release 14 (and AutoCAD LT 97/LT 98), which first came out over a decade ago, in early 1997. If you're using AutoCAD 2006 or earlier, you're limited to two file formats back. On the off chance you need to go back farther than that, go to www.autodesk.com/dwg and download a copy of Autodesk DWG TrueView — a conversion program that does not require AutoCAD or AutoCAD LT to be installed — and use it to save back to AutoCAD R14 DWG format.

If you receive a DWG file that was saved with a newer release than the one you're currently using, you can use Autodesk DWG TrueView to save the DWG file to a file format that you can open with your release of AutoCAD.

Seeing the LT

As most people quickly discover, AutoCAD is an expensive program. To soften the blow, several years ago Autodesk introduced a release of AutoCAD called AutoCAD LT that contained less functionality. An old rule called the 80-20 rule states that you get 80 percent of the functionality for 20 percent of the price. Nowadays, the 20 percent is more like 40 percent of the price of AutoCAD, but it's still a good deal if you're looking for a primarily 2D drafting program.

Mostly, this means if you never do (or never plan to do) 3D work in AutoCAD, you may — emphasis on *may* — be able to get away with AutoCAD LT and save some cash. In other parts of this book, I tell you more about AutoCAD LT. Watch for the icons in the margins and read the AutoCAD LT–specific notes to see whether you're in that category. From experience, I can safely say that if you have never used AutoCAD before, you will never miss most of the features that are not carried over from AutoCAD to AutoCAD LT. However, if you're a proficient AutoCAD user, and you find yourself in a new office that has AutoCAD LT rather than AutoCAD, there may be dozens of features you will sorely miss.

I tell you much more about the differences between AutoCAD and AutoCAD LT in Book IV.

Using AutoCAD's Latest-and-Greatest Feature Set

When I say *using AutoCAD's feature set,* I mean *really* using the program's features. It's all too common for offices to introduce new releases of AutoCAD to the drawing office without giving proper training or even demonstrations of new features to the people who have to use it. As a result, many drafters continue using the latest release in exactly the same way they used AutoCAD five or ten years ago. Through lack of interest (and because you're reading this book, I'm sure *you* do not fall into that category) or more likely lack of time, many AutoCAD users simply bypass features that can make them more efficient.

For example, it's very common to read the AutoCAD forums and see questions from people asking how to turn off this or that feature — often features such as the right-click shortcut menus that specifically relate to the command being run.

In this book I focus on some of the major new and enhanced features of recent releases, such as creating 3D solids (new in AutoCAD 2007), Multileaders (new in AutoCAD 2008), and Action Recorder (which is making its first appearance in AutoCAD 2009). I also make a strong pitch on using many of the other enhancements that have been introduced in recent releases.

AutoCAD 2009 is the release for those who have wanted to get into customizing AutoCAD but have been turned off by needing to know a programming language. These users will see their dreams start to come true in the form of Action Recorder. Along with Action Recorder, there are many enhancements for 2D and 3D users. Here's a brief rundown of what's new:

◆ Navigating a 3D model is now easier than before with the introduction of the ViewCube and SteeringWheels.

◆ The user interface has received a face-lift in the form of a new enhanced status bar, the addition of a menu browser, and a ribbon that is similar to the one found in Microsoft Office 2007.

◆ Properties for objects in a drawing can be accessed and queried by using the new Quick Properties panel and rollover tooltips.

◆ Actions can be recorded with Action Recorder to reduce the number of repetitive tasks that would normally need to be performed manually.

◆ Named views can be assigned movement and used to navigate a drawing through ShowMotion.

◆ Open drawings and layouts can be navigated visually with the help of thumbnails displayed in Quick View.

◆ Support to publish DWFx files has been added, which allows you to view and print DWFx files by using Windows Vista or Windows XP with the XPS Viewer.

◆ Layers can be accessed by using a modeless user interface which allows you to see layer changes automatically without the need to click Apply first.

Alas, LT still does not do 3D, so some of the nifty new features are not part of the package. However, LT has some new features (which have been available in AutoCAD for several releases).

Some of the new enhancements in AutoCAD LT this release are

◆ Fields are no longer limited to being only viewed; you can now create fields by using the FIELD command. Because AutoCAD LT does not support sheet sets, fields specific to sheet sets are not available for insertion.

◆ True color support has been added, allowing you to assign a true color to an object in the form of an RGB/HSL color or a Color Book color.

◆ Raster images can now be attached to a drawing file through the External References palette.

◆ You can create nonrectangular viewports on a layout and clip a rectangular viewport by using the VPCLIP command.

You can find more details on all these features throughout the rest of the book.

Chapter 3: Navigating the AutoCAD Interface

In This Chapter

✔ Starting AutoCAD

✔ Taking a quick tour around the AutoCAD window

✔ Talking (and listening) to AutoCAD

✔ Taking command

✔ Exploring program options

✔ Calling for Help

*H*ow do I start thee? Let me count the ways . . ." (with apologies to Elizabeth Barrett Browning).

So, let me count the ways. . . .

Starting the Application

As with all good Windows programs — and AutoCAD is a very good Windows program — you can make your drawings appear on-screen in numerous ways.

For a start, there's the . . . er, Start button, the one that Mick and the Rolling Stones sang about way back when Bill Gates launched Windows 95 on an unsuspecting world. To get to AutoCAD 2009 (or AutoCAD LT 2009), you click Start⇨(All) Programs⇨Autodesk⇨AutoCAD 2009⇨AutoCAD 2009. (You can tell you're at the end of the line because the last *AutoCAD 2009* has a unique program icon rather than a generic folder icon beside it.) Figure 3-1 shows the Windows Vista Start menu gradually revealing AutoCAD's program icon.

The Start button works, but one thing that working in Windows has taught us is to be efficient, and click-click-click-click-clicking is not the most direct way to go about opening the drawing editor. Wouldn't you know it — Microsoft and Autodesk between them have come up with several alternatives called — what else — shortcuts.

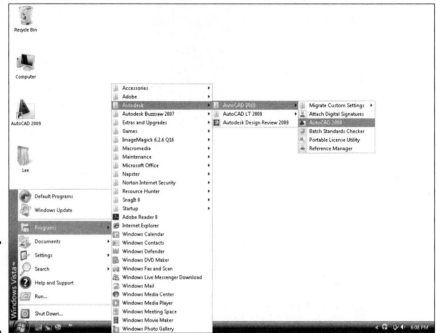

Figure 3-1:
Starting
AutoCAD
with the
Start button.

Creating Start menu shortcuts

If you're using Windows Vista or the Windows XP–style Start menu (as opposed to the Windows NT/2000–style Classic Start menu), you may have a large AutoCAD 2009 button in the left column — the *top-level menu* in Windows parlance — that lets you click once to start the program (see Figure 3-2).

This section of the Start menu can be used for the shortcuts to the programs that you commonly use. You can remove these icons by right-clicking them and choosing Remove from This List.

To add an AutoCAD shortcut to the top-level Start menu, right-click an existing AutoCAD shortcut icon and choose Pin to Start Menu. If you're using the Windows 2000, Windows XP, or Windows Vista Classic Start menu, you can still put a shortcut to AutoCAD on your Start menu by dragging the AutoCAD shortcut icon to your Start button (see Figure 3-3).

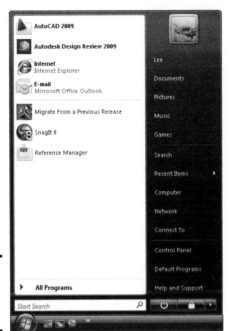

Figure 3-2:
Windows
Vista's Start
menu.

Figure 3-3:
The
Windows
Vista's
Classic Start
menu.

Using desktop shortcuts

By default, AutoCAD creates a shortcut on your desktop when you install the program. If you'd like more control over where AutoCAD opens — that is, where it's going to save your files or where it will look for files to open — you can modify the desktop shortcut so that it directs AutoCAD to a specific *Start In* folder. The following steps explain how:

1. **Right-click the AutoCAD icon on your desktop.**

All recent releases of AutoCAD create a desktop icon by default. Unless you've renamed it, yours will say "AutoCAD 2009" (or earlier).

2. **Choose Properties from the shortcut menu.**

A Properties window for the desktop icon appears, with the Shortcut tab current and the text in the Target field highlighted.

3. **Press Tab to highlight the text in the Start In field, and then type the path to your chosen folder.**

By default, the Start In folder is identified as UserDataCache, which actually points to a hidden folder under AutoCAD's install folder but saves new drawings to the My Documents folder, which can be confusing. It's best to create a new folder such as C:\DRAWINGS or to create a new folder under your My Documents folder that is used to store just drawing files. Note that the folder must exist before you can modify the shortcut.

4. **Click OK to save the changes to the icon.**

The icon is now configured to open in — and save to — the specified folder, but there's another thing you have to do from inside AutoCAD.

5. **Double-click the icon to start AutoCAD.**

AutoCAD starts, but it's still wired to the My Documents folder. You need to modify a system variable to rewire the program.

6. **Type REMEMBERFOLDERS and press Enter, and then type 0 and press Enter to change the setting of 1 to 0.**

When REMEMBERFOLDERS is set to 1 (the default), AutoCAD ignores the Start In folder specified in the desktop shortcut.

You can copy your desktop icon multiple times and set a different Start In folder for each one. Using a *Start In* folder is helpful when you are working on a few different projects and would like to avoid switching back and forth between the folders in which the projects are stored while opening and saving files.

Accessing files from Windows Explorer

If you need to work on drawings from multiple projects that may be in different folders all over your hard drive, sometimes it's easier to find the files in Windows Explorer than in AutoCAD's Open Drawing dialog box. (Okay, I find Windows Explorer handier than the My Computer window because you can more easily move from folder to folder.) Double-clicking a drawing file will open that file in AutoCAD.

Touring the AutoCAD Interface

As far as Windows programs go, AutoCAD 2009 is average in complexity. In fact, compared with its first Windows release (Release 12 for Windows), it's a marvel of simplicity. If you have a nodding familiarity with other Windows programs, you will not have any difficulty navigating AutoCAD's interface.

Title bars

AutoCAD (and most other programs as well) has three levels of title bars. The program itself has a title bar, each drawing window has a title bar, and individual ribbon panels, ribbon tabs, and palettes have their own title bars. Figure 3-4 gives you a sampling.

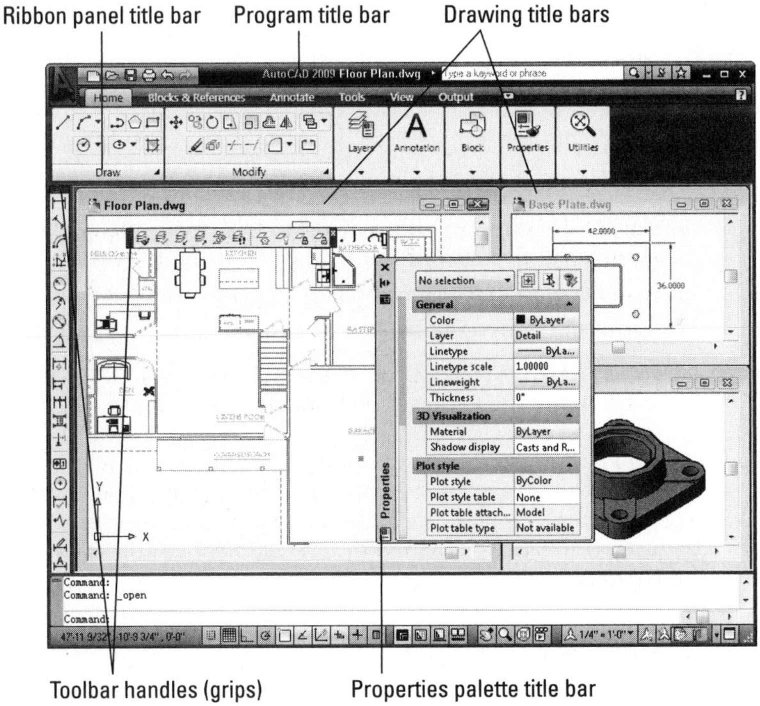

Ribbon panel title bar   Program title bar   Drawing title bars

Figure 3-4:
A whole mess of title bars.

Toolbar handles (grips)   Properties palette title bar

All three levels of title bars have more or less the same function:

✦ The *program title bar* tells you the name of the program, which you know already.

✦ The *drawing title bar* tells you the name of the drawing file you're working on and, optionally, its full path on your computer.

> ✦ The *ribbon panel* or *tab*, or the *palette* title bar tells you the name of a collection of tools.

The ribbon bar is a new interface element that organizes tools into panels and tabs. The ribbon bar in AutoCAD is similar to the one found in the applications that are part of Microsoft Office 2007.

Similarly, you can control the placement and state of most elements — the application and document windows, toolbars, and palettes — using the following actions:

> ✦ Double-click the program title bar to toggle between a maximized or windowed application window.

> ✦ Double-click the drawing title bar to switch a windowed drawing file to maximized within the application window. (This, of course, is a one-way trip, because after the file is maximized, it no longer has a title bar.)

> ✦ Double-click the handle on a toolbar or a palette's title to toggle between docked or floating locations. (To float a docked toolbar, double-click the handles at the left side or top.)

> ✦ Place the mouse pointer over an edge or corner of any unmaximized window or toolbar, or any undocked palette, to resize it.

> ✦ Click the X button at the top right (sometimes top left) to close a palette, toolbar, drawing window, or AutoCAD itself. If you've made any changes to a file, you'll be prompted to save your work first.

AutoCAD menus and menu browser

AutoCAD 2009 uses two menu interfaces: the menu browser and the standard menu bar (see Figure 3-5). The standard menu bar that was displayed in previous releases is not displayed by default.

To open the menu browser, click the Menu Browser button in the upper-left corner of AutoCAD's application window. After the menu expands in the menu browser, run your mouse pointer down the menu to select a command or expand one of the submenus (for example, File, Edit, or View). The first five or six menus are common to most Windows programs.

The menu browser is a new interface element that allows you to recover a little more of that precious commodity that you can never have enough of when working with AutoCAD, screen real estate. The menu browser in AutoCAD is similar to the one found in the applications that are part of Microsoft Office 2007.

Quick Access toolbar

Menu Browser

Menu bar

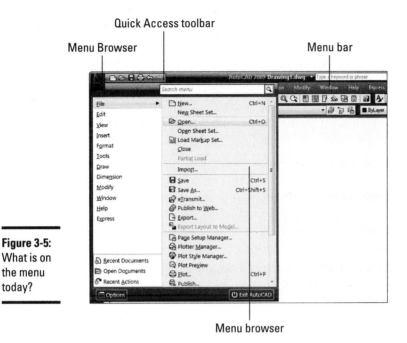

Figure 3-5:
What is on
the menu
today?

Menu browser

The second menu interface, the standard menu bar, was displayed in previous releases of AutoCAD but is not displayed by default in AutoCAD 2009. To
display the menu bar, right-click the Quick Access toolbar next to the Menu
Browser button and select Show Menu Bar. The menu bar is also displayed
by default if you make the AutoCAD Classic or AutoCAD LT Classic workspace current by clicking the Workspace Switching icon on the status bar
and choosing AutoCAD Classic (or AutoCAD LT Classic) from the menu that's
displayed. I cover the Workspace Switching button on the status bar later in
this chapter. For more information on workspaces, see Chapter 2 of Book IX.

Menus contain most of the commands you'll need in AutoCAD, but not all
commands are accessible this way. You may have to click a button on a toolbar or the ribbon, or even (oh, gasp, the horror!) type a command.

AutoCAD's menus are arranged as follows:

✦ **File:** Create new or open existing files; print or publish drawings; add
   plotters or plot styles; access utility commands; close the program

✦ **Edit:** Undo and redo; cut, copy, and paste; select objects; erase objects;
   find text in the drawing

   Oddly enough, AutoCAD's editing commands are not located on the Edit
   menu — you'll find them on the Modify menu. Watch out especially for
   Copy because there's one on each menu and they do different things!

✦ **View:** Redraw or regenerate the display; pan and zoom; create viewports; set viewpoints for 3D drawings; set render and viewport shading options

✦ **Insert:** Add blocks, raster images, and external references; insert objects from other programs; create hyperlinks

✦ **Format:** Establish layers, colors, linetypes, and lineweights; set appearance properties for text, dimensions, tables, and multileaders; establish drawing limits

✦ **Tools:** Display the Options dialog box or palettes to control drawing settings; edit blocks; use CAD standards; access customization tools

✦ **Draw:** Create primitive and complex objects; add text and hatching; define blocks and tables; create 3D surface and solid models (not in AutoCAD LT)

✦ **Dimension:** Add dimensions; format dimension styles

✦ **Modify:** Edit . . . er, modify existing drawing objects; check or match object properties

✦ **Express:** Additional tools and commands to create and modify all types of drawing objects (not in AutoCAD LT)

The Express menu is added as an option during the installation of the program. I strongly recommend that you install the Express Tools when you install AutoCAD. By default Express Tools is selected to be installed, but if you do not want to install it you can disable the feature during the install. Express Tools is available in only AutoCAD — not AutoCAD LT. I tell you more about the Express Tools in Book IX.

✦ **Window:** Cascade or tile open drawing windows; manage workspaces; lock down interface; select other open drawings

✦ **Help:** Access the built-in Help system; run the New Features Workshop; access help on the Web

AutoCAD toolbars

AutoCAD 2009 has 38 toolbars (not including the Express Tools toolbars), most of which are closed by default. When you start AutoCAD for the first time and choose AutoCAD Classic as your workspace, you see the Standard, Styles, Workspaces, Layers, and Properties toolbars docked at the top of the screen, between the menu bar and the drawing area. Docked at the left is the Draw toolbar, and at the right, the Modify and Draw Order toolbars. Assuming you installed the Express Tools, you might also see the three Express Tools toolbars floating near the top of the drawing area (see Figure 3-6).

Workspaces   Properties

Standard   Layers   Styles

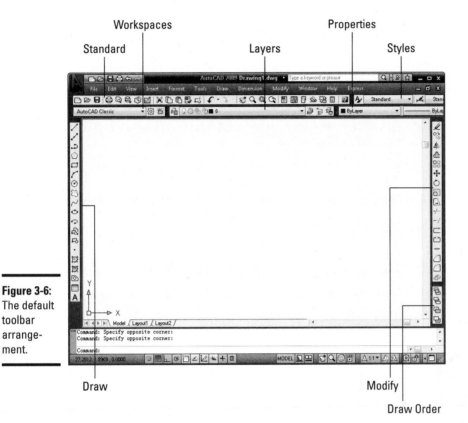

Figure 3-6:
The default
toolbar
arrange-
ment.

Draw   Modify

Draw Order

Stop and take a deep breath, you're not seeing things; some icons have been altered in this release. However, you will get through the transition to draft another day.

Unlike the menu system, toolbars contain a subset of AutoCAD's commands. Toolbars can be customized easily — I show you how in Book IX — and are a highly efficient way of working with the program.

You already know how to close toolbars. (*Hint:* It starts with an X.) The easiest way to open toolbars is to put your mouse pointer over any tool button and *right*-click. (Don't left-click or you'll run the command.) AutoCAD displays a list of toolbars; just select the one you want to open.

When you right-click a toolbar button, you see a listing of the toolbars that share the same menu as the toolbar you right-clicked; to see the toolbars in all loaded menus, right-click a button on the Quick Access toolbar and choose Toolbars (or on the menu browser or menu bar, click Tools menu⇨ Toolbars). From the Toolbars submenu, click the name of a loaded menu and then the toolbar you want to display.

To save constantly opening and closing toolbars, or having so many toolbars open that you can't see the drawing window, you can open a bunch and then save them as a workspace. I tell you how in Book IX.

Quick Access toolbar

The Quick Access toolbar (see Figure 3-7) is similar to one of AutoCAD's standard toolbars, except it can't be undocked. This toolbar allows you to quickly access a set of commands no matter what other user interface elements (toolbars, menus, palettes, or ribbon panels) are displayed. By default, the Quick Access toolbar contains the following commands, from left to right:

✦ **New:** Create a new drawing based on a template or from scratch.

✦ **Open:** Open a previously saved drawing file.

✦ **Save:** Save the current drawing. If the drawing was not previously saved, the Save Drawing As dialog box is displayed so you can enter a name and specify a location for the drawing file.

✦ **Plot:** Plot a drawing to a named plotter or an electronic file.

✦ **Undo:** Undo the most recent command or action.

✦ **Redo:** Undo the most recent undo operation.

Figure 3-7:
Commands
are just a
click away
with the
Quick
Access
toolbar.

Quick Access toolbar

The Quick Access toolbar is new to AutoCAD 2009 and is similar to the one found in the applications that are part of Microsoft Office 2007.

You can customize the commands that are displayed on the Quick Access toolbar. I tell you how in Book IX.

Palettes

AutoCAD 2004 introduced palettes, and they have become increasingly sophisticated with each release. Some dialog boxes from earlier releases, such as Object Properties & Layers, have been converted to palettes. Palettes have the advantage of staying open on-screen while you do other things (see Figure 3-8).

Ribbon tab

Ribbon   Ribbon panel   Layer palette

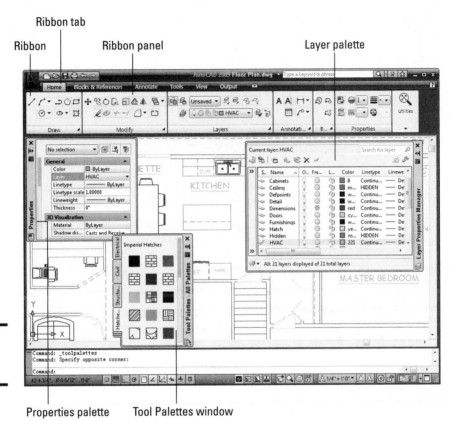

Figure 3-8:
A pile of
palettes.

Properties palette   Tool Palettes window

You open and close palettes by clicking their tool buttons on the ribbon bar
or a toolbar, from the menu system, or with a Ctrl+key combination indicated in the following list. AutoCAD has the following palettes:

✦ **Ribbon:** An interface that allows you to access commands that are
grouped by task, using panels and tabs. A panel organizes individual
commands, and tabs organize individual panels. The ribbon is a new
interface that expands on the Dashboard palette, which was introduced
in AutoCAD 2007. The ribbon can be docked horizontally along the top
of the program or vertically along the left or right side.

✦ **Properties:** Lists all properties of selected objects, including layer, color,
coordinates, and style (Ctrl+1). For more on object properties, see
Chapter 5 of this minibook.

✦ **Layer:** Use to create and manage the layers in a drawing. You can make
changes to the layers of a drawing in real time without having to apply
the changes first. For more on layers, see Chapter 4 of this minibook.

◆ **Tool Palettes window:** Use to access frequently used blocks, hatch patterns, and commands (Ctrl+3). For more on tool palettes, see Book VI.

◆ **QuickCalc:** Just like the one in your desk drawer, only it works with stuff you've drawn as well as with numbers (Ctrl+8). I cover AutoCAD's nifty built-in calculator in Book VI.

◆ **External References:** Manages the external reference files that are attached to a drawing (drawing (xref), raster image, DWF, or DGN files). I give you the scoop on working with external reference drawings, raster images, and DWF and DGN underlays in Book VI.

◆ **Sheet Set Manager:** Set up drawing sets by project for printing and electronic distribution (Ctrl+4). I tell you all about sheet sets and Sheet Set Manager in Book VII.

◆ **Markup Set Manager:** Review electronic markups of DWF files and incorporate necessary changes (Ctrl+7). Check out Book VIII for more on this feature.

◆ **AutoCAD DesignCenter:** Use to copy objects from one drawing to another (Ctrl+2). I tell you more about DesignCenter in Book VI.

◆ **Lights:** Lists all the lights in the current drawing that are used when rendering. (Not in AutoCAD LT.) I take a look at creating lights in Book V.

◆ **Materials:** Use to create and manage the materials in a drawing that are used when creating a rendering. (Not in AutoCAD LT.) I cover creating and using materials in Book V.

◆ **Visual Styles:** Use to create and manage the visual styles in a drawing that affect the appearance of the 3D objects in the current view. (Not in AutoCAD LT.) I explain the purpose of visual styles in Book V.

◆ **Advanced Render Settings:** Controls the settings used to create a rendering of a 3D model. (Not in AutoCAD LT.) I look at rendering in Book V.

◆ **DBConnect Manager:** Connect AutoCAD drawings with external database files (Ctrl+6). This is an esoteric area of AutoCAD, and I do not cover it in this book. (Not in AutoCAD LT.)

Anchoring and docking palettes allows you to keep the drawing window clear of floating palettes. (Docked palettes? Anchored palettes? Could there be some sailors at Autodesk?) An anchored palette is a combination of a docked palette (which does not keep moving around on you) and a palette that is set to auto-hide (which rolls up out of the way when you're not using it). To anchor any palette, right-click its title bar and choose Allow Docking. Then right-click the title bar again and choose Anchor Left < or Anchor Right >. The palette collapses and anchors its title bar along the left or right edge of the application window.

Okay, at this point you're probably dying to know what Ctrl+9 and Ctrl+0 do, so go ahead and try them. And do not panic when parts of your screen disappear — these keypresses are toggles, so just press Ctrl+9 again to bring back the command window, and press Ctrl+0 again to restore all your toolbars, palettes, title bars, and other screen components. I tell you about the command window shortly, in "The floating command window" section.

Pressing Ctrl+0 issues a command called CLEANSCREENON, which maximizes the program window, turns off the program title bar, all toolbars and palettes, and hides the Windows taskbar. This maximizes your screen real estate but leaves you with only the menu system and the keyboard to work with. Press Ctrl+0 again to run the CLEANSCREENOFF command to restore the previous state of the interface.

Drawing area

That big black (or maybe white) area that occupies almost 90 percent of AutoCAD's application window is the drawing window. Everything you draw goes here. Each drawing consists of two different spaces and each can have its own appearance. The two different spaces are model and paper. *Model space* is where you create the objects that represent the object you're drafting, typically in full scale; whereas *paper space* is where you go to lay out your drawing for plotting.

Keeping with the space theme, you can think of the model and paper spaces as parallel universes. I tell you a lot more about these two spaces in Chapter 5 of this minibook. At this time, you just need to recognize this part of the screen. The double-headed arrow in the lower-left corner of the drawing window (see Figure 3-9) is called the UCS icon. When it looks like this, you're in *model space*. And that is where you should be when you're drawing your buildings, valves, or bridges.

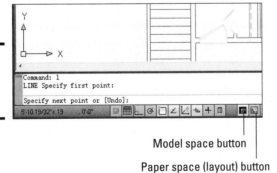

Figure 3-9:
The model
space UCS
icon.

Model space button

Paper space (layout) button

If your UCS icon looks like the one in Figure 3-10, you're in the other space — paper space. Paper space is also referred to as a *layout*, and a drawing can contain many different layouts to control the plotting of a drawing. This is where you put your drawing's title block, add notes and dimensions, and such. If your screen looks like Figure 3-10 rather than Figure 3-9, click the Model button on the application window's status bar or the Model tab at the bottom left of the drawing area to switch to model space.

Model and layout tabs

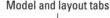
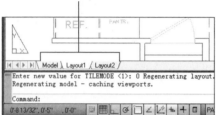

Figure 3-10:
The paper
space UCS
icon.

To display the Model and layout tabs, right-click the Model or Paper space button on the status bar and choose Display Layout and Model Tabs. If you want to remove the Model and layout tabs along the bottom of the drawing window (to save some additional drawing real estate), right-click one of the tabs and choose Hide Layout and Model Tabs. The Model and layout tabs are hidden and a Model and Layout button is added to the application window's status bar.

Crosshairs

The on-screen mouse pointer takes on two different appearances when you're working in AutoCAD: one when working in 2D and a second appearance when working in 3D. When you move the mouse outside the drawing window, it looks like the standard arrow pointer you see everywhere else in Windows. When you're inside the drawing window, it turns into a pair of lines that intersect at right angles, with a small square box (called the *pickbox*) where they cross. You can change the length of the crosshairs in the Options dialog box.

You also see the pickbox — without the crosshairs — when you're selecting objects. Many users find the default size (3 pixels square) too small, and I concur. To change the size of the pickbox, type **PICKBOX,** press Enter, and then set a new value. I find a 5-pixel-square pickbox a good compromise.

The floating command window

The *command line* — also known as the command *prompt* — is one of the things that makes AutoCAD *AutoCAD*. It's a throwback to earlier days, before dialog boxes, toolbars, and pull-down menus were a glint in Bill Gates's eye. The command line lives inside the *command window,* that area of text near the bottom of your screen.

AutoCAD is one of the few graphics programs where you still type — not just numbers and distances, but command names and options. Unlikely as it may seem (but obvious to grizzled AutoCAD old-timers), communicating with AutoCAD through the keyboard is one of the most efficient ways to interact with the program.

When you are new to AutoCAD, though, it's not an obvious thing to remember. That is why most CAD classrooms have a sign in big red letters that says *Watch the command line!* AutoCAD 2006 made a slight lurch into the 21st century with something called *dynamic input.* When enabled, AutoCAD displays interactive tooltips near the cursor; these show you a lot — but not all — of the command line information. You may still need to look down at the bottom of the screen to get the whole story. And if you're using AutoCAD 2005 or an earlier release, WATCH THE COMMAND LINE!

In AutoCAD 2006 and later you can turn the command window off and on with the Ctrl+9 toggle. I have even seen books that recommend that you turn it off, but I think this is a bad idea. The dynamic input tooltips do not show you everything that the command window does, so even if you are using AutoCAD 2006 or later, and at the risk of repeating myself . . . *watch the command line!* Maybe if I ask nicely it will help reinforce getting into a good habit of doing so, so *Please watch the command line.*

I tell you a bit more about the command window a few paragraphs from here. So you can stop watching it until then.

The status bar

At the bottom of the application window is the status bar. The status bar contains three elements. At the left side is the coordinates display, which shows the x-, y-, and z-values of wherever your crosshairs happen to be at a given moment. By default, the coordinates update as you move your mouse around. Also by default, the coordinate values are displayed as decimal numbers with four places of precision. If you change to a different type of drawing unit (I describe units in Chapter 4 of this minibook), the format of the coordinates changes to match the drawing's new unit type. To the right of the coordinates readout is a set of buttons where you can easily toggle a range of drafting modes such as snap, grid, and object snap. Table 3-1 lists the different drafting status toggles found on the status bar.

Table 3-1	Status Bar — Drafting Status Toggles	
Button	*Name*	*Description*
16.5000, 9.5000 , 0.0000	Coordinates	Toggles between the different coordinate display settings.
	Snap Mode	Toggles rectangular or polar snapping on and off.
	Grid Display	Toggles the display of the grid on and off.
	Ortho Mode	Toggles ortho mode on and off.
	Polar Tracking	Toggles polar tracking on and off.
	Object Snap	Toggles running object snaps on and off.
	Object Snap Tracking	Toggles object snap tracking on and off.
	Allow/Disallow Dynamic UCS	Toggles dynamic UCS on and off. (AutoCAD only)
	Dynamic Input	Toggles dynamic input on and off.
	Show/Hide Lineweight	Toggles the display of lineweights on and off.
	Quick Properties	Toggles the display of the Quick Properties panel on and off.

Many of the tools on the status bar are not just toggles that turn a setting on or off. They also allow you to access the settings for the various drafting tools they represent. To change the settings of a particular drafting tool, right-click its status bar button and choose Settings from the menu that appears. This displays a dialog box that you can use to change the behavior of the drafting tool.

AutoCAD 2009 and AutoCAD LT 2009 by default display a graphic for each of the drafting status toggles. You can right-click one of the drafting status toggle buttons and choose Use Icons to switch between the graphical and text buttons.

The Quick Properties panel allows you to access a defined set of properties for selected objects. You use the Quick Properties panel the same way you use the Properties palette, except you can customize the properties displayed for each object type. I talk more about using the Quick Properties panel in Chapter 2 of Book II, and how to customize which properties are displayed in Chapter 3 of Book IX.

Just to the right of the drafting status toggles are four clusters of buttons. Table 3-2 explains what each of these buttons is used for.

Table 3-2	**Status Bar — Drawing Navigation, Annotation Scaling, and User Interface Controls**	
Button	*Name*	*Description*
MODEL PAPER	Model or Paper Space	Toggles between the Model and Paper space, and switches Paper space layouts. If the layout tabs are not displayed, three buttons are displayed that allow you to switch between the Model and Paper spaces and switch between the different Paper space layout tabs.
	Minimize/Maximize and Viewport Navigation	Toggles between maximized and minimized viewport states and allows you to switch between different viewports.
	Quick View Layouts	Displays the Quick View layouts interface, which allows you to navigate to, plot, or publish a layout.
	Quick View Drawings	Displays the Quick View Drawings interface, which allows you to navigate the open drawings in the current session and to a layout in the open drawing.
	Pan	Allows you to reposition the view of the objects in the current viewport.
	Zoom	Allows you to increase or decrease the magnification of the current view.
	SteeringWheels	Displays the Steering Wheels.
	ShowMotion	Displays the ShowMotion interface, which allows you to navigate the named views in the current drawing. (AutoCAD only.)

(continued)

Table 3-2 *(continued)*

Button	Name	Description
	Lock/Unlock Viewport	Locks or unlocks a viewport so the scale assigned to the viewport can't or can be changed.
1/4" = 1'-0"	Viewport Scale	Displays and allows you to set the scale for the current viewport.
	Synchronize Annotation Scale	Indicates that the scale for the viewport is different from its annotation scale.
1:1	Annotation Scale	Allows you to set the current annotation scale, which is used to assign an annotation scale to the current viewport or define the scale for new annotation objects.
	Annotation Visibility	Toggles the display of objects that have been assigned an annotation scale. When on, it shows the annotative objects for all scales and not just the current scale. When off, only the objects assigned the current annotation scale are displayed.
	Automatically Add Scales	Toggles whether or not scales are automatically assigned to annotation objects.
	Workspace Switching	Allows you to switch between workspaces saved in the main and enterprise CUI files, and to change the workspace settings.
	Toolbar/Window Lock	Allows you to control whether toolbars and dockable windows (palettes) can be moved (floated) around the screen, or whether they are stationary (docked).

Finally, at the right end of the status bar, comes the status bar tray. You should see anywhere from three to more icons here; their functions are listed in Table 3-3.

Table 3-3	Status Bar — Tray Icons	
Button	*Name*	*Description*
	Performance Tuner	Allows you to access The Performance Tuner log and dialog box. (AutoCAD only.)
	Plot Notification	Allows you to access information about recent plotted files and to receive information about a job that is being processed in the background.
	Trusted Autodesk DWG	Allows you to identify whether the current drawing was created with an application developed by Autodesk or a non-Autodesk product.
	External Reference Notification	Allows you to identify that External Reference drawings are contained in the drawing and notifies you when the files have been updated and need to be reloaded. The notification balloon allows you to reload the file that has changed without needing to open the External Reference palette.
	CAD Standards Notification	Allows you to identify that a drawing has CAD Standards associated with it, access the CAD Standards tools, and receive notifications when the drawing becomes out of sync with the associated CAD Standards files. (AutoCAD only.)
	Unreconciled New Layers	Allows you to identify which layers have been recently added to the drawing and have not been reconciled yet.
	Data Link	Allows you to identify that a table object in the drawing is linked to a data source. If the original information that the table points to is changed, you'll be notified that the table has become out of sync.

(continued)

Table 3-3 *(continued)*

Button	Name	Description
	Validate Digital Signatures	Allows you to identify whether the current drawing has been digitally signed, and if the digital signature is valid.
	Application Status Bar Menu	Allows you to toggle the display of the drawing status bar and control the display of other buttons on AutoCAD's status bar.
	Clean Screen	Allows you to enable or disable Clean Screen.

AutoCAD supports two status bars: application and drawing. By default, only the application status bar is enabled and displays the buttons and tray icons that I previously mention in this section. You can turn on the drawing status bar, which displays a subset of the tray icons and status bar options specific to each open drawing below the drawing window. To display the drawing status bar, click the Application Status Bar menu and choose Drawing Status Bar.

Communicating with Your Software

So now you know what everything is . . . but what do you do with it? You see at the beginning of this chapter that there are a few ways to start AutoCAD. Now you're about to discover that you can do just about anything in multiple ways in AutoCAD, beginning with how you speak AutoCADese.

The command line

Not to be confused with the LINE command, the *command line* is the place where AutoCAD talks back to you (see Figure 3-11). Sometimes it just echoes what you type (it's easy to assume that it's not very bright), but more often it engages you in a helpful — if occasionally cryptic — dialog box.

Typically, you start your conversation with AutoCAD by issuing a command. If you want to draw something new, AutoCAD usually starts by asking where you would like it to start. You choose a point, and then AutoCAD asks how big you want it. You tell AutoCAD, and the program draws the object.

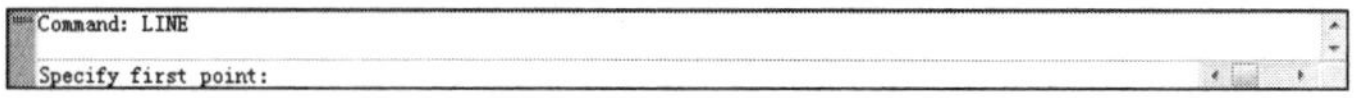

Figure 3-11:
The LINE
command
on the
command
line in the
command
window.

```
Command: LINE
Specify first point:
```

If you want to edit something that is already there, you issue a command —
for example, MOVE. AutoCAD asks you to select the objects to move. You
select them and press Enter to confirm your selection. The command now
starts prompting — for example, the MOVE command prompts for a base
point (a *from* point) and a second point (a *to* point).

You can switch off the display of the command window, but I think that is a
bad idea. There is just not enough feedback from dynamic input alone. The
best thing to do is to use both, the command line and dynamic input together.

Dynamic input

You might have the wrong impression about dynamic input by the way I
have talked about it, but truth be told it's a great addition to AutoCAD. The
issue is that it changes the way you think about working with AutoCAD when
entering values or choosing coordinate points, so it will probably be easier
for the newbies than it is for the old-timers to adjust to the feature.

When dynamic input is enabled (by clicking the Dynamic Input button on the
status bar), AutoCAD displays tooltips near the crosshairs whenever a command is active or you move the crosshairs across the drawing window. When
AutoCAD is expecting you to choose a point, the tooltip displays a constantly
updating coordinate readout (x and y coordinates only). If AutoCAD needs
more information, such as the radius of a circle, you can type the desired
value into the tooltip.

Dynamic input is highly configurable. Right-click the Dynamic Input button
on the status bar and choose Settings to display the Dynamic Input tab of
the Drafting Settings dialog box. You can turn options on and off here and
further refine them by clicking the Settings buttons under Enable Pointer
Input and Enable Dimension Input.

Dialog boxes

AutoCAD has two types of dialog boxes — modal and modeless. *Modal* dialog boxes are the regular, old dialogs you see in every Windows program. They pop up whenever you save a new drawing, or want to format your units, or make some drawing settings. *Modal* dialog boxes such as Save, Open, and Plot take command of AutoCAD. You can't do anything else while one of these dialog boxes is open.

Modeless dialogs *can* stay open while you do other things in AutoCAD. They're so unique, in fact, that they're not even called dialog boxes. They're called *palettes,* and you've already found out a thing or two about them. AutoCAD has over a dozen modeless dialog boxes — or palettes — and I highlight their importance at appropriate places in the text.

Running AutoCAD Commands

Even when you execute commands by using menus from the menu browser, menus from the menu bar, or toolbars, there are still significant differences between AutoCAD and other Windows applications.

Grasping the AutoCAD difference

The fundamental difference with AutoCAD is that AutoCAD expects you to take part in a conversation. When you tell the program you want to move something, AutoCAD asks what you want to move, where you want to move it from, and where you want to move it to.

Most of this conversation takes place in dialog boxes and the dynamic input tooltips. One of the delights of AutoCAD is the number of different ways the program has for doing what you ask it to do. All I can do at this point is refer you to the chapters to come (starting with the early chapters of Book II).

Repeating a command

Oftentimes in AutoCAD, you want to perform the same action on different objects. You might, for example, want to move a bunch of linework to a different layer, and then move a bunch of text to a third layer.

Pressing Enter or pressing the spacebar at a blank command prompt repeats the last command. You can also right-click and choose the last command from the top of the shortcut menu.

You can press the up-arrow key to retrieve the previous command. If you continue to press the up-arrow key, you can step back even farther in the list of previously used commands in the drawing. To run the command, press Enter.

A nifty feature was added to AutoCAD 2004's Options dialog box, and you can use it in any 2004 or later release of AutoCAD or AutoCAD LT. On the User Preferences tab, in the Windows Standard Behavior area, click the Right-Click Customization button. In the dialog box, select the Turn on Time-Sensitive Right-Click box. Click Apply & Close, and then click OK. Now, if you right-click within a quarter-second (the default value in the dialog box), you get a carriage return, just as if you had pressed the Enter key or spacebar. If you keep the right mouse button pressed down for longer than a quarter-second, you get whatever Windows shortcut menu is appropriate to the current command.

Book I Chapter 3

Navigating the AutoCAD Interface

Canceling a running command

To cancel a command, simply press Esc. If you're a long-time user of AutoCAD, and have been away for . . . well, a long time, you may be used to pressing the Ctrl+C combination that issued a Cancel in all DOS releases of AutoCAD. If you're not one of those grizzled old-timers, you know that Ctrl+C copies selected objects to the Windows Clipboard. Whatever your origins, remember that Esc cancels whatever is happening in the drawing window.

Invoking transparent commands

Most AutoCAD commands are meant to be run without interruption. You would not, for example, start drawing a line and then decide in the middle of the line sequence that you wanted to draw a circle. Well, maybe you would, but trust me, it's not very efficient.

Other times, however, it's efficient to run one command inside another. For example, you might be placing a very long linear dimension, and you would like to be able to zoom in closely on one end of the object to be dimensioned, and then zoom in closely again on the other end.

You can do this with AutoCAD's display commands, as well as with some of the drafting settings, because these commands can be run *transparently*. A transparent command is one that can be executed in the middle of another command.

You may, for example, be in the middle of creating a linear dimension when you realize you're zoomed out too far and are unable to choose the defining points accurately; so you go to the Standard toolbar or ribbon bar and choose one of the Zoom commands. You execute the Zoom command, and when you're done, AutoCAD takes you back to the command you were running. The same thing happens with toolbars and ribbon panels — just click a button, and your top-level command is suspended while the secondary command executes.

AutoCAD system variables

Not everyone uses AutoCAD the same way. Despite its hundreds of commands, users want those commands to operate in specific ways. AutoCAD accommodates with an array of system settings — called *system variables* — that cover nearly all the bases. Many system variables are toggles — they have a value of either 0 or 1, meaning they're either enabled or disabled. For example, the system variable MIRRTEXT controls what happens to text when a group of drawing objects is mirrored. If MIRRTEXT is enabled (that is, set to 1), any text in the group is also mirrored — it reads backward on the screen. If MIRRTEXT is set to 0, the objects, including the text object, are all mirrored, but the text itself is not mirrored, so it reads the right-way around instead of appearing backwards. However, the justification of the text is altered, resulting in left-justified text being right justified after being mirrored.

Other system variables can have different settings (more than simply off and on), and still others can store values that remain intact until they're replaced with new values.

For information on AutoCAD's system variables, go to the online help.

You can mimic this behavior at the command prompt by typing an apostrophe before the command. The apostrophe is a sign to AutoCAD that what follows is to be executed transparently. Many commands can be run transparently, including most of the display commands. Go ahead and experiment: Just type an apostrophe and then the name of a command, and see what happens.

Reaching for AutoCAD Help

I hope that the *AutoCAD 2009 & AutoCAD LT 2009 All-in-One Desk Reference For Dummies* will answer most of your questions about using AutoCAD. Nevertheless, there will be times when you want to go to the source of all that is AutoCAD. Here are some ways of accessing AutoCAD's Help system:

✦ At a blank command prompt, enter **?**

✦ From the Help menu, choose Help

✦ Press the F1 function key at any time

✦ From the command prompt, type **HELP**

Using built-in Help

Most of the time, AutoCAD's Help system is *context sensitive*. If you're in the LINE command and press F1 (or choose Help⇨Help), the Help system will launch and take you to information about the LINE command.

You can get context-sensitive help at the command line, too, by entering an apostrophe and then a question mark (that is, '?).

Tooltips

Tooltips are by far one of the most basic methods of getting help from a software program. AutoCAD is no different; tooltips are used throughout the user interface and provide information about a command button on a toolbar, an object in a drawing, or a control in a dialog box. To display a tooltip, you simply point the cursor at the command button on a toolbar or almost any other object and let the cursor hover over the object for a moment. After a brief period, a small box appears with text that explains what the object is or does in the case of a command button or control if it is clicked. Figure 3-12 shows a few of the different tooltips found in AutoCAD.

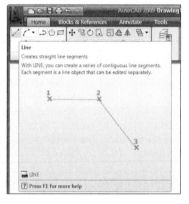

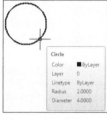

Figure 3-12:
Help is available right at the tip of the cursor.

Tooltips in AutoCAD 2009 have been greatly enhanced over what was available in previous releases. Tooltips now display information about the object in the drawing window below the crosshairs, as well controls in dialog boxes. In previous releases, to access the explanatory text for a control in a dialog box, you had to click the ? in the upper-right corner of the dialog box and then click the control; now you just let the cursor hover over the control.

Following is an overview of the different tooltips in AutoCAD:

✦ **Command and dialog box tooltips:** Tooltips that display information about a button or control on a toolbar or ribbon panel, a menu item on the menu browser, and controls in a dialog box.

✦ **Extended tooltips:** Extended tooltips go above and beyond just displaying plain textual messages. Extended tooltips are used to provide additional information about a command or control in a dialog box. When the cursor continues hovering over a command or control after the tooltip is initially displayed, the tooltip expands to reveal additional information about the object. If an object has an extended tooltip assigned to it, the additional text and even images related to the object are displayed.

✦ **Rollover tooltips:** Tooltips that display the values for a specified set of properties for an object when the crosshairs hover over an object in the drawing window. To find out more about how to customize which properties are displayed on a rollover tooltip, see Book IX, Chapter 3.

✦ **Other tooltips:** Some of the other tooltips display a thumbnail of a drawing layout when the Model and Layout tabs are displayed, preview images and details for a sheet in Sheet Set Manager, and the descriptions of the fields in the Properties palette.

For more on controlling the display of many of the different tooltips that are in AutoCAD, see Book IX, Chapter 2.

When a tooltip is displayed, and Press F1 for More Help is displayed in the tooltip; do as it asks and press F1 to find out more about the user interface element. The online Help system opens and displays a topic related to the object associated with the tooltip.

InfoCenter

InfoCenter (see Figure 3-13) replaces what was called the Info Palette and combines the functionality of the Communication Center in one place. The InfoCenter is located in the upper-right corner of AutoCAD on the title bar and allows you to search for information in the online Help system as well as get information from your favorite blogs or Web sites that post content in an RSS (Really Simple Syndication) file format. If you find a specific topic or entry of interest, you can flag it as a favorite, which allows you to easily go back to the topic at a later date.

Search button Communication Center

InfoCenter Search Field   Favorites

Figure 3-13: InfoCenter is your one-stop shop for getting help from AutoCAD.

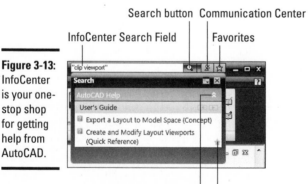

Expand/collapse section Link to Favorites toggle

Finding online resources

Much as I would like to think this book is all you'll ever need, I recognize that there are millions of one-off requirements that no book can possibly cover comprehensively. One of the best resources available is Autodesk's own discussion groups. To locate the discussion groups on Autodesk's Web site, go to www.autodesk.com, click Communities and then click Visit the Discussion Groups to find your way to a shopping list of discussion groups based on AutoCAD (or AutoCAD LT). You can also do a search on the keywords *Discussion Groups*.

Book I
Chapter 3

Navigating the
AutoCAD Interface

Chapter 4: All about Files

In This Chapter

✔ **Reviewing AutoCAD's file types**

✔ **Starting a new drawing**

✔ **Saving your drawing**

✔ **Saving to different file types**

✔ **Opening existing drawings**

✔ **Closing windows**

✔ **Passing File Management 101**

✔ **Backing up**

AutoCAD not only needs hundreds of files to keep itself going, it also generates more files than you can shake a mouse at. All these files are important, but none is more important than DWG — the drawing file itself.

In this chapter I cover all the important files that you are likely to run into — and one or two that you are not likely to run into but should still know what they are.

It's also important that both AutoCAD and you are able to *find* the files you both need to work together. AutoCAD can usually take care of itself; after it's initially installed, all the files the program needs are in appropriate places. But *you* need to be able to find your drawing files too, and AutoCAD by itself is not much help there. Left alone, it will save *all* your drawings in your My Documents folder. It's up to you to organize your storage space, and I give you some ideas at the end of the chapter about how to go about getting organized.

File Types in AutoCAD

AutoCAD's drawing (DWG) files contain everything that you draw, and a bit more besides. In addition to all those lines, arcs, circles, text, and dimensions, your DWG files also contain:

+ Style definitions for things such as dimensions and text

+ Properties associated with any graphical objects, such as color, layer, and linetype

✦ Layer definitions, each of which includes such things as default color, linetype, plot style; whether or not the objects on the layer are printed/plotted

Not contained in the DWG file itself, but necessary for it to display properly, are associated files that define the fonts used by the text and dimension styles, hatch and linetype patterns, plot-style tables, and more. I cover those associated files in more detail a few paragraphs from now.

A lot of file interaction is going on when you work in AutoCAD. An important aspect of drafting in AutoCAD — or any CAD system — is having a good version of your drawing to fall back on, in case bad things happen to it. Luckily, AutoCAD by default creates a backup version of a drawing file every time a drawing is saved. When you use the Save command, AutoCAD makes a copy of your drawing (let's call it FOO.DWG) and renames the copy FOO.BAK. After the backup is created, AutoCAD takes all the changes that you've made and that are stored in memory, and spoons them into a drawing file. When it's finished remembering everything, it saves a new version of FOO.DWG.

Not all programs will do this for you, but AutoCAD does, as long as you do not tell it not to. I cover that a bit more later in the chapter.

One thing that puzzles new users to AutoCAD is the fact that not all the data needed to generate a drawing is included in the drawing file. Problems do not arise if you open your drawings only on your own computer, but they can crop up if you ever have to send your drawings to someone else. If that someone else — a client, a contractor, your teacher, or your boss — does not have all the same files on his or her computer that you did on your computer when you made the drawing, then the drawing is not going to look the same as it did for you when you drew it.

Here are some of the files external to your DWG file that must be available on every computer on which the drawing will be opened:

✦ **Fonts (SHX or TTF or both files):** AutoCAD comes with over 70 vector font files (SHX extension). These fonts are installed in AutoCAD's own subfolders in the Program Files folder (usually) on your C: drive. AutoCAD can also use TrueType (TTF) fonts, which are part of Windows itself and which live in the Fonts folder of your operating system. I tell you more about fonts in Book III.

Be careful about using nonstandard fonts — either SHX fonts that did not come with AutoCAD or TTF fonts that did not come with the Windows operating system. If you have to send your drawings to someone whose computer does not have the fonts you used, AutoCAD will substitute any missing font with the specified alternate font. Typically when AutoCAD uses an alternate, the accuracy of the drawing is not compromised but it will not look the same as it did on your machine.

✦ **Hatch patterns (PAT files):** Hatch pattern files are used to generate the cross-hatching that indicates which objects are cut in a section view or specific areas on maps or plans. (By default, AutoCAD uses a file named acad.pat; AutoCAD LT's version is named acadlt.pat.) Hatching is covered in depth in Book III.

✦ **Linetype patterns (LIN files):** Linetype pattern files are used to control the pattern that linework appears in. This file defines noncontinuous linetypes such as center, dashed, and hidden, which are used in standard drafting. (By default, AutoCAD uses a file named acad.lin; AutoCAD LT's version is named acadlt.lin.) I talk about linetypes in Chapter 6 of this minibook.

The acad and acadlt hatch pattern and linetype definition files are for use with imperial units. If you are working in metric units, you use the acadiso.pat (acadltiso.pat) and acadiso.lin (acadltiso.lin) files. If you start your drawings correctly, these files are available automatically.

✦ **Plot-style tables (CTB or STB files):** Plot styles are collections of settings that tell your output device (a highfalutin' way of saying printer) what thickness drawing objects should be plotted at, or what properties are to be assigned to drawing objects when plotting a drawing. (Don't worry about plotting for now — I cover it in much greater depth in Book VII. You can worry about it then!) Plot-style *tables* are the files where all the plot styles live, and AutoCAD needs to find them or your drawing will not plot properly. Plotting in AutoCAD is like printing in other Windows-based applications, except you are working with larger pages than 8½ x 11 (A4) and 11 x 17 (A3).

✦ **Image files:** AutoCAD can display and print raster images that are placed in drawing files, but the files do not become part of the drawing file itself. If AutoCAD can't find them (say, you forget to send them with the drawing file), you get a rectangle showing the name of the missing file instead. I cover working with raster image files in Book VI.

✦ **Other DWG files:** You can attach drawings to other drawings so you do not have to keep redrawing the same things over and over again. Those attached drawings are called external references (or xrefs for short). The idea is that if you change something in a referenced drawing, it automatically changes in all drawings to which it is attached. It's a useful feature, but it can be complicated to understand at first (don't worry — I reveal all in Book VI!). The point here is that if AutoCAD can't find the referenced drawing file, you get another one of those missing file messages in addition to a helpful string of text that appears in the drawing to let you know that a referenced drawing is missing.

✦ **Underlay files:** In recent releases, the number of external files that you can reference has increased. In addition to being able to attach raster images and xrefs (drawing files), you can attach Design Web Format (DWF and DWFx) files and MicroStation DGN files. I explain how underlay files work in Book VI.

Support for publishing and attaching DWFx files is new in AutoCAD 2009. I talk more about the benefits of DWFx later in Book VIII.

To summarize, if you are sharing drawings with others outside your office

✦ You usually do not have to worry about the font, hatch pattern, or line-type files if you are using the standard fonts and patterns that come with AutoCAD.

✦ You may have to worry about plot-style tables if you are using custom ones.

✦ You usually do have to worry about images and external references because you create those files so they're not part of AutoCAD.

You can use the eTransmit feature to package your drawing files and all the files that your drawings are dependent on before sharing them with a client. I cover eTransmitting drawings in Book VII.

Starting a New Drawing

If all that information seems a little daunting at this point, do not worry — all will be revealed in these pages. In the meantime, it's just possible that you might want to get your hands dirty and draw something. So let's take a look at a trio of ways to start a new drawing in AutoCAD.

If you are using AutoCAD out of the box (AutoCAD veterans call this the "out-of-the-box experience"), when you click New on the Quick Access toolbar, you get the Select Template dialog box (see Figure 4-1). The New button starts the NEW command.

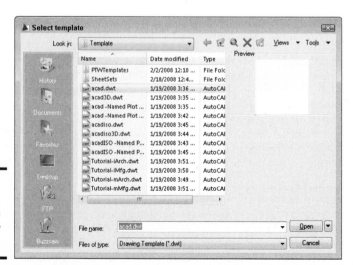

Figure 4-1:
Select a template to start a new drawing.

An alternate command that you can use instead of NEW is called QNEW. Who knew? Here is what QNEW can do for you. If you do not change any settings in AutoCAD, using QNEW always displays the Select Template dialog box like the NEW command does. Now, if you always start a drawing by using the acad.dwt template (not the best idea, but read on), you have to click acad.dwt, and then click Open. That can get a bit tedious. But if you go into the Options dialog box and click the Files tab, you can identify a default template file (maybe even acad.dwt). Doing so will tell AutoCAD to start a new drawing by using the specified template every time. I explain how to assign a template to the QNEW command in Book VIII.

A further wrinkle in starting a new drawing occurs if the system variable called STARTUP is enabled. By default, STARTUP is disabled or set to 0; for more on system variables, see the sidebar "AutoCAD system variables" in Chapter 3 of this minibook.

If STARTUP is enabled (or set to 1), the first time you start AutoCAD you see a Startup dialog box (see Figure 4-2).

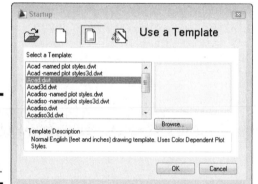

Figure 4-2:
The Startup
dialog box
you see if
STARTUP=1.

From this dialog box, you can choose to open an existing drawing or start a new drawing in one of three ways: starting from scratch, using a template, or employing a wizard. After the first drawing in an AutoCAD session has been opened by using any of these methods, subsequent uses of the QNEW command will display the Create New Drawing dialog box. This dialog box looks suspiciously like the Startup dialog box — it gives you the same three choices for starting a new drawing, but the icon for opening an existing drawing is dimmed.

The STARTUP system variable must be set to 1 for the Startup and Create New Drawing dialog boxes to appear when you start AutoCAD or when you use the QNEW command. If you see the Select Template dialog box only when you start AutoCAD or use QNEW, your STARTUP variable is disabled.

I suggest you leave STARTUP set to 0, because the other options for starting a new drawing — that is, from scratch or using a wizard — are much less efficient, as I explain now.

Starting from scratch

When you start a new drawing from scratch, you are starting AutoCAD with no preconfigured settings. The drawing has no layers other than Layer 0, nor does it have any text styles, table styles, multileader styles, or dimension styles other than STANDARD, and no predefined layouts. When you choose this option, you really do start from scratch, and you must spend a fair amount of time making settings that you could easily make once and save in a template file. I explain the importance of template files later in this chapter.

For simple sketching or working out design ideas, it's okay to start from scratch, but when you are working on production drawings, it's a lot more efficient to use a template. But even starting from scratch is better than using a wizard.

Using a wizard

Wizards are often powerful and mystical, but the drawing setup wizard is a few tricks short of being truly magical. I do not mean to disparage all wizards — AutoCAD has many useful wizards — but the wizard available for starting a new drawing for you is not one of them. You can choose from two wizards: Quick and Advanced (see Figure 4-3).

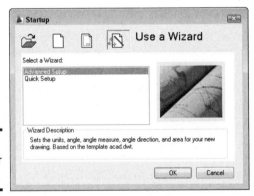

Figure 4-3: Choose your wizard.

The problem with the wizards — both of them — is that the settings they control for you are not useful. Both wizards will set these values:

✦ **Units:** Choose the format and precision for your linear drawing units (see Figure 4-4). Regardless of the format you choose, the units are based on inches if you live in the U.S. or millimeters if you live outside the U.S.

✦ **Area:** Specify the drawing area by its length and width. You arrive at the correct figures by multiplying the intended plot scale of the drawing by the dimensions of the paper on which it will be plotted.

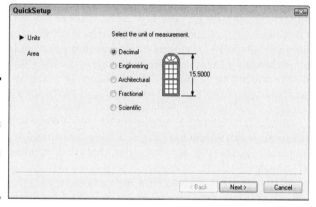

Figure 4-4:
Both wizards (this is the Quick one) ask you to select the unit type.

In addition to units and area, the Advanced Setup wizard also sets these values:

✦ **Angle:** Choose the format and precision for angular measure. The default type of angular measure (and the easiest by far for most people to work with) is decimal degrees.

✦ **Angle measure:** Specify where in the circle 0 degrees lies. By default, 0 degrees lies due east. If you do not have a compass handy, you can also think of this direction as 3 o'clock, or to the right in a dead horizontal alignment.

✦ **Angle direction:** Specify whether angles are measured in a clockwise or counterclockwise direction. By default, angles are measured in a counterclockwise direction, so if 0 degrees lies on an east-pointing horizontal axis, 90 degrees is straight up, 180 degrees is horizontal pointing west (9 o'clock for you clock watchers), and 270 degrees is straight down.

Nearly all major industries go with the AutoCAD defaults for angular measure — that is, 0 degrees is on an easterly horizontal axis and angles are measured in a counterclockwise direction. One exception to this rule is in surveying, where 0 degrees usually points north and angles are measured in a clockwise direction. But if you are not a surveyor (and maybe even if you are), do not change the settings for angular measure from their defaults, because it can make editing the drawing a nightmare.

The problem with a drawing setup wizard is that there are so many settings that define a drawing it's impossible to capture them all in a single wizard. By far your best bet is to use one of the drawing templates that AutoCAD provides or create your own drawing template with the settings that you'll want to use when creating a new drawing. I talk briefly about using drawing templates next and go into more detail about drawing templates in Book VIII.

Using a drawing template

Drawing templates are drawing files with collections of settings and styles already defined. You should regard the settings that come with AutoCAD as starting points; some of them may be very close to what you want, but you need to add the other 5 or 10 percent yourself.

Drawing templates *are* drawing files — the only difference is the last letter of the file extension: DWG for regular drawing files and DWT for drawing templates. By default, AutoCAD is configured to look for drawing templates in the Documents and Settings folder for the current user profile, although you can tell the program to look elsewhere. If your company has several drafters, you may want to create a single set of drawing templates and share them from a single location on the network, if one is available.

AutoCAD comes with just a little over ten drawing templates, but do not worry, you do not have to go through them all to find a useful one! Nearly half of them come in two versions, one configured for color-dependent plot styles and one for named plot styles (I explain more about plot styles in Book VII.)

Unless you are told otherwise by your boss or teacher, you should probably choose one of the color-dependent plot-style drawing template files. Color dependent means the colors of the objects in the drawing determine how thick the linework will be plotted. Named plot styles, on the other hand, are independent of object color, and are specific properties applied to those objects. I recommend that you stick with color-dependent plot styles because AutoCAD has used this system since the 1980s to plot drawings, and not all objects support named plot styles. But I have more to say about all of that in Book VII.

Following are the types of drawing templates:

✦ **Standard drawing templates:** AutoCAD comes with several standard drawing templates that are good for both 2D and 3D drawings. The drawing templates are basic, but they lay a good foundation. Two drawing templates are available for imperial units (acad.dwt and acad -Named Plot Styles.dwt), and two drawing templates are available for metric units (acadiso.dwt and acadISO -Named Plot Styles.dwt). Both acad.dwt and acadiso.dwt are designed for color-dependent plot styles; the other two drawing templates, as their name implies, are designed for named plot styles. The drawing templates that come with AutoCAD LT are acadlt.dwt, acadlt -Named Plot Styles.dwt, acadiso.dwt, and acadltISO -Named Plot Styles.dwt.

✦ **3D drawing templates:** These drawing templates have some settings specific to 3D modeling. Four 3D drawing templates are available: two imperial (acad3D.dwt and acad -Named Plot Styles3D.dwt) and two metric (acadiso3D.dwt and acadISO -Named Plot Styles3D.dwt). Because AutoCAD LT does not support 3D modeling, no 3D drawing templates come with the program.

✦ **Miscellaneous drawing templates:** In addition to the standard and 3D drawing templates, four other drawing templates can be used as a starting point for creating your own drawing templates if you are in the architectural or mechanical disciplines.

Which drawing template should you use? That is a trick question because you should use your own drawing templates and not the ones that come with AutoCAD. Remember that the supplied drawing templates are just starting points. You'll need to customize them to make them truly useful time-savers. I recommend that you take some time and create a drawing template that holds all your company's styles and settings.

Saving a Drawing

I do not have to tell you that it's important to save often. Everyone has their own little formula for saving: every hour, every 15 minutes, on the solstice and equinox (and I *sincerely* hope you are not in the last category!).

Okay, let's get serious for just a moment. How often should you save your work? A great mantra to keep in mind — or maybe even print and pin to the wall over your desk — is, "How much work am I prepared to lose?" You may have just completed a complicated polar array of a gazillion objects, but it's still three minutes away from your quarter-hourly save. Forget the clock — click that Save button right now! That is how often you should save.

Saving files in AutoCAD can be a little complicated. (By now, you were probably expecting that, right?) There are three commands for saving files: SAVE, SAVEAS, and QSAVE, but they all fall naturally to hand (or to tool button, to be more accurate).

Save

AutoCAD does have a command called SAVE, and the Windows-standard Ctrl+S key combo works here too. But doing a Ctrl+S or clicking the Save button or menu item does not run the SAVE command. It runs one of two other commands: SAVEAS, which displays the Save Drawing As dialog box, or the QSAVE command, which does not display anything.

Save As

If your drawing is unnamed — if the title bar says [Drawing 15.dwg], it's unnamed — pressing Ctrl+S or clicking Save in some form runs the SAVEAS command. SAVEAS opens the Save Drawing As dialog box (see Figure 4-5).

Places list   Save in list

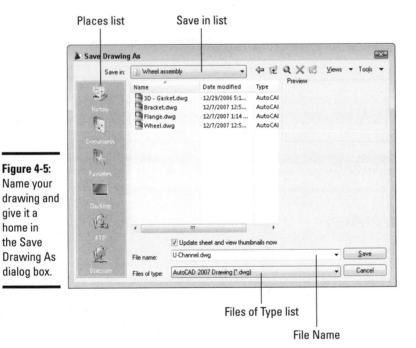

Figure 4-5:
Name your
drawing and
give it a
home in
the Save
Drawing As
dialog box.

Files of Type list

File Name

In this dialog box, you can enter three pieces of information:

+ **Save in:** Use this drop-down list to navigate to the folder where you want to store the drawing. The list box below the Save in list shows all drawings stored in the current folder.

+ **File name:** Enter a name for the drawing. I will have more to say about naming files at the end of the chapter.

DXF: The neutral format

DXF, drawing interchange format, is the officially sanctioned method for exporting AutoCAD drawing data to other CAD or graphics programs, or for importing vector graphics from other programs into AutoCAD. Autodesk publishes the DXF specification but keeps DWG proprietary. DXF should produce a close representation of a DWG file, but some data types do not translate well; typically drawing geometry is translated better than some of that geometry's object properties. Because DXF is Autodesk's specification, it's up to other software developers to code their programs to support it properly. In other words, if your illustration program will not import a DXF file, the fault is more likely to be the illustration program's than Autodesk's.

DXF files are created through the Save Drawing As dialog box. In the Files of Type drop-down list,

you can choose from four flavors of DXF: AutoCAD 2007, AutoCAD 2004, AutoCAD 2000/LT 2000, and AutoCAD Release 12/LT2. You can open DXF files through a similar Files of Type drop-down list in the Select File dialog box.

For users of AutoCAD 2004, 2005, and 2006, DXF is one way (the only way, using plain AutoCAD) of converting a drawing back to Release 14 or earlier. AutoCAD 2007 and later *can* save back to Release 14 DWG format. If you're using one of those older releases, you can download a copy of Autodesk DWG TrueView from Autodesk's Web site that will let you save back to R14 DWG. If you need to go further back than that, you really do need to use R12 DXF.

✦ **Files of type:** You want to save a drawing, right? Well, there are drawings, and there are drawings. You can save your work as a DWG in the current format or go back up to three versions of the DWG file format. If you have to go back further than that, you can save in Release 12 DXF format. Finally, you can save your drawing as a drawing template (DWT) file, or a drawing standards (DWS) file.

The current DWG version is AutoCAD 2007 which is used for AutoCAD 2007, 2008, and 2009. The prior DWG version was AutoCAD 2004, which was used by AutoCAD 2004, 2005, and 2006. The one prior to that was AutoCAD 2000, which was used by AutoCAD 2000, 2000i, and 2002. And before that came AutoCAD R14 (used by that release only). So, if need be, you can save your work in a DWG format that can be read by a release of AutoCAD first released in 1997. For more on file formats and releases, see Chapter 2 of this minibook.

You can use the Places list to quickly access named locations and folders that you commonly use to store drawings. If you frequently use drawings from a specific folder, you can add it to the Places list. To add a folder to the Places list, simply drag and drop a folder listed in the files area of the Save Drawing As dialog box.

QSAVE

After all those Save and Save As options, QSAVE should come as a relief, because it has no options. As noted, if a drawing is unnamed, clicking the Save button on the Quick Access toolbar or pressing Ctrl+S displays the Save Drawing As dialog box, which presents a plethora of options.

After the drawing is named, clicking the Save button or menu or pressing Ctrl+S runs the QSAVE command. QSAVE has no dialog box; in fact, it may look as if nothing happened. QSAVE simply resaves the named drawing file in the same location, with the same file name, and as the same type of file, all without additional input from you. Any guesses what the *Q* in QSAVE stands for?

If you are working in an environment with some older and newer releases of AutoCAD, you can specify the default DWG file format that you save to each time a drawing is saved. To set the default DWG file format, select the desired format from the Save As drop-down list on the Open and Save tab of the Options dialog box.

Opening an Existing Drawing

Opening an existing drawing does not present quite so many possible alternatives as creating a new one does. All you have to know is where the drawing is, and if you practice good file-management techniques, that should not be a problem.

Open command

Clicking the Open button on the Quick Access toolbar or using the Ctrl+O key combination displays the Select File dialog box, as shown in Figure 4-6.

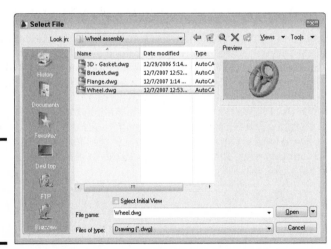

Figure 4-6:
Select files to open in the . . . er, Select File dialog box.

The default file type in the Files of Type drop-down list is Drawing (*.dwg). Unlike the Save As dialog box, which gives you a number of DWG versions to save the drawing to, only one DWG option is listed in the Select File dialog box. This is because AutoCAD can open *any* DWG file saved in the current or older file format.

Your other choices of file types to open through the Select File dialog box are

✦ **Standards (*.dws):** A DWS file is a regular drawing file that contains settings and properties that you want to use as a base standard for a project or for all your drawings. You can use the CAD Standards options from Tools on the menu browser to configure a DWS file and to review your current drawing to make sure it complies with the standards.

✦ **DXF (*.dxf):** Autodesk's neutral and nonproprietary version of the DWG format used for transferring drawing data into and out of AutoCAD. For more information, see the sidebar "DXF: The neutral format."

✦ **Drawing Template (*.dwt):** A DWT file is a regular drawing file that contains settings, properties, and drawing objects that you want to use in all the drawing files of a project. Using a template means you do not have to keep making changes to the settings or drawing those objects over and over again.

Be careful when opening DWT files, as you may inadvertently make unwanted changes that will show up whenever you try to start a new drawing based on that DWT.

Can't find a drawing file? Funny . . . you knew where it was yesterday, right? Luckily, AutoCAD has a dandy but well-concealed utility in the Select File dialog box. To find Find, click the Tools button on the Select File dialog box's toolbar, and choose Find from the menu; the Find dialog box opens. Optionally, enter a file name or a partial file name, and lickety-split, AutoCAD will turn up files that meet your criteria. (If lickety-split does not happen, try changing the Look In location to the root folder.) Entering no file name in the Named text box will return all drawings in the selected folder and subfolders if the Include Subfolders option is selected (see Figure 4-7). Highlight the file you are after in the list and click OK. The Select File dialog box reappears with the selected file in the File name box, ready to open.

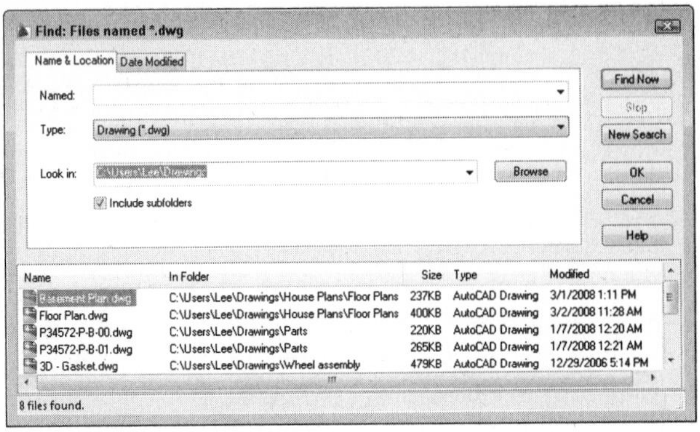

Figure 4-7:
Finding files
through the
Select File
dialog box's
Tools⇨Find.

Recent drawings

Often you might work on the same drawing during the course of a week or a project. In releases of AutoCAD before AutoCAD 2009, you might have used the History option under the Places list, which was slow and clunky. The menu browser allows you to access a list of recent drawing files (see Figure 4-8). To display a list of recently opened drawings, click the Menu Browser button in the upper-left corner of AutoCAD and hover the cursor over Recent Documents (a drawing is a form of a document). You can sort the list of recently opened drawings by name, date, and type. You can also control the size of the preview of each drawing in the list.

Figure 4-8:
Which
drawings
have I
worked on
recently?
There's no
more
guessing
with the
Recent
Documents
option.

Using Windows Explorer

When you can't quite remember where you put that danged drawing, the Find function in AutoCAD's Select File dialog box works well, but not many people know about it. *Everyone*, however, knows Windows Explorer and the Search tool on the Windows Start menu. If the drawing was created in AutoCAD 2006 or later, you can even search on words that are part of drawing text. This is not the place to explain the Search function in Windows Vista, XP, or 2000 — if you do not know how to use it, click Help on the Start button.

After you've searched and found the drawing, you can open it and start AutoCAD at the same time.

And a double-click to open

You can always use Windows Explorer to open your drawings. Simply double-click to open them in AutoCAD.

One potential drawback of double-clicking in Explorer arises if you have more than one release of AutoCAD on your computer. If you are a one-person shop, that may sound unlikely, but lots of big organizations will have two releases of AutoCAD on their systems while they're transitioning from one release to the next. Such a company might have seats of both AutoCAD and AutoCAD LT, or "vanilla" AutoCAD alongside a vertical product such as AutoCAD Architecture, AutoCAD Mechanical, or AutoCAD P&ID. When you double-click a drawing file in Explorer, the drawing opens with the last-used version of the software, and that may not be what you want at all. If you have only one version of AutoCAD, no problem, but if you have access to several versions, do not do the double-click thing — start your AutoCAD of choice first, and then use the Open dialog box.

What a drag (and drop)

Perhaps a better way of using Windows Explorer with AutoCAD is dragging and dropping files into an already running instance of AutoCAD (especially if you have more than one version on your system).

Be careful where you drop though. If you drag and drop a drawing from Explorer into an open AutoCAD drawing, the dragged-and-dropped drawing will be inserted into the already open drawing as a block. If you want to open a drawing from Explorer by dragging, make sure you do the dropping in an area of AutoCAD outside the drawing window, as shown in Figure 4-9.

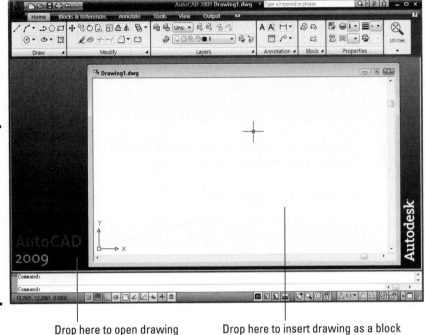

Figure 4-9:
To open a drawing from Explorer, be sure to drop it into an empty part of the graphics area.

Drop here to open drawing   Drop here to insert drawing as a block

The Multiple-Drawing Environment

All 21st-century releases of AutoCAD support multiple documents. Big deal, you say — every Windows program can open multiple documents. Well, it *is* a big deal if you are a grizzled old-timer, because for several releases, AutoCAD was one of the few Windows programs that did *not* support multiple documents.

Having several drawings open at once means that you can easily copy objects from drawing to drawing by using the Windows Clipboard. AutoCAD's Window menu lets you arrange several drawings within the application window, either by cascading them in an overlapping array or by tiling them so each drawing window is visible.

In addition to using the Window menu on the menu browser or menu bar, you can also use the Open Documents item listed at the bottom of the menu browser to switch between open drawings. Hover the cursor over the Open Documents item to display a list of all the open drawings in AutoCAD, and then click one of the drawings to make it the current drawing. You can also click the Quick View Drawings button on the application status bar to open the Quick View tool to switch between one of the open drawings, save and close an open drawing, and switch to one of the layouts in an open drawing. The Quick View tool can also be used to create and open a drawing.

When the Quick View tool is active and if you have a mouse with a scroll wheel on it, you can change the size of the previews for the drawing or layouts. To change the size of the previews, hover the cursor over the preview and scroll the wheel on the mouse while holding down the Ctrl key.

If you're like me, you'll most likely prefer to have as much of your drawing visible as possible. In AutoCAD, just like in other Windows programs, you can have several drawings open and maximized at once. To switch between them, use the Ctrl+Tab key combination.

A few add-on programs for AutoCAD can't handle multiple documents; they will function only if one and only one drawing is open at a time. AutoCAD has a system variable named SDI (Single Document Interface) that you can enable if you have one of these ornery add-ons. Set SDI to 1 to disable multiple drawings or to 0 to allow multiple drawings. Note that it's highly unlikely that you'll need to change this variable, and if you do, the add-on's documentation should tell you so.

Closing Windows

Closing AutoCAD windows is just like closing files in other applications. All the window types that you look at in Chapter 3 have Close buttons on their title bars. You can simply click the Close button on a toolbar or palette to shut it down.

To *open* toolbars, right-click over a button — it doesn't matter which — in any open toolbar to see a shortcut menu of all AutoCAD toolbars. If you're after one of the Express Tools toolbars, you need to right-click the Quick Access toolbar. Choose Toolbars⇨EXPRESS and then the toolbar you want to open. To open a palette, go to the menu browser and choose Tools⇨Palettes and then the palette you want to open. After you've been working with the program a while, try to memorize the Ctrl+key shortcuts; it's much more efficient toggling Ctrl+1 to open and close the Properties palette, for example, than to keep opening the menu browser and Tools menu.

If you click the Close button on a drawing window or the Close button on the AutoCAD title bar, and you have unsaved changes, the program displays an alert box like the one in Figure 4-10. Click Cancel to go back and save your changes, click No to close the drawing without saving changes, or click Yes to save the changes and *then* close the drawing. If your drawing is unnamed, the Save Drawing As dialog box appears.

Figure 4-10:
Keep it or
toss it?
AutoCAD
asks
whether you
want to
save
changes
before
closing.

File Management for AutoCAD

Now that you know what all those files are, how to create new drawings, how to open existing ones, and how to close everything down, you need to think about effective file management. When you want to open an existing drawing file, the Find utility in the Select File dialog box is all very well and good, but it's not efficient. It's much better if you *know* where you put those drawings so you do not waste time looking for them. It's a lot like taking all those papers that are in piles on your desk and neatly storing them in file folders in your filing cabinet.

The best approach here is to have a comprehensive organizational scheme that covers both naming and storage.

Naming drawing files

If you are working on your own, and you produce your own hard-copy versions of one-off drawing files, you can name your drawings pretty well anything you like. If you are an employee in a design or engineering firm, however, or a student taking a course, you'll probably need to pay attention to the file-naming conventions in your organization.

Typically, drawings are seldom one-off — it's rare that something can be manufactured or constructed by using a single drawing. When you start dealing with drawing sets, you need to pay attention to a naming scheme that keeps all associated files together in your file folders. Individual companies may have their own system. In the United States, professional organizations, such as the American Institute of Architects and the Construction Specifications Institute, produce nonmandatory guidelines for naming CAD files. Following the AIA file-naming specification may give you drawing names such as A-FP01 or C-SP04, but even if you do not know the system, a quick check in the guidelines will tell you that you're looking at the first sheet of Architectural Floor Plans, or the fourth sheet of Civil Site Plans.

For more information on these and other file-naming protocols, visit these Web sites:

✦ American Institute of Architects, www.aia.org

✦ Construction Specifications Institute, www.csinet.org

✦ National CAD Standard, www.nationalcadstandard.org

Storing your files

Files go in folders, and it makes as much sense to name your folders sensibly as it does to name your files in a useful way. If you belong to an organization, the file storage protocols will already be set up. You'll probably be saving to a network — in predefined folders that you may not be able to modify.

If you are on your own, come up with a system that will help you find files quickly. Obviously, storing files by project is a sensible first step. If you are *really* busy (lucky you!), you might consider having the year as a top-level folder, and then individual projects down a level. Using a similar subfolder structure can help you find those files, even if it does entail drilling down a bit. For example, if you design houses, you might have a standard series of folders named Details, Elevations, Floor Plans, Schedules, Sections, and Site Plans and residing under each project (see Figure 4-11).

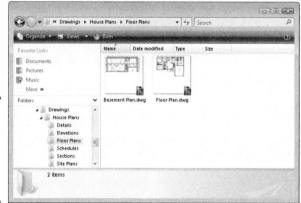

Figure 4-11:
A typical file storage system for a residential designer.

Backing Up Is Hard to Do . . .

. . . but losing a file you've spent two days working on is even harder. It's not a matter of *if* you ever need to call on your backups; it's a matter of *when*. Hardware is pretty reliable these days, but disks do fail. Remember that IBM, or Dell, or HP, or whoever it was that you bought your computer from chose the lowest bidders as their suppliers.

I'm not talking about your BAK files now, the ones I explained at the beginning of this chapter. AutoCAD's own backup files are all well and good, but they're not adequate for a backup system.

The likeliest thing to go is your hard drive, and luckily, that is what backup solutions are meant to protect. Invest in backup hardware; there are many solutions to choose from out there, so fire up your trusty search engine and see what you can find on the Web. Among your choices are the following:

✦ **External hard drives:** Especially practical if you have more than one computer. Some drives are especially designed as backup units and come with software that lets you schedule and automate backups.

You can also use the built-in Backup utilities that come with Windows Vista, Windows XP, and Windows 2000.

✦ **Tape drives:** Tape is fairly obsolete now, and I do not recommend buying a new tape backup unit. But if it's all you have, it's better than nothing!

✦ **Removable disks:** The best known of these devices is Iomega's Zip Drive; the drives themselves can be internal or external, and the proprietary disks come in 100MB, 250MB, and 750MB capacities.

✦ **CD-Rs and DVD-Rs:** Compact Disc-Recordable and Digital Versatile Disc-Recordable disks are cheap and efficient means to backing up data up to about 700MB. Most computers purchased in the last five years come with CD-RW drives, so the investment here is minimal.

✦ **Blu-ray and HD-DVDs:** CDs and DVDs are nice, but with file size and project complexity increasing, it might be time to think about the next generation of compact discs for data storage. Blu-ray and HD-DVDs are pretty new in the computing space compared to other formats but have been used for high-definition movies for the past few years. Although hardware costs are still high for these media formats, the amount of storage space can justify the cost differences. Blu-ray discs can hold about 50GB, while an HD-DVD can hold 30GB of data.

✦ **USB memory keys:** A great idea, and now amazingly cheap. These pen-sized devices plug into a spare USB port and are seen by Windows Vista and Windows XP as just another drive.

How often should you back up your hard drive? It's worth revisiting that earlier question: "How much work do I want to lose?" Now, I'm not suggesting that you run a full system backup every 15 minutes, but once a day, at the end of the day, is not excessive. If your hard drive does crash at your afternoon coffee break, you might have lost your day's work, but you can always use yesterday's backup.

If you have one.

Chapter 5: Basic Tools

In This Chapter

✓ Drawing lines

✓ Drawing circles

✓ Changing viewpoints by panning and zooming

✓ Erasing and unerasing objects

✓ Undoing and redoing actions

In this chapter, I look at some of AutoCAD's primitive drawing objects. That is not an insult to the cavemen who might still be walking among us; by *primitive* I mean *basic* drawing elements such as lines, arcs, and circles. I get to complex drawing objects, such as polylines in Book II, multiline text, tables and dimensions in Book III, and blocks in Book VI.

The purpose of this chapter is to show you how to draw stuff as simply as possible. Remember that the purpose of a CAD drawing is to convey technical information accurately and precisely (and those two words do not mean the same thing!). This chapter shows you how to draw primitives but does not show you the best way to manage and apply object properties. When you create your own drawings, you need to pay attention to precision as well as object properties such as color, linetype, and layer, which all affect the output of the drawing.

Drawing Lines

Lines are the second most-basic object you can create in AutoCAD. Lines are geometrically defined in AutoCAD by two coordinate points that are used as the start and endpoint of the line. The only thing simpler than a line is a point object, which is defined by a single set of coordinate values. (Do not be too concerned about coordinates at this point — I tell all in Chapter 7 of this minibook.)

Lines are the fundamental building blocks of most types of drawing, especially if you work in architecture or general building design. If you do mechanical drafting, you may draw as many circular shapes as straight ones (in that case, do I have a paragraph coming up for you — hang on tight!). If you do civil-engineering drawings or mapping, you're probably lucky if you see a straight line once every six months. But whatever kind of drafting you do, at some point you'll need to draw lines.

You would think that a line is a line is a line, wouldn't you? But not when it comes to CAD in general and AutoCAD. What looks like a line may or may not be a *line* — meaning a line object. Straight, linear-looking thingies on your drawing screen may also be *polyline* objects, or components of a *multi-line* object. They may even be part of a *table* object. I cover all the various types of lines later in the book, but what I cover here is the primitive line object.

You draw primitive line objects with a command called . . . wait for it . . . LINE! You can start this command in a number of ways:

+ **Ribbon:** On the ribbon, click the Home tab⇨Draw panel⇨Line.

+ **Menu browser:** Click the Menu browser button. On the menu browser, click Draw⇨Line.

+ **Menu bar:** On the menu bar, click Draw menu⇨Line.

+ **Toolbar:** On the Draw toolbar, click the Line tool.

+ **Keyboard input:** Type **LINE** (either uppercase or lowercase, it does not matter which; as I explained in the Introduction, I show proper command names in all uppercase in this book). When you finish typing the command, press Enter.

+ **Command alias:** More typing (actually, *less* typing). Type **L** and press Enter.

+ **Tool palettes:** You find the LINE command (and a few others) on the Draw tab of the Tool palettes. If you do not see the tab, right-click the title bar of the Tool Palettes window and choose either 3D Make or All Palettes.

AutoCAD offers a large number of command aliases that can be used as an alternative to typing the full name of a command or using one of the user interface elements to start a command. L is the alias for the LINE command, so typing either **LINE** (the full command name) or **L** (the command alias) and then pressing Enter both do the same thing: They run the LINE command. You can probably figure out a lot of aliases for yourself: C for CIRCLE, A for ARC, Z for ZOOM, and so on. For a complete list of AutoCAD's command aliases, on the menu browser or menu bar click Tools menu⇨Customize⇨Edit Program Parameters (acad.pgp) to open the program parameters file in Windows Notepad or your configured text editor. If you're using AutoCAD LT, click Tools menu⇨Customize⇨Edit Program Parameters (acadlt.pgp).

The following procedure uses the ribbon to start the LINE command and draws a line by using two random points in the drawing window:

1. **On the ribbon, click Home tab⇨Draw panel⇨Line.**

AutoCAD starts the LINE command. The command displays the prompt:

```
Specify first point:
```

2. **Specify the first point of the line by clicking a point in the drawing window.**

AutoCAD starts drawing a line from the point you chose. As you move the cursor, a *temporary line segment* (see Figure 5-1) joins the first point with the crosshairs. AutoCAD prompts:

```
Specify next point or [Undo]:
```

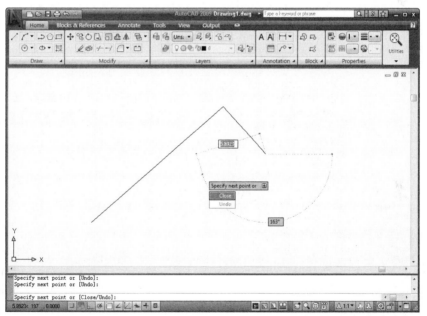

Figure 5-1:
Primitive lines (you have to start *somewhere*).

The second prompt displays a command option inside a pair of square brackets. To enter a command option at the command line, type the uppercase letter or letters of the option. In this case, typing **U** and pressing Enter runs the LINE command's Undo option; this option undoes the previous line segment and backs up AutoCAD to the line's start point.

If you're using dynamic input (that is, when Dynamic Input is enabled on the status bar), a downward arrow in the dynamic input tooltip is displayed when command options are available. Press the down-arrow key when you see the downward arrow on the dynamic input tooltip to access the available command options. Because command options are not displayed as part of the dynamic input tooltip, tooltip looks like the following when you're prompted for the next point of the line:

```
Specify next point or
```

3. **Specify additional points by clicking them in the drawing window.**

Notice that AutoCAD does not end the LINE command after you've drawn a single line. You can keep clicking points in the drawing window, and AutoCAD will keep adding line segments to your drawing.

After you click a third point, the command line changes slightly:

```
Specify next point or [Close/Undo]:
```

Two options appear inside the pair of square brackets for the command prompt. The Undo option is still available, but a new option called Close appears as well.

4. **Press C and then press Enter to close the shape.**

AutoCAD locates the next point based on the first point you chose after the LINE command was started. By using the Close option, you can make a closed triangular or polygonal shape. AutoCAD ends the LINE command and returns you to a blank command line.

Refer to Figure 5-1 to see the command in process; notice the command line and the dynamic input tooltip, both showing command options.

 TIP

When you enter **C** to create a closed shape, what you end up with is a series of separate line objects. If you click your mouse pointer on top of any line segment, you see that only that part of the shape is selected. In Book II, I look at another entity type called a *polyline,* where all the line segments form a single continuous object.

Creating Circles

 Circles, like lines and every other drawing object in AutoCAD, are mathematically defined. Lines are defined by the coordinates of their endpoints. Circles are defined by the coordinates of the center point and a specified numeric value for the radius.

The default method of drawing circles in AutoCAD is by selecting a center point on-screen and then entering a number for the radius. But you can draw circles in a half-dozen ways. Figure 5-2 shows these options on the Draw menu.

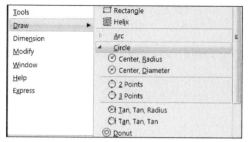

Figure 5-2:
You can
draw circles
in six
different
ways.

The options are

+ **Center, Radius:** Select a center point in the drawing window, and then either enter a value for the radius or drag a second point from the center point to indicate the radius. This is the default method for drawing circles.

In this case, *default* means what happens when you start the CIRCLE command without specifying a command option.

+ **Center, Diameter:** Select a center point in the drawing window, and then either enter a value for the diameter or drag a second point from the center point to indicate the diameter. Because it's a diameter distance that you're dragging, the second point is twice as far from the center as the circumference.

+ **2 Points:** Specify two points in the drawing window; the two points are treated as endpoints of the diameter of the circle.

+ **3 Points:** Specify three points in the drawing window; a circle is drawn through the selected points.

+ **Tan, Tan, Radius:** Select two existing objects, and then enter a value for the radius. AutoCAD draws a circle tangent to the two selected objects with the specified radius (assuming such a circle is possible).

+ **Tan, Tan, Tan:** Select three existing objects and, geometry permitting, AutoCAD draws a circle tangent to all three of them. This one is not really an option of the CIRCLE command but a special macro that uses the 3 Points option in combination with the Tangent object snap.

Any of these options will create a circle, but which one you choose depends on the drawing geometry and the information you have. For example, if you're given the requirement for a circle of diameter 29.57137, it's easier to use the CIRCLE command's Diameter option than it is to dig out your calculator and divide 29.57137 by 2 to get the radius.

The following steps use the ribbon to start the CIRCLE command, and then draw a circle by using the Diameter option:

1. On the ribbon, click Home tab⇨Draw panel⇨Circle flyout⇨Circle, Radius.

AutoCAD starts the CIRCLE command. The command displays the prompt

```
Specify center point for circle or [3P/2P/Ttr (tan tan
    radius)]:
```

If you want to use one of the available options, enter **3P** for a 3-point circle, **2P** for a 2-point circle, or **T** to use the Tan, Tan, Radius option. You need to type the uppercase letters of the command option you want. For 2-point and 3-point, press P after the 2 or 3, or AutoCAD thinks you're trying to enter a numeric coordinate location. If you're using dynamic input, press the down-arrow key to access the available command options.

2. Specify the center point.

AutoCAD places the center of the circle and drags a rubber-band line between the center point and the crosshairs; the command displays the prompt

```
Specify radius of circle or [Diameter]:
```

If you simply choose a point or enter a value at this point, AutoCAD interprets the input as the radius. If you want to use the Diameter option, you must let AutoCAD know.

3. Press D and then press Enter.

Entering D lets AutoCAD know you want to use the Diameter option of the CIRCLE command. The command displays the prompt

```
Specify diameter of circle:
```

4. Enter a numeric value for the diameter and press Enter, or drag the crosshairs to indicate a length equivalent to the diameter and then click.

AutoCAD draws the circle.

The steps in this and the preceding section show how to draw two of the simplest object types in AutoCAD. The procedures used to draw most objects in AutoCAD are basically similar. I look at drawing other kinds of objects in Chapter 1 of Book II.

Taking a Closer Look

One of the great advantages of AutoCAD is that you work on an infinitely large drawing sheet — so large, in fact, that you could design a solar system full size! With a drawing sheet that size, though, you need to be able to get up close to the drawing objects to add detail. Enter the display commands.

There are three broad categories of display commands: ZOOM, PAN, and VIEW. I look at all of them in detail in Book II. Here, I show you just enough of the basics so you can navigate around your drawing (or one of AutoCAD's sample drawings).

I begin with the two realtime navigation commands, RTZOOM and RTPAN. They're called *realtime commands* because you can see the view of the drawing change in real time as you use the commands.

Checking out realtime zoom

Using realtime zoom allows you to increase or decrease the magnification of the objects in a drawing. To make drawing objects appear larger, you zoom in; to make them appear smaller, you zoom out.

When you zoom in to or out of a drawing, you make drawing objects look larger or smaller by moving your viewpoint farther away or closer, respectively. You're not changing the size of the objects themselves. When I cover the Modify commands in Book II, you discover the SCALE command, which allows you to make objects smaller or larger by changing their size.

You can initiate realtime zoom in a number of ways. Perhaps the easiest is to click the Zoom button on the application status bar and then press Enter.

When you start either Realtime Zoom or Realtime Pan, the crosshairs are replaced by a magnifying glass cursor or a hand cursor, respectively. Right-clicking displays a shortcut menu that lets you switch from Zoom to Pan and vice versa. The shortcut menu has three other options of the ZOOM command, as well as a link to the 3DORBIT command if you're using AutoCAD and not AutoCAD LT. For the time being, I focus on the flat two-dimensional world, but I cover 3DORBIT in Book V, Chapter 3.

Using realtime pan

Panning in a drawing changes the view without changing the magnification. To initiate realtime pan, click the Pan button on the application status bar. A right-click while in Realtime Pan mode displays the same shortcut menu as Realtime Zoom, although there are no specific panning options.

To zoom and pan in a drawing, follow these steps:

1. **Open a drawing.**

   You can open one of your own drawings, the drawing you created in Chapter 1 of this minibook, or a sample drawing such as Architectural — Annotation Scaling and Multileaders.dwg found in the \Program Files\ AutoCAD 2009\Sample folder (or the \Program Files\AutoCAD LT 2009\ Sample folder for those using AutoCAD LT 2009).

2. **Click the Model tab at the lower-left corner of the drawing window or the Model button on the application status bar.**

   Realtime panning and zooming work in layouts as well as in the Model tab, but to keep it simple for now, we'll stay with the Model tab. I cover Model and layout tabs (also known as model space and paper space) in the Chapter 6 of this minibook.

3. **Click the Zoom button (the one with the magnifying glass) on the application status bar and then press Enter.**

   You can't use any other command while using realtime zoom or pan. The command prompt displays

   ```
   Press ESC or ENTER to exit, or right-click to display
       shortcut menu.
   ```

4. **Move the magnifying glass cursor to the middle of the drawing window, and then hold the left mouse button and drag the cursor downward, and then upward.**

   Dragging the magnifying glass cursor upward increases the magnification of the current view, making the drawing objects appear closer; dragging it downward decreases the magnification of the current view, making drawing objects appear farther away.

5. **Right-click to display the shortcut menu shown in Figure 5-3 and choose Pan.**

	Exit
	Pan
✓	Zoom
	3D Orbit
	Zoom Window
	Zoom Original
	Zoom Extents

Figure 5-3: The shortcut menu in real time.

The magnifying glass cursor changes to the hand cursor; you're now in realtime pan mode, just as if you had started the Pan Realtime command from the application status bar.

6. **Hold down the left mouse button and drag the cursor to pan the drawing back and forth, or up and down around the display.**

You can toggle back and forth between realtime panning and zooming by right-clicking at any time and choosing the other mode.

7. **Right-click and choose Zoom Original to return to the original view of the drawing, before you started the Realtime Zoom command.**

This is a quick way to get back to where you started, in case you get lost with all the panning and zooming. I describe the other two Zoom options on the shortcut menu — Zoom Window and Zoom Extents — in Book II, Chapter 3.

8. **Right-click and choose Exit.**

The hand cursor or magnifying glass cursor is replaced by the standard AutoCAD crosshairs, and the command line looks like this:

```
Press ESC or ENTER to exit, or right-click to display
    shortcut menu.
Command:
```

These are only the very basics of panning and zooming from the Zoom (or Pan) button on the application status bar. I cover the remaining zoom options — and there are several — in Book II.

Modifying Objects

AutoCAD provides three ways to modify objects:

✦ **Starting a command, and then selecting objects:** The technical term for this form of editing is *verb/noun selection.* You specify what you want to do — such as erase objects — and then specify what objects you want to perform the action on.

✦ **Selecting objects, and then starting a command:** The technical term for this form of editing is *noun/verb selection.* You specify what objects you want to perform an action on and then you specify the action you want to perform.

✦ **Grip editing:** When you select an object by clicking it and no command is active, you see one or more little blue boxes on the object. These are called *grips.* If you click one of the blue boxes (called cold grips), it turns red (or hot) and you can access a range of editing commands without needing to start a command first. Book II is the place to go for more information on modifying objects with grips.

For now, I'm going to stick with the most basic way of modifying objects — start a Modify command, and then select the objects to modify. If you master only one of these three methods, this is the one, because every Modify command supports modifying objects in this way. Not all the Modify commands allow you to first select objects and then start a command — noun/verb selection — and even fewer work with grips.

Erasing and Unerasing Stuff

 When you're not creating objects or navigating a drawing, you'll be spending the majority of your time modifying objects that you've already drawn. *Modifying* means copying, stretching, rotating — and getting rid of mistakes. Mistake is such a harsh word that I prefer saying "alterations that others feel should be made to a design" — after all, a mistake is often a matter of opinion and can sometimes lead to design innovation.

Using the digital eraser

You can do a wide range of things with objects in your drawing. You can move them, copy them, rotate them, scale them, and mirror them. But maybe they're objects that were used for constructing other objects or features that are no longer needed. In this case, anything you want to remove, delete, expunge, annihilate . . . erase them. Here's how:

1. **Open a drawing.**

You can open one of your own drawings, the drawing you created in Chapter 1 of this minibook, or a sample drawing such as Architectural — Annotation Scaling and Multileaders.dwg found in the \Program Files\ AutoCAD 2009\Sample folder (or the \Program Files\AutoCAD LT 2009\ Sample folder for those using AutoCAD LT 2009).

2. **Click the Model tab at the lower-left corner of the drawing window or the Model button on the application status bar.**

Again, this will go more easily if the Model tab is current.

3. **On the ribbon, click Home tab⇨Modify panel⇨Erase.**

AutoCAD starts the ERASE command. The command displays the following prompt:

```
Select objects:
```

4. **Select two or three objects by clicking each one.**

5. **AutoCAD highlights the objects by displaying them in dashed linework and displays the prompts:**

```
Select objects: 1 found
Select objects: 1 found, 2 total
Select objects: 1 found, 3 total
Select objects:
```

AutoCAD continues adding objects that you select to the current selection set. I talk more about selecting objects in Book II, Chapter 2.

6. **When you finish selecting objects to erase, press Enter.**

The selected objects are erased from the drawing.

These steps are typical for any modifying operation in AutoCAD. The most important thing to remember is that you must press Enter when you finish selecting objects to complete the command or proceed to the next prompt.

Unerasing objects

Everyone makes mistakes, from time to time, including erasing objects in a drawing that *really* shouldn't have been erased. Although you can't easily unerase something that occurred in the real world, AutoCAD is more forgiving and allows you to unerase objects that you have unintentionally removed.

Like most Windows-based programs, AutoCAD has an UNDO command (covered in the next section). The problem with UNDO is that you can't selectively skip over a bunch of stuff to get back to the action that you really want to undo. Say, for example, that you erased a wall and then drew a new wall in a different place, and then copied some bathroom fixtures, and then zoomed and panned — and then you realized you never should have erased that original wall in the first place. AutoCAD will let you undo back to just before that crucial erasure. Unfortunately, it will also undo the pan, the zoom, the copied bathroom fixtures, and the new wall drawn in a different place that you really want to keep, all before it will undo that erasure.

There's a little-known command that is appropriately named OOPS. It's little known because it doesn't appear in the user interface on a toolbar, menu, or any other place. You have to *know* it's there, and you have to type the command at the command prompt. OOPS performs one single task: It unerases the last thing you erased. So, in the scenario I just mentioned, if you had entered OOPS instead of undoing all the previous commands, the view you got by panning and zooming, and those copied bathroom fixtures as well as that new wall would all be retained, and the wall that you never should have erased would be restored — because it was the last thing you erased, and that is exactly what OOPS is for. Remember OOPS. Write it down on a yellow sticky note and stick it up on your monitor. If anyone asks, you can tell them it's your mantra.

Ready . . . Undo, Undo, Redo . . .

Like all good Windows programs, AutoCAD has Undo and Redo functions. However, the UNDO command in AutoCAD is more complex than the one in most other programs. You can undo the most recent action or multiple actions, and it offers many more options as well.

The simplest way to run UNDO is to use the Windows Ctrl+Z shortcut. You can also type **U** at the command prompt and press Enter, or click the Undo button on the Quick Access toolbar.

If you enter UNDO at the command prompt and press Enter, you get the full-blown UNDO command. The command prompt looks like this:

```
Current settings: Auto = On, Control = All, Combine = Yes,
    Layer = Yes
Enter the number of operations to undo or
    [Auto/Control/BEgin/End/Mark/Back] <1>:
```

I have more to say about UNDO in Book II.

Right next door to the Undo button on the Quick Access toolbar is the Redo button. In the latest versions of AutoCAD, you can redo multiple undos — great if you need to redo multiple undo operations.

Chapter 6: Setting Up Drawings

In This Chapter

✔ Establishing drawing units

✔ Understanding systems of measure

✔ Establishing drawing limits

✔ Understanding scale and scale factors

✔ Choosing between model space or paper space

✔ Working with layers

✔ Understanding object properties

✔ Establishing standards

✔ Creating templates

AutoCAD is much more than an electronic sketchpad. Technical drawings — as I'm sure you're aware — need to be accurate, precise, neat enough to be read easily, and standardized. Chapter 7 covers precision drawing techniques. This chapter explains how to set up drawings and introduces a number of ways to ensure standardization — ways that help you draw more efficiently and make all the drawings you create look similar to one another.

Choosing Units of Measurement

In this book, when I discuss units of measurement in AutoCAD, I'm not talking about *systems* of measurement. It's important to keep those two separate.

Globally speaking, two main *systems* of measurement are in use today. *Imperial* or *English* measurement is based on inches, and *metric* measure is based on the meter (or metre, if you live outside the United States).

Several releases back, AutoCAD used the measurement units of *English* and metric. Starting with AutoCAD 2000, the terminology switched from *English* to *Imperial* units. Although English and Imperial liquid measurements have some slight differences, these differences are likely not to bother most AutoCAD users who deal in linear and angular measure. For example, a U.S. pint has 16 ounces and a U.K. pint has 20 ounces, but a foot in both countries contains 12 inches. Come to think of it, maybe it *would* bother the U.K. AutoCAD user who has just ordered a pint of Guinness in the U.S.!

The metric system is being adopted in virtually every country in the world, but some are taking longer than others to embrace it. The biggest holdout — if you haven't guessed it already — is the United States. Rumor has it, in fact, that the United States, Liberia, and Myanmar are the last countries in the world using English (or is that Imperial?) units.

Talking about units in AutoCAD can be confusing. It's worth establishing some definitions before I get to the nitty-gritty:

✦ **Units:** *Units* is a generic term in AutoCAD, and it can cause a lot of confusion to both newbies and experienced users; it's best if you state specifically what *kind* of units you mean.

   • **Real-world units:** Real-world units are the units you measure things with every day. These units may be inches or miles, or millimeters or kilometers, or yards or nautical miles. Real-world units are established components of a uniform *system of measure* such as the metric system.

   • **AutoCAD units:** AutoCAD, like all CAD programs, works by crunching numbers, and numbers generally don't have real-world units attached to them — they're just numbers. AutoCAD units can be formatted so that they look like real-world units, but internally, they're just numbers that represent an angle or a linear distance. A line 1 unit in length might represent two different lengths due to how units are represented in the drawing, but measure the same length virtually. A line 1 unit long could represent 1 inch or 1 mile.

✦ **Unit types:** There are two types of AutoCAD units: *linear* and *angular*.

✦ **Unit formats:** Each of the two unit types can be formatted in one of five ways, as shown in Table 6-1.

✦ **System of measure:** Globally, the most widely used *system of measure* is the metric system. Locally (if you're a North American, that is), the English (or Imperial) system of measure is much more widely used. These are the two systems of measure I focus on in this book, and I assume the vast majority of readers are on the same pages.

Table 6-1		AutoCAD Unit Formats	
Linear	*Example*	*Angular*	*Example*
Architectural	1'–3 1/2"	Decimal degrees	90.000
Decimal	15.500	Deg/Min/Sec	90d0'0"
Engineering	1'–3.500"	Grads	100.000g
Fractional	15 1/2	Radians	1.571r
Scientific	1.550E+01	Surveyor	N or N0d00'00.0"E

Regarding Table 6-1:

✦ All linear examples are equivalent to one another, and all angular examples are equivalent to one another.

✦ *Architectural units* in AutoCAD mean feet and fractional inches. Of course, architects outside the United States and Canada will have to configure decimal units if they want to work in metric units.

✦ *Surveyor units* in AutoCAD mean quadrant bearings (for example, North 30 degrees West), but quadrant bearings are used only by American surveyors. Surveyors in other parts of the world work in whole circle bearings in either decimal degrees (for example, 120.000°) or Deg/Min/Sec (for example, 120d00' 00.0").

✦ The default precision for Angular units is zero places; Table 6-1 shows the results of setting three places of precision.

Despite the large number of choices, chances are you'll be working in either architectural (feet-and-fractional inches) or decimal linear units, and decimal degree or possibly deg/min/sec angular units.

Don't be fooled by those foot-and-inch marks you see if you configure AutoCAD to display architectural or engineering units. AutoCAD uses inch marks on every unit, and whenever it reaches 12 of those, it adds a foot value and foot mark. It may look like 1'–4 1/2" to you, but to AutoCAD it's just 16.500.

If you're working in architectural units, remember that AutoCAD represents linear values in an inch. If you want to enter 6", entering **6** is enough. If you want to enter 6', you need to include the foot mark. If you don't use a foot mark, AutoCAD assumes that you want to use inches.

AutoCAD units

AutoCAD ignores the differences between metric and English/Imperial units because it doesn't actually work in either. In AutoCAD, the fundamental unit is . . . the *unit*. It's up to you, the AutoCAD user, to determine what kind of real-world units AutoCAD units represent.

Unless specifically labeled otherwise, AutoCAD's drawing templates have their units *format* (not their units *type*) set to decimal units, with four places of precision. Those decimal units can represent any real-world unit you want, such as decimal inches, decimal meters, or decimal miles.

When you set the format for units in the Drawing Units dialog box, you control the display of units in the coordinate display on the status bar, the Properties palette, the command line, and the dynamic input tooltip when you draw new objects or query existing ones. You do *not* affect the display of dimension values. To see how to format dimension values, see Book III.

Imperial or metric

Despite the previous discussion on AutoCAD units versus real-world units, you still need to determine upfront whether you're working in metric or Imperial (or is it English?) units. Remember, as far as AutoCAD is concerned, a unit is a unit is a unit.

Choosing a metric or Imperial default beforehand can make your drafting more efficient. Why? Because if you start a drawing with Imperial defaults, AutoCAD is automatically configured to use the Imperial hatch pattern and linetype definition files, and if you start out with metric defaults, AutoCAD is automatically configured for the metric equivalents.

AutoCAD uses external definition files for its hatch patterns and linetype patterns. For hatch patterns, AutoCAD has two files, acad.pat and acadiso.pat. Similarly for linetype pattern definitions, the two files are named acad.lin and acadiso.lin. (The equivalent files in AutoCAD LT are acadlt.pat, acadltiso.pat, acadlt.lin, and acadltiso.lin.) I discuss using linetypes later in this chapter. See Book III, Chapter 3 for more on applying hatch patterns closed objects in a drawing.

Here's how to determine whether to start with a metric-defaults drawing or an Imperial-defaults drawing template:

✦ To set Imperial defaults, start with the acad.dwt (acadlt.dwt in AutoCAD LT) template. To set metric defaults, start with the acadiso.dwt (acadltiso.dwt) template.

✦ Start with no template by clicking the down arrow to the right of the Open button in the Select Template dialog box. Choose Open with No Template — Imperial to create a drawing using the Imperial default settings; choose Open with No Template — Metric to create a drawing using the metric default settings.

System variables

You need to know about two system variables, especially if you work in both Imperial and metric systems of measure. If you work exclusively in one or the other, it still doesn't hurt to know about them, but you can file them in a dustier, less-visited part of your brain. (For more on system variables, see Chapter 3 of this minibook.)

✦ **MEASUREMENT:** This variable allows the values of either 0 (Imperial units) or 1 (metric units). The MEASUREMENT variable is stored in each drawing, which means that you can work with drawings based in either Imperial or metric units.

✦ **MEASUREINIT:** This variable also allows the values of either 0 (Imperial units) or 1 (metric units). MEASUREINIT is stored in the system registry and determines whether drawings started from scratch (without a template) call on the acad (acadlt) or acadiso (acadltiso) pattern and linetype files.

As long as you start your drawings from the appropriate template files (that is, acad.dwt or acadlt.dwt for Imperial units, or acadiso.dwt or acadltiso.dwt for metric units), the MEASUREMENT system variable is set correctly automatically. The value of the MEASUREINIT variable is set when you install AutoCAD; by default, it's set to 0 for Imperial units if you live in the United States, and 1 for metric units if you live anywhere else in the world.

Setting units in your drawing

The following steps show how to set architectural linear units and deg/min/sec angular units for your current drawing:

1. **On the menu browser, click Format menu⇨Units.**

AutoCAD displays the Drawing Units dialog box (see Figure 6-1).

2. **In the Length area, click the Type drop-down list box and then choose Architectural.**

The Precision drop-down list box and Sample Output display change to show feet and fractional inches.

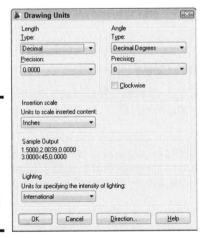

Figure 6-1:
Format the display of drawing units in the Drawing Units dialog box.

3. **In the Length area, click the Precision drop-down list box and choose the desired precision format.**

   The acceptable range of values is 0'–0" to 0'–0 1/256".

   You are not setting dimension format here. You never see a drawing dimensioned to the nearest 256th of an inch, but you might want to see more precision when you're drawing.

   For now, ignore the drop-down list box in the Insertion Scale area; I cover insert units in Book VI. Also, ignore the drop-down list in the Lighting area for now; I cover lighting in Book V.

4. **In the Angle area, click the Type drop-down list box and choose Deg/Min/Sec.**

   The Precision list box and Sample Output display change to show degrees-minutes-seconds.

5. **In the Angle area, click the Precision drop-down list box and choose the desired precision format.**

   Setting the maximum precision in the drop-down list formats angular units to degrees, minutes, and seconds to four decimal places.

The Clockwise check box allows you to define the direction in which angles are measured. By default, angles are measured in a counterclockwise direction — 0 is to the right, 90 is up, 180 is to the left, and 270 is down in a drawing. The angular direction of 0 degrees can also be changed in the Direction Control dialog box, which is displayed by the Direction button located at the bottom of the Drawing Units dialog box.

Setting Limits for Your Drawings

Well, you don't want your drawings staying out all night, do you? Or borrowing the car and leaving it in the impound lot?

Okay, the limits that you establish for your kids will not have the same effect on AutoCAD. In AutoCAD, the limits of a drawing define the working area of a drawing. But you've already seen in Chapter 2 of this minibook that you have an unlimited drawing area in AutoCAD, so why does it now have limits?

It may not make a lot of sense to pay strict attention to limits when you can change those limits whenever you want. In fact, limits are an historical artifact in AutoCAD and have a somewhat limited use on modern systems.

All the same, it's not a bad idea to know how big your drawing area is, even though it can be infinitely large and infinitely flexible. That's because sooner or later you're going to want to print that drawing, and that means you're going to have to fit it onto a piece of paper.

The theory behind limits is that you set your drawing limits according to the sheet size on which you'll eventually plot your drawing. So if you're drawing a mouse pad, you might set your drawing limits to $11 \times 8\ 1/2$ inches so that the limits represent a letter-size sheet. If you're drawing a fax machine, you set the drawing limits to 36×24 inches, to represent a D-size sheet.

Here are some other reasons to set limits for your drawing:

✦ **Defining the grid:** AutoCAD can display a grid of horizontally and vertically aligned dots over an area in a drawing. This grid can help keep you aware of the relative sizes of what you're drawing and the size of the printed drawing. I cover the grid in detail in Chapter 7 of this minibook, but for now, the key point is that the grid will be displayed over the area defined by the drawing limits.

✦ **Zooming:** One option of the ZOOM command is All, which changes the viewpoint of the drawing so you see everything within the drawing limits in the drawing window. This can be useful if you want to see some white space (or black space, depending on the background color of the drawing window) around your drawing objects.

✦ **Plotting:** If you want to plot a drawing from the Model tab (I discuss the Model tab in the "Lost in Space: Model or Paper?" section later in this chapter, and I cover plotting drawings in Book VII), one of the options is Limits. Choosing Limits plots everything within the defined limits of the drawing.

Pay attention to the order of those values. In AutoCAD, the horizontal dimension always comes before the vertical, so a 24×36-inch sheet would be aligned in portrait (long side vertical) mode, and a 36×24-inch sheet would be aligned in landscape (long side horizontal) mode.

So far so good, but it gets a little more complicated when you start drawing things that *won't* fit on a sheet of paper at their full size — no matter how big the paper is. For more on scaling, see the "Understanding Drawing Scale" section a bit later on in this chapter.

You specify the drawing limits by entering coordinates for the lower-left and upper-right corners of the drawing area. The following procedure shows you how to set your drawing's limits:

1. **On the menu browser, click Format menu⇨Drawing Limits, or type LIMITS at the command prompt and press Enter.**

    AutoCAD starts the LIMITS command. The command displays the prompt

    ```
    Reset Model space limits:
    Specify lower left corner or [ON/OFF] <0.0000,0.0000>:
    ```

2. **Press Enter to accept 0,0 as the lower-left corner, or type a different two-dimensional coordinate value and press Enter.**

It's a good idea to accept the default value (0,0) for the lower-left limit. 0,0 is the origin of the coordinate system. Chapter 7 covers the coordinate system in detail.

AutoCAD then prompts

```
Specify upper right corner <12.0000,9.0000>:
```

3. **Type a new value in coordinates for the upper-right corner of the drawing limits and then press Enter, or press Enter to accept the current value.**

Understanding Drawing Scale

Just now, I talked about drawing mouse pads and fax machines, objects you can carry around easily and that will fit on a letter-size or D-size drawing sheet. Most of the time, however, you're going to be drawing things that won't fit very well, or won't fit at all, on a sheet of paper. To make your drawing objects fit on the sheet, you use a scale factor when plotting a drawing.

You know that AutoCAD has an infinitely large sheet of virtual paper at its disposal. You've just found out that if your virtual drawing sheet isn't big enough, you can just make it bigger by altering the drawing limits. This is a great system — until you have to produce a hard copy of your drawing.

Scaling on the drawing board

In manual drafting, you're given a sheet of paper on which to lay out a drawing. Assume that it's an ISO A1 sheet that measures 841 × 594mm. By the time you've taken margins and room for a border and title block into account, you're left with a drawing area of, say, 550mm × 475mm.

Now suppose that you've been given a floor plan to draw. The building measures 45 meters × 70 meters. Obviously, you're not going to draw that building full size on an A1 sheet. You need to figure out a reduction factor that lets you draw your detailed plan of the building to an approved drafting scale and fit it on the sheet. You decide that the floor plan will fit on the sheet at a scale of 1:20. So you dig out your drafting scale, flip it around to the 1:20 scale, and start laying out your sheet.

When drawing manually, you scale everything down as you draw. Otherwise, things won't fit on the page. The opposite is true when working with AutoCAD.

Scaling in AutoCAD

You already know that in AutoCAD, you draw things full size, so that's how you've drawn your 45 × 70-meter floor plan. You're also given an A1 sheet on which to produce your drawing.

In AutoCAD, you have two ways to produce your drawing, which (you have calculated) needs to end up at a scale of 1:20 on the paper drawing:

✦ **Plot from model space:** When plotting from model space, you tell the PLOT command to output the drawing at a scale of 1:20. Most of the time you'll be plotting from a layout, so don't worry too much about this method.

✦ **Plot from a layout:** A layout represents a blank, physical sheet of paper on which you lay out your drawing sheet. The floor plane is still drawing on the Model tab, but outputting the drawing to paper is done from a layout tab. On a layout tab you create a viewport — in effect, a hole in the drawing sheet through which you can view your floor plan in model space. You apply a scale of 1:20 *to the viewport.* You then tell the PLOT command to plot the drawing at 1:1.

Is your head hurting? I have just tossed a bunch of terms at you that you may not have come across before: *model space, layout,* and *viewport.* Don't worry — I cover the differences between model space and layouts (paper space) in the next section of this chapter. All I wanted to get across here is the different methods of scaling between manual and AutoCAD drafting.

Scale factors

What both systems — manual drafting and CAD — have in common is *scale factor.* Whichever method you use to end up with a 1:20 scale plotted drawing, a scale factor is involved. Now, prepare for your head to hurt again, because I'm going to do some math. To calculate the scale factor of any given scale, you take the inverse of the scale ratio itself.

Okay, this calls for some examples. The metric system is about as simple as it gets, because a drawing with a scale of 1:20 has a scale factor of 20. A scale of 1:50 has a scale factor of 50, and 1:100 has a scale factor of 100.

It gets a little more complicated with Imperial scales, because you're typically dealing with scales such as 1/4"=1'-0" or 1"=20'. You'll notice that these scales have units, and here's what really messes things up: They have different units on each side of the equal sign. Before you can calculate the scale factor, you have to find the scale's ratio, and for that, you need to make both sides of the equation have the same units.

As an example, take the drawing scale 1/8"=1'-0". To find the ratio, first convert both sides of the equation to the same units; you arrive at 1/8"=12".

Next, multiply both sides of the equation so that you're dealing with whole numbers; in this case, multiplying both sides by 8 gives you 1"=96". The scale can also be expressed as 1:96, and so the scale factor is 96. (The metric system is a lot easier, isn't it?)

Table 6-2 lists some common scales and their corresponding scale factors (the math has already been done for you).

Table 6-2	Common Scales and Scale Factors	
Drawing Scale	*Ratio*	*Scale Factor*
1"=500'	1:6000	6000
1"=200'	1:2400	2400
1"=100'	1:1200	1200
1"=50'	1:600	600
1"=20'	1:240	240
1"=10'	1:120	120
1/16"=1'–0"	1:192	192
1/8"=1'–0"	1:96	96
1/4"=1'–0"	1:48	48
1/2"=1'–0"	1:24	24
1"=1'–0"	1:12	12
1 1/2"=1'–0"	1:8	8
3"=1'–0"	1:4	4
12"=1'–0"	1:1	1
1:100	1:100	100
1:50	1:50	50
1:20	1:20	20
1:10	1:10	10
1:5	1:5	5
1:2	1:2	2
1:1	1:1	1

Using scale factors to establish drawing settings

You use the drawing scale factors that you've just worked out to establish a number of drawing settings. These include

+ **Drawing limits:** Multiply the scale factor by the dimensions of your plot sheet to arrive at the limits. For example, if you're going to print your drawing on a D-size sheet (36 × 24 inches) at a scale of 1/4"=1'-0", multiply both sheet dimensions by the scale factor of 48. This gives you an area of 1728 inches by 1152 inches, so you would set the upper-right corner of the limits to 1728,1152 (or 144",96").

✦ **Dimension scale:** All dimension sizes and spaces are set to their actual plotted size. Text, for example, may be 2.5mm high. But 2.5mm text would be invisible next to a wall that is 70 meters long. If you're dimensioning in model space, you set the dimension scale factor equivalent to the drawing scale factor. I cover dimensions in Book III, Chapter 2.

✦ **Text height:** Some drawing text goes in model space — and once again, text that's specified as 1/8" high will be a speck beside a 200' wall. Multiply the desired text height times the drawing scale factor to arrive at a model space text height that won't be a speck; in this case, you multiply 1/8" times the drawing scale factor of 48, and tell AutoCAD to make your text 6" high. I cover text in Book III, Chapter 1.

✦ **Hatch pattern scale** and **linetype scale:** Drawing scale affects the appearance of the dash lengths and gaps for hatch patterns and linetypes. I cover hatch patterns in Book III, Chapter 3, and linetypes later in this chapter.

✦ **Viewport scale:** You use drawing scales to affect the size of objects in a viewport located on a layout. I cover viewports in Book VII, Chapter 1.

Lost in Space: Model or Paper?

It's possible to print your drawing from the Model tab, but it's much more convenient to print from a layout. To do so, you must understand some of the differences between model space and paper space, where layouts live.

✦ **Model space:** This is the drawing environment that corresponds to the Model tab. Model space can represent an infinitely large, three-dimensional area in which you create "real" objects. These objects are referred to as the model, whether they're 2D or 3D. Every drawing entity that represents a real object is created in model space. Because only one model space exists, AutoCAD provides only one Model tab. On the Model tab, you can see only objects in model space.

✦ **Paper space:** This is the drawing environment that corresponds to the Layout tabs. Paper space is also referred to as paper space layout or as layout space. Although model space represents the real 1:1 space where you create your models, paper space represents the 2D drawing sheet that you create to document them. Any objects you add to your model to document it — for example, title block, notes, dimensions, and section marks — can generally be found on a paper space layout. (Notable exceptions are center lines and hatching.) Because you may want to create more than one drawing sheet from a model, you can have an infinite number of layouts in a drawing file.

✦ **Layout:** This is the tabbed environment where you create plottable drawing sheets. The layout represents what will be plotted to paper. In addition to title blocks, notes, and dimensions, layouts include *viewports* —
  windows cut through the paper so you can see the model. A layout can
  contain a single viewport, or several viewports that examine different
  areas of the model at the same or different scales. On the layout tabs, you
  can see objects in model space and paper space, but you can select
  objects only in one space or the other — never both at the same time.

Every AutoCAD drawing must have a Model tab and at least one layout tab.

Create the objects that represent the real object on the Model tab. Then create
layout tabs and viewports as needed to output your model. For more
on layouts and viewports, see Book VII.

A Layered Approach

Layers are your principal tool for controlling information in an AutoCAD
drawing. Layers are like transparent overlays in manual drafting, where you
assemble different combinations of overlays to present different types of
information.

On an architectural drawing, for example, one drawing can contain the walls,
furniture layout, and ceiling grid with light fixtures and diffusers, as shown in
Figure 6-2. If each type of information is on its own layer, you can generate a
floor plan drawing by turning on the walls and furniture layers, and turning
off the ceiling layer. Then you can turn off the furniture layer and turn on the
ceiling layer to generate a new drawing, a reflected ceiling plan.

Layers are used also to segregate different drawing components. For **example**, dimensions usually go on their own layer, as does text, the drawing
border, and any title-block information.

Figure 6-2:
Turn layers
off and on to
generate
different
sheets from
the same
drawing file.

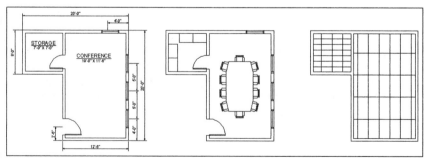

Layers must be created before they can be used. AutoCAD creates layer names automatically as you add layers, but it gives them names like Layer 1, Layer 2, Layer 3, and so on. It's a good idea to give your layers sensible names as you create them. Layer names can be up to 255 characters long (which is pretty impractical!).

One process for setting up and using layers in a drawing follows:

1. **Create the layers you need.**

2. **Assign color and linetype properties as required.**

3. **Set the desired layer current.**

4. **Draw stuff.**

Anything you draw from this point on will be placed on the layer you made current, until such time as you make another layer current.

All AutoCAD drawings contain a layer named 0, which can't be renamed or deleted. I recommend that you do not actually draw anything on Layer 0; instead, you should create layers specifically for the objects that you add to a drawing. Layer 0 has special properties when you create blocks, which I go into in Book VI. Another special layer is named DEFPOINTS; this layer is created the first time you add a dimension to a drawing and, like Layer 0, can't be deleted. I explain dimensions in Book III.

The Layer Properties Manager dialog box has been replaced with a modeless version (a palette) in AutoCAD 2009. You can now create and control the visibility and properties of layers in real time with the use of the new Layer Properties Manager palette.

Creating layers

The following steps explain how to use the Layer Properties Manager palette to create layers in any drawing file.

1. **On the ribbon, click Home tab⇨Layers panel⇨Layer Properties.**

AutoCAD displays the Layer Properties Manager palette (see Figure 6-3).

2. **Click the New Layer button to add a new layer definition.**

AutoCAD adds a new layer named Layer 1 to the layer list. The layer name is highlighted, so you can type a new name to replace AutoCAD's generic label.

Delete Layer

New Layer | Set Current

Figure 6-3:
Manage,
manipulate,
and modify
your layers
in the Layer
Properties
Manager
palette.

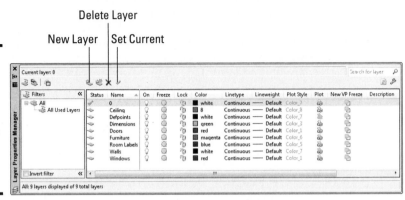

3. **Type a new layer name (for example, Wall), and press Enter.**

   Give your layers sensible names. If you're doing simple floor plans, it's enough to have layers named Wall, Door, Window, Appliance, and so on. Whatever you do, don't accept the default values of Layer 1, Layer 2, and so on, or you'll have no idea which objects are on which layer!

4. **Continue adding layer names as required.**

   If you keep pressing Enter, you can keep adding (and renaming!) new layers.

5. **Click the Set Current button to make a layer the current layer.**

   Only one layer at a time can be current, and anything you draw is created on the current layer.

   If you select a layer in the layer list before clicking the New Layer button, the new layer created will be based on the selected layer. So the new layer will share the same color, linetype, lineweight, plot style, plottable state, and all other properties and states. This makes it easier to create multiple layers that are almost the same with the exception of a few properties.

Defining layer properties

After you create layers, you can assign various states and properties to them. Setting layer properties ensures that objects drawn on a given layer take on the proper color, linetype, lineweight, and plot style.

Unless you have a really good reason to avoid doing so, use layers to control the appearance of objects. It's possible to set the color and other properties of individual objects, but it's usually a bad idea unless you know what you're doing and have a good reason. Applying explicit colors and other properties to objects can make them difficult to edit when the need arises because you can't tell which layer objects are located on.

Layer properties include

+ **Color:** When a color is assigned to a layer, objects drawn on that layer take on that color. Set layer color by accessing the Select Color dialog box through the Layer Properties Manager palette. Color also controls the plot style assigned to a layer when a drawing uses color-dependent plot styles. I cover plot styles in Book VII.

+ **Linetype:** Most AutoCAD objects have the default linetype, which is a solid, continuous line. However, some drafting conventions require the use of noncontinuous linetypes (sometimes called *dash-dot* linetypes), such as center lines and hidden lines. You can assign a linetype to a layer by using the Select Linetype dialog box through the Layer Properties Manager palette. I cover linetypes later in this chapter.

+ **Lineweight:** Lineweight refers to the visible width of lines in the drawing window. When drawings are plotted correctly, the output shows different line thicknesses — thin lines for dimensions, thick lines for borders, medium lines for object lines and text, and so on. But when displayed in the drawing window, objects usually appear with a single-line thickness. You can assign a lineweight to a layer by using the Lineweight dialog box through the Layer Properties Manager palette.

+ **Plot style:** If your drawing is configured to use named plot styles, you can assign an already existing plot style to a layer. If your drawing is set up to use color-dependent plot styles, the Plot Style column in the Layer Properties Manager palette is dimmed; the only way to change a plot style here is to change the layer color. Plot styles are not something you need to be concerned with at this moment; I cover them in detail in Book VII.

+ **Description:** This is text that explains what a layer might be used for. Although it's an optional property for a layer, it can help when sharing drawings with contractors or clients because it helps them understand the general purpose of a layer in a drawing.

Viewports offer additional control over layer properties. When a viewport on a layout tab is active, you can override a layer's color, linetype, lineweight, or plot style. Layer overrides are specific to only that viewport. So you can have a single layer with multiple property values in a drawing if layer overrides are applied to different viewports. I cover applying layer overrides to viewports in Book VII.

You can also access the Select Color, Select Linetype, and Lineweight dialog boxes by entering the appropriate command names at the command prompt or by choosing Color, Linetype, or Lineweight from the Format menu on the menu browser or menu bar. But doing those things does *not* set a layer property — it does something potentially more damaging. It sets the default color, linetype, or lineweight that will be used when you create new objects, regardless of the current layer and its settings, from that point forward.

When objects are allowed to take on the properties of the layers on which they are drawn, those properties are said to be *By Layer.*

Setting layer modes

In addition to layer properties, which have a wide range of possible settings, you can choose from a series of layer modes, which are toggles with only two possible settings (see Figure 6-4).

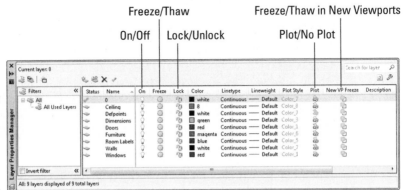

Figure 6-4: Toggle layer modes by clicking their icons.

The five layer modes are

✦ **On/Off:** Objects on the layer are visible if the mode is on (the light bulb is switched on) and invisible if the mode is off (the light bulb is switched off).

Strangely enough, the current layer can be turned off; it's even possible to draw on a layer that's turned off, as long as it's current. So if you start drawing lines that don't appear in the drawing window, check to make sure that the layer is not turned off or frozen.

✦ **Freeze/Thaw:** Objects are visible if the layer is thawed or invisible if the layer is frozen. The difference between Off and Frozen is that frozen layers are not included when AutoCAD regenerates the objects in the current drawing. A glowing sun indicates a thawed layer, and a snowflake means a layer is frozen. You can't set a frozen layer as current.

If you frequently need to use a layer but want to hide the objects when they are not needed on the screen, turn off the layer instead of freezing it. When you turn the layer back on, AutoCAD doesn't need to regenerate the objects in the current drawing. Also, objects on a frozen layer can't be selected when you use the All option at the Select objects prompt. I cover regenerating a drawing in Book II, Chapter 3; I cover the All option for selecting objects in Book II, Chapter 2.

✦ **Lock/Unlock:** When a layer is locked, you can see the objects on the layer, you can select the objects, and you can even draw on the layer. But you can't edit objects on a locked layer. A padlock icon in Layer Properties Manager or the Layer list indicates whether a layer is locked. You can identify if a layer is locked in the drawing window by the presence of a padlock icon next to the crosshairs when the crosshairs are hovering over an object on a locked layer.

To make it easier to identify which layers are locked and unlocked, you can fade locked layers into the background. To turn on locked layer fading, expand the Layers panel (by clicking its title area) on the Home tab of the ribbon. Then click the Locked Layer Fading toggle and adjust the percentage by which you want the layers to appear faded. A value of 0 percent means objects on a locked layer are not faded; a value greater than 0, up to 90 percent, indicates the amount the objects on the locked layer are faded into the background.

✦ **Plot/NoPlot:** You can set this layer mode so that objects on the selected layer are visible but will not appear on a plot or print preview.

✦ **Freeze/Thaw in New Viewports:** Controls which layers are frozen or thawed for each new viewport that is created on a layout tab. I discuss this option in greater detail in Book VII.

Another mode is available when a viewport is active on a layout tab. When a viewport is active, you can freeze a layer or set of layers specific to that viewport. I cover this additional option in Book VII.

Modifying layer settings

You can access the Layer Properties Manager palette at any time by clicking the Home tab on the ribbon and then clicking Layers panel⇨Layer Properties, or by typing **LA** at the command prompt and pressing Enter. You don't have to create all your layers when you start a new drawing; you can add (or remove) layers at any time in the drawing's life.

Nonetheless, the most efficient way of setting up and managing layers in any drawing is to create them all at once and make the appropriate property and layer stats while you're creating them.

Setting layer color

The following steps explain how to modify layer properties and settings in the Layer Properties Manager palette:

1. **Open the Layer Properties Manager palette if it's not already open.**

   On the ribbon, click Home tab⇨Layers panel⇨Layer Properties.

2. **Select the layer whose color you want to change.**

   To select multiple layers, hold down the Ctrl key to select multiple layers at a time, or hold down the Shift key to select a range of layers.

3. **Click the color swatch in the Color column for the selected layer.**

   AutoCAD displays the Select Color dialog box (see Figure 6-5).

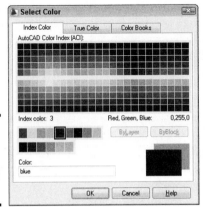

Figure 6-5:
AutoCAD's
standard
colors — all
255 of them.

4. **With the Index Color tab current, select one of the large color swatches near the bottom left of the dialog box, and then click OK to close the dialog box.**

   The foreground color of the sample rectangles in the lower-right corner of the dialog box changes to the selected color. AutoCAD closes the Select Color dialog box and returns to the Layer Properties Manager palette. The layer shows the new color and name under the Color column.

For more information on using colors in AutoCAD, see the "Using AutoCAD's color systems" section later in the chapter.

Setting linetype

There's a wrinkle to setting linetypes in an AutoCAD drawing. Unlike colors, which are always available, noncontinuous linetypes are defined in an external file that goes by one of these file names:

+ **acad.lin:** The default linetype definition file, designed for use with Imperial units and based on inches.

+ **acadiso.lin:** The default linetype definition file designed for use with metric units and based on millimeters.

✦ **acadlt.lin:** The AutoCAD LT version of acad.lin. (Prior to AutoCAD 2007, this file was named aclt.lin.)

✦ **acadltiso.lin:** The AutoCAD LT version of acadiso.lin. (Prior to AutoCAD 2007, this file was named acltiso.lin.)

For an explanation of the different linetype definitions, see the "Using linetypes" section later in the chapter.

You can load linetypes as a separate step, before you create your layers, by clicking Format➪Linetype from the menu browser or menu bar to display the Linetype Manager dialog box. Alternatively, you can follow these steps to access Linetype Manager from the Layer Properties Manager palette:

1. **If the Layer Properties Manager palette is not already open, open it.**

On the ribbon, click Home tab➪Layers panel➪Layer Properties. AutoCAD displays Layer Properties Manager.

2. **Select the layer whose linetype you want to change.**

3. **In the Linetype column, click the name of the current linetype (by default Continuous).**

AutoCAD displays the Select Linetype dialog box. By default, only the Continuous linetype is loaded.

4. **Click Load to display the Load or Reload Linetypes dialog box.**

Load or Reload Linetypes displays all linetypes defined in the current linetype definition file (see Figure 6-6).

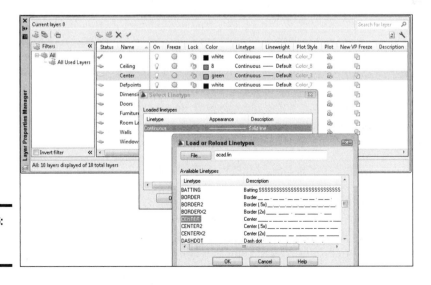

Figure 6-6:
Linetypes
galore.

5. **Scroll through the list and select the linetypes to load, and then click OK.**

   Hold the Ctrl key to select more than one linetype or hold down the Shift key to select a range of linetypes to load. The Load or Reload Linetypes dialog box closes, and the focus returns to the Select Linetype dialog box.

6. **Select the linetype you want to assign to the selected layer in the Layer Properties Manager palette, and then click OK.**

   The Select Linetype dialog box closes, and the selected linetype is assigned to the layer (see Figure 6-7).

Figure 6-7:
Many clicks later, a linetype is assigned.

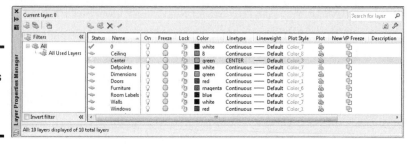

Setting lineweight

Lineweights are like colors — they're always present and available, unlike linetypes which have to be loaded into the drawing before they can be assigned.

Lineweight is a display property that shows a representation of the relative thickness of different drawing objects. Lineweight works differently in model space and paper space:

✦ In model space, lineweight is based on a number of pixels, so that no matter how close you zoom in — or how far you zoom out — linework always appears to have the same visual thickness.

✦ In paper space, lineweight is part of the representation of the paper drawing. If you put linework on a paper drawing under a magnifying glass, the lines appear thicker, and that's exactly how it works in paper space — as you zoom in, the lines appear thicker.

The following steps explain how to assign a lineweight to a layer:

1. **If the Layer Properties Manager palette is not already open, open it.**

   On the ribbon, click Home tab⇨Layers panel⇨Layer Properties.

2. **Select the layer whose lineweight you want to change.**

3. In the Lineweight column, click the word Default.

AutoCAD displays the Lineweight dialog box (see Figure 6-8).

Figure 6-8:
Scroll to set
a default
lineweight
for your
layer.

4. Scroll down the list to find the desired lineweight.

Because plotter pens were traditionally sized in millimeters, AutoCAD's lineweights are also displayed in millimeters whether metric or Imperial units are configured.

5. Select the lineweight you want to assign to the selected layer in the Layer Properties Manager palette, and then click OK.

The Lineweight dialog box closes and focus returns to the Layer Properties Manager palette.

Assigning lineweights to layers is only half the story. You also need to click the Show/Hide Lineweights (or LWT) button on the status bar to display lineweights in the drawing window. When the button is selected, lineweight display is enabled; when the button is not selected, all geometry appears in the default line width, which is 1 pixel in size.

The lineweight property can be applied to the output of a drawing that is generated when plotting, as well as to the visual representation of drawing objects. I tell you more about that in Book VII.

Setting layer modes

As already noted, the layer modes are toggles that let you control the following: layer visibility, the layers that are recalculated when AutoCAD regenerates a drawing, whether the objects on a visible layer can be edited, whether the objects on a visible layer are plotted, and whether a layer is frozen by default when a new viewport is created on a layout.

The following procedure runs through the five layer modes in the Layer Properties Manager palette:

1. **If the Layer Properties Manager palette is not already open, open it.**

   On the ribbon, click Home tab⇨Layers panel⇨Layer Properties.

2. **Select a layer whose modes you want to modify.**

3. **To toggle a layer's visibility on or off, click the light bulb icon in the On column.**

4. **To freeze a layer so that it's not recalculated when the display is regenerated, click the sun icon in the Freeze column. To thaw a layer, click the snowflake icon.**

5. **To lock or unlock a layer to prevent or allow the objects on the layer to be edited, click the padlock icon in the Lock column.**

6. **To prevent or allow objects on a layer to be printed, click the Printer icon in the Plot column.**

7. **To freeze a layer in new viewports created on layouts, click the sun icon in the New VP Freeze column. To have the layer thawed in new viewports, click the snowflake icon.**

   I discuss this option in greater detail in Book VII.

The Layer Control drop-down list

You use the Layer Properties Manager palette to modify layer properties, including color, linetype, lineweight, and plot style. You can also turn layer modes off and on in the Layer Properties Manager palette, but if the latter is all you need to do, there's a more efficient way than opening and closing a palette.

The Layers panel contains a drop-down list of all the layers in a drawing (see Figure 6-9).

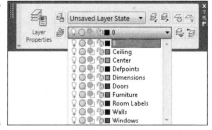

Figure 6-9:
Switch layer modes in the Layer Control drop-down list.

You can click the down arrow (or inside the list box) to expand the list, and then perform any of the following actions:

+ Set a layer current by clicking the layer name.

+ Turn layer visibility off or on by clicking the light bulb.

+ Freeze or thaw a layer by clicking the sun or snowflake.

  You can't freeze the current layer.

+ Lock or unlock a layer by clicking the padlock.

+ Freeze or thaw a layer for new viewports by clicking the sun or snowflake over a rectangle. I discuss this mode in greater detail in Book VII.

After you change the mode, click anywhere outside the Layer Control list to close the list and return focus to the drawing.

Because the Layer Control drop-down list shows a color tile for each layer, you might think you can click it to change a layer's color, but you're wrong. Color is a property, and properties can be changed only in the Layer Properties Manager palette.

Layer tools

AutoCAD provides a wide variety of tools that allow you to select an object and display only the objects on that layer or freeze a layer just by selecting an object in the drawing. These additional tools can be found on the Layers panel of the Home tab on the ribbon. The commands that start each layer tool are listed in the parentheses next to the tool name.

+ **Layer States Manager (LAYERSTATE):** Layer States Manager allows you to save and restore layer states. This tool allows you to create a snap-shot of the layers in a drawing that you receive from a client, and then restore the layers to the way they were when you received the drawing before sending it back to the client.

+ **Make Object's Layer Current (LAYMCUR):** Make Object's Layer Current allows you to select an object in the drawing window and set the object's layer as the current layer.

+ **Layer Walk (LAYWALK):** Layer Walk allows you to dynamically step through all the layers in a drawing to see the objects placed on those layers, without forcing you to freeze or thaw or turn layers off and on.

+ **Layer Match (LAYMCH):** Layer Match allows you to select objects in the drawing that should be moved to a different layer based on the layer a selected object is already on.

✦ **Change to Current Layer (LAYCUR):** Change to Current Layer allows you to select an object in a drawing and set the selected object to the current layer.

✦ **Copy Objects to New Layer (COPYTOLAYER):** Copy Objects to New Layer allows you to move selected objects to another layer or a new layer.

✦ **Layer Isolate (LAYISO):** Layer Isolate allows you to turn off all layers except the ones selected.

✦ **Isolate Layer to Current Viewport (LAYVPI):** Isolate Layer to Current Viewport freezes the layer in all viewports except the active viewport.

✦ **Layer Unisolate (LAYUNISO):** Layer Unisolate restores the layers that were hidden or locked with the Layer Isolate tool.

✦ **Layer Off (LAYOFF):** Layer Off allows you to turn off a layer by selecting an object that is on that layer.

✦ **Turn All Layers On (LAYON):** Turn All Layers On turns on all layers that are currently marked as off.

✦ **Layer Freeze (LAYFRZ):** Layer Freeze allows you to freeze a layer by selecting an object that is on that layer.

✦ **Thaw All Layers (LAYTHW):** Thaw All Layers thaws layers that are currently marked as frozen.

✦ **Layer Lock (LAYLCK):** Layer Lock allows you to lock a layer by selecting an object on that layer.

✦ **Layer Unlock (LAYULK):** Layer Unlock allows you to unlock a layer by selecting an object on that layer.

✦ **Layer Merge (LAYMRG):** Layer Merge allows you to move all the objects on one layer to another layer.

✦ **Layer Delete (LAYDEL):** Layer Delete allows you to delete all the objects on a layer and then purge the layer from the drawing.

Object Properties

In AutoCAD, all objects have properties. Every object in a drawing is created on a layer. Layers can have a number of properties assigned to them, and anything drawn on a specific layer takes on the color, linetype, lineweight and other "by layer" properties of that layer.

In addition to the properties that an object inherits from its layer, an object can have the following properties:

+ Color
+ Linetype
+ Lineweight
+ Plot style

Layers in AutoCAD, but not AutoCAD LT, have an additional property that is not managed through the Layer Properties Manager palette. A material name can be attached to a layer by using the Material Attachment Options dialog box (MATERIALATTACH command). I cover materials in Book V, Chapter 6.

Object properties can be assigned directly (or *explicitly*) to objects, or they can be assigned to layers. For example, on a floor plan you might have a bunch of blue doors. The color blue may have been assigned to each individual door, in which case the color will be listed as *Blue*. Or the color blue may have been assigned to the layer on which the doors were drawn, in which case the color is listed as *BYLAYER*.

Is one method better than the other? I certainly think so. For example, you may draw a floor plan in which you want all the doors to be blue. Then you decide they should be green instead. If you changed the doors explicitly, you would have to go through the drawing and select each and every door, and then open the Properties palette and change their color to green. Alternatively, you can just open the Layer Properties Manager palette and change the color of the Door layer from blue to green. Obviously, one of these processes is easier than the other.

When objects do not have explicit colors or other properties set, they take on the properties of the layer they are placed on.

I strongly advise you not to change the properties of objects in a drawing, but instead to leave their color, linetype, lineweight, and other properties set to BYLAYER. Applying explicit changes to objects can make them difficult to edit because you can't tell on which layer the objects are located.

Using AutoCAD's color systems

In AutoCAD drafting, color has two main functions, neither of which is producing color drawings:

✦ Color helps you differentiate objects from one another in the drawing window. When you assign colors to layers, you can tell immediately if something is on the wrong layer if it doesn't show up in the color you expect.

✦ Using the traditional color-dependent plotting system, the colors of objects determine the thickness of the plotted linework.

Since AutoCAD 2004, you can use three color systems:

✦ **ACI Color Index:** The original and genuine 255 colors that have always been part of AutoCAD (refer to Figure 6-5).

✦ **True Color:** A range of over 16 million colors you can set by dragging sliders or entering RGB (Red Green Blue) or HSL (Hue Saturation Luminance) values.

✦ **Color Books:** A set of predefined color palettes that are often used in graphic arts and desktop publishing. You can choose colors from the DIC, Pantone, and RAL color systems.

You use True Color or Color Books colors to try and match a specific material color if you're creating materials for rendering in AutoCAD only. For most drafting purposes, the 255 standard colors on the ACI Color Index tab are adequate.

Usually AutoCAD gets a new feature or both AutoCAD and AutoCAD LT get the same feature, but in this release AutoCAD LT gets a feature that AutoCAD has had since AutoCAD 2004. In AutoCAD LT 2009, you can now assign a True Color or Color Books color to an object or layer. No longer is AutoCAD LT limited to just having support for only the 255 ACI Color Index colors.

Using linetypes

The four linetype files (acad.lin and acadiso.lin, and their acadlt equivalents) include 45 linetype definitions, broken down as follows:

✦ **24 AutoCAD standard linetypes:** 8 basic patterns (border, center, dash-dot, dashed, divide, dot, hidden, and phantom) each in 3 spacing variants; for example, BORDER has normal spacing of its dash and dot elements; BORDER2's elements are half the size of BORDER's; BORDERX2's elements are twice the size of BORDER.

✦ **14 ISO 128 linetypes conforming to ISO/DIS 12011 specification:** These are rarely used; I recommend that you stick with the 24 standard line-types, for Imperial or metric drafting.

✦ **7 complex linetypes:** These include symbols or text as well as dash-dot line patterns. Linetypes include fence lines, railroad tracks, and batt insulation.

In addition to these 45 linetypes, the acadiso.lin and acadltiso.lin files include an additional 14 JIS linetypes. Although the preceding linetypes will work for either Imperial or metric drafting, the JIS linetypes are for metric work only. And I *still* recommend using the 24 standard linetypes for most drafting in metric or Imperial. If you find that the linetypes that come with AutoCAD do not cover what you need to represent a linetype in a drawing, you can create your own custom linetypes. I cover creating custom linetypes in Book IX, Chapter 4.

Linetypes are loaded into a drawing by using the Select Linetypes dialog box (from the menu browser or menu bar, click Format⇨Linetypes). I cover load-ing linetypes earlier in this chapter under the section "Setting linetype."

Setting Up Standards

In this chapter, I discuss many of the settings you can use to enhance your AutoCAD drawings. You may have observed that AutoCAD provides a number of settings, and if you're like me, the last thing you want to do is go through setting up layers each and every time you create a new drawing.

The good news is, you don't have to!

In Chapter 3 of this minibook, I discuss the various file types available in AutoCAD, and explain how to create a drawing by using a drawing template (DWT) file. I point out that the default drawing templates are fine, but that you probably want to add settings (and maybe even objects) to make them *really* useful.

Everything that I discuss in this chapter — from layers to linetypes to text and dimension styles — can be created and saved in a drawing template so that they're available to you in every drawing you start from that drawing template. After going through this chapter, you know that you can add quite a few settings to a drawing template to save yourself a great deal of effort for future drawings. In the chapters ahead, I look at annotation, inserting blocks, and other features that will enhance the usability of your drawing templates as well.

Chapter 7: Precision Tools

In This Chapter

✔ **Defining precision versus accuracy**

✔ **Understanding coordinate systems**

✔ **Entering coordinates**

✔ **Using direct distance entry**

✔ **Using drawing modes, object snaps, and point filters**

✔ **Using object snap tracking**

*T*he purpose of creating technical drawings, or *drafting,* is to convey enough information to a builder or fabricator so that he or she can construct or manufacture whatever it is that you've just technically drawn . . . er, drafted.

Manual drawings are as precise as the drafter can make them, which means as precise as a mechanical pencil dragged against a parallel rule or drafting machine. They're good enough to get the job done because the dimensions are going to confirm sizes and notes.

Dimensioning can be a major job in manual drafting, and luckily, you have an extra tool at your disposal with AutoCAD: You can add dimensions by clicking objects or selecting points. AutoCAD extracts the dimension value and adds the correct text to the dimension. Now, if you are precise in your drafting, the dimension values will be perfect, but if you are sloppy . . . you may be hearing from the builder that you've asked to locate a wall 12'–6 29/256" from the corner!

This chapter tells you how to make use of AutoCAD's built-in drafting aids to create accurate and precise drawings.

Understanding Accuracy and Precision

You probably hear a lot of sloppy word usage in the technical-drawing field. One of the most common offenses is the idea that *accuracy* and *precision* mean the same thing. They're different, and here's how:

✦ **Precision** means the degree of fineness of measurement. AutoCAD is capable of extremely high levels of precision — and can create drawings much more precisely than, say, a building or a highway could ever be constructed.

✦ **Accuracy** refers to the relationship between what is being drafted and reality. You can create the most precise drawings of which AutoCAD is capable, but if the surveyor got the field measurements wrong, or you read the field notes incorrectly, your drawing is not going to be accurate to reality.

Although accuracy is important, precision is the order of the day when you work with AutoCAD. Here's the skinny on AutoCAD's drafting aids:

✦ **Coordinate input:** Create drawing objects by specifying the x-, y-, and z-coordinates that locate them in 2D (or 3D) space.

✦ **Direct distance entry:** Locate new points relative to a point you've just entered by dragging the mouse pointer to show direction and then entering a value for the distance.

 ✦ **Grid and snap:** Drafting modes you can toggle on and off; grid is a purely visual aid, but snap is a precision input method.

 ✦ **Ortho and polar:** Additional drafting modes that can be toggled on/off; when turned on, ortho mode forces the crosshairs to move horizontally or vertically only, and polar tracking guides the crosshairs along preset angles.

 ✦ **Object snaps:** Locate points that fall at precise locations on an object (such as endpoints and midpoints of lines, or centers and quadrant points of circles).

 ✦ **Object snap tracking:** Use object snap points on existing objects to locate a new point in a drawing that does not fall on an existing object.

Through a combination of these drafting aids, you can create drawings far more precise than the most skillful manually drafted drawing. And what you'll quickly find as you gain experience is that drawing precisely is easier than drawing sloppily.

Understanding Coordinate Systems

In an AutoCAD drawing, everything is located in 2D (or 3D) space by a set of Cartesian, or x,y ($-z$), coordinates. Cartesian coordinates are named after the French philosopher Rene Descartes, who's probably better known for his saying, "I think, therefore I am."

Descartes believed that you could tease out the meaning of anything through a system of reasoning modeled on the certainty of mathematics. One of the side benefits of his mathematical thinking (arguably a more useful one than the system of reasoning) was the coordinate system named after him. Described simply, everything in 3D space can be located from a predefined origin by counting the number of units in each of the three directions between the object and the origin.

The 2D coordinate system — for the time being, I'll stick with 2D to keep things simple — is defined by a horizontal axis and a vertical axis. By convention, the horizontal axis is called the *x* axis, and the vertical axis is called the *y* axis. The *x* axis and *y* axis intersect at the *origin* of the coordinate system. The two axes define a plane called, naturally enough, the *xy plane*. The coordinates of any point are its distances from the origin along the *x* axis and the *y* axis, and the coordinates are expressed in the form *x,y*. For example, the coordinate pair 5,4 would indicate a point lying 5 units to the right of the origin along the *x* axis, and 4 units above the origin along the *y* axis.

The 3D coordinate system adds a third axis, the *z axis* (which is pronounced *zed-axis* outside the United States). The *z* axis also passes through the origin, and is perpendicular to the *xy* plane. I've more to say about the *z* axis in Book V.

The *x* and *y* axes divide the *xy* plane into four quadrants. Points located in the two quadrants to the right of the *y* axis have positive *x* coordinates; points to the left of the *y* axis have negative *x* coordinates. Points located in the two quadrants above the *x* axis have positive *y* coordinates, and points in the quadrants below the *x* axis have negative *y* coordinates. Figure 7-1 illustrates the 2D coordinate system.

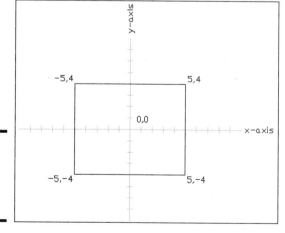

Figure 7-1:
The
Cartesian
coordinate
system.

To keep coordinates simple, most drawings are created in the upper-right quadrant. This locates the origin (0,0) at the lower-left corner of the drawing area so that all coordinate values can be positive numbers. The lower-left corner of the limits of a drawing usually starts at the origin, and is why the default lower-left corner is set to 0,0.

The world coordinate system

Everything you draw in AutoCAD is created in an infinitely large drawing space, and can be located by *x* and *y* coordinates. The default coordinate system in AutoCAD is called the *world coordinate system*, or WCS. Many AutoCAD users spend their whole careers drafting in the WCS. Unless you're working in 3D, there's little reason to change the WCS to a *user coordinate system* (or UCS), but it can be done if necessary. For more on working in 3D and the user coordinate system, see Book V.

The icon in the lower-left corner of the drawing area in Figure 7-1 is the UCS icon, and it's a handy device for recovering your bearings if you ever lose them. Figure 7-2 shows several variations in the icon's appearance. The box at the intersection of the two arrows means you're in the WCS.

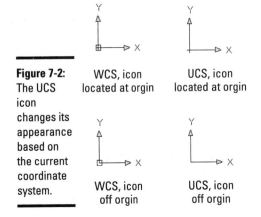

Figure 7-2: The UCS icon changes its appearance based on the current coordinate system.

WCS, icon located at orgin

UCS, icon located at orgin

WCS, icon off orgin

UCS, icon off orgin

If the UCS icon is set to display at the origin, it will move around the drawing area as the view of the drawing is panned and zoomed. If the icon is set to display *off* the origin, it will always appear at the lower-left corner of the drawing area.

By default AutoCAD displays the UCS icon at the origin. This can be distracting if you're only working in the WCS. The following steps explain how to control the UCS icon's display:

1. **On the ribbon, click View tab⇨UCS panel (expand the panel by clicking the panel's title area)⇨Display UCS Icon.**

The display of the UCS icon is toggled on and off based on its current state.

2. **On the ribbon, click View tab⇨UCS panel⇨Origin.**

3. **Specify a new point to move the UCS icon to 0,0,0 in the drawing, or to the lower-left corner of the drawing area.**

You can control the appearance and size of the UCS icon by using the UCS Icon dialog box. (On the menu browser or menu bar, click View menu⇨ Display⇨UCS Icon⇨Properties). If you are the nostalgic type, you can even make the UCS icon look the way it did in AutoCAD 2000 and earlier releases.

The display and position of the UCS icon is saved in the drawing. If you create a drawing template, you can set the UCS icon to display off the origin. Each drawing created with the drawing template will display the UCS icon in the position specified in the drawing template.

Entering coordinates

The standard way of feeding coordinates to AutoCAD is by typing them at the command prompt and pressing Enter. Five types of coordinate entries are commonly used in AutoCAD:

✦ Absolute x,y coordinates

✦ Relative x,y coordinates

✦ Relative polar coordinates

✦ Spherical coordinates

✦ Cylindrical coordinates

The first three types work in both 2D drafting and 3D modeling. The last two — spherical and cylindrical coordinates — are alternative ways of entering 3D coordinates and work in 3D only. These two coordinate-input methods are covered in Book V.

Entering absolute x,y coordinates

You enter absolute coordinates as pairs of numbers separated by a comma, like this: x,y. No spaces, just the comma (this is AutoCAD, not English punctuation!). The x value is always expressed first, and then the y value is represented. If you see a third value — for example, x,y,z — the z coordinate is representing a 3D point.

To draw a square by using absolute *x,y* coordinates from the command line, follow these steps:

1. **On the status bar, click Dynamic Input (DYN) to disable dynamic input.**

The Dynamic Input (DYN) button is disabled when it is not highlighted or not pushed in.

2. **On the ribbon, click Home tab⇨Draw panel⇨Line.**

The LINE command starts and displays the prompt

```
Specify first point:
```

3. **Type** 3,3 **and press Enter.**

The command displays the prompt

```
Specify next point or [Undo]:
```

4. **Type** 6,3 **and press Enter.**

The command displays the prompt

```
Specify next point or [Undo]:
```

5. **Type** 6,6 **and press Enter, and then type** 3,6 **and press Enter, and then type** C **and press Enter.**

The command line appears as follows:

```
Specify next point or [Undo]: 6,6
Specify next point or [Close/Undo]: 3,6
Specify next point or [Close/Undo]: C
```

To draw a square by using absolute *x,y* coordinates with dynamic input, follow these steps:

1. **On the status bar, click Dynamic Input (DYN) to enable dynamic input.**

You can tell that the Dynamic Input (DYN) button is enabled because it is highlighted or pushed in.

2. **On the ribbon, click Home tab⇨Draw panel⇨Line.**

The LINE command starts and displays the prompt

```
Specify first point:
```

3. **Type** 3,3 **and press Enter.**

The command displays the prompt

```
Specify next point or [Undo]:
```

The # (pound sign) tells dynamic input that the coordinate value entered is absolute and not the default relative coordinate value. If you do not enter # before the coordinate pair, dynamic input will process the value as a relative coordinate value. I discuss controlling the behavior for entering coordinate values for the second or next point in the "Dynamic input and coordinate entry" section later in this chapter.

4. **Type #6,3 and press Enter.**

The command displays the prompt

```
Specify next point or [Undo]:
```

5. **Type #6,6 and press Enter, and then type #3,6 and press Enter, and then type** C **and press Enter.**

The command line appears as follows:

```
Specify next point or [Undo]: 6,6
Specify next point or [Close/Undo]: 3,6
Specify next point or [Close/Undo]: C
```

You might use absolute coordinates if you're working on a site plan, and the surveyor has supplied you with coordinates of parcel corners. Drawing this way satisfies the need for precision, but you'd have to do a lot of calculating to figure out the absolute coordinates of every point in the drawing. It's much handier to use relative coordinates, which I cover next.

Entering relative x,y coordinates

Where absolute coordinates are always based on the origin of the drawing (that is, 0,0), relative coordinates are based on the last point entered. Input of the coordinates themselves is the same as for absolute *x,y* coordinates, but you tell AutoCAD that the location you're entering is based on the last point by typing an @ symbol before the coordinates — for example, entering **@5,4** makes a new point 5 units to the right and 4 units above the last point, not the origin.

To draw a square by using relative *x,y* coordinates from the command line, follow these steps:

1. **On the status bar, click Dynamic Input (DYN) to disable dynamic input.**

The Dynamic Input (DYN) button is no longer highlighted or pushed in.

2. **On the ribbon, click Home tab⇨Draw panel⇨Line.**

The LINE command starts and displays the prompt

```
Specify first point:
```

3. **Type 5,5 and press Enter.**

The command displays the prompt

```
Specify next point or [Undo]:
```

4. **Type** @5,0 **and press Enter.**

The command displays the prompt

```
Specify next point or [Undo]:
```

The @ symbol tells AutoCAD that the next point is relative to the point you just entered rather than the origin. From this point, AutoCAD draws a line 5 units in the *x* direction and 0 units in the *y* direction.

5. **Type** @0,5 **and press Enter, and then type** @-5,0 **and press Enter, and then type** C **and press Enter.**

Create vertical or horizontal lines by specifying 0 as the relative *y* or *x* coordinate. Draw lines to the left of or below the last point by specifying negative coordinate values.

The command line appears as follows:

```
Specify next point or [Undo]: @0,5
Specify next point or [Close/Undo]: @-5,0
Specify next point or [Close/Undo]: C
```

To draw a square by using relative *x,y* coordinates with dynamic input, follow these steps:

1. **On the status bar, click Dynamic Input (DYN) to enable dynamic input.**

The Dynamic Input (DYN) button is highlighted or pushed in.

2. **On the ribbon, click Home tab⇨Draw panel⇨Line.**

The LINE command starts and displays the prompt

```
Specify first point:
```

3. **Type** 5,5 **and press Enter.**

The command displays the prompt

```
Specify next point or [Undo]:
```

4. **Type** 5,0 **and press Enter.**

The command displays the prompt

```
Specify next point or [Undo]:
```

When using dynamic input, and its default behavior, you do not have to enter the @ symbol because it automatically assumes that you want to use relative coordinate values for the second or next points. If you enter @5,0 for the coordinate value, dynamic input will still process the value as relative.

5. **Type** 0,5 **and press Enter, and then type** -5,0 **and press Enter, and then type** C **and press Enter.**

Create vertical or horizontal lines by specifying 0 as the relative *y* or *x* coordinate. Draw lines to the left of or below the last point by specifying negative coordinate values. Notice that even though you did not enter the @ symbol, dynamic input added it for you when it sent the coordinate value to the command line.

The command line appears as follows:

```
Specify next point or [Undo]: @0,5
Specify next point or [Close/Undo]: @-5,0
Specify next point or [Close/Undo]: C
```

In my experience, this is one of the least-used methods of coordinate input. Luckily, you have another way of entering relative coordinates, one that makes much more sense than either of the preceding two: relative polar coordinates.

Entering relative polar coordinates

Relative polar coordinates are like relative *x,y* coordinates in that both use the @ symbol to tell AutoCAD to draw a line from the last point, not from the origin. They're different from relative *x,y* coordinates in that the two values are distance and angle, rather than offsets along the *x* and *y* axes. AutoCAD knows that you're entering polar coordinates because instead of a comma, you type a left angle bracket (also known as the less than symbol). Luckily, the left angle bracket is on the same key as the comma you use for *x,y* coordinates; you just need to also remember to hold down the Shift key.

For example, entering @5,30 at a LINE command prompt tells AutoCAD to draw a line segment 5 units in the *x* direction and 30 units in the *y* direction from the last point. Entering @5<30 tells AutoCAD to draw a line 5 units in length at an angle of 30 degrees. Obviously, the results are going to be very different, so if you want polar, don't forget to Shift!

To draw a square by using relative polar coordinates from the command line, follow these steps:

1. **On the status bar, click Dynamic Input (DYN) to disable dynamic input.**

The Dynamic Input (DYN) button is disabled when it is not highlighted or not pushed in.

2. **On the ribbon, click Home tab⇨Draw panel⇨Line.**

The LINE command starts and displays the prompt

```
Specify first point:
```

3. Type 9,9 **and press Enter.**

The command displays the prompt

```
Specify next point or [Undo]:
```

4. Type @7<0 **and press Enter.**

Remember, the @ symbol means *relative to the last point.* Type the distance, type — remember that Shift key! — the left angle bracket, type the angle, and press Enter.

AutoCAD draws a line 7 units long, at an angle of 0 degrees.

Chapter 4 of this minibook explains that by convention in AutoCAD, 0 degrees lies in the direction of the positive *x* axis, and angles are measured in a counterclockwise direction.

The command displays the prompt

```
Specify next point or [Undo]:
```

5. Type @7<90 **and press Enter, and then type** @7<180 **and press Enter, and then type** C **and press Enter.**

With relative polar coordinates, you're always entering positive values.

The command line appears as follows:

```
Specify next point or [Undo]: @7<90
Specify next point or [Close/Undo]: @7<180
Specify next point or [Close/Undo]: C
```

To draw a square by using relative polar coordinates with dynamic input, follow these steps:

1. On the status bar, click Dynamic Input (DYN) to enable dynamic input.

The Dynamic Input (DYN) button is highlighted or pushed in.

2. On the ribbon, click Home tab⇨Draw panel⇨Line.

The LINE command starts and displays the prompt

```
Specify first point:
```

3. Type 9,9 **and press Enter.**

The command displays the prompt

```
Specify next point or [Undo]:
```

4. Type 7<0 **and press Enter.**

Remember, you do not need to use the @ symbol when using the default settings of dynamic input. Type the distance, the left angle bracket, angle, and press Enter. If you enter @7<0 for the coordinate value, dynamic input will still process the value as relative.

AutoCAD draws a line 7 units long, at an angle of 0 degrees.

The command displays the prompt

```
Specify next point or [Undo]:
```

5. **Type** 7<90 **and press Enter, and then type** 7<180 **and press Enter, and then type** C **and press Enter.**

   With relative polar coordinates, you're always entering positive values.

   The command line appears as follows:

```
Specify next point or [Undo]: @7<90
Specify next point or [Close/Undo]: @7<180
Specify next point or [Close/Undo]: C
```

Most users find that relative polar coordinates are the most logical method of coordinate entry for use with the second or next point when creating or modifying objects in AutoCAD. You don't need to calculate displacements in the *x* and *y* directions; distances are actual distances.

So far so good, but AutoCAD has one more little trick up its sleeve that makes polar coordinates even easier. Read on . . .

Direct distance entry

An elaboration (actually a simplified method) of relative polar coordinates is called *direct distance entry,* or DDE. When you enter relative polar coordinates, you specify distance and angle, typing no fewer than four keystrokes, two of which also require that you hold down the Shift key.

When using DDE, you enter the distance only. You specify the angle by dragging the crosshairs on the screen. Not much hunting and pecking, and no holding down the Shift key.

"Waaaaait a minute," you say. "How *precise* can dragging the crosshairs to specify an angle be?" The answer, of course, is not very precise at all, *if* you're simply dragging the crosshairs without using the precision aids that AutoCAD provides. Ortho mode and polar tracking (both discussed shortly) help here: *Ortho* forces the crosshairs to move at angles of 0, 90, 180, and 270 degrees. *Polar tracking* is similar to ortho mode but is more flexible; you can specify any angle you like. Also, it doesn't force the crosshairs to follow those preset angles; it jumps to a specified angle and displays a tooltip to show your tracking (see Figure 7-3).

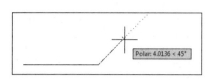

Figure 7-3: Now you're tracking! Polar tracking helps ensure precise angular input.

To draw a square by using direct distance entry, follow these steps:

1. On the status bar, click Ortho Mode (ORTHO) to enable ortho mode.

Ortho mode forces any lines you draw to be horizontal or vertical. I discuss ortho mode later in this chapter.

2. On the ribbon, click Home tab⇨Draw panel⇨Line.

The line command starts and displays the prompt

```
Specify first point:
```

3. Type 15,15 **and press Enter.**

The command displays the prompt

```
Specify next point or [Undo]:
```

4. Drag the crosshairs to the right, and then type 9 **and press Enter.**

It doesn't matter how far you drag the crosshairs — you're providing AutoCAD with an angle, not the distance. AutoCAD draws a horizontal line to the right with a length of 9 units.

The command displays the prompt

```
Specify next point or [Undo]:
```

5. Drag the crosshairs upward, type 9, **and press Enter. Then drag to the left, type** 9, **and press Enter. Finally, type** C **and press Enter.**

With relative polar coordinates, you always enter positive values. The command line appears as follows:

```
Specify next point or [Undo]: @7<90
Specify next point or [Close/Undo]: @7<180
Specify next point or [Close/Undo]: C
```

When you can use it, DDE is a terrific keystroke saver.

Dynamic input and coordinate entry

I introduce dynamic input in Chapter 3 of this minibook. Dynamic input was first introduced in AutoCAD 2006, and many have started to use it more and more with each release. Dynamic input provides several enhancements over entering coordinate values at the command line or using ortho mode and polar tracking. By default, dynamic input uses relative coordinates automatically when entering a second or next point, doing away with the need of the @ symbol.

If you turn off Dynamic Input (DYN) mode, AutoCAD still accepts input at the command line or through picking points in the drawing window, but if you're using dynamic input, relative coordinates are specified by default. And if you want to enter absolute coordinates by using dynamic input, you must use the # symbol as the prefix.

Dynamic input also offers some of the flexibility found in ortho mode and polar tracking through the use of dimension input tooltips that are displayed when specifying coordinate points. The dimension input tooltips allow you to lock the current input to a specific distance or angle or both. You control the behavior of the coordinate input for the second or next point through the use of dimension inputs on the Dynamic Input tab of the Drafting Settings dialog box.

To change the settings for dynamic input, follow these steps:

1. **On the status bar, right-click Dynamic Input (DYN) and choose Settings.**

   AutoCAD displays the Drafting Settings dialog box with the Dynamic Input tab current (see Figure 7-4).

2. **In the Pointer Input area, click Settings.**

   AutoCAD displays the Pointer Input Settings dialog box (Figure 7-5).

3. **In the Format area, select Relative Coordinates.**

   Selecting Relative Coordinates sets dynamic input to use relative coordinate values unless the # symbol is entered for the second or next point; this is the default option. When Relative Coordinates is set, you do not need to enter @ to use a relative coordinate value. If absolute is chosen, you must enter @ to use relative coordinate values.

   If you select Polar Format, AutoCAD defaults to the use of relative polar coordinates when both Relative Coordinates and Polar Format are enabled. When Polar Format is enabled, you must type a , (comma) to use Cartesian coordinate values. If Cartesian Format is chosen, you must type < (angle symbol) to use polar formats.

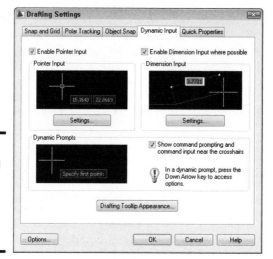

Figure 7-4:
Configuring
dynamic
input in the
Drafting
Settings
dialog box.

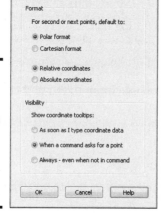

Figure 7-5:
Controlling
the format
used for the
second and
next point
when using
dynamic
input.

4. **Under Visibility, select When a Command Asks for a Point.**

   Selecting When a Command Asks for a Point displays dynamic tooltips
   only when a command is active; this is the default option. The option
   Always — Even When Not in a Command displays the dynamic input
   tooltip with the current coordinate location of the crosshairs when no
   command is active. The other setting, As soon as I Type Coordinate
   Data, displays dynamic tooltips only when you start typing a value.

5. **Click OK.**

   AutoCAD closes the Dimension Input Settings dialog box and returns to
   the Drafting Settings dialog box.

6. On the Dynamic Input tab, under the Dimension Input area, click Settings.

AutoCAD displays the Dimension Input Settings dialog box (see Figure 7-6).

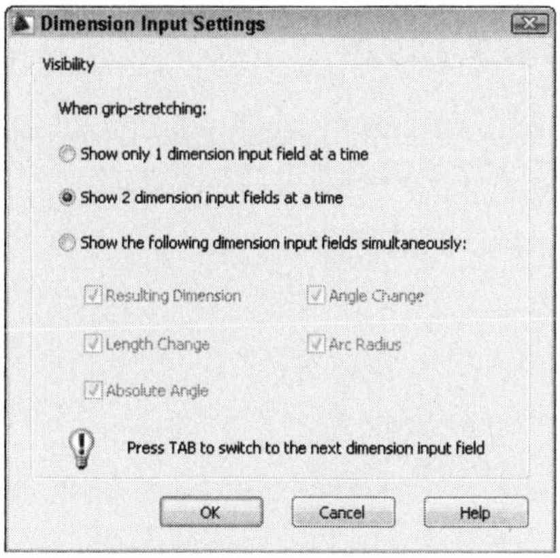

Figure 7-6:
Controlling the display of dimension input fields.

7. In the Dimension Input Settings dialog box, under the Visibility area, select Show 2 Dimension Input Fields at a Time.

This lets up to two dynamic input tooltips be displayed at a time; this is the default option. For example, when using the LINE command, a tooltip for distance and a second tooltip for angle are displayed. Not all commands support two dynamic tooltips; for example, the CIRCLE command displays only a distance tooltip for the radius/diameter of the circle.

When Show 1 Dimension Input Fields at a Time is set, only the primary dimension tooltip is displayed. The last option, Show the Following Dimension Input Fields Simultaneously, allows you to control which dimension input tooltips you want to display when specifying a point.

8. Click OK.

AutoCAD returns to the Drafting Settings dialog box.

9. In the Drafting Settings dialog box, click Drafting Tooltip Appearance.

AutoCAD displays the Tooltip Appearance dialog box, which allows you to control the color scheme, size, and transparency for the dynamic input tooltips.

10. In the Tooltip Appearance dialog box, make the desired changes to the appearance of the tooltips and click OK.

AutoCAD returns to the Drafting Settings dialog box.

11. **In the Drafting Settings dialog box, click OK.**

AutoCAD returns to the drawing window.

To draw a square by using the dimension input of dynamic input, follow these steps:

1. **On the status bar, click Dynamic Input (DYN) to enable dynamic input.**

The Dynamic Input (DYN) button is highlighted or pushed in.

2. **On the ribbon, click Home tab⇨Draw panel⇨Line.**

The LINE command starts and displays the prompt

```
Specify first point:
```

3. **Type** 9,3 **and press Enter.**

The command displays the prompt

```
Specify next point or [Undo]:
```

4. **Type** 6 **and press Tab.**

A lock now appears in the distance input tooltip, indicating that the distance dimension value is set. The angle input tooltip becomes active. Also notice that as you drag the crosshairs in the drawing window, the line segment is locked to 6 units.

5. **Type** 0 **and press Tab.**

A lock now appears in both the distance and angle input tooltips (see Figure 7-7). The distance input tooltip becomes active. Also notice that as you drag the crosshairs in the drawing window, the line segment is locked to 6 units and at an angle of 0.

Figure 7-7:
Locking input values for dimension tooltips.

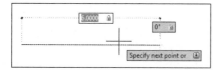

6. **Click in the drawing window to create the line.**

The command displays the prompt

```
Specify next point or [Undo]:
```

7. Type 6 **and press Tab, type** 90 **and press Tab, and then press Enter to create the line.**

The command displays the prompt

```
Specify next point or [Close/Undo]:
```

8. Type 6 **and press Tab, and then click Ortho Mode on the status bar to turn on ortho mode. Then drag to the left and click to create the line.**

The command displays the prompt

```
Specify next point or [Close/Undo]:
```

9. Type C **and press Enter.**

The command ends and completes the box.

Setting Grid and Snap

AutoCAD's grid is helpful for getting your bearings in a drawing but is not (strictly speaking) a precision aid. As I explain in Chapter 6 of this minibook, AutoCAD can display a nonplotting grid of horizontally and vertically aligned dots over the drawing area. This grid can help keep you aware of the relative sizes of what you are drawing — and their size on the plotted drawing. It also gives you a visual cue when you are drawing outside the established drawing limits.

If you're working in Isometric mode, the grid adjusts itself to a 30-60-90 angular alignment rather than horizontal and vertical. I do not cover isometric or other forms of 2D pictorial drafting in this book.

You can toggle the grid off and on with the Grid Display (GRID) button on the status bar or by pressing the F7 function key. You can set grid spacing at the command prompt, but it's easier to use the Drafting Settings dialog box, as I describe in a few paragraphs.

If you're zoomed way out in a drawing and turn on the grid, you may see the following message displayed at the command line:

```
Grid too dense to display
```

This message is not an error — it just means that the grid spacing is too small for AutoCAD to display at the current zoom ratio. Either zoom in closer (if you need to see the grid) or change the grid spacing (as I explain in just a moment).

Snap constrains the movement of the crosshairs to a specific increment; when snap is enabled, the crosshairs can no longer move freely about the drawing area but jump to points on an invisible grid. Snap, like grid, is toggled off and on by clicking the Snap Mode (or SNAP) button on the status bar, or by pressing the F9 function key. Also like the grid, snap can be set to Isometric mode. And finally, a polar snap is available when you have polar tracking turned on. (I discuss polar tracking in the next section.)

The following steps explain how to specify settings and enable snap and grid in the Drafting Settings dialog box:

1. **Move the crosshairs around the screen and look at the Drawing Coordinates area on the status bar.**

   If the Snap Mode (SNAP) button on the status bar is not selected, the crosshairs move freely in the drawing window, and the current location of the crosshairs is shown in the Drawing Coordinates area.

2. **On the status bar, click Snap Mode (SNAP) and Grid Display (GRID) so both buttons are highlighted or pressed in.**

   The grid turns on (it may be a little hard to see) and the crosshairs now jump from location to location. The Drawing Coordinates area continuously updates with the current location of the crosshairs and shows that the crosshairs move in constant increments.

3. **Right-click either the Snap Mode (SNAP) or Grid Display (GRID) button and choose Settings.**

   The Drafting Settings dialog box appears with the Snap and Grid tab active (see Figure 7-8).

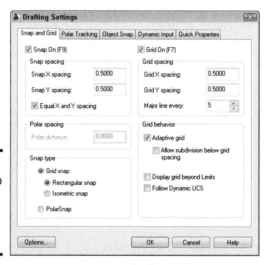

Figure 7-8:
Setting snap and grid in the Drafting Settings dialog box.

4. **In the Grid Spacing area, enter values for the *x* (horizontal) and *y* (vertical) spacing of the grid.**

   Entering the *x* spacing first causes the same value to appear in the *y* spacing box. For different *x* and *y* spacing, enter a new value in the *y* spacing box.

5. **To configure rectangular snap: In the Snap Spacing area, enter values for the *x* and *y* spacing.**

   As with setting grid spacing, entering a value for *x* spacing causes the same value to appear as the *y* spacing.

7. **To set up snap and grid for isometric drawing: In the Snap Type area, select Grid Snap and then select Isometric Snap.**

   When isometric snap is enabled, both grid and snap adjust from horizontal and vertical to 30-60-90 angles.

8. **If you're using polar tracking, select PolarSnap in the Snap Type area.**

   Selecting PolarSnap disables the settings in the Snap Spacing area and enables the Polar Spacing area in which you can enter a polar distance.

9. **Select the Snap On or Grid On check boxes to enable or disable snap or grid mode.**

10. **Click OK.**

    AutoCAD returns to the drawing window. The grid is displayed and the crosshairs snap to the specified x and y snap spacing.

It's not actually necessary to open the Drafting Settings dialog box to toggle snap and grid off and on — just use the status bar buttons or F7/F9 function keys.

You can change the snap origin and snap angle used for rectangular snap mode. The snap origin controls the starting point for a hatch pattern when using the HATCH command. I cover the HATCH command in Book III, Chapter 3. The snap angle rotates the snap points and the grid based on the specified angle. The crosshairs also rotate to match the entered angle.

Understanding Ortho and Polar Tracking

Ortho mode and polar tracking are two precision drafting aids that force the crosshairs to a specific angle. Ortho mode has been part of AutoCAD since the very beginning. When ortho mode is on, you can draw lines or choose points horizontally or vertically *only* along a vector based on the previous selected point. This is handy, but most drawings could use some consistent angular guidance beyond 90-degree increments. Polar tracking allows you to draw lines along specified angles other than in 90-degree increments.

Using ortho mode

Ortho mode could hardly be simpler. There are no settings to change; it's either on or it's off. If you find yourself drawing lots of horizontal and vertical lines, it's perfect for creating right-angled linework. To toggle ortho mode off and on, click the Ortho Mode (ORTHO) button on the status bar or use the F8 function key.

Using polar tracking

It's a rule in AutoCAD (and in life!) that with flexibility comes complexity. Polar tracking is a lot more flexible than ortho mode, and polar tracking has a ton more options than ortho mode (hey, *one* more option would be a lot more!).

You can right-click the Polar Tracking (POLAR) button on the status bar. From the shortcut menu, you can change the current polar angle by selecting one of the standard or additional angles that you added.

Options can make things feel more complex and even more confusing than necessary by using the same words for features that seem similar but are actually different. *Tracking* is one of those words. In this section I describe *polar* tracking, where AutoCAD displays "tracking vectors" to show you when you're on a preset polar tracking angle. At the end of this chapter I discuss *object snap* tracking (after I have told you what object snaps are, of course!). With object snap tracking, you use points on existing objects to find new points in a drawing that do not exist on other objects.

Simple stuff first: To enable polar tracking, click the Polar Tracking (POLAR) button on the status bar or press the F10 function key.

Where ortho mode forces you to draw horizontal and vertical lines and nothing else, polar tracking gently guides you along the right path by displaying a tooltip and a tracking vector to verify that you're heading the right way. All in all, polar is a kinder, gentler — and did I say more flexible? — version of ortho mode.

The default angle setting for polar tracking is 90 degrees, which means you can use it instead of ortho mode. Having polar tracking turned on with the default setting means that you can draw at any angle, but you see a tooltip when you're on a horizontal or vertical path.

Polar tracking and ortho mode can't both be on at the same time; enabling one disables the other. If you're like many experienced drafters, you may consign ortho mode to the virtual trash can.

The following steps explain how to configure and use polar tracking:

1. **On the status bar, click the Polar Tracking (POLAR) button so it is not highlighted or pressed in.**

2. **Start the LINE command, pick a start point, and then move the crosshairs around the drawing window.**

There is no restriction or input on where you pick the next point of the line.

3. **On the status bar, right-click the Polar Tracking (POLAR) button and choose Settings.**

AutoCAD displays the Drafting Settings dialog box with the Polar Tracking tab current (see Figure 7-9).

Figure 7-9:
Configuring polar tracking in the Drafting Settings dialog box.

4. **In the Polar Angle Settings area, select the Increment Angle (angles and their multiples that you want to track on-screen) drop-down list and then one of the available angles.**

Standard subdivisions of 90 degrees appear in the drop-down list. AutoCAD also recognizes multiples of increment angles; for example, if you select 45 degrees from the list, AutoCAD also locks on 135, 225, and 315 degrees.

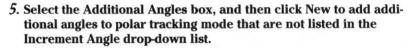

5. **Select the Additional Angles box, and then click New to add additional angles to polar tracking mode that are not listed in the Increment Angle drop-down list.**

AutoCAD does *not* track multiples of Additional Angles you enter; if you enter 16.87 degrees, polar tracking will recognize that angle only, not 33.74 degrees or other multiples of the original.

6. **In the Object Snap Tracking Settings area, choose which tracking vectors you want to appear when using object snap tracking to find points.**

Select Track Orthogonally Only (the default setting) to display only horizontal and vertical tracking vectors, or Track Using All Polar Angle Settings to display all the Increment and Additional angles you specified in the Polar Angle Settings area. Note that this has an effect only if the Object Snap Tracking (OTRACK) button is enabled. I cover object snap tracking at the end of this chapter.

Although object snap tracking settings appear on the same tab as polar tracking angles, they're independent of one another. Regardless of whether you choose Track Orthogonally Only or Track Using All Polar Angle Settings, when you're drawing stuff, all tracking angles show up. The object snap tracking settings only kick in if you're actually tracking from one object snap point to another — that is, the Object Snap Tracking (OTRACK) button on the status bar is enabled. Are you lost yet? Don't worry; I discuss object snaps in the following section and object snap tracking at the end of the chapter.

7. **In the Polar Angle Measurement area, choose how the polar angles are to be measured.**

Selecting Absolute is the least likely to get you lost because the tracking angles are the same as the angular measure you set up in the Units dialog box; that is, 0 degrees is to the right, 90 degrees is straight up, and so on. Selecting Relative to Last Segment would display a vector at, say 45 degrees to the last line, which will probably not be the same as the absolute angle of 45 degrees.

When you're familiar with the system, of course, it's fine to temporarily set Polar Angle measurement relative to the last segment. But I think it's a good idea to use Absolute until you are familiar with the feature. If you want, experiment with the Relative to Last Segment option to see which option you prefer.

8. **Select the Polar Tracking On check box to enable polar tracking.**

9. **Click OK.**

AutoCAD returns to the drawing window.

10. **Move the crosshairs around the drawing window again.**

Notice that the crosshairs snap to the angle listed under the Increment Angles drop-down list and any angles listed under the Additional Angles list box.

The Polar Snap setting in the Snap Type area and the Polar Distance in the Polar Spacing area allow you to snap to points along the tracking vector at a specified distance.

Clicking the Options button in the Drafting Settings dialog box takes you to the Drafting tab of AutoCAD's Options dialog box. For the time being, you don't need to change any settings here — the defaults all work fine. I cover the Options dialog box in detail in Book IX.

Working with Object Snaps

Up until now, you've been relying on AutoCAD's coordinate system to locate points and draw objects. That's fine, but if calculating and entering coordinates were the only way of drawing accurately, you'd probably run screaming back to a drafting board. After you use coordinates to get some objects drawn, you can start using another important feature: object snaps.

Object snaps let you pick a precise point on an existing object; the point you pick depends on which Object Snap mode you select.

Object Snap modes are different from object to object, depending on the object type. For example, lines have endpoint and midpoint object snaps, circles have center and quadrant object snaps, and arcs have endpoints, midpoints, centers, *and* quadrants.

You can right-click the Object Snap (OSNAP) button on the status bar and turn on and off different running object snaps from the shortcut menu.

New users often get confused by snap and object snap. *Snap* is a status bar toggle that forces the crosshairs to jump from preset snap interval to interval. Snap is available whether or not objects are in the drawing. *Object snap* lets you find exact points on existing objects, such as the center of a circle or the insertion point of a piece of text. Snap doesn't need objects, but object snap does.

You can use object snaps in two ways: They can be on and available all the time, in which case they're referred to as *running object snaps,* or you can select the ones you want from a toolbar, shortcut menu, or the command prompt, for one click only. These are referred to as *single object snaps,* or object snap *overrides.* Because there are some extra wrinkles involved in setting up running object snaps, I'm going to deal with object snap overrides first.

Table 7-1 lists the Object Snap modes and how you use them.

Table 7-1		**Object Snap Modes**	
Button	*Marker*	*Function*	*Description*
	—	Temporary TRACK point	Sets a temporary point by using object snap tracking
	—	FROM	Sets a temporary reference point from which you specify an offset
	□	ENDpoint	Locates the endpoints of lines, arcs, elliptical arcs, splines, or polyline segments
	△	MIDpoint	Locates the midpoints of lines, arcs, elliptical arcs, splines, or polyline segments
	✕	INTersection	Locates the intersection of two or more objects
	⊠	APParent INTersection	Locates the visual intersection of two objects that are on different planes but appear to intersect in the drawing window
	—	EXTension	Projects a temporary vector from the end of a line, an arc, an elliptical arc, or a polyline segment along which you can pick a point
	○	CENter	Locates the center of circles, arcs, elliptical arcs, or polyline arc segments
	◇	QUAdrant	Locates the quadrant points of a circle, an arc, elliptical arc, or polyline arc segment
	○	TANgent	Locates the point of tangency on circles, arcs, elliptical arcs, splines, or polyline arc segments
	⊥	PERpendicular	Locates a point perpendicular to an object

Button	Marker	Function	Description
		PARallel	Lets you draw a line parallel to another line through any point
		INSertion	Locates the insertion point of text, block insertions, or external references
		NODe	Locates a point object, corners of the bounding box for a multiline text object, or the start points of the extension lines for dimensions
		NEArest	Locates a point on an object closest to the crosshairs
	—	NONe	Temporarily disables all running object snaps for one selection
	—	OSNAP settings	Displays the Object Snap tab of the Drawing Settings dialog box

Some object snap modes require two picks to set and therefore can't be used as running object snaps. For example, you can find a point midway between two unconnected points by choosing Mid Between 2 Points (M2P or MID2) from the shortcut menu or keyboard, but you can't set it as a running object snap.

Hardcore typists can use the keyboard to set object snap overrides by entering the capitalized letters in the table. To find the apparent intersection of two objects, for example, you can enter **APPINT** or type **END** to select the endpoint of an object.

You can use the OSMODE system variable to set multiple running object snaps at once. To find out more about the OSMODE system variable, type **OSMODE** at the command prompt and press F1 to open the related topic in AutoCAD's Command Reference guide.

For AutoCAD LT users, the Parallel and Extension object snaps were first made available in AutoCAD LT 2007.

The following steps explain how to use object snaps:

1. **On the status bar, right-click the Object Snap (OSNAP) button and choose Settings.**

AutoCAD displays the Drafting Settings dialog box with the Object Snap tab current (see Figure 7-10).

2. **Click the Clear All button.**

All the object snaps are unchecked.

3. **In the Object Snap Modes area, select Endpoint and then click OK.**

Endpoint is set as the only running object snap and AutoCAD returns to the drawing window.

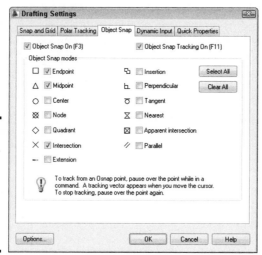

Figure 7-10:
Snap to it . . .
set running
object
snaps in the
Drafting
Settings
dialog box.

4. **On the ribbon, click Home tab⇨Draw panel⇨Line.**

The LINE command starts and displays the prompt

```
Specify first point:
```

5. **Type** 2,5 **and press Enter.**

The command displays the prompt

```
Specify next point or [Undo]:
```

6. **Type** @5<90 **and press Enter twice.**

A line 5 units in length is drawn and the LINE command ends.

7. **Start the LINE command again.**

8. **Position the crosshairs near the start point of the line that you just drew. When the Endpoint object snap marker is displayed, click in the drawing window.**

The first point of the line is started at the endpoint of the previous line.

9. **Type @5<0 and press Enter.**

The command displays the prompt

```
Specify next point or [Undo]:
```

10. **Type** MID **and press Enter.**

The command displays the prompt

```
Specify next point or [Undo]: mid of
```

The Midpoint object snap is used as an override for the Endpoint running object snap.

11. **Position the crosshairs near the middle of the first line that was drawn. When the Midpoint object snap marker is displayed, click in the drawing window.**

You should get an object that resembles a triangle on a stick, like the one shown in Figure 7-11.

12. **Press Enter to end the LINE command.**

Figure 7-11:
Results of using both running and override object snaps.

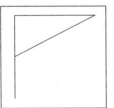

Using Point Filters

Sometimes it's useful to use part of a location's coordinates to locate a point in a drawing. You can find the center of a circle by using object snaps. But suppose you want to find the precise middle point of a square. Squares and rectangles don't have "centers" in the same way that circles do.

Using *point filters* (also known as *dot filters* or *xy filters*), you can locate a new point by combining the *x* coordinate from one point with the *y* coordinate from another (and, if you're working in 3D, the *z* coordinate from a third). It's a complicated system, and it takes some practice, but if you feel like taking the AutoCAD Point Filter Challenge, follow these steps to draw a circle at the center of a rectangle:

1. **Open a drawing containing a rectangular area in which you want to draw a circle, or create a new drawing and draw a rectangle.**

2. **On the status bar, right-click the Object Snap (OSNAP) button and choose Settings. Make sure that Midpoint object snap is selected and click OK.**

3. **On the ribbon, click Home tab⇨ Draw panel⇨Circle, Radius.**

   The CIRCLE command starts and displays the prompt

   ```
   Specify center point for circle or [3P/2P/Ttr (tan tan
       radius)]:
   ```

4. **Hold down the Shift key, right-click, and choose Point Filters to open the list shown in Figure 7-12.**

Figure 7-12:
Use the
shortcut
menu to
select point
filters.

5. **Choose .X.**

   The command displays the prompt

   ```
   .X of
   ```

6. **Move the crosshairs over a horizontal side of the rectangle and click when you see the Midpoint object snap marker.**

   The command displays the prompt:

   ```
   .X of (need yz):
   ```

7. **Move the crosshairs over a vertical side of the rectangle and click when you see the Midpoint object snap marker.**

   AutoCAD locates the center point of the circle at a new point generated from the *x* coordinate of the first picked point and the *y* coordinate of the second.

Working with Object Snap Tracking Mode

No, OTRACK is not the name of the Irish railway system. Sure and begorrah, OTRACK is much more useful than that. OTRACK is short for *object snap tracking,* an AutoCAD feature that lets you locate new points based on object snap points on existing objects.

Object snap tracking automates the point filter process I describe earlier. For example, here's how you use object snap tracking to place a circle in the exact center of a rectangle:

1. **Open a drawing containing a rectangular area in which you want to draw a circle, or create a new drawing and draw a rectangle.**

2. **On the status bar, right-click the Object Snap Tracking (OTRACK) button and choose Settings to display the Drafting Settings dialog box, and make sure that the Midpoint object snap is selected.**

   You can also right-click the Object Snap (OSNAP) button and choose Midpoint if it is not selected.

3. **Select the Object Snap On and Object Snap Tracking On check boxes, and then click OK.**

   You can also click the Object Snap (OSNAP) and Object Snap Tracking (OTRACK) buttons to enable both modes.

4. **On the ribbon, click Home tab⇨Draw panel⇨Circle flyout⇨Circle, Radius.**

   The CIRCLE command starts and displays the prompt

   ```
   Specify center point for circle or [3P/2P/Ttr (tan tan
       radius)]:
   ```

5. **Move the crosshairs to the middle of a horizontal side of the rectangle.**

   The Midpoint object snap marker appears.

6. **Rest the crosshairs over the object snap marker for a moment but don't click.**

   When you move the crosshairs, you should see a tracking vector passing through the object snap marker.

7. **Without clicking, move the crosshairs to the middle of a vertical side of the rectangle.**

8. **When the object snap marker appears, rest the crosshairs over it for a moment.**

   Now when you move the crosshairs, you should see two tracking vectors, one running through each of the midpoints.

9. **Move the crosshairs until the two tracking vectors are aligned vertically and horizontally (see Figure 7-13), and then click to set the center point of the circle.**

   If dynamic input mode is enabled, you also get confirmation that you're on the money in the dynamic input tooltip.

Figure 7-13: Finding the "center" of a square by using object snap tracking.

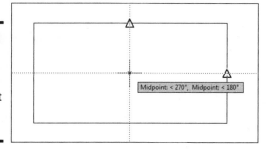

Midpoint: < 270°, Midpoint: < 180°

For AutoCAD LT users, object snap tracking was first made available in AutoCAD LT 2007.

Book II

2D Drafting

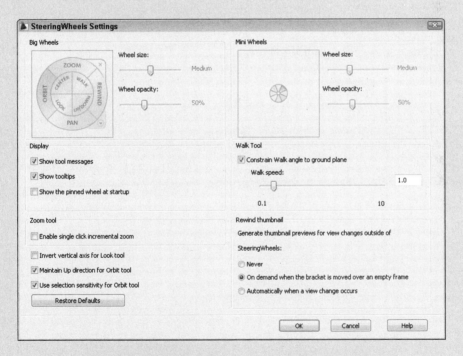

Set a course across drawings and through models
as the venture into AutoCAD is set to begin.

Contents at a Glance

Chapter 1: Drawing Objects **157**

Locating and Using the Drawing Tools 157
Let's Get Primitive 161
Creating Construction Geometry 166
Without a Trace...169
A Bit Sketchy...170
Drawing Parallel Lines 171
Complex Curves 174
Complex Objects and Shapes 178

Chapter 2: Modifying Objects **185**

Setting Selection Options 185
Selecting Objects...187
AutoCAD's Editing Commands 193
Coming to Grips with Grips 213

Chapter 3: Managing Views **215**

A Zoom of One's Own 219
Pan in a Flash..224
Get a Grip on the Wheel and Hang On...226
Name That View 228
Having AutoCAD Put on a Show 232
To Regen or to Redraw . . . That Is the Question 234

Chapter 1: Drawing Objects

In This Chapter

✔ **Using drawing tools**

✔ **Creating primitive objects**

✔ **Understanding construction objects**

✔ **Creating trace objects**

✔ **Sketching objects**

✔ **Drawing parallel lines**

✔ **Drawing complex curves**

✔ **Drawing complex objects and shapes**

*W*elcome to Book II. It's time to get primitive! No, I'm not asking you to move into a tree in the backyard and howl at the moon. In this chapter, I introduce AutoCAD's *primitive objects* — or the *basic objects* if you will — and the drawing commands for creating them. Primitive objects in AutoCAD are lines, arcs, circles, and points.

After I explore the primitive heart of AutoCAD, I look at some of its more complex object-creation tools. These include polylines, multilines (double lines if you're using AutoCAD LT), and some obscure entities such as traces and 2D solids.

As I explain in Book I, you can interact with AutoCAD in several ways. You can start most drawing commands from the Draw panel, the toolbar, or the menu, or by typing the command name (or its short-form *alias*) at the keyboard. In nearly all cases, using any of these methods to start a command initiates a dialog with AutoCAD.

Locating and Using the Drawing Tools

Table 1-1 tells you where to find all the drawing commands AutoCAD provides, as well as what you can do with these commands. We don't cover the commands in this order; just think of this table as a handy reference chart. In the interests of fairness and democracy, Table 1-1 lists commands in alphabetical order by command name, not by popularity or frequency of use. Depending on the drawings that you create, LINE, ARC, and CIRCLE are probably going to be the commands you will use the most.

Table 1-1			AutoCAD's 2D Drawing Tools		
Icon	*Ribbon*	*Draw Toolbar*	*Draw Menu*	*Command Name (Alias)*	*Function*
	Home⇨ Draw panel⇨Arc	Arc	Arc	ARC (A)	Draws circular arc objects.
	Blocks & References⇨ Attributes panel⇨ Define Attributes	—	Block, Define Attributes	ATTDEF (ATT)	Defines attributes to be included in block definition. Attributes are covered in Book VI.
	Blocks & References⇨ Block panel⇨ Create	Make Block	Block, Make	BLOCK (B)	Defines a block from drawing objects. Blocks are covered in Book VI.
	Home⇨ Draw panel's title bar⇨Boundary	—	Boundary	BOUNDARY (BO)	Creates a polyline or a region from edges of a closed area. For more on Boundary, see Book III.
	Home⇨Draw panel⇨Circle	Circle	Circle	CIRCLE (C)	Draws circle objects.
—	—	—	Double Line	DLINE (DL)	Draws double parallel lines. (AutoCAD LT only.)
	Home⇨ Draw panel's title bar⇨Donut	—	Donut	DONUT (DO)	Draws a circular polyline object specifying the inside and outside diameter.
	HomeDraw panel⇨Ellipse flyout⇨Axis, End	Ellipse	Ellipse⇨Axis, End	ELLIPSE (EL)	Draws ellipse objects.
	Home⇨Draw panel⇨Ellipse flyout⇨Elliptical Arc	Ellipse Arc	Ellipse⇨Arc	ELLIPSE (EL)	Draws elliptical arc objects.

Icon	Ribbon	Draw Toolbar	Draw Menu	Command Name (Alias)	Function
	Home⇨Draw panel's title bar⇨Gradient	Gradient	Gradient	GRADIENT (GD)	Applies a gradient fill pattern to closed areas. Gradients are covered in Book III.
	Home⇨Draw panel⇨Hatch	Hatch	Hatch	HATCH (H)	Applies a solid or predefined pattern to closed areas. Hatches are covered in Book III.
	Home⇨Draw panel⇨Line	Line	Line	LINE (L)	Draws straight line objects between two points.
	—	—	Multiline	MLINE (ML)	Draws multiple parallel lines. (AutoCAD only.)
A	Annotate ⇨ Text panel⇨ Multiline Text	Multiline Text	Text⇨ MultilineText	MTEXT (MT)	Draws multiline annotation text objects. Text is covered in Book III.
	Home⇨ Draw panel⇨ Polyline	Polyline	Polyline	PLINE (PL)	Draws connected linear or arc segment objects.
	Home⇨ Draw panel's title bar⇨Point flyout⇨Point	Point	Point	POINT (PO)	Draws point objects.
	Home⇨Draw panel⇨Polygon	Polygon	Polygon	POLYGON (POL)	Draws regular closed polygonal polylines.
	Home tabDraw panel's title bar⇨Ray	Ray	Ray	RAY (—)	Draws infinite-length construction lines starting from a single point.
	Home⇨Draw panel⇨Rectangle	Rectangle	Rectangle	RECTANG (REC)	Draws closed rectangular polyline objects.

Book II Chapter 1

Drawing Objects

(continued)

Table 1-1 *(continued)*

Icon	Ribbon	Draw Toolbar	Draw Menu	Command Name (Alias)	Function
	Home⇨Draw panel⇨Region	Region	Region	REGION (REG)	Creates a single closed object from nested objects.
	Home⇨Draw panel's title bar⇨ Revision Cloud	Revision Cloud	Revision Cloud	REVCLOUD (—)	Draws revision clouds.
—	—	—	—	SKETCH (—)	Draws freehand sketches as poly-lines or multiple line objects.
	Home⇨3D Modeling panel's title bar⇨2D Solid	—	Modeling⇨ Meshes⇨2D Solid	SOLID (SO)	Draws 3- or 4-sided solid-filled shapes. Not related to 3D solids.
	Home⇨Draw panel's title bar⇨ Spline	Spline	Spline	SPLINE (SPL)	Draws freeform spline curve objects.
	Annotate⇨ Tables panel⇨ Table	Table	Table	TABLE (TB)	Draws table objects specifying rows and columns. Tables are covered in Book III.
	Annotate⇨ Text panel⇨ Single Line Text	—	Text⇨Single Line Text	TEXT (T)	Draws single-line annotation text objects. Text is covered in Book III.
—	—	—	—	TRACE (—)	Draws single segment lines with width.
	Home⇨Draw panel's title bar⇨ Construction Line	Construc-tion Line	Construction Line	XLINE (XL)	Draws an infinite-length construction line through specified points.
	Home⇨ Draw panel's title bar⇨Wipeout	—	Wipeout	WIPEOUT (—)	Draws closed polygons that mask the objects below it.

If a command can be executed only by typing its name (that is, it has no tool button or menu item), it's not going to be used that frequently; SKETCH and TRACE are in this category.

In this chapter, I'm not going to cover every single drawing command in extensive detail — if you need to know more about a command I suggest using the online Help system. The Command Reference has an alphabetical listing of every command and details about each command's options. To access the Command Reference, choose Help⇨Help or press the F1 key. Click the Contents tab, and then click the plus sign beside Command Reference.

Sometimes you have to dig down into the Help system to find a command. You can get to a command much faster by typing the command you need additional help on and pressing Enter. After the command is started, press F1 to open the online Help system to the topic on the command. You can also position the cursor over a command on the ribbon, toolbar, or menu browser and press F1 when the tooltip is displayed.

Let's Get Primitive

AutoCAD's primitive object types are lines, circles, arcs, and points. Each of these object types takes very little input to define. A line is defined by two endpoints, arcs and circles by their center points and radii, and points by a single set of coordinates.

In this section, I look at the four commands that create these four primitive object types. The commands are (which should not be much of a shock) LINE, CIRCLE, ARC, and POINT.

Keeping to the straight and narrow

The LINE command creates a line object. In AutoCAD, a line object is defined with two endpoints. You use the LINE command to draw straight lines from point to point to point. The LINE command continues prompting for points until you explicitly end the sequence by pressing Enter or Esc. Whichever method you choose to start the command, the first prompt that is displayed is

```
Specify first point:
```

Pick a point in the drawing window, or use an object snap (see Book I for more information on using object snaps) to find a precise point on an existing object, or type a pair of *x,y* coordinates to locate the starting point of the line. After you pick the first point, the command displays the prompt

```
Specify next point or [Undo]:
```

Specify the second and next points by using the methods just described. If you make a mistake, or change your mind after you specify the second point, enter U (for *Undo*) and press Enter to undraw the previous line segment. As you continue to add line segments, you can enter U and press Enter at any time to undo the last line segment you drew.

Command options appear inside square brackets. To select a command option, type the uppercase letter in the option and press Enter.

Specify subsequent points in the same manner as the first points. After you pick the third point (that is, after you have two line segments), the command displays the prompt

```
Specify next point or [Close/Undo]:
```

There are now two options, Undo and Close. After you've drawn two line segments, you can create a closed shape by entering C and pressing Enter. If you're using dynamic input, you can select Close from the dynamic display (see Figure 1-1). This draws one last line segment from the last point you specified to the original starting point, which was specified when you started the LINE command. To stop drawing line segments and exit the LINE command, press Enter or Esc or the spacebar, or right-click and choose Enter from the shortcut menu.

In Book I, I talk about relative coordinates and how AutoCAD interprets the @ symbol as relative to the last point you picked. You can use the @ symbol by itself to tell AutoCAD you want to use the last point you picked in the drawing window or entered by using coordinates. For example, if you enter @ at the *Specify first point:* prompt, AutoCAD starts the line at the last point entered.

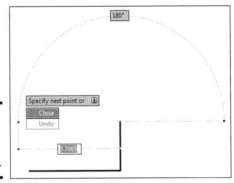

Figure 1-1:
Drawing
lines
dynamically.

Going around in circles

Circles are one of the basic objects that can be created in AutoCAD, although you may not create them quite as often as you create arcs. I'm going to talk about circles before I talk about arcs because circles are simpler to draw. Even so, you can create circles in five ways — six, if you use the ribbon or menus. Figure 1-2 shows the menu browser with all six options.

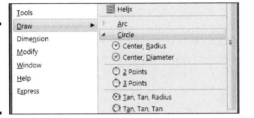

Figure 1-2:
How many
ways can
you draw a
circle?

On the ribbon, click Home⇨Draw panel⇨Circle flyout⇨Center, Radius, which is the default method for drawing circles. the Circle, Radius option is the default method used for creating a circle when you click Circle on the Draw toolbar, or type CIRCLE or its alias C and press Enter.

If you start the command by using the default option, the command displays the prompt

```
Specify center point for circle or [3P/2P/Ttr (tan tan
    radius)]:
```

At this point, you can locate the center point by specifying a point in the drawing window or by entering coordinates for the center point, or you can choose one of the three options inside the square brackets.

If you specify a center point, the command displays the prompt

```
Specify radius of circle or [Diameter]:
```

Another choice to make! You can either enter a value for the circle's radius or specify a point in the drawing window to define the circle's radius, or you can enter **D** and press Enter to choose the diameter option. If you enter a value or specify a point, the circle is drawn based on the specified values. If you enter **D** and press Enter, the command displays the prompt

```
Specify diameter of circle:
```

If this is the first circle you've drawn in this session, no previous or default value is shown at the command line. If you've drawn a previous circle, a default value (the last-entered radius) is shown inside the angle brackets.

You can also draw circles by specifying two points that represent the endpoints of a line representing the diameter of the circle, or by specifying three points that lie on the circumference of the circle. And yet another way you can draw circles is by selecting two objects your circle should be tangent to, and then entering a radius.

The Draw panel on the ribbon offers a sixth method that actually invokes a macro; instead of prompting you to enter a radius after you've selected the first two objects for tangency, AutoCAD asks you to select a third object.

Arcs of triumph

If you thought a half-dozen ways of drawing circles was a lot, you haven't seen anything yet! There are no fewer than 11 ways to draw arcs. Worse, the default method — 3 points — is the construction method for creating arcs that you're least likely to encounter. Figure 1-3 shows the Arc command options available through the Draw menu on the menu browser.

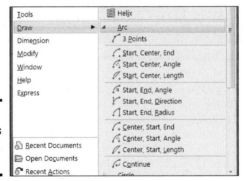

Figure 1-3:
Eleven ways
to draw
an arc.

While you're getting familiar with the program, it's easiest to use the Draw panel on the ribbon's Home tab to choose the option you want. The nine central options on the Arc flyout of the Draw panel are all based on start points and center points, and then each has variations of endpoint, included angle, direction, length, or radius.

On the ribbon, click Home⇨Draw panel⇨Arc flyout. Then click Start, Center, End, for example, to preset the command options so that the three points you enter are indeed interpreted as the starting point, the center point, and the ending point.

One little gotcha is that by default, arcs are drawn in a counterclockwise direction. Figure 1-4 shows how you control the way your arcs are drawn.

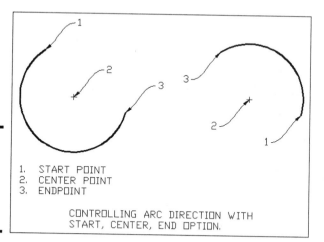

Figure 1-4: Arc direction by default is counter-clockwise.

1. START POINT
2. CENTER POINT
3. ENDPOINT

CONTROLLING ARC DIRECTION WITH START, CENTER, END OPTION.

You're probably aware that pressing Enter or the spacebar, or right-clicking and choosing Enter, repeats the last command. What these actions don't do is repeat the last command options you chose. Instead, they repeat the command with its default options. In the case of ARC, that will give you a 3-point arc, where the three points you pick are the starting and ending points and a random point somewhere along the arc itself. Most of the time this is not what you want.

The point of the exercise

After all that arcane arc knowledge, you're probably ready for something simple. You're in luck — the simplest of all objects that can be created is at hand. Points are defined in the drawing by an *x-, y-, z*-coordinate location. You create a point object by using one of the methods for starting the POINT command in Table 1-1 and then specifying a point in the drawing window; you need to do nothing else.

Although I've been talking about *x,y* coordinate pairs, in fact every object in a drawing is located by an *x-, y-, z*-coordinate triplet. In most cases for 2D drafting, the value of the *z* coordinate is 0.

Although I'm dealing with 2D objects in this part of the book, the point object is pretty one dimensional. Because points have no length or width, they can be small and hard to see. The default appearance for the point object is a single pixel, but you can change the appearance to something more visible by following these steps:

1. From the menu browser or menu bar, click Format⇨Point Style.

AutoCAD displays the Point Style dialog box (see Figure 1-5).

2. Select one of the point styles by clicking its icon.

The selected point style is globally applied to all point objects in the drawing; you can have only one point style per drawing.

3. Specify the size of the point objects, and then click OK.

Set the point size as either a percentage relative to the screen size or in absolute units. If you set the point size in absolute units, the point objects appear larger or smaller as you zoom in or out; if you set the point size relative to the screen size, point objects stay the same size as you zoom in or out.

As I mention, the default point style is a single pixel. Click the top-left icon in the Point Style dialog box to select it. The next icon to the right is no display at all — that's right, you can create point objects that you can't see. Setting the point style to nothing is ideal if you don't want the point objects to appear when plotting a drawing.

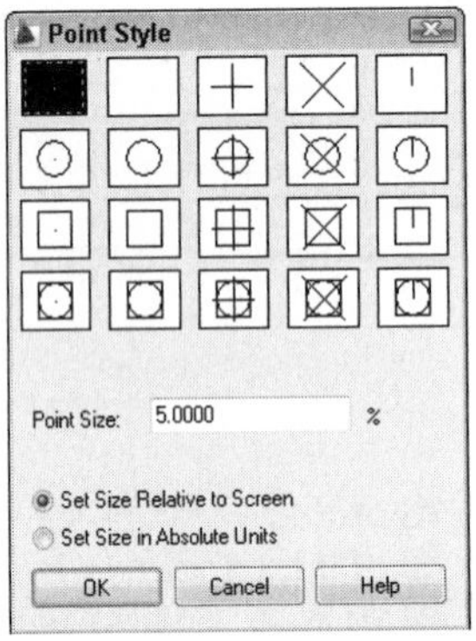

Figure 1-5:
Style your points in the Point Style dialog box.

Creating Construction Geometry

In spite of snap mode, ortho mode, polar tracking, and object snaps, many drafters use the software the same way they drew things with pencils and T squares — they draw temporary construction geometry to line things up and project drawing features from one view to another. AutoCAD has a couple of construction geometry tools that help with this process: *construction lines* and *rays*.

Xlines for X-men

You create construction lines (commonly known as *xlines*) with the XLINE command. Xlines (and rays) are unlike any other object in AutoCAD in that they have infinite length.

Create a separate layer for your construction lines so you can easily turn them off and on when you want to see your objects in the drawing without all the visual noise. Construction lines and rays will plot, so be sure to turn off the layer before you plot your drawings.

Although xlines look a lot like lines, they do not have endpoints, so you have to construct your xlines accordingly. The following steps explain how to create a series of vertical xlines, as shown in Figure 1-6:

1. **Turn on appropriate object snaps.**

This is an important step; because you're going to be aligning your xlines with existing drawing objects, it's important that you place them precisely.

**Book II
Chapter 1**

Drawing Objects

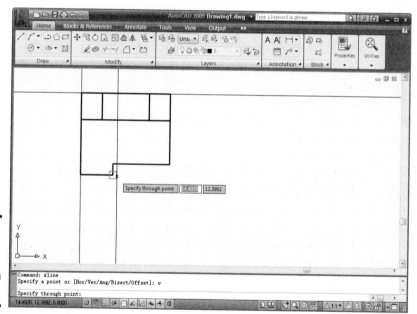

Figure 1-6:
Laying down construction lines.

2. **Start the XLINE command by using one of the methods in Table 1-1.**

   The command displays the prompt

   ```
   Specify a point or [Hor/Ver/Ang/Bisect/Offset]:
   ```

3. **Type the uppercase letter of the option you want. In this case, type V and press Enter.**

   When you respond to the prompt, it doesn't matter whether you type an uppercase or lowercase letter. The command displays the prompt

   ```
   Specify through point:
   ```

4. **Use the appropriate object snap mode and pick a point in the drawing window through which you want the xline to pass.**

   The XLINE command continues to prompt for points for new xline objects until you press Enter or Esc.

If you want to lay down a whole bunch of xlines at different angles, don't select a command option first. Your new xlines will pass through the point you pick, but you'll be able to set the angle by picking in the drawing window. This is an efficient method of laying out construction lines for a drawing if you have polar mode turned on and the correct object snaps enabled.

A little ray of sunshine

The most significant difference between a ray and a construction line is that a ray has one endpoint and extends infinitely away from that endpoint, but a construction line has no endpoints and therefore extends infinitely in both directions.

The following steps explain how to create rays:

1. **Turn on the appropriate object snaps and enable ortho mode or polar tracking as necessary.**

   As noted, construction lines and rays need to be created precisely to be of any use.

2. **Start the RAY command by using one of the methods mentioned in Table 1-1.**

   The command displays the prompt

   ```
   Specify start point:
   ```

3. **Use the appropriate object snap mode and pick a point in the drawing window where you want the ray to start.**

   The command displays the prompt

   ```
   Specify through point:
   ```

4. **Again, use the appropriate object snap mode and pick a point in the drawing window through which you want the ray to pass.**

   The RAY command continues to prompt for points for new ray objects until you press Enter or Esc.

When should you use rays and when should you use xlines? Xlines are easier to construct, because they need only a through point, whereas rays need a start point and a through point. Really, the only advantage of rays is having slightly less clutter on your screen — they disappear off only one side of the screen instead of two.

For more on construction lines and rays, check out the User's Guide in the Online Help system. On the menu browser, click Help⇨Help⇨User's Guide, and then navigate to Create and Modify Objects⇨Draw Geometric Objects⇨ Draw Construction and Reference Geometry⇨Draw Construction Lines (and Rays).

Without a Trace

Because the *AutoCAD 2009 & AutoCAD LT 2009 All-in-One Desk Reference For Dummies* is nothing if not comprehensive, I'm going to cover the TRACE command. As Table 1-1 shows, TRACE isn't accessible through the user interface or command alias. The TRACE command, which creates trace objects (is that pattern settling in yet?), is a prime example of AutoCAD's attic. It's really hard to throw anything away, even though it's been 15 years since it might have been one of the key commands in the program.

Traces had a function once. They were used in the preparation of printed circuit boards (or PCBs). Traces are more or less like lines with one significant difference: Traces, like one or two other object types I'm going to cover shortly, can have width. As with the LINE command, you can keep picking points and AutoCAD will continue making traces, automatically cleaning up the intersections as it goes.

Traces offer no benefits over polylines. (I cover polylines a bit later.) Traces can't have curved segments (polylines can). The TRACE command lacks Close and Undo options like those in the LINE command. You can't even see traces as you draw them.

I'm not going to tell you not to experiment with TRACE — who knows, you may find a unique use for that castoff in AutoCAD's attic. For a very brief description of the command, look up TRACE in the index of the online Help system. Figure 1-7 shows you some sample traces.

Book II
Chapter 1

Drawing Objects

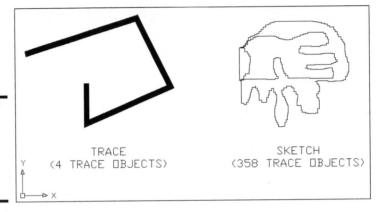

TRACE
(4 TRACE OBJECTS)

SKETCH
(358 TRACE OBJECTS)

Y
X

Figure 1-7:
Sketching
with
Picasso
(and some
traces).

A Bit Sketchy

Another command from yesterday is the SKETCH command. Like TRACE, SKETCH isn't accessible from the user interface or the command alias. You have to type the whole command name to start it. The SKETCH command doesn't create its own entity type; the end product of a SKETCH sequence is either a polyline or a whole bunch of teeny lines.

In its earliest days, AutoCAD had no commands for freehand sketching. Enter the SKETCH command. Unless you use it every day (and I'm sure not many people do that), SKETCH takes some getting used to because it works unlike any other AutoCAD command. Follow these steps and you'll see what I mean:

1. **At the command prompt, type** SKETCH **and press Enter to start the command.**

   The command displays the cryptic prompt

   ```
   Record increment <0.1000>:
   ```

   Unlike with LINE, ARC, or CIRCLE, you don't have to select or enter points while you're sketching — simply moving the crosshairs creates the sketched entities. The prompt is telling you that any mouse movements greater than 0.1 units will be recorded. Change this value now if you want longer or shorter movements to be turned into drawing entities.

2. **Press Enter to continue.**

   The command displays this prompt (even more cryptic than the first one, if that is possible)

```
Sketch.   Pen eXit Quit Record Erase Connect .
```

Sketch is ordering you to do something, unlike most commands that ask you to tell them what to do.

3. **Click the left mouse button to start sketching. Click again to stop sketching.**

   Clicking the left mouse button toggles Sketch mode between <Pen down> and <Pen up>. Simply moving the crosshairs a minimum of 0.1 units (or whatever record increment you specified) creates sketched entities. The SKETCH command ignores object snaps, and it ignores the right mouse button.

The system variable SKPOLY determines whether SKETCH creates polyline objects or gazillions of separate lines. The default value of SKPOLY is 0, which will generate many many many line objects. Setting SKPOLY to 1 tells AutoCAD to create polylines from the connected sketch segments.

Drawing Parallel Lines

If you're drawing something such as the floor plan of a house, you need parallel lines to represent the walls. The LINE command gives you a single line, which you then need to offset or copy to get a pair of lines that can represent a wall. Both AutoCAD and AutoCAD LT have commands for drawing parallel lines, but they're different in each program.

AutoCAD LT provides a command called *DLINE* that enables you to draw double lines. You specify a thickness, or separation distance, and then draw. The DLINE command creates pairs of line objects that can be edited or erased separately. The DLINE command is not included in AutoCAD. For more on using DLINE, see Book IV.

Multilines (which are not included in AutoCAD LT) are multiple parallel lines that can have different properties from one another. A multiline can have up to 16 elements. You create multiline objects with the MLINE command and edit them with the MLEDIT command, which provides a set of special tools that are specific to multilines. I cover editing multilines in Chapter 2 of this minibook.

Multilines definitely belong in the ranks of AutoCAD's complex objects. To use multilines effectively, you need to be able to create and edit the multiline styles that format the multiline objects. And you need to be able to edit them in the unique way that they require. Many AutoCAD users don't like using multilines because of their perceived inflexibility.

Figure 1-8 shows one example of a multiline object. Using the LINE command, it would take 24 separate lines (and a lot of editing) to get the same result.

The following steps show you how to create a simple multiline shape:

1. **Start the MLINE command by using one of the methods in Table 1-1.**

The command displays the prompts

```
Current settings: Justification = Top, Scale = 1.00,
    Style = STANDARD
Specify start point or [Justification/Scale/STyle]:
```

2. **If you want to change Justification from the current value, type J.**

Justification is either Top, Zero, or Bottom, and refers to where the multi-line elements are located relative to where you pick your locations. Zero justification centers the multiline elements on the points you pick. If Justification is Top, and you draw your multilines from left to right, the points you pick will be at the top element of the multiline. If you draw a closed shape with multilines, drawing clockwise with Top justification places the outermost element on the pick points. Logically, choosing Bottom justification does the reverse.

If you find the MLINE command's justification labeling confusing, you'll probably have better luck if you choose one justification (for example, Top) and one direction (for example, clockwise), and stick to it.

3. **To change Scale from the current setting, type S.**

The default value of 1.0 draws multilines exactly as specified. So if your multiline style has two lines with a 1-inch separation, that's how far apart they'll be in your drawing. If you want to use this multiline style to represent a 6-inch-wide wall, you change the scale factor to 6.

Rather than trying to do everything with a single multiline style, consider creating styles for real objects by using real dimensions. For example, if you want a 6-inch-wide wall, define the wall style so that the lines are 6 inches apart. That way you don't have to even think about the Scale option.

4. Type ST **to switch the current multiline style to another style.**

The new style must already exist in the drawing; you can't create a new multiline style from the MLINE command.

5. **Pick a start point or enter coordinates.**

The remaining prompts are identical to those for the LINE command. The MLINE command continues drawing multiline segments until you press Enter or Esc to terminate the command. After the second pick, there's an Undo option, and after the third pick, a Close option.

Because multilines are single objects, they must be created according to a defined multiline style. By default, every AutoCAD drawing contains a multiline style definition called *Standard*. The default Standard style is used to create pairs of continuous parallel lines.

That's how you create multiple lines with multilines. As for why you may want to use multilines, I leave that up to you but offer the following list of multiline shortcomings:

✦ A sequence of multilines, such as the foundation drawing example, is a single AutoCAD object, and therefore difficult to edit; frequently users create parallel lines with multilines and then explode them to individual lines. (I discuss the EXPLODE command in Chapter 2 of this minibook.)

✦ Multilines can't have curved segments. If you're laying out a floor plan and need curved walls, for example, you have to exit the command and draw the curved segments with regular lines and arcs.

✦ Multiline styles can't be modified if there are any multiline objects drawn with that style in the drawing. If you want a slightly different style, you have to create a similar-looking multiline style and then re-create the lines.

✦ You can't change the style of an existing multiline object in the Properties palette as you can with other object types defined by styles.

✦ Editing multilines requires a specialized set of tools and its own dialog box (although in AutoCAD 2005 and later you can use some regular editing commands on multilines).

✦ It can be nonintuitive — not to say, downright tricky — to define multiline styles.

Complex Curves

Splines are smooth curves that pass near or through a series of control points. A spline object can form a closed or an open shape. An *ellipse* is a symmetrical, oval shape that can be closed or open (if it's open, technically it is no longer an ellipse but an elliptical arc — but AutoCAD still classifies an elliptical arc as an ellipse). Ellipses are defined by a center point, a major axis, and a minor axis. In its early days, AutoCAD could only approximate spline curves and ellipses by creating polyline objects. (I say more about polylines a little later.) More recent versions of AutoCAD have acquired the math skills to create what are known as Non-Uniform Rational B-Splines — or NURBS to their friends.

Lucy, you have some splining to do!

 AutoCAD can create two types of splines; one type is the spline-fit polyline, which I discuss in the next section. Industrial designers use splines to give form to organic shapes, while a surveyor might use splines for contour lines. Splines are created with the SPLINE command and are defined by an arbitrary number of control points. Depending on your needs, you can eyeball your splines or calculate the coordinates of their control points for absolute precision.

The following steps show you how to create splines and describe the options of the SPLINE command:

1. **Start the SPLINE command by using one of the methods in Table 1-1.**

The command displays the prompt

```
Specify first point or [Object]:
```

2. **Pick a point in the drawing window, or enter coordinates to specify a precise start point for the spline.**

If you type **O** at this prompt, you can select a spline-fit polyline to convert to a NURBS spline. To create a spline-fit polyline, you must use the Spline option of the PEDIT command. For more on the PEDIT command, look up PEDIT in AutoCAD's online Help system.

3. **Pick another point in the drawing window, or enter coordinates for the second point.**

The command displays the prompt

```
Specify next point or [Close/Fit tolerance] <start
    tangent>:
```

4. **Type F to specify a Fit tolerance.**

Fit tolerance determines how closely the spline object is defined based on the coordinate points specified (see Figure 1-9). The default value of 0 forces the spline to pass precisely through the control points. Values greater than 1 allow the curve to pass that point within that tolerance value.

You can use the Properties palette to adjust the Fit tolerance for the spline if you specify a value that does not look right. I cover the Properties palette in Chapter 2 of this minibook.

5. **To create a closed spline, type C and press Enter.**

AutoCAD makes its best guess at closing the spline shape, but needs one more piece of information from you. The command displays the prompt

```
Specify tangent:
```

You can either pick a point in the drawing window to set the tangency direction or simply press Enter to accept the default tangent direction.

6. **To create an open spline, press Enter to accept the default choice, and specify a start and end tangent direction.**

The command displays the prompts

```
Specify start tangent:
Specify end tangent:
```

For each prompt, pick points in the drawing window, enter coordinates, or simply press Enter to accept the default tangency directions.

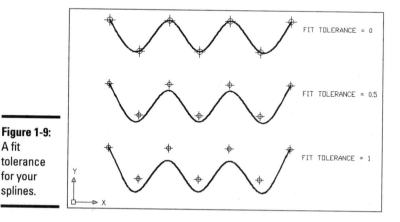

Figure 1-9:
A fit
tolerance
for your
splines.

Solar ellipses

Ellipses, like splines, are created as NURBS curves. Unlike splines, ellipses are closed, symmetrical shapes. Elliptical arcs are similar to ellipses, except that they're open.

Drawing ellipses

AutoCAD provides two methods for drawing ellipses. You can define the ellipse by locating the two endpoints of its first axis and one endpoint of its second. Or you can locate the center of the ellipse and then one endpoint on each of its axes. The following steps show you how to create an ellipse:

1. **Start the ELLIPSE command by using one of the methods in Table 1-1.**

   The command displays the prompt

   ```
   Specify axis endpoint of ellipse or [Arc/Center]:
   ```

2. **To draw an ellipse based on its center, pick a point or enter coordinates to specify the first endpoint of the first axis.**

   The command displays the prompt

   ```
   Specify other endpoint of axis:
   ```

3. **Pick a second point or enter coordinates for the second endpoint of the first axis.**

   The command displays the prompt

   ```
   Specify distance to other axis or [Rotation]:
   ```

   You have three choices here: You can specify a point by picking or typing a coordinate pair (the default method); you can specify a distance (that is, the length of the second axis); or you can use the Rotation option to specify an angle between the two axes.

   Acceptable angle values range between 0 and 89.4 degrees. The higher the rotation angle, the flatter the ellipse, and a 0 degrees rotation will generate a circular ellipse.

4. **To draw an ellipse by using the default method, pick a third point above or below the first axis, or enter a coordinate pair.**

   The ellipse is added to the drawing.

Drawing elliptical arcs

Drawing elliptical arcs is almost the same as drawing ellipses, except two additional values are needed to specify the angles for the ellipse. The following steps explain how to draw an elliptical arc by using the default method:

1. **Start the ELLIPSE command with the Arc option by using one of the methods in Table 1-1.**

Using one of the user interface elements such as the ribbon or menu allows for the most direct route to this function, which is actually an option of the regular ELLIPSE command. The command displays the prompt

```
Specify axis endpoint of elliptical arc or [Center]:
```

Book II Chapter 1

The Elliptical Arc command is actually a command macro that's programmed to automatically choose the Arc option of the ELLIPSE command. The second line takes you to the first step of drawing a regular ellipse.

Figure 1-10 shows the Arc option of the Ellipse submenu on the menu browser. If you are a dedicated keyboarder or use AutoCAD LT, you must type the **A** (for Arc option).

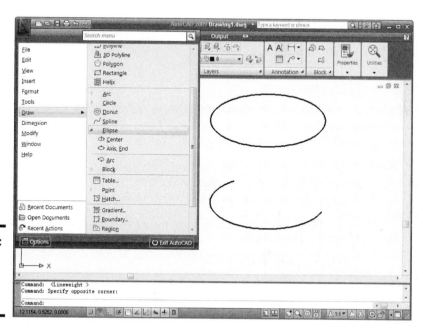

Figure 1-10: Elliptical arcs are on today's menu.

2. **Pick points in the drawing window to specify the first and second endpoints of the first axis, and the endpoint of the second axis.**

   The command displays the prompts

   ```
   Specify other endpoint of axis:
   Specify distance to other axis or [Rotation]:
   ```

   The final prompts allow you to set the internal angle of the elliptical arc.

3. **Pick points in the drawing window to specify the starting and ending points of the elliptical arc.**

   The command displays the prompts

   ```
   Specify start angle or [Parameter]:
   Specify end angle or [Parameter/Included angle]:
   ```

For information on the Parameter option (which doesn't do much that simply picking endpoints can't handle), refer to the ELLIPSE command on the Index tab of the online Help.

Complex Objects and Shapes

The last selection of commands and objects covered in this chapter are more complex than most of those covered previously. Some, like polylines, are extremely useful. Others, like 2D solids, are a lot less so.

2D solids

The first thing to be said about 2D solids is that they're not 3D solid objects. I talk about working in 3D in Book V. Here I briefly discuss another entity type, the 2D solid. *Solid* here refers to a solid-*filled* 2D outline.

A long, long time ago, AutoCAD couldn't create solid-filled areas. If you wanted the effect, you had to use the SOLID command. A big drawback is that 2D solids can have only three or four sides — no more. So you might have had to create dozens of 2D solids to fill a randomly shaped area. The other problem with 2D solids is that their three or four sides are always straight.

Ninety-nine times out of one hundred, you can get the effect you need with the HATCH command or a polyline with width. (I discuss hatching in Book III and polylines in the next sections.) If you still think you need 2D solids, refer to the SOLID command in the online Help.

Rectang, Polygon, Donut

No prizes for guessing what kinds of things that commands named RECTANG, POLYGON, and DONUT make. (Actually you *may* have to guess, but I don't have any prizes for you!)

All three commands make polyline objects. A polyline is a very useful type of object that can be used to draw any shape, as long as each part is connected to the other.

Rectangles

 The RECTANG command creates four-sided closed polylines with horizontal and vertical sides. Command options allow you to draw rectangles in different ways. You can

+ Locate two diagonal corners.

+ Locate one corner, and then enter values for area and the length of one side.

+ Locate one corner, enter values for length and width, and then specify direction.

+ Locate one corner, specify a rotation angle, and then locate the other corner.

In addition, before you pick the first point, you can

+ Set chamfer or fillet values so that all four corners are automatically chamfered or filleted.

 In drafting, a *chamfer* is a straight line that forms the transition between two 2D objects that meet at an angle; one example is a beveled edge at a corner. A *fillet* is a curved transition between two 2D objects; an example is a rounded edge at a corner.

+ Set a width value so the sides of the rectangle have a 2D width.

+ Set elevation and thickness values for the rectangle if you're working in 3D. I discuss setting the elevation and thickness in Book V, Chapter 4.

Polygons

 Polygons, like rectangles, are closed polyline objects. Unlike rectangles, by default polygons are regular: They have equal length sides and equal internal angles.

If you want to draw irregular polygons, use the PLINE command.

The POLYGON command draws regular polygons of a minimum of three and a maximum of 1024 sides. After specifying the number of sides for your polygon, there are three options:

✦ **Edge:** Locate an endpoint of the first edge, and then pick or enter a value to locate the second endpoint.

✦ **Inscribed:** Locate the center of an imaginary circle, and then specify its radius. AutoCAD draws the polygon so that the corners touch the circumference of the circle (the circle is not actually drawn).

✦ **Circumscribed:** Locate the center of an imaginary circle, and then specify its radius. AutoCAD draws the polygon so that the sides are tangent to the imaginary circle.

Donuts

Now for the biggest disappointment of the whole chapter. No, AutoCAD does not generate snack food when you run the DONUT command. Trust me — it's better that way.

AutoCAD donuts are solid-filled polylines (as opposed to jelly-filled pastries). When you create donuts in AutoCAD, you specify an inside and an outside diameter, and then locate them by picking a center point.

A common use for donuts (the AutoCAD flavor, anyway) is in structural engineering drafting where you need to draw round reinforcing steel in a cross section. You can specify an inside diameter of 0 to create a solid-filled donut. Just like asking for "plain" at the coffee shop.

Polylines

A polyline is a single object that consists of one or (more usefully) multiple linear or curved segments. You create open or closed regular or irregular polylines with the PLINE command. Just like the LINE command, PLINE continues adding line (or arc) segments until you terminate the command. Unlike the case with LINE, the objects you create with the PLINE command are single entities. Figure 1-11 shows geometry created with each command. The LINE command (on the left) created six connected but separate line objects. The PLINE command (on the right) created one single object.

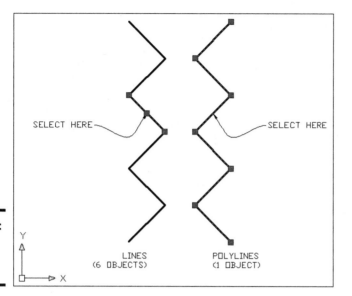

Figure 1-11:
Drawing
polylines
(and lines).

The following sequence from the command prompt shows how the polyline in Figure 1-12 was drawn:

```
Command: _pline
Specify start point: 40,20
Current line-width is 0.0000
Specify next point or [Arc/Halfwidth/Length/Undo/Width]: W
Specify starting width <0.0000>: 0
Specify ending width <0.0000>: 2
Specify next point or [Arc/Halfwidth/Length/Undo/Width]:
    @4<180
Specify next point or
    [Arc/Close/Halfwidth/Length/Undo/Width]: @4<180
Specify next point or
    [Arc/Close/Halfwidth/Length/Undo/Width]: W
Specify starting width <2.0000>: 2
Specify ending width <2.0000>: 4
Specify next point or
    [Arc/Close/Halfwidth/Length/Undo/Width]: @4<180
Specify next point or
    [Arc/Close/Halfwidth/Length/Undo/Width]: W
Specify starting width <4.0000>: 4
Specify ending width <4.0000>: 0.5
Specify next point or
    [Arc/Close/Halfwidth/Length/Undo/Width]: @8<180
Specify next point or
    [Arc/Close/Halfwidth/Length/Undo/Width]: W
Specify starting width <0.5000>: 0.5
Specify ending width <0.5000>: 0
```

```
Specify next point or
    [Arc/Close/Halfwidth/Length/Undo/Width]: A
Specify endpoint of arc or
[Angle/CEnter/CLose/Direction/Halfwidth/Line/Radius/Second
    pt/Undo/Width]: @12<270
Specify endpoint of arc or
[Angle/CEnter/CLose/Direction/Halfwidth/Line/Radius/Second
    pt/Undo/Width]: <Press Enter to end the command>
```

Figure 1-12:
Constructing
a polyline.

Ahhhh . . . Wipeout

No, you have not crossed the boundaries of time and space to find yourself on a beach with surfers. AutoCAD supports an object known as a *wipeout* that can be used to mask objects in a drawing. You define a wipeout similar to how you create a polyline — except a wipeout must be a closed object. As you pick points or enter coordinate values, the command automatically shows what the object will look like as a closed object by showing the last segment drawn from the current location of the crosshairs to the first point specified.

As mentioned, you can use wipeouts to mask objects. They can be handy for creating electrical or P&ID symbols, where you might draw a series of lines to represent circuits or piping. With the wipeout as part of the symbol, any objects under the wipeout are not displayed in the drawing so you don't need to worry about trimming a line to the symbol.

Figure 1-13 shows an example of using a wipeout object as a mask for the table-top of a conference table. Notice that on the left, no wipeout element is used and you see the chairs extend under the table, while on the right, the wipeout object makes the part of the chair under the tabletop appear to disappear.

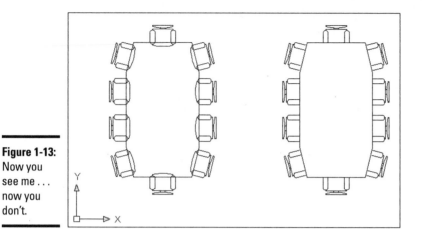

Figure 1-13:
Now you
see me . . .
now you
don't.

To create a wipeout object, you use the WIPEOUT command. Use one of the methods mentioned in Table 1-1 to start the WIPEOUT command. Then you pick points or enter coordinate values to define the shape of the wipeout. When you have finished defining the shape of the wipeout, just press Enter or Esc. You can also enter **P** when the WIPEOUT command is first started to convert a closed polyline to a wipeout object. You can choose to keep or discard the original polyline object.

If the polyline is not closed, you can select the polyline and display the Properties palette. In the Properties palette, set the polyline's Closed property to Yes. I cover the Properties palette in Chapter 2 of this minibook.

By default wipeout objects display their edges. To turn on or off the display of the edges of all wipeout objects, use the Frame option of the WIPEOUT command. Turning off the frame for wipeouts can help to keep the display of objects in your drawing cleaner.

Chapter 2: Modifying Objects

In This Chapter

✓ **Setting selection options**

✓ **Selecting objects**

✓ **Using object groups**

✓ **Editing objects**

✓ **Editing objects by using grips**

Most of the work you do in any CAD drawing file involves modifying existing objects. You may need to move objects from one part of the drawing to another, or you may need to copy them from one part of a drawing to another, or even from one drawing to another. "Draw once, reuse as much as possible" should be your mantra when you work in AutoCAD.

Of course, before you can edit an object, you have to tell AutoCAD which object you want to work with. Sounds simple enough, but you can select objects by using a bewildering number of methods. AutoCAD's Options dialog box is the place to begin setting your choices for object selection, and that's where I start in this chapter.

Setting Selection Options

Before I get to the actual selecting and then editing of objects, I need to briefly explain the options on the Selection tab of the Options dialog box (see Figure 2-1).

The six settings in the lower-left corner determine how you select objects:

✦ **Noun/verb selection:** When checked (the default) allows you to select objects for editing before you start an editing command. See "Object selection modes" later in this chapter for more information.

✦ **Use Shift to add to selection:** When not checked (the default), selecting items one after another adds them to the *selection set;* to remove items from the selection set, hold down the Shift key and select them. When checked, press the Shift key to add objects to the selection set; clicking a selected object removes it from the set.

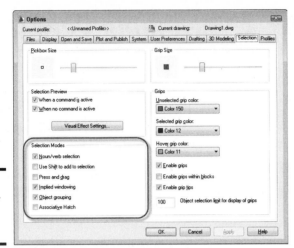

Figure 2-1:
Select your
selection
modes.

Selection set refers to any selected objects that are ready to be edited. Only one selection set can be active at a time, and when you make a new selection, the old selection set is replaced. A selection set can contain any number of objects, even including everything in the drawing. It's also possible to save a selection set as a named group — see the later section "Object groups."

✦ **Press and drag:** When not checked (the default), you click once to set one corner of a selection box and then click again to set the other corner. (For more on selection boxes, see "Selecting multiple objects" later in this chapter.) When checked, you use Windows-standard pressing and dragging with the left mouse button to set the selection box.

✦ **Implied windowing:** When checked (the default), picking a point away from any object starts an automatic selection box. Moving the mouse to the left creates a crossing box, and moving it to the right creates a window box. I explain the difference in the "Selecting multiple objects" section.

✦ **Object grouping:** When checked (the default), clicking one object that belongs to a defined object group selects every other object in that group. When not checked, other group members are not selected when one member is selected. See "Object groups" for more information.

✦ **Associative hatch:** When not checked (the default), selecting a hatch object selects only the hatch. When checked, selecting a hatch object also selects the boundary used to create it.

Figure 2-1 and this list point out the default selection settings. The following sections assume that these are the current settings. If you get different results when you try some of these methods, open the Options dialog box and make sure that the settings jibe with mine.

Selecting Objects

You must decide two things when you see some drawing objects that need editing:

✦ How many objects do you want to modify? If there are several, are they adjacent to one another, or are they scattered all over the drawing?

✦ How do you want to modify the objects? Do you want to select the objects first, or do you want to start the command first, and must you start the command first in some cases? Or would you rather use another method altogether? (For the last, I'm referring to object grips, which I discuss near the end of the chapter.)

The first thing you have to work out is whether you want to perform an action on one single object or modify a group of separate objects. Selecting a single object is (to use some technical language) a no-brainer — you just click it with the pickbox, and it's selected.

Book II
Chapter 2

Modifying Objects

The little square box at the intersection of the crosshairs is called the *pickbox,* and whenever it's visible, you can use the crosshairs to select objects. The pickbox disappears from the crosshairs in any command in which you're being prompted to select a point. (And the crosshairs disappear from the pickbox when AutoCAD asks you to select an object.) By default, the pickbox measures 3 pixels square; you can alter the size by using the Pickbox Size slider on the Selection tab of the Options dialog box (refer to Figure 2-1), or by typing PICKBOX at the command prompt and specifying a new value.

Selecting multiple objects

If you start your editing process by selecting one of the Modify commands, AutoCAD prompts you to select objects. Use one of the following techniques to do so:

✦ To select a single object, position the pickbox over the object and click.

✦ To invoke an automatic window selection box, pick a point above and to the left of the objects you want to select, and then move the crosshairs up and down and to the right to create a window box around the objects.

✦ To invoke an automatic crossing selection box, pick a point above and to the right of the objects you want to select, and then move your crosshairs up and down and to the left to create a crossing box around the objects.

✦ To invoke any other option, enter the capitalized parts of the option name as follows: Last, ALL, Fence, WPolygon, CPolygon, Add, Remove, and Previous.

Table 2-1 lists all the selection modes provided by AutoCAD. You can invoke any mode by typing the uppercase letters for the option (for example, F for Fence, ALL for All).

Table 2-1	AutoCAD's Selection Modes
Mode	*Description*
Window	Prompts for the first corner and then the other corner of a rectangular selection window. Only objects *completely within* the selection window will be selected. Window boxes are indicated by continuous border lines and by default a semitransparent blue fill.
Crossing	Prompts for the first corner and then the other corner of a rectangular selection window. Objects *completely within or crossed by* the selection window will be selected. Crossing boxes are indicated by dashed border lines and by default a semitransparent green fill.
WPolygon	Prompts you to draw an irregular shape around the objects you want to select by picking points; after you've picked at least two points, the boundary becomes self-closing. Only objects completely within the WPolygon boundary polygon will be selected. WPolygon boundaries are indicated by continuous lines and by default a semitransparent blue fill.
CPolygon	Prompts you to draw an irregular shape around the objects you want to select by picking points; after you pick at least two points, the boundary becomes self-closing. Objects either entirely within or crossed by the CPolygon boundary are selected. CPolygon boundaries are indicated by dashed lines and by default a semitransparent green fill.
Fence	Prompts you to draw a series of line segments through the objects to select. All objects touched by the Fence line will be selected.
ALL	Selects everything in the drawing except objects on frozen or locked layers, and objects in paper space if you are in model space or objects in model space if you are in paper space. (Refer to Book I for more information on model and paper space.)
Last	Selects the last object created *that's visible in the current display.* (This may not necessarily be the last object added to the drawing.)
Previous	Reselects the last selection set created. Only the most recent selection set can be recalled by using the Previous option, until a new selection set is created. The new set then becomes the most recent selection set.
Add	Lets you continue to add objects to a selection set. (You can add to the selection set also by simply picking more objects.)
Remove	Removes selected objects from a selection set. (You can remove selected objects from the selection set also by holding down the Shift key and picking them.)

Figure 2-2 shows the results of selecting objects by using Window, Crossing, WPolygon, CPolygon, and Fence modes.

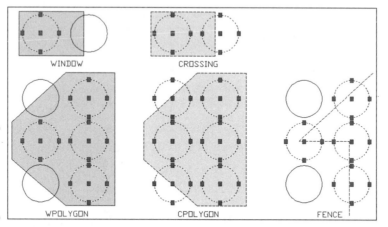

Figure 2-2:
Picking your way through AutoCAD objects.

Book II
Chapter 2

Modifying Objects

 In addition to selecting objects directly by using the different selection modes I just mentioned, you can select objects also based on object type or a specific property value. For example, you can select all the circles in a drawing with a radius of 0.5 units. To select objects based on type or property values, you can use Quick Select or object filters created with the FILTER command. These are advanced topics that I cover in Bonus Chapter 5 on the Web, at www.wiley.com/go/autocad2009aio.

 When no command is active, you can use the key combination Ctrl+A to select all objects in the drawing that are not frozen. You can also right-click over the drawing window and choose Deselect All or press Esc to unselect all the selected objects when no command is active.

 At times, you may need to select overlapping objects. To select overlapping objects, you position the pickbox over the object and then hold down the Shift key while pressing the spacebar to cycle through the overlapping objects below the pickbox. When the object that you want to select is highlighted, click in the drawing window.

Object selection modes

You can select objects for editing in two ways:

✦ **Verb-noun editing:** Start the desired edit command, and then select the objects you want to modify.

✦ **Noun-verb editing:** Select the objects you want to modify, and then start the specific edit command.

You're probably wondering if this is AutoCAD or Grade 6 English. Don't worry; this is just the terminology that was chosen to distinguish the two methods.

The following steps show you how to use each mode. As an example, I've chosen the ERASE command because it's one of the most commonly used commands in AutoCAD, but the majority of the modifying commands work with either mode:

1. **In a new, blank drawing, draw some lines, circles, or other objects, or open a drawing containing a number of objects.**

2. **Type ERASE at the command prompt and press Enter.**

I cover other methods of starting the ERASE command in Table 2-2 later in this chapter.

To use verb-noun editing, first start the editing command. The command displays the prompt

```
Select objects:
```

3. **Move the crosshairs so that they're on top of an object, and then click.**

The command line displays

```
Select objects: 1 found
Select objects:
```

4. **Move the crosshairs until they're not on top of an object, and then click.**

With Implied Windowing turned on (see the previous section, "Setting Selection Options"), move the mouse to the left to start a crossing selection box, or move it to the right to start a window selection box. The command display the prompt

```
Select objects: Specify opposite corner:
```

5. **Move the mouse to the right so that the blue window selection box entirely surrounds an object or move it to the left so that the green selection box crosses some objects, and click.**

The command displays the prompts

```
Select objects: Specify opposite corner: 2 found, 3
   total
Select objects:
```

6. **Press Enter twice to finish selecting objects and to complete the command.**

AutoCAD continues prompting you to select more objects until the cows come home. Or until you press Enter to complete the command — which, I hope, you'll do first.

Still got some objects left to erase? Good! (If not, click the Undo button on the Quick Access toolbar to get some of them back.)

7. **Make sure that no command is active, and then use any selection method you like to choose some objects.**

   If you need to, press Esc a couple times to make sure no command is active. When no command is active, you can still select commands to create a selection set. The command line displays the prompts

   ```
   Command:
   Command: Specify opposite corner:
   ```

8. **Type** ERASE **at the command prompt and press Enter.**

   The selected objects are erased from the drawing and the command line displays the prompts

   ```
   Command: e
   ERASE 3 found
   Command:
   ```

Selection preview

Now that you know how to select objects in a drawing, you should know about a feature known as selection preview. *Selection preview* allows you to visually see what object you are about to select and to identify which objects might be grouped together or are part of a complex object. As you move the pickbox over an object, the object by default is highlighted and appears in a heavier lineweight and dashed linetype. You can control whether selection preview is used when no command is active and while a command is active by using the Selection tab of the Options dialog box under the Selection Preview area (refer to Figure 2-1).

You can control how objects are highlighted, which objects are highlighted, and the fill applied to crossing and window selections by clicking the Visual Effect Settings button under the Selection Preview area. Clicking this button displays the Visual Effect Settings dialog box (see Figure 2-3). Make any desired changes and click OK to return to the Options dialog box.

Figure 2-3:
The visual effects of selection preview take the mystery out of which objects you are about to select.

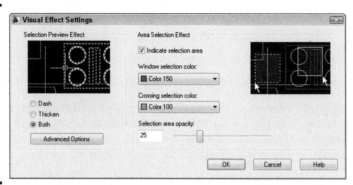

Object groups

The final object selection topic to mention is object groups. You know that selection sets can be recalled for subsequent edits, but only until you select a new object or bunch of objects — then the new bunch will overwrite the previous set.

The *object groups* feature lets you save a selection set with a name so that you can recall it at any time. You can have as many object groups as you want, and individual objects can belong to more than one group at a time. When object grouping is turned on, selecting one member of a group selects the entire group; when grouping is off, selecting a group member selects only the one you picked. You can turn object grouping off and on at the Selection tab of the Options dialog box (see the previous section, "Setting Selection Options," for details). An easier way exists, however; Ctrl+Shift+A toggles object grouping off and on.

The following steps explain how to create an object group:

1. **Type** GROUP **and press Enter.**

   The GROUP command is available only at the command prompt. The Object Grouping dialog box appears.

2. **In the Group Identification area, enter a name in the Group Name box, and optionally enter a description in the Description box.**

   All groups must have a valid name before you can select objects; a group name can be a maximum of 31 characters and can't contain spaces or special characters such as #%&*. The description is optional.

3. **In the Create Group area, select Selectable if it is not selected, and then click New.**

   The Selectable option makes the group so it can be selected in the drawing. The command line displays the prompts

   ```
   Select objects for grouping:
   Select objects: Specify opposite corner: 2 found
   Select objects:
   ```

4. **When you're finished selecting objects, press Enter.**

   You are returned to the Object Grouping dialog box (see Figure 2-4).

5. **Click OK to finish creating the group and close the dialog box.**

AutoCAD LT does support groups, but it uses a different, and more limited, procedure from regular AutoCAD. Rather than with the Object Grouping dialog box, AutoCAD LT does its group work with Group Manager. For more on working with groups in AutoCAD LT, see Book IV.

Figure 2-4:
A newly
made object
group.

AutoCAD's Editing Commands

Table 2-2 lists AutoCAD's most common editing commands and tells you
where to find them and what they do. As with the drawing commands in the
preceding chapter, we don't cover the commands in this order (which, in
case you're wondering, is alphabetical by command name). You'll find most
of these commands on the Modify toolbar and menu and a few on the
Standard toolbar and Edit menu. There's also a Modify II toolbar, which contains some of the more specialized editing commands.

To display closed toolbars, right-click any tool button and choose a toolbar
from the shortcut menu. If the toolbar shows a check beside its name, it's
already open.

We cover an additional set of commands for editing text and dimensions in
Book III. I also discuss 3D editing commands in Book V.

Table 2-2		**AutoCAD's Editing Commands**			
Icon	*Ribbon*	*Toolbar*	*Menu*	*Command Name (Alias)*	*Function*
	Home⇨ Modify panel's title bar⇨Array	Modify, Array	Modify⇨ Array	ARRAY (AR)	Duplicates objects in a circular or rectangular pattern.
	Home⇨ Modify panel's title bar⇨Break at Point				

(continued)

Table 2-2 (continued)

Icon	Ribbon	Toolbar	Menu	Command Name (Alias)	Function
	Home⇨ Modify panel⇨Break	Modify, Break at Point Modify, Break	Modify⇨ Break	BREAK (BR)	Breaks selected objects into separate objects at selected points.
	Home⇨ Modify panel⇨ Fillet/Chamfer flyout⇨Chamfer	Modify, Chamfer	Modify⇨ Chamfer	CHAMFER (CHA)	Applies a beveled corner to intersecting objects.
	Home⇨ Modify panel's title bar⇨ Change Space	—	Modify⇨ Change Space	CHSPACE	Moves objects between model space in a viewport on a layout tab and paper space.
	Home⇨ Modify panel⇨ Copy	Modify, Copy	Modify⇨ Copy	COPY (CO)	Duplicates selected objects.
	Home⇨ Utilities panel⇨ Copy flyout⇨ Copy Clip	Standard, Copy	Edit⇨Copy	COPYCLIP	Copies objects to the Windows Clipboard.
	Home⇨ Cut	Standard, Cut	Edit⇨Cut	CUTCLIP	Moves objects from the drawing to the Windows Clipboard.
	Home⇨Modify panel⇨Draw Order flyout	Draw Order	Tools⇨ Draw Order	DRAWORDER (DR)	Controls the order in which objects are displayed in the drawing. The top-most objects are drawn over other objects.
	Home⇨ Modify panel⇨ Erase	Modify, Erase	Modify⇨ Erase	ERASE (E)	Removes selected objects.
	Home⇨ Modify panel⇨ Explode	Modify, Explode	Modify⇨ Explode	EXPLODE (X)	Breaks complex objects into individual objects.
	Home⇨ Modify panel⇨ Extend	Modify, Extend	Modify⇨ Extend	EXTEND (EX)	Lengthens an object by extending to another selected object.
	Home⇨ Modify panel⇨ Fillet/Chamfer flyout⇨Fillet	Modify, Fillet	Modify⇨ Fillet	FILLET (F)	Applies a fillet or round to intersecting objects.

Icon	Ribbon	Toolbar	Menu	Command Name (Alias)	Function
—	—	—	—	GROUP (G)	Creates object groupings.
	Home⇨ Modify panel's title bar⇨Edit Hatch	Modify II, Hatch Edit	Modify⇨ Object⇨ Hatch	HATCHEDIT (HE)	Modifies the properties and boundaries of a hatch object.
	Home⇨ Modify panel's title bar⇨Join	Modify, Join	Modify⇨ Join	JOIN (J)	Connects selected discontinuous objects.
	—	—	Modify⇨ Lengthen	LENGTHEN (LEN)	Changes the length of open objects.
	Home⇨ Properties panel⇨Match Properties	Standard, Match Properties	Modify⇨ Match Properties	MATCHPROP (MA)	Applies the properties of one object to other objects.
	Home⇨ Modify panel⇨ Mirror	Modify, Mirror	Modify⇨ Mirror	MIRROR (MI)	Creates a mirrored version of an original or a copy.
	Home⇨ Modify panel⇨ Move	Modify, Move	Modify⇨ Move	MOVE (M)	Relocates selected objects.
	—	—	—	MREDO	Reverses a selectable series of Undos.
	Home⇨ Modify panel⇨ Offset	Modify, Offset	Modify⇨ Offset	OFFSET (O)	Creates a duplicate object based on a specified distance.
—	—	—	—	OOPS	Unerases the last erased objects.
	Home⇨ Utilities panel⇨ Paste flyout⇨ Paste	Standard, Paste	Modify⇨ Edit⇨Paste	PASTECLIP	Pastes objects from the Windows Clipboard.
	Home⇨ Modify panel's title bar⇨Edit Polyline	Modify II, Edit Polyline	Modify⇨ Object⇨ Polyline	PEDIT (PE)	Modifies geometric properties of the selected polyline.

(continued)

Table 2-2 *(continued)*

Icon	Ribbon	Toolbar	Menu	Command Name (Alias)	Function
	View⇨ Palettes panel⇨Properties Properties	Standard, Properties	Modify⇨ Properties	PROPERTIES (PR)	Lists and changes object properties.
	—	Standard, Redo	Modify⇨ Edit⇨Redo	REDO	Reverses the last Undo.
	Home⇨ Modify panel⇨ Rotate	Modify, Rotate	Modify⇨ Rotate	ROTATE (RO)	Rotates the selected object around a base point.
	Home⇨ Modify panel⇨ Scale	Modify, Scale	Modify⇨ Scale	SCALE (SC)	Resizes objects from a base point by a given factor.
	Home⇨ Modify panel's title bar⇨Set to ByLayer	—	Modify⇨ Change to ByLayer	SETBYLAYER	Changes the specified properties of the objects to ByLayer.
	Home⇨Modify panel's title bar⇨Edit Spline	Modify II, Edit Spline	Modify⇨ Object⇨ Spline	SPLINEDIT (SPE)	Modifies the geometric properties of the selected spline.
	Home⇨ Modify panel⇨ Stretch	Modify, Stretch	Modify⇨ Stretch	STRETCH (S)	Allows you to resize objects by dragging them.
	Home⇨ Modify panel⇨ Trim	Modify, Trim	Modify⇨ Trim	TRIM (TR)	Shortens an object by removing a part of the object based on other selected objects.
	—	Standard, Undo	Modify⇨ Edit⇨Undo	U	Reverses the last single action.
	—	—	—	UNDO	Reverses a selectable series of actions.
—	—	—	—	XPLODE (XP)	Breaks complex objects into individual objects and set properties after exploding.

Removing stuff

Everybody makes mistakes, and now it's time to clear away the evidence. I present the simplest-to-use of all of AutoCAD's editing commands: ERASE. I hope it's not your most frequently used command, but it doesn't really matter whether it is or not — you're not going to rub a hole in your screen by erasing AutoCAD objects too frequently.

Here are some ways to erase objects from your drawing:

✦ On the menu browser or menu bar, click Modify➪Erase, select the undesirables, and then press Enter.

✦ On the menu browser or menu bar, click Edit➪Delete, select the undesirables, and then press Enter.

✦ On the Modify toolbar, click the Erase tool, select your objects, and then press Enter.

✦ Select the objects to remove and then press Delete.

✦ Select the unwanted objects, right-click, and select Erase.

Book II Chapter 2

Modifying Objects

Relocating and replicating

Most commands require more direction than simply selecting objects and clicking a button or pressing a key. The first set of commands I look at allow you to relocate and duplicate existing drawing objects.

MOVE

Moving objects requires three sets of input: the objects you want to move, a point to move them from, and another point to move them to.

Using noun-verb editing for simple commands such as MOVE and COPY saves keystrokes. You don't want to overwork those pinkies, do you?

The following steps explain how to move objects by using noun-verb editing:

1. **Select a single object, or select several objects by using one of the multiple selection methods described in the section "Selecting multiple objects."**

The objects are highlighted and the grips for each object are displayed. Don't worry about the grips (all those blue boxes and wedges) — I discuss them near the end of the chapter.

2. **Start the MOVE command by using one of the methods in Table 2-2.**

Use object snaps or other precision aids if you need to. If you're simply moving objects relative to their current location, it doesn't matter where you pick. The command displays the prompt

```
Specify base point or [Displacement] <Displacement>:
```

The command shows you the number of objects that were selected, and then tells you what to do next — it wants you to specify a *base point* ("take these things *from here*"). If you didn't select objects in Step 1 first, the Select objects prompt would be displayed asking you to select objects first before prompting you for a base point. Select the objects to move and then press Enter.

3. **Pick a point in the drawing window or enter coordinates as the base point.**

Sometimes you should pick a precise point for the base point, but if you're moving or copying something only a relative distance, it doesn't matter where you pick. The command displays the prompt

```
Specify second point or
<use first point as displacement>:
```

4. **Pick a second point or enter coordinates for the destination of the selected objects.**

Remember, "second point" means "put it here." The selected objects are moved and you're returned to a blank command prompt.

Even the simplest commands can throw you for a loop. You may get unexpected results if you press Enter in response to the *Specify second point* prompt. Pressing Enter tells AutoCAD to look at the *coordinates* of the first point and use those values as the *displacement* for the second point. I can pretty well guarantee this is not what you want or will expect to happen.

COPY

When you use verb-noun editing, editing in AutoCAD is much more obviously a two-step process: You select the objects, press Enter, and carry on with the command. This is a good time to demonstrate the difference between selecting objects before and after a command is started because the MOVE and COPY commands are pretty much the same.

The COPY command allows you to duplicate existing objects within a drawing, and the COPYCLIP command allows you to copy objects to the Windows Clipboard. You want to use COPYCLIP to copy objects between open drawings; you should use the COPY command when creating copies of objects in a particular drawing. After objects are copied to the Windows Clipboard, you use the PASTECLIP command to create new objects based on those from the Clipboard. Don't confuse these two copy commands.

Use the following steps to copy objects, using the COPY command and verb-noun editing:

1. **Start the COPY command by using one of the methods in Table 2-2.**

The command displays the prompt

```
COPY
Select objects:
```

2. **Select the objects you want to copy by using any object selection method.**

If you choose a window or crossing, the command displays the prompts

```
Specify opposite corner: 4 found
Select objects:
```

3. **Press Enter when you're finished selecting objects to copy.**

The first prompts for COPY are exactly the same as for MOVE. What's different is that I show how to copy objects by using verb-noun selection, and I showed how to move objects by using the noun-verb mode.

After you press Enter to finish selecting, AutoCAD prompts

```
Specify base point or [Displacement/mOde]
    <Displacement>:
```

4. **Pick a point in the drawing window or enter coordinates as the base point.**

Again, use object snaps or other precision aids if you need to. If you're simply copying objects relative to their current location, it doesn't matter where you pick. After you've picked the first point, the command displays the prompt

```
Specify second point or
<use first point as displacement>:
```

5. **Pick a second point or enter coordinates for the destination of the selected objects.**

You can enter relative coordinates, or use direct distance entry (see Book I, Chapter 7) or any precision method (where appropriate), or eyeball a point. For example, typing **@2.85<0** makes a copy of the selected objects 2.85 units to the right of the originals.

The command displays the prompts

```
Specify second point or
<use first point as displacement>: @2.85<0
Specify second point or [Exit/Undo] <Exit>:
```

6. Continue making additional copies or exit the command.

By default, AutoCAD continues offering to make copies until you tell it to stop. To exit the command, press Enter, the spacebar, or Esc, or type **E** and press Enter.

By default the COPY command operates in multiple-copy mode, which means you keep specifying points to copy the selected objects. If you want the COPY command to operate in single-copy mode, you set the COPYMODE system variable to 1.

MIRROR

MIRROR creates a mirrored version of the selected objects, or it can create a mirrored copy. Instead of picking a base and second point as you do with MOVE and COPY, with MIRROR you pick two points that define an imaginary mirror. The selected object is "reflected" on the other side of the mirror line. The final MIRROR prompt asks if you want to retain or delete the selected objects, known as the *source objects*.

The following steps demonstrate using the MIRROR command in verb-noun mode:

1. Start the MIRROR command by using one of the methods in Table 2-2.

AutoCAD does its usual "Select objects" thing. By now you know the ropes — select some objects and press Enter. The command displays the prompts

```
Select objects: Specify opposite corner: 4 found
Select objects: Specify first point of mirror line:
```

If it doesn't matter where the objects get mirrored to, just pick a random point in the drawing window. Do the same for the second point. More often than not, though, it *does* matter. If that's the case, make use of some of the precision drafting aids I discuss in Book I, Chapter 7. In this example, the selected objects need to be mirrored precisely about the middle of the rectangle.

2. Hold down the Shift key and right-click to display the object snap shortcut menu. Choose Midpoint and pick a horizontal edge of the rectangle when you see the triangular object snap marker.

The command displays the prompt

```
Specify second point of mirror line:
```

3. **Hold the Shift key if ortho mode is disabled and click a second point directly above or below the first point.**

   You need to be precise for the second point, too. Holding Shift temporarily invokes ortho mode; when you move the crosshairs, they will lock horizontally or vertically and remain that way until you release the Shift key (see Figure 2-5). The command displays the prompt

```
Erase source objects? [Yes/No] <N>:
```

4. **Type Y or N and press Enter to erase or retain the source objects.**

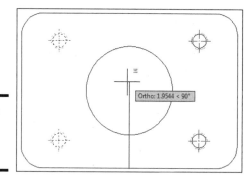

Figure 2-5:
Mirroring
objects
precisely.

OFFSET

 OFFSET, like COPY, duplicates selected objects, but it's more rigorous in where it lets you put those duplicates. It also doesn't make exact copies; different object types offset in different ways. Figure 2-6 shows the results of offsetting different entity types. You can OFFSET lines, arcs, circles, splines, ellipses, and polylines.

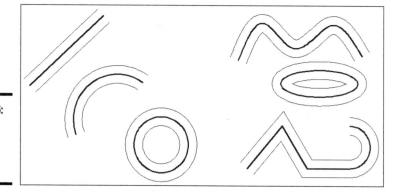

Figure 2-6:
Offsetting
different
object
types.

The following steps explain how to use OFFSET with the verb-noun editing mode:

1. **Start the OFFSET command by using one of the methods in Table 2-2.**

The command displays the prompts

```
Current settings: Erase source=No  Layer=Source
    OFFSETGAPTYPE=0
Specify offset distance or [Through/Erase/Layer]
    <Through>:
```

2. **Optionally, type E to erase the source object or type L to change the new object's layer from the same layer as the source object to the current layer, and press Enter.**

When offsetting objects, you can specify an offset distance or pick a *Through point* in the drawing window. Logically enough, choosing the Through option offsets the object through the point you pick in the drawing. The first time you run OFFSET in a drawing, the default value is <Through>.

3. **Press Enter to use the Through point option.**

The command displays the prompt

```
Select object to offset or [Exit/Undo] <Exit>:
```

If you simply pick a point, without pressing Enter to confirm the <Through> option, the command assumes you really want to enter an offset distance and you will be prompted for a second point. The distance between the two points is used as the offset distance value.

4. **Select a single object to offset.**

You can specify only one object at a time; that is, you can't select a group of wall lines and offset them all in the same step. If you specified Through, the command displays the prompt:

```
Specify through point or [Exit/Multiple/Undo] <Exit>:
```

For precise locations, use object snaps when picking through points. The command creates a new version of the selected object through the point you picked, and it continues prompting for additional offsets and through points.

5. **When you finish offsetting, press Enter to return to a blank command prompt.**

If you enter a distance, you need to make an additional pick to specify which side of the source object you want the new object to be created on. The following steps show the process:

1. **Start the OFFSET command by using one of the methods in Table 2-2.**

The command displays the prompts

```
Command: OFFSET
Current settings: Erase source=No  Layer=Source
   OFFSETGAPTYPE=0
Specify offset distance or [Through/Erase/Layer]
   <Through>:
```

2. **Type an offset distance value and press Enter.**

The command displays the prompt

```
Select object to offset or [Exit/Undo] <Exit>:
```

3. **Select the single object you want to offset.**

Because two possible directions could be used to offset the selected object, the OFFSET command wants you to specify in which direction you want to create the offset object by displaying the prompt

```
Specify point on side to offset or [Exit/Multiple/Undo]
   <Exit>:
```

It doesn't matter precisely where you pick, just so it's clearly on one side or the other of the source object.

4. **When you finish offsetting, press Enter to return to a blank command prompt.**

Figure 2-7 shows the effect of offsetting a set of joined linework. The closed shape on the left is a single polyline, and the shape on the right is drawn as separate lines with the LINE command. For this kind of result, it's obviously best to use a polyline rather than separate lines — you'll end up with no intersection cleanup.

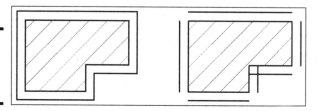

Figure 2-7:
Offsetting
polylines
and lines.

ARRAY

COPY makes multiple copies of objects by default. If it doesn't matter where the copies go, the COPY command is fine. However, if you need your ducks in rows (and in columns, or even in a circle), the ARRAY command is for you.

ARRAY creates regular patterns of selected objects in either *rectangular* (rows and columns) or *polar* (circular) arrangements. The following steps explain how to create a rectangular array:

1. **Start the ARRAY command by using one of the methods in Table 2-2.**

The Array dialog box appears. Figure 2-8 shows the dialog box config-ured for rectangular arrays.

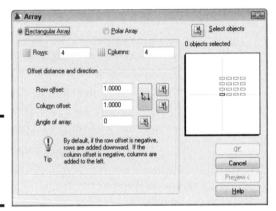

Figure 2-8:
Setting a
rectangular
array in a
dialog box.

2. **Make sure to choose the Rectangular Array option (at the top of the dialog box) and then click the Select Objects button.**

The dialog box closes, allowing you to select objects to array.

3. **Select one or more objects to array, and then press Enter to finish selecting.**

The dialog box reappears.

4. **Specify the number of rows or columns or both, the row and column offsets, and (optionally) a rotation angle for the array.**

If you want a single row or a single column, specify 1 in the appropriate box. Also, even though you're making copies of a source object, the number of rows and columns must include the number of copies you want *plus* the source object.

You can also use the buttons beside the Row offset, Column offset, and Angle of array boxes to specify distances and angles. Clicking any of the buttons temporarily closes the dialog box and lets you pick points in the drawing.

5. **Click Preview to make sure that your ducks (or objects) are in a row.**

   A preview of the resulting array based on the values entered is displayed. You can freely pan and zoom in the drawing to see the arrayed objects.

6. **Right-click in the drawing window to accept the array as it appears and to finish the command, or click or press the ESC key to return to the Array dialog box.**

In AutoCAD 2009 and AutoCAD LT 2009, you can now pan and zoom when previewing the array before accepting it.

Choosing a polar array changes the look of the Array dialog box, as shown in Figure 2-9. To create a polar array, you specify the objects to array, and then you specify a center point, the number of items and angle to fill, and whether the selected objects should be rotated as they're arrayed.

Rotating and resizing

The next set of commands modifies objects by changing their size or orientation in the drawing.

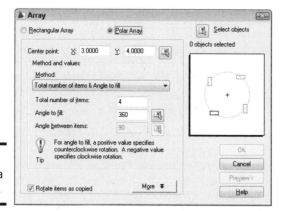

Figure 2-9:
Setting up a polar array.

Book II
Chapter 2

Modifying Objects

ROTATE

ROTATE spins the objects you select around a base point based on an angle value, or by defining a reference angle and then an angle value. A typical ROTATE command sequence looks like the following:

```
Command: ROTATE
Current positive angle in UCS:  ANGDIR=counterclockwise
    ANGBASE=0
Select objects: 3 found
Select objects:
Specify base point: 0,0
Specify rotation angle or [Copy/Reference] <0>: 32
```

After pressing Enter at the last prompt, the selected objects are rotated.

You use the Copy option to create a copy of the selected objects and then rotate the copied objects instead of rotating the original objects that you select.

SCALE

SCALE proportionately resizes selected objects about a base point. You specify a numeric scale factor or define a reference to specify the new size. The procedure is similar to that for ROTATE: Select your objects, specify a base point, and then specify a scale factor.

You use the Copy option to create a copy of the selected objects and then scale the copied objects instead of scaling the original objects that you select.

Use the SCALE command if you need to convert a drawing done in millimeters so that you can work on it in inches, or vice versa. If you scale a drawing based in inches by a factor of 25.4, the distance values (including the dimensions) will be equivalent to true distances in millimeters. If you have to go the other way, scale the drawing by a factor of 0.03937.

STRETCH

STRETCH stretches but also compresses. Perhaps it should be called STRETCHANDSHRINK? Create a crossing window through the objects you want to stretch and then specify a base point and a second point just like you do with the MOVE and COPY commands. Objects that are fully in the cross window are moved and not stretched.

LENGTHEN

LENGTHEN changes the length of lines, splines, arcs, and open polylines. Start the LENGTHEN command and then choose the object you want to lengthen (or shorten). The length of the object changes based on the option you specify at the command prompt. It's easier to adjust the length of some objects by using grips, which I discuss near the end of this chapter.

Breaking, mending, and blowing up real good

AutoCAD has let you break objects for years and years. And what's *really* great is that you never have to pay for the stuff you break. Recent releases also let you fix things (well, a few things, under very particular conditions). But sometimes, there's just no alternative to blowing things up.

BREAK

BREAK is a tricky command to master because you really, really have to keep a watch on the command prompt. The normal function of BREAK is to remove a chunk of an object, such as remove a piece of a line to make two lines with a gap between them, or remove a piece of a circle to turn it into an arc. The following steps describe how to use BREAK to create a gap in an object:

1. **Start the BREAK command by using one of the methods in Table 2-2.**

You can use this command only in verb-noun mode. The command displays the prompt to select an object. When you have done so, the prompt reads

```
Specify second break point or [First point]:
```

BREAK's default behavior is to use the point where you selected the object as the first point of the break. The second point is the other end of the break; after the second pick, the command breaks the object and then returns to a blank command prompt. This is usually not a precise way of working, so most of the time you should use the First point option.

2. **Type F and press Enter to specify the First point option.**

The command displays the prompt

```
Specify first break point:
```

Use your favorite precision technique to pick the exact point where the break should start. The command then displays the prompt

```
Specify second break point:
```

Pick again to specify the second break point. AutoCAD removes the portion of the object between the first and second points.

Use Break at Point to break an object into separate pieces without creating a gap between them — the objects meet endpoint-to-endpoint. Break at Point is a command macro; you can achieve the same result by starting the BREAK command and then entering the @ symbol at the Specify second break point: prompt, but this way requires less typing.

JOIN

JOIN enables you to combine separate objects into single ones, as long as some fairly stringent criteria are met. For starters, all objects must lie on the same plane. Separated lines to be joined must be collinear. Arcs and ellipses must be concentric. Lines and arcs can be joined to a polyline as long as you select a polyline first. JOIN is another command that can be used only in verb-noun mode.

EXPLODE

EXPLODE breaks up complex objects into their individual primitive elements. You can explode polylines, as well as multiline text, dimensions, tables, and blocks. (I discuss multiline text, dimensions, and tables in Book III and blocks in Book VI.) If you use EXPLODE on a polyline, the separate entities (that is, lines and arcs) end up on the same layer as the original polyline.

A related command called XPLODE explodes complex entities and gives you a range of options you can set for the exploded objects.

Double-barrel commands

Love and Marriage. Horse and Carriage. Trim and Extend. Even though they don't rhyme, TRIM and EXTEND do work in similar fashion, so I discuss them together here. And while I'm at it, I'll talk about CHAMFER and FILLET as well.

TRIM and EXTEND

TRIM and EXTEND use existing geometry to modify other geometry. The TRIM command lets you cut objects by selecting other objects that cross them. The EXTEND command lets you lengthen objects by selecting other objects that you want them to reach.

The following steps and Figure 2-10 describe how to use TRIM to shorten and extend objects:

1. **Start the TRIM command by using one of the methods in Table 2-2.**

In this two-part command, you first select the objects you want to trim with your temporary pair of scissors. The command displays the prompts

```
Current settings: Projection=UCS, Edge=None
Select cutting edges ...
Select objects or <select all>:
```

The first prompt line displays the current command settings. To change
the Projection or Edge setting, use the command options that appear
after you've finished selecting your cutting edges. The second line tells
you that the objects you're going to select will be used as the cutting
edges.

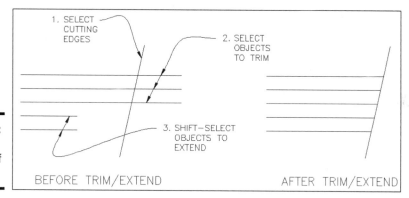

Figure 2-10:
The long
and short of
TRIM.

2. **At the *Select objects* prompt, use any object selection method to
   select linework or other drawing objects as the cutting edges, or press
   Enter to select all visible objects as cutting edges.**

   After you finish selecting objects to use as the cutting edges, the command displays the prompt

```
Select object to trim or shift-select to extend or
[Fence/Crossing/Project/Edge/eRase/Undo]:
```

3. **On the object that you want to trim, pick a point on the side of the cutting
   edge that you want to get rid of, or choose one of the command options.**

   TRIM and EXTEND are such close relatives that you can actually run
   EXTEND from within TRIM, and vice versa. To do so, simply hold down
   the Shift key and select the objects you want to extend or trim.

FILLET and CHAMFER

FILLET and CHAMFER offer methods of finishing off intersecting objects. CHAMFER creates a straight beveled edge between two nonparallel objects. FILLET creates a curved transition (actually an arc object) between two nonparallel objects. FILLET can also create a semicircular connection between parallel lines. Figure 2-11 shows a typical intersection after filleting and chamfering.

Holding down the Shift key when creating the fillet or chamfer creates a clean intersection, as shown at the right of Figure 2-10. This is like setting the fillet radius or chamfer distances to 0.

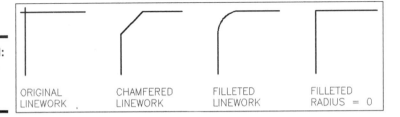

Figure 2-11: Cornering your intersections.

ORIGINAL LINEWORK   CHAMFERED LINEWORK   FILLETED LINEWORK   FILLETED RADIUS = 0

Specialized commands

Most of the commands I've discussed so far can work on any type of object; for example, you can trim or extend lines, arcs, or polylines. Some object types are sufficiently complex that they require unique editing commands. These specialized editing commands allow you to modify the geometric properties of hatches, polylines, and splines, and they can be found when the Modify panel is expanded on the Home tab of the ribbon (see Figure 2-12). Along with these specialized editing commands, two other unique commands come in handy from time to time based on the objects in the drawing.

Change Space   Draw Order

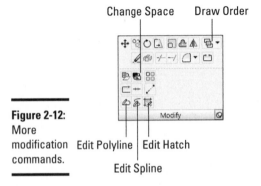

Figure 2-12: More modification commands.

Edit Polyline | Edit Hatch

Edit Spline

These five commands for modifying graphic objects are as follows:

✦ **Draworder:** Invokes the DRAWORDER command; move objects in front of or behind other objects.

✦ **Change Space:** Invokes the CHSPACE command; move objects between model space in a viewport on a layout tab and paper space.

✦ **Edit Hatch:** Invokes HATCHEDIT command; modify pattern, scale, and other properties of existing hatch objects.

✦ **Edit Polyline:** Invokes PEDIT command; modify width, linetype generation, curve type, and other properties of existing polyline objects.

✦ **Edit Spline:** Invokes SPLINEDIT command; modify curve type, vertexes, and other properties of existing spline objects.

For additional information on these commands, refer to AutoCAD's online Help system.

Changing properties

All the edit commands I've looked at so far have involved modifying or duplicating objects in some form or other. But sometimes you may just want to change an object's layer or find out how long something is.

MATCH PROPERTIES

MATCHPROP is AutoCAD's magic wand. Match properties copies object properties (linetype, color, layer, text or dimension style, and so on) from one object to one or more other objects, simply click the source object and then the objects you want to change. You can use the Settings option to specify which general property values are copied from one object to another along with some special formatting properties that are specific to certain object types.

PROPERTIES

PROPERTIES displays a window (or palette) of its own (see Figure 2-13) in which you can see a list of every property (editable or not) of the selected object or objects.

The Properties palette is a dockable window. Unlike dialog boxes, dockable windows can stay open while you're working in the drawing. And by double-clicking their title bars, you can *dock* them — that is, anchor them — at the left or right edges of the display.

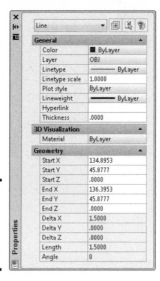

Figure 2-13:
Checking out the Properties palette.

Quick Properties

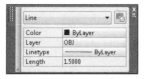

The Quick Properties panel (see Figure 2-14) is a customizable version of the Properties panel that lets you control which properties are displayed by object type. When the Quick Properties (QP) button on the application status bar is enabled, the Quick Properties panel is displayed when you select an object or objects.

Figure 2-14:
Quickly access object properties with the Quick Properties panel.

The Quick Properties panel is new in AutoCAD 2009 and makes accessing properties easier than using the Properties palette.

The Quick Properties panel can float over the drawing window or be docked on the ribbon. To change where the Quick Properties panel is displayed, right-click the panel and choose Location Mode⇨Cursor or Float. You use the Customize User Interface (CUI) editor to control the display of the properties on the Quick Properties panel. To display the CUI editor, click the Customize button on the Quick Properties panel. I cover using the CUI editor to customize the user interface in Book IX, Chapter 3.

SETBYLAYER

SETBYLAYER changes all general property overrides of selected objects to ByLayer. You can use the Settings option to control which properties are set to ByLayer. The properties that you can change to ByLayer are color, linetype, lineweight, material, and plot style. I covered general properties in Book 1, Chapter 5.

Changing your mind

I introduce you to UNDO in Book I and point out a little-known but useful command called OOPS. Remember: OOPS restores the last things you erased. UNDO undoes the last operation. Refer to Book I if you need a refresher on the difference.

Coming to Grips with Grips

When you select objects, not only do they highlight, they also sprout little blue boxes called *grips*. You can perform a number of editing operations by clicking these grips and then following the prompts that are displayed at the command line (or the dynamic input tooltip if you're using it — and if you've forgotten what dynamic input is, have a look at Book I, Chapter 3).

By default, grips appear as solid blue squares at specific points on selected objects. Grip locations often correspond with object snap points, but they're not the same. To make a grip active, move the crosshairs over the grip and click. You know it's selected when its color changes from blue to a dark red (see Figure 2-15).

Selecting a grip activates the grip-edit mode. The grip turns red to show that it's active. As soon as a grip becomes active, the command prompt is replaced by a series of five grip-edit commands. When a grip is active, you can choose the grip-edit commands and options in any of these ways:

✦ Press Enter or the spacebar to cycle through the five commands. If you go past the one you want, keep pressing Enter until it reappears. To select an option, type its capitalized letter.

Red grip   Blue grip

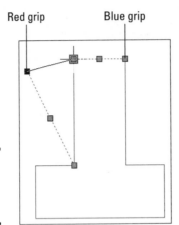

Figure 2-15:
A gripping
way of
editing.

✦ Right-click and choose the command or option from the shortcut menu.

✦ If dynamic input is enabled, you can use the down-arrow key (on the keyboard) to choose an option, although you must choose the grip-edit command by right-clicking or pressing Enter or the spacebar.

If you're using the keyboard, activating a grip replaces the command line with the grip-edit commands. They look like this:

```
** STRETCH ** <Stretch to point>/Base point/Copy/Undo/eXit:
** MOVE ** <Move to point>/Base point/Copy/Undo/eXit:
** ROTATE ** <Rotation angle>/Base
   point/Copy/Undo/Reference/eXit:
** SCALE ** <Scale factor>/Base
   point/Copy/Undo/Reference/eXit:
** MIRROR ** <Second point>/Base point/Copy/Undo/eXit:
** STRETCH ** ... and round and round you go.
```

Each grip-edit command has options to change the base point or make multiple copies. The **ROTATE** and **SCALE** options also let you use reference options.

Grips also have an automatic object snap; as soon as you move your cursor close to a grip, it jumps to the precise control point.

Chapter 3: Managing Views

In This Chapter

✔ **Zooming in and out of your drawings**

✔ **Panning around your drawings**

✔ **Using SteeringWheels to navigate the drawing**

✔ **Going back to where you were with named views**

✔ **Viewing a drawing in motion**

✔ **Updating the display**

*W*hen you draw things in AutoCAD, you draw them at full size. If you're drawing the cross section of a 2 x 4 (or a 38 x 89 for our metrically inclined friends), you can look at it full size, so that the screen width is the same as the width of the actual piece of lumber. If your monitor is big enough, you can even view a 2 x 12 (38 x 286) on your screen at its real size. Sooner rather than later, though, it becomes uneconomical to keep getting a bigger monitor as you need to draw bigger things.

Luckily, the ZOOM command lets you increase or decrease the magnification of your drawing objects through a number of options, which I discuss in this chapter. In addition to zooming in and out of drawings, you should know some other display commands — PAN, NAVSWHEEL, VIEW, AND NAVSMOTION — because they'll come in handy as you navigate your drawings.

PAN lets you move around in the drawing without changing the magnification. The NAVSWHEEL command combines the ZOOM and PAN commands into a single user interface that will remind you of a steering wheel in a car. The VIEW command displays a dialog box in which you can save and restore named views. NAVSMOTION command allows you to visually access named views quickly from the status bar without using a dialog box.

Table 3-1 lists AutoCAD's 2D display commands in alphabetical order, together with how they can be accessed from the user interface and general descriptions of what they do.

Table 3-1				AutoCAD's 2D Display Commands	
Icon	*Ribbon*	*Toolbar*	*View Menu*	*Command Name, Option (Alias)*	*Function*
—	—	—	Aerial View	DSVIEWER	Displays the Aerial Viewer window. (See later in this chapter for details.)
▢▢▢ ▶	—	—	ShowMotion	NAVSMOTION (MOTION)	Displays the ShowMotion interface, which allows you to restore a saved view or create a new one. You can also play back the motion assigned to a view.
◉	Home tab⇨ View panel⇨ Steering- Wheels	—	Steering- Wheels	NAVSWHEEL (WHEEL)	Displays a wheel that contains a set of navigation tools that you can access from a single interface.
—	—	—	—	NEWSHOT (NSHOT)	Displays the New View/Shot Properties dialog box with the Shot Properties tab current. The dialog box allows you to create new named views with motion.

Icon	Ribbon	Toolbar	View Menu	Command Name, Option (Alias)	Function
—	—	—	—	NEWVIEW (NVIEW)	Displays the New View/Shot Properties dialog box with the View Properties tab current. The dialog box allows you to create new named views.
	Home tab⇨ Utilities panel⇨Pan	Standard, Pan Real-time	Pan⇨ Realtime	PAN (P)	Allows you to dynamically drag the drawing in the drawing window without changing the magnification of the drawing.
	—	—	Pan⇨Point	-PAN (-P)	Allows you to move the drawing in the drawing window by defining the displacement of the view by clicking two points.
	—	—	Redraw	REDRAW (R)	Refreshes the display.
—	—	—	—	REDRAWALL (RA)	Refreshes the display of all viewports.
—	—	—	Regen	REGEN (RE)	Recalculates the drawing database, and then redraws the graphics.

(continued)

Table 3-1 *(continued)*

Icon	*Ribbon*	*Toolbar*	*View Menu*	*Command Name, Option (Alias)*	*Function*
—	—	—	Regen All	REGENALL (REA)	Recalculates the drawing database, and then redraws the graphics in all viewports.
—	—	—	—	REGENAUTO	Enables or disables automatic regenerations.
	—	View, Named Views	Named Views	VIEW (V)	Displays the View Manager dialog box, which allows you to add or modify named views or set them as current.
—	—	—	—	VIEWRES	Controls the visual smoothness of curved objects in the current viewport.
	Home tab⇨ Utilities panel⇨Zoom flyout⇨ Realtime	Standard, Zoom Realtime	Zoom⇨ Realtime	ZOOM, Realtime (Z)	Starts the Realtime option of the ZOOM command.
—	Home tab⇨ Utilities panel⇨Zoom flyout	Standard (Zoom flyout)	Zoom	ZOOM (Z)	Displays the full Zoom flyout or submenu.
	Home tab⇨ Utilities panel⇨Zoom flyout⇨ Previous	Standard, Zoom Previous	Zoom⇨ Previous	Zoom, Previous (Z)	Replaces the current drawing view with the previous view.

As you see from the table, there aren't individual aliases for each option of the ZOOM command. Without custom programming (unavailable in AutoCAD LT), the quickest keyboarding options are to type **Z,** press Enter, and then type the key letter for the option and press Enter again.

As you can see in Figure 3-1, the View menu of the menu browser has many other viewing commands than those listed in Table 3-1, and that's because I cover only the 2D viewing commands here. The other commands on the View menu that are not covered in this chapter are related to 3D viewing, and I discuss them in Book V.

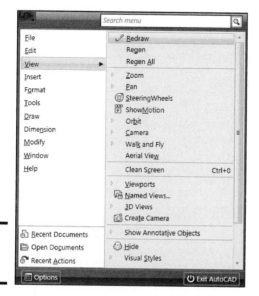

Figure 3-1:
A menu
to view.

A Zoom of One's Own

Zooming in closer and zooming out farther away should be simple enough, right? But this is AutoCAD, where little is as simple as it seems. There's a host of options for the ZOOM command (some simpler than others), and Table 3-2 sets them out for you.

Table 3-2		ZOOM Command Options
Icon	*Option*	*Description*
	Zoom Window	Pick two corners to define a rectangular window. AutoCAD zooms in on the defined rectangular area.
	Zoom Dynamic	Combines both panning and zooming (like Realtime Pan and Zoom). Somewhat difficult to master, and made somewhat obsolete by the Realtime options.

(continued)

Table 3-2 *(continued)*

Icon	Option	Description
	Zoom Scale	Specify a zoom factor relative to the current display, the entire drawing, or paper space scale (usually 1:1).
	Zoom Center	Pick a point or enter coordinates for the center of the view, and then enter a magnification value.
	Zoom Object	Select an object; the display zooms in on the selected object which fills the drawing window.
	Zoom In	Zooms in on the objects in the drawing by a factor (default is 2x). Same as using ZOOM Scale and entering 2x as the scale factor.
	Zoom Out	Zooms out by a factor (default is .5x). Same as using ZOOM Scale and entering 0.5x as the scale factor.
	Zoom All	Zooms out to display the objects in the drawing limits. If the drawing objects fall outside the limits, the option zooms to show those objects (that is the command works the same as ZOOM Extents).
	Zoom Extents	Zooms out to display all drawing objects on nonfrozen layers in the current drawing space.

ZOOM Previous, another command option, has its own button on the user interface. Most ZOOM options are available from the Zoom flyout on several available user interface elements. There's also a separate Zoom toolbar, but unless you have acres and acres of screen real estate, it's probably more space efficient to use the flyout on the ribbon or the Standard toolbar.

In case you have not encountered them before, a flyout button is distinguished by a tiny — and I do mean tiny — black arrow in its lower-right corner. Clicking any button that has one of those arrows displays a subset of buttons that start commands. Figure 3-2 shows the effect of clicking the down arrow next to the Zoom flyout on the Utilities panel (which is on the Home tab of the ribbon). Clicking and holding down the mouse button over a flyout on a toolbar allows you to select one of the commands on the flyout. To choose a command, run your mouse pointer down the button to the one you want, and then click or release the mouse button for a flyout on a toolbar.

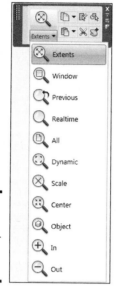

Figure 3-2:
Hidden
treasures —
the Zoom
flyout.

You can zoom in and out of your drawings by using one of three methods:

✦ **Wheel mouse:** The simplest method of all: Just scroll the mouse wheel
forward or back to zoom in or out of your drawing. By default, scrolling
the wheel away from you zooms in, and scrolling the wheel toward you
zooms out.

✦ **Realtime zoom (and pan):** Start the command from a right-click menu or
use the Zoom Realtime or Pan Realtime buttons from one of the user
interface elements. Press and drag to change the view visually in the
drawing window.

✦ **Regular ZOOM command options:** Choose a specific command option
from the menu browser or menu bar by clicking View menu⇨Zoom, or
by clicking the Zoom flyout on the Zoom toolbar or Utilities panel on the
Home tab of the ribbon. The regular options do not zoom in real time —
you have to complete the command before the view changes.

When you use one of the options of the ZOOM command other than
Realtime, AutoCAD performs a smooth transitioning effect between the
current view and the final view based on the input values provided. You
can control when and how the transition effect happens by using the
VTOPTIONS command.

Wheeling through your drawing

Although there are lots of powerful options for the ZOOM command, both regular and real time, sometimes simple is good. I honestly cannot get through the day without using a wheel mouse. If you don't have one, drop what you're doing and go get one now!

Here are some of the reasons I like using a mouse with a wheel:

✦ You can adjust the rate at which you zoom in and out as you scroll the mouse wheel with the ZOOMFACTOR system variable. The default value is 60, which means that each time you scroll you are 60 percent closer in or farther out.

✦ Starting with AutoCAD 2007, you can reverse the scroll direction of the mouse wheel in the Options dialog box. On the 3D Modeling tab, select the Reverse Mouse Wheel Zoom option. This works for 2D drafting as well as 3D modeling.

✦ Press down on the wheel and move the mouse to pan around the drawing window.

✦ Double-click the scroll wheel to zoom out far enough to show everything in the drawing. (This is called a *ZOOM Extents* in AutoCAD and is covered later in this chapter.)

Before you start scrolling to zoom in, move the crosshairs to the part of the drawing you're most interested in seeing. As you scroll, that location will be the center of the zoomed-in view.

Realtime zooming

Realtime zooming and panning are two halves of the same command. (I cover PAN Realtime in the following section.)

The following steps explain how to move around a drawing by using this command:

1. **Open a drawing that contains some objects that you may want to have a closer look at.**

If you're new to AutoCAD and don't have any suitable drawings yet, you can open one of the sample drawings from the C:\Program Files\ AutoCAD 2009\Sample folder (or C:\Program Files\AutoCAD LT 2009\ Sample folder for AutoCAD LT users).

2. **On the status bar, click the Zoom button and press Enter.**

(The Zoom button is the one with the magnifying glass and the plus and minus sign.) The crosshairs change to a magnifying glass cursor with plus and minus signs, as shown in the middle of Figure 3-3. The command displays the prompt

```
Press ESC or ENTER to exit, or right-click to display
    shortcut menu.
```

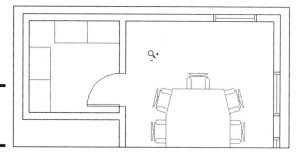

Figure 3-3:
Zooming in
real time.

3. **Hold down the left mouse button and drag the magnifying glass cursor upward. Release the mouse button when you have finished zooming in.**

As you drag upward, you zoom in closer to the drawing.

4. **Press and drag again, this time moving the cursor downward. Release the mouse button when you have finished zooming out.**

Your view of the drawing zooms back out.

5. **Take the third choice: Right-click to display the shortcut menu (see Figure 3-4).**

6. **Choose one of the menu options or select Exit to end realtime zooming and return to a blank command prompt.**

Figure 3-4:
Shortcut to
a new view.

The shortcut menu (refer to Figure 3-4) presents the following options:

✦ **Exit:** Exit the Realtime Pan and Zoom commands and return to the command prompt.

✦ **Pan:** Press and drag the left mouse button to shift the current view of the drawing without zooming in or out.

✦ **Zoom:** Press and drag the left mouse button to change the magnification of the objects in the current view.

✦ **3D Orbit:** View a 3D model from different viewpoints (AutoCAD only). I talk about it more in Book V.

✦ **Zoom Window:** The cursor icon changes to an arrow and a box (see Figure 3-5). Press and drag to create a rectangular window; the display zooms in to the area defined by the rectangle.

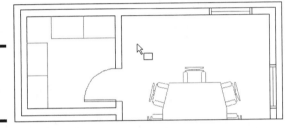

Figure 3-5:
Zoom me
a realtime
window.

✦ **Zoom Original:** If you change your mind about a Realtime Zoom Extents you just performed, Zoom Original undoes it for you, restoring the previous view.

✦ **Zoom Extents:** Zooms far enough out so you can see all objects in the drawing.

PAN and ZOOM can be run as *transparent* commands. A transparent command can be started in the middle of another command; for example, you might start drawing with the LINE command and realize the next point is off the screen. Without leaving the LINE command, you can click PAN or some of the ZOOM buttons and change your view. When you end the PAN or ZOOM command, the LINE command resumes where you left off. You can run PAN and ZOOM transparently from the command prompt by typing an apostrophe (') before the command name. When you use the wheel mouse to pan and zoom, the commands are executed transparently without needing to use the apostrophe (').

Pan in a Flash

The PAN command lets you change the view of your drawing without changing its magnification. You can pan around in your drawing in four ways — that is, to look at different parts of your drawing at the same magnification or elevation:

✦ **Realtime panning:** Pressing and dragging when the PAN Realtime command is active lets you visually shift the display of the drawing.

✦ **Realtime panning with a wheel mouse:** Pressing and holding the left mouse button down while moving the mouse lets you visually shift the display of the drawing.

✦ **Panning by displacement:** The old-style PAN command, where you pick a base point for your view change on-screen, and then pick a second point in the drawing that you want to see in the picked-point location. This one's as hard to use as it is to explain!

✦ **Scroll bars:** As in every Windows program, drag the slider bar, click either side of it, or click the arrows at the end of the scroll bars.

 You can start realtime panning by using a number of options (it seems as though there are *always* a number of options). The following steps explain them:

1. **Open a drawing that contains some objects that you may want to have a closer look at, and zoom in on them.**

Obviously, panning isn't going to achieve much if you're zoomed all the way out in a drawing!

2. **On the status bar, click the Pan button.**

(The Pan button has four arrows pointing in opposite directions.) The crosshairs change to the hand cursor, as shown in the middle of Figure 3-6.

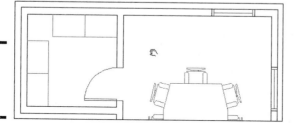

Figure 3-6:
Give us a
hand with
this pan.

3. **Press and hold the left mouse button, and drag the hand icon around the screen. Release the mouse button when you have finished panning.**

The display pans in real time (meaning you can see the objects in the current view move on-screen as you move the mouse).

4. **Right-click the drawing window to display the Realtime shortcut menu and choose Exit.**

AutoCAD returns to a blank command prompt. Note that you can also switch from realtime panning to realtime zooming with this menu.

Alternative ways to start realtime panning are

✦ At the command prompt, type **P** and press Enter.

✦ Press and drag with the mouse wheel (or the middle mouse button, if you have a three-button mouse).

✦ With no command active and nothing selected, right-click anywhere in the drawing and choose Pan from the default shortcut menu.

Be sure that no objects are selected and no command is active if you try this last method — otherwise the Zoom and Pan options will not appear on the menu.

To pan by using the mouse wheel or middle mouse button, the system variable MBUTTONPAN must be set to a value of 1. I cover working with system variables in Book I, Chapter 3.

Get a Grip on the Wheel and Hang On

Do not let go of the wheel or AutoCAD might spin out of control — okay maybe not the same type of wheel that you might find in your automobile, but AutoCAD does have a SteeringWheels feature. SteeringWheels is a user interface that follows, or tracks, the movement of the cursor. It contains a variety of navigation tools that allow you to change the display of the drawing.

The SteeringWheels feature is new in AutoCAD 2009 and primarily targeted at navigating 3D models. Those using AutoCAD LT get only the 2D Navigation wheel; users of AutoCAD get the 2D Navigation wheel along with three other types of wheels designed for primarily 3D navigation.

In AutoCAD, the 2D Navigation wheel is accessible only when working with a layout by default. However, if you set the NAVSWHEELMODE system variable to a value of 3 before starting the NAVSWHEEL command, you can use the 2D Navigation wheel in model space as well. Because AutoCAD LT supports only the 2D Navigation wheel, the 2D Navigation wheel is displayed in model space and on layout tabs.

In this section I talk about the basics of SteeringWheels and the 2D Navigation wheel. I describe the other wheels in Book V when I cover navigating 3D models. Figure 3-7 shows what the 2D Navigation wheel looks like and the tools on it.

Wedge   Close button

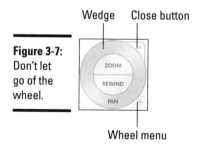

Figure 3-7:
Don't let
go of the
wheel.

Wheel menu

To display the 2D Navigation wheel, you use the NAVSWHEEL command; refer
to Table 3-1 to see how to start the command or click the SteeringWheel
button on the status bar. When you start the NAVSWHEEL command, the
following prompt is displayed:

```
Right-click to display the shortcut menu. Press ESC or
    ENTER to exit.
```

To close the 2D Navigation wheel, you can click the Close button or press
Esc or Enter.

The 2D Navigation wheel is divided into three wedges — a wedge is simply a
section of the main area of the wheel. The three wedges hold the Pan, Zoom,
and Rewind tools. Both the Pan and Zoom tools work similarly to the
Realtime Pan and Zoom tools that I discuss previously. To use one of the
tools on a wedge, position the cursor over the wedge and press and hold
down the mouse button. Then drag in the drawing window to pan or zoom.

The third wedge is the Rewind tool. The Rewind tool is similar to the Previous
option of the ZOOM command, except Rewind allows you to restore a previous view visually through the use of the Rewind user interface (UI) (see
Figure 3-8). If you click and drag over the Rewind wedge, the Rewind UI
appears, displaying a thumbnail of the previous views in the drawing that
can be restored. The current position in the Rewind history is indicated by
the orange brackets. You can restore the 20 most recent view changes. If you
click the Rewind wedge only, the previous view is restored.

Figure 3-8:
I missed
that. Can
you rewind
that please?

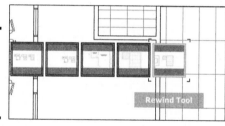

If you're using AutoCAD, not AutoCAD LT, you can control how wheels are displayed by clicking the Wheel menu (the button with the down arrow on the wheel) and choosing SteeringWheels Settings to display the SteeringWheels Settings dialog box (see Figure 3-9).

Figure 3-9:
Changing the appearance and behavior of Steering-Wheels with the Steering-Wheels Settings dialog box.

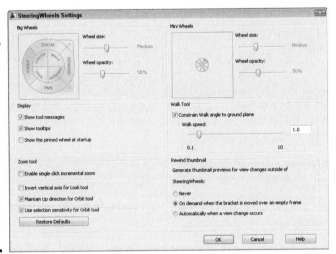

Name That View

So if panning and zooming are that powerful and flexible, what more do you need? Why should you find out about named views, anyway?

Imagine you're on the phone to a subcontractor for your project, and you're discussing part of a drawing. You both have the same drawing open (you can tell that from the drawing title!) but you have to refer to a specific area that you've spent a long time detailing. The conversation could go something like this:

"OK, zoom in to the room labeled *Seminar Area.* No, the one beside the office corridor. No, the other corridor, the one by the elevators. NO, NOT those elevators, the ones on the other side of the floor. OK, now zoom in on. . . ."

Or, it could go like this:

"OK, restore the view named *Seminar Room NE detail.*"

You can save a lot of frustration for yourself — as well as for others who need to use your drawings — if you set up named views of important areas.

Along with making it easier to navigate a drawing, creating named views also makes it easier to plot and set up layouts. You can plot named views from the Model tab with the PLOT command, or assign a named view to a viewport on a layout tab. Named are used also for working with sheet sets as well. I cover plotting and working with layouts in Book VII, Chapter 3; while I take a closer look at sheet sets in Book VII.

Creating views

The setup for saving named views has changed over recent releases of AutoCAD and AutoCAD LT. The View Manager dialog box has undergone some minor changes to support new animation properties (see Figure 3-10). The new animation properties are supported only in AutoCAD (sorry AutoCAD LT users).

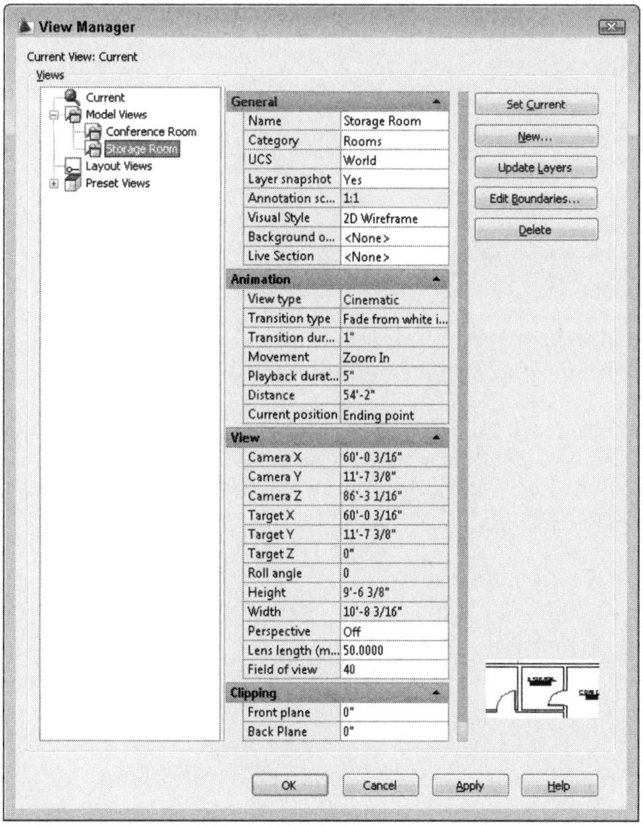

Figure 3-10:
The View Manager dialog box is used to create and organize named views.

View Manager

Current View: Current

Views
- Current
- Model Views
  - Conference Room
  - Storage Room
- Layout Views
- Preset Views

General

Name	Storage Room
Category	Rooms
UCS	World
Layer snapshot	Yes
Annotation sc...	1:1
Visual Style	2D Wireframe
Background o...	<None>
Live Section	<None>

Animation

View type	Cinematic
Transition type	Fade from white i...
Transition dur...	1"
Movement	Zoom In
Playback durat...	5"
Distance	54'-2"
Current position	Ending point

View

Camera X	60'-0 3/16"
Camera Y	11'-7 3/8"
Camera Z	86'-3 1/16"
Target X	60'-0 3/16"
Target Y	11'-7 3/8"
Target Z	0"
Roll angle	0
Height	9'-6 3/8"
Width	10'-8 3/16"
Perspective	Off
Lens length (m...	50.0000
Field of view	40

Clipping

Front plane	0"
Back Plane	0"

Set Current
New...
Update Layers
Edit Boundaries...
Delete

OK Cancel Apply Help

The following steps explain how to create, restore, and modify named views, beginning with steps that work in all recent releases of AutoCAD:

1. **Zoom into and pan around your drawing until you're looking at the area you want to save as a named view.**

   You *can* define an area without displaying it exactly as you want to see it, but for now, do the zooming and panning.

2. **Start the VIEW command by using one of the methods in Table 3-1.**

   The View Manager dialog box appears.

3. **Click New.**

   The New View/Shot Properties dialog box (see Figure 3-11) is displayed if you're using AutoCAD; the New View dialog box is displayed if you're using AutoCAD LT.

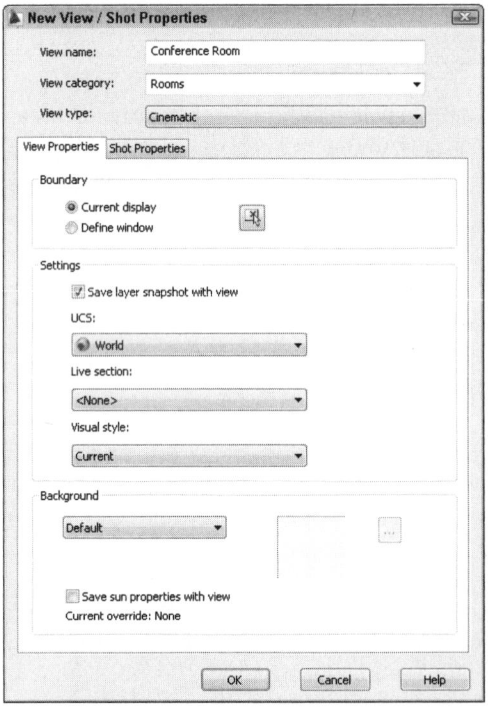

Figure 3-11:
You use the New View/Shot Properties dialog box to create named views.

4. **Type a name for the new view in the View Name list box.**

5. **In the boundary area, click the Current Display option if it's not selected already.**

If you want to define the area of your view within the current view, click Define Window in the Boundary area. Then when prompted to define the area, pick two corners. Ignore the other settings for now.

6. **Click OK.**

The View Manager dialog box shows the newly created view in its list box, under the Model Views or Layout Views node in the tree view of the Views area.

7. **Click OK.**

The location and magnification of the named view are now stored as part of the drawing file. You can restore the view at any time. Try it with these next two steps.

8. **Perform a ZOOM Extents to restore the overall view of your drawing.**

To zoom to the extents of the drawing, on the application status bar, click Zoom. Then at the command prompt type **E** and press Enter.

9. **On the ribbon, click View tab⇨Viewports panel. Select the name of the view to set current by clicking the down arrow on the View drop-down list and then select the named view.**

The selected named view is displayed in the drawing area. You can also open the View Manager dialog box again and select the view you want to restore and then click Set Current.

Other view options

You can associate layer settings with a named view. For example, you may want to restore a view of part of a complex assembly, but you only want to see the objects drawn on certain layers. The following steps explain how:

1. **Zoom into the area you want to save as a named view.**

2. **Turn on (or thaw) the layers you want to see, and turn off (or freeze) the ones you don't.**

Set the appropriate layer visibility states before you save the named view. For information on working with layers, see Chapter 6 of Book I.

3. **Follow Steps 2 through 5 from the preceding section.**

Open the View Manager dialog box, and then the New View dialog box. Give the view a name and make sure the Current Display option is selected.

4. **Select the Save Layer Snapshot with View option.**

Selecting this box means that when you restore this view, the current layer visibility states will also be restored.

Saving a layer snapshot is the default setting. Make sure you really want to save the layer settings before clicking OK, because your previous layer settings are not restored when you change views.

5. Click OK.

You return to the View Manager dialog box.

6. Click OK.

The named view is saved and you return to the drawing window.

You can easily change the boundaries of a view in the View Manager dialog box. Just select the view you want to edit in the list and click Edit Boundaries. AutoCAD shows you a grayed-out view of your drawing with the currently defined view highlighted in white. Then pick two corners to define a new view area.

View Manager lists *layout views* as well as regular model views. Sheet views are named views associated with viewports in drawing layouts as part of AutoCAD's sheet set feature.

The third category of view, after model views and layout views, is preset views. These are intended for 3D use and serve no purpose in 2D drafting. I have more to say about these preset views in Book V.

Having AutoCAD Put on a Show

AutoCAD can show you more about your model than ever before by adding motion to a named view. Prior to AutoCAD 2009, named views were used for navigating a drawing, placing views on a sheet of a sheet set, or plotting a section of a drawing. Now with AutoCAD 2009, named views can tell — I mean show — you a story of the model.

With the introduction of the ShowMotion user interface (see Figure 3-12), you can restore a named view quickly and easily through a series of thumbnails versus a dialog box or the View Control. Along with restoring named views, you can also add motion to the named views that you create so an animation can be played back when the view is restored. Named views don't need to have motion assigned to them to appear in the ShowMotion user interface. ShowMotion isn't available in AutoCAD LT.

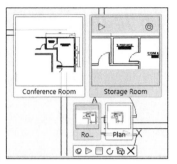

Figure 3-12:
Bringing named views to life with Show-Motion.

After you create a named view in a drawing, you can restore it by using ShowMotion or you can create new named views directly from ShowMotion. Either way, you use the New View/Shot Properties dialog box to create the named view. You assign motion to a named view by choosing a view type other than Still from the View Type drop-down list. Then you specify the properties for the shot on the Shot Properties tab (see Figure 3-13). After you assign the motion and create the named view, you display ShowMotion by using the NAVSMOTION command or by clicking ShowMotion on the status bar.

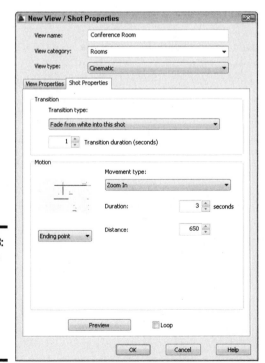

Figure 3-13:
Getting the desired shot with the New View/Shot Properties dialog box.

To Regen or to Redraw . . . That Is the Question

To regen or to redraw that is the question. If the great William Shakespeare had been an AutoCAD user, he might have had the same quandary as well. At times you'll need to update the display of the drawing window and you'll need to perform either a *redraw* or a *regen.* AutoCAD in recent releases is pretty good about identifying when it needs to update the display by using a redraw or a regen so there are no sudden productivity gaps.

So what is the difference between the two? AutoCAD maintains in memory how a drawing should look for each open drawing. As you add objects to the drawing window, AutoCAD keeps track of those objects in and out of the current view. A *redraw* simply refreshes the display by indicating to AutoCAD that it's okay to clear the screen and display a representation of the graphics it has been keeping track of without the need to recalculate the display again.

A *regeneration* — or *regen* as it is most commonly known — tells AutoCAD to discard the display it has in memory and start all over again. AutoCAD recalculates how all the objects should be displayed by looking at the information in the DWG file that it has open in memory. A redraw can be done quickly without any productivity lost, but a regeneration can take several seconds to several minutes based on the size of the drawing. (Usually a regen takes a matter of seconds, not minutes.)

You use the REDRAW command to redraw the display of the current viewport and the REDRAWALL command to redraw the display of all viewports in the current drawing. The REGEN command recalculates the display of the current viewport, and the REGENALL command recalculates the display of all viewports. When you use REDRAWALL and REGENALL, they affect tiled viewports on the Model tab and floating viewports on layouts.

Book III

Annotating Drawings

The 5th Wave   By Rich Tennant

©RICHTENNANT

"After Leroy sketched it out with CAD, Ronnie made the body from what he learned in Metal Shop, Sisy and Darlene's Home Ec. class helped them in fixing up the inside, and then all that anti-gravity stuff we picked up off the Web."

Contents at a Glance

Chapter 1: Text: When Pictures Just Won't Do 237

Text in AutoCAD 237
Fonts 244
Working with Text Styles 245
Creating Single Line Text 249
Working with Multiline Text.......................................252
Creating Multiline Text 253
Editing Text 258
Turning the Tables 259
Finding Text and Spell Checking 264

Chapter 2: Dimensioning 267

Understanding What a Dimension Is Made Of............267
Types of Dimensions..269
Creating New Dimensions as Associative 270
Using and Creating Dimension Styles 271
Creating Dimensions..283
Editing Dimensions 293
Leaders 296
Working with Geometric Tolerances 301

Chapter 3: Hatching Your Drawings 303

Adding Hatch Patterns and Fills.................................304
Working with Hatch Patterns and Solid Fills 309
Using Gradient Fills...310
Editing Hatch Patterns and Fills................................311

Chapter 4: Scaling Mt. Annotation 313

The What, With, and Why of Annotation Scaling........313
Making Styles and Objects Annotative.......................314
Adding and Removing Annotation Scales 317
Controlling the Annotation Scale for Output..............319

Chapter 1: Text: When Pictures Just Won't Do

In This Chapter

✔ Types of text in AutoCAD

✔ Controlling text appearance

✔ Creating and using text styles

✔ Using single-line and multiline text

✔ Editing text

✔ Creating tables

You know the old saying about a picture being worth a thousand words? I've done some digging and discovered that with the current exchange rate and cost of living increases, a picture is now worth 3,712 words!

However, text is important, too. It's a lot simpler — and more precise — to specify a manufacturer and part number in numbers and letters than it is to try to draw the darned thing from every angle. And until you can teach your drawings to talk, adding text is a necessary part of drafting in AutoCAD.

In this chapter, I look at creating and editing text in AutoCAD drawings.

Text in AutoCAD

In AutoCAD, little is as simple as it can be. Take drawing text, for instance. AutoCAD has not one but two kinds. You use one if you want to enter single characters or short lines of text, and the other if you want to write a novel — or at least some general notes. The first type is called *single-line text,* and the second (wait for it . . .) is called *multiline text* (Autodesk also refers to the latter as *paragraph text*).

An AutoCAD drawing has other kinds of text as well:

✦ **Leaders:** Leaders are drawing notes that include a line with an arrow at one end that points to a drawing object. You create leaders by using a few dimensioning commands. I cover leaders in Chapter 2 of this minibook.

✦ **Dimension values:** Dimension values appear as text and are formatted according to a text style, but they're not text objects — they're an integral part of dimension objects. (I cover text styles later in this chapter, and dimensions in Chapter 2 of this minibook.)

✦ **Attributes:** Attributes are pieces of text attached to a block. What makes them different from regular text is that the text is variable and can be changed for each instance of the block that's inserted into the drawing. I cover blocks and attributes in Book VI.

✦ **Tables:** Tables are another type of textlike object. Prior to AutoCAD 2005, you had to construct tables (for bills of material, drawing lists, and so on) by creating a grid using lines and then carefully filling in the spaces with text. Table objects automate the process; the text part is defined with text styles, just like multiline text.

✦ **Fields:** Fields are placeholders for textual data. You can place fields in tables, in attributes, or in both single-line and multiline text objects. Fields contain changeable data such as file name, date last saved, and drafter.

I describe each of these types of text or textlike objects in the chapters of this minibook.

Getting familiar with text terminology

Before I go on, I need to define a few terms:

✦ **Text:** *Text* usually refers to an AutoCAD object, either a single line of text (also called a text string) or a paragraph (called multiline text or mtext in AutoCAD). TEXT is also an alternate command name for DTEXT, the command used to enter single-line text.

✦ **Style:** *Style* refers to a named definition of the way your text appears when you place it in your drawing. Included in a style definition are the font, height, width factor, and obliquing angle, and whether it will be drawn backwards, upside down, or vertically. The style also defines whether the text created using the style supports annotation scaling. STYLE is also the name of the command used to create text styles. Text justification and rotation are not defined in a style; they're applied when you start the DTEXT or MTEXT command. AutoCAD also supports styles for other types of objects besides text, such as dimensions, tables, and multileaders.

✦ **Justification:** *Justification* refers to the direction that text flows from the start point, and how subsequent lines of text align below the first line. Left-aligned or left-justified text is the default in AutoCAD. I explain more about the many justification options later in this chapter.

✦ **Font:** *Font* refers to the appearance of the letters, numbers, and symbols. AutoCAD supports two types of font:

- AutoCAD shape (or vector) fonts
- Windows TrueType fonts

I go into more detail on both font types later in the chapter. For now, understand that you must use a font file to define a style, and you must have a style before you can create text objects.

If AutoCAD can't find the font files used to create text, the drawing won't load or display properly. A large number of add-on fonts are available for AutoCAD. However, you should use only the font files that come with AutoCAD or Windows, in case you ever need to send your drawings to other offices.

Will that be one line or two?

Every version of AutoCAD from the very first right up to AutoCAD 2009 has provided single-line text. The idea is that you type a line of text and press Enter, and then press Enter again to end the command. You end up with a single object — the single line of text.

You can create multiple lines of text by simply typing another line after each press of the Enter key; you end the sequence by pressing Enter on a blank line.

But picture this scenario. You've carefully laid out your drawing sheet, and you've allowed a 4-inch wide space along the right side of the sheet for your general notes. You add 40 or 50 lines of general notes as single-line text, which means that you have 40 or 50 individual text objects.

Now your boss comes along and tells you you're going to have to squeeze those notes into a 3-inch wide column so you can add some more details. Your mission — should you choose to accept it — is to edit each and every line, removing a word or two from the end of the first line and adding it to the second, and then removing two or three words from the second and adding them to the third . . . and on, and on, and on.

There ought to be a better way, and there is, although it didn't show up until AutoCAD Release 13. When you create multiline (or paragraph) text, you define a width for your text block by specifying a value or picking two points on-screen. Multiline text wraps from one line to the next, just like your friendly word processor.

Book III
Chapter 1

Text When Pictures
Just Won't Do

There are plenty of differences between single-line and multiline text:

✦ Single-line text has fewer formatting options, so it's simpler to create and edit. Multiline text has many, many formatting options, so it's much more complicated to create and edit.

✦ To place single-line text in a drawing, you simply pick a start point and type. To place multiline text, you specify two diagonal corners of a temporary bounding box; the lines of text are placed inside.

✦ Single-line text appears character by character as you type. To type a second line of text below the first, press Enter and continue typing. Press Enter on a blank line to exit the command. You enter multiline text in a special dialog box called the in-place text editor. AutoCAD automatically wraps lines of text based on the width of the bounding box you specify when you start the command.

✦ You create single-line text with the DTEXT or TEXT commands. You create multiline text with the MTEXT command.

Why are there two commands for creating single-line text? Remember that this is AutoCAD, where nothing is simple. By default, single-line text is created with the DTEXT command. TEXT is now an alias for the DTEXT command; typing either at the command line runs DTEXT. But the folks at Autodesk hate to throw anything away, so the old TEXT command is still there in the latest releases. To run it, put a hyphen in front: -TEXT. Go ahead and try it, and see why nobody uses it any more!

Single-line text is much more limited than multiline text in its formatting possibilities. You can define a few properties such as a single font or a preset height in a text style, but that's about it. You can go crazy in formatting multiline text, changing things such as font, size, and color, and structuring text in columns. Later in this chapter, I explain how to add and change the appearance of both types of text.

So how do you choose which type to use? The usual advice is to use single-line text for things such as letters or numbers inside grid bubbles or keynotes, and for short one-liners such as view titles and scales. Use multiline text for anything longer — certainly for anything longer than a couple of lines.

Justification

Justification (or alignment) refers to the look of a block of text on a drawing or page. If you're used to a word processor, you're probably familiar with the standard text justification options. Most text is left justified, like in this book. You may prefer center-justified text for headings and titles. (Not me, I keep to the left!) Rarely, you even see right-justified text, which means the right margin of a block of text is neatly lined up, and the left margin is ragged.

Many books (although very few drawings) use fully justified text, where both right and left margins line up tidily.

All these word processor options have their counterpart in AutoCAD. But because AutoCAD is AutoCAD, it can't leave well enough alone. It has six justification options that you can apply to single-line text (see Figure 1-1) and nine options that you can use with multiline text.

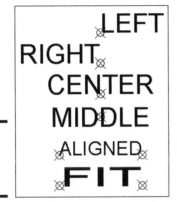

Figure 1-1:
Justifying
single-line
text.

Justifying single-line text

The single-line justification options probably make more sense to most people because the line of text starts (or at least is based on) the insertion point you pick. Left and right justified are plain enough, but the other options need a bit of explanation:

✦ **Center:** The point you pick is the middle point of the text's baseline; the text flows equally to the left and right from this point. Use this option for a title that you want centered under a drawing view.

✦ **Middle:** The text you enter is centered both horizontally and vertically about the point you pick. Use this option if you want to locate a letter or number in the center of a keynote or grid bubble.

✦ **Align:** You specify two points for this option, and the text you enter starts at the first point and ends at the second point. Aligned text maintains the height you enter, so characters are stretched or compressed to fill the space.

✦ **Fit:** Similar to align in that you pick two points, but instead of maintaining height and changing proportions, fit text maintains the proportions and changes the height to fill the space.

If it's absolutely essential that you have fully justified text (that is, straight margins at both left and right ends), either Align or Fit is for you. Be aware, however, that they're rare in AutoCAD drawings.

These six options are not the only justification choices for single-line text; it can also be justified to any of the additional nine options described in the next section, "Justifying multiline text." However, multiline text can't be justified by using any of the six options described here.

Justifying multiline text

Multiline text is treated as a single object, and the insertion point is either a corner, or the midpoint of a side, or the absolute middle of the bounding box. Figure 1-2 shows the same block of text with the nine justification options. In addition to these options, the text of a multiline text object can also use paragraph alignment options, which are left, center, right, justified, and distributed.

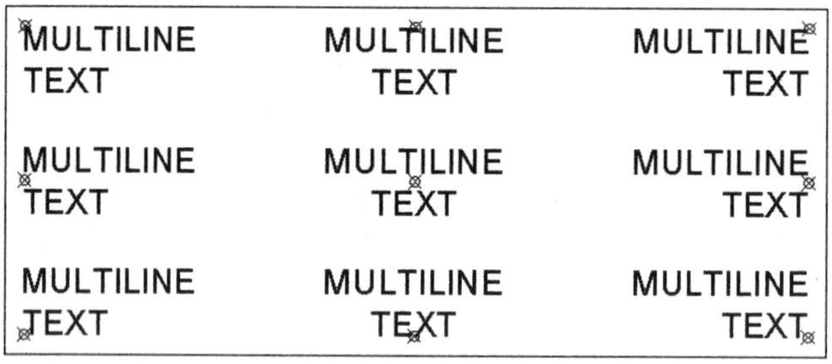

MULTILINE TEXT	MULTILINE TEXT	MULTILINE TEXT
MULTILINE TEXT	MULTILINE TEXT	MULTILINE TEXT
MULTILINE TEXT	MULTILINE TEXT	MULTILINE TEXT

Figure 1-2: Nine ways to multiline.

Where should text go?

In Book I, I introduce the two spaces that exist in every AutoCAD drawing file. Let's do a quick recap:

✦ **Model space** is an infinitely large 3D environment where you create the "real stuff" that you're drawing. This is where you draw your house plans or highways full size.

✦ **Paper space,** which is accessible as a layout, represents your drawing sheet, a 2D environment where you add the documentation that describes the "real stuff." This is where you place your border and title block, general notes, view titles, and symbols such as section marks and north arrows.

These are just guidelines, of course. A kazillion drawings out there (I know because I have counted every single one of them) are drawn entirely in model space or have dimensions and text in model space.

In think that most text belongs in model space because of how drawing data is exchanged not only with AutoCAD, but with other CAD-based programs. When you export, import, insert, or reference a drawing file, only the objects in model space on the Model tab are brought in or over because that's where all the important stuff is.

Scaling text for model space

In releases prior to AutoCAD 2008, it was a pain to figure out what size text had to be created when you drew something at full scale but plotted it to a another scale. Say that you've drawn a floor plan, and you want to put a title under it, with the scale below that, as shown in Figure 1-3. Your office standard says that titles are 3/16" high, and the scale reference should be 3/32" high. The issue of calculating text heights has been resolved with the introduction of annotation scaling, which I describe in Chapter 4 of this minibook. But you should understand how to calculate text height manually because you might have to work in existing drawings that do not use annotation scaling.

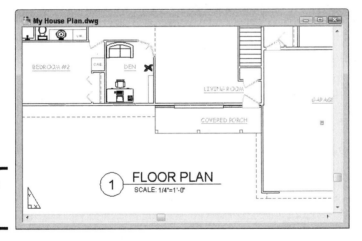

Figure 1-3:
A drawing
view title.

To make your floor plan fit on a drawing sheet, you're going to have to scale it — say, to 1/4"=1'–0". The scale factor here is 48 (refer to Book I, Chapter 6 for more on how to calculate scale factors). When you print your drawing, that 8" wall is going to measure a little over 1/8" wide on the page. So text that's 3/16" high will be a teeny speck on the hard copy of the drawing. To make your text visible and in conformance with your office standard, you need to multiply 3/16" by the drawing scale factor. In this example, you'd multiply 3/16 by 48 for a result of 9. When entering the text for the view title, you need to make it 9" high. A similar calculation shows that the scaled annotation needs to be 4 1/2" high.

If you do a lot of this sort of thing, you probably have a cheat sheet table (like Table 1-1, for example) with drawing scale factors applied to different printed text heights.

Table 1-1	Scale Factors for Model Space Text Height		
Drawing	*Scale Factor*	*Large Text* (3/16" / 5 mm)	*Small Text Scale* (3/32" / 2.5 mm)
1/16"=1'–0"	192	3'–0"	1'–6"
1/8"=1'–0"	96	1'–6"	9"
1/4"=1'–0"	48	9"	4 1/2"
1/2"=1'–0"	24	4 1/2"	2 1/4"
1"=1'–0"	12	2 1/4"	1 1/8"
3"=1'–0"	4	3/4"	3/8"
12"=1'–0"	1	3/16"	3/32"
1:100	100	500 mm	250 mm
1:50	50	250 mm	100 mm
1:20	20	100 mm	50 mm
1:10	10	50 mm	25 mm
1:5	5	25 mm	10 mm
1:2	2	10 mm	5 mm
1:1	1	5 mm	2.5 mm

Adding text to paper space

Did you say you wanted 3/16" text for your titles and 3/32" text for the scale annotations? If you put these on your layouts in paper space, the text heights will always be the same — 3/16" and 3/32" — regardless of the scale of any views in the layout. Still want to put that text in model space?

Fonts

A *font* is a character set that controls the look of the formatted text. AutoCAD uses fonts as part of a text style definition (I discuss text styles in the next section). You have literally thousands of fonts at your disposal. Some come with AutoCAD; some come as part of the Windows operating system; some come with different software programs that may also live on your computer. Remember, though, that you are drafting, not doing desktop publishing or authoring Web sites. (Or maybe you are doing desktop publishing or authoring Web sites, but, if so, you're definitely using the wrong program!) In short, don't get carried away with ransom note– or medieval manuscript–style text. Your job is to present the text data on your drawing clearly.

Types used by AutoCAD

Modern versions of AutoCAD can use two font types:

✦ **Shape (.SHX) fonts:** These fonts come with AutoCAD and work only with AutoCAD. Shape (or vector) fonts are made up of line segments and are more efficient than TrueType fonts.

✦ **TrueType fonts:** These fonts come with Windows. They give you lots of fancy options but can slow down AutoCAD performance in common tasks such as panning, zooming, and object selection.

Using fonts in drawings

You can use the default font you get when you start entering text the first time you open AutoCAD, or you can configure the fanciest TrueType font on your system. I advocate a middle road, nearer the first option than the second. My advice is to keep it simple and stick with AutoCAD's shape fonts — preferably the ones that come with the program.

There's a healthy aftermarket for SHX fonts, but they nearly always come with a license that prevents you from distributing the font file to others. The same applies to TrueType fonts that you purchase or obtain through installing other software programs. If your drawing is opened on a computer that doesn't have the fonts you've used, AutoCAD substitutes the missing font with an alternate font and displays a message that a font substitution has been made.

Two system variables control this font substitution process. FONTALT specifies a single font to use when AutoCAD can't find designated fonts. FONTMAP specifies the name of a mapping file that lists specific substitute local fonts for missing TrueType, Shape, and Postscript PFB fonts. (AutoCAD supported Postscript fonts for only one release, but probably hundreds of thousands of drawings out there use them.) For more information on how to configure these two variables, see the online Help index.

Working with Text Styles

Before you can add text to a drawing, you must have a text style — and luckily, every AutoCAD drawing contains at least one text style. The default templates include two basic text styles named Annotative and Standard. Text created with the Standard style uses the Arial TrueType font, which is different from the clunky looking font that AutoCAD has used in previous releases called txt.shx. The named Annotative style is a direct copy of the Standard style, except it is designated for use when creating annotative objects. Both styles are defined with a height of 0, which means you're prompted to specify a text height at the command prompt when creating a single-line or multiline text object.

A *text style* is a collection of settings that are stored in the drawing file itself. Text style definitions include a designated font file, a height, and — depending on the chosen font — options such as width factor and obliquing angle. Text styles are also used to designate whether the text objects using that text style are all annotative text objects, unless the Annotative property has been set for an individual text object, which essentially override the style's annotative behavior. I cover annotation scaling in Chapter 4 of this minibook.

Because text styles are created and saved inside a drawing file, they're not necessarily available in all your drawing files. If you create new text styles and save them in a template (DWT) file, they become available in every new drawing you start from that template. If you've created a nifty text style and want to use it in another existing drawing file, you can use DesignCenter to copy it from one file to another.

If you're sufficiently seasoned, feel free to modify the Standard style. If you're new to AutoCAD, I suggest you leave the Standard style alone and instead create a new style of your own. That way, if you mess it up badly, you can always go back to the Standard style and start again.

The following steps explain the process:

1. **On the ribbon, click Annotate tab⇨Text⇨Text Style (or on the menu browser or menu bar, click Format menu⇨Text Style).**

The Text Style dialog box displays the properties of the current and all available text styles (see Figure 1-4).

2. **Click New and enter a style name (for example,** MyNewStandard**) in the New Text Style dialog box, and then click OK.**

The New Text Style dialog box closes and you return to the Text Style dialog box. The new style starts as a clone of whatever the current style is set to.

3. **In the Font area, click the down arrow next to the Font Name drop-down list to display a list of all available fonts.**

The list contains all TrueType fonts installed in your Windows Fonts folder and all AutoCAD shape fonts.

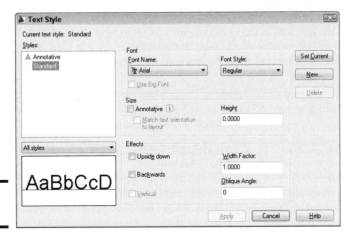

Figure 1-4:
Get stylin'.

4. Select a font from the list.

AutoCAD shape fonts are indicated by a teeny pair of dividers and display the SHX file extension. Windows TrueType fonts show a double-T icon and no file extension.

The Roman Simplex font (romans.shx) is probably the most popular font in AutoCAD because it combines efficiency with a much more pleasing appearance than the default txt.shx font.

5. Click Apply and then Close to save the new text style definition and set it current.

The Text Style dialog box closes. The new text style is now the current style and will be used for all text added to the drawing until it's changed to a different style.

The remaining options in the Text Style dialog box modify the style definition in the following ways:

✦ **Font Style:** If a TrueType font has style options (usually bold, italic, and bold italic), they appear in this list. Vector (.shx) fonts don't have options, so the list is dimmed.

✦ **Use Big Font:** "Big fonts" (is that an unhelpful name or what?) are special vector fonts used in Asian language drawings. Regular font files contain uppercase and (usually, but not always) lowercase letters, numbers, and most of the symbols you see on your keyboard. Asian languages use many more characters than that, and big font files contain the definitions for those additional characters. For more information on big fonts, look up Big Font file in the online Help system index.

✦ **Annotative:** This option determines if the text placed in the drawing with the text style is annotative. When a text style is annotative, the resulting height of the text is determined by the viewport's current annotation scale and the height at which you want the text to be drawn when plotted.

✦ **Match text orientation to layout:** When the text style is annotative, this option causes the text to orientate itself based on the current orientation of the layout on which the text is visible.

✦ **Height** and **Paper Text Height:** When the text style is not annotative, the value entered is used to determine the actual height of the text. So a value of 4" is 4" in model space but might plot smaller when displayed in a viewport on a layout based on the scale of the viewport it is visible in. When the text style is annotative, the text height can look consistent on both the Model tab and a paper space layout due to the annotation scales assigned to the viewport and text objects. If a text style is defined with a height of 0, you're prompted to specify a height each time you add text to the drawing. You can save this step (and help standardize your drawings) by defining a height. I go into greater detail about annotation scaling in Chapter 4 of this minibook.

Most of the time, it doesn't matter whether you set the text height as part of the style definition or leave it at 0 and enter a height every time. But one situation where it does matter is when you define a text style to use with your dimensions. In this case, the text height *must* be set to 0 or your dimension styles won't work properly. I explain all about dimensioning in Chapter 2 of this minibook.

✦ **Upside down** and **Backwards:** (What, no inside out?) These two text effects are self-explanatory. You might use Backwards if you were going to print on the back side of one-sided drafting film. I have bent over backwards to figure out when you might want upside-down text, but I haven't come up with a reason other than maybe doing vinyl lettering or creating injection molds.

✦ **Vertical:** The characters are horizontal, but the text string is vertical, like a movie marquee. Unless you're designing movie theaters, you're not likely to use this option. It's not available with TrueType fonts, nor with many shape fonts.

✦ **Width Factor:** This option allows you to change the width of the characters in a text string. Values of less than 1 compress the text, and values greater than 1 expand it.

If you set the width factor of the text style for dimensions to somewhere between 0.75 and 0.85, you'll be able to make dimension text fit between extension lines that might otherwise be forced outside them. For more on dimensioning, see Chapter 2 in this minibook.

✦ **Oblique angle:** This is for do-it-yourself italic! You specify an angle to apply a slope to the characters. Positive angles slope the characters to the right, and negative angles slope characters to the left. If you do any isometric drafting, you'll want to use this effect.

✦ **Preview:** The Preview window shows you a sample of your text style that changes as you fiddle with the properties.

You don't need to open the Text Style dialog box if you just want to change text styles. You can use the Annotate tab on the ribbon, which contains drop-down listings of text styles and dimension styles and various other styles. Just click the drop-down list and select the style to make a different one current. The buttons adjacent to the drop-down lists open the respective style definition dialog boxes. You can also use the controls and buttons on the Styles toolbar if you're using the AutoCAD Classic (or AutoCAD LT Classic) workspace, which doesn't display the ribbon by default. The AutoCAD Classic workspace displays toolbars and the menu bar for accessing commands instead of the ribbon. To set the AutoCAD Classic workspace current, on the status bar click Workspace Switching⇨AutoCAD Classic.

Creating Single Line Text

The following steps show you how to add multiple lines of single-line text to a drawing.

**Book III
Chapter 1**

**Text: When Pictures
Just Won't Do**

1. **On the ribbon, click Annotate tab⇨Text panel⇨ Single Line Text (or on the menu browser or menu bar, click Draw menu⇨Text⇨Single Line Text).**

The following prompt is displayed at the command line:

```
Current text style:  "Standard"  Text height:  0.2000
    Annotative:  No
Specify start point of text or [Justify/Style]:
```

At this point, you can change the justification or style of your text input. To stay with the default justification (aligned left) and style (Standard), skip to Step 5.

2. **To change the text justification:**

a. **At the command prompt, type J and press Enter.**

The following prompt is displayed at the command line:

```
Enter an option [Align/Fit/Center/Middle/Right/TL/TC/
    TR/ML/MC/MR/BL/BC/BR]:
```

b. **To change justification from the default (left justified), enter the uppercased letter of the option and press Enter.**

For example, type **M** and press Enter to set your text input to middle justified in the drawing. You have a lot of options here — I discuss text justification earlier in the chapter.

AutoCAD does not retain changes to text justification. If you want to place a number of middle-justified text objects, you need to specify the Middle option for each one.

3. To change the text style, type S **and press Enter.**

The prompt below is displayed at the command line:

```
Enter style name or [?] <Standard>:
```

The current text style name is shown inside angle brackets. Just press Enter to keep using the current style. If you want to switch to a different style and you know its name, type it now and press Enter. The new text style must already be defined in the current drawing. I cover text styles earlier in this chapter.

4. For a list of text styles defined in the current drawing, do the following:

a. At the command prompt, type ? **and press Enter.**

This prompt is displayed:

```
Enter text style(s) to list <*>:
```

The default option is the asterisk wild card.

b. Press Enter and AutoCAD lists all text styles defined in the current drawing together with their style properties.

```
Text styles:
Style name: "Notes"       Font typeface: ArchStencil
   Height: 0.0000  Width factor: 1.0000  Obliquing
   angle: 0
   Generation: Normal
Style name: "Standard"    Font files: txt.shx
   Height: 0.0000  Width factor: 1.0000  Obliquing
   angle: 0
   Generation: Normal
```

AutoCAD ends this command prompt sequence by redisplaying the current text style name and resuming the regular DTEXT command prompts:

```
Current text style: "Standard"
Current text style:  "Standard"  Text height:  0.2000
   Annotative:  No
Specify height <0.2000>:
```

5. To specify the text height, either press Enter to accept the default height, or type a new value for the text height and then press Enter.

You see the Specify height prompt only if your current text style is defined with a height of 0 (the default Standard text style is so defined). You can accept the default or enter a new text height here.

After you entered the desired text height, the following prompt is displayed:

```
Specify rotation angle of text <0>:
```

6. To specify the rotation angle, press Enter to accept the default value, or enter a new rotation angle.

Rotation angle refers to the angle of the whole text string, not to the slant of the individual characters, which is called the *obliquing angle* (see Figure 1-5). For horizontal text, leave the rotation angle at 0 degrees. Rotation angle is set when you're placing single-line or multiline text; obliquing angle is part of the text style definition.

Figure 1-5:
Rotation and obliqueness.

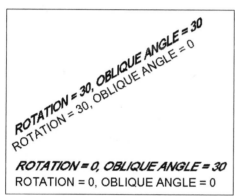

After a whole lot of prompting, you're finally ready to start adding text to the drawing! The crosshairs change to a text box to let you know that AutoCAD is indeed ready for some text.

7. Type your text.

When you want to break a line and continue on the next line, press Enter and continue typing. As you enter text, you can change the settings used for the in-place text editor, insert fields, perform find and replace operations, and much more by right-clicking. To find out about these additional features, press F1 while the in-place text editor is displayed. I cover working with fields, spell checking, and finding and replacing text later in this chapter.

8. When you finish adding single-line text, press Enter on a blank line to return to the command line.

Working with Multiline Text

 As if single-line text wasn't bad enough, multiline text introduces even more levels of complexity! Many longtime users were slow to adopt multiline text because of the complexities, and really, you can get most annotation jobs done with single-line text. So why bother?

A few tasks that you need to do every so often are extremely difficult to achieve with single-line text. I've already talked about word wrap in multiline text, which lets you shift the space required by a block of notes by simply grabbing the grips of the text object and dragging them to a new location.

Nicely aligned numbered or bulleted lists are hard to create by using single-line text because proportionally spaced fonts (and nearly all AutoCAD fonts are proportionally spaced) make lining things up virtually impossible. Creating columns of text is also difficult with single-line text but can be accomplished with just a few clicks with multiline text.

Finally, a font's full character set (that is, nonalphanumeric symbols) is readily accessible in multiline text. Single-line text offers just a few special characters that you have to enter with special codes.

I hope the advantages of multiline text encourage you to hang in there with it. The final bit of advice is this: If you master only one kind of text in AutoCAD, make it multiline text!

You create both single-line and multiline text in an *in-place text editor.* In-place means that the text you create in the editor will appear in the drawing in exactly that place at exactly that size when you finish creating the text and close the editor as long as you're not zoomed out to a point where you may not be able to visually read the text. If you're zoomed out too far, the text in the in-place editor will not appear at the actual size that it will be inserted into the drawing.

For single-line text, the in-place editor is simply a Windows-style text box. For multiline text, the in-place editor is more elaborate, consisting of two components: the in-place text editor (see Figure 1-6) and either the Multiline Text tab on the ribbon or the Text Formatting toolbar (which is displayed only when the ribbon is not shown).

When creating a multiline text object, you can control the formatting of the text for the object in the following ways:

✦ **Multiline Text ribbon panel:** The ribbon panel contains a multitude of drop-down lists and buttons that would do a word processor proud. Set justification, color, or style; add symbols or fields; and fine-tune character or line spacing.

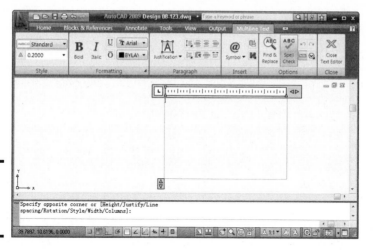

Figure 1-6:
The
multiline
text editor.

♦ **Text Formatting toolbar:** The toolbar contains the same plethora of drop-down lists and buttons that are on the Multiline Text ribbon panel. The Text Formatting toolbar is displayed only when the ribbon is not displayed or the MTEXTTOOLBAR system variable is set to a value of 1.

♦ **Bounding box with ruler:** The text you type appears in the bounding box. You can set margin and tab stops in the ruler by dragging the pointers, just like in a word processor. If you don't see a ruler atop the bounding box: On the ribbon or the top row of the Text Formatting toolbar, click Options panel⇨Ruler .

Creating Multiline Text

The following steps show you how to add a multiline text object to a drawing:

1. **On the ribbon, click Annotate tab⇨Text panel⇨ Multiline Line Text (or on the menu browser or menu bar, click Draw menu⇨Text⇨Multiline Text).**

The standard crosshairs change to plain crosshairs and ghosted text in the current style and height. The current text style name, height, and whether the text style is annotative are displayed in the command line. The command displays the following prompt:

```
Current text style:  "MyNewStandard"  Text height:
    2.6654  Annotative: No
Specify first corner:
```

You can control the ghosted text that is displayed when you first start the MTEXT command by changing the text string of the MTEXTJIGSTRING system variable. Type **MTEXTJIGSTRING** at the command prompt and type the text string you want to display with a maximum of 10 characters. Then press Enter to accept the new text string.

2. **Pick the first corner of the bounding box.**

   The default multiline text justification is Top Left, so the first point you pick will be the upper-left corner of the text object. The following prompt is then displayed at the command line:

   ```
   Specify opposite corner or [Height/Justify/Line
       spacing/Rotation/Style/Width/Columns]:
   ```

3. **Enter a command option or pick the second corner.**

   Enter the uppercase letter of the option to change text height, justification, line spacing, rotation, style, or the overall width of the text box. To retain all the default settings, pick the opposite corner of the text box. The command prompt disappears, and the in-place text editor is displayed with the bounding box. If the ribbon is displayed, the contextual Multiline Text panel is displayed. If the ribbon is not displayed, the Text Formatting toolbar is displayed.

   The bounding box sets only the width of the multiline text object. It does not control the object's height — it will expand as necessary to include all the text you enter.

4. **Type your text.**

   The text you type flows across the bounding box. When the text reaches the opposite side, it wraps automatically to the next line, just like your favorite word processor.

5. **To indicate that you have finished entering text, click outside the in-place editor.**

   The in-place text editor closes. You can also press Ctrl+Enter or click Close Text Editor on the ribbon or Text Formatting toolbar.

Formatting options

The various panels on the ribbon's Multiline Text tab (refer to Figure 1-6) and the Text Formatting toolbar enable you to perform many of the functions of a full-featured word processor. You can change the style, font, height, and any number of other properties of your multiline text object. See the online Help system for a full description of each formatting option — while the in-place text editor is displayed, press F1. The online Help system opens to the In-Place Text Editor topic.

A multiline text object can be created using only one text style. If you type some text, change the style, and type some more, the entire multiline text object changes to the new style. You can get the effect of different styles by highlighting some text and changing the font, height, color, and so on.

Numbered and bulleted lists

Another advantage of multiline text is that it supports bulleted and numbered lists. This feature is especially useful for creating general drawing notes, as shown in Figure 1-7.

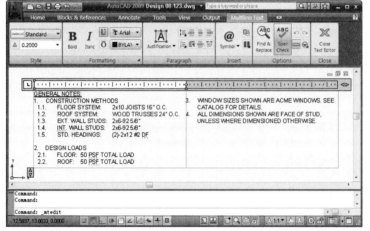

Figure 1-7:
Tabs, indents, and automatic numbering set to create numbered lists.

AutoCAD automates the process of creating numbered lists almost completely. Here's how:

1. **Follow Steps 1 through 3 in the previous section, "Creating Multiline Text."**

2. **Type a title; for example,** GENERAL NOTES.

   If you want your title underlined, click Underline on the Formatting panel in the Multiline Text tab on the ribbon or Text Formatting toolbar before you type the title, and then click Underline again to turn it off.

3. **Press Enter to go to the next line.**

   Press Enter again if you want to leave a little more space between the title and the body of the text.

4. **Right-click inside the in-place text editor and choose Bullets and Lists⇨Numbered. Also select Allow Auto-List, Use Tab Delimiter Only, and Allow Bullets and Lists if they are not already selected.**

The number 1 followed by a period appears on the current line, and the cursor jumps to the tab stop visible in the ruler at the top of the in-place text editor's ruler.

Numbered places numerals followed by periods in front of items in a list. *Lettered* places uppercase or lowercase letters followed by periods in front of list items. (*Bulleted* places bullet characters in front of list items.) *Auto-list* enables automatic numbering — each time you press Enter to move to a new line, the number of the bulleted list increments by one. *Use Tab Delimiter Only* means you must press the Tab key to move to the tab stop.

5. **Type the text corresponding to the current number or bullet.**

   As AutoCAD wraps the text, the second and subsequent lines align with the tab stop — that is, the text is automatically indented.

6. **To move to the next line, press Enter at the end of the paragraph.**

   Just like creating numbered lists in a word processor, AutoCAD automatically inserts the next number at the beginning of the new paragraph, with everything perfectly aligned (refer to Figure 1-7).

7. **Type the text corresponding to the next number or bullet, and then press Enter at the end of the paragraph to move to the next line.**

8. **Repeat Steps 5 through 7 for each subsequent numbered or bulleted item.**

9. **When you finish creating the numbered list, press Enter and then right-click in the in-place text editor. Choose Bullets and Lists⇨Off.**

10. **Enter any additional text. Then click outside the in-place editor.**

Controlling the flow of text

When you create a multiline text object, you can control the width of the object but not its height. The object's width affects how and when the text flows, or wraps, automatically. In addition, you can use columns to control the flow of the text (refer to Figure 1-7). Multiline text objects support static and dynamic columns.

When you define the behavior of columns for a multiline text object, you can specify the number of columns, the height for the columns, the width for each column, the gutter width, and the overall total width of the multiline text object. Text automatically flows between the columns based on the dimensions specified or when you insert a column break. You set the column settings by right-clicking in the in-place editor and choosing Columns⇨ Columns Settings. Make the desired column settings in the Column Settings dialog box and click OK. You can also adjust the width, gutter, and height for columns by using the controls on the ruler and outside the boundary box of the in-place text editor.

Fields, masks, and other multiline text delights

I haven't exhausted the features of the multiline text editor yet, and two especially useful ones are fields and background masks. The in-place text editor also offers a panoply of little functions and utilities that come in handy from time to time.

The convention in drafting is that text in a drawing is uppercase at all times. One way to avoid having to keep the Shift key pressed down is to use the Caps Lock key. But when you finish typing text and want to log into your network, if you forget to turn off Caps Lock, you get an error message. The in-place text editor has a great solution for you. Right-click the in-place text editor and choose AutoCAPS. Everything you type in the in-place text editor when creating multiline text will be in uppercase, without using Caps Lock. If you do forget and start typing text only to find out that you entered the text in lowercase, do not reach for the Backspace key. Instead highlight the text, right-click, and choose Change Case⇨UPPERCASE. The highlighted text is now all in uppercase.

Fields

Fields are placeholders for changeable data that updates automatically — such as the author of a drawing and when it was created, last saved, or plotted. This data comes from drawing properties, objects in a drawing, system variables, or a sheet set (sheet sets are not available in AutoCAD LT). To display the Field dialog box, right-click in the in-place text editor and choose Insert Field. Fields can also be inserted into single-line text objects. For more information on inserting and updating fields, refer to the online Help system.

Background masks

Sometimes you just have to place a note on top of drawing objects, and invariably, it looks bad. If you use multiline text for your note, you can mask the background drawing data so that the text displays clearly. Follow these steps:

1. **In a drawing containing some graphic objects, add some multiline text on top of the drawn objects.**

2. **Right-click inside the in-place text editor and choose Background Mask.**

   The Background Mask dialog box appears.

3. **Select Use Background Mask.**

   The remaining dialog box options become accessible.

4. **Set a Border Offset factor.**

This value, which must be between 1 and 5, controls the distance beyond the text object that the mask extends. When set to 1, the mask is tight to the text object.

5. In the Fill Color area, either select Use Drawing Background Color or click the drop-down list to select a color for the mask.

If you don't want bright red rectangles all over your drawing, make sure you select the Use Drawing Background color box.

6. Click OK and then exit the in-place text editor (see Figure 1-8).

Figure 1-8:
Masking the background of your text.

Editing Text

After you've created either single-line or multiline text, editing it is a straightforward exercise. As you might expect, there are two editors for the two types of text. So how do you know which editor to use? Easy — AutoCAD chooses for you if you double-click the text.

Editing single-line text

I've already pointed out all the formatting options available for multiline text, and if those are what you need, it's multiline text for you. Your editing options are fewer with single-line text, but for simple text, they should be more than ample.

Both types of text use an in-place text editor, where the text appears inside an edit box at the size and location it appears in the drawing. Simply double-click a string of single-line text to display it in the in-place editor. All you can change here is the value of the text itself. If you need to change other properties such as style, justification, or height, select the text and make changes in the Properties palette.

If you're an old hand at AutoCAD and you absolutely can't function with the in-place text editor for new single-line text, you can restore the pre-AutoCAD 2006 Edit Text dialog box by setting the DTEXTED system variable to 1.

Editing multiline text

Double-clicking a multiline text object also opens its in-place editor, but as you've already seen, it's an editor with a lot more bells and whistles. I cover most of the options in the earlier sections on creating multiline text. To change all or parts of the text, select as you would in a word processor and apply your changes. Then click outside the in-place editor to indicate that you've finished editing the text.

Single-line text isn't allowed to have anything that paragraph text doesn't also have, so an MTEXTED system variable lets you revert to the previous editor. To do so, type **MTEXTED** and press Enter; then type **OldEditor** and press Enter. The old editor still has the same toolbar and ruler, but the bounding box doesn't display the selected text at its actual size or location.

Fiddling with text can be a tedious task, and lots of little-known commands and functions let you do your tweaking more efficiently. Two such commands let you adjust text height and justification in different ways:

✦ **SCALETEXT:** Suppose you have a whole bunch of annotation objects in your drawing, and you want to reduce the size of them all. The SCALE command requires a lot of selecting and moving, but SCALETEXT scales each text object about its own insertion point, so the text stays where it ought to.

✦ **JUSTIFYTEXT:** If you change the justification of text in the Properties palette or the in-place text editor, the insertion point stays put and the text moves. JUSTIFYTEXT lets you change the justification by keeping the position of the text where it is and moving the insertion point.

Turning the Tables

Table objects were introduced in AutoCAD 2005. Before then, if you needed to add a table — say a bill of materials, or a door schedule, or a drawing list — you were in for some work; drawing lines, adding text, moving lines, and aligning everything at the end. AutoCAD's tables can start at the top and flow downward, as they do in most of the examples mentioned. They can also be anchored at the bottom and flow upward, which is the typical fashion for things like revision blocks. Tables can contain regular text, blocks, or fields.

Setting the table with styles

Tables, like text and dimensions, are defined according to styles. Every drawing has at least one table style waiting to be called on. The default templates contain a table style called (what else?) Standard, which also references the Standard text style. The following steps explain how to create a table style:

1. **On the ribbon, click Annotate tab⇨Tables panel⇨ Table Style (or on the menu browser or menu bar, click Format menu⇨Table Style).**

   The Table Style dialog box appears, showing on the left a list of all table styles defined in the current drawing, and on the right a preview of the current style settings. You can select an existing table style to set it current, to modify it, or to delete it; however, you can't delete the Standard style.

2. **Click New to create a new table style.**

   The Create New Table Style dialog box appears.

3. **Enter a name for the new style; for example, Door Schedule.**

   If you have more than one style defined, you can use the drop-down list to select an existing table style as the prototype for the new style.

4. **Click Continue.**

   The New Table Style dialog box opens, again with a preview of the current settings — except they're displayed on the left this time (see Figure 1-9).

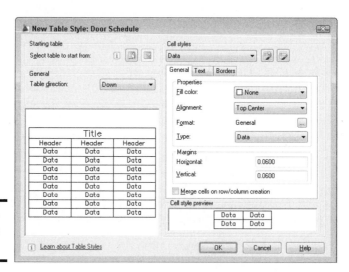

Figure 1-9:
Setting the table.

A table style has up to three parts: title, column headings, and data. Each part of the table can be formatted with a cell style, and each part of a table style has one default style. The settings for formatting a cell style are on the three tabs to the right of the dialog box (General, Text, and Border). When you insert a table, you have the ability to control which cell style is applied to the title, column headings, or data of the table. In other words, your table can contain the data only; the data and column heads; the data and a table title; or the data, column heads, and a title.

5. **In the Cell Styles area, select Data from the drop-down list. Change the settings for the cell style by using the General, Text, and Border tabs located below the Cell Styles drop-down list.**

   The Cell Style Preview updates as you change settings for the cell style. If you need to, click the Create a New Cell Style button (under the Cell Styles area and just to the left of the Cell Styles drop-down list along the top of the dialog box) to add additional cell styles that you might want to use. The Margins area on the General tab allows you to increase or decrease the space between the table text and the lines. Cell styles can also contain cell formatting, which allows you to represent values as currency or with a specific precision,

6. **Repeat Step 5 for the Header and Title cell styles, or any of the other cell styles in the drawing that you'll be using to create a new table.**

7. **In the General area (on the left), specify whether the table direction should be Down (the default) or Up.**

8. **Click OK to close the New Table Style dialog box.**

   You return to the Table Style dialog box. The new table style is automatically set current.

Creating and editing tables

After the table style is created, you use the TABLE command to add a table object to the drawing. The following steps show how:

1. **On the ribbon, click Annotate tab⇨Tables panel⇨ Table (or on the menu browser or menu bar, click Draw menu⇨Table).**

   The Insert Table dialog box appears (see Figure 1-10).

2. **In the Table Style drop-down list, select a table style or click the Launch the Table Style Dialog button located under the Cell Styles area to create a new table style.**

   The Preview area displays a preview of a table with the current cell styles that are set under the Set Cell Styles area.

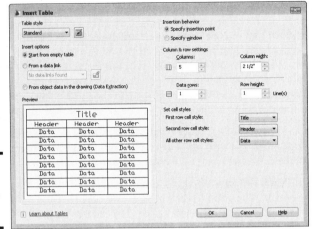

Figure 1-10:
Rows and
columns for
a table.

3. **In the Insertion Options area, select Start from Empty Table.**

   The Start from Empty Table option gives you a table with no data in it. If you have a spreadsheet that contains values for your table, you can choose the From a Data Link option instead, or you can use the From Object Data in the Drawing (Data Extraction) option if you want to create a table based on the properties of objects in the drawing along with block attribute values. I cover working with Data Links in the "Link me up Scotty" section later in this chapter. For information on using object properties and attribute values to populate a table, look up the DATAEXTRACTION command on the Index tab of AutoCAD's online Help system.

4. **In the Insertion Behavior area, select Specify Insertion Point or Specify Window.**

   Specify Insertion Point is the preferable option because it maintains the height and width settings you set in the table and text styles. Choosing Specify Window squeezes or stretches the table into the rectangular area you define.

5. **Specify the number of columns and data rows.**

   Data Rows excludes the rows for the title and column headings.

6. **Adjust the column width and row height as required.**

   One or the other pair of these options is dimmed if you choose Specify Window in Step 4. If you're using a table style that was created by using an existing table, you have the option to specify what values and formatting are applied to the new table in the Table Options area, which will be displayed below the Column & Row Settings area.

7. Click OK.

The empty table is placed in the drawing. The Multiline Text panel is displayed on the ribbon (or the Text Formatting toolbar appears if the ribbon is not displayed), and the first column cell is highlighted, ready for text input.

8. Enter the table title, column headings, and data.

It's now a matter of simply filling in the spaces. Imagine creating a table like that with the TEXT and LINE commands! If you want to input the text later, just click outside the highlighted cell.

You can use the Tab and arrow keys to navigate to cells in a table, and use Alt+Enter to force a new line in a table cell.

9. Click outside the table to indicate that you have finished entering text.

To add table data, or to edit what's already there, double-click inside the table cell. You can format individual cells in a table by clicking the cell and then changing its properties by using the Properties palette. You can also manipulate the properties of all the cells in a row or column by clicking the row or column on the Table Indicator that's displayed along the top and left side of the table.

Combine tables and fields to automatically populate a drawing title block or revision block. Field data updates automatically when the data source changes.

Table cells can also contain blocks, so you can create a drawing legend with graphic symbols in one column and a description of what they stand for in another column.

You can export the values in a table to a CSV file by using the TABLEEXPORT command.

Link me up Scotty

As mentioned, you can create a new table in a drawing, or create a table based on the properties of the objects and attributes of blocks in a drawing. You can also link a spreadsheet to a drawing as a Data Link and then control what sheets or cells from the spreadsheet are displayed in the table. You use the DATALINK command to display Data Link Manager, which allows you to link to a Microsoft Excel spreadsheet. By linking to a spreadsheet, you have the ability to pull values from the spreadsheet into your drawing or push values from AutoCAD to the spreadsheet after it is linked.

This bidirectional workflow makes it more natural to work with spreadsheets than using OLE or performing a Paste Special to get the data into AutoCAD and then the TABLEEXPORT command to get it back to the spreadsheet. When you link to the spreadsheet, you have the option of AutoCAD retaining the full and relative path to the spreadsheet file or none, which is important when sharing drawings outside your company. After you link to the file, you have the option to link to a sheet in the spreadsheet, a named range if one is defined, or a range of cells. After the Data Link has been defined, you then use the TABLE command to bring the values that you're linking to in the spreadsheet into AutoCAD.

In the Insert Table dialog box, you use the From a Data Link option in the Insert Options area and then select one of the configured data links. The row and column information is defined already for you based on how the data link was set up. After the table is created, you will know that it's defined by using a data link because when it's selected and the crosshairs hover over the table, an icon of two chain links appear locked together. If a padlock icon appears when you select a cell, it indicates that the contents, the format, or both are locked. If you right-click and choose Locking, you can turn locking on or off so the cell can be modified. If you make changes to the table, be sure to update the spreadsheet if you want the changes reflected in the data source. You can also update the table in the drawing as well as from the data source. To update the data source or the table, you use the DATALINKUPDATE command.

Finding Text and Spell Checking

As you work in a drawing and add more and more annotation, the chances of finding a specific annotation object go down and the chances of making a spelling mistake go up. The FIND command displays the Find and Replace dialog box, which allows you to search for a text string in the entire drawing, selected objects, or the current space (layout). Along with finding a text string, you can also replace the matching text string if an instance of the text string you're searching for is found. The More Options button in the Find and Replace dialog box gives you access to settings that determine how the search for a text string is carried out and which annotation objects (single-line text, dimensions, hyperlink, and others) will be searched for a text string match. The in-place text editor used for single-line and multiline text offers simplified find and replace options that are accessible by right-clicking the in-place text editor and choosing Find and Replace.

Because to err is human but to misspell is unforgiving in this age of computers, AutoCAD helps you fix spelling mistakes through the use of the SPELL command. The SPELL command displays the Check Spelling dialog box which allows you to spell check the entire drawing, selected objects, or the current space (layout). When AutoCAD encounters a spelling mistake, you're provided with a list of words that might be the correct spelling. You can also enter a replacement value yourself. You can add words that your company normally uses to the dictionary so AutoCAD understands that the word is not misspelled each time you run the spell checker.

You can also access the spell checker in the in-place text editor when working with multiline text objects. If you misspell a word, the in-place editor lets you know by underlining the misspelled word in red, which is similar to what Microsoft Word does. To correct the misspelled word, right-click it to access a list of suggested corrections (the list of corrections appears at the top of the menu).

**Book III
Chapter 1**

Text: When Pictures
Just Won't Do

Chapter 2: Dimensioning

In This Chapter

✔ Understanding what makes up a dimension

✔ Discovering the different types of dimensions available

✔ Defining and using dimension styles

✔ Adding dimensions

✔ Modifying dimensions

✔ Leading with leaders

✔ Constructing geometric tolerances

Dimensions are a form of annotation that provides information about the size or angle of a part so you know how it should be manufactured or constructed. Typically, dimensions provide information on the length of a part, the diameter of a hole, callouts in the form of leaders, or the allowable tolerances that a machined part can have before it might fail. In this chapter, you find out how to create and work with dimensions, leaders, and geometric tolerances.

AutoCAD and AutoCAD LT offer a number of dimension-related commands to help convey your design ideas to the people who are doing the construction (in the case of a building) or manufacturing (in the case of a machine part). Just as text styles manage the appearance of text in a drawing, dimension styles do the same thing for dimensions and multileader styles for multileaders. Dimension styles allow you to visually define how dimensions appear in a drawing, but they are more complex than text styles. Multileader styles control how a multileader is created, the type of annotation object that is used for the content of the multileader, and how it visually looks in the drawing. Both dimension styles and multileader styles also use text styles to help format the way the text in the objects appear.

Understanding What a Dimension Is Made Of

Dimensions are made from lines, arcs, multiline text, single-line text, 2D solids, points, and blocks. Hands down they're one of the most complex objects in AutoCAD or AutoCAD LT because of how they work and the many options that are available to control how they appear in a drawing. Dimensions are made up of several subobjects or components that define what the dimension looks like. Some of the subobjects that define a dimension are extension lines, dimension lines, arrowheads, dimension text, and origin points.

Before you begin creating dimensions, you should understand some of the common terminology that is used to call out the different parts of a dimension (see Figure 2-1). Although each dimension type has its purpose, they do share some things in common.

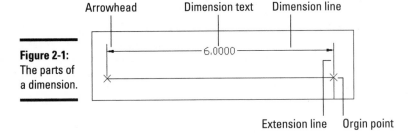

Figure 2-1:
The parts of
a dimension.

Here are the five main parts of a dimension:

✦ **Origin point:** An origin point defines the measurement value for the dimension text and is a small nonprinting point attached to the dimension. Origin points are typically placed on an object and allow you to move or reposition a dimension that may need to be updated.

✦ **Extension line:** An extension line extends up to the dimension line and arrowheads, and indicates which feature or points on an object are being dimensioned. An extension line typically has a gap between it and the origin point of the dimension object and extends past the dimension line. The gap helps show that the dimension is not part of the object.

✦ **Arrowhead:** An arrowhead appears at the end of a dimension line and indicates where a dimension starts and ends. Arrowheads can be displayed as open or closed arrows, architectural ticks, dots, or user-defined arrows, among other arrowhead styles.

✦ **Dimension line:** A dimension line is typically displayed between the extension lines and goes outward from the center of the dimension object toward the extension line. Based on where the dimension text is placed, the dimension line may appear broken or on the outside of the extension lines.

✦ **Dimension text:** Dimension text provides the value of measurement with which the dimension was created and can be formatted in a variety of ways. Some of the formatting options are the units of measurement, the type of decimal separator that is used, and how the value should be rounded. You can also override the dimension text with your own text string or add additional notes to the dimension string.

Each of the parts of a dimension can be formatted globally by using dimension styles or formatted individually by using *dimension overrides*. I talk more about dimension styles and dimension overrides later in this chapter.

Types of Dimensions

Dimensions are a special type of block that AutoCAD treats differently from the blocks that you can create and insert into drawings; I cover blocks later in Chapter 1 of Book VI. Because dimensions are a special type of object, you interact with them differently. Dimensions can be created so that if the object that was dimensioned is changed, the dimension is updated automatically. Dimensions can also be created so that they are exploded after they have been created (which is not recommended because you won't be able to quickly update the dimension when the geometry in the drawing changes). They can also be created so that if the original object that is dimensioned is modified, the dimension doesn't update. No matter what type of dimension you create, they all look the same, but you edit them in different ways.

Associative dimensions

Associative dimensions are created as a single object — so when you select any part of the dimension, the entire dimension is selected. An associative dimension is linked to the original object that was dimensioned, so when the original object is modified, the dimension is updated accordingly. Modifying the original dimensioned object by moving, rotating, stretching, or scaling it will cause the dimension to be update automatically. Fully associated dimensions were first introduced in AutoCAD 2002; before AutoCAD 2002, associated dimensions meant that the dimension was all one object and had no association with the dimensioned object.

Nonassociative dimensions

Nonassociative dimensions, like associative dimensions, are created as a single object. But unlike associative dimensions, nonassociative dimensions are not linked to the original dimensioned object and therefore are not updated when the original dimensioned object is modified. If you select both the dimension and the original dimensioned object, you can update both objects based on the modify command being used. Before AutoCAD 2002, nonassociative dimensions were referred to as associative dimensions because they were a single object instead of individual objects. You can use the DIMREASSOCIATE command to change nonassociative dimensions into associative dimensions. See the "Associating dimensions" section later in this chapter for more information.

Book III
Chapter 2

Dimensioning

Exploded dimensions

An exploded dimension looks just like an associative or nonassociative dimension except it's made up of individual 2D objects and not just one single object, which makes it hard to update. I recommend that you don't create exploded dimensions because it can lead to inaccuracies in the dimension text. If you really need to create an exploded dimension, it is best to create an associative dimension and then use the EXPLODE command on the dimension.

Creating New Dimensions as Associative

To specify whether new dimensions are created as associative or non-associative, you can select or deselect the Make New Dimensions Associative option in the Associative Dimensioning section on the User Preferences tab (see Figure 2-2).

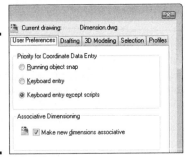

Figure 2-2:
Specifying newly created dimensions as associative.

Follow these steps to determine whether new dimensions should be created as associative or nonassociative.

1. **Right-click the drawing window and choose Options.**

2. **In the Options dialog box, click the User Preferences tab.**

3. **In the Associative Dimensioning section, select or deselect the Make New Dimensions Associative option.**

If you select the option, all new dimensions are created as associative.

The setting to create new dimensions as associative is saved in the drawing. When you get a drawing from a vendor or client, be sure that the setting is set to create new dimensions as associative.

4. **Click OK.**

The change is saved and the Options dialog box is closed.

As you can see from the Options dialog box, even Autodesk tries to discourage you from creating exploded dimensions. However, if you need to create new dimensions as exploded dimensions, you can set the DIMASSOC system variable to a value of 0. Setting DIMASSOC to a value of 1 creates nonassociative dimensions and a value of 2 (the default value) creates associative dimensions.

Using and Creating Dimension Styles

Dimensions contain a large number of display options. Both AutoCAD and AutoCAD LT use dimension styles to contain groups of settings that control the appearance of dimensions. Dimension styles tell AutoCAD and AutoCAD LT how the dimension and extensions lines, dimension text, and arrowheads should be displayed for any dimension created in a drawing. When a dimension style is updated, all dimensions referencing that dimension are updated, unless you have applied an override at the dimension object level.

Working with Dimension Style Manager

 Dimension styles are stored in a drawing file and are referenced by every dimension created in the drawing. Each dimension that's created can reference a different dimension style, but it always references a dimension. You create, modify, and manage dimension styles through the Dimension Style Manager dialog box (see Figure 2-3), which is displayed with the DIMSTYLE command.

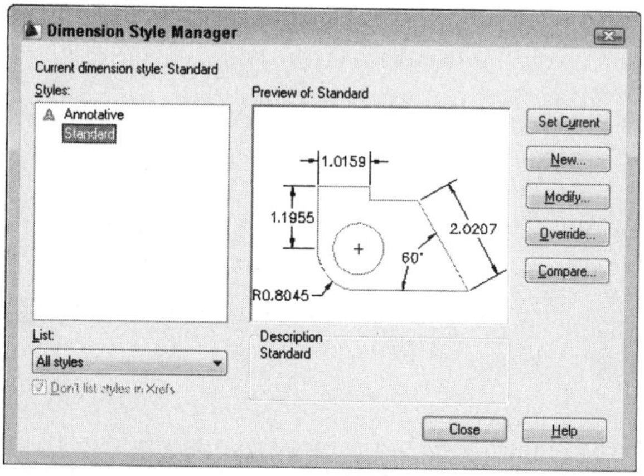

Figure 2-3:
The Dimension Style Manager dialog box.

To start the DIMSTYLE command and display the Dimension Style Manager dialog box, do one of the following:

✦ On the ribbon, click Annotate tab⇨Dimensions panel⇨Dimension Style.

✦ On the menu browser or menu bar, click Format or Dimension menu⇨ Dimension Style.

✦ On the Styles or Dimension toolbar, click the Dimension Style button.

✦ At the command prompt, type **DIMSTYLE** or **D** and press Enter.

Creating a dimension style

Dimension styles can only be created from a style that already exists in the drawing; by default, each drawing contains a dimension style called Standard (imperial units) or ISO-25 (metric units). Dimension Style Manager is used to create the new dimension style and then allows you to make any necessary property changes to the style. The following steps create a new dimension style:

1. **Start the DIMSTYLE command by using one of the preceding methods.**

The Dimension Style Manager dialog box (refer to Figure 2-3) is displayed.

2. **Click New.**

The Create New Dimension Style dialog box (see Figure 2-4) is displayed.

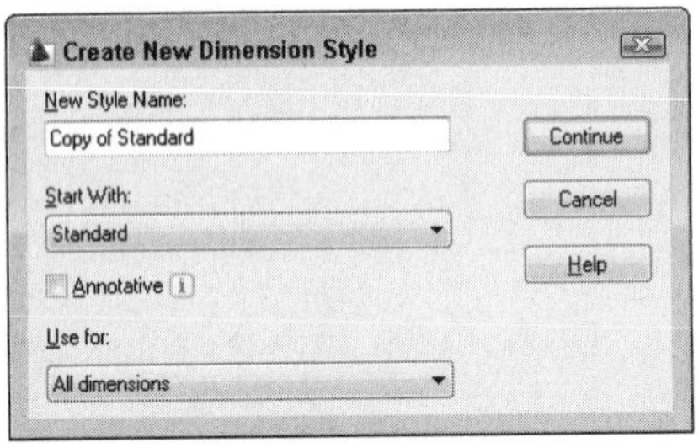

Figure 2-4: Creating a new dimension style.

3. **In the New Style Name text box, enter a name for the dimension style that you're creating.**

The name entered is used to set the dimension style current when you want to create new dimensions using that dimension style.

4. **In the Start With drop-down list, select the dimension style on which you want to base the new dimension style.**

The dimension style on which you base the new dimension style will be identical to the one you're creating until you make changes to the new dimension style.

5. **(Optional) Select the Annotative option.**

   This tells AutoCAD that the dimension style supports annotation scaling. If you choose to not select the option now, you can select the Annotative option on the Fit tab of the New Dimension Style or Modify Dimension Style dialog box later. I cover working with annotation scaling in Chapter 4 of this minibook.

6. **In the Use For drop-down list, select All Dimensions.**

   This drop-down list allows you to create substyles for a dimension style. Substyles allow you to define specific characteristics for certain types of dimensions that can be created by using a single dimension style. Substyles are used when the parent dimension style is used.

7. **Click Continue.**

   The New Dimension Style dialog box is displayed so you can change the settings of the new dimension style.

8. **Adjust the properties of the dimension style or the substyle as necessary.**

9. **Click OK.**

   The New Dimension Style dialog box closes and the dimension style is saved in the drawing. You return to the Dimension Style Manager dialog box.

10. **Click Close.**

    The Dimension Style Manager dialog box closes.

Stylizing dimensions

The New Dimension Style dialog box allows you to define how dimensions in a drawing look when they're created. The New Dimension Style dialog box is divided into seven tabs, which help to organize the properties of a dimension style by characteristics. As you change the properties for the dimension style, the preview of the dimension style in the upper-right corner of the dialog box is updated.

The Lines tab

The Lines tab (see Figure 2-5) allows you to define the display of dimension and extension lines. On the Lines tab, you can specify the color, the linetype, the lineweight, which extension and dimension lines are suppressed, and some spacing/offset values that help to define what a dimension should look like when assigned the dimension style.

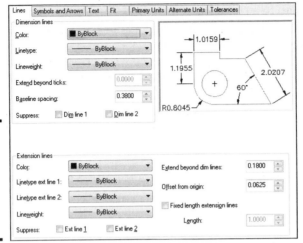

Figure 2-5:
The Lines tab of the New Dimension Style dialog box.

The Symbols and Arrows tab

The Symbols and Arrows tab (see Figure 2-6) allows you to define the characteristics of the terminators and symbols for dimensions. On the Symbols and Arrows tab, you can specify the type of arrowheads that are used, how center marks are drawn, the symbol that should be used for arc length dimensions, the jog angle for jogged radial dimensions, the height of the jog for linear jogged dimensions, and the size of the break when you break dimensions based on the geometry that passes through them.

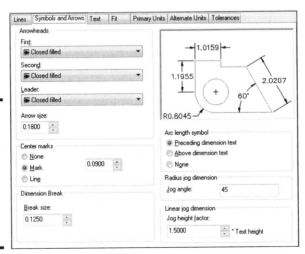

Figure 2-6:
The Symbols and Arrows tab of the New Dimension Style dialog box.

The Text tab

The Text tab (see Figure 2-7) allows you to define how dimension text is placed along the dimension line and how it appears. On the Text tab, you can specify the color, text style, background fill color, and height, as well as some other properties that affect how text is created, placed, and aligned with the dimension line.

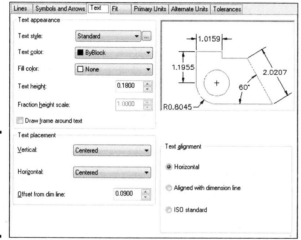

Figure 2-7:
The Text tab of the New Dimension Style dialog box.

**Book III
Chapter 2**

Dimensioning

If you assign a text style that has a specified text height to a dimension style, the text height specified on the Text tab is overridden by the value specified in the text style. For the best control, use a height of 0 when defining a text style.

The Fit tab

The Fit tab (see Figure 2-8) allows you to define how dimension text and arrowheads are placed between extension lines. You can specify how dimension text and arrowheads are placed in relation to the amount of space between the extension lines; the scale of dimension text in model space and on a layout tab, and whether the dimension style is annotative; whether dimension text is placed with a leader; and whether a dimension line should be drawn between the extension lines.

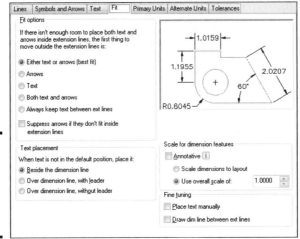

Figure 2-8:
The Fit tab of the New Dimension Style dialog box.

The Primary Units tab

The Primary Units tab (see Figure 2-9) allows you to define how the measurement value displayed in the dimension text should be formatted. On the Primary Units tab, you can specify how dimension text is formatted, including decimal separators, rounding factor, measurement units, prefix and suffix for the dimension text, measurement scale factor, and how leading and trailing zeros are displayed. The settings affect linear, radial, and angular measurement values for dimensions.

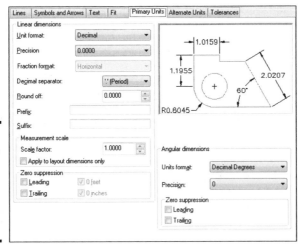

Figure 2-9:
The Primary Units tab of the new Dimension Style dialog box.

The Alternate Units tab

The Alternate Units tab (see Figure 2-10) allows you to define how alternate measurements appear as part of the dimension text. You can control whether an alternate measurement value is placed with the primary measurement value. Typically, alternate units are used when you want to display dimensions with both imperial and metric values. The Alternate Units tab contains options that are used for the formatting of the alternate measurement text and its placement.

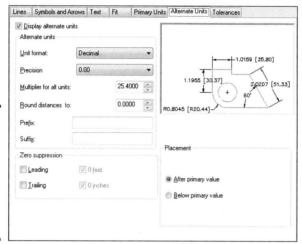

Figure 2-10:
The Alternate Units tab of the new Dimension Style dialog box.

The Tolerances tab

The Tolerances tab (see Figure 2-11) allows you to define how tolerances appear as part of the dimension text. Dimension text tolerances are much different from the geometric tolerance object, which I talk about later in this chapter. On the Tolerances tab, you specify the type of tolerance that's displayed with the dimension text; the format of the tolerance, including precision, upper limits, and lower limits; and how leading and trailing zeros are suppressed. The settings affect linear, radial, and angular measurement values for dimensions.

Defining the scale for dimensions

You have to determine the appropriate scale for a dimension style, similar to what you do with text objects. However, instead of using the same method to calculate the height of text you follow a slightly different process that varies slightly depending on whether you're plotting from the Model tab or a paper space layout.

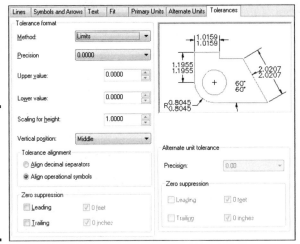

Figure 2-11:
The Tolerances tab of the New Dimension Style dialog box.

When plotting from the Model tab, you normally follow this formula when creating multiline or single-line text unless you're using annotation scaling, which I explain in Chapter 4 of this minibook:

plot scale factor * desired text height when plotted = text height to use

To calculate the scale for dimensions, you use the formula

plot scale factor * desired text height when plotted = final text height

But instead of using the resulting value, which is final text height, you use the plot scale factor as the dimension scale factor and the desired text height as the text height for the dimension style.

To set the dimension scale for a dimension style, you display the dimension style in the Modify Dimension Style dialog box, and then click the Fit tab. In the Scale for Dimension Features area, uncheck Annotative if it is checked and select Use Overall Scale. Then enter the plot scale for the drawing in the text box to the left of Use Overall Scale. The desired height for text when plotted is entered into the Text Height text box on the Text tab.

When plotting from a paper space layout, you just set the Text Height option on the Text tab to the desired height when plotted and select Scale Dimensions to Layout in the Scale for Dimension Features area on the Fit tab. Really what you are doing is setting a dimension scale that allows AutoCAD to control the scale as needed for the dimensions. Annotation scaling, although it requires some effort to set up, simplifies the scaling process for text and dimensions, among other annotation objects in AutoCAD.

Dimension variables

AutoCAD and AutoCAD LT hide many of their complex workings in the latest releases. In earlier releases of AutoCAD, when dimensions were introduced, you had to know a lot of system variables specific to dimension styles. Even to this day, you can still access the system variables specific to the current dimension style and make changes to them through script files to set up a dimension style. By changing the values of the dimension system variables in this way, you create an override for the current dimension style that's applied to each new dimension created in the drawing — unless you use the –DIMSTYLE command with its Save option.

You can get a list of the dimension system variables by doing the following:

1. **At the command prompt, enter** SETVAR **and press Enter.**

The following prompt is displayed:

```
Enter variable name or [?]:
```

2. **At the prompt, type ? and press Enter.**

The following prompt is displayed:

```
Enter variable(s) to list <*>:
```

3. **At the prompt, type DIM* and press Enter.**

The system variables specific to the current dimension style are displayed in the AutoCAD Text window (or AutoCAD LT Text window if you're using AutoCAD LT).

4. **Press Enter to continue listing additional system variables that are related to the current dimension style.**

5. **Press ESC to end the SETVAR command, and then type the name of the dimension system variable at the command prompt.**

You're prompted for the new value.

6. **Enter the new value and press Enter.**

The value is updated accordingly.

By changing the value of a system variable, you're invoking a dimension style override for the current dimension style. To save the changes to the current dimension style, type **–DIMSTYLE** at the command prompt and press Enter. At the Enter a Dimension Style Option prompt, type **S** and press Enter. Then when prompted for the name of the dimension style, enter the name of the current dimension style and press Enter. Because the style is being redefined, when prompted to redefine the style, type **Y** and press Enter.

If you need help with what values you can use with a system variable, enter the name of the system variable and press Enter. When the system variable is prompting you for a new value, press F1 and the online Help for that system variable opens. This also works well for commands that are in progress and other system variables.

Setting a dimension style current

Dimension styles need to be set current to be assigned to a new dimension when it's created. AutoCAD and AutoCAD LT allow you to set a dimension style current in several ways. The most common ways of setting a dimension style current follow:

✦ On the ribbon, click Annotate tab⇨Dimensions panel⇨Dimension Styles drop-down list and then select the dimension style.

✦ On the Styles or Dimension toolbar, click the Dimension Styles drop-down list and select the dimension style.

✦ In the Dimension Style Manager dialog box, double-click the dimension style in the Styles list box, or select the dimension style in the Styles list box and click Set Current.

Modifying a dimension style

At times, you may find that a dimension style needs to be updated. This could be due to changes to the current CAD standards that your company uses or even requirements that dimensions be provided with specific arrow-heads or formatting for a client. You're already familiar with creating a dimension style, so you'll find that modifying one is not that much different.

Dimension styles are modified through the Dimension Style Manager dialog box. In the Styles list box, select the dimension style that you want to change and click Modify. The Modify Dimension Style dialog box is displayed, which is identical to the New Dimension Style dialog box. Make the desired changes and then click OK to save the changes to the dimension style and to close the Modify Dimension Style dialog box. Any dimensions using the modified style are automatically updated to reflect the changes.

Dimension style overrides

Dimension style overrides allow you to make property changes to the current dimension style without creating a new dimension style. Style overrides can cause some confusion in a drawing when creating new dimensions, though, unless you know that a style override is currently in use. To create a style override, you change one of the dimension style variables, or click the

Override button in the Dimension Style Manager dialog box and make the property changes that you want to be part of the style override.

Only new dimensions that are created with the style override current take on the values of the changed properties. So you can draw dimensions using different text fit options, for example, to better accommodate the placement of dimension text for some of the dimensions in a drawing. Overrides are best done at the individual dimension object level by using the Properties palette so that you don't accidentally create more dimensions than you need with the specific overrides in place. Selecting a dimension in a drawing allows you to override any property of a dimension object through the Properties palette (see Figure 2-12). This makes it easier to get the correct override that you want to use instead of setting it through the Dimension Style Manager dialog box.

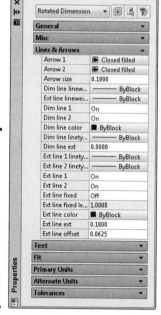

Figure 2-12: The Properties palette allows you to override dimension style properties at the object level.

Dimension style overrides can be merged into the parent dimension style from which the override was created by right-clicking the <Style Overrides> text in the Dimension Style Manager dialog box and choosing Save to Current Style. Only one dimension style override can exist in a drawing at a time, and switching to another dimension style discards the style overrides unless they are saved to the dimension style.

Dimension substyles

Dimension substyles are different from editing dimension styles and style overrides because the substyle limits which properties you can edit based on the substyle that's created. Dimension substyles are created just like a new dimension style, except you select one of the dimension types in the Use For drop-down list in the Create New Dimension Style dialog box, and you don't need to specify a name for the dimension style. To modify a dimension substyle, select the substyle below the dimension style that the substyle is part of and click the Modify button.

Renaming a dimension style

A dimension style can be renamed by using the Dimension Style Manager or Rename dialog box (on the ribbon, click Tools tab⇨Drawing Utilities control panel⇨Rename), but style overrides and substyles can't be. To rename a dimension style by using the Dimension Style Manager dialog box, select the dimension style in the Styles list box and press F2. The in-place editor appears and allows you to change the dimension style's name. You can also right-click the dimension style you want to rename and choose Rename to display the in-place editor and enter a new name. To rename a dimension style in the Rename dialog box, start the RENAME command and select Dimension Styles from the Named Objects list. In the Items list, select the dimension style you want to rename. Then in the Rename To box, enter the new name for the Dimension style and click the Rename To button. Click the OK button after you finish renaming dimension styles or other named objects.

Deleting a dimension style

Dimension styles, substyles, and style overrides can be deleted from a drawing through the Dimension Style Manager dialog box when they are not being used. To delete a dimension style, a substyle, or style override, right-click the dimension style in the Styles list box and choose Delete. When the AutoCAD or AutoCAD LT message is displayed, click Yes to confirm the deletion.

The PURGE command can also be used to remove any unused dimension styles from a drawing. For more information on purging dimension styles and other named objects from a drawing, see Chapter 5 of Book VI.

Comparing dimension styles

You can compare two dimension styles to see what properties are different between them. To compare two dimension styles, display the Dimension Style Manager dialog box and click Compare to display the Compare Dimension Styles dialog box. In the Compare drop-down list, select a dimension style, substyle, or the current style override. Then in the With drop-down list, select the dimension style, substyle, or the current style override.

The property differences between the two selected styles are displayed in the list box in the lower portion of the dialog box. You can click the Copy to Clipboard button to copy the list of differences to the Windows Clipboard so they can be pasted into another Windows application. Click Close to return to Dimension Style Manager.

Importing a dimension style

Dimension styles should be part of the drawing template that you use to create new drawings with. At times, you may not want to place a dimension style in the drawing template that you use, but that doesn't mean you have to create the dimension style every time you need it either. You can use DesignCenter to drag and drop dimension styles from one drawing to another. For more information on using DesignCenter, see Chapter 4 of Book VI.

Creating Dimensions

AutoCAD and AutoCAD LT allow you to create many types of dimensions to communicate overall design concepts: Dimensions are used to measure the distance between two points, the radius or diameter of a curved object, the location of a feature such as a hole, and more. The important thing to note about dimensions is which ones you need and how to create them. This section covers the different kinds of dimensions that you can create in AutoCAD and AutoCAD LT. Table 2-1 lists the commands you use to create and modify dimensions.

Table 2-1   **AutoCAD's Dimensioning Commands**

Icon	Ribbon Annotate⇨ Dimension Panel	Dimension Toolbar	Dimension Menu	Command Name (Alias)	Function
	Dimension flyout⇨Linear	Linear	Linear	DIMLINEAR (DLI)	Creates a linear dimension that measures a distance between two points
	Dimension flyout⇨Aligned	Aligned	Aligned	DIMALIGNED (DAL)	Creates an aligned dimension that measures a distance between two points
	Dimension flyout⇨Jog Line	Jogged Linear	Jogged Linear	DIMJOGLINE (DJL)	Adds a jog line to the dimension line of a linear or aligned dimension
	Continued Dimension flyout⇨Baseline	Baseline	Baseline	DIMBASELINE (DBA)	Creates a string of dimensions that continue from the same origin point
	Continued Dimension flyout⇨Continue	Continue	Continue	DIMCONTINUE (DCO)	Creates a string of dimensions that continue from the last origin point of the previous dimension
	Dimension flyout⇨ Angular	Angular	Angular	DIMANGULAR (DAN)	Creates a dimension that measures an angle of measurement
	Dimension flyout⇨ Arc Length	Arc Length	Arc Length	DIMARC (DAR)	Creates a dimension that measures the length along a curve

Icon	Ribbon Annotate⇨ Dimension Panel	Dimension Toolbar	Dimension Menu	Command Name (Alias)	Function
	Dimension flyout⇨ Radius	Radius	Radius	DIMRADIUS (DRA)	Creates a dimension that measures the radius of a curved object
	Dimension flyout⇨Diameter	Diameter	Diameter	DIMDIAMETER (DDI)	Creates a dimension that measures the diameter of a curved object
	—	Jogged	Jogged	DIMJOGGED (DJO)	Creates a radial dimension that has a different origin point other than the center point on the curved object
	Expand the Dimension panel⇨ Center Mark	Center Mark	Center Mark	DIMCENTER (DCE)	Creates inter-secting line segments that designate the center point of a curved object
	Dimension flyout⇨Ordinate	Ordinate	Ordinate	DIMORDINATE (DOR)	Creates a dimension that displays either the X or Y coordinate position in the drawing relative to the current UCS
	Quick Dimension	Quick Dimension	Quick Dimension	QDIM	Allows you to place multiple dimensions at a time based on the selected geometry
	Expand the Dimension panel⇨Oblique	Dimension Edit	Oblique or Align Text submenu	DIMEDIT	Allows you to edit the dimen-sion text for a selected dimension

(continued)

Book III
Chapter 2

Dimensioning

Table 2-1 *(continued)*

Icon	Ribbon Annotate⇨ Dimension Panel	Dimension Toolbar	Dimension Menu	Command Name (Alias)	Function
	Expand the Dimension panel⇨ Text Angle	Dimension Text Edit	Align Text⇨ Angle	DIMTEDIT	Allows you to edit the placement of the dimension text for a selected dimension
—	—	—	—	DIMDIS-ASSOCIATE	Removes the association between the selected dimension and the objects that it currently dimensions
	Expand the Dimension panel⇨ Reassociate	—	Reassociate Dimensions	DIMRE-ASSOCIATE	Re-creates the association between a dimension and an object in the drawing
	Break	Dimension Break	Dimension Break	DIMBREAK	Creates breaks in a dimension based on the objects that pass through the dimension or extension lines
	Adjust Space	Dimension Space	Dimension Space	DIMSPACE	Allows you to equally space or align dimensions of the same kind
	Inspect	Inspection	Inspection	DIMINSPECT	Adds an inspection block to a dimension which states the frequency with which the measured value should be checked on the manufactured part

Linear and aligned dimensions

Linear dimensions are the most commonly used dimensions: They are used to measure an object or two points horizontally or vertically in a drawing. You can use linear dimensions to measure the distance between straight segments of lines or polylines, the chord length of an arc, or the diameter of a circle, which can be created horizontally, vertically, or rotated (see Figure 2-13). Linear dimensions are created by using the DIMLINEAR command. To start the DIMLINEAR command, refer to the methods outlined in Table 2-1.

Figure 2-13: Different linear dimensions that can be created with the DIMLINEAR command.

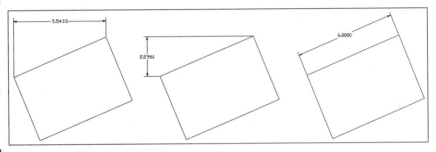

Aligned dimensions are similar to linear dimensions except they are not created orthogonally based on the origin points picked and they measure the actual distance between the origin points picked, rather than the horizontal or vertical distance. Aligned dimensions are created by using the DIMALIGNED command, and its command prompts are nearly identical to the DIMLINEAR command. To start the DIMALIGNED command, refer to the methods outlined in Table 2-1.

Book III
Chapter 2

Dimensioning

The following steps create a linear dimension:

1. **Start the DIMLINEAR command by using one of the methods in Table 2-1.**

2. **At the prompt, pick a point for the first origin point of the dimension or press Enter to select an object to dimension.**

If you select a point, the prompt *Specify second extension line origin* is displayed. If you press Enter, the prompt *Select object to dimension* is displayed.

When specifying points for the origins of dimensions, use object snaps to make sure that the dimensions are created with the correct measurement.

3. **If the Specify second extension line origin prompt is displayed, pick a point for the second origin point of the dimension. If the Select object to dimension prompt is displayed, select an object to dimension in the drawing.**

4. At the prompt, pick a point to place the dimension or specify one of the available options.

The dimension is placed and the command ends. The options Mtext, Text, and Angle affect the value of the dimension text or how the dimension text is rotated. The options Horizontal, Vertical, and Rotated affect how the dimension is created in the drawing and the measurement value that is calculated.

You can add a jog line to a linear or aligned dimension that is used to indicate the actual distance between the origin points in a dimension in a drawing rather than the measured distance. This allows you to dimension very long objects without actually showing the entire length of the object in the drawing. To add or remove a jog line, you start the DIMJOGLINE command and select a linear or aligned dimension. When a jog line is added to a dimension, you can select the dimension and use grip editing to reposition the jog line. To start the DIMJOGLINE dimension, use one of the methods in Table 2-1.

Baseline and continued dimensions

Baseline dimensions allow you to create a string of dimensions (see Figure 2-14) that continue from the first origin point of the previous linear, aligned, angular, or ordinate dimension. Typically, you place the first dimension and then follow it up by creating baseline dimensions, but you have the option of creating baseline dimensions by selecting an existing dimension in a drawing. Baseline dimensions are created by using the DIMBASELINE command. To start the DIMBASELINE command, refer to the methods in Table 2-1.

Figure 2-14:
Baseline
and
Continued
dimensions
based on a
linear
dimension.

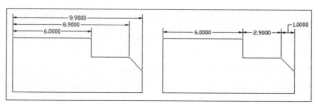

Baseline dimensions   Continued dimensions

Continued dimensions allow you to create a string of dimensions that continue from the second origin point of the previous linear, aligned, angular, or ordinate dimension. As with baseline dimensions, you commonly place the first dimension and then follow it up by creating the continued dimensions, but you have the option of creating continued dimensions by selecting an existing dimension in a drawing. Continued dimensions are created by using the DIMCONTINUE command, and its options are identical to the DIMBASE-LINE command. To start the DIMCONTINUE command, refer to the methods outlined in Table 2-1.

The following steps explain how to create a baseline dimension:

1. **Start the DIMBASELINE command by using one of the methods in Table 2-1.**

   The command line displays

   ```
   Specify a second extension line origin or [Undo/Select]
       <Select>:
   ```

2. **At the prompt, pick a point for the second origin point of the dimension or press Enter to select a new base dimension.**

   The command line displays

   ```
   Specify a second extension line origin or [Undo/Select]
       <Select>:
   ```

   If you press Enter once, the prompt *Select base dimension* is displayed, which allows you to select a dimension to use as the base dimension for creating more baseline dimensions.

Angular dimensions

Angular dimensions (see Figure 2-15) allow you to show the angular measurement of objects in a drawing. The angular measurement might be based on the endpoints of an arc, the angular relationship between two straight segments, the center of a circle and another angle, or two vertexes that define an angle. Angular dimensions are created by using the DIMANGLUAR command. To start the DIMANGLUAR command, refer to the methods outlined in Table 2-1.

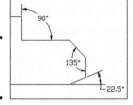

Figure 2-15:
Angular
dimensions.

The following steps explain how to create an angular dimension based on two lines:

1. **Start the DIMANGULAR command by using one of the methods in Table 2-1.**

The command line displays

```
Select arc, circle, line, or <specify vertex>:
```

2. At the prompt, select a line segment.

The command line displays

```
Select second line:
```

3. At the prompt, select another line segment.

The command line displays

```
Specify dimension arc line location or
    [Mtext/Text/Angle/Quadrant]:
```

4. At the prompt, pick a point to place the dimension or specify one of the command's options.

The dimension is placed and the command ends.

Arc length dimensions

 Arc length dimensions (see Figure 2-16) are similar to angular dimensions, except instead of measuring an angle, they measure the length of an arc or an arc segment of a polyline. Based on how an arc needs to dimensioned, you might use the arc length dimension over an angular or linear dimension. Arc length dimensions are created by using the DIMARC command. To start the DIMARC command, refer to the methods outlined in Table 2-1.

Figure 2-16:
Arc length
dimensions.

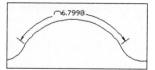

Radius, diameter, and jogged dimensions

AutoCAD offers four types of dimensions that are used to dimension the radius or diameter of a circle or an arc, or place a center mark or center lines at the center point of a circle or an arc. Figure 2-17 shows the results of using the DIMRADIUS, DIMDIAMETER, DIMCENTER, and DIMJOGGED commands on a circle or an arc.

Radius dimensions

 Radius dimensions display an uppercase *R* prefixed to the measurement value to designate that the measurement is for the radius and not the diameter of an arc or a circle. When a radius dimension is placed, an optional center mark is also displayed so you know the center of the object that is being dimensioned. Radius dimensions are created by using the DIMRADIUS command. To start the DIMRADIUS command, refer to the methods outlined in Table 2-1. After the DIMRADIUS command is started, select the arc or circle to dimension and the point for the placement of the dimension text.

Figure 2-17: Radius, diameter, and jogged dimensions along with center marks and a set of center lines.

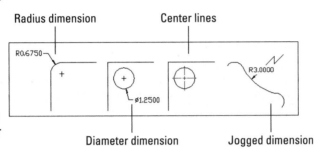

Diameter dimensions

Diameter dimensions are similar to radius dimensions except they're used to measure the diameter of an arc or a circle. The two dimensions look almost identical, except the diameter dimension displays a diameter symbol in front of the measurement value. Diameter dimensions are created by using the DIMDIAMETER command. To start the DIMDIAMETER command, refer to the methods in Table 2-1. After the DIMDIAMETER command starts, select the arc or circle to dimension and the point for the placement of the dimension text.

Jogged dimensions

Like a radius dimension, a jogged dimension allows you to show the radius of an arc or a circle, except instead of the dimension automatically indicating the center of the object, you specify a different location in the drawing for the center override location of the jogged dimension. When a jogged dimension is placed, zigzag lines are displayed on the dimension line to indicate that the dimension is not being dimensioned from the center of the object. Jogged dimensions are created by using the DIMJOGGED command. To start the DIMJOGGED command, refer to the methods in Table 2-1. After the DIMJOGGED command starts, select the arc or circle to dimension, the center override location, the location of the dimension line, and then the location of the jog.

Center marks

Center marks allow you to place a mark or set of lines at the center of an arc or a circle. The lines that are created are not a single dimension object but a bunch of separate line objects. The type of center mark created is based on the settings in the Center Mark area of the Symbols and Arrows tab in the New/Modify Dimension Style dialog box. Center marks are automatically created when you place radius and diameter dimensions, but you want to place center marks at the center of circles when placing linear dimensions to indicate that you are dimensioning to the center of the circle. Center marks are created by using the DIMCENTER command. To start the DIMCENTER command, refer to the methods in Table 2-1. After the DIMCENTER command starts, select an arc or a circle to create the center mark or center lines at the center point of the selected arc or circle.

Ordinate dimensions

Ordinate dimensions (see Figure 2-18) allow you to place the x and y coordinate value of a feature or specific point in a drawing. Each ordinate dimension represents either an x or a y value, but not both. Ordinate dimensions are not a commonly used type of dimension, but you might find them on shop drawings, which are used to manufacture parts. Ordinate dimensions are created by using the DIMORDINATE command. To start the DIMORDINATE command, refer to the methods in Table 2-1.

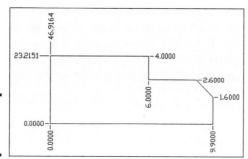

Figure 2-18:
Ordinate
dimensions.

When you create ordinate dimensions, they are based on the origin of the current user coordinate system (UCS). (For more information on the User Coordinate System, see Chapter 2 of Book V.) Usually a point on an object in the drawing is designated as 0,0. To do that, you need to specify a new origin for the current UCS. To specify a new origin, start the UCS command and then pick the point in the drawing that you want to set as the current 0,0 value. To undo the moving of the origin, use the World option of the UCS command.

The Quick Dimension command

The Quick Dimension command allows you to quickly place a number of dimensions in a drawing by selecting multiple objects. The QDIM command allows you to create linear, continuous, staggered, baseline, ordinate, radius, and diameter dimensions. The dimensions that the QDIM command creates are identical to the dimension objects that you can create by using one of the other related dimension commands, such as DIMLINEAR to create linear dimensions or DIMBASELINE to create baseline dimensions. To start the QDIM command, refer to the methods in Table 2-1.

The QDIM command is not available in AutoCAD LT.

Trans-spatial dimensions

Trans-spatial dimensions are not something you find in a science fiction novel, but instead are a feature of AutoCAD that allows you to dimension objects that are visible through a floating viewport and exist in model space. Trans-spatial dimensions allow you to place on layouts dimensions that accurately measure the objects they are dimensioning, but this brings up the question of where dimensions should be placed.

You should generally do dimensioning in model space (using the Model tab), but at times, you may find it beneficial to dimension objects that are in model space through a viewport. One of the benefits to dimensioning objects on a paper space layout in releases of AutoCAD before AutoCAD 2008 was to avoid having multiple dimensions and dimension styles so you could display dimension text and arrowheads at the correct size based on the scale of the viewport. Using different dimensions and dimension styles is no longer an issue with the introduction of annotation scaling in AutoCAD 2008.

Although you can place dimensions on a paper space layout, it can lead to some issues when trying to insert or reference a drawing into another drawing. When inserting or referencing a drawing, only the objects on the Model tab are brought in, resulting in lost or missing dimensions that might be crucial to the design. If you still want to place dimensions on a paper space layout, you must set the scale used for the dimension style to a value of 1.

Before you attempt to take on dimensioning on a paper space layout, I recommend that you stick to dimensioning in model space for a while.

Editing Dimensions

Dimensions are edited in slightly different ways, depending on what part of the dimension object you want to edit. In this section, I explain some of the common ways to edit dimensions.

Adding overrides to a dimension

At times, you may need to make adjustments to the location of an arrowhead, change the position and formatting of text, or change the dimension style of a dimension. The Properties palette allows you to override specific properties of a dimension object that are also defined by the dimension style assigned to the dimension object. Along with using the Properties palette, you can also select dimensions and right-click to access some of the commonly used dimension overrides. From the right-click shortcut menu, you have the option to flip arrowheads individually so they are on the inside or outside of an extension line, change the precision formatting of dimension text, change the current dimension style for the dimension object, change the position of the dimension text along the dimension line, or add or delete annotation scales assigned to the dimension.

Editing the dimension text

Dimension text can be edited to add a prefix or suffix to a measurement value to denote a typical dimension or quantity. You can edit the text of a dimension by using the DDEDIT command, or change the Text Override, Dim Prefix, and Dim Suffix properties with the Properties palette.

If you use the DDEDIT command, note that the measurement value is displayed with a background fill color. If the measurement text is not displayed with a background fill color, a text override has been applied. To add the true measurement value back into a dimension's text, add the text <> to the in-place text editor. The <> text string will be automatically resolved and the actual dimension's measured value will be displayed.

AutoCAD offers two commands that are specifically used for editing dimension text: DIMEDIT and DIMTEDIT. DIMEDIT allows you to change the dimension text displayed for a dimension, the placement of dimension text, and the angle of the extension lines for the dimension. DIMTEDIT is used to move and rotate dimension text. If you need additional help with these commands, refer to AutoCAD's online Help system.

Using grips to edit dimensions

Grips are one of the most powerful editing methods that AutoCAD offers, and you can use them to edit dimensions. With grips, you can reposition dimension text, change the placement of the dimension line along the extension lines, and move the origin points of a dimension. Moving the origin points can cause the dimension to become nonassociative; however, you can make the dimension associative again by using the DIMREASSOCIATE command, which I mention in the next section "Associating dimensions." If you use grips to stretch both the dimension and the object the dimension is associated to, the dimension remains associative to the object.

Associating dimensions

Dimensions, at times, can wander off and disassociate themselves from the original object to which they were dimensioned. Dimensions can become disassociated through the use of the DIMDISASSOCIATE command, or a dimension might break its associativity after being modified. If a dimension becomes disassociated, you can try counseling, or save yourself a visit to the psychologist and use the DIMREASSOCIATE command. The DIMREASSOCIATE command allows you to respecify the origin points of selected dimension objects, making them once again associative to the objects in a drawing. The DIMREASSOCIATE command can be used to convert pre-AutoCAD 2002 dimensions to fully associative dimensions.

AutoCAD and AutoCAD LT do a pretty good job of watching for changes to objects in a drawing, and making sure their associated dimensions are kept up-to-date. If a dimension seems to be confused after you update an object, you can kick-start it by using the DIMREGEN command. This forces the dimension object to update if it's still associative.

Breaking and spacing dimensions

Placing dimensions in a drawing can take some time to ensure that non-dimension objects do not pass through the extension or dimension lines of a dimension, or to equally space and align dimensions with other dimensions in a drawing. The DIMBREAK and DIMSPACE commands help with breaking, equally spacing, and aligning dimensions. The DIMBREAK command allows you to break extension and dimension lines based on where objects intersect the dimension, without having to explode the dimension. The DIMSPACE command allows you to equally space linear and aligned dimensions without having to first erase the dimensions and then create them again by using the DIMBASELINE command. You can also align linear, aligned, and angular dimensions as long as you select dimensions of the same type and use a spacing value of 0. Figure 2-19 shows dimensions before and after using the DIMBREAK and DIMSPACE command. Notice that on the image on the right, the breaks in the extension lines of the dimensions and the dimensions have been equally spaced.

**Book III
Chapter 2**

Dimensioning

Figure 2-19: Those are the breaks and give them some space.

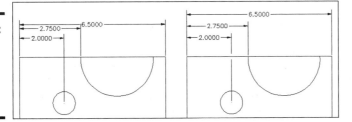

Inspecting dimensions

To help lower the costs of manufactured goods, companies have been increasing their use of outside suppliers located all around the globe. When working with new suppliers or even existing suppliers with new products, you typically need to increase quality assurance checking. AutoCAD allows you to add inspection symbols to a dimension.

An inspection symbol includes the dimension value and the rate at which the dimension should be validated against the part produced off the assembly line. As quality goes up, you might choose to reduce the rate at which the part needs to be verified. Along with the dimension value and the rate for the inspection, you can choose the shape of the frame for the inspection symbol and add a label. Figure 2-20 shows an example of a linear dimension with an inspection rate and label on the left side of the image. Inspection symbols are added and removed from a dimension with the DIMINSPECT command, which displays the Inspection Dimension dialog box (see Figure 2-20).

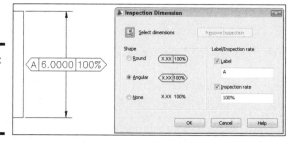

Figure 2-20:
Ensuring quality through inspection.

Leaders

Leaders are used to point to and call out a feature in a drawing. Figure 2-21 shows a couple of examples of leaders that can be created in AutoCAD. A leader typically has an arrowhead at one end pointing to an object in the drawing; the other end has text, an object, a block, or a tolerance object. The leader can contain any of the arrowheads that dimensions can, and the leader line can contain as many straight or spline segments as you want.

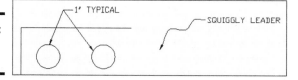

Figure 2-21:
Leaders of the pack.

AutoCAD allows you to create two types of leaders: multileaders and legacy (or standard) leaders. Multileaders offer more flexibility, such as associative annotation and support scaling. Legacy leaders do not support annotative annotation, which means the leader and the text are separate objects.

Make way for multiple leaders

Starting with AutoCAD 2008, leaders were overhauled and now provide better flexibility. The new type of leader object that was introduced with AutoCAD 2008 was multileader. Multileaders work like dimensions in that they get their display and behavior characteristics from styles and are associative objects, which means that they know what they are pointing at in the drawing. So if the object they are pointing at is modified, the leader remains pointing to that same object after the object is modified (unless the object is deleted). Multileaders, as the name suggests, can have more than one arrow pointing at objects in a drawing, with a single annotation object or even multiple annotation objects.

Multileader styles

Multileader styles control the behavior of the MLEADER command and the way a multileader object looks. You use the MLEADERSTYLE command to display the Multileader Style Manager dialog box, which allows you to create, modify, and manage all the multileader styles in a drawing. (The Multileader Style Manager dialog box will remind you of the Dimension Style Manager dialog box.) In the Multileader Style Manager dialog box, you click New to create a new multileader style or select an existing style in the Styles list and then click Modify.

After you create a new multileader style or modify an existing style, the New/Modify Multileader Style dialog box (see Figure 2-22) is displayed.

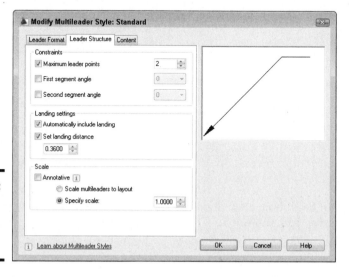

Figure 2-22:
Leaders
never had
so much
style.

The New/Modify Multileader Style dialog box contains three tabs that control the appearance of the multileader object, the type of annotation that is used with the multileader style, and how the multileader should be created with the MLEADER command. The three tabs of the dialog box are as follows:

✦ **Leader Format:** Controls the general properties of the multileader object such as type (straight, spline, or none), color, linetype and lineweight, arrowhead style and size, and the break size when breaks are added to the leaders of the multileader object.

✦ **Leader Structure:** Controls how the multileader object is created with the MLEADER command. You can control the maximum number of points the multileader object can have, the angle for the first and second segments, whether a landing is created and its size, and the scale of the multileader object. Like dimension scale, the scale controls the size of all the elements of the multileader object, and you can specify that the multileader style supports annotation scaling.

✦ **Content:** Controls the type of annotation that the multileader uses: multiline text, block, or none. Based on the type of annotation that will be used, you specify the text properties for the multiline text, the block that should be used, and how the annotation should be attached to the multileader object when the annotation is to the left or right of the multileader object.

To display the Multileader Style Manager dialog box, you use the MLEADER-STYLE command. To start the MLEADERSTYLE command, do one of the following:

✦ On the ribbon, click Annotate tab⇨Multileaders panel⇨Multileader Style.

✦ On the menu browser or menu bar, click Format menu⇨Multileader.

✦ On the Multileader toolbar, click the Multileader Style button.

✦ At the command prompt, type **MLEADERSTYLE** or **MLS** and press Enter.

Multileader styles need to be set current to be assigned to a new multileader when it is created. AutoCAD and AutoCAD LT allow you to set a multileader style current in several different ways. The most common ways of setting a multileader style current follow:

✦ On the ribbon, click Annotate tab⇨Multileaders panel⇨Multileader Styles drop-down list.

✦ On the Styles or Multileader toolbar, click the Multileader Styles drop-down list.

✦ In the Multileader Style Manager dialog box, double-click the multileader style in the Styles list box, or select the multileader style in the Styles list box and click Set Current.

For information on each of the settings in the New/Modify Multileader Style dialog box, refer to AutoCAD's online Help system.

Multileaders

After you create a multileader style and set one current, you're ready to create the multileader object. How you create the multileader object depends on the settings of the current multileader style. To create a multi-leader, you use the MLEADER command. Multileaders typically are made up of an arrowhead, straight or curved (spline) segments, a landing, and some form of content. Figure 2-23 shows the different parts of a multileader.

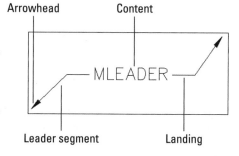

Figure 2-23: Parts of a multileader.

Multileaders are created by using the MLEADER command. To start the MLEADER command, do one of the following:

✦ On the ribbon, click Annotate tab⇨Multileaders panel⇨Multileader.

✦ On the menu browser or menu bar, click Dimension menu⇨Multileader.

✦ On the Multileader toolbar, click the Multileader button.

✦ At the command prompt, type **MLEADER** or **MLD** and press Enter.

The following procedure explains how to create a multileader object based on two leader points, a landing, and a multileader style that uses Mtext for its content:

1. **Start the MLEADER command by using one of the methods in the preceding list.**

The following prompt is displayed:

```
Specify leader arrowhead location or [leader Landing
    first/Content first/options] <Options>:
```

2. **At the prompt, specify the point for the leader of the multileader object in the drawing.**

   The following prompt is displayed:

   ```
   Specify leader landing location:
   ```

3. **At the prompt, specify the point in the drawing for the landing.**

   If the multileader style is designed to use Mtext for its annotation type, the In-Place Text Editor is displayed. If the multileader style is not designed to use Mtext but rather a block or no content, the block is inserted near the end of the landing or the command just ends if no content is configured for the style.

4. **Enter the designated text string and click outside the In-Place Text Editor.**

   The Multileader object is placed and the command ends.

Modifying multileaders

Multileaders can be modified by using many of the common editing commands, such as COPY, MOVE, and MIRROR. You can also use grips to edit the placement of the text or block of the multileader, where the leaders on a multileader point to, and the location and length of the landing. You can also use the DIMBREAK command with multileaders to add gaps to the segments and landings of multileaders to avoid issues with the objects that made up the design in your drawing. In addition to these commands, three additional commands are specific to working with multileaders:

✦ **MLEADEREDIT:** Adds and removes leaders from a multileader object. By adding additional leaders, you can use one annotation object to point to one or more features that need the same callout.

✦ **MLEADERALIGN:** Aligns multileaders.

✦ **MLEADERCOLLECT:** Combines multiple multileaders that contain blocks into a group with a single leader.

For information on each of the multileader specific editing commands, refer to AutoCAD's online Help system.

Legacy leaders

Legacy leaders are the leader objects that you could create prior to AutoCAD 2008 and still can create. If you're still using the QLEADER command to create your leaders, you're missing out on the benefits that multileaders offer. If you've been out of the loop for a bit and happen to even be using the legacy LEADER command, you want to make sure you jump onboard with multileaders as soon as you can because they truly do make editing and using leaders much easier.

I have to admit, though, if you are creating a simple AutoLISP routine or script file, adding a leader to a drawing by using the LEADER command is easier than using the MLEADER command. However, you may want to invest some time in using the MLEADER command for your customizing and programming needs because it will make the user of the customization or program much happier. To find out more about the QLEADER and LEADER commands, refer to AutoCAD's online Help system.

I cover some of the basics of AutoLISP in Bonus Chapter 4, which you can download from www.wiley.com/go.autocad2009aio.

Working with Geometric Tolerances

Geometric tolerances allow you to create a series of what are called *feature control frames*. Feature control frames can contain symbols, tolerance values, datum references, and projected tolerance zone values (see Figure 2-24). Geometric tolerances are used for mechanical drawings and vary based on the standards you need to follow, such as ANSI (American National Standards Institute), ISO (International Standards Organization), or JIS (Japanese Industrial Standards).

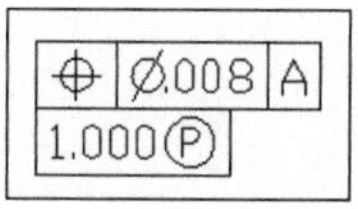

Figure 2-24:
The
Geometric
tolerance.

Geometric tolerances are created by using the TOLERANCE command. To start the TOLERANCE command, follow one of these methods:

✦ On the ribbon, click Annotate tab⇨Dimensions panel⇨Panel's title bar⇨Tolerance.

✦ On the menu browser or menu bar, click Dimension menu⇨Tolerance.

✦ On the Dimension toolbar, click the Tolerance button.

✦ At the command prompt, type **TOLERANCE** or **TOL** and press Enter.

When you start the TOLERANCE command, the Geometric Tolerance dialog box (see Figure 2-25) is displayed.

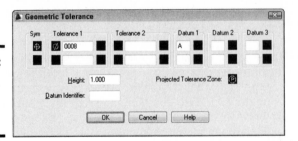

Figure 2-25:
The
Geometric
Tolerance
dialog box.

In the dialog box you can specify the tolerances, datum references, symbols, and projected tolerance zone value you need reflected in the geometric tolerance. After you click OK, you are prompted for the insertion point of the geometric tolerance object. You can modify geometric tolerances by using grips, the DDEDIT command, and the common modifying commands. If you need help, refer to AutoCAD's online Help system.

Chapter 3: Hatching Your Drawings

In This Chapter

✔ Adding hatch patterns and fills

✔ Using hatch patterns and solid fills

✔ Working with gradient fills

✔ Editing hatch patterns and fills

*I*n this chapter, you discover hatch patterns and fills and how to create and edit them. Hatch patterns and fills are used to communicate section cuts of a design, represent construction materials, and add depth to a drawing so it doesn't look flat. AutoCAD and AutoCAD LT offer two types of hatches: hatch patterns and solid fills. Hatch patterns are made up of line segments that are stored in pattern files, whereas solid fills are a single color and are not made up of line segments. AutoCAD offers an additional hatch type called gradient fills.

A *gradient fill* is similar to a solid fill except it's a blend of one color with a tint, or two colors, to give the illusion of depth and realism to a 2D drawing. Hatching allows you to quickly add a visual representation of floor tiles, shingles, or shakes on a roof for an architectural drawing. For a mechanical drawing, you might use a hatch pattern that creates diagonal lines to represent the part of a model that's shown cut through for a section view.

Hatch objects are created by default as a single object and are associative like dimensions. Hatch objects are created associative to the objects that form the closed boundary in which the hatch object is created. Keeping a hatch object associative allows it to be automatically updated when the boundary changes. Hatch objects can also be created nonassociative, which keeps the hatch object from being updated when the boundary changes. Hatch objects can be exploded if they are created with a hatch pattern other than a solid or gradient fill.

Starting with AutoCAD 2008, you can make hatch objects annotative, which affects the scale applied to a hatch pattern. I cover working with annotative scaling in Chapter 4 of this minibook. Figure 3-1 shows a drawing that uses hatch patterns and fills to indicate the materials used for the exterior of a building.

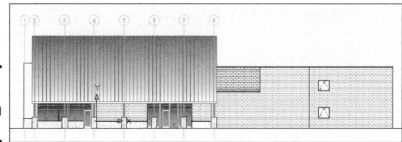

Figure 3-1:
Hatch
patterns and
fills.

Adding Hatch Patterns and Fills

Hatch objects are created by using the Hatch and Gradient dialog box (see Figure 3-2) or the Hatch dialog box if you're using AutoCAD LT. The Hatch and Gradient dialog box allows you to specify which hatch pattern or fill should be used to hatch (or fill) a closed boundary (or area). Based on the type of hatch (or fill) you are creating, you might need to specify a pattern, a scale, an angle, and other settings.

Figure 3-2:
The Hatch
and
Gradient
dialog box
with the
Hatch tab
active and
expanded.

More Options

Many different settings control how the resulting hatch object looks after it's created. Most of the commonly used settings for creating and editing hatch objects are displayed by default, but if you want to access some of the more advanced settings, click the More Options button.

Adding hatch to a drawing

The first few times you add fills and patterns by hatching closed boundaries in a drawing can be confusing, but that is to be expected because many factors in a drawing and the dialog box can affect how a hatch object is created. When you want to create a hatch object, make sure that the area you want to hatch is closed — meaning all lines, arcs, and so on that define a boundary are either connected end to end or overlapping each other. Hatch objects are created by using the Hatch and Gradient dialog box, which is displayed with the HATCH command.

To start the HATCH command and display the Hatch and Gradient dialog box, follow one of these methods:

✦ On the ribbon, click Home tab⇨Draw panel⇨Hatch.

✦ On the menu browser or menu bar, click Draw menu⇨Hatch.

✦ On the Draw toolbar, click the Hatch button .

✦ At the command prompt, type **HATCH** or **H** and press Enter.

The following procedure explains how to create a hatch object by using a predefined hatch pattern:

1. **Draw a circle or use other drawing commands to create a closed boundary.**

2. **On the ribbon, click Home tab⇨Draw panel⇨Hatch.**

The Hatch and Gradient dialog box is displayed.

3. **In the Type and Pattern section, select Predefined in the Type drop-down list.**

The controls that are used with a predefined hatch pattern are enabled.

4. **In the Pattern drop-down list, select one of the predefined hatch patterns.**

A preview of the selected hatch pattern is displayed in the Swatch area below the Pattern list. You can also click the Ellipsis button to the right of the Pattern list to display the Hatch Pattern Palette dialog box (see Figure 3-3). This dialog box allows you to visually select predefined hatch patterns that come with the software or custom ones that you might create yourself or download from the Internet.

5. **In the Angle and Scale section, specify an angle for the hatch pattern by selecting a predefined value or entering a value in the Angle drop-down list.**

6. **Specify a scale for the hatch pattern by selecting a predefined value or entering a value in the Scale drop-down list.**

**Book III
Chapter 3**

Hatching Your Drawings

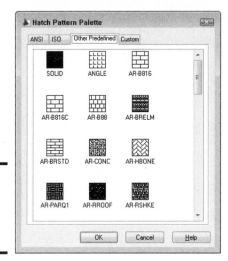

Figure 3-3:
The Hatch
Pattern
Palette
dialog box.

7. **In the Boundaries section, click Add: Pick Points.**

Focus is brought to the drawing window and the Hatch and Gradient dialog box is closed while you pick points inside closed boundaries. The prompt *Pick internal point or [Select objects/remove Boundaries]:* is displayed.

Picking points can increase the time it takes to hatch a closed boundary in a complex drawing. To more efficiently add hatching to a drawing, you can click the Add: Select Objects button and select objects that form a closed boundary instead of picking points with the Add Pick Points button.

8. **At the prompt, click inside a closed boundary to define the boundary for the hatch object.**

The boundary is calculated, and you're prompted for additional closed boundaries. If the boundary is not closed or the boundary can't be calculated, a message box is displayed (see Figure 3-4).

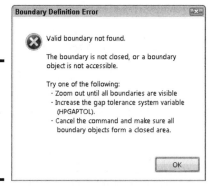

Figure 3-4:
The
Boundary
Definition
Error
message
box.

The system variable HPGAPTOL specifies whether a tolerance value is used when calculating a closed boundary with objects that don't form a completely closed boundary. The value can also be specified under the Gap Tolerance section when the Hatch and Gradient dialog box is expanded.

9. **Press Enter to accept the selected boundaries and to return to the Hatch and Gradient dialog box.**

10. **Click Preview.**

   The hatch object is displayed in the drawing.

11. **Press Esc to return to the Hatch and Gradient dialog box to make changes or press Enter to create the hatch object.**

   The hatch object is created and you're returned to the drawing window.

Hatching and tool palettes

After you've successfully created a hatch object in a drawing (and are finished jumping up and down with glee), you can create hatch tools on a tool palette of that hatch object so you can create new hatch objects with the same settings in a drawing later. You create a hatch tool by dragging and dropping a hatch object from a drawing onto a tool palette. The hatch tool is created based on the properties and settings of the hatch object. To use a hatch tool that's on a tool palette, click the tool and then click inside a closed boundary, or drag and drop the tool over a closed boundary. For more information on tool palettes, see Book VI, Chapter 4.

Hatching and DesignCenter

Hatch objects and hatch tools can be created from hatch pattern files by using DesignCenter. To create a hatch object or a hatch tool, browse to a location where you store your hatch pattern (.pat) files with DesignCenter. Double-click the hatch pattern file, and then drag and drop the hatch pattern over a closed boundary or over a tool palette. After the hatch tool is created on a tool palette, you can then right-click and choose Properties to change the general properties for the hatch tool and any hatch-specific properties.

Advanced settings for additional control

The Hatch and Gradient dialog box offers a number of options to control how a hatch object is created and how the boundary for a hatch object is generated. These options can be found in the Hatch Origin and Options sections and under the extended section of the Hatch and Gradient dialog box.

Being annotative

Like text and dimensions, hatch objects can be annotative, which controls the scale of a hatch pattern based on the current annotation scale or viewport

Book III
Chapter 3

Hatching Your
Drawings

scale. As the annotation scale for the current view or viewport increases, so does the scale of the hatch object if it's designated as annotative; this ensures that the hatch object is always displayed correctly based on the current annotation or viewport scale. I cover working with annotative scaling in Chapter 4 of this minibook.

Specifying the origin of a hatch object

The Hatch Origin section allows you to define the base point in the drawing from which the hatch pattern is calculated. By default, the origin point of the drawing is used, rather than a point in the closed boundary. The Specified Origin option allows you to select a point in the drawing that should be used for the origin of the hatch pattern assigned to the hatch object. Specifying an origin point allows you to make the appearance of hatch patterns predictable. This is important if you're using hatch patterns for creating tiles, bricks, and siding on a house; for example, you want to make sure that you have a full run of bricks at the bottom of a house, and not just have the pattern appear to be generated randomly. By designating the lower corner of the elevation, you can get the bricks to start in a consistent and predictable way.

Island detection

Island detection is used when calculating the closed boundary for a hatch object. An *island* is defined as an interior boundary located inside the outer boundary of a closed boundary. To access the island detection settings, you have to click the More Options button, which is located to the right of the Help button of the Hatch and Gradient dialog box. Figure 3-5 shows examples of the three island detection options:

✦ **Normal:** The outer detected boundary is hatched, but hatch is turned off for any detected island until another island is detected.

✦ **Outer:** Only the outer detected boundary is hatched; no hatch is applied to islands inside the boundary calculated.

✦ **Ignore:** All islands are ignored and the hatch fills the entire area defined by the outer boundary.

Figure 3-5:
Island
detection
settings.

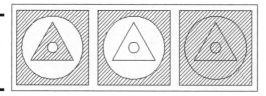

The Remove Boundaries button under the Boundaries area of the Hatch and Gradient dialog box allows you to remove and add islands to adjust the boundary of a hatch object when it is being edited.

Others settings available for defining a hatch object

Some additional settings allow you to specify a factor that should be used when defining a boundary that might not be completely closed. Another setting allows you to create separate hatch objects for each closed boundary that is defined when selecting objects or picking points to define boundaries. Another nice feature is to define the order in which the hatch object is displayed on-screen with respect to the objects that define its boundary. For additional information on the options of the Hatch and Gradient dialog box, see the online Help system.

The OSOPTIONS system variable allows you to control whether object snaps can be used with hatch objects. If the system variable is set to a value of 1 or 3, object snaps are ignored for hatch objects.

Working with Hatch Patterns and Solid Fills

Hatch patterns and solid fills are the most commonly used types of hatches. AutoCAD and AutoCAD LT offer three types of hatch patterns that you can use when adding hatch to a drawing: predefined, user defined, and custom.

Predefined patterns

AutoCAD and AutoCAD LT come with a number of predefined patterns; AutoCAD comes with the files acad.pat for imperial drawings and acadiso.pat for metric drawings, while AutoCAD LT comes with the files acadlt.pat for imperial drawings and acadltiso.pat for metric drawings. To use a predefined hatch pattern or solid fill, select Predefined in the Type drop-down list. The Pattern drop-down list becomes enabled, which allows you to select a pattern in its list. Alternatively, click the ellipsis button to the right of the Pattern drop-down list to select a pattern visually from the Hatch Pattern Palette dialog box.

The system variable MEASUREMENT is used to control which hatch pattern and linetype files are used for imperial or metric drawings. If MEASUREMENT is set to a value of 0, the imperial files are used; a value of 1 indicates that the metric files should be used.

User-defined patterns

User-defined hatch patterns are not common because they just don't offer much more than what the predefined hatch patterns offer. When defining a user-defined hatch pattern, you specify the spacing and angle of lines that

Book III Chapter 3

Hatching Your Drawings

run parallel or perpendicular to each other. One of the nice things about user-defined hatch patterns is that you specify the spacing of the lines in drawing units rather than a scale factor. To create a user-defined hatch pattern, select User Defined in the Type drop-down list. After User Defined is selected, set the angle and spacing values and specify whether double lines should be created.

Custom hatch patterns

Custom hatch patterns are typically supplemental patterns that offer something that is not available from the predefined hatch patterns that come with the application. Custom hatch patterns are usually much more complex than just a series of lines that can be generated as a user-defined pattern. Custom hatch pattern files must be placed in one of the support paths defined under the Files tab of the Options dialog box.

To use a custom hatch pattern, select Custom in the Type drop-down list and then click the Ellipsis button next to the Custom drop-down list to display the Hatch Pattern Palette dialog box. The Custom tab is set current and displays the hatch patterns that AutoCAD or AutoCAD LT automatically found in the support paths. Select the custom pattern and set the options for the pattern just like you would a predefined pattern. For more information on creating custom hatch patterns, see Book IX, Chapter 4.

Using Gradient Fills

Gradient fills were added to AutoCAD 2004 to replace the fills that users had previously been creating with external paint applications. Gradient fills are created based on a choice of one color and a tint value or two colors, the direction of the color shift, whether the gradient is centered, and its angle. Gradient fills are created from the Gradient tab of the Hatch and Gradient dialog box (see Figure 3-6).

Creating a gradient fill isn't much different from creating a hatch object that uses a predefined, user-defined, or custom pattern. After the basic characteristics of the gradient fill have been defined, you define the boundary for the hatch in the same way you create one of the hatch types from the Hatch tab.

Gradient fills can't be *applied* with AutoCAD LT but are displayed in AutoCAD LT with no problems.

If a drawing is saved back to AutoCAD 2002 or earlier versions, gradient fills are displayed as a solid fill. The color of the solid fill is based on the closest ACI color to the first color of the gradient fill.

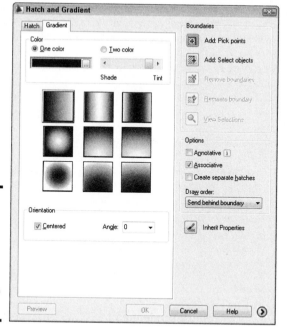

Figure 3-6:
The Hatch
and
Gradient
dialog box
with the
Gradient tab
active.

Editing Hatch Patterns and Fills

 Editing a hatch object is similar to editing a text object or other objects. Double-clicking a hatch object starts the HATCHEDIT command, which allows you to edit a hatch object. Alternatively, you can start the HATCHEDIT command by selecting and right-clicking a hatch object and choosing Hatch Edit from the shortcut menu. The HATCHEDIT command displays the Hatch Edit dialog box, which is identical to the Hatch and Gradient dialog box, except some of the options used only for creating a hatch object are disabled. Make the necessary changes and click OK to apply the changes.

 The MATCHPROP command is great for making one or more hatch objects look the same by copying the properties from one hatch object to another. Use the Settings option of the MATCHPROP command to specify which general properties of an object are copied between objects and whether the special properties of a hatch object are also copied from the selected source object.

Chapter 4: Scaling Mt. Annotation

In This Chapter

✔ Understanding annotation scaling

✔ Making styles and objects annotative

✔ Adding and removing an annotation scale

✔ Outputting a drawing with annotative objects

Annotation plays a large role in technical drawings, whether that annotation is in the form of single-line or multiline text, dimensions, or hatching. Up until AutoCAD 2008, it was difficult to control the display of annotation in a drawing. If you plotted from the Model tab, you scaled up your annotation objects so they plotted at the correct size, the same with plotting annotation in a viewport on a paper space layout. However, if you placed text on a layout, you created the text at its actual plotted size. This was fairly simple, but after you started using viewports on a layout that contained different scales for the objects on the Model tab, you ended up with text in one viewport larger than text in the other viewport, which made things look nonuniform. Many users worked around this problem by creating multiple annotation objects at different sizes and different layers, and then controlling which annotation layer was displayed in the different viewports. Autodesk's answer to this problem is annotation scaling, which you might at first find confusing mainly because of the way we had to deal with annotation since the dawn of AutoCAD.

In this chapter I take you through working with annotation objects and using annotation scaling. If you have existing drawings that you work with, you might have to continue calculating the height of annotation objects, but for your new drawings you should seriously consider using annotation scaling.

The What, With, and Why of Annotation Scaling

Annotation scaling helps to simplify the issue of coming up with a text height for the annotation objects in a drawing. For example, you might want a text object to be 1/8" high on a drawing that's plotted at 1/4" = 1'–0". To determine the text height of the annotation object, you take the decimal equivalent of 1/8" (which is 0.125) and multiple it by the result of dividing 12" by the decimal equivalent of 1/4" (which is 0.125) — in other words

0.125 * (12 / 0.25) which results in a value of 6. You would use 6" for the height of the text on the Model tab so it would be plotted at a height of 1/8" when the drawing was plotted at a scale of 1/4" = 1'–p.

Wouldn't it be easier to select 1/4" = 1'–0" as the current annotation scale and enter a height of 1/8" because that is what you want the text to be plotted at anyway? With annotation scaling it is truly just that easy. You draw the text at the scale and height you want, and AutoCAD does the rest. By using annotation scaling, you can also control when the text is displayed by not assigning annotation objects certain scales.

Now that you know what annotation scaling is and why you want to use it, the last question is: What can annotation scaling be used with? Annotation scaling can be used with the following styles and objects in a drawing:

+ Attributes
+ Block definitions
+ Block references
+ Dimension styles
+ Dimensions
+ Geometric tolerances
+ Hatches
+ Multileader styles
+ Multileaders
+ Single-line and multiline text
+ Text styles

To make using annotation scaling as easy as possible, I recommend creating block definitions or styles for text, dimensions, and multileaders that are set up as annotative. That way, any blocks or annotation objects in the drawing referencing those styles are annotative and use the current annotation scale.

Making Styles and Objects Annotative

Because so many types of objects utilize annotation scaling, I feel it is best to have one central location to explain how to work with each of the different styles and objects. This approach hinges on knowing how to create each of the different types of styles and objects, so you'll probably find yourself coming back to this chapter more than once.

Annotative styles and block definitions

When you create or modify a text, dimension, or mulitleader style or block definition, you have the option of making it annotative. When you make a style or block definition annotative, all new objects that are placed with that style current or that reference the block definition are annotative. If a non-annotative style is made annotative, only new objects created with the style current or new inserts of the block definition will be annotative and all existing objects will remain nonannotative. So aside from a few differences with properties in the settings, you are telling AutoCAD that the annotative property for the text, dimension, multileader, or block reference should be turned on, which removes the manual step of having to do it yourself by using the Properties palette.

The following explains how to make text styles, dimension styles, multi-leader styles, and block definitions annotative:

✦ **Text styles:** On the menu browser or menu bar, click Format menu⇨Text Style. In the Text Style dialog box, select Annotative in the Size area. For more information on text styles, see Chapter 1 of this minibook.

✦ **Dimension styles:** On the menu browser or menu bar, click Format menu⇨Dimension Style. In the Dimension Style Manager dialog box, select Annotative in the Create New Dimension Style dialog box when creating a new dimension style, or select Annotative in the Scale for Dimension Features area on the Fit tab in the Modify Dimension Style dialog box. For more information on dimension styles, see Chapter 2 of this minibook.

✦ **Multileader styles:** On the menu browser or menu bar, click Format menu⇨Multileader Style. In the Multileader Style Manager dialog box, select Annotative in the Create New Multileader Style dialog box when creating a new multileader style, or select Annotative in the Scale area on the Leader Structure tab in the Modify Multileader Style dialog box. For more information on multileaders styles, see Chapter 2 of this minibook.

✦ **Block definitions:** On the menu browser or menu bar, click Draw menu⇨Block⇨Make. In the Block Definition dialog box, select Annotative in the Behavior area and create a new block by selecting an insertion point and objects for the block among other settings, or select an existing block definition in the Name drop-down list and select Annotative in the Behavior area. For more information on defining blocks, see Chapter 1 of Book VI.

316 *Making Styles and Objects Annotative*

Annotative objects

Using annotative styles and block definitions is the easiest way to go, but unfortunately not all objects that support annotation scaling use styles. You might also come across the situation of working with existing annotation objects in a drawing that need to use annotation scaling.

When placing multiline text, hatches, and attributes, you can designate the object created as being annotative by doing the following:

✦ **Multiline text:** When creating a multiline text, on the ribbon click Multiline Text tab⇨Style panel⇨Annotative (or click the Annotative button on the Text Formatting toolbar when the ribbon is not displayed). When the button is highlighted, the multiline text object will be created as annotative. For more information on creating multiline text, see Chapter 1 of this minibook.

✦ **Hatches:** When creating a hatch, select Annotative in the Options area in the Hatch and Gradient dialog box (or Hatch dialog box in AutoCAD LT). For more information on creating hatch objects, see Chapter 3 of this minibook.

✦ **Attributes:** When creating an attribute, select Annotative in the Text Settings area in the Attribute Definition dialog box. I cover creating attributes in Chapter 1 of Book VI.

If you forget to create the annotation object as being annotative or with some objects you do not have the object to create the object as being annotative, which is the case for geometric tolerances, you can use the Properties palette. To make annotation objects annotative through the Properties palette, follow these steps:

1. **Select the annotation objects for which you want to enable the annotative property.**

2. **Right-click the drawing window and choose Properties.**

3. **In the Properties palette, select the Annotative property.**

4. **Click the down arrow in the drop-down list that appears to the right of the Annotative field and choose Yes.**

   After an object is annotative, the Annotative Scale property is accessible from the Properties palette. For most objects, except hatches, single-line text, multiline text, and attributes, the Annotative property is located in the Misc category in the Properties palette. The Annotative property for hatches is in the Pattern category, and the Annotative property for single-line text, multiline text, and attribute objects is under the Text category.

5. **Click the X in the Properties palette to close it.**

After an object is annotative, a small icon appears next to the crosshairs when the crosshairs hover on top of it. If an annotative object has one scale assigned to it, the icon appears as a side view of an architectural scale. If more than one annotation scale is assigned to the annotative object, the icon appears as two architectural scales (see the upcoming Figure 4-2).

Using the Properties palette to make annotation objects annotative has its downside. If you select objects that are of different types, you will not be able to change the Annotative property to Yes. A way around this is to use the CHANGE command, which is a lot more forgiving in what you select. After you select the objects you want to make annotative, type **P** for the Properties option and press Enter. Then at the *Enter property to change* prompt, type **A** and press Enter. You will be prompted to make the objects annotative. Type **Y** and press Enter. AutoCAD sifts through the selected objects and sets the objects annotative that can be annotative and ignores the other ones.

Adding and Removing Annotation Scales

When you create your annotative annotation object, you want to make sure that the scale at which you want the object to be created is set current. For example, if you'll be plotting your drawing at 1/4" = 1'–0" make sure that you set 1/4" = 1'–0" as the current annotation scale. To do so, click the Annotation Scale button on the status bar to display a list of available scales. Select the scale you want to set current, and any new annotative annotation objects added to the drawing will automatically be assigned that scale.

If an object needs to have more than one scale, you have two choices. You can manually add the additional scales that the annotation object might need or you can let AutoCAD handle the task for you. When you add scales manually, you control which annotation objects should have the additional annotation scales; AutoCAD assigns the additional scales to all annotation objects that are currently annotative in the drawing.

To manually add scales to an annotation object, you use the OBJECTSCALE command, which displays the Annotation Object Scale dialog box (see Figure 4-1). From here, you can add scales to or remove scales from the selected annotative objects. If you select an annotative object and right-click, you can add or remove the current annotation scale by choosing Annotative Object Scale⇨Add Current Scale or Annotative Object Scale⇨Add Delete Scale.

If you don't want to worry about assigning multiple scales to annotation objects as you switch between different annotation scales, click the Automatically Add Scales to Annotative Objects button on the status bar. When the lightning bolt has color, the option is enabled and when you change the annotation scale by using the Annotation Scale button on the status bar, the new scale is assigned to all annotative objects in the drawing.

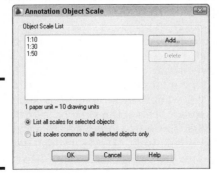

Figure 4-1:
Putting annotation objects on the scale.

To add annotation scales to an annotative object, follow these steps:

1. **Select the annotation objects to which you want to add an annotation scale.**

2. **Right-click the drawing window and choose Annotative Object Scale⇨ Add/Delete Scales.**

The Annotation Object Scale dialog box is displayed (refer to Figure 4-1).

3. **Click Add.**

The Add Scales to Object dialog box is displayed.

4. **Select the scales to add to the annotative object and click OK.**

You return to the Annotation Object Scale dialog box and the selected scales are added to the Object Scale List area.

5. **Click OK.**

To delete a scale, follow Steps 1 and 2 in the preceding list and then do the following:

1. **In the Object Scale List area, select the scales you want to remove and then click Delete.**

2. **Click OK.**

When an annotative object has more than one annotation scale assigned to it, you can see all the different representations of the annotative object by clicking the Annotation Visibility button on the status bar so that the light bulb on the button is yellow. Then when you select the annotative object, all of its different representations are displayed as faded objects (see Figure 4-2). This allows you to see where each representation is currently located in the drawing. You can move each scale representation of the annotative object by setting the appropriate annotation scale current and then using grips to move the annotation object. Using the standard modifying techniques on the annotation object moves all representations of the annotative object uniformly.

Figure 4-2:
Seeing
double,
triple,
oh my.

TIP

If you have wandering representations of the annotative objects in your drawing, you can use the ANNOREST command and select the annotative objects to reset the positions of the scaled representations.

Controlling the Annotation Scale for Output

Now that you have assigned scales to your annotative objects, I'm sure you are wondering what you need to do to get the scales to work when plotting or publishing your drawing. When using the PLOT command from the Model tab, you set current the annotation scale that matches the scale at which you'll be plotting your drawing. If the plot scale and the annotation scale don't match, AutoCAD displays the Plot Scale Confirm dialog box. If you want to continue plotting the drawing, click Continue. Or click Cancel and change the plot scale or annotation scale as needed. If you select Fit to Paper in the Plot Scale area, AutoCAD assumes you know what you're doing and plots the drawing.

When plotting from a layout tab, there's no annotation scale for AutoCAD to be concerned with because the floating viewports on the layout control the annotation scale for each viewport. When setting up the floating viewports on a layout, make sure that the annotation scale and the viewport scale of a viewport are set to the same scale factor. To set the viewport scale, select the viewport and click the Viewport Scale button on the status bar. In the scale list that's displayed, select the scale for the viewport. Doing this typically changes both the annotation and viewport scales for the selected viewport. However, if they are not the same, click the Annotation/Viewport Scale Synchronization button just to the left of the Viewport Scale button on the status bar. Then just plot the layout tab as you normally do. Any annotative objects that do not match the selected scale are not displayed in the view-port because there is no graphical representation for the object.

For more information on plotting and floating viewports, see Chapters 1 and 3 of Book VII.

It's a good idea to set the MSLTSCALE system variable to a value of 1, the default value, to make sure that linetypes on the Model tab are scaled correctly, based on the current annotation scale. Other settings to check when creating annotative objects are the system variables DIMSCALE and MLEADERSCALE. DIMSCALE and MLEADERSCALE should both be set to 0 when using annotation scaling, and are by default when you create a new annotative dimension or multileader style.

Book IV

LT Differences

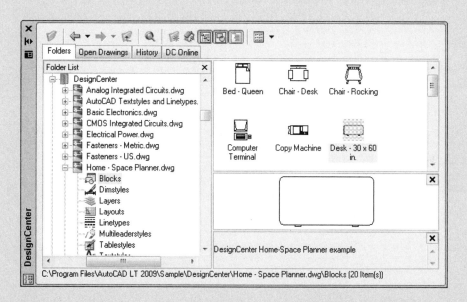

AutoCAD LT offers many of the same features found in AutoCAD, such as DesignCenter, which allows you to reuse named objects from existing drawings.

Contents at a Glance

Chapter 1: The LT Difference 323

Understanding the Boundaries and Limitations of AutoCAD LT............323
Determining Whether AutoCAD or AutoCAD LT Is Best for You.............329

Chapter 2: Extending AutoCAD LT 331

Customizing AutoCAD LT 331
Object Enabler Technology 334
Additional Utilities Available from Autodesk 335
Companion Products from Autodesk 336
Third-Party Custom Solutions 337

Chapter 3: Mixed Environments 339

Using AutoCAD LT and AutoCAD in the Same Office..............................339
Making the Trip from AutoCAD to AutoCAD LT 341

Chapter 1: The LT Difference

This minibook of the *AutoCAD 2009 & AutoCAD LT 2009 All-in-One Desk Reference For Dummies* takes a look at the differences between AutoCAD and AutoCAD LT. If you are considering purchasing AutoCAD or AutoCAD LT, you should understand what the strengths and weaknesses of the two programs are before making your final decision. Or maybe you already have AutoCAD LT and want to know what you might be missing out on by not having AutoCAD. In this minibook, I try to give you a good understanding of the differences between the two programs.

Understanding the Boundaries and Limitations of AutoCAD LT

AutoCAD LT is a scaled-back version of AutoCAD targeted at companies that create only 2D drawings and can't (or don't want to) afford the higher price of AutoCAD. AutoCAD LT is what Autodesk refers to as an AutoCAD OEM (Original Equipment Manufacturer) program: AutoCAD OEM is simply the AutoCAD platform or engine with some features removed and others added to make a new program without the need to reinvent the wheel — or re-create the program, in this case. Using AutoCAD as the basis for AutoCAD LT guarantees that the files created in AutoCAD can be read by AutoCAD LT without any problems.

AutoCAD LT contains roughly 80 percent of the functionality of AutoCAD for about roughly 20 percent of the price. Most of the features that don't make it into AutoCAD LT are based on project collaboration, 3D, and the ability to create custom programs — or add-ons as they are known in the world of AutoCAD. Autodesk removes these features from the program to justify the cost difference between the two programs. For the price, AutoCAD LT is an outstanding value and ensures that you will be able to communicate with others who use AutoCAD. However, because you can't create or use custom programs with AutoCAD LT, you can't do much to change or improve on the drafting workflow that doesn't already come with the program through custom add-ons as you can with AutoCAD.

So what exactly are the differences between the two programs? The programs have a number of major and minor differences. Here is a list summarizing many of the differences between the two programs:

✦ **User interface:** For the most part, the user interfaces of AutoCAD and AutoCAD LT are identical (see Figure 1-1). Both programs take advantage of the Windows platform by using common user interface elements that can be found in most Windows-based applications. These common user interface elements are

- Ribbon

- Menu browser, pull-down menus, and shortcut menus

- Quick Access toolbar and floating/dockable toolbars

- Status bar

- Dialog boxes

- Floating/dockable windows — palettes

Some of the common AutoCAD-related UI elements, such as the Text window, command line window, and dynamic input are present in both AutoCAD and AutoCAD LT. AutoCAD LT lacks some of the palettes found only in AutoCAD, such as dbConnect Manager, Sheet Set Manager, and others that are specific to visualizing 3D models. For more information on the AutoCAD and AutoCAD LT user interfaces, see Book I, Chapter 3.

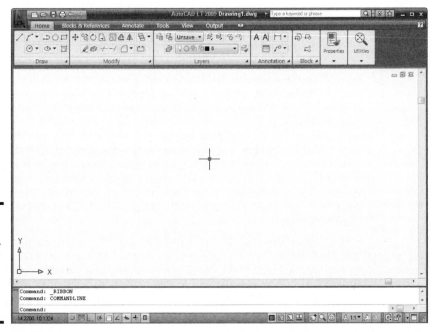

Figure 1-1:
The
AutoCAD LT
user
interface
out of
the box.

✦ **2D drafting:** The foundation of both applications is 2D drafting, so both programs are similar in the features and commands that are available for it. A few features do stand out as different, however:

- AutoCAD supports the ability to create multilines with the MLINE command, whereas AutoCAD LT has a command called DLINE instead. Both commands allow you to create parallel lines, but the DLINE command is much easier to work with.

- Groups are created and managed differently in the two programs. AutoCAD LT offers an easier-to-use interface and is dockable, versus the older dialog box interface that comes with AutoCAD.

- You can't edit an Xref in-place in AutoCAD LT like you can in AutoCAD.

- Xrefs can't be opened directly from the External References palette in AutoCAD LT. Instead you have to browse to the drawing file and open it with AutoCAD.

- AutoCAD provides utilities for managing attributes in a block and synchronizing attribute changes in a block when all blocks in a drawing have the same name.

- Xrefs can be clipped with the XCLIP command in AutoCAD but not in AutoCAD LT.

For more information on 2D drafting, see Book II, Chapters 1 and 2; for more information on working with layouts, see Book VII, Chapter 1.

✦ **Annotation/dimensioning:** The annotation and dimension features of the two programs are very similar, for the most part. A few notable differences are

- AutoCAD LT lacks the ability to create gradient fills.

- The QDIM command is missing from AutoCAD LT, which helps to improve productivity by allowing you to quickly place multiple dimensions at a time in a drawing.

- You can create Fields with AutoCAD LT, but they do not offer the same functionality found in AutoCAD, such as working with sheet sets.

- AutoCAD LT provides a basic utility for extracting attributes, whereas AutoCAD allows you to extract the values of attributes and generate the extracted data as a table.

For more information on annotating and dimensioning a drawing, see Book III.

✦ **3D modeling:** For the most part, 3D drawing in AutoCAD LT is nonexistent. Sure, you can create wireframe models, but you can't create surface or solid models. AutoCAD LT does offer some limited properties that do allow you to create pseudo-3D objects or objects that appear to be 3D, such as giving an object thickness or drawing objects at different Z elevations. The 3D modeling capability is one of the defining features that makes AutoCAD LT different from AutoCAD.

When modeling solids in AutoCAD, you can use a feature called dynamic UCS, which moves the UCS to the face of the 3D solid located under the crosshairs. AutoCAD LT also doesn't support the ability to create a helix, or offer true 3D modifying commands to move, rotate, align, or mirror objects in 3D.

For more information on 3D modeling in AutoCAD and AutoCAD LT, see Book V.

✦ **Viewing/navigation:** AutoCAD LT offers basic ways to view a drawing compared to AutoCAD. Most of the available ways of viewing a drawing in AutoCAD LT are

- Realtime zoom and pan, window, extents, previous, and others

- Named and preset views

- VPOINT and DDVPOINT commands

- Toggling between Perspective and Parallel view

- SteeringWheels

AutoCAD allows you to view and navigate a drawing the same way that AutoCAD LT does, with these added navigation features:

- 3D orbit to rotate the camera around objects in the model

- Walk and fly through navigation features

- Swivel and adjust the distance from the camera

- Camera objects

- Navigate named views with motion by using ShowMotion

- Four SteeringWheels

- ViewCube to visually change between preset views and orbit the model

For more information on viewing and navigating a drawing with AutoCAD and AutoCAD LT, see Chapter 3 of Book II and Chapter 4 of Book V.

✦ **Visualization/rendering:** Visualizing a 3D drawing is basic in AutoCAD LT compared to AutoCAD. AutoCAD LT allows you to display a drawing in 2D wireframe, shaded, or as a hidden line drawing. AutoCAD LT doesn't support rendering, the creation of walkthroughs or an animation, and the use of visual styles.

For more information on visualization and rendering of a drawing in both AutoCAD and AutoCAD LT, see Chapters 3 and 6 of Book V.

✦ **Collaboration/sharing:** Both AutoCAD and AutoCAD LT can be used to create drawings for a project, but AutoCAD offers features that allow better project collaborating or sharing of design ideas. Both support the ability to open and save files to FTP sites and work with the project collaboration site Buzzsaw. You can put drawings on the Web through the Publish to Web feature and send sets of drawings via eTransmit. Where the two differ is in the Sheet Set Manager, Publish, and Drawing Security features.

- You can't create 3D DWF and 3D DWFx files from AutoCAD LT.

- Sheet Set Manager is not part of AutoCAD LT, so you can't use it to share projects with AutoCAD and AutoCAD LT users.

- Drawings can't be secured with passwords when using AutoCAD LT.

- 3D models cannot be rendered with AutoCAD LT, so if you receive a 3D model you can't create a rendered image to share with others.

For more information on publishing drawings and project collaboration with AutoCAD and AutoCAD LT, see Books VII and VIII.

✦ **Data exchange:** If you're working with vendors or clients that use different drafting packages other than AutoCAD or AutoCAD LT, you might run into exchange problems if you're using AutoCAD LT. AutoCAD LT doesn't offer as many file export and import options as AutoCAD does. If you're using AutoCAD LT, you can't import or export the following file formats:

- 3D DWF file (export)

- 3D DWFx file (export)

- ACIS file (import and export)

- Stereolithograph file (export)

- Encapsulated PS file (export)

- 3D Studio file (import and export)

- Drawing Exchange Binary file (import)

For more information on exchanging drawings in other file formats other than DWG and DXF from AutoCAD and AutoCAD LT, see Chapter 4 of Book VIII.

✦ **CAD standards:** Both AutoCAD and AutoCAD LT allow you to manage CAD standards through the use of drawing template files, layers, styles (text, point, dimension, and tables), and blocks just to name a few. However, AutoCAD supplies a few additional tools that are not part of AutoCAD LT to make sure that everyone is following the same standards. These additional CAD standards tools are

- CAD Standards Manager

- Batch CAD standards

- Layer Translator

**Book IV
Chapter 1**

The LT Difference

For more information on using CAD standards with drawings created in AutoCAD and AutoCAD LT, see Chapters 1 through 3 of Book VIII.

✦ **Customization/programming:** Outside of 3D modeling, the ability to customize and program AutoCAD are key differences between AutoCAD and AutoCAD LT. Although AutoCAD LT does support customization to a certain extent, it doesn't support Action Recorder or programming languages and platforms such as AutoLISP/Visual LISP, VB/VBA, C++/ObjectARX, and .NET. This makes it impossible to get the same level of productivity out of AutoCAD LT that you can with AutoCAD. Many third-party applications run inside AutoCAD to help with things such as block management, attribute extraction, modifying objects, and even programs that connect to external data sources.

For more information on customizing and programming AutoCAD and AutoCAD LT, go to www.wiley.com/go/autocad2009aio.

✦ **Additional utilities:** AutoCAD offers many features that are improvements to older versions or features that are not available at all in AutoCAD LT. Some of these features are

- dbConnect Manager, which allows you to link objects in a drawing to a table in a database

- Express Tools, which contains additional tools that help with a variety of tasks in AutoCAD

- Reference Manager, an external utility that allows you to update the paths for external referenced files and quickly identify whether files are missing for a set of drawings

- Multiple user profiles, which are used to store different drafting settings and file paths

For more information on extracting and editing attributes in blocks, see Chapter 1 of Book VI; for more information on Express Tools, see Chapter 4 of Book IX.

✦ **Software deployment:** AutoCAD allows you to create a customizable install by using the Network Deployment wizard and manage software licenses with a license manager. AutoCAD LT doesn't offer network deployment and license management, which can help to control the costs of the software. For example, if you have five drafters, but only three are typically working in AutoCAD at a time, you can get away with buying only four network licenses.

The license manager hands out licenses until none are left to hand out. If no additional licenses are available, the fifth user gets a message that says all licenses have been checked out. After a user closes out of

AutoCAD, the license is returned to the license manager and becomes available for the next person. The Network Deployment wizard allows you to streamline installing AutoCAD by allowing you to specify settings such as user profile names, custom support paths, and files that should be used by default.

Determining Whether AutoCAD or AutoCAD LT Is Best for You

Now that you have an idea of what the differences are between AutoCAD and AutoCAD LT, you have to decide which one is right for you. It really depends on what you are doing: 2D drafting, 3D modeling, plotting drawings, or reviewing comments. Here are six questions that should help you to determine whether AutoCAD or AutoCAD LT would work best for you. This list doesn't provide all the possible questions that can help to determine which is best for you, but it should be enough to get you going in the right direction. Keep in mind that you have to consider what your current needs are and what your future needs might be:

1. Are the drawings you create or work with 2D only?

   If so, you might think about using AutoCAD LT.

2. Do some of the drawings that you create or work with contain 3D objects, or will you need to supply renderings to any of your clients?

   If so, you might think about using AutoCAD. AutoCAD LT doesn't support rendering or the creation of 3D objects. You might also want to consider using AutoCAD LT and Autodesk Viz if your 3D needs are centralized around presentations.

3. Will you be doing nothing more than some light drafting, plotting, and reviewing of DWG files?

   If so, you might think about using AutoCAD LT unless you need to plot renderings. If you just need to plot 2D drawings or know someone in the office who does, you can download DWG TrueView 2009 from Autodesk's Web site for free. I cover DWG TrueView 2009 in Chapter 2 of this minibook.

4. Do you need or want to run third-party applications to extend the functionality that comes with the program?

   If so, you need to use AutoCAD and not AutoCAD LT because AutoCAD LT doesn't support certain forms of customization and programming languages.

5. Do you plan on working with a variety of clients and vendors?

If so, consider using AutoCAD and not AutoCAD LT. AutoCAD offers a number of collaboration features that can make working with vendors and clients much easier. Some of the features that make collaborating with AutoCAD easier are CAD standards and sheet sets. If you choose to use AutoCAD LT, you can still work with vendors and clients, but you might have some additional hurdles that you will need to plan for. Vendors have a tough time working with the lowest common denominator, AutoCAD LT in this case, if you're missing out on productivity features.

6. What is your budget for software?

If you have a small budget and you do only 2D only drawings, the best choice is AutoCAD LT. Another solution you might consider is to buy a single seat of AutoCAD and the other seats as AutoCAD LT if you are primarily doing 2D only drawings. This would allow you to at least see what those with AutoCAD created when you receive drawings or what they will see when you send drawings back. You can always upgrade to a full seat of AutoCAD later if you need to as well.

If you have a medium or large budget, you might consider buying AutoCAD and using the license manager to allow you to buy fewer licenses than you have staff. You can then add new licenses later as needed. If your budget simply allows you to buy what you need, you could buy a license of AutoCAD for each user in your office and be done with it. (And hey, if you feel extremely generous, I can always use a license or two as well!)

No matter whether you plan on using AutoCAD or AutoCAD LT, remember that you will be using the most popular CAD drafting package on the market and will be able to communicate by using the DWG file format. Using the DWG file format is important because almost all the products that Autodesk develops can either create or read a DWG file, and many other CAD-drafting packages on the market can at least read a DWG file, which makes DWG a popular exchange file format as well.

Chapter 2: Extending AutoCAD LT

In This Chapter

✔ **Customizing AutoCAD LT**

✔ **Understanding object enabler technology**

✔ **Finding out about utilities available from Autodesk**

✔ **Discovering companion products from Autodesk**

✔ **Getting third-party custom solutions**

*T*his chapter takes a look at extending AutoCAD LT. Extending AutoCAD LT is similar to extending AutoCAD, but the choices you have are more limited. What exactly do I mean by extending AutoCAD LT? *Extending* means adding custom functionality beyond what comes out of the box. Extending could be creating a custom toolbar, or it could be a way to save drawing files so they can be used in companion programs that allow you to perform a specific task. In this chapter, you look at how you can customize AutoCAD LT, discover what object enablers are, and find out what utilities are available from Autodesk and third-party developers.

Customizing AutoCAD LT

Although it's true that AutoCAD LT lacks many of the methods of customization that AutoCAD offers, it does still offer some nice customization options. As mentioned in Chapter 1 of this minibook, AutoCAD LT doesn't support programming languages such as AutoLISP/Visual LISP, VB/VBA, VB .NET, C#, or C++ with ObjectARX or Action Recorder. Even without the capability to use programming languages and Action Recorder to extend AutoCAD LT, you can create script files, custom linetypes and hatch patterns, blocks, and menu customization, and use a few other customization methods.

It's all in the script

Script files are ASCII or plain-text files that are created with a text editor such as Notepad. Script files contain command and command option sequences and are used to reduce the number of repetitive or redundant steps in a workflow. Script files can be used to perform drawing cleanup after a drawing is created or to do some initial drawing setup. Here is an example of a script file that creates a layer called Bolt, creates a hexagon with a radius of 1" at the coordinates 5,5, and then performs a zoom extents:

```
-layer m bolt c 5
polygon 6 5,5  1
zoom e
```

For more information on creating and using script files, see Chapter 4 of Book IX.

Linetype and hatch patterns

AutoCAD LT comes out of the box with a variety of linetypes and hatch patterns that are used in architectural and mechanical drawings. Although quite a few patterns are available, chances are you might need others that don't come with the program. Linetype and hatch patterns are stored in ASCII or plain-text files and can be created or modified with the use of a text editor such as Notepad. The CENTER linetype definition is shown here:

```
*CENTER,Center ____ _ ____ _ ____ _ ____ _ ____ _ ____
A,1.25,-.25,.25,-.25
```

For more information on creating custom linetypes and hatch patterns, see Chapter 4 of Book IX.

Blocks and DesignCenter

Blocks are one of the most powerful features in AutoCAD LT. Blocks allow you to create and define geometry once and reuse it in as many drawings as you need. The DesignCenter palette (see Figure 2-1) allows you to access and place blocks in a drawing, as well as access other named objects in previously created drawings and add them to your current drawing. For more information on creating and using blocks, see Chapters 1 and 2 of Book VI, and for information on DesignCenter, see Chapter 3 of Book VI.

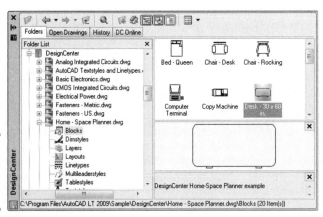

Figure 2-1:
The DesignCenter palette.

Tool palettes

The Tool Palettes window (see Figure 2-2) allows you to organize reusable content so you can access it quickly. Tool palettes can contain blocks and external references, tools that allow you to create tables and hatch patterns, and commands. For more information on creating and using tool palettes, see Chapter 3 of Book VI.

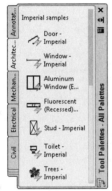

Figure 2-2:
The Tool
Palettes
window.

Changing the user interface with the CUI Editor

AutoCAD LT supports the Customize User Interface (CUI) Editor, which allows you to create and modify toolbars, menus, ribbon panels, and tabs, shortcut keys, double-click actions, and other user interface elements. For more information on creating and modifying user interface elements, see Chapter 2 of Book IX.

Diesel

Diesel is an interesting form of customization in AutoCAD LT. It allows you to display values in the status bar area, and it can be used to create conditional statements for command macros when customizing the user interface with the CUI Editor. AutoCAD LT uses Diesel in several of its own command macros to determine the current state of the application before running a specific command. For example, when you use the shortcut key Ctrl+0, which toggles Clean Screen on and off, AutoCAD LT looks to see what the current state of Clean Screen is, on or off, and executes the correct command to change the current state. For more information on using Diesel with the status bar or menu customization, see Chapter 2 of Book IX.

**Book IV
Chapter 2**

**Extending
AutoCAD LT**

Command aliases

Command aliases are frequently used to quickly execute a command from the command line. Instead of typing the command's full name, you can type a few letters to start it instead. Many of the popular commands have command aliases assigned to them right out of the box, but you can create or modify command aliases in the ACADLT.PGP file by using a text editor such as Notepad. For more information on creating and modifying command aliases, see Chapter 1 of Book IX.

Desktop icons

Desktop icons are great for starting an application, but they offer so much more capability than that. AutoCAD LT allows you to use *command line switches* for changing the behavior of AutoCAD LT when you start it from a desktop icon. For more information on modifying a desktop icon with command line switches, see Chapter 1 of Book IX.

Object Enabler Technology

Object enablers have been around since AutoCAD R14 but were first supported in AutoCAD LT with AutoCAD 2000i. Object enablers allow you to view custom objects that are not part of the program by default. Often, you hear about object enablers when you work with drawings created in some of the AutoCAD-based vertical products such as Autodesk Building Systems (ABS) or AutoCAD Architecture (formally known as Architectural Desktop — ADT). An object enabler is a series of files that AutoCAD LT loads on demand when it detects the use of specific custom objects; this allows for the objects to be displayed in their original form and to be plotted correctly instead of not appearing at all or only being shown somewhat accurately in the drawing.

AutoCAD LT ships with a few commonly used object enablers for other Autodesk products. But you may need to obtain other object enablers based on the objects created in a drawing so they can be properly displayed. Object enablers are developed by Autodesk so that any new object types that their programs might create can be displayed and plotted. Third-party developers also create object enablers that work with the custom objects that their programs add to a drawing.

Autodesk posts its object enablers on its Web site at www.autodesk.com/ enablers/. If an object in a drawing requires an object enabler and one is not available for the object, the drawing object is still displayed in most cases, so the drawing can still be viewed and plotted, but the object in the drawing is known as a proxy graphic. A *proxy graphic* is a graphical representation of the original object in a drawing that's displayed in an older release or when the object enabler is not installed. Proxy graphics were once called *zombies* back in AutoCAD R13. (How fitting for a release numbered 13!)

In the Options dialog box, in the Live Enabler Options section of the System tab, you can select the Check Web for Live Enablers option to allow AutoCAD LT to automatically download object enablers as they are needed based on the objects in the drawings you have open.

Additional Utilities Available from Autodesk

Even though AutoCAD LT doesn't allow for the loading of custom applications directly into the application, Autodesk provides some utilities that run outside AutoCAD LT to help with some processes. Some utilities are used to convert drawings from one drawing file format to another, and others give you the capability to view and mark up DWF files created with the PLOT or PUBLISH commands.

DWG TrueView 2009

DWG TrueView 2009 allows you to convert an AutoCAD or AutoCAD-based drawing file so that it can be opened with AutoCAD R14 and later. DWG TrueView 2009 can be used to save drawing files to the latest release or even save them back to an older version (which comes in handy if you need to send drawings to a vendor who might still be using an older release). DWG TrueView 2009 doesn't require AutoCAD LT to be installed on the computer before it can be used because it's a standalone application. Along with saving DWG files to an earlier release, you can also view, plot, and publish DWG and DXF files. For more information on saving drawing files, see Chapter 3 of Book VIII.

Viewers

Autodesk supports two viewers that allow you to view DWF, DXF, and DWG files. If you're creating DWF files, you should look them over before sending them out. To do this, AutoCAD LT comes with a free DWF viewer called Autodesk Design Review 2009, which allows you to view 2D and 3D DWF files, measure distances between points, and create markups. For more information on creating DWF files and Autodesk Design Review 2009, see Chapter 4 of Book VIII.

As I mention in the preceding section, DWG TrueView 2009 allows you to view DWG and DXF files. It's a great alternative to buying a copy of AutoCAD LT if someone just needs to view and plot drawing files.

**Book IV
Chapter 2**

Extending
AutoCAD LT

Companion Products from Autodesk

Autodesk has a huge portfolio of applications for the design community. Many of these applications are designed to be integrated solutions with other applications it sells. AutoCAD LT is no different, and the drawing files it creates can be used in other applications that Autodesk offers. Autodesk also offers many software packages that help improve productivity. Most of the packages require the use of AutoCAD and not AutoCAD LT, but in this section I describe some of the ones that you can use with AutoCAD LT.

Autodesk Symbols 2000

Autodesk Symbols 2000 is a library of ready-to-use blocks that are useful whether you do architectural, mechanical, or electrical drawings. More than 12,000 symbols are available for use through DesignCenter after the symbols have been installed. To find more information about Autodesk Symbols 2000, visit the Autodesk Web site at www.autodesk.com/symbols.

Autodesk VIZ 2008

Autodesk VIZ 2008 is a program that allows you to create complex 3D objects, apply materials to them, add lights, and then generate a rendered image or an animation. You can use the objects that you create in your 2D drawings from AutoCAD LT in Autodesk VIZ to create a 3D model for visualization purposes. If having the ability to create renderings and animations is important for your business, and you don't need the ability to create or use custom add-ons for AutoCAD, you might think about buying AutoCAD LT and Autodesk VIZ instead of a single copy of AutoCAD. Autodesk VIZ allows you to create stunning visual effects and photo-realistic renderings. Autodesk VIZ 2008 retails for about $1,900. To find out more information about Autodesk VIZ 2008, visit the Autodesk Web site at www.autodesk.com/viz.

Autodesk Impression

Autodesk Impression is a relatively new program developed by Autodesk. It brings back the look and feel of hand-drawn illustrations that was lost when the industry went to CAD. Impression allows you to create presentation drawings from DWG and DWF files. After your drawing is open, you can fill closed areas, insert blocks, and stylize your linework from the DWG or DWF file so it looks like it was drawn with a marker or pencil. AutoCAD LT comes with part of Impression built into the program, which can be accessed from the Output tab on the ribbon. To find more information about Autodesk Impression, visit the Autodesk Web site at www.autodesk.com/impression.

Third-Party Custom Solutions

Although Autodesk's portfolio of applications is large, one of the company's keys to success has been its large development community, which builds even more applications on or around Autodesk products. Most of the applications by third-party developers are created to run on top of AutoCAD or one of the AutoCAD-based vertical products and not AutoCAD LT. Some companies create applications that run outside AutoCAD LT that allow you to view DWG and DWF files online through Java-based applications, or to access block libraries. Many of these types of applications can be found by using your Web browser and search engine.

Block utilities/libraries

One of the most time-consuming things about starting to use AutoCAD LT is that you have to create your own block libraries. To save time, you can download block libraries or symbols from the Internet. Many are out there for you to use — it's just a matter of finding them.

Table 2-1 lists some of the different Web sites that contain block utilities or symbol libraries that you can use with AutoCAD LT. Some are free; others aren't.

Table 2-1	URLs to Block Utilities/Libraries	
Web Site	*URL*	*Description*
AutoCAD Block	www.autocadblock.com	Lists symbol libraries and utilities that contain symbols for architectural, landscaping, and mechanical drawings. Some of the symbol libraries are free, and others start at about $99.
CADdepot	www.caddepot.com	Lists a wide range of 2D and 3D symbols for a variety of industries. Most of the symbols on the site are free for downloading after registering on the site; some symbols and utilities might need to be purchased. Symbols and utilities for purchase are available in a wide range of prices.
CADOPOLIS.COM	www.cadopolis.com	Lists symbols and utilities that contain a wide range of 2D and 3D symbols for a variety of industries. Symbols and utilities are available for free and for purchase. Symbols and utilities for purchase are available in a wide range of prices.

Book IV Chapter 2

Extending AutoCAD LT

(continued)

Table 2-1 *(continued)*

Web Site	URL	Description
CADToolsOnline.com	www.cadtoolsonline.com	Lists symbol libraries for architectural and piping drawings. Some of the symbol libraries are free, while others have a price range of $60 and up based on the number of users and the type of library.

Viewers

A number of third-party applications allow you to view DWG, DXF, and DWF files all in the same application; many allow you to view images and other file formats as well. Most of the third-party viewers aren't free, but if you shop around, you can find a reasonably priced version. You can find viewers in all shapes and sizes: from PC and Mac desktops to server applications. Table 2-2 lists some viewers available from third-party developers.

Table 2-2	URLs to Block Utilities/Libraries	
Web Site	**URL**	**Description**
AutoVue	www.cimmetry.com	Supports the widest range of document and file formats. You can view AutoCAD drawing, DXF, DWF, PDF, image, and Office files, and many others. Pricing is available only by request.
Brava! Viewer	www.bravaviewer.com	Comes in different styles and allows you to view Word, Excel, AutoCAD drawing, PDF, and DWF files plus many others in a single application. It also supports markups that can be saved in an XML file. Prices range from about $30 to $350.
CADViewer	www.cadviewer.com	A Java-based CAD viewing tool that supports AutoCAD drawing, DXF, and PDF files, and some other file types. Pricing is available only by request.
Microspot DWG Viewer	www.microspot.co.uk	An application that runs on an Apple Macintosh computer and allows you to view, annotate, and print DWG and DXF files. Price is about $55.

Chapter 3: Mixed Environments

In This Chapter

✓ Using AutoCAD LT and AutoCAD in the same office

✓ Exchanging drawing files between AutoCAD LT and AutoCAD

*I*n this chapter, I look at issues you encounter when you use AutoCAD LT and AutoCAD in the same environment, or when you open drawings created in AutoCAD with AutoCAD LT. Although AutoCAD LT and AutoCAD both create DWG files and are both developed by Autodesk, that doesn't mean both see the same things in the same way. If you read the first two chapters of this minibook, you already know that there are differences between AutoCAD and AutoCAD LT. If you exchange drawings between the two programs, you will discover even more differences.

Using AutoCAD LT and AutoCAD in the Same Office

AutoCAD and AutoCAD LT are developed with the needs of many different users in mind, which sometimes means that an office ends up using both programs. If you already use AutoCAD in your office and are considering purchasing copies of AutoCAD LT to control costs, you should pay close attention to this section.

Budgeting

When it comes to budgeting, the first thing you may say is, "That's not my job." But it is, when you think about it: You're the one who supports or uses the application. Everyone plays an intricate part in making the best decision for your department or the company you work for. Three main things to consider during budgeting are hardware, software, and training for AutoCAD and AutoCAD LT. Being on the same release of AutoCAD and AutoCAD LT can make things run more smoothly than if everyone is on different releases, so you'll want to keep in mind how much upgrades will cost and even new seats that you may need in the upcoming year. To help make budgeting for upgrades easier, Autodesk offers an annual subscription program.

As you upgrade your software, keep in mind that your hardware needs may change. Having the right hardware is key to ensuring that AutoCAD runs efficiently. Leasing computers on a two- to three-year cycle can help with budgeting and ensure that you're always using some of the most current hardware.

The final piece of the puzzle is training, which is covered in the next section.

Training

Properly trained drafters help to ensure the creation of quality drawings. AutoCAD and AutoCAD LT by themselves are not enough to create a good drawing; it also takes time and a disciplined drafter committed to following company CAD standards. Training not only helps to ensure quality drawings but can also make sure that drawings are communicated properly to internal departments and external vendors. Training can be performed by an external company or an internal member of the drafting department. You shouldn't assume that everyone knows and understands the company's CAD standards or how to communicate designs with internal or external resources. It's always good to have refresher courses on company procedures and the software you use.

Communication

Communication is important in every aspect of the drafting process: from capturing a client's idea into a drawing to making sure that vendors have the right information to bid on a project. Properly communicating company CAD standards is vital to making a mixed office run smoothly because a process that works on AutoCAD might not necessarily work on AutoCAD LT. Because AutoCAD LT lacks some of the features of AutoCAD, AutoCAD LT should be used as the basis for any company CAD standards. In the same way, those who use AutoCAD LT need to communicate what is not working for them back to those creating drawings with AutoCAD. A communication breakdown sometimes occurs when AutoCAD users don't realize that a certain function isn't supported by AutoCAD LT and users of AutoCAD LT don't report the issue.

Environment

Although AutoCAD and AutoCAD LT are very similar, they are slightly different in the interfaces and commands they offer. Just because people know AutoCAD fairly well, don't automatically assume that they will be proficient at using AutoCAD LT. Some features that they routinely use in AutoCAD may not be available in AutoCAD LT, which can lead to some frustration. It's easier for a user to go from AutoCAD LT up to AutoCAD than it is for a user of AutoCAD to move down to AutoCAD LT.

Customization

AutoCAD and AutoCAD LT share some commonalities when it comes to customization. To make sure that upgrading and supporting the two programs is as easy as possible, place all custom files in networked locations so they can be shared between the two programs. Files such as scripts, custom linetypes, and hatch pattern files are easily shareable between the two programs because they are not product- or release-specific (as long as you do not use commands for features that are only in AutoCAD), whereas CUI files, standard linetype, and hatch pattern files are specific to each program. You can share CUI files between AutoCAD and AutoCAD LT if you create custom CUI files and load them as partial CUI files. Also keep in mind that AutoCAD LT does not support programming, so a command in a shared CUI file can't reference a custom command that is defined in a custom program file. Blocks and drawing templates are program neutral, so you can safely create blocks and drawing templates that can be shared between both programs.

Installation and deployment

Installing and deploying AutoCAD and AutoCAD LT are somewhat different based on the type of licensing you have or plan on purchasing. AutoCAD can be deployed by using a license manager that distributes licenses, which makes it easy to manage the number of licenses in use. AutoCAD LT doesn't support this option. Both AutoCAD and AutoCAD LT support standalone and multiseat deployment installation options. AutoCAD LT doesn't support the use of profiles, so you need to manually add or change any support paths that are necessary so that each one can locate company standard files such as templates and blocks.

Making the Trip from AutoCAD to AutoCAD LT

Exchanging drawings created in AutoCAD with those who use AutoCAD LT can be a challenge at times, based on which features you're using. If you use AutoCAD and are sharing drawings with someone who uses AutoCAD LT, you don't have to do anything special. However, you might need to show some restraint in using certain features if it's important for those on AutoCAD LT to be able to modify your drawings. In the next sections, I've gathered some of the key areas that you should know about if you are an AutoCAD LT user and work on drawings created in AutoCAD. I also cover issues for those of you who use AutoCAD and send out drawings to vendors that might be using AutoCAD LT.

2D drafting

AutoCAD allows you to create multilines. *Multilines* are a series of parallel lines that can have different colors and linetypes for each parallel line segment making up the object. They are commonly used for streets, showing the main part of the road and any offsets that the municipality or city requires from the road, and can also be used for floor and basement plans of buildings. When a drawing with multilines is opened in AutoCAD LT, you don't have any control over the object other than changing its standard object properties and being able to grip edit the object. If you need to make changes to the lines themselves, you have to explode the multiline object, which can be frustrating to the individual who originally sent you the drawing if you need to send it back to them.

Another issue that you have to deal with is the clipping of blocks and external references. AutoCAD LT displays the clipping frame, but you can't remove the clipping unless you remove the external reference object and reattach it. Figure 3-1 shows an external reference without a clipping boundary (on the left) and the same external reference with a clipping boundary (on the right). AutoCAD LT can also make it hard to tell whether an external reference has been clipped unless the frame is left on. For more information on multilines, see Chapter 1 of Book II; for more information on external references, see Chapter 3 of Book VI.

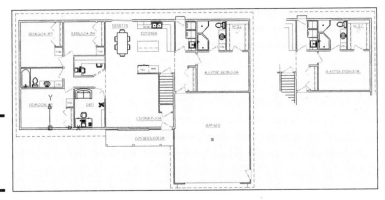

Figure 3-1:
Clipped external references.

3D modeling

The ability to work with drawings that contain 3D solids and surfaces is limited in AutoCAD LT. In AutoCAD, you have many ways to modify 3D solids and surfaces, such as through the use of grips and the SOLIDEDIT command; these are not available in AutoCAD LT. AutoCAD LT doesn't allow you to create and modify 3D solids and surfaces besides using basic modifying commands such as move, copy, and rotate. You are limited to changing only general properties of 3D solids and surfaces, such as their color, what layer they are on, and other general properties available for all object types. However, a 3D solid or surface can be exploded into wireframe models that are made up of regions or 2D objects.

If a drawing has a section plane and Live Section is enabled for the section plane, it won't look the same in AutoCAD LT as it does in AutoCAD (see Figure 3-2). The Live Section is not displayed, but the section plane will exist in AutoCAD LT, so if the drawing is saved and reopened in AutoCAD, it looks just like it did before it was opened in AutoCAD LT.

For more information on 3D solids and surfaces, see Chapters 4 and 5 of Book V and Bonus Chapter 1 on the Web at www.wiley.com/go/autocad2009aio.

Figure 3-2:
Live Section
enabled in
AutoCAD
(left), and
how it looks
in AutoCAD
LT (right).

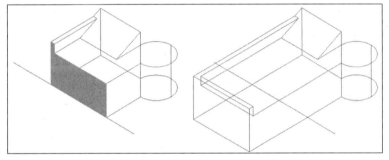

Annotation

AutoCAD and AutoCAD LT have few differences in annotation. The two main differences that you have to be concerned about when exchanging drawing files between AutoCAD and AutoCAD LT are gradient fills and fields. Both gradient fills and fields are displayed in AutoCAD LT without any problems, but gradient fills and fields with sheet set values can't be created or edited. If you use the HATCHEDIT command on a gradient fill, it turns into a solid fill. If you change the boundary associated with a gradient fill, it continues to exist as a gradient fill in the drawing.

Fields are used to associate properties of a drawing file or an object in the drawing with text, multiline text, a table cell, or an attribute. Fields can help make sure that information remains in sync when something is changed in the drawing or an object is modified. Based on the type of field, it displays the last value or updates according to changes in the drawing file. You can change the value of a field as long as it is not associated with a sheet set because AutoCAD LT does not support sheet sets. For more information on

**Book IV
Chapter 3**

**Mixed
Environments**

hatch in a drawing, see Chapter 3 of Book III; for more information on fields, see Chapter 1 of Book III.

Viewing

Cameras are displayed as glyphs in AutoCAD and are accessible from either the drawing window or the View Manager dialog box. AutoCAD LT doesn't display camera glyphs in the drawing, but it does list the camera in the View Manager dialog box. AutoCAD LT also doesn't support several properties that are available for a named view in AutoCAD. These properties are for things such as backgrounds and live sections, which are not supported in AutoCAD LT. AutoCAD LT also does not support motion assigned to a named view and ShowMotion.

Visualization

Drawings created with AutoCAD can contain a variety of additional objects and settings that really don't do anything in AutoCAD LT: One example is lights. Lights appear in the drawing and can be selected and modified via grips, but you can't alter their properties. Because AutoCAD LT lacks the ability to do renderings, you won't be able to use any material assignments that are on objects or be able to modify the materials stored in a drawing file. This can cause problems if a viewport on a layout tab is set up to use the Realistic visual style that AutoCAD offers. For the most part, all visual styles are supported by AutoCAD LT, with the exception of Realistic (see Figure 3-3). The visual styles can't be changed, but if they are assigned to a viewport on a layout tab, they will be displayed correctly.

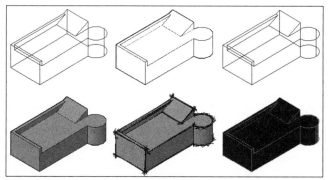

Figure 3-3:
Visual styles saved with a drawing are displayed in AutoCAD LT.

CAD Standards

The CAD Standards feature of AutoCAD uses Drawing Standards (DWS) files that are associated with the drawing file, but AutoCAD LT doesn't use or know about these files. This isn't a problem with AutoCAD LT because the feature doesn't exist in LT, but it can become a nightmare if you work on a set of drawings and use the eTransmit feature to repackage them to send off to someone else. Because AutoCAD LT doesn't know about these types of files, it doesn't know enough to inform you that they might be missing or are needed when sending off a set of drawings.

Collaboration and sharing

Collaboration plays a large role in designing a building, creating a machine, or engineering a bridge. All these things and many more don't just happen by themselves: They require collaboration. AutoCAD allows you to create a sheet set with all the drawing files related to a project and maintain links from model views to drawing layouts. AutoCAD LT doesn't support the use of sheet set (DST) files because it doesn't have the Sheet Set Manager palette, so any values that reference part of the sheet set file through fields can't be updated. If a field value needs to be changed, it must be replaced with plain text, which causes problems if it is reopened later in AutoCAD.

Book V

3D Modeling

Contents at a Glance

Chapter 1: Introducing the Third Dimension .349

Understanding the Different Types of 3D Models 350
Entering Coordinates above the x,y Plane..351

Chapter 2: Using the 3D Environment 357

Setting Up AutoCAD for 3D 357
Understanding What the UCS Icon Is Telling You 362
Using the Coordinate System for 3D Drawing 365

Chapter 3: Viewing in 3D 369

Expressing Your Point of View...369
Orbiting around a 3D Model 373
Navigating a 3D Model..375
Hugging the Corners with the Steering Wheels......................................376
Cube with a View...377
Adding Color and Style to a 3D Model..378

Chapter 4: Moving from 2D to 3D 381

Working with Regions 381
3D Polylines and Helixes 384
Creating 3D Objects from 2D Objects...385
Creating 2D Objects from 3D Objects...388
3D Modify Commands 390

Chapter 5: Working with Solids 393

Creating Solid Primitives...393
Editing Solids 399

Chapter 6: Rendering: Lights, Camera, AutoCAD! 403

Lighting a Scene 403
Getting the Right Look with Materials..409
Setting Up a Backdrop 410
Rendering the Final Scene...411

Chapter 1: Introducing the Third Dimension

In This Chapter

✔ Understanding the different types of 3D models

✔ Entering coordinates above the *x,y* plane

This book of the *AutoCAD 2009 & AutoCAD LT 2009 All-in-One Desk Reference For Dummies* takes you on a journey to a whole new dimension. I'm talking about not traveling through space or time, but rather giving your drawing some depth or height based on how you look at it. AutoCAD is a powerful 2D drafting tool, but it also sports a nice set of tools for 3D modeling. AutoCAD LT, unlike its older counterpart, has limited 3D drafting, visualization, and viewing capabilities. Most of what is discussed in the chapters of this minibook is geared toward only AutoCAD; but some things apply to AutoCAD LT, and I point those out to you along the way.

Most drafters think and feel most comfortable when drafting in 2D; this makes 3D modeling seem foreign and often more difficult than it really is. 3D modeling is not all that difficult — much of what was covered in previous minibooks applies to 3D drafting.

AutoCAD allows you to create three types of 3D models: wireframe, solid, and surface. AutoCAD LT is capable of creating and editing only wireframe models, but you can use it to view solid and surface models.

Throughout the chapters in this minibook, you see how to select points above the *x,y* coordinate plane, and how to adjust and manipulate the coordinate system to more easily use drafting commands. After you have mastered selecting points in the drawing and working with the coordinate system, I take you on a tour of some of the navigation and viewing commands that AutoCAD and AutoCAD LT offer for viewing 3D models. After you have the basics under your belt, I show you how to use many of the different modeling and editing commands that are used with solids and surfaces. To close out the minibook, I touch on the concepts of creating renderings from AutoCAD. 3D modeling in AutoCAD is a huge area of the program, and would take an entire book to cover everything efficiently — actually, there is a companion book that covers 3D modeling in AutoCAD, titled *AutoCAD 2008 3D Modeling Workbook For Dummies*.

Understanding the Different Types of 3D Models

AutoCAD and AutoCAD LT allow you to create and view drawings that are created as wireframe, surface, or solid models. These different types of models each have their own strengths and weaknesses:

✦ **Wireframe model:** Wireframe models are created with the use of 2D objects such as lines, arcs, polylines, and circles with no thickness. The 2D objects are drawn in 3D space by using full *x, y,* and *z* coordinates, not just *x-* and *y*-coordinate values. Wireframe models are not intended to be used for visualization because they do not have any surface area that allows them to hide objects beyond the geometry that they represent. Wireframe models provide for a great starting point when creating surface models. Figure 1-1 shows a cube with a hole drawn as a wireframe model and displayed with the HIDE command. You can think of a wireframe model as being much like a wire hanger or a bird cage.

Figure 1-1:
Wireframe model of a cube with a hole in the center.

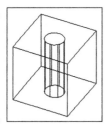

✦ **Surface model:** Surface models are created from 3D objects called faces. Faces can be made up of three or four points. Unlike wireframe models, surface models can be used for visualizing a design. However, based on the type of visualization, such as a hidden line drawing, some cleanup might be necessary to hide the edges of faces that form a visible side of the model. AutoCAD offers several commands that allow you to create and manipulate surfaces. Figure 1-2 shows the same cube with a hole drawn in it as shown in Figure 1-1, with the exception that it was drawn as a surface model. The HIDE command shows each surface and edge visible from the current viewpoint of the surface model. You can think of a surface model as being much like a cardboard shipping box: It's hollow on the inside but from the outside it looks like a solid object because it's a fully closed object.

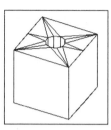

Figure 1-2:
Surface model of a cube with a hole in the center.

✦ **Solid model:** Solid models are created from 3D objects called *solids* which come in two forms: primitives and compound. Solid objects are much more flexible than faces and 2D objects for creating wireframe and surface models. Solid objects can be created and modified through a number of commands in AutoCAD. These commands allow you to create primitive objects such as cubes, spheres, and cones, and then combine them to form compound objects. Unlike surfaces, solids do have mass and therefore are not hollow, which allows you to capture information about them. Solids are much easier to work with than surfaces. Figure 1-3 shows a cube with a hole drawn as a solid model and displayed with the HIDE command. The HIDE command shows the surfaces and edges of the solid model. You can think of a solid model as being much like a block of solid wood: It is not hollow on the inside unless you do something to it.

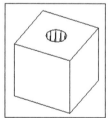

Figure 1-3:
Solid model of a cube with a hole in the center.

Entering Coordinates above the x,y Plane

Everything you've read up to this point has been using the *x*- and *y*- coordinate values. This is all about to change as you step in a new direction with the *z* coordinate. Most of AutoCAD's commands are not true 3D commands; this means that commands such as PLINE, which is used to create polylines, can be used to draw a polyline only at a single *z* height (or elevation) for all its vertices. Out of what are known as the traditional 2D commands, only the LINE command allows you to specify two different *z* heights for the start and end points of the line object that is being created.

Manually inputting coordinates

Chapter 7 of Book I explains how to input relative and absolute coordinates for 2D drafting. Both of these coordinate input formats are great for 3D modeling as well. The only difference that you'll find when working in 3D is the need to enter a *z* coordinate value. Along with those coordinate input formats, the relative polar coordinate input is expanded to include two additional formats called *cylindrical* and *spherical,* which are specific to 3D modeling. Of course, you can use object snaps, point filters, and object snap tracking when creating and modifying 3D objects.

You can input coordinate values through the use of direct distance entry and the using of dynamic input. Both of these are covered in Chapters 3 and 7 of Book I.

Absolute x, y, and z coordinates

Working with absolute coordinates in 3D is just like inputting them for 2D, except you add the *z* coordinate. You supply the coordinate input in the format *x,y,z*. Following is an example of using the LINE command to draw a line in 3D by using absolute coordinate entry:

```
Command: line
Specify first point: 0,0,0
Specify next point or [Undo]: 2,3,7.25
```

Relative x, y, and z coordinates

Working with relative coordinates in 3D is just like when inputting them for 2D, except you add the *z* coordinate. You supply the coordinate input in the format of *@x,y,z*. An example of using the LINE command to draw a line in 3D by using relative coordinate entry is

```
Command: line
Specify first point: 2.125,7,-3
Specify next point or [Undo]: @0.5,0.125,7
```

Cylindrical coordinates

Cylindrical coordinates is the first of two coordinate input formats based on relative polar coordinates used in 3D. You supply the coordinate input in the format *@XYdistance<angle,Z*. Following is an example of using the LINE command to draw a line in 3D by using cylindrical coordinate input:

```
Command: line
Specify first point: 0,0,0
Specify next point or [Undo]: @5<45,2
```

Figure 1-4 shows the results in AutoCAD.

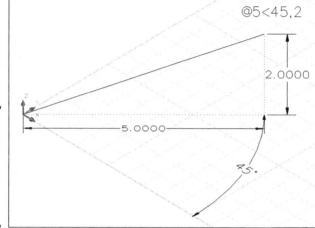

Figure 1-4:
Line created
in 3D by
using
cylindrical
coordinate
input.

Cylindrical coordinate input doesn't work well when dynamic input is enabled. I recommend turning it off by clicking the Dynamic Input (or DYN) button on the status bar area or by pressing F12.

Spherical coordinates

Spherical coordinates is the second coordinate input format based on relative polar coordinates used in 3D. You supply the coordinate input in the format of *@XYdistance<angle<anglefromXY*. An example of using the LINE command to draw a line in 3D by using spherical coordinate input is

```
Command: line
Specify first point: 0,0,0
Specify next point or [Undo]: @5<30<30
```

Figure 1-5 shows the results in AutoCAD.

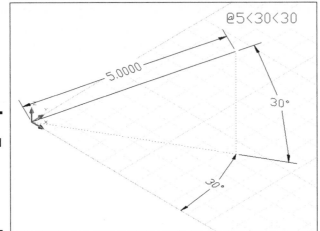

Figure 1-5:
Line created
in 3D by
using
spherical
coordinate
input.

Point filters

You can use point filters to construct coordinate values based on existing points on an object whether it's in 2D or 3D. Three point filters are specific to 3D modeling: *xy, xz,* and *zy.* Point filters can be typed at the command prompt, selected from the Object Snap shortcut menu by pressing and holding down the Shift key while right-clicking, or right-clicking and choosing Snap Overrides. Here's an example of using the LINE command to draw a line in 3D by using the *xy* point filter entry:

```
Command: line
Specify first point: specify a point or a coordinate value
Specify next point or [Undo]: type .xy and press enter
of specify a point or a coordinate value
(need Z): specify a point or a Z height value
```

Object snaps

Object snaps are a great way to ensure that you have the precise point you want in the drawing. AutoCAD has a toggle that controls whether the *z* height of the point you select by using an object snap or the current elevation value is used. (I cover changing the current elevation later in this chapter.) To switch between these two behaviors, follow these steps:

1. **Right-click over the command line window, and choose Options.**

   The Options dialog box appears.

2. **In the Options dialog box, click the Drafting tab.**

3. Click the Replace Z Value with Current Elevation check box.

When you select the Current Elevation check box, AutoCAD substitutes the z height that was obtained from the object snap with the current elevation. When the check box is not selected, AutoCAD uses the z height of the coordinate specified from the object snap.

AutoCAD LT does not have the Replace Z Value with Current Elevation option.

Object snap tracking and moving orthogonally

Object snap tracking can be used above the current x,y plane. Object snap tracking allows you to track points in the z direction. When using object snap tracking in the z direction, AutoCAD provides feedback in the form of tooltips when you are moving in the positive or negative z direction. Figure 1-6 shows an example of the tooltip displayed in AutoCAD when using object snap tracking in 3D.

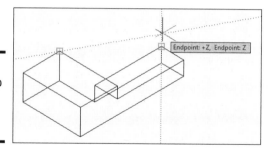

Figure 1-6:
Object snap tracking in the Z direction.

You can use ortho mode in 3D just like in 2D, with the addition of being able to constrain the movement of the crosshairs in the positive and negative z directions. When you drag the crosshairs up or down after specifying the first point when ortho mode is enabled, you're specifying the next point in the z direction. A tooltip is displayed to tell you which direction from the first point you're moving in.

AutoCAD LT does support the use of object snap tracking in 3D, but it does not the use ortho mode to constrain the movement of the crosshairs in the z direction.

Elevation . . . going up

Specifying a z height when entering coordinates is not the only way to draw objects above the x,y plane; you can specify a default z height for all new objects as they are created. If you're drawing a bunch of objects that need a specific *z* height, this can be an efficient way to ensure that they are placed at the correct height. You use the ELEV command to specify the default *z* height used for new objects as they are created. The specified value is used only if you don't use object snaps; if you use object snaps, the *z* height of the object snap is used by default. See the "Object snaps" section, presented earlier in this chapter, for more information.

To set a new elevation value, type **ELEV** at the command prompt and enter a new elevation value at the *Specify new default elevation <0.0000>:* command prompt. Then at the *Specify new default thickness <0.0000>:* command prompt, press Enter or enter a thickness value. I cover using thickness in Chapter 4 of this minibook.

Instead of changing the current elevation, you can use a custom UCS (user coordinate system) to create objects at a specific elevation. I cover the user coordinate system and the world coordinate system in Chapter 2 of this minibook.

Chapter 2: Using the 3D Environment

In This Chapter

✔ Setting up AutoCAD for 3D

✔ Understanding what the UCS icon is telling you

✔ Changing the coordinate system for 3D drawing

Chapter 1 of this minibook covers the three types of 3D models you can create with AutoCAD and AutoCAD LT, as well as how to enter coordinates above the *xy* (or working) plane in the *z* direction. This chapter helps you get a grasp of the 3D environment in AutoCAD and AutoCAD LT. I take a look at some of the key settings and features that help you work efficiently with 3D models. Some of these settings are for getting the most out of your computer investment by enabling hardware acceleration if it is available. You can also change other settings to control the appearance of the grid, the background color, and more in the drawing window.

One of the keys to becoming an efficient drafter with AutoCAD is to understand what the UCS icon is indicating, and in 3D drafting that is no different. The UCS icon provides you with information on which way is up or down in your model, and the direction of the *x, y,* and *z* axes. You can also modify the coordinate system to draw 2D objects on a different plane. 2D objects are always drawn on the *xy* (or working) plane, so by changing the direction or elevation of the plane you can draw 2D objects on a new plane.

Setting Up AutoCAD for 3D

AutoCAD and AutoCAD LT offer various display, hardware, and drafting options that all play different roles when working with 3D. Properly configuring and understanding all these options can make modeling easier. Because AutoCAD LT doesn't support the creation of surface and solid models, many of these options are not available in LT. I point out the differences as I go along.

Orienting yourself in the drawing window

The drawing window is where you create, modify, and view 3D models. Based on how you are viewing a model, the background color, grid display, and crosshairs change in the drawing window. You can customize the display settings for the drawing window through the Drawing Window Colors dialog box (see Figure 2-1). To display the Drawing Window Colors dialog box, click the Colors button under the Window Elements section on the Display tab of the Options dialog box. The Options dialog box can be displayed by clicking Tools menu⇨Options on the menu browser or menu bar.

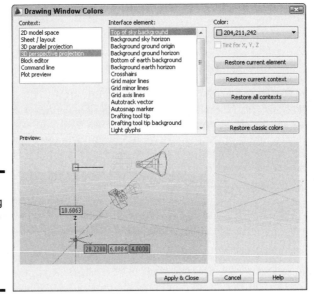

Figure 2-1: Customizing the appearance of the drawing window for 3D.

When working in 3D, you can view a 3D model in parallel or perspective projection. The projection mode (or context) you are currently in affects the display of the model as well as the colors used for various window elements in the drawing window. In AutoCAD LT, only one context, called hidden, is related to 3D drafting.

The following steps explain how to adjust the background color of the drawing window and the color tinting used for the crosshairs under the 3D parallel projection context (or the hidden context if you're using AutoCAD LT):

1. **Right-click the drawing window (with no command active) and choose Options.**

The Options dialog box is displayed.

2. **In the Options dialog box, click the Display tab.**

3. **In the Window Elements section, click Colors.**

   The Drawing Window Colors dialog box is displayed.

4. **In the Context list, select 3D Parallel Projection (or Hidden if you're using AutoCAD LT).**

   The Preview at the bottom of the dialog box updates to show the current colors that the interface elements are set to and which interface elements are available.

5. **In the Interface Element list, select Uniform Background (or Background if you're using AutoCAD LT).**

   The Color drop-down list displays the current color.

6. **Click the Color drop-down list and select White.**

   The color white will be assigned to the background of the drawing window.

7. **In the Interface Element list, select Crosshairs.**

   The Color drop-down list displays the current color, and the Tint for X, Y, Z (or X, Y in AutoCAD LT) check box becomes enabled.

8. **Select the Tint for X, Y, Z check box below the Color drop-down list.**

   The Tint for X, Y, Z (or X, Y) option is used to tint the crosshairs with the colors of red, green, and blue to represent the different axes. The X axis is always represented by the color red, Y by green, and Z by blue (in AutoCAD only). The tinting is by default enabled for the different 3D contexts.

   If you like the color tinting of the crosshairs, you can enable it for the other contexts that are not used for 3D.

9. **Click Apply & Close.**

   The changes are saved and the Drawing Window Colors dialog box closes.

10. **Click OK.**

    The changes are saved and the Options dialog box is closed.

If you or someone you know is colorblind or sensitive to the colors red, green, or blue, you may want to turn off the tinting for the crosshairs because the specific colored axes can disappear from view.

Customizing crosshairs and dynamic input

You can customize the display of the crosshairs and dynamic input for working in 3D in AutoCAD only. These changes go beyond being able to change the size of the crosshairs or even the tinting of the different axes of the crosshairs. These options allow you to enable the display of labels on the crosshairs so you know which direction x, y, and z are without having to display the UCS icon. You can also control whether the z direction is indicated on the crosshairs as well. If you use dynamic input and manually enter points, you can control the display of an additional input field for entering z-coordinate values. You can change these options under the 3D Crosshairs and Dynamic Input sections of the 3D Modeling tab in the Options dialog box. The 3D Modeling tab is not available in AutoCAD LT.

Using workspaces to switch between 2D and 3D drafting

AutoCAD and AutoCAD LT come with a feature called Workspaces. *Workspaces* were introduced in AutoCAD 2006 and play a role in efficiently switching between different task-based drafting tools. I talk about working with workspaces in Chapter 2 of Book IX.

AutoCAD 2009 comes with a workspace named 3D Modeling. This workspace displays many of the common ribbon panels and panels specific to 3D modeling and the Tool Palettes window. The menu bar, all toolbars, and the layout tabs at the bottom of the drawing window are hidden by default in this workspace. To switch to the 3D Modeling workspace, on the status bar at the bottom of AutoCAD choose Workspace Switching➪3D Modeling.

Introducing toolbars and ribbon tabs for 3D

AutoCAD comes with a number of toolbars and ribbon tabs that contain 3D-related tools for creating, editing, and navigating your drawings.

✦ The **Modeling toolbar** contains tools for creating 3D solid objects and some of the more common editing tools.

✦ The **Solid Editing toolbar** contains tools that are used for editing individual faces and edges of a 3D solid.

✦ The **ribbon,** shown in Figure 2-2, enables you to access many of the different commands for creating, editing, navigating, and visualizing 3D models. These commands are organized on different tabs:

   • The Home tab has tools that allow you to create, modify, and view 3D objects.

   • The Visualize tab has tools that allow you to add lighting, materials, and visual styles to a model.

   • The View tab has tools that allow you to work with the UCS, viewports, and 3D palettes.

   • The Output tab has tools that allow you to render a 3D model.

Figure 2-2:
The ribbon
gives you
quick access
to a variety
of 3D-related
tools.

AutoCAD provides other toolbars and palettes that are useful for working
with various aspects of 3D. Many of these palettes and toolbars are discussed in later chapters of this minibook.

The ribbon is new in AutoCAD 2009 and allows you to access both 2D and
3D drafting commands, along with other 3D features. The ribbon can also be
found in AutoCAD LT 2009 but does not display 3D-related commands.

Accelerating your hardware

AutoCAD can use either software or hardware acceleration to display the
graphics in the drawing window. AutoCAD LT, however, does not support
hardware acceleration. By default, AutoCAD will attempt to use hardware
acceleration (because some graphics cards are not designed for CAD applications, AutoCAD may default to software acceleration right out of the gate).
AutoCAD might choose to use software acceleration based on your current
graphics driver; you can check to see if a later driver for your graphics card
is available by visiting the AutoCAD Certification Web site
(www.autodesk.com/autocad-graphicscard).

When you first start AutoCAD, the program evaluates your graphics card
and determines whether it can properly support hardware acceleration. If it
can, it informs you that your hardware is capable of this. At times your
graphics card might not support all features that use hardware acceleration,
so AutoCAD tweaks its display settings a little to help optimize regenerations
and the overall display quality of the objects in the drawing window. This
process is called *adaptive degradation.*

The Adaptive Degradation and Performance Tuning dialog box (see Figure
2-3) allows you to change the display options and toggle between the use
of software and hardware acceleration. To open this dialog box, open the
Options dialog box and click Performance Settings under the 3D Performance
section of the System tab. Click Manual Tune to toggle open the Manu
Performance Tuning dialog box, which allows you to enable hardware acceleration and change the options related to using hardware acceleration, such
as Full Shadow and Smooth Line display.

Figure 2-3:
Performance
tuning
AutoCAD
can help
it prrrr like
a kitten.

Understanding What the UCS Icon Is Telling You

The UCS icon is similar to a tour guide that helps you to stay on the right path (rather than the left I guess). The UCS icon doesn't tell you to stay with the tour and to keep up, but it does help you find the positive *x*, *y*, and *z* axes. It's important to know in which direction these axes are going when creating objects. It can get frustrating when you can't get your objects created in the right direction.

Orientating yourself with the UCS icon

The UCS icon can be strange at times depending on how you're viewing the drawing and whether you're in model or paper space. The UCS icon is a drafter's survivalist tool, much like any good hikers or campers venturing into the woods will have a compass with them. AutoCAD and AutoCAD LT display different UCS icons for different situations; understanding these situations is necessary to help maximize the use of the user coordinate system, which I talk about later in this chapter. The UCS icon lets you know how the coordinates you type at the command prompt are affected. The appearance of the UCS icon is affected by the current visual style or whether the current view is displayed as hidden or shaded. I talk about visual styles, hiding, and how to apply shading to a model in Chapter 3 of this minibook.

Model space and 2D wireframe visual style

When you're looking down at the *xy* (or working) plane, the UCS icon shows the positive direction for the *x* and *y* axes. If the current view of the *xy* (or working) plane is from an angle like one of the preset isometric views, you'll see the *x, y,* and *z* axes called out. Figure 2-4 shows the UCS icon as it appears when looking at the *xy* (or working) plane straight on and from an angle. If you don't see a box at the intersection of the *x* and *y* indicators, this informs you that you are not looking at the drawing from the world coordinate system but instead at a user-defined coordinate system, as shown in the rightmost image of the UCS icon.

Figure 2-4:
UCS icon
displayed in
model space
with 2D
wireframe
visual style.

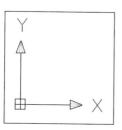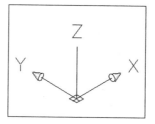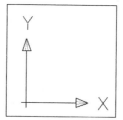

Model space and a 3D visual style

When you're looking down at the *xy* (or working) plane, the UCS icon shows the positive direction for the *x* and *y* axes, and the *z* direction coming toward or moving away from you. If the current view of the *xy* (or working) plane is from an angle like one of the preset isometric views, you'll see the *x, y,* and *z* axes called out. Figure 2-5 shows the UCS icon as it appears when looking at the *xy* plane straight on and from an angle.

Figure 2-5:
UCS icon
displayed
in model
space with
one of the
3D visual
styles.

Paper space layout

On a paper space layout, the UCS icon appears as a triangle and indicates the directions of the positive *x* and *y* axes only (see Figure 2-6). You can't change the display angle of a paper space layout because this layout is used to represent a virtual piece of paper and is not used for modeling.

Figure 2-6:
UCS icon
displayed
on a paper
space
layout.

Controlling the display of the UCS icon

The UCS icon by default has a 3D appearance to it and is displayed with a specific size, color, and location. You can tailor the display of the UCS icon with the UCS Icon dialog box (see Figure 2-7) and the 3D Modeling tab of the Options dialog box. To display the UCS Icon dialog box: From the menu browser or menu bar, choose View menu⇨Display⇨UCS Icon⇨Properties.

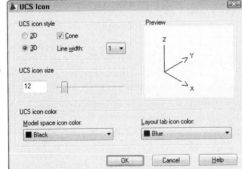

Figure 2-7:
You can
change the
appearance
of the UCS
icon here.

You can control where and if the UCS icon is displayed on-screen by using the following options:

✦ **Hide/Show the UCS icon:** You can toggle the display of the UCS icon. On the menu browser or menu bar, click View menu⇨Display⇨UCS Icon⇨On.

✦ **Display the UCS icon at the origin:** You can toggle the display of the UCS icon at the origin of the drawing. On the menu browser or menu bar, click View menu⇨Display⇨UCS Icon⇨Origin. If the UCS can't be displayed at the origin, AutoCAD places it in the lower-left corner of the drawing window.

✦ **Display the UCS icon in 2D or 3D visual styles:** You can control whether the UCS icon is displayed when the model is being viewed with a 2D or 3D visual style. This option is available only in AutoCAD, and not in

AutoCAD LT. To control the display of the UCS icon in 3D, display the Options dialog box, click the 3D Modeling tab, and uncheck the Display in 3D Model Space — Display UCS Icon check box in the Display ViewCube or UCS Icon section. In the same section, you can also control the display of the UCS icon in 2D model space by selecting or not selecting the Display UCS Icon in 2D Model Space option.

Using the Coordinate System for 3D Drawing

The coordinate system in AutoCAD is powerful and can be mysterious at times. When you are drawing in 2D, you don't worry too much about altering the coordinate system. When working in 3D, it becomes important to know how to properly alter and use the coordinate system. By altering the coordinate system, you can draw objects going in different directions or on the sides of other objects. For example, you can draw an object on the *xy* (working) plane and then move or rotate the object into place, but that would take some effort. By relocating the origin and direction of the coordinate system, you can draw the object as if the object were on the *xy* (working) plane.

Right-hand rule for left-brained people

When you first look at the coordinate system in 3D, you may feel a little overwhelmed, which is understandable. After all, the UCS can be moved and rotated. So at times you may not know which way you are heading in the *z* direction or which way around an axis is the positive angle of rotation. AutoCAD provides a method called the *right-hand rule* that you can apply when you need to figure out the direction of positive *z* and the positive angle of rotation.

To identify the positive *z* axis with the right-hand rule, you place the back side of your right hand toward the monitor so that your palm is facing you. Take your thumb and point it in the direction of the positive *x* axis, and then take your index finger and extend it out so it forms a right angle with your thumb. Make sure that your index finger points in the direction of the positive *y* axis. Bend your middle finger toward you so it makes a right angle with your index

finger. Your middle finger now indicates the positive direction of the *z* axis. To identify the direction of positive rotation around an axis in 3D space, point your thumb on your right-hand in the positive direction of the axis and then curl your fingers. The direction that your fingers curl in indicates the positive direction of rotation around that axis.

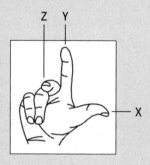

Understanding the coordinate system

AutoCAD has two coordinate systems: *world* and *user*. You use both coordinate systems when creating new objects in a drawing.

World coordinate system (WCS)

The world coordinate system, or WCS, is a fixed coordinate system that all objects in a drawing are stored and defined to. By default in 2D views, the x axis runs horizontal (left and right) and the y axis runs vertical (up and down). Positive x is to the right and positive y is up. Unlike the user coordinate system, the WCS can't be moved or redefined.

User coordinate system (UCS)

The user coordinate system, or UCS, is a movable coordinate system and is much more flexible for creating and editing objects. The UCS affects coordinate entry, drafting aids (object snap tracking, dynamic input, grid, and others), and the orientation of dimensions and text.

Adjusting the UCS

AutoCAD offers a variety of ways to create and save custom UCSs for future use. When you want to create a new UCS, you have some options as to how you want to create it, such as by selecting three points in the drawing to indicate origin, positive x, and positive y, or selecting an object. After you specify a new UCS, you can decide to save it for future use by giving it a name.

Commanding the UCS

The user coordinate system can be changed through the use of the UCS command. To make it easy to create a new UCS, AutoCAD offers a number of options that you can choose from the New UCS submenu under the Tools menu on the menu browser. The New UCS submenu has 11 choices, but the command prompt offers a few more. I've listed some of the most commonly used options of the UCS command to get you started. After the option is specified, follow the displayed prompts. For more information on using the UCS options, refer to AutoCAD's online Help system.

✦ **World:** Changes the UCS to match the world coordinate system.

✦ **Face:** Allows you to align the UCS to the face of a 3D solid.

✦ **View:** Creates a new UCS by rotating the xy plane to being perpendicular to your current viewing direction.

✦ **3 Point:** Allows you to specify a new origin for the UCS and designate the positive direction for both the x and y axes.

Using named UCSs

If you find yourself going back to a particular UCS to create or edit objects, you might consider saving the UCS for future use. To save a UCS that you created, you use the UCSMAN command, which displays the UCS dialog box (see Figure 2-8). The UCS dialog box lets you save and restore named UCSs on the Named UCSs tab, customize the distance between the *xy* plane of the six orthographic coordinate systems (top, bottom, front, back, left, and right) on the Orthographic UCSs tab, and control some of the save and display settings for UCSs on the Settings tab.

In AutoCAD 2009, you can also use ViewCube to create and restore named UCSs. ViewCube is a new modeless feature that allows you to not only work with named UCSs but also identify and change the current orientation of a model. I cover ViewCube more in Chapter 3 of this minibook.

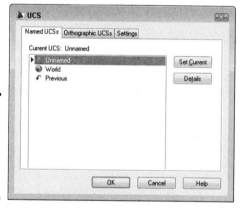

Figure 2-8:
Saving a custom UCS with the UCS dialog box.

The following steps create a UCS by rotating the UCS 45 degrees around the *z* axis and then save it by using the UCS dialog box:

1. **On the ribbon, choose click View tab⇨UCS panel⇨Z.**

The command displays the prompt

```
Specify rotation angle about Z axis <90>:
```

2. **Type 45 and press Enter.**

The UCS is rotated 45 degrees. Now any object drawn at 0 degrees is actually drawn at 45 degrees.

3. **On the ribbon, click View tab⇨UCS panel⇨Named.**

The UCS dialog box is displayed.

4. **In the UCSs list, select Unnamed.**

The Unnamed UCS is the current UCS in the drawing and is listed at the very top of the list.

5. **Right-click Unnamed and choose Rename from the shortcut menu.**

An in-place editor is displayed that allows you to change the UCSs name.

6. **Type a new name for the UCS and press Enter.**

The Unnamed UCS is renamed with the name you entered.

7. **Click OK.**

The UCS dialog box closes and the UCS is saved in the drawing. To use a saved UCS, open the UCS dialog box and then select the saved UCS from the list and click Set Current.

Using the dynamic UCS feature

Setting up a UCS takes a bit of effort and can be distracting if you need to create one just to draw an object on the side of a 3D object. AutoCAD allows you to create a UCS on-the-fly by using the dynamic UCS feature. This feature can save you a great deal of time and is easy to toggle on and off by clicking the dynamic UCS (or DUCS) button on the status bar. For example, when dynamic UCS is turned on, you can start the CYLINDER command and position the crosshairs over one of the faces of a box to draw a hole in the box. The face that is being tracked is highlighted, and when you click to start drawing the cylinder, the UCS jumps to the face until you are finished with the command. Figure 2-9 shows the use of the dynamic UCS in action.

Figure 2-9:
Dynamic
UCS makes
creating
objects
directly on
solids easy.

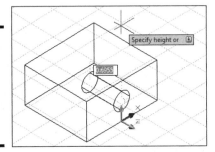

Dynamic UCS is not available in AutoCAD LT 2009.

Chapter 3: Viewing in 3D

In This Chapter

✔ **Establishing a different view of a 3D model**

✔ **Orbiting around a 3D model**

✔ **Navigating a 3D model**

✔ **Adding a touch of visual style to a 3D model**

*I*n this chapter, I immerse you into the world of 3D in AutoCAD as I explain how to navigate and view 3D models. AutoCAD and AutoCAD LT offer a number of ways to view 3D models. These include basic preset views as well as more sophisticated viewing tools, such as orbit and walk, which are available only in AutoCAD. After you have a model displayed the way you want, you can apply a visual style or a shade mode to make the objects appear hidden or shaded, respectively, on-screen.

Expressing Your Point of View

AutoCAD offers what seems like an endless number of ways to view a 3D model, while AutoCAD LT offers a basic set of 3D navigation tools for viewing a 3D model. I cover all the available 3D navigation tools in this section.

Using preset views

Both AutoCAD and AutoCAD LT offer some standard preset views that can help you view different sides of a 3D model quickly. The presets include being able to view a 3D model from the top, left, and southeast. If the presets don't offer what you need, you can use the Viewpoint Presets dialog box to get a little more control over the viewpoint.

Specifying a standard view preset

AutoCAD and AutoCAD LT have a total of ten preset views. Six of these preset views are parallel (or orthographic) to the current UCS — top, bottom, left, right, front, and back — and four are isometric views — southwest (SW) isometric, southeast (SE) isometric, northeast (NE) isometric, and northwest (NW) isometric. The presets are available in several ways:

♦ From the 3D Views submenu on the View menu on the menu bar or menu browser

♦ From the Preset Views node under the Views tree in the View Manager dialog box

♦ On the ribbon or the View toolbar, by clicking Home tab⇨View panel⇨Views drop-down list

Select one of the presets to start the VIEW command and use the option that matches the chosen preset.

The ViewCube allows you to set preset views as current by clicking one of its corners, faces, or edges. I cover the ViewCube later in this chapter. It is not available in AutoCAD LT.

Changing with the Viewpoint Presets dialog box

The Viewpoint Presets dialog box (see Figure 3-1) gives you more control over the viewing angle than the preset views do. To display the Viewpoint Presets dialog box, from the menu browser click View menu⇨3D Views⇨ Viewpoint Presets. To change the angle, select either the Absolute to WCS or Relative to UCS option. Specify the angle from the x axis by entering a value in the From: X Axis text box or by selecting the angle on the dial itself. After you set the x axis, specify the angle from the xy (working) plane by entering a value in the From: XY Plane text box or from the dial on the right. Values above 0 allow you to look down on the model; values below 0 allow you to look up at the model as if you were looking up at a building.

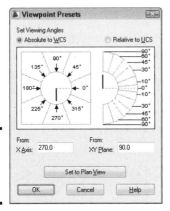

Figure 3-1:
Control the viewing angle.

Finding your way with the compass and tripod

The preset views and the Viewpoint Presets dialog box are nice, but they don't provide a visual way to set a viewpoint. The VPOINT command allows you to see the current UCS via an axis tripod and a circular display known as the *compass* in the upper-right corner of the drawing window (see Figure 3-2). This allows you to specify the angle from the *x* axis and *xy* plane like the Viewport Presets dialog box does but is also visual and interactive. Although changing the viewpoint is visually done on-screen rather than by using a dialog box, it can still be a bit confusing.

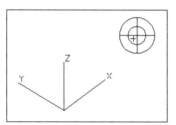

Figure 3-2:
Using the tripod and compass for navigation.

To select an angle above 0, keep the small crosshairs in the inner circle, which represents a positive *z* axis (the outer circle represents a negative *z* axis). Where the inner and outer circles meet is 0, or no change in the *z* axis direction. The compass and tripod are the most advanced 3D navigation tools in AutoCAD LT. But if you're using AutoCAD, you'll most likely never want to use them, preferring the newer and better tools that I explain later in this chapter.

Cameras

Cameras are similar to named views, with the exception that they have a graphical representation in a model and can be updated via the Properties palette. Along with using the Properties palette, you can also edit a camera's properties through the View Manager dialog box. The graphical representation of a camera is referred to as a glyph. *Glyphs* allow you to manipulate the object they represent (in this case a camera) by using standard modify commands such as MOVE, COPY, and ERASE, along with grip editing.

AutoCAD LT does not support the creation or use of cameras. Cameras also do not appear in the drawing window when a drawing file containing cameras is opened.

Creating a camera

To create a camera, you use the CAMERA command. To start the CAMERA command, do one of the following:

✦ On the menu browser or menu bar, click View menu⇨Create Camera.

✦ On the ribbon or the View toolbar, click Home tab⇨View panel⇨Create Camera.

✦ In the Tool Palettes window, click the Cameras palette and then one of the camera tools.

As you create a camera, you are prompted for the location of the camera and a target point. After the camera is created, you can change its name, location, height, target, lens, or clipping, or switch to the cameras view. After the camera is created, the glyph is displayed in the drawing.

You can control the display of camera glyphs in AutoCAD by using the system variable CAMERAGLYPH. Set CAMERAGLYPH to 0 to turn off the display of camera glyphs, and 1 to turn on the display.

Adjusting the view of a camera

To adjust the view of a camera, you select its glyph in the drawing and then adjust it by using the grips that are displayed. The grips let you adjust the distance between the camera and target, along with the lens length of the camera. When a camera is selected, the Camera Preview dialog box (see Figure 3-3) should be displayed, which lets you see what the camera is seeing without switching to the camera's view. If the Camera Preview dialog box isn't displayed when you select a camera in the drawing, right-click and select View Camera Preview on the shortcut menu.

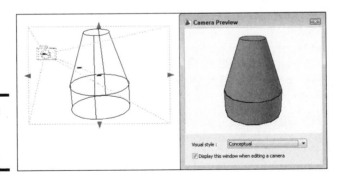

Figure 3-3:
Editing a
camera in
the scene.

Perspective versus parallel

AutoCAD and AutoCAD LT can display a 3D model in parallel view, which makes a 3D model appear flat and without depth, or in a perspective view, which makes a 3D model seem to disappear into the distance and have depth. Figure 3-4 shows a rectangle displayed in both parallel and perspective view. When you look at objects in real life, you see things in a perspective view. To enable perspective view in a drawing, type **PERSPECTIVE** at the command prompt and press Enter, and then type **1** and press Enter. Perspective view is available only when a visual style or shade mode other than 2D wireframe is active. We talk about visual styles and shade mode later in this chapter.

Figure 3-4:
A rectangle in both parallel and perspective view.

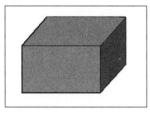
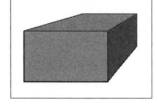

Parallel view   Perspective view

Orbiting around a 3D Model

AutoCAD comes with many commands that allow you to navigate around a 3D model. Being able to rotate the viewpoint around a 3D model allows you to quickly see things from a different angle and make the necessary edits. The ability to rotate the viewpoint around a 3D model is called *orbiting,* like what planets do around the sun. Orbiting is done along a circular path; the rotation point is different based on the orbit command you choose to use. To access the 3D orbit commands, do one of the following:

✦ On the menu browser or menu bar, click View menu⇨Orbit and then click one of the Orbit commands.

✦ On the ribbon or the Orbit toolbar, click Home tab⇨View panel⇨Orbit flyout and then click one of the Orbit commands.

AutoCAD LT does not support the 3D orbit commands.

Table 3-1 lists the three 3D orbit commands available in AutoCAD.

Table 3-1		3D Orbit Commands
Icon	*Command*	*Description*
⟟	3DORBIT	Constrained Orbit sets the target to a stationary point at the center of the objects you are viewing when the 3DORBIT command starts. Dragging horizontally moves the camera along the current *xy* (working) plane, and dragging vertically moves the camera along the *z* axis.
⊘	3DFORBIT	Free Orbit sets the target of the view to the center of the displayed arcball. The arcball (see Figure 3-5) controls how the view is rotated around its center rather than the center of the objects you are viewing. Dragging inside the arcball allows you to freely rotate the model, whereas dragging on the outside of the arcball rolls the model perpendicular to the screen. Clicking and dragging in the left or right quadrants (small circles) causes the model to rotate around the vertical axis of the arcball, and clicking and dragging in the top or bottom quadrants (small circles) causes the model to rotate around the horizontal axis of the arcball.
⊘	3DCORBIT	Continuous Orbit is similar to Constrained Orbit in the way it works, except you can send the model into a continuous orbit that lasts until you stop it.

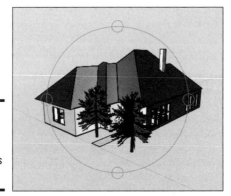

Figure 3-5:
The Free Orbit command is active.

While one of the 3D orbit commands (or any of the other 3D navigation commands that I mention in the next section) is active, you can right-click and access the Navigation Modes menu (see Figure 3-6). This menu allows you to switch between parallel and perspective projection modes, between different visual styles, or even to other navigation commands without having to exit one command to start another. You can also switch to a different navigation command by pressing the number next to it in the Other Navigation Modes submenu.

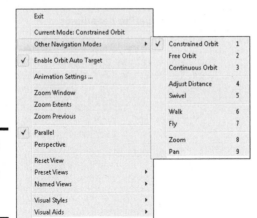

Exit			
Current Mode: Constrained Orbit			
Other Navigation Modes ▶	✓ Constrained Orbit	1	
✓ Enable Orbit Auto Target	Free Orbit	2	
	Continuous Orbit	3	
Animation Settings ...			
	Adjust Distance	4	
Zoom Window	Swivel	5	
Zoom Extents			
Zoom Previous	Walk	6	
	Fly	7	
✓ Parallel	Zoom	8	
Perspective	Pan	9	
Reset View			
Preset Views ▶			
Named Views ▶			
Visual Styles ▶			
Visual Aids ▶			

Figure 3-6:
The
Navigation
Modes
menu.

If you hold down the Shift key *first* and then press and hold down the middle mouse button, you can temporarily switch to 3DORBIT. Pressing and holding the middle mouse button and then pressing the Shift key temporarily places you in orthogonal pan mode.

If the drawing contains a lot of objects, you can select a small set of the objects to isolate them before starting one of the 3D orbit commands. This can help with performance in larger drawings because only the selected objects appear while the 3D orbit command is in use.

Navigating a 3D Model

AutoCAD offers other 3D navigation commands besides the 3D orbit commands. Chapter 5 of Book I describes the ZOOM and PAN commands; both of these commands also have specific 3D versions, but you can still use other zoom options such as window and extents. However, some additional commands are specific for 3D navigation. These commands, listed in Table 3-2, make it feel like you are right in your drawing. The 3D navigation commands can be accessed from the following:

✦ On the menu browser or menu bar, click View➪Camera➪Walk and Fly

✦ On the 3D Navigation toolbar, click Camera flyout➪Walk and Fly flyout.

AutoCAD LT does not support the 3D navigation commands listed in Table 3-2.

Table 3-2		3D Navigation Commands
Icon	*Command*	*Description*
	3DPAN	Allows you to interactively drag the view vertically, horizontally, and diagonally.
	3DZOOM	Allows you to move the camera closer to or farther away from the target, making objects appear closer or farther away.
	3DDISTANCE	Allows you to pull or push yourself in and out of the drawing by making objects come closer or go farther away from you.
	3DSWIVEL	Allows you to change the target of the view you are currently looking at in the drawing. This makes it feel as though you are turning your head around in the drawing to view other objects while standing in a single spot.
	3DFLY	Allows you to interactively change the view of the drawing as you "fly" through it. You leave the *xy* plane and feel as though you are above the drawing.
	3DWALK	Allows you to interactively change the view of the drawing as you "walk" through it. You remain on the *xy* plane and feel as though you are walking through the drawing.

When using one of the 3D navigation commands, you can right-click and choose a different navigation mode from the shortcut menu.

Hugging the Corners with the SteeringWheels

The SteeringWheels feature integrates several 2D and 3D navigation tools into a single user interface. I cover working with the 2D Navigation wheel, the only wheel in AutoCAD LT, in Chapter 3 of Book II. AutoCAD has three additional wheels, which contain 3D navigation tools:

+ **View Object:** Center a model in the drawing window, zoom in and out, or orbit around a model.

+ **Tour Building:** Move the viewpoint forward and backward, look around, and change the elevation of the viewpoint up and down.

+ **Full Navigation:** Access most of the tools on the 2D Navigation, View Object, and Tour Building wheels in addition to walking or flying through a model.

All the wheels offer the Rewind tool, which I describe in Chapter 3 of Book II. To display one of the 3D-related wheels, start the NAVSWHEEL command and then right-click. From the menu, choose Full Navigation Wheel, or Basic Wheels⇨View Object Wheel or Tour Building Wheel. The 3D wheels can also be displayed in a smaller (or mini) version, which can be selected by right-clicking and choosing one of the options that starts with *Mini*.

When using a tool from a 3D wheel, you'll see indicators that display the current value and possible range of values along with tool messages that help you with the type of input that is being requested to use the tool. Many of the 3D navigation tools work similarly to their 3D command counterparts; for example, the orbit and walk tools are similar to 3DORBIT and 3DWALK. To find out more about the specific tools on the wheels, see AutoCAD's online Help. To display help specific to the wheels, right-click when a wheel is displayed and choose Help from the shortcut menu.

Cube with a View

AutoCAD comes with a new feature called the ViewCube. (The feature is not available in AutoCAD LT.) The ViewCube (see Figure 3-7) is an interactive modeless tool that provides visual feedback about the current viewpoint. It also allows you to set a preset view current, orbit the model, restore a named UCS, and define and restore the Home view of a model.

Home icon

Figure 3-7:
The
ViewCube
identifies
the current
viewpoint
and more.

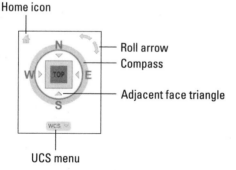

Roll arrow
Compass

Adjacent face triangle

UCS menu

To change the view of the model by using the ViewCube, you click a corner, a face, or an edge. Figure 3-8 shows what the ViewCube looks like after one of the three different areas on the ViewCube is clicked. The faces, edges, and corners allow you to switch to one of 26 preset views. In addition to clicking the ViewCube to set a preset view, you can click and drag the ViewCube to orbit the model. Dragging the ViewCube gives you more freedom in defining the viewpoint of the model. When you click a face on the ViewCube to define an orthographic view, you can click the roll arrows to rotate the view 90 degrees or you can click one of the adjacent face triangles to switch to the adjacent orthographic view indicated by the triangle.

Figure 3-8:
ViewCube
offers 26
preset
views.

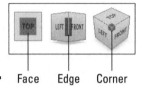

Face   Edge   Corner

The Home view of a model is a new concept in AutoCAD 2009. It's a special view that you can define so you have a known reference view in the model. The Home view can be used for the thumbnail preview of the drawing file when it's saved and can be restored from the ViewCube or SteeringWheels shortcut menu. To define the Home view, select the view you want by using the ViewCube or one of the other 3D navigation tools that AutoCAD offers, and then right-click the ViewCube and choose Set Current View as Home. To restore the Home view, right-click and choose Home, or click the Home icon.

You can use the Home view for the thumbnail when saving a drawing file by clicking the Thumbnail Preview Settings button on the Open and Save tab of the Options dialog box. Then select Use Home View in the Drawing section in the Thumbnail Preview Settings dialog box; make sure the Save a Thumbnail Preview Image option is also selected.

In addition to changing the view of a model, you can do the following:

✦ Change the current projection mode by choosing Parallel, Perspective, or Perspective with Ortho Faces. The Perspective with Ortho Faces option uses perspective projection unless a face view is active, in which case parallel projection is used. The other two options work as I describe earlier in the chapter.

✦ You can control the behavior and display of the ViewCube by using the ViewCube Settings option. When the option is selected, the ViewCube Settings dialog box is displayed.

Adding Color and Style to a 3D Model

Looking at drawings displayed in 2D and 3D wireframe can make it difficult to visualize what is in there. AutoCAD and AutoCAD LT offer a few options to help you see what all those lines actually look like. AutoCAD uses *visual styles* to display geometry so you only see the objects that are in front of others. AutoCAD LT does not support visual styles but instead has a feature called *shade modes*. Shade modes were available in releases of AutoCAD prior to AutoCAD 2006 to hide faces that are beyond those closest to the current viewpoint.

Visual styles in AutoCAD

Visual styles allow you to see your drawing in a hidden, shaded, or semirendered state. Visual styles are available from the Visual Styles Manager palette or the Visual Styles panel on the Visualize tab of the ribbon. To display the Visual Style Manager palette (see Figure 3-9) you use the VISUALSTYLES command. To start the VISUALSTYLES command: From the menu browser or menu bar, choose Tools menu➪Palettes➪Visual Styles. Double-click one of the available visual styles to set it current. You can also make a custom visual style and make changes to it by changing its properties in the lower part of the palette. You can set a visual style current when drawing to give you a sense of which lines you might want to snap to.

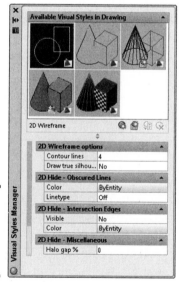

Figure 3-9:
Visual styles
give a 3D
model
personality.

Figure 3-10 shows the Visual Styles (left) and Edge Effects (right) panels on the Visualize tab of the ribbon. These panels contain a variety of controls that allow you to change visual styles, enable *x*-ray mode to see through faces, control how faces and edges are displayed, and even control the display of shadows in a scene. To find more about visual styles, see AutoCAD's online Help.

Figure 3-10:
The Visual
Styles and
Edge Effects
panels of
the ribbon.

Shademode in AutoCAD LT

AutoCAD LT doesn't support the use of visual styles, but you can do a few
things to get a similar effect when viewing a 3D model. AutoCAD LT offers a
command called SHADEMODE, which allows you to view a model in 2D wireframe or hidden line view. SHADEMODE is similar to a visual style in most
ways, except you can't customize its appearance. AutoCAD LT also offers
the SHADE command, which allows you to shade a 3D model based on the
colors that the objects are assigned, and you can use the HIDE command to
display a 3D model in a hidden line view. The SHADE and HIDE commands
are available from the View menu on the menu browser or menu bar. Type
SHADEMODE at the command prompt and then select the option you
want to use.

Chapter 4: Moving from 2D to 3D

In This Chapter

✔ Working with regions

✔ Understanding 3D polylines and helixes

✔ Creating 3D objects from 2D objects

✔ Creating 2D objects from 3D objects

✔ Using 3D modify commands

*N*ow that you know how to get around a drawing, it's time to create some objects. You start by creating 2D objects. (Yes, you read that correctly: 2D objects.) Although the result you want is a 3D model, you don't have to create everything by using just 3D objects. Taking what you already know about creating 2D objects and applying that knowledge to 3D modeling helps you feel more comfortable with using and working in 3D. AutoCAD also provides some tools that help you create 2D objects from a 3D model so you can generate the necessary shop drawings to get the model built.

At the end of this chapter, I cover some of the common 3D modify commands to help position, rotate, mirror, and array 3D objects. Most of this chapter applies to AutoCAD only (not AutoCAD LT) and is designed to give you an overview of the different commands that allow you to go from 2D to 3D and back again. (An entire book could be written on just working with AutoCAD 3D alone, and actually has been: *AutoCAD 2008 3D Modeling Workbook For Dummies.*) For more information on the commands in this chapter, refer to AutoCAD's online Help.

Before you read any farther, you'll want to set the 3D Modeling workspace current if it's not already. To do so, on the status bar choose Workspace Switching⇨3D Modeling. The 3D Modeling workspace allows you to access many of the 3D-related commands and settings from the ribbon.

Working with Regions

Regions are 2D objects that are created from closed shapes — or loops. A *loop* is a set of objects such as lines and arcs that form a closed object but are not necessarily closed objects themselves, such as circles, polylines, or splines. You can create a region from polylines, lines, arcs, circles, elliptical arcs, ellipses, and splines. Regions can be great for creating complex areas to hatch, and can be used to create 3D objects. You can obtain the centroid (the center point of the mass or volume of a region), the moment of inertia (the value used to calculate distributed loads), and other information about a region by using the MASSPROP command, like you can with 3D solids. For more information on the MASSPROP command, see the section "Getting more information about regions," later in this chapter.

Creating regions

Because regions are created from existing objects in a drawing, you first must create the closed objects or loops and then use the REGION command to generate a region from them. A region is created for each selected closed object or loop. You can start the REGION command on the menu browser or menu bar by clicking Draw menu⇨Region, on the ribbon by clicking Home tab⇨Draw panel⇨Region, or on the Draw toolbar by clicking the Region button. An example of the REGION command follows, along with the objects that were selected (see Figure 4-1):

```
Command: _region
Select objects: Select the closed objects or loops
Specify opposite corner: 8 found
Select objects: Press Enter
6 loops extracted.
6 Regions created.
```

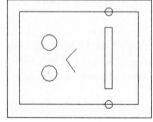

Figure 4-1:
Closed objects converted to regions.

When you use the REGION command (and some of the other commands covered in this chapter), the original objects that you select to create the region or 3D object from are deleted automatically. To keep the original objects from being deleted, set the DELOBJ system variable to a value of 0.

Modifying regions

Regions are interesting objects because they are no longer 2D objects, nor are they 3D objects, so you modify them in a slightly different way. Although regions are not 3D objects, you can use some of the 3D modify commands on them. If you want to remove a portion of a region with another region, you don't use the TRIM command; instead, you use the SUBTRACT command. You can use the EXPLODE command to convert a region back to 2D objects.

Union

Union allows you to combine two or more regions into a single region. In this way, you can create complex 2D objects that can later be extruded to create a 3D object. A great example of this is a metal plate that is used to keep an object in place or the side panel of a desk. You can start the UNION command on the menu browser or menu bar by clicking Modify menu⇨ Solid Editing⇨Union, on the ribbon by clicking Home tab⇨Solid Editing panel⇨Boolean flyout⇨Union, or on the Solid Editing toolbar by clicking the Union button. After the UNION command is started, select the regions to combine.

Subtract

Subtract removes a region from another region that it intersects or overlaps. This allows you to create holes, slots, or notches in regions before you extrude them to create a 3D object. You can start the SUBTRACT command on the menu browser or menu bar by clicking Modify menu⇨ Solid Editing⇨Subtract, on the ribbon by clicking Home tab⇨Solid Editing panel⇨Boolean flyout⇨Subtract, or on the Solid Editing toolbar by clicking the Subtract button. After the SUBTRACT command is started, select the regions to subtract from and then select the regions to subtract.

Intersect

Intersect allows you to keep only the closed area where two regions overlap or intersect. Using intersect is much more common when you are working with 3D solids. You can start the INTERSECT command on the menu browser or menu bar by clicking Modify menu⇨Solid Editing⇨Intersect, on the ribbon by clicking Home tab⇨Solid Editing panel⇨Boolean flyout⇨Intersect, or on the Solid Editing toolbar by clicking the Intersect button. After the INTERSECT command is started, select the regions you want to create a new region from, based on where all the selected regions intersect each other.

Getting more information about regions

Regions are complex objects that you can use to construct 3D solids or 2D objects for calculating additional information for a design, such as area and perimeter. The MASSPROP command allows you to obtain more information about a 2D region or 3D solid than what the LIST command displays. To start the MASSPROP command from the menu browser or menu bar, click Tools menu⇨Inquiry⇨Region/Mass Properties. An example of the MASSPROP command is

```
Command: _massprop
Select objects: Select a region(s)
Specify opposite corner: 1 found
Select objects: Press Enter
--------------- REGIONS ---------------
Area:                        37.3681
Perimeter:                   26.4645
Bounding box:        X: 15.9560  --  24.1580
                     Y:  6.3739  --  11.4041
Centroid:            X: 19.7700
                     Y:  9.0755
Moments of inertia:  X: 3150.3487
                     Y: 14801.8030
Product of inertia:  XY: 6725.9145
Radii of gyration:   X:  9.1818
                     Y: 19.9025
Principal moments and X-Y directions about centroid:
                     I: 68.9979 along [0.9864 0.1644]
                     J: 199.8441 along [-0.1644 0.9864]
Write analysis to a file? [Yes/No] <N>: Press Enter
```

3D Polylines and Helixes

Although a line object is not commonly thought of as a 3D object, a line can have a different starting and ending *z* coordinate value, which makes it a 3D command. The 3DPOLY command allows you to draw 3D polylines, and the HELIX command allows you to create 2D and 3D spirals. 3D polylines and helixes, like line objects, can also have varying *z* coordinate values without the need to change the current user coordinate system (UCS). For more information on the UCS, see Book V, Chapter 2.

3D polyline

3D polylines are similar to their 2D counterparts, except they support only straight segments and you can specify a different *z* coordinate value for the start and endpoint of a segment. You use the 3DPOLY command to create a 3D polyline. You can start the 3DPOLY command on the menu browser or menu bar by clicking Draw menu⇨3D Polyline, on the ribbon by clicking Home tab⇨Draw panel⇨3D Polyline, or on the Draw toolbar by clicking the 3D Polyline button.

Helix

You can use helixes to create 2D and 3D spirals, shown in Figure 4-2, which might be used to represent springs, coils, or even doorstops. To create a 2D helix, use a height value of 0. To create a helix (2D or 3D spiral) you use the HELIX command. You can start the HELIX command on the menu browser or menu bar by clicking Draw menu⇨Helix, on the ribbon by clicking Home tab⇨Draw panel⇨Helix, or on the Modeling toolbar by clicking the Helix button.

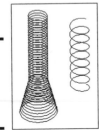

Figure 4-2:
Helixes can be used to create springs.

Creating 3D Objects from 2D Objects

AutoCAD's roots started with 2D drafting. That continues to be the primary focus of the program, but Autodesk has shifted to making sure that 3D is a key part of the program as well. Because AutoCAD started off being a 2D drafting package, you can take your knowledge of 2D drafting to create 3D objects with it. This section discusses many of the different commands that allow you to convert existing 2D objects into 3D objects. Some work with 2D profiles, whereas others might require you to first create a region or some sort of closed object. Everything in this section applies to AutoCAD only, with the exception of the Thickness section.

Thickness

Thickness is a property of most 2D objects, such as lines and circles. When you change the thickness of a 2D object, you are creating a surface out of the object, or a set of surfaces. These surfaces hide objects behind them, unlike wireframe models. If you add thickness to a circle, a cylinder is created that is capped on the top and bottom. Changing the thickness of a pline that has a width is a quick way to create a 3D wall. Thickness is also a system variable that can be set by typing **THICKNESS** at the command prompt and entering a new value. The current value of the THICKNESS system variable is assigned to each new object that is created.

Extrude

Extrude allows you to take an open or a closed 2D object and create a solid or surface out of it. When you extrude a closed 2D object such as a polyline, a spline, an ellipse, a circle, or a region, you create a solid. If you extrude an open 2D object such as a polyline, a spline, a line, an arc, or an elliptical arc, you create a surface. Figure 4-3 shows the results of extruding an open and a closed object. You can extrude a face on a solid by holding down the Ctrl key and selecting the face when asked to select objects to extrude.

Figure 4-3:
The results of extruding open and closed objects.

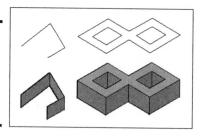

After you select the objects or faces you want to extrude, you specify a distance and direction to create the extrusion in. During the extrusion, you can select a path to extrude along, which can be a 2D object or an edge of a solid or surface. You can start the EXTRUDE command on the menu browser or menu bar by clicking Draw menu⇨Modeling⇨Extrude, on the ribbon by clicking Home tab⇨3D Modeling panel⇨Extrude, or on the Modeling toolbar by clicking the Extrude button.

 If you want to keep the original object that is used to create the extruded object, set the DELOBJ system variable to a value of 0.

Loft

 Loft allows you to create a solid or surface based on a series of specified cross sections. The cross sections are used to define the profile that is generated, and you must use a minimum of two cross sections for the loft. If you use open objects for the cross sections, the resulting loft is a surface; if you use closed objects for the cross sections, the resulting loft is a solid. You can loft objects along a path by using guides or just the selected cross sections (see Figure 4-4). You can start the LOFT command on the menu browser or menu bar by clicking Draw menu⇨Modeling⇨Loft, on the ribbon by clicking Home tab⇨3D Modeling panel⇨Loft, or on the Modeling toolbar by clicking the Loft button.

Figure 4-4:
The results of lofting objects, using only cross sections.

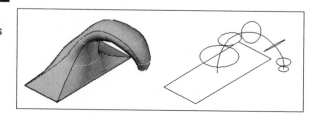

Sweep

Sweep is similar to Loft except you use a single cross section rather than two or more. The cross section defines the generated profile. If you use an open object for the cross section, the resulting sweep is a surface; if you use a closed object for the cross section, the resulting sweep is a solid. You sweep the selected objects along a path (see Figure 4-5). You can start the SWEEP command on the menu browser or menu bar by clicking Draw menu⇨Modeling⇨Sweep, on the ribbon by clicking Home tab⇨3D Modeling panel⇨Sweep, or on the Modeling toolbar by clicking the Sweep button.

Figure 4-5:
The results of sweeping objects along a path.

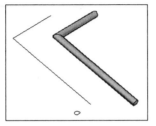

Revolve

Revolve allows you to create a solid or surface based on selected objects and a specified axis that they should revolve around. If you use open objects, the resulting revolve is a surface; if you use closed objects, the resulting revolve is a solid. You revolve the selected objects around an axis and specify the angle at which you want the objects to be revolved (see Figure 4-6). You can start the REVOLVE command on the menu browser by clicking Draw menu⇨Modeling⇨Revolve, on the ribbon by clicking Home tab⇨3D Modeling panel⇨Revolve, or on the Modeling toolbar by clicking the Revolve button.

Figure 4-6:
The results of revolving objects along an axis.

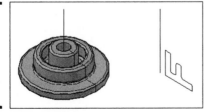

Creating 2D Objects from 3D Objects

AutoCAD allows you to make the transition from 2D to 3D without having to completely abandon what you already know about 2D drafting. Wouldn't it be nice to be able to create a 2D representation of a 3D model that you spent numerous hours creating? You're in luck: AutoCAD comes with commands that allow you to take a 3D model and generate a 2D representation of a given view. After you have a 2D representation of the 3D model, you can then add any dimensions and notes necessary for construction or manufacturing.

Flatshot

Flatshot allows you to create a block that contains 2D objects based on the current view of a 3D model. By creating the 3D model first, you can create a block that contains only the objects that are visible in a view, or include the obscured lines in a different color or linetype (see Figure 4-7). Flatshot looks for all 3D objects in the current view and ignores all 2D objects. To start the FLATSHOT command, on the ribbon, click Home tab⇨Solid Editing panel's title bar⇨Flatshot.

Figure 4-7: The results of creating three different views from one model with Flatshot.

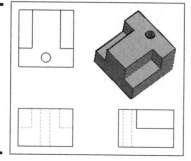

Section Plane

With Section Plane, you can cut a 3D solid without actually altering the object itself to generate a 2D or 3D object based on the geometry along the defined plane (see Figure 4-8). This allows you to quickly create different views of a model to help manufacture it or even assemble it. Unlike Flatshot, a Section Plane can go through an object and generate a 2D representation of the objects along the Section Plane.

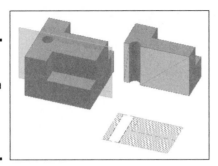

Figure 4-8:
The results
of creating a
2D and 3D
object from
a Section
Plane.

To create a 2D or 3D representation of the objects along a plane, you first start the SECTIONPLANE command on the menu browser or menu bar by clicking Draw menu⊏⊅Modeling⊏⊅Section Plane, or on the ribbon by clicking Home tab⊏⊅Solid Editing panel's title bar⊏⊅Section Plane.

After the Section Plane has been created, you have various options to control how the objects around the Section Plane are displayed. The display options can be accessed from the right-click shortcut menu or the Properties palette. To generate a 2D or 3D object from the Section Plane, you use the Generate Section/Elevation dialog box, which you display by clicking the section plane and choosing Generate 2D/3D Section from the shortcut menu.

Solid Draw, Solid View, and Solid Profile

Three older commands called Solid Draw (SOLDRAW), Solid View (SOLVIEW), and Solid Profile (SOLPROF) work similarly to the Flatshot (FLATSHOT) and Section Plane (SECTIONPLANE) commands. These three commands allow you to generate views of 3D models, but they work only in a layout with viewports. Solid Profile allows you to create a profile of a 3D object out of 2D objects, which can be helpful if you want to create an exploded view of a part for an illustration guide.

Solid View and Solid Draw are used with each other. You use Solid View to create a viewport and a specific set of layers; after the viewport is created, you display the 3D objects in the viewport that you want to convert to 2D objects with the Solid Draw command. Start the Solid Draw command and select the viewport. All hidden objects are placed on a specific layer along with other objects and layers that are created from the command (see Figure 4-9). To start the commands on the menu browser or menu bar, click Draw menu⊏⊅Modeling⊏⊅Setup⊏⊅Drawing, View, or Profile. On the ribbon, click Home tab⊏⊅3D Modeling panel's title bar⊏⊅Solid Draw, Solid View, or Solid Profile.

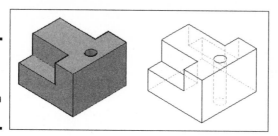

Figure 4-9:
The results
of using
SOLPROF on
a 3D object.

3D Modify Commands

Meshes, surfaces, and solids that make up 3D models can be modified
by using all the modify commands that you already know, such as ERASE,
MOVE, and ROTATE. However, AutoCAD also offers some modify commands
that are designed specifically for working in 3D. These specialized 3D
commands can be used on meshes, solids, surfaces, and even 2D objects.
You can locate all these commands on the menu browser or menu bar by
clicking Modify menu⇨3D Operations, or on the ribbon by clicking Home
tab⇨Modify panel.

3D Move

The 3D Move command allows you to move selected objects along the *xy*
(working) plane and in the *z* direction. This command uses what is called
a *grip tool* to allow you to restrict or constrain movement along an axis
(see Figure 4-10). The command prompts are identical to the MOVE command, so using the 3D Move command should feel familiar. You can start
the 3DMOVE command on the menu browser or menu bar by clicking
Modify menu⇨3D Operations⇨3D Move, on the ribbon by clicking Home
tab⇨Modify panel⇨3D Move, or on the Modeling toolbar by clicking the
3D Move button.

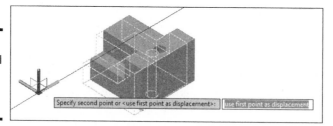

Figure 4-10:
The grip tool
for the
3DMOVE
command.

3D Rotate

The 3D Rotate command allows you to rotate selected objects along the *x*, *y*, or *z* axis. Like the 3D Move command, the 3D Rotate command uses a grip tool to allow you to restrict or constrain the rotation along an axis (see Figure 4-11). The command prompts are similar to the ROTATE command, with a few slight differences: You need to pick an axis for rotation, and then a start and end angle rather than just a rotation angle. You can start the 3DROTATE command on the menu browser or menu bar by clicking Modify menu⇨3D Operations⇨3D Rotate, on the ribbon by clicking Home tab⇨Modify panel⇨3D Rotate, or on the Modeling toolbar by clicking the 3D Rotate button.

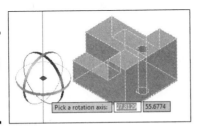

Figure 4-11:
The grip tool for the 3DROTATE command.

Align

The Align command can be used to align 2D and 3D objects based on one, two, or three pairs of points. Based on the number of point pairs that you select and how they are selected, the Align command might move or rotate or both move and rotate the selected objects into place. You start the ALIGN command on the menu browser or menu bar by clicking Modify menu⇨3D Operations⇨Align.

3D Align

The 3D Align command is an improved version of the ALIGN command that includes some additional options, including the ability to copy the selected objects instead of just moving and rotating them, and the ability to use dynamic UCS with the command. You can start the 3DALIGN command on the menu browser or menu bar by clicking Modify menu⇨3D Operations⇨3D Align, on the ribbon by clicking Home tab⇨Modify panel⇨3D Align, or on the Modeling toolbar by clicking the 3D Align button.

3D Mirror

The 3D Mirror command allows you to mirror objects along the xy plane like the standard MIRROR command does. But you can also specify the mirror plane by using a number of additional methods to define it: by three points, an existing object in the drawing, a previously defined mirror plane, the z axis, the current view, the xy plane, the yz plane, and the zx plane. The three-point option is the most common and is the default option. You can start 3DMIRROR command on the menu browser or menu bar by clicking Modify menu⇨3D Operations⇨3D Mirror, or on the ribbon by clicking Home tab⇨Modify panel⇨3D Mirror.

3D Array

The 3D Array command allows you to array objects along the xy plane (rows and columns) like the ARRAY command does, but it also allows you to array objects in the z direction (levels). You can create both rectangular and polar arrays with the 3D Array command just like you can with the ARRAY command. The 3D Array command doesn't use a nice dialog box like the ARRAY command does, so entering the correct values can be hard the first few times until you get used to the prompts. You can start the 3DARRAY command by clicking Modify menu⇨3D Operations⇨3D Array, on the ribbon by clicking Home tab⇨Modify panel⇨3D Array, or on the Modeling toolbar by clicking the 3D Array button.

Chapter 5: Working with Solids

In This Chapter

✔ Creating solid primitives

✔ Editing solids

In the previous chapter, I covered many of the commands that allow you to take the knowledge that you already have about 2D drafting and apply it to 3D modeling. In this chapter, you discover many of the 3D commands that allow you to create and edit 3D objects. AutoCAD allows you to create 3D objects known as primitives. *Primitives* are basic objects such as boxes, cones, and spheres that you can use to create complex objects. You also find out about additional modifying commands that are used to manipulate 3D solids.

Creating Solid Primitives

AutoCAD offers a pretty good variety of primitive 3D objects that you can use to create complex models. The primitive objects help to form the foundation of 3D modeling in AutoCAD: You can combine primitives together or even manipulate a primitive so that its edges are filleted, to shell or hollow out the inside of a 3D solid, and much more. Table 5-1 lists the commands that are used to create solid primitives.

Table 5-1		AutoCAD's Solid Primitives Commands			
Icon	*Ribbon*	*Toolbar*	*Menu*	*Command Name (Alias)*	*Function*
	Home tab⇨ 3D Modeling panel⇨ Polysolid	Modeling, Polysolid	Draw⇨ Modeling⇨ Polysolid	POLYSOLID (PSOLID)	Creates a 3D solid that is similar to a 2D polyline with a height
	Home tab⇨ 3D Modeling panel⇨3D Primitives flyout⇨Box	Modeling, Box	Draw⇨ Modeling⇨ Box	BOX	Creates a cube or 3D rectangle

(continued)

Table 5-1 *(continued)*

Icon	Ribbon	Toolbar	Menu	Command Name (Alias)	Function
	Home tab⇨ 3D Modeling panel⇨3D Primitives flyout⇨ Wedge	Modeling, Wedge	Draw⇨ Modeling⇨ Wedge	WEDGE (WE)	Creates a cube or 3D rectangle that has a height of zero along one side
	Home tab⇨ 3D Modeling panel⇨3D Primitives flyout⇨Cone	Modeling, Cone	Draw⇨ Modeling⇨ Cone	CONE	Creates a 3D object that has a circular or elliptical base and a height with a top radius that is equal to 0 or greater
	Home tab⇨ 3D Modeling panel⇨3D Primitives flyout⇨ Sphere	Modeling, Sphere	Draw⇨ Modeling⇨ Sphere	SPHERE	Creates a 3D object that has the same circumference in all directions
	Home tab⇨ 3D Modeling panel⇨3D Primitives flyout⇨ Cylinder	Modeling, Cylinder	Draw⇨ Modeling⇨ Cylinder	CYLINDER (CYL)	Creates a 3D object that has a circular or an elliptical base and top that have the same radius
	Home tab⇨ 3D Modeling panel⇨3D Primitives flyout⇨Torus	Modeling, Torus	Draw⇨ Modeling⇨ Torus	TORUS	Creates a circular 3D tubular object
	Home tab⇨ 3D Modeling panel⇨3D Primitives flyout⇨ Pyramid	Modeling, Pyramid	Draw⇨ Modeling⇨ Pyramid	PYRAMID (PYR)	Creates a 3D object that has a polygon-shaped base and a top radius of 0 or greater that is the same shape as the base unless the radius of the top is set to 0

Polysolid

A polysolid is similar to a 2D polyline, except it has a single uniform width and height when it is created. Polysolids are great for creating 3D walls when making a conceptual model of a building (see Figure 5-1) or for modeling rectangular duct work. To start the POLYSOLID command, use one of the methods in Table 5-1. After you start the POLYSOLID command, you can draw a polyline-like object that allows you to create both straight and curved segments. If you already have lines, arcs, and polylines in your drawing, you are able to convert those to solids with the Object option of the POLYSOLID command. You are also able to specify the height, width, and justification for the new solid object.

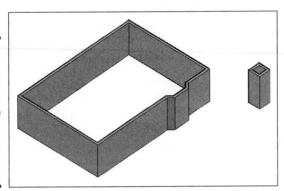

Figure 5-1:
The outline of a 2D floor plan converted to 3D walls with the POLYSOLID command.

Box

A box is a six-sided object that is either a cube or a 3D rectangle. A box can be used for virtually anything from a table (see Figure 5-2) to a door or even a building in the background of a conceptual model. To start the BOX command, use one of the methods in Table 5-1. After specifying the first corner or the center of the box, you can then finish defining the base of the box by selecting the opposite corner, by creating a cube, or by defining its length. Based on the option you select, you may need to define the box's height.

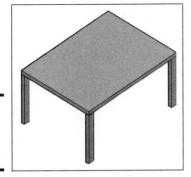

Figure 5-2:
A table created from boxes.

Wedge

A wedge is half a box diagonally from an upper edge to a lower edge (essentially a box that has a height of 0 on one edge). A wedge might be useful for creating a ramp, a roof slope, or even a slice of chocolate cake. Figure 5-3 shows some of the different sizes of wedges that can you can create with the WEDGE command. To start the WEDGE command, use one of the methods in Table 5-1. After specifying the first corner or the center of the wedge, you can then finish defining the base of the wedge by selecting the opposite corner, by creating a cube, or by defining its length. Based on the option selected, you may need to define the wedge's height.

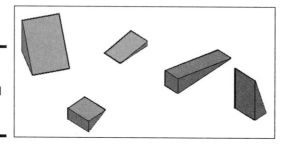

Figure 5-3:
Some
shapes and
sizes of
wedges.

Cone

A cone is an object with a circular base that has either a point or a flat top. The base of a cone can be larger than its top and even be elliptical rather than circular. You might use a cone for a handle or pull, a cup, or a planter. Figure 5-4 shows some of the sizes and types of cones that you can create with the CONE command. To start the CONE command, use one of the methods in Table 5-1. After specifying the center of the cone's base, you specify the radius or diameter of the base and then its height.

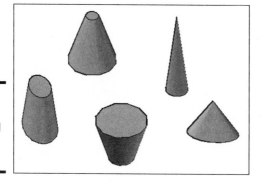

Figure 5-4:
Some
shapes and
sizes of
cones.

Sphere

A sphere is a full circular object that is created from the center of the object. The sphere is one of two types of 3D solids that are created half above and half below the current *xy* (working) plane (see Figure 5-5). Torus (which I discuss later in this chapter in the "Torus" section) is the other type of 3D solid created above and below the current *xy* (working) plane. To start the SPHERE command, use one of the methods in Table 5-1. After specifying the center of the sphere, you specify its radius or diameter.

Figure 5-5:
A sphere.

Cylinder

A cylinder is a circle or an ellipse with height and is commonly created from the center of the object. Cylinders can be used to represent a variety of features in a model, like the legs of a table or chair, glasses, or a shaft for a gear. Figure 5-6 shows some of the different sizes and types of cylinders that can be created with the CYLINDER command. To start the CYLINDER command, use one of the methods in Table 5-1. After specifying the center of the cylinder's base, you specify the radius or diameter of the base and then its height.

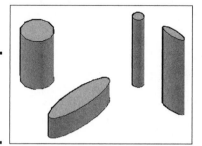

Figure 5-6:
Different
shapes and
sizes of
cylinders.

Torus

A torus is a 3D tubular object, similar to a cake donut, which is created from the center of the object. The torus, like the sphere, is created half above and half below the current *xy* (working) plane (see Figure 5-7). To start the TORUS command, use one of the methods in Table 5-1. After specifying the center of the torus, you specify its radius or diameter, and then the radius or diameter of the tube.

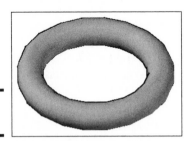

Figure 5-7:
A torus.

Pyramid

A pyramid is similar to a cone, except rather than a circular base, it has a polygon-shaped base that can have from 3 to 32 sides and either a point or a flat top with the same number of sides as the base. You might use a pyramid for the top of a building, the base of a street sign, or even a light fixture. Figure 5-8 shows some of the sizes and shapes of pyramids that you can create with the PYRAMID command. To start the PYRAMID command, use one of the methods in Table 5-1. After you specify the center or the edge of the pyramid's base, you specify the radius or use the inscribed option, and then its height.

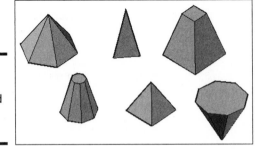

Figure 5-8:
Different shapes and sizes of pyramids.

Editing Solids

You can edit a solid in many ways, and some of these ways are not always easy to recognize. AutoCAD allows you to select a solid and use grip editing to modify certain characteristics of a solid, perhaps its height or base size. Along with being able to edit solids directly with grips, you can also manipulate faces and edges of a solid with the SOLIDEDIT command and by using the Ctrl key when selecting objects. You can edit a solid in many other ways, such as using the TRIM and FILLET commands.

Solid editing

The SOLIDEDIT command allows you to modify a face, an edge, or the entire body of a 3D solid. Based on how you want to edit a 3D solid, different options are available. Many of the options that are part of the SOLIDEDIT command are on the Solid Editing toolbar, the flyouts on the Solid Editing panel of the Home tab on the ribbon, or the Solid Editing submenu of the Modify menu on the menu browser or menu bar.

Table 5-2 lists the options of the SOLIDEDIT command and their uses.

Table 5-2	SOLIDEDIT Command Options	
Icon	*Command Option*	*Description*
	Edge, coLor	Allows you to specify a different color for an edge on a 3D solid.
	Edge, Copy	Allows you to create copies of the selected edges on a 3D object. The copied edges result in 2D objects such as lines and arcs.
	Face, Extrude	Allows you to extrude a selected face away or into the 3D solid that it belongs to.
	Face, Move	Allows you to move a selected face on a 3D solid. This works great for moving holes or notches in a face.
	Face, Offset	Allows you to offset a selected face on a 3D solid.
	Face, Delete	Allows you to delete a selected face, fillet, or chamfer on a 3D solid.
	Face, Rotate	Allows you to rotate a selected face on a 3D solid.

(continued)

Table 5-2 *(continued)*

Icon	Command Option	Description
	Face, Taper	Allows you to taper a selected face on a 3D solid. Tapering a face causes it to flare out based on the specified axis and angle provided.
	Face, coLor	Allows you to specify a different color for a face on a 3D solid.
	Face, Copy	Allows you to create copies of the selected faces on a 3D solid. The copied edges result in 2D regions being created for each selected face.
—		Face, mAterial Allows you to select faces on a 3D solid and apply a material to them.
	Body, Imprint	Imprints a 2D or 3D object onto a 3D solid. The object to be imprinted must intersect one or more faces of the 3D solid that it is to be imprinted on. After the object has been imprinted onto the solid, you can then extrude the new face that is created if the imprinted object creates a closed area on the 3D solid.
	Body, cLean	Scrubs the 3D solid and cleans up any redundant edges, vertices, and unused geometry.
	Body, seParate solids	Creates separate 3D solid objects based on any dis jointed volumes of a 3D solid; this does not separate Boolean objects with a single volume.
	Body, Shell	Hollows out a 3D solid based on a specified wall thickness. A positive offset distance creates the shell to the inside of the perimeter; a negative value creates the shell to the outside of the perimeter.
	Body, Check	Performs a validation on the 3D solid object to determine whether it is valid with ShapeManager.

Using grips to edit 3D solids

Grips are a powerful way to edit objects such as lines and arcs. You can also use grips to edit some of the characteristics of a 3D solid after it has been created in a drawing. To edit a 3D solid by using grips, select the 3D solid with no active command and then select the grip you want to use. Some grips allow you to change the overall size of the 3D solid, whereas others allow you to change part of the 3D solid such as its base or top in the case of a cone. Figure 5-9 shows a cone selected and its grips displayed.

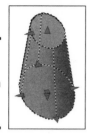

Figure 5-9:
Grips
displayed on
the selected
cone.

Starting with AutoCAD 2007, grip editing was greatly improved for editing 3D solids. In prior releases, you could use grips only to move 3D solids, but now you can modify a 3D solid after it's been created. The Properties palette also allows you to edit the properties of a 3D solid after it's been created in a drawing.

Complex solids

3D solids can be combined to form a complex object by using the UNION command. Along with being able to union 3D solids, you can also subtract 3D solids from a 3D solid with the SUBTRACT command. A 3D solid can also be created based on the intersection of two or more 3D solids with the INTERSECT command. For more information on these commands, see Chapter 4 of this minibook and the online Help system.

Filleting and chamfering

3D solids, just like 2D objects, can be filleted and chamfered. You use the FILLET and CHAMFER commands that you're already familiar with. Figure 5-10 shows a solid that has had its edges filleted and chamfered. To remove a fillet or a chamfer from a solid, you use the Delete Faces option of the SOLIDEDIT command.

Figure 5-10:
A 3D solid
before and
after it was
filleted and
chamfered.

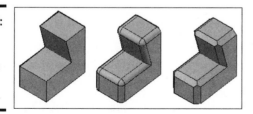

Slice

At times, you may want only a portion of the 3D solid for your model. In these cases, you can use the SLICE command. You can slice a 3D solid by using a planar object such as a circle, an ellipse, a 2D polyline, or a surface. You can keep both halves of the solid after it has been sliced, or whichever side you want to keep. Figure 5-11 shows a solid that has been sliced in half.

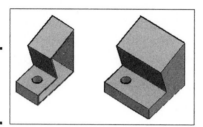

Figure 5-11:
A 3D solid sliced in half.

You can start the SLICE command on the menu browser or menu bar by clicking Modify menu⇨3D Operations⇨Slice, or on the ribbon by clicking Home tab⇨Solid Editing panel's title bar⇨Slice. After you specify the 3D solid to slice, you specify the axis or object you want to use as the cutting plane and then decide which part of the resulting object to keep.

Chapter 6: Rendering: Lights, Camera, AutoCAD!

In This Chapter

✏ **Adding lights into a scene**

✏ **Placing materials on objects**

✏ **Setting a background for a view**

✏ **Rendering a scene**

After you understand how to navigate, visualize, create, and edit 3D solid or surface models, you're ready to take your 3D model through the process of being rendered. *Rendering* allows you to visually present a concept to clients so they have an idea of what the final product will look like when it is manufactured or built. Hidden line and shaded views can help the client visualize a 3D model, but they lack the depth and realism that can really sell a concept. Before you generate a rendering, you add lights, materials, and a background to your 3D model. These visuals all help bring realism to a 3D model by making it look as much as possible like the final product. This chapter applies to AutoCAD only (sorry AutoCAD LT users) and is designed to be an overview of lights, materials, backgrounds, and rendering a model. For more information on these topics, refer to AutoCAD's online Help system.

Lighting a Scene

Lighting is a key to making your model — also known as a scene — look realistic because it generates variations of color in your model. Objects closest to the light source appear brighter and objects farther from the light source appear darker, giving your model depth. This is what happens in real life with light that comes from the sun or from a light bulb. AutoCAD offers three distinct types of lights: default lights, user lights (point, spotlight, web, and distant), and sunlight. All of these types of lights, except the default lights, can cast shadows. To help manage the creation and editing of lights, you use the Lights, Sun, and Time & Location panels on the ribbon, the Sun Properties palette, and the Lights in Model palette.

Default lights

Prior to AutoCAD 2007 there was a single default light, which always shone in the direction of the current view. Since AutoCAD 2007, there has been the option to use two default lights to help bring the level of lighting up and to balance the lighting on each side of the model. Default lighting does not cast shadows, so you should not use it for the final render, but it might be good enough for generating conceptual renderings. You do have some control over the brightness and contrast of the default lighting with the slider controls that are available when the Lights panel on the ribbon is expanded (see Figure 6-1).

Figure 6-1:
The Lights panel on the ribbon.

The DEFAULTLIGHTINGTYPE system variable controls whether you use one or two default distant lights. A value of 0 indicates to AutoCAD that one default light should be used, while a value of 1 indicates that two default lights should be used. Default lighting is enabled when the DEFAULTLIGHTING system variable is set to a value of 1.

User lights

User lights are lights that you add to a scene. When you place user lights in a scene, you need to disable the default lights that AutoCAD automatically creates when a drawing is open. AutoCAD supports two classifications of lights: generic and photometric. Generic lights give you more flexibility to determine how light is emitted from a user defined light, but photometric lights make it easier to represent lighting that you find in the real world. The LIGHTINGUNITS system variable determines whether generic or photometric lights are used when creating and modifying lights. When LIGHTINGUNITS is set to 0, generic lights are used. When LIGHTINGUNITS is set to 1 or 2, photometric lights are in use; 1 indicates American lighting units and 2 indicates International lighting units.

User lights come in four distinct types of lights:

+ **Point light:** A point light emits light in all directions, but the light decays or falls off the farther you get from the light. The falloff defines at what point no more light is emitted; by defining the falloff value of the light, you can reduce rendering time. You can think of a point light as similar to a candle or a lamp. Figure 6-2 shows four objects illuminated by a single point light. Point lights can be created with or without a target location. You create point lights by using the POINTLIGHT and TARGETPOINT commands.

Figure 6-2:
Point light
emitting
light and
casting
shadows on
objects in a
scene.

 ✦ **Spotlight:** A spotlight emits light in a specific direction in a cone shape and allows you to define the hotspot — the brightest part of the light — and the falloff of the light. A spotlight is like track lighting, recessed lighting, or a flashlight. Figure 6-3 shows four objects illuminated by a single spotlight. Spotlights can be created with or without a target location. You use the SPOTLIGHT and FREESPOT commands to create spotlights.

Figure 6-3:
Spotlight
emitting
light and
casting
shadows on
objects in a
scene.

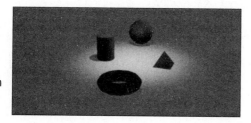

✦ **Weblight:** A weblight is a cross between a point and spotlight, but a weblight provides light distribution like you would find in the real world. Web lights always attenuate or support light falloff. One thing that makes weblights different from the other types of lights is that you can use them Web files containing photometric data provided by various lighting vendors. Figure 6-4 shows four objects illuminated by a single weblight. Weblights can be created with or without a target location. You create weblights by using the WEBLIGHT and FREEWEB commands.

Figure 6-4:
Weblight emitting light and casting shadows on objects in a scene.

 ✦ **Distant light:** A distant light emits light in a specific direction but doesn't have a hotspot or a falloff like a point light, spotlight, or weblight. A distant light is like the sun because it emits light all over every object that it's exposed to, so it's great for backdrop lighting that comes from behind a camera to fill a room with nondirect light. Figure 6-5 shows four objects illuminated by a single distant light. You use the DISTANTLIGHT command to create a distant light.

Figure 6-5:
Distant light emitting light and casting shadows on objects in a scene.

Don't use a distant light when using photometric lighting. If you decide to ignore AutoCAD's warning, be sure to turn down the intensity factor of the light.

When you add your first user-defined light to a scene, you're prompted by a task dialog box asking you to disable default lighting if it's not already disabled. Click Turn Off the Default Lighting command link to disable default lighting. You can toggle the use of default lighting on the ribbon by clicking Visualize tab⇨Lights panel⇨Default Lighting.

You can use the light commands that I previously mention in this section to create lights or you can use the LIGHT command. You can start the LIGHT command on the ribbon by clicking Visualize tab⇨Lights panel⇨ Lights flyout, or on the menu browser or menu bar by clicking View menu⇨ Render⇨Light and then one of the available options. After a light has been added to the scene, you can modify it with the Properties palette and by using grip editing.

Point lights, spotlights, and weblights can be selected and edited directly in a scene because a glyph is displayed to show where the light is located. Distant lights do not have associated glyphs. (A *glyph* is a nonprinting object displayed in a scene that enables you to modify an object that is not part of the actual model, such as a light or a camera.)

You can control the display of glyphs for lights by using the LIGHTGLYPHDISPLAY system variable. A value of 0 turns off the display of light glyphs, and a value of 1 displays light glyphs. You can also expand the Lights panel on the Visualize tab of the ribbon and click Light Glyphs.

If the scene is complex or you need to select a distant light in the scene, you need to use the Lights in Model palette (see Figure 6-6). The Lights in Model palette allows you to select, delete, and access the Properties palette for editing the selected light(s). To display the Lights in Model palette, use the LIGHTLIST command. You can start the command on the menu browser or menu bar by clicking Tools menu⇨Palettes⇨Lights, on the ribbon by clicking View tab⇨3D Palettes panel⇨Lights in Model, or on the Lights toolbar by clicking the Light List button.

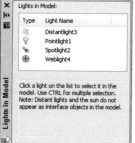

Figure 6-6: The Lights in Model palette.

The LIGHTSINBLOCKS system variable controls whether lights in blocks are used when rendering. When LIGHTSINBLOCKS is set to 0, lights in a block are disabled and not used when rendering. A value of 1 indicates to AutoCAD that lights in blocks should participate in the rendering process.

Sunlight

The ability to add light that is similar to sunlight is great for outdoor scenes or for indoor scenes with light coming in through a window. Sunlight is controlled through the Sun Properties palette (see Figure 6-7) and the Geographic Location dialog box (see Figure 6-8). Both interfaces allow you to designate the position of the sun based on the city that your scene is nearest to in the physical world, or at a specific latitude and longitude. You can also designate the northern direction of the scene to make sure that light is emitting on the scene as it would after it was built.

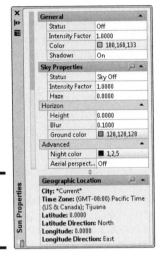

Figure 6-7:
The Sun
Properties
palette.

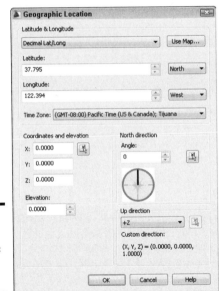

Figure 6-8:
The
Geographic
Location
dialog box.

With AutoCAD 2009 you can import location information from KML and KMZ files and import a location from Google Earth. You also still have the option of using the Geographic Location dialog box to define a location on Earth.

Getting the Right Look with Materials

Materials help to give your objects that special touch of realism, whether they're made up of metal, glass, plastic, or wood. Materials allow you to make the objects in a scene appear more convincing to the viewer. The MATERIALS command is used to display the Materials palette (see Figure 6-9), which allows you to create and edit materials based on a variety of properties such as transparency, shininess, or simply a color. After the material is created, you then apply it to the objects in your scene. Here are the three ways you can associate a material to objects in a scene:

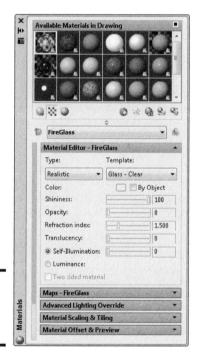

Figure 6-9:
The
Materials
palette.

+ **Materials by Layer:** Materials can be assigned to objects globally throughout a scene by assigning the material to a layer. Use the MATERIALATTACH command to assign a material to a layer in the scene.

+ **Materials by Object:** Materials can be assigned to individual objects in the scene by using the MATERIALASSIGN command and selecting the object or objects that you want to assign the material to or by changing the Material property of an object through the Properties palette.

✦ **Materials by Face:** Materials can be assigned to an individual face of a 3D solid by holding down the Ctrl key while using the MATERIALASSIGN command, or by using the SOLIDEDIT command and assigning a material, using the Material option under the Face option.

Setting Up a Backdrop

Backgrounds allow you to fill what looks like empty space beyond the 3D model in your scene. The background of a named view can be defined as a solid color, a gradient that consists of two or three colors, an image file, or a sky with a sun (only available when using photometric lighting). To set the background of a named view, change the Background Override property of the view in View Manager. To find more about working with named views, see Chapter 3 of Book II.

In View Manager, select the view whose background you want to change from the Views tree. You can only select views that are under the Model Views and Layout Views nodes. Next, under the General section, select the Background Override property. Then select the Background Override drop-down list and choose Solid, Gradient or Image to display the Background dialog box (see Figure 6-10) or Sun & Sky to display the Adjust Sun & Sky Background dialog box (see Figure 6-11). Specify the desired options in the dialog box and click OK. To set the view current and use the new background, select the view from the Views tree and click Set Current. When you exit the dialog box, the background is displayed along with the view that was selected.

With AutoCAD 2009 you can, once again, type BACKGROUND at the command prompt and press Enter to display the Background dialog box. This option was removed a few releases ago and has been reintroduced in this release.

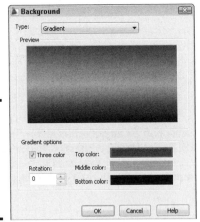

Figure 6-10:
The Background dialog box with Gradient selected.

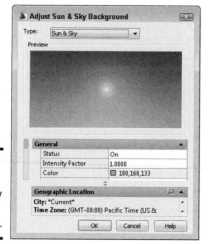

Figure 6-11:
Defining
Sun and Sky
for the
background.

Rendering the Final Scene

After you create your 3D model, put lights in the scene, create and apply materials, and put a background in the current view, you're ready to put it all together through the rendering process. During the rendering process, AutoCAD gathers all the materials and applies them to the objects and faces of your 3D model and calculates the light emitted in the scene and shadows. Rendering takes place by default in the Render Window dialog box (see Figure 6-12). You can start the RENDER command on the menu browser or menu bar by clicking View menu⇨Render⇨Render, on the ribbon by clicking Output tab⇨Render panel⇨Render, or on the Render toolbar by clicking the Render button.

Instead of rendering the entire scene to the Render Window, you can use the RENDERCROP command and specify the part of the current view that you want to render. This is a great way to test the lighting and shadows in a specific area of a scene without having to render everything. The rendering happens directly in the current viewport. You can start the RENDERCROP command on the ribbon by clicking Output tab⇨Render panel⇨Region.

When you create a rendering, you can select from five render presets to help speed up the rendering process. A render preset can be selected from the drop-down list on the Render panel of the Output tab on the ribbon. Render presets range from quick renderings with draft settings, which makes your objects appear grainy, to a presentation-quality preset, which can significantly increase rendering times while increasing the quality of the rendered output.

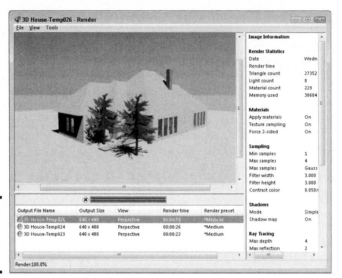

Figure 6-12:
The Render
Window
dialog box.

If the render presets don't offer the look you want, you can choose Manage Render Presets from the render presets drop-down list. Then you can create a copy of one of the render presets and customize it the way you want to. You can also use the Advanced Render Settings palette (see Figure 6-13) to customize and create a custom render preset. When you have the rendering settings that you want, you can then output the rendering to an image file from the Advanced Render Settings palette or the Render Window dialog box.

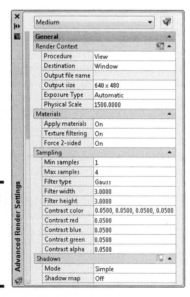

Figure 6-13:
The
Advanced
Render
Settings
palette.

In addition to rendering to a still image with the RENDER command, you can create a basic walkthrough of your model by using the ANIPATH command. The ANIPATH command displays the Motion Path Animation dialog box, which allows you to create a camera that moves around a fixed point or follows a path. As the command hints by its name, you can create an animation that can give your presentation an added edge over still images. When you create the animation, you can choose from the AVI, MPEG, and WMV file formats, the size and length of the animation, and the visual style that should be used. You can start the ANIPATH command on the menu browser or menu bar by clicking View menu⇨Motion Path Animations, on the ribbon by clicking Tools tab⇨ Animations panel⇨Animation Motion Path. To find out more about creating animations and rendering, see AutoCAD's online Help system.

Book VI

Advanced Drafting

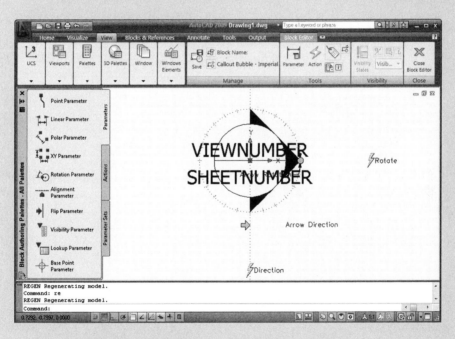

Blocks, parameters, and actions . . . Oh my.

Contents at a Glance

Chapter 1: Playing with Blocks 417

Working with Reusable Content 417
Creating Blocks 418
Inserting Blocks 422
Managing Blocks 424
Enhancing Blocks with Attributes 427

Chapter 2: Dynamic Blocks 433

What Makes a Block Dynamic? 433
Block Editor Environment 434
Going Dynamic 439
Using Dynamic Blocks 446
Dynamic Blocks in Older Releases 448

Chapter 3: External References 449

Blocks versus External References 449
Working with External References 450
Raster Images 462
DWF and DWFx Underlays 466
DGN Underlays 470
Draw Order 475
Object Linking and Embedding (OLE) 475
Managing External References Outside AutoCAD 476

Chapter 4: Organizing Your Drawings 479

Why Bother to Organize Drawings? 479
Using the Windows Clipboard 480
AutoCAD DesignCenter 482
Using the Tool Palettes Window 486

Chapter 1: Playing with Blocks

In This Chapter

✔ **Creating blocks**

✔ **Inserting blocks**

✔ **Managing blocks**

✔ **Using attributes to store information**

This minibook of the *AutoCAD 2009 & AutoCAD LT 2009 All-in-One Desk Reference For Dummies* takes a look at creating and managing reusable content. Reusable content is content that needs to be created only once and then can be used in many different drawings. The ability to reuse content was a huge advantage for those early drafters that dared to venture into the unknown world of CAD so many years ago. If you've ever had the pleasure of drafting on a board, you may have used plastic templates for things such as circles, furniture in a house plan, and mechanical fasteners. Those plastic templates allowed you to draw the same objects over and over without drawing them completely from scratch each time. As you will find out, blocks are AutoCAD's equivalent to plastic drafting templates, except they are much more powerful.

Working with Reusable Content

AutoCAD allows you to create geometry templates called blocks. A *block* is an object that is made up of many different objects and given a name to reference when you want to place the block in a drawing. Blocks are great for providing a consistent look to your drawings. You may have already used a block in your drawings for a border that contains a project name, date, and other information that relates to a particular drawing. Blocks can be defined with static or dynamic geometry, and contain elements called attributes, which can be used to store static text or allow users to enter their own text value. Attributes allow you to assign a varying text value that identifies a feature of the physical object that the block represents or to store information about the drawing. An attribute can have a different value for each block with the same name inserted into a drawing. Attributes are often used to store costing, descriptions, room numbers, and other information that you might want to extract out of a drawing. The extracted attribute information can be imported into an external application, such as Microsoft Excel, or even placed on a drawing as a table object.

Blocks are not the only form of reusable content in AutoCAD. AutoCAD can reference entire drawings and other files into a drawing, called *external referencing*. When a drawing file is referenced into another drawing, it is referred to as an *xref*. Xrefs allow you to share drawings with others who may need to ensure that their drawings match up with yours. For example, you can share a floor plan with the building systems contractor and the landscaper at one time. If the floor plan is used as an xref, the next time the drawing is opened by the contractors, the updates are displayed (of course, the contractors need the updated drawing file). AutoCAD is also capable of referencing raster images and DWF, DWFx, and DGN files.

Drawings often display schedules. Sometimes drafters create this information in a word processor or spreadsheet program. AutoCAD allows you to copy and paste content from Windows-based applications through the use of the Windows Clipboard, but doing so causes the information to become static. AutoCAD can keep some of this information dynamic through the use of Object Linking and Embedding (OLE).

Being able to reuse content has advantages, but being able to access that content quickly makes it even more valuable. AutoCAD provides two interfaces that allow you to organize and access content quickly; these interfaces are called DesignCenter and Tool Palettes window. For more information on DesignCenter and the Tool Palettes window, see Chapter 4 of this minibook.

Creating Blocks

Creating a block isn't all that difficult after you have the objects created that you want to combine into a block. Blocks can contain the same drawing and annotation objects that you add to a drawing file, such as rectangles, circles, arcs, dimensions and multiline text. Objects that are part of a block look just like individual objects drawn in a drawing.

AutoCAD allows you to create a block directly from the objects in a drawing without the need of doing much more. To create a block, you use the BLOCK command to display the Block Definition dialog box (see Figure 1-1). When you create a block, you need to know three things:

+ **Name:** The text string is used to identify the block and is used when inserting the block into the drawing.

+ **Base point:** The base point of a block helps place it into the drawing when you are inserting it. This point is usually established on an object that's selected when creating the block, but you don't have to use the same point to insert the block.

+ **Selected objects:** The objects used to define the way the block looks and behaves when inserted into a drawing.

Figure 1-1:
The Block
Definition
dialog box.

AutoCAD provides other options beyond these three that can be specified in the Block Definition dialog box, but the others alter the behavior of the block when it's placed into the drawing and aren't required to create a block. I explain the additional options available when creating a block in the "Exploring some advanced options" section later in this chapter.

Accessing the Block Definition dialog box

To start the BLOCK command and display the Block Definition dialog box, use one of the following methods:

✦ On the ribbon, click Blocks & References tab⇨Block panel⇨Create.

✦ On the menu browser or menu bar, click Draw⇨Block⇨Make.

✦ On the Draw toolbar, click the Make Block button.

✦ At the command prompt, type **BLOCK** or **B** and press Enter.

Follow these steps to create a block:

1. **Add the geometry to your drawing that you want to use to define a block.**

If you want to control the visibility of the objects within the block later, be sure to place the objects on specific layers so that they can be turned on and off or frozen and thawed.

2. **Use one of the methods just listed to initiate the BLOCK command.**

The Block Definition dialog box appears (refer to Figure 1-1).

3. **In the Name combo box, enter a meaningful name.**

The name entered must be unique from other blocks that already exist in the drawing, or you end up redefining the existing block with the new geometry, which might not be what you want to do. The name entered must be less than 255 characters.

4. **In the Base Point area, either click the Pick Point button and select a point in the drawing or enter a coordinate value for the base point in the X, Y, and Z text boxes.**

   The point that you specify will be used as the base point of the block or its insertion point. Usually this point is on the geometry that's being selected to define the block.

   If you clicked the Pick Point button in the Base Point area, you are returned to the drawing window. Specify a point in the drawing to use as the base point for the block. After you select the base point for the block in the drawing window, you return to the Block Definition dialog box.

5. **In the Objects area, click the Select Objects button.**

   You're returned to the drawing window once again so you can select the objects that you want to add to the block.

6. **In the drawing window, select the objects you want to add to the block. Press Enter to complete selecting objects and return to the Block Definition dialog box.**

   The objects you select can be text, lines, circles, and even other blocks. Any object you can select can be added to the block. You can use the QuickSelect button to the right of the Select Objects button to filter objects by specific property values.

7. **In the Block Definition dialog box in the Objects area, click one of the Select Objects modes.**

   The different object modes affect what happens to the selected objects after the block is created:

   - **Retain:** The selected objects remain in the drawing.

   - **Convert to block:** The selected objects are removed from the drawing, but the new block is inserted in the same location as the original selected objects.

   - **Delete:** The selected objects are removed from the drawing after the block is created.

8. **Deselect the Open in Block Editor option (at the bottom of the dialog box) for now; I cover that option in a little bit.**

   AutoCAD 2006 introduced the Block Editor environment for editing blocks and adding dynamic properties and actions. If the Open in Block Editor is selected, the block is opened in the Block Editor when the Block Definition dialog box is closed.

9. **Click OK.**

   The Block Definition dialog box closes. Results vary based on the objects selected, the selected objects mode, and the other settings chosen.

Creating geometry on Layer 0 (zero) is usually a "no-no" in AutoCAD, but when geometry is added to a block that's on Layer 0, it takes on the properties of the layer that the block is inserted on. This is a great way to check and see whether a block happens to be on the correct layer.

Exploring some advanced options

The preceding section covered the basic options in the Block Definition dialog box that you need to create a block. In this section, I cover the other options, because some of them can be used to enforce CAD standards. The following list describes some of the more advanced options and fields in the Block Definition dialog box:

+ **Block unit:** Specifies the units in which the block is being created. This setting affects how the block is inserted into the drawing. If the block is created in the units of Inches and inserted into a drawing that is specified as Millimeters, AutoCAD scales the block accordingly. If Block unit is set to Unitless, the scaling of the block is controlled by the Insertion Scale options in the Options dialog box under the User Preferences tab.

+ **Annotative:** When selected, the block is annotative and is scaled based on the current annotative scale of model space or of a viewport object on a layout tab. For more information on annotation scaling, see Chapter 4 of Book III.

+ **Match block orientation to layout:** When selected, the orientation of the block matches the layout's orientation.

+ **Scale uniformly:** When selected, the block can only be scaled equally along all axes. The option is available when the Annotative option is not enabled.

+ **Allow exploding:** When selected, the block can be exploded by using the EXPLODE command. For more information on the EXPLODE command, see Chapter 2 of Book II.

+ **Description:** The description is used in different interfaces in AutoCAD that can display the block; some of these interfaces are DesignCenter and the Tool Palettes window.

+ **Hyperlink:** Allows you to specify a hyperlink for the entire block. The hyperlink can be used to link a view or layout in the drawing, an external location such as a file, or a Web site via a URL to a block. You can access the hyperlink by holding down the Ctrl key and clicking the block when you see the icon of the globe and a chain link.

+ **Open in block editor:** When selected, the block is opened into the Block Editor for further editing after the Block Definition dialog box is closed.

Inserting Blocks

 AutoCAD stores blocks in what is called the *block definition table*. The block definition table is used to hold information and settings about the block. To display the block in the drawing after you create it, you need to insert a reference of the block definition from the table. An inserted block in the drawing is known as a *block reference* because it refers to its definition in the block table. To insert a block into the current drawing file, you use the INSERT command, which opens the Insert dialog box (see Figure 1-2). The INSERT command can insert a block from within the current drawing or an entire drawing file as a block. It just depends on where the information you want to insert into the drawing is located.

Figure 1-2: The Insert dialog box is used to create a reference to a block definition.

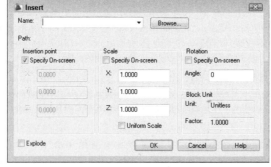

To start the INSERT command and display the Insert dialog box, use one of the following methods:

✦ On the ribbon, click Blocks & References tab⇨Block panel⇨Insert.

✦ On the menu browser or menu bar, click Insert menu⇨Block.

✦ On the Draw or Insert toolbars, click the Insert Block button.

✦ At the command prompt, type **INSERT** or **I** and press Enter.

To insert a block into a drawing, follow these steps:

1. **Start the INSERT command by using one of the previously listed methods.**

   The Insert dialog box appears (refer to Figure 1-2).

2. **In the Insert dialog box, either click the down arrow on the Name drop-down list and select the block that is defined in the drawing to insert, or click the Browse button to insert a drawing as a block.**

The selected name is displayed in the text box of the Name drop-down list. If you clicked the Browse button, the Select Drawing File dialog box appears. If the block has a preview saved with it, the preview appears to the right of the Browse button.

3. **If you clicked the Browse button, in the Select Drawing File dialog box, browse and select the drawing file that you want to insert as a block. Click Open.**

   The name of the selected drawing file is displayed in the text box of the Name drop-down list and the path to the drawing is displayed just below the drop-down list.

4. **In the Insert dialog box in the Insertion Point area, select or deselect the Specify On-Screen option. If deselected, enter the coordinate value for the insertion point of the block in the X, Y, and Z text boxes.**

   If Specify On-Screen is selected, you will be prompted for the insertion point of the block during the block insertion process after the Insert dialog box is closed.

5. **In the Scale area, select or deselect the Specify On-Screen option. If deselected, enter the scale for the x, y, and z axes in the text boxes. If Uniform Scale is selected, you can enter a scale only in the X axis text box and the value is automatically assigned to the two other axes.**

   If Specify On-Screen is selected, you will be prompted for the scale of the block during the block insertion process. If the block was created with the Scale Uniformly option selected, the Uniform Scale option is disabled and selected (forcing you to use only uniform scale).

6. **In the Rotation area, select or deselect the Specify On-Screen option. If deselected, enter the rotation angle in the Angle text box.**

   If Specify On-Screen is selected, you are prompted for the rotation angle of the block during the block insertion process.

7. **In the Block Unit area, all you have to do is verify the current insertion units and scale that you want applied to the block.**

   The Unit value is based on the current setting of the INSUNITS system variable. This variable specifies the drawing's current units for inserted blocks. The Factor value is the result of the unit used when the block was created and the current value of INSUNITS. To change the current INSUNITS value, close the Insert dialog box and type **INSUNITS** at the command prompt. Then enter the corresponding integer for the insertion units you want. For more information, look up INSUNITS in AutoCAD's online Help.

8. **At the bottom of the Insert dialog box, select or deselect if you want the block to be exploded after it is inserted into the drawing.**

   If the Allow Exploding option was deselected in the Block Definition dialog box when the block was created, the Explode option is disabled.

9. **Click OK.**

The Insert dialog box closes, and you are returned to the drawing window. The INSERT command may still be running, based on whether you selected any of the Specify On-Screen options for the insertion point, scale, or rotation. Specify the prompts as required. Here are the three possible prompts:

```
Specify insertion point or [Basepoint/Scale/Rotate]:
Specify scale factor <1>:
Specify rotation angle <0>:
```

You can create custom toolbars, menus, or ribbon panels to help insert blocks. If you do create custom commands and place them on toolbars, menus, or ribbon panels, you need to use the –INSERT command rather than the INSERT command for the menu macro. The –INSERT command runs from the command prompt instead of displaying a dialog box.

When inserting a block, you can specify its rotation and scale by using the Properties palette if it's displayed before you specify the insertion point of the block. Using the Properties palette this way allows you to change the dynamic properties of a block before it's inserted. I cover dynamic properties of blocks in Chapter 2 of this minibook.

Managing Blocks

Blocks are a powerful feature of AutoCAD and no doubt you will be using them as often as you can. AutoCAD offers several tools and commands for managing blocks. Some of the ways to manage blocks in a drawing are as follows:

✦ Rename a block definition

✦ Redefine a block definition

✦ Purge a block definition

✦ Export a block definition to a drawing file

Renaming a block definition

You can rename blocks by using the RENAME command. Follow these steps to rename a block:

1. **At the command prompt, type** RENAME **and press Enter. Or on the ribbon, click Tools tab⇨Drawing Utilities panel⇨Rename.**

The renamed dialog box appears.

2. **In the Named Objects list, select Blocks.**

3. **In the Items list, select the block that you want to rename.**

The name of the selected block in the Items list is displayed in the Old Name text box.

4. **In the text box directly below the Old Name text box, type the new name and click Rename To.**

5. **Rename additional blocks if necessary, and then click OK to exit the Rename dialog box.**

Redefining a block definition

You can redefine (or edit) a block definition. In releases before AutoCAD 2006 and AutoCAD LT 2007, you insert a block and then explode it. After exploding it, you make the necessary changes to the geometry and then reblock it by using the BLOCK command again. Or you might use the REFEDIT command, which allows you to open a block or an xref so the geometry can be modified. Some issues with using the REFEDIT command can be overcome with the BEDIT command. I cover the REFEDIT command in Chapter 3 of this minibook.

AutoCAD LT does not support the REFEDIT command.

Redefining a block in AutoCAD 2006 and AutoCAD LT 2007 became so much simpler with the introduction of the Block Editor. The Block Editor allows you to edit a block in its own drawing window. You use the BEDIT command to start the Block Editor. Follow these steps to edit a block definition with the Block Editor:

1. **In the drawing window, select the block that you want to redefine.**

2. **Right-click and select Block Editor from the shortcut menu.**

   The block definition is opened in the Block Editor.

3. **In the Block Editor, make your changes to the existing geometry or add geometry as you normally do when working in the drawing window.**

4. **On the ribbon, click Close Block Editor to exit the Block Editor.**

5. **When prompted to save the changes, click Yes.**

   You're returned to the drawing window, and the references to the edited block are updated.

Purging a block definition

You can completely remove blocks that are not being used and will never be used by using the PURGE command and Purge dialog box. Follow these steps to purge a block definition from a drawing:

Book VI
Chapter 1

Playing with Blocks

1. Before you can purge a block, you must remove all inserted references of the block.

2. At the command prompt, type PURGE and press Enter. Or on the ribbon, click Tools tab⇨Drawing Utilities panel⇨Purge.

3. In the Purge dialog box, double-click the All Items node if it is not already expanded, and then expand the Blocks node.

   The block definitions that can be purged appear.

4. Select the block and click Purge.

   The Confirm Purge dialog box is displayed.

5. In the Confirm Purge dialog box, click Yes.

   The block definition is removed from below the Blocks node and from the drawing. The Confirm Purge dialog box is displayed if you selected the Confirm Each Item to Be Purged option (near the bottom of the Purge dialog box).

6. Click Close to exit the Purge dialog box.

To quickly purge all unused named objects from a drawing, select the Purge Nested Items option and deselect the Confirm Each Item to Be Purged option in the Purge dialog box. Then click Purge All. This purges all nested named objects out of a drawing, without stopping to prompt and ask whether you really want to remove the item.

Exporting a block definition

Blocks created by using the BLOCK or BEDIT commands are defined only in the current drawing, but many times you will want to be able to access the block from other drawings. The Write Block dialog box, shown in Figure 1-3, is used to export a block from the current drawing and make a new drawing file based on a selected block. The Write Block dialog box is displayed with the WBLOCK command. You can also use DesignCenter to insert blocks stored in a drawing; I cover DesignCenter in Chapter 4 of this minibook.

Follow these steps to export a block definition to a new drawing file:

1. At the command prompt, type WBLOCK and press Enter.

2. Under the Source area of the Write Block dialog box, select Block.

   All the controls under the Source area except for the drop-down list become disabled.

3. From the drop-down list, select the block you want to export.

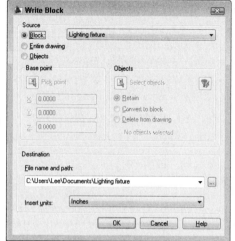

Figure 1-3:
The Write
Block dialog
box is used
to export a
block
definition.

4. **Specify a file name and path in the File name and path text box under the Destination area or click the Ellipsis button to specify a path and name by using a dialog box.**

   If the Ellipsis button is clicked, the Browse for Drawing File dialog box appears. Browse to the location where you want to create the new drawing file and enter a name. Click Save after you have specified the new folder location and file name, and return to the Write Block dialog box.

5. **In the Write Block dialog box, specify the insertion units for the new drawing by selecting one of the options from the Insert units drop-down list.**

   AutoCAD applies the insertion units to the drawing and uses them when the drawing is inserted into another drawing.

6. **Click OK to export the block as a new drawing and to close the Write Block dialog box.**

You can create a new drawing instead of using the WBLOCK command. To define the insertion point that should be used when inserting a drawing into another drawing, use the BASE command or the INSBASE system variable. Either the BASE command or INSBASE system variable allows you to re-define the insertion point that is used for inserting a drawing as a block.

Enhancing Blocks with Attributes

Blocks can store custom information, and that information can later be extracted to an external file or a table object (AutoCAD only). To store custom information with a block, you use an attribute. You use attributes to hold information in a block such as a part number, a description or even project-related information. You will often find that title blocks contain attributes, which allows the user to edit all the attributes at one time instead of individually as you have to do with text or multiline text. Attributes may appear like standard text objects, but they're much more than that. You can change the text value of attributes when they're part of a block.

Adding an attribute to a block definition

Attributes are added to a block in the same way you add other types of geometry, such as lines or arcs. First you add an attribute to the drawing and then you add the attribute to the block. When an attribute is added to a drawing, it is known as an *attribute definition*. The attribute definition is stored in the block definition and is used to describe what the actual attribute of the block reference should be like. When a block is inserted into the drawing, attributes are added to each block reference that contains attribute definitions. To create an attribute definition, you use the ATTDEF command to display the Attribute Definition dialog box (see Figure 1-4).

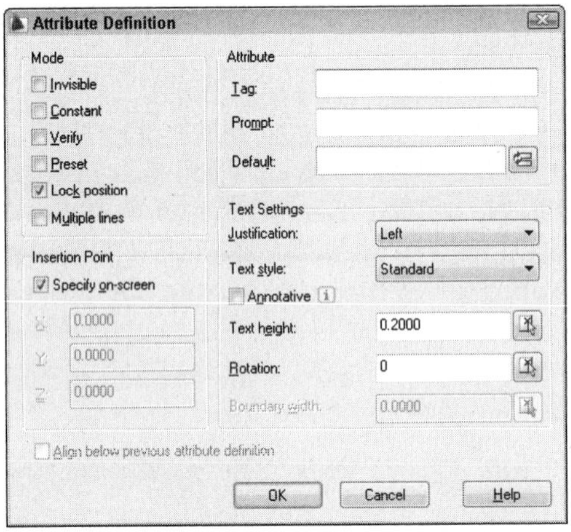

Figure 1-4:
Creating an attribute definition.

To start the ATTDEF command and display the Attribute Definition dialog box, follow one of the following methods:

✦ On the ribbon, click Blocks & References tab⇨Attributes panel⇨Define Attributes.

✦ On the menu browser or menu bar, click Draw menu⇨Block⇨Define Attributes.

✦ At the command prompt, type **ATTDEF** or **ATT** and press Enter.

The following steps explain how to create an attribute definition and then add it to a block:

1. **Add the geometry to your drawing that you want to use to define a block.**

2. **Start the ATTDEF command by using one of the methods previously listed.**

The Attribute Definition dialog box appears (refer to Figure 1-4).

3. **In the Mode area, select the options that you want to use for the attribute definition.**

Attributes can have six modes:

**Book VI
Chapter 1**

Playing with Blocks

- **Invisible:** When selected, the attribute is invisible. By default, the attribute is visible. If an attribute is invisible, you can set the ATTMODE system variable to a value of 2 to display all invisible attributes in a drawing.

- **Constant:** When selected, the attribute has a fixed value which is assigned to all blocks and can't be changed unless you use a command such as BEDIT or BATTMAN.

- **Verify:** When selected, you're prompted to verify that the value entered is correct for the block being inserted into a drawing.

- **Preset:** When selected, the default value is automatically assigned to the block when it's inserted into a drawing.

- **Lock position:** When selected, the attribute can't be moved by using grips. You use this mode also when you want to control the placement of the attribute with dynamic properties. I cover working with dynamic properties in Chapter 2 of this minibook.

- **Multiple lines.** When selected, the attribute supports multiple lines of text instead of a single line of text.

4. **In the Attribute area, specify the attribute's tag, prompt, and default value.**

The tag is the value you see on-screen before the attribute is added to a block. The prompt is what the user sees at the command prompt, in the Edit Attributes or the Enhanced Attribute Editor (AutoCAD only), when inserting or editing the attribute values of a block. The default value defines the value that the attribute has when it's inserted in a drawing. The default value can be a plain text string that contains field values or can be defined with special multiline formatting.

5. **In the Insertion Point area, select or deselect the Specify On-Screen option. If it's deselected, enter the coordinate value for the insertion point of the block in the X, Y, and Z text boxes.**

If Specify On-Screen is selected, you will be prompted for the insertion point of the attribute after you click OK to close the Attribute Definition dialog box.

6. **In the Text Settings area, specify the attribute's justification, text style, height, rotation, and boundary width (if Multiple lines in Mode area is selected).**

Justification of the attribute controls how the value of the attribute appears at its insertion point. The text style controls the font and other text characteristics used for the tag and value of the attribute. Height specifies the height of the text, and rotation controls the rotation angle after the attribute is created. Both the height and rotation properties have buttons that can be used to specify a distance or angle by using points in the drawing. Boundary width defines the width of the bounding box for the attribute text when the attribute is set to Multiple lines; you can enter a number or click Boundary width to pick a distance in the drawing. The Annotative check box controls whether the attribute scales based on the current annotation scale or matches the orientation of the block.

7. **Initially, the Align below Previous Attribute Definition check box is de-selected. Select the option if you have inserted an attribute in your drawing and want the next one placed below the one previously created.**

When selected, the attribute is positioned below the previously created attribute.

8. **Click OK.**

The Attribute Definition dialog box closes, and you're returned to the drawing window. The ATTDEF command might still be running, depending on whether you selected the Specify On-Screen options for the insertion point. If you need to specify an insertion point for the attribute definition, the following prompt is displayed:

```
Specify start point:
```

9. **Start the BLOCK command and create the block as you normally do — just don't forget to add the attribute.**

When you insert a block with attributes or edit the attribute values, you're prompted to edit the attribute values in a specific order. The order of the attributes is determined by the order they're selected when the block is created. Select each attribute in the order you want them to be displayed when the block is inserted or edited.

Inserting a block with attributes

You insert a block with attributes the same way you insert a block without attributes, except after the block has been inserted into the drawing, you're prompted to change the values for the attributes contained in the block with the Edit Attributes dialog box (see Figure 1-5) or at the command line. You're not prompted for attributes that are flagged as constant or preset.

The ATTDIA and ATTREQ system variables affect how a block with attributes is inserted. ATTDIA controls the display of the Edit Attributes dialog box or the command prompt for entering values for attributes when a block with attributes is inserted. ATTREQ enables or suppresses the prompts for entering values for attributes when a block with attributes is inserted.

Edit Attributes

Block name: ARCHBDR-D

Drawn By

Checked By

Drawing Date

Drawing Scale

Page Number

Page Number(out of)

Project Name

Page Title

[OK] [Cancel] [Previous] [Next] [Help]

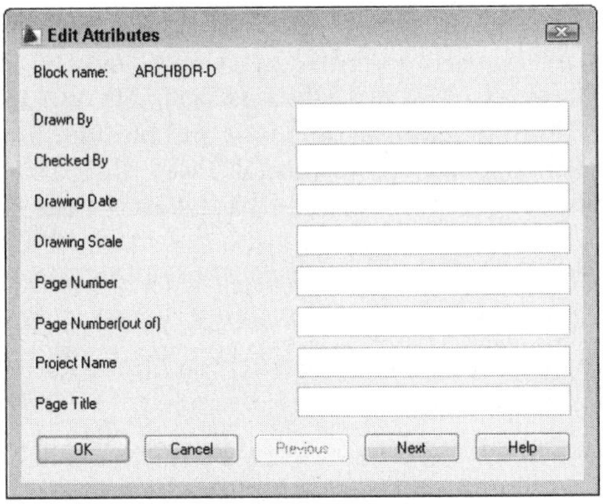

Figure 1-5:
Editing attribute values after a block is inserted.

Editing an attribute's value in a block

You can edit an attribute's value for a block by using the Properties palette, the Edit Attributes dialog box (ATTDEF), or the Enhanced Attribute Editor (EATTEDIT) — this works with AutoCAD only. The easiest way to edit an attribute value is to double-click the attribute you want to edit or a block that contains attributes. Doing so launches the default Attribute Editor. Make the changes to the values of the attributes in the dialog box that is displayed.

Managing attributes in blocks

When you redefine blocks with attributes, you need to be aware of something. When you use the BMAKE or BEDIT command to update a block with attributes, only the changes to the objects in the block are reflected in the drawing unless the block contains attributes that are defined as constant. Any redefined block containing nonconstant attributes will take some extra effort to get them to update correctly in the drawing. If you redefine a block and add or change the properties of the attributes for a block, you must do one of the following:

✦ Delete and reinsert the block so all the attributes and property changes are used as part of the block reference.

✦ Use the ATTSYNC (Attribute Synchronize) command. Using this command ensures that all the existing blocks in the drawing are updated. (This command is available only in AutoCAD.)

 ✦ The BATTMAN (Block Attribute Manager) command allows you to modify the properties of attributes in a block. You can use this command to change the order in which the attributes appear when edited along with other properties such as color, layer, and even text style. (This command is available only in AutoCAD.)

Extracting attribute data from blocks

 You can extract attributes from a drawing by using the Attribute Extraction dialog box (ATTEXT), which you can find in both AutoCAD and AutoCAD LT, or the Data Extraction Wizard (EATTEXT), which is available only in AutoCAD. Attributes can be extracted to external data files and brought into your favorite spreadsheet or database program, or in AutoCAD you can extract attribute values and create a table object that summarizes all like values. For information on extracting attributes out of your drawing, see the online Help topics Extract Data from Block Attributes or Extract Block Attribute Data (Advanced), which you can access from the Contents tab of the online Help system. Choose User's Guide⇨Create and Modify Objects⇨Create Use Blocks (Symbols)⇨Attach Data to Blocks (Block Attributes).

Chapter 2: Dynamic Blocks

In This Chapter

✔ Understanding what makes a block dynamic

✔ Adding parameters and actions to a block

✔ Working with visibility states

✔ Understanding what happens to dynamic blocks in older releases

*I*n Chapter 1 of this minibook, I discuss how to create and manage blocks with and without attributes. The types of blocks that you create by using the BLOCK command and any blocks that were created prior to AutoCAD 2006 or AutoCAD LT 2007 are known as a *static blocks* or *legacy blocks* (Blocks version 1.0). AutoCAD 2006 and AutoCAD LT 2007 introduced a new type of block called a *dynamic block* (Blocks version 2.0). Static blocks are altered primarily through placement, rotation, overall scaling, and the editing of attribute values. Dynamic blocks enhance static blocks by adding a new level of editing. Dynamic blocks allow you to stretch the geometry of a block in one direction and confine the distance that the block can be stretched by a set of incremental values. This chapter focuses on how to add dynamic behavior to a block.

What Makes a Block Dynamic?

Dynamic blocks are static blocks with some new tricks — you might not be able to teach your old dog new tricks, but blocks are eager to learn. Dynamic blocks are created in the Block Editor, which is displayed with the BEDIT command. Dynamic blocks can contain custom properties that are defined by adding parameters and actions to the block. Parameters and actions bring blocks to life by allowing you to rotate, move, or modify objects within each instance of a block. If you want to move objects within a static block, you have to explode the block and then reblock it with a different name or use in-place reference editing (REFEDIT command); otherwise, reblocking the block with the same name changes all the instances of that block in the drawing.

Dynamic blocks allow you to assign the following actions to objects within a block:

✦ Move

✦ Scale

✦ Stretch

+ Polar Stretch

+ Rotate

+ Flip (or Mirror)

+ Array

+ Lookups

After parameters and actions have been assigned to a block, the block doesn't look any different until you select it when no command is running. Based on the type of parameters added to the block, you see different types of grips appear. Some of these grips appear in the form of circles, arrows, and triangles (see Figure 2-1).

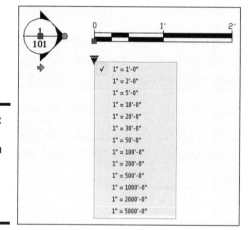

Figure 2-1:
Dynamic blocks can display different types of grips.

Block Editor Environment

The Block Editor, shown in Figure 2-2, was mentioned briefly in Chapter 1 of this minibook because it can be opened when creating a block with the Block Definition dialog box. The Block Editor is a special instance of the drawing window that allows you to work with a block definition in the same way that you work with a drawing file. The Block Editor also allows you to add parameters and actions to a block definition to change the way it behaves after an instance of the block is inserted into the drawing. Unlike the main window, the Block Editor doesn't allow you to use some commands, such as BLOCK, REFEDIT (AutoCAD only), and PLOT, and it doesn't contain layout tabs or buttons because blocks don't contain layouts.

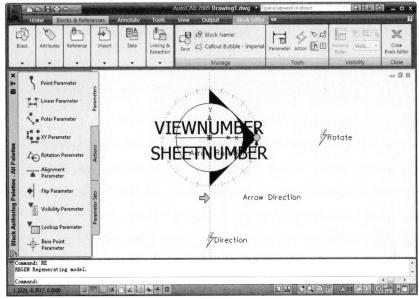

Figure 2-2:
The Block
Editor is
used to
modify block
definitions.

After you open the block definition, you can add or remove geometry, add or remove parameters and actions, and work with attributes. You can also capture block and custom properties by using fields with attribute definitions in the block.

Components of the Block Editor

Even though the Block Editor is similar to a standard drawing window, it still uses some specialized interfaces. When the Block Editor is active, three additional panels are added to the ribbon and organized on the Block Editor tab (see Figure 2-3). The Block Editor ribbon tab is displayed only when the Block Editor is active. These ribbon panels contain tools that you use to enhance a legacy block or modify a dynamic block.

Here is a list of what you can accomplish from the Block Editor tab:

✦ **Save:** Saves the changes made to the block definition.

✦ **Save As:** Displays the Save Block As dialog box and allows you to save the block definition as a new block.

✦ **Block Editor:** Displays the Edit Block Definition dialog box and allows you to open a different block definition from inside the Block Editor.

✦ **Block Definition Name:** Displays the name of the open block definition.

✦ **Parameter:** Starts the BPARAMTER command and allows you to add a parameter without using the Block Authoring palettes.

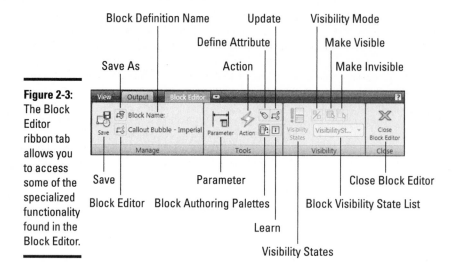

Figure 2-3:
The Block Editor ribbon tab allows you to access some of the specialized functionality found in the Block Editor.

♦ **Action:** Starts the BACTION command and allows you to add an action without using the Block Authoring palettes.

♦ **Define Attribute:** Starts the ATTDEF command and displays the Attribute Definition dialog box, allowing you to add an attribute definition to the block definition.

♦ **Update:** Starts the REGEN command to update the display of text, arrowheads, grips, and a few other display elements in the Block Editor. (These elements are based on the current zoom factor of the block in the drawing window.)

♦ **Block Authoring Palettes:** Displays or hides the Block Authoring Palettes window.

♦ **Learn:** Starts the New Features Workshop.

♦ **Visibility States:** Displays the Visibility States dialog box so you can create, edit, or delete visibility states from the block.

♦ **Visibility Mode:** Controls the current visibility of objects in the Block Editor that have been assigned to a Visibility State.

♦ **Make Visible:** Starts the BVHIDE command and allows you to display objects that are currently invisible in the current visibility state.

♦ **Make Invisible:** Starts the BVHIDE command and allows you to hide objects from the current visibility state.

♦ **Block Visibility State List:** Specifies which visibility state is current.

♦ **Close Block Editor:** Closes the Block Editor and prompts you to save any changes made.

You use the Block Authoring Palettes window (see Figure 2-4) to add parameters and actions to a block. By using the parameters, you define custom properties for the open block definition. After a parameter is added to a block, in most cases you must associate an action with the parameter for it to be usable. Actions define which geometry is associated with a parameter and what happens when the parameter is used with grip editing. The Block Authoring Palettes window has three tabs. One contains the available parameters and another contains the available actions. The final tab contains both parameters and actions in what are called *parameter sets*. If you're new to creating dynamic blocks, the parameter sets can help you work more quickly by combining many of the common parameter and action combinations into easy-to-use tools.

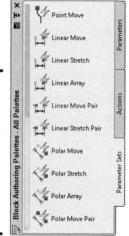

Figure 2-4:
The Block Authoring Palettes window contains parameters and actions for dynamic blocks.

Editing a block definition

To start the Block Editor, you use the BEDIT command. The BEDIT command displays the Edit Block Definition dialog box (see Figure 2-5). From the Edit Block Definition dialog box, you select a block from the list to edit or enter a name in the text box to create a new block. The Edit Block Definition dialog box displays a preview of the block that is selected from the list and its associated description. If the preview displays a small lightning bolt in the lower-right corner, the selected block is a dynamic block. This indicator is displayed in many of the different interfaces and dialog boxes where block previews are displayed.

When set to 0, the BLOCKEDITLOCK system variable allows you to edit blocks by using the BEDIT command. When set to a value of 1, it doesn't allow the BEDIT command to be started and, in turn, restricts the modifying of a block's dynamic properties.

Figure 2-5:
Use the Edit
Block
Definition
dialog box
to open a
block
definition for
editing.

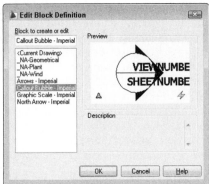

To start the BEDIT command and display the Edit Block Definition dialog box, use one of the following methods:

✦ On the ribbon, click Blocks & References tab⇨Block panel⇨Block Editor.

✦ On the menu browser or menu bar, click Tools menu⇨Block Editor.

✦ On the Standard or Standard Annotation toolbar, click the Block Editor button.

✦ At the command prompt, type **BEDIT** or **BE** and press Enter.

✦ Select a block and right-click. From the shortcut menu, select Block Editor. This option automatically opens the selected block's definition in the Block Editor.

The following steps explain how to modify a block with the Block Editor:

1. **Start the BEDIT command by using one of the methods described in the preceding list.**

The Edit Block Definition dialog box appears.

2. **Select a block from the list and click OK.**

The selected block is opened in the Block Editor.

3. **Make the necessary changes to the block.**

4. **On the Block Editor ribbon tab, click Close panel⇨Close Block Editor.**

A message box asks you to save your changes.

5. **Click Yes to save the changes.**

Clicking Yes closes the Block Editor and saves the changes made to the block definition. If you click No, the Block Editor closes and the changes are discarded, and if you click Cancel, you remain in the Block Editor.

If you add or remove attributes from the block definition, the changes are not reflected in the block references that currently exist in the drawing until you erase and reinsert the blocks. If you're using AutoCAD and not AutoCAD LT, you can use the ATTSYNC command to update the attributes of the block references in the drawing.

Going Dynamic

When you have a block open in the Block Editor, you can add parameters and actions to your block. Most parameters require an action for them to be used. AutoCAD offers ten parameters for you to place in the drawing; three do not require an associated actions.

Table 2-1 lists the available parameters and the actions that can be associated with them.

Book VI Chapter 2

Dynamic Blocks

Table 2-1	Parameters and Actions	
Parameter	*Description*	*Actions*
Point	Defines a point in the block so you can move or change the geometry associated with the point.	Move Stretch
Linear	Modifies geometry in a block along a linear path.	Array Move Scale Stretch
Polar	Modifies geometry in a block along a polar path.	Array Move Scale Stretch Polar Stretch

(continued)

Table 2-1 *(continued)*

Parameter	Description	Actions	
XY	Modifies geometry in a block across a horizontal and vertical distance.	Array	Move
		Scale	Stretch
Rotation	Rotates geometry in a block around a given point	Rotation	
Alignment	Aligns a block so it is perpendicular or tangent to the geometry that it is being inserted next to	No action required.	
Flip	Mirrors the entire block along a reflection line.	Flip	
Visibility	Controls the display of geometry contained within a block. Also can be used to have one block that might display multiple different views or styles of similar geometry.	No action required	
Lookup	Creates a table with a list of values that match up with a custom property.	Lookup	
Base Point	Redefines the insertion point of a block.	No action required	

Adding parameters

You add parameters to a block by using the Block Authoring Palettes or the BPARAMETER command. The following steps explain how to add a point parameter to a block:

1. **Open an existing block with the Edit Block Definition dialog box, or create a new block with the Block Definition dialog box and make sure that the Open Block in Editor option is selected.**

For information on the Edit Block Definition dialog box, see the "Editing a block definition" section earlier in this chapter. For information on the Block Definition dialog box, see Chapter 1 in this minibook.

2. **In the Block Editor, if the Block Authoring Palettes interface is not displayed, on the ribbon click Block Editor tab⇨Tools panel⇨Block Authoring Palettes.**

3. **In the Block Authoring Palettes window, click the Parameters tab and then click the Point Parameter tool.**

   The Parameters tab is displayed and the BPARAMETER command starts with the Point option.

4. **At the Specify parameter location prompt, specify a point in the drawing window for the parameter to reference, or choose one of the available options by right-clicking and selecting the option from the shortcut menu.**

   The command line displays the prompt

   ```
   Command: _BParameter Point
   Specify parameter location or
       [Name/Label/Chain/Description/Palette]:
   ```

5. **At the Specify label location prompt, specify the location in the drawing where you want to place the label for the parameter.**

   The command line displays the prompt

   ```
   Specify label location:
   ```

   The label is a visual reference to the parameter. The label is used in the Block Editor, the Properties palette, and to reference the property in a field. The parameter will be displayed with a yellow box that contains an exclamation point in it; this is because no action has been associated with the parameter yet.

6. **In the drawing window, select the parameter that was just placed and right-click. From the shortcut menu, choose Properties.**

   The Properties palette appears with the parameter's properties.

7. **In the Properties palette, change the properties in the Property Labels, Geometry, and Misc areas to change the behavior of the parameter.**

   The Properties palette allows you to control the different properties associated with each parameter type. The properties vary based on each parameter. To find out about each property, see the online Help topic Add Dynamic Behavior to Blocks, which you can access from the Contents tab of the online Help system. Choose User's Guide⇨Create and Modify Objects⇨Create Use Blocks (Symbols).

8. **On the ribbon, click Block Editor tab⇨Manage panel⇨Save.**

**Book VI
Chapter 2**

Dynamic Blocks

You remain in the Block Editor so you can continue adding parameters or actions as needed.

9. **On the ribbon, click Block Editor tab⇨Close panel⇨Close Block Editor to exit the Block Editor.**

Adding actions

You add actions to a block by using the Block Authoring Palettes or the BACTIONTOOL command. To add a move action to a point parameter, follow these steps:

1. **Open an existing block with the Edit Block Definition dialog box, or create a new block with the Block Definition dialog box and make sure that the Open Block in Editor option is selected. If you create a new block, you need to first add a parameter to the block before you can add an action (see the preceding section for information on adding a parameter).**

   For information on the Edit Block Definition dialog box, see the "Editing a block definition" section earlier in this chapter. For information on the Block Definition dialog box, see Chapter 1 in this minibook.

2. **In the Block Editor, if the Block Authoring Palettes interface is not displayed, on the ribbon click Block Editor tab⇨Tools panel⇨Block Authoring Palettes.**

   The Block Authoring Palettes window appears.

3. **Click the Actions tab and then click the Move Action tool.**

   The Parameters tab is displayed and the BACTIONTOOL command starts with the Point option.

   The command line displays the prompt

   ```
   Command: _BActionTool Move
   Select parameter:
   ```

4. **At the Select parameter prompt, select the parameter that you want to associate with the action.**

   After the parameter is selected, this prompt is displayed at the command line:

   ```
   Specify selection set for action
   Select objects:
   ```

5. **In the Block Editor, select the objects that you want to associate with the action, and press Enter when you have finished selecting objects.**

   The following prompt appears at the command line:

   ```
   Specify action location or [Multiplier/Offset]:
   ```

6. **Specify a point in the Block Editor for the action, or choose one of the available options by right-clicking and choosing the option from the shortcut menu.**

   The point that you specify should be near the parameter so that you know which actions are associated with each parameter. The actual placement has no bearing on how the action works. After you create the action, the yellow box with an exclamation point in it near the parameter disappears. This indicates that the parameter is now associated with an action.

7. **Select the action that was just placed and right-click. From the shortcut menu, select Properties.**

   The Properties palette appears, showing the action's properties.

8. **In the Properties palette, change the properties in the Geometry, Overrides, and Misc areas to change the behavior of the parameter.**

   The Properties palette allows you to control the behavior of an action. The properties vary based on the selected action.

9. **On the ribbon, click Block Editor tab⇨Manage panel⇨Save.**

   You remain in the Block Editor so you can continue adding parameters or actions as needed.

8. **On the ribbon, click Block Editor tab⇨Close panel⇨Close Block Editor to exit the Block Editor.**

Using parameter sets

Parameter sets simplify the process of adding parameters and actions individually by combining the two into a streamlined process. To use a parameter set, display the Block Authoring Palettes window while in the Block Editor and click the Parameter Sets tab. When the Parameter Sets tab is active, click the parameter set you want to use and follow the prompts that are displayed.

Visibility states

You use visibility states to control the display of geometry within a block. This can be a great advantage when you're doing drawings and need to change out a block from one to another. For example, you may have a plumbing drawing that uses several types of valves. You can use one block to represent six types of valves. In releases prior to AutoCAD 2006 or AutoCAD LT 2007, you had to erase the block from the drawing and then find the other block to insert, which takes time. You can accomplish this task much more quickly by using dynamic blocks and visibility states. The Visibility States dialog box, shown in Figure 2-6, allows you to create, rename, delete, set current, or change the order of a visibility state for a block.

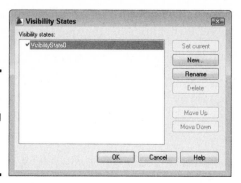

Figure 2-6:
Managing
and creating
visibility
states in
one place.

Follow these steps to add a visibility parameter in a block:

1. **Open an existing block with the Edit Block Definition dialog box, or create a new block with the Block Definition dialog box and make sure the Open Block in Editor option is checked.**

   For information on the Edit Block Definition dialog box, see the section "Editing a block definition" earlier in this chapter. For information on the Block Definition dialog box, see Chapter 1 in this minibook.

2. **In the Block Editor, if the Block Authoring Palettes interface is not displayed, on the ribbon click Block Editor tab⇨Tools panel⇨Block Authoring Palettes.**

   The Block Authoring Palettes window appears.

3. **Click the Parameters tab and then click the Visibility Parameter tool.**

   The Parameters tab is displayed, and the BPARAMETER command starts with the Visibility option:

   ```
   Command: _BParameter Visibility
   Specify parameter location or [Name/Label
       /Description/Palette]:
   ```

4. **At the Specify parameter location prompt, specify a point in the drawing window for the visibility parameter, or select one of the available options by right-clicking and selecting the option from the shortcut menu.**

5. **In the drawing window, select the parameter that was just placed and right-click. From the shortcut menu, choose Properties.**

   The Properties palette appears, showing the parameter's properties.

6. **In the Properties palette, change the properties in the Property Labels, Geometry, and Misc areas to change the behavior of the parameter.**

Follow these steps to define a new visibility state and associate geometry in the block to the visibility state for a block:

1. **On the ribbon, click Block Editor tab⇨Manage panel⇨Save.**

The Visibility States dialog box appears (refer to Figure 2-6).

2. **Click New.**

The New Visibility State dialog box appears (see Figure 2-7).

Figure 2-7:
Defining a new visibility state.

3. **In the Visibility State Name text box, type a name.**

You use the name to select and manage the visibility state when the block is inserted into a drawing.

4. **In the Visibility Options for New States area, select one of the three options.**

These options control the display of the geometry in the drawing. You can hide or show all the objects in the block, or leave the objects as they appear, based on the current visibility state.

5. **Click OK.**

The New Visibility State dialog box is closed, and you're returned to the Visibility States dialog box. The new visibility state is listed in the list box.

6. **In the Visibility State dialog box, click OK.**

The Visibility State dialog box is closed, and you're returned to the Block Editor.

7. **In the Block Editor, select the visibility state you want to modify in the Visibility State drop-down list on the Visibility panel on the Block Editor tab of the ribbon.**

The visibility state is set current.

8. **Click Block Editor tab⇨Visibility panel⇨Make Visible or Block Editor tab⇨Visibility panel⇨Make Invisible.**

If you click Make Visible, all the geometry currently marked as invisible is displayed but appears faded so you know which geometry can be marked visible again. If you click Make Invisible, only the visible geometry is displayed, allowing you to select which should not be displayed.

9. **In the Visibility State drop-down list, click the visibility state that you want to use as the default state.**

The selected visibility state will be the one that is displayed when the block is initially inserted into the drawing.

10. **On the ribbon, click Block Editor tab⇨Manage panel⇨Save.**

You remain in the Block Editor so you can continue adding parameters or actions as needed.

11. **On the ribbon, click Block Editor tab⇨Close panel⇨Close Block Editor to exit the Block Editor.**

Using Dynamic Blocks

You use and modify dynamic blocks similar to how you use a static (or legacy) block, including the methods for inserting blocks, editing attributes, and manipulating properties through the Properties palette. In this section, I describe the differences between the two.

Inserting a dynamic block

 Dynamic blocks are inserted into the drawing just like you insert a static (or legacy) block. You can use the Insert dialog box by starting the INSERT command and dragging and dropping blocks from the DesignCenter or the Tool Palettes window. Chapter 4 of this minibook discusses the DesignCenter and the Tool Palettes window. If you use the Tool Palettes window to insert a dynamic block, you can specify the value for each of its custom properties before the block is inserted into the drawing. You can also use the Properties palette to specify the values for dynamic properties as you drag a block on-screen.

While the block is being dragged on-screen, you can toggle through the points at which parameters are referencing in the dynamic block. These points are called the *insertion cycling order*. You can specify the insertion cycling order while you are in the Block Editor by using the Insertion Cycling Order dialog box (see Figure 2-8), which is displayed with the BCYCLEORDER command. Pressing the Ctrl key while dragging a block on-screen toggles through the various insertion cycling points in the block.

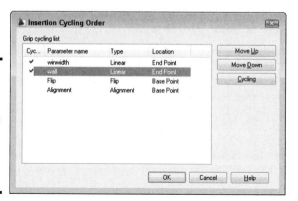

Figure 2-8:
Defining
insertion
cycling for a
block can
make
inserting it
easier.

Modifying a dynamic block

The key benefit of a dynamic block is that after you finish adding the parameters to a block and associating actions to each parameter that needs one, you can modify the block without exploding it after it is inserted into the drawing. This allows you to take advantage of attributes in your drawing, which would not be possible if you exploded the block.

Using a dynamic block's custom grips

To modify a dynamic block, you select the block to enable its grips and manipulate the geometry assigned to the parameter and action. You can also use the Properties palette to manipulate custom properties of a dynamic block in the Custom area. Select the custom property in the Properties palette and change its value. Some custom properties can be reference points, rotation angles, or a list of values.

Resetting a dynamic block

You might want to reset a dynamic block to its initial state; you could reinsert the block which requires unnecessary work. AutoCAD allows you to reset a dynamic block to its initial state by using the Reset Block option from the shortcut menu that appears when you select a block and right-click. Doing so resets only the custom properties of the block and none of the attribute values.

The RESETBLOCK command allows you to reset multiple block references at a single time.

Dynamic Blocks in Older Releases

When a DWG file is saved to an older release (with the exception of AutoCAD 2006 and later), dynamic blocks appear as if they are static blocks. A dynamic block when listed in a release prior to AutoCAD 2006 shows as an anonymous block, which is a name that is assigned by AutoCAD and not the same name that the block is given when it is created. The custom properties don't work in an older release because the release doesn't understand the information. If the block is left unaltered in an older release after it is saved to a previous version of the DWG file format, the dynamic properties of the block will work again when the drawing is reopened in AutoCAD 2006 or later. If the dynamic block contains fields in its attributes, AutoCAD displays the field values with their last updated value.

Because dynamic blocks are relatively new, older applications that are used to extend AutoCAD and work with blocks may not work correctly with dynamic blocks. You should test each application that manipulates blocks with dynamic blocks. If the application doesn't work correctly, contact the vendor of the application to see if an updated version is available.

Chapter 3: External References

In This Chapter

✔ **Understanding the differences between blocks and external references**

✔ **Using external references (xrefs)**

✔ **Referencing raster images**

✔ **Understanding DWF and DWFx underlays**

✔ **Understanding DGN underlays**

✔ **Controlling object display with draw order**

✔ **Using object linking and embedding (OLE)**

✔ **Managing external references from outside AutoCAD**

The first two chapters of this minibook explain how to create and work with blocks. Blocks form the cornerstone of reusable content in drawings. In this chapter, you read about external references and how you can use them to improve communication and keep file size down. External references are used to link DWG, DWF, DWFx, DGN, and raster image files into a drawing. By linking these files into the drawing, you have the most up-to-date geometry or image displayed. Some types of external references allow you to snap directly to the geometry that they reference.

AutoCAD LT 2009 now allows you to not only view raster images that are attached to a drawing file but also to attach raster images to a drawing file.

Blocks versus External References

Blocks are groups of objects that are assigned a user-defined name. The definition of a block is stored in a drawing file, and when a change is required, the block needs to be redefined. This can be a problem if the block is contained in a number of different drawings. *External references* maintain a link to a file outside a drawing that contains drawing objects or a raster image; the contents of the file are not actually part of the drawing file that they are being referenced into.

An external reference in a drawing file contains the location of the external file on disk, the file name of the referenced file, and its insertion point, scale, and angle of rotation. When you open a drawing that contains references to external files, the external files are reloaded as long as AutoCAD can locate them. This makes external references ideal for creating plans of a building that spans multiple drawings or drawings that can benefit from the use of geometry stored in other drawings. A floor plan for a building is an ideal example of how external references might be used because it is not uncommon for a floor plan to be the base drawing for other drawings that might be used for a reflected ceiling grid or for building systems such as HVAC or sprinklers.

Working with External References

 You work with external references through a single interface called the External References palette (see Figure 3-1). This palette allows you to attach, detach, reload, unload, and access the details of the various types of supported external references. You use the EXTERNALREFERENCES command to display the External References palette.

Figure 3-1:
The External References palette is used to manage attached DWG, DWF, DWFx, DGN, and raster image files.

The controls along the top of the palette allow you to attach an external reference, reload external references that are currently attached, or launch Help. The File References area is the main portion of the palette and displays which files are referenced into the current drawing. This area allows you to control how you view the referenced files in the palette, either in the default list view, which just shows which files are referenced, or the tree view, which displays the relationship between the parent (or host) drawing and all the files that are currently being referenced. The lower portion of the palette displays details or a preview about the selected reference in the File References area.

To start the EXTERNALREFERENCES command and display the External References palette, do one of the following:

✦ On the ribbon, click View tab➪Palettes panel➪External References.

✦ On the menu browser or menu bar, click Tools menu➪Palettes➪External References or Insert menu➪External References.

✦ On the Reference toolbar, click the External References button.

✦ At the command prompt, type **EXTERNALREFERENCES** or **ER** and press Enter.

Path to success with xrefs

AutoCAD allows you to reference a drawing file into another drawing. The drawing that is being referenced is referred to as an *xref,* which is short for *external reference.* When a drawing is referenced into another drawing, all the styles contained in the referenced file are maintained, so the drawing looks just like it would if you opened the file. Attaching an xref is similar to inserting a block, except you need to specify an attachment and a path type. There are two different attachment types for xrefs: attachment and overlay. The following list explains the two attachment types:

✦ **Attachment:** Attachment type xrefs are displayed if the host drawing file in which they are contained is referenced into another drawing file.

✦ **Overlay:** Overlay type xrefs are not displayed if the host drawing file in which they are contained is referenced into another drawing file.

When an xref is attached to a drawing, you can control how AutoCAD stores the path information to the source file associated with the xref. There are three different path types for xrefs:

✦ **Full path:** Maintains an absolute path to the file, which includes the drive letter and all folders. This option is the least flexible because it requires the drawings to be placed in specific locations in order for AutoCAD to find them.

✦ **Relative path:** Only the path relative to the parent (or host) drawing is maintained with the xref. This option is more flexible than Full path if your xrefs are stored in subfolders above or below the parent drawing.

✦ **No path:** No path information is maintained with the xref. AutoCAD looks in the parent (or host) drawings folder for the xrefs. This option is the easiest to maintain because it looks for the xrefs in the same folder as the parent drawing. Even though it is the easiest to use, it doesn't allow for much in the form of organization as the other two options do.

Book VI Chapter 3

External References

When AutoCAD loads an xref, it first looks in the folder that the external file was in when it was attached, based on the specified path type. From there, it looks in the following locations in the order listed:

✦ The current folder of the parent (or host) drawing

✦ The project search paths specified under the Project Files Search Path node on the Files tab of the Options dialog box, or the PROJECTNAME system variable (AutoCAD only)

✦ The support search paths specified under the Support File Search Path node on the Files tab of the Options dialog box

✦ The path specified in the Start-in property of the shortcut used to start AutoCAD or AutoCAD LT

Attaching an xref

Xrefs are attached to a drawing through the External References palette or the XATTACH command. During the attachment process, you need to determine the type of attachment that should be used, where in the drawing the xref should be placed, its scale and rotation, and the path type that should be used. When the xref is attached, all its named objects are suffixed with

`|filename`

For example, if a drawing file named 1234 - Floor Plan contained a layer called TitleBlock, and the file was referenced into another drawing, the layer would be named TitleBlock|1234 — Floor Plan.

To start the XATTACH command and display the External Reference dialog box, do one of the following:

✦ On the ribbon, click Blocks & Reference tab ⇨Reference panel⇨DWG.

✦ On the menu browser or menu bar, click Insert menu⇨DWG Reference.

✦ On the Reference or Insert toolbar, click the Attach Xref button.

✦ At the command prompt, type **XATTACH** or **XA** and press Enter.

✦ On the External References palette, right-click the File References area and choose Attach DWG from the shortcut menu.

To attach a DWG reference to a drawing file, follow these steps:

1. **Start the XATTACH command by using one of the methods in the preceding list.**

The Select Reference File dialog box is displayed.

2. **Browse to and select the drawing file that you want to attach. Click Open.**

The Select Reference File dialog box closes, and the External Reference dialog box appears (see Figure 3-2). The path to and the name of the file you selected appear in the Found In and Saved Path fields, respectively. The Name drop-down list allows you to select a previously attached drawing file, and Browse allows you to specify a different drawing file to reference.

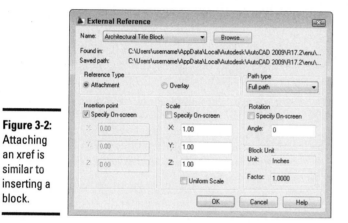

Book VI Chapter 3

External References

Figure 3-2:
Attaching
an xref is
similar to
inserting a
block.

3. **In the Reference Type area, specify the type of attachment for the xref.**

You can select either Attachment or Overlay.

4. **In the Path Type area, specify the path format that should be maintained when attaching the xref.**

You can select Full Path, Relative Path, or No Path. If you want to use the Relative Path option, the drawing that the xref is being attached to must be saved first. For more information on the available path options, see "Path to success with xrefs" earlier in this chapter.

5. **In the Insertion Point area, select or deselect the Specify On-Screen option. If it's deselected, enter the coordinate value for the insertion point of the block in the X, Y, and Z text boxes.**

If Specify On-Screen is selected, you're prompted for the insertion point of the xref after you click OK to close the External Reference dialog box.

6. **In the Scale area, select or deselect the Specify On-Screen option. If it's deselected, enter the scale for the X, Y, and Z axes in the text boxes, but if Uniform Scale is selected, you can enter a scale only in the X axis text box.**

If Specify On-Screen is selected, AutoCAD prompts you for the scale of the xref after you click OK to close the External Reference dialog box.

7. **In the Rotation area, either select or deselect the Specify On-Screen option. If it's deselected, enter the rotation angle in the Rotation text box.**

If Specify On-Screen is selected, you're prompted for the rotation angle of the xref after you click OK to close the External Reference dialog box.

8. **In the Block Unit area, verify the current insertion units and scale that will be applied to the block.**

The Unit value is based on the current setting of the INSUNITS system variable, which specifies the drawing's current units for inserted blocks. The Factor value is the result of the unit used when the xref was created and the current value of INSUNITS.

To change the current value of INSUNITS, close the External Reference dialog box and use the UNITS command to display the Units dialog box. In the Units dialog box, select the desired insertion unit from the drop-down list in the Insertion Units area and then click OK.

9. **Click OK.**

The External Reference dialog box closes, and AutoCAD returns to the drawing window. The XATTACH command may still be running depending on whether you selected any of the Specify On-Screen options for the insertion point, scale, or rotation. The following prompts might be displayed:

```
Specify insertion point or
    [Scale/X/Y/Z/Rotate/PScale/PX/PY/PZ/PRotate]:
Enter X scale factor, specify opposite corner, or
    [Corner/XYZ] <1>:
Enter Y scale factor <use X scale factor>:
Specify rotation angle <0>:
```

External reference notification

AutoCAD offers a notification system for various features. External references are part of this notification system. You can see when a drawing has an xref attached to it by the appearance of the Manage Xrefs icon in the status bar tray. When a change occurs to one of the attached external references, the icon changes and a notification balloon is displayed (see Figure 3-3). Click the link in the notification balloon to reload the external references that have changed.

Figure 3-3:
Stay informed with the External Reference notification.

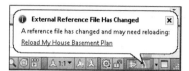

The External Reference notification can be turned on and off with the XREFNOTIFY system variable (AutoCAD only). The default value is 2, which displays the balloon and changes the icon to reflect a change to one of the xrefs. Instead of completely disabling the notification, you may want to use the TRAYSETTINGS command to control how long the notification is displayed.

Editing an xref

Xrefs can be edited by using many of the common modify commands, but there are also some unique commands that are available for modifying xrefs. There will be times when you'll want to make changes directly to the drawing file that's being referenced; in these cases, AutoCAD allows you to edit the xrefs in-place or open them in a drawing window. The commands that allow you to perform these editing operations are REFEDIT and XOPEN.

The REFEDIT and XOPEN commands are not available in AutoCAD LT.

Editing a reference in-place

Starting the REFEDIT command displays the Reference Edit dialog box (shown in Figure 3-4) and allows you to edit an xref or block in-place. AutoCAD opens the xref or block for modification right where it's inserted in the drawing. This can be great when you want to modify the xref or block based on surrounding objects in the drawing. When an xref or block is being edited in-place, some commands are not available, such as SAVE, BEDIT, and EXPORT.

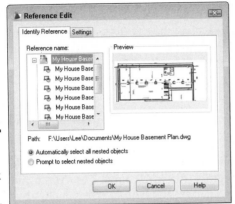

Figure 3-4:
Editing an
xref or block
in-place.

To start the REFEDIT command and display the Reference Edit dialog box, use one of the following methods:

✦ On the ribbon, click Blocks & References tab⇨References⇨Edit In-Place.

✦ On the menu browser or menu bar, click Tools menu⇨Xref and Block In-Place Editing⇨Edit Reference In-Place.

✦ On the Refedit toolbar, click the Edit Reference In-Place button.

✦ At the command prompt, type **REFEDIT** and press Enter.

✦ Select an xref, right-click, and choose Edit Xref In-Place from the shortcut menu.

✦ Double-click the xref.

The following steps explain how to edit an xref in-place:

1. **Use one of the previously mentioned methods to start the REFEDIT command.**

The following prompt is displayed at the command line:

```
Select reference:
```

2. **At the prompt, select the xref you want to edit in-place.**

The Reference Edit dialog box is displayed (refer to Figure 3-4).

3. **On the Identify Reference tab, select the Automatically Select All Nested Objects option.**

This option selects all the objects in the xref, even any attributes that it may contain.

4. **Click the Settings tab to specify the additional settings you want to use during in-place editing.**

It's best to have the following options selected:

- **Create Unique Layer, Style, and Block Names:** All layers and styles used by the objects in the block have unique names while the in-place editing session is active.

- **Lock Objects Not in Working Set:** Locks all objects in the drawing that are not part of the selected block.

This way, you can easily identify which objects you are working with. The Display Attribute Definitions for Editing option controls whether attributes in the block definition are displayed during the in-place editing session.

5. **Click OK.**

The Reference Edit dialog box closes and the Edit Reference tab is displayed on the ribbon (or the Refedit toolbar is displayed if the ribbon is not displayed). The ribbon and toolbar contain tools specific for editing an xref in-place. All the objects that are not part of the xref are faded, which allows you to identify which objects are in the xref.

6. **Modify the objects you want to change.**

You can add and remove objects from the xref. (On the ribbon, click Edit Reference tab⇨Edit Reference panel⇨Xref and Block, Add to Working Set or Xref and Block, Remove from Working. Or click the Add to Working Set or Remove from Working Set button on the Refedit toolbar.)

7. **On the ribbon, click Edit Reference tab⇨ Edit Reference panel⇨Save Changes (or Save Reference Edits on the Refedit toolbar) to save any changes made.**

A message box appears asking you to confirm the changes you made to the xref.

8. **In the AutoCAD message box, click OK to save the changes made.**

The changes are committed back to the xref, and the in-place editing session is closed. The xref is reloaded automatically.

The degree to which the background objects are faded is controlled by the XFADECTL system variable. By default, the setting is 50.

Opening a reference

The XOPEN command (on the menu browser or menu bar, click Tools menu⇨ Xref and Block In-place Editing⇨Open Reference; or on the External References palette, right-click a DWG reference and choose Open) open an xref in its own drawing window, which enables you to use any editing commands without the limitations of the REFEDIT command. After you save the changes to the file that's open for editing, the External Reference Notification is displayed, which allows you to reload the external reference by clicking the link.

Clipping an xref

Clipping an xref enables you to control how much of the xref is displayed. When working with large xrefs, loading the file can take a while. By clipping an xref, you can reduce the amount of time it takes to load a drawing. The XCLIP command controls the clipping boundary of an xref. The XCLIP command has the following options:

+ **ON:** Enables the clipping for an xref.

+ **OFF:** Disables the clipping for an xref.

+ **Clipdepth:** Controls the distance of the front and back clipping planes from the clipping boundary. The option has the suboptions Front, Back, Distance, and Remove.

+ **Delete:** Removes the clipping boundary for an xref.

+ **Generate Polyline:** Creates a polyline object based on an xref's clipping boundary.

+ **New boundary:** Adds a clipping boundary to the xref. You can create a clipping boundary by picking two points (rectangular), creating a closed polyline object by picking two or more points (polyline), or selecting a closed polyline object. You can also invert how the objects of the xref are displayed when the clipping boundary is created.

The XCLIP command is available only in AutoCAD. If you open a drawing that contains a clipped xref in AutoCAD LT, the clipped boundary is maintained.

To start the XCLIP command, use one of the following methods:

+ On the ribbon, click Blocks & References⇨Reference panel's title bar⇨Clip Xref.

+ On the menu browser or menu bar, click Modify menu⇨Clip⇨Xref.

+ On the Reference toolbar, click the Clip Xref button.

+ At the command prompt, type **XCLIP** or **XC** and press Enter.

+ Select an xref, right-click, and choose Xref Clip from the shortcut menu.

Clipping a drawing reference (xref)

The following steps explain how to clip an xref based on a rectangular boundary:

1. **Start the XCLIP command by using one of the methods in the preceding list.**

   The following prompt appears at the command line:

   ```
   Select objects:
   ```

2. At the prompt, select the xref that you want to clip and press Enter.

The following prompt appears at the command line:

```
Enter clipping option
[ON/OFF/Clipdepth/Delete/generate Polyline/New
    boundary] <New>:
```

3. Press Enter to accept the default option of creating a new boundary.

The following prompt appears at the command line:

```
Specify clipping boundary:
[Select polyline/Polygonal/Rectangular/Invert clip]
    <Rectangular>:
```

4. Press Enter to accept the default option of creating a rectangular clipping boundary.

The following prompt appears at the command line:

```
Specify first corner:
```

5. Specify the first corner and then the opposite corner of the rectangular clipping boundary. The points should be outside the area of the xref that you want left visible.

The command ends, and the xref is clipped based on the specified rectangle.

The boundary that appears when you use the XCLIP command can be controlled on the menu browser or menu bar by clicking Modify menu⇨ Object⇨External Reference⇨Frame. By default, the frame is hidden.

Even though the XCLIP command is intended to be used with xrefs, you can also use it to clip blocks.

Editing a clipped xref

You can modify the clipped boundary of an xref by running the XCLIP command again, or selecting the clip boundary and using grips to modify what is displayed. You can use the XCLIP command to replace the clipping boundary that is already assigned to the xref, remove the clip boundary, or turn the clip boundary on or off. When grips are active for a clip boundary, you can resize and adjust the boundary by moving the grip points or click the arrow grip to invert the clipping boundary.

If you set the XCLIPFRAME system variable to a value of 0, you can't use grips to modify the clip boundary of an xref. If you set XCLIPFRAME to a value of 1, you can modify the clip boundary of an xref.

Increasing the performance of xrefs

When you're working with a number of xrefs or working with large xrefs, you can do a few things to help increase performance. If you're no longer using some of the attached xrefs, the best thing to do is unload or detach the xref through the External References palette. Unloading an xref keeps the link to the external drawing file, but keeps all references to the xref in the drawing and doesn't just load the objects from the file into memory. To unload an xref, select the xref in the File References area, right-click, and choose Unload from the shortcut menu. You can use the Reload option from the shortcut menu to load the xref back into the drawing if you need it later. Detaching an xref severs the link to the external drawing file, and removes all references of the xref from the drawing file.

Another way to increase the performance of working with Xrefs is to use a process called demand load. *Demand loading* improves the overall performance of working with xrefs by loading only the part of the drawing that's needed. Demand loading can be changed by selecting an option from the Demand Load Xrefs drop-down list in the External References (Xrefs) section on the Open and Save tab of the Options dialog box. AutoCAD provides three options for demand loading:

✦ **Disabled:** Demand loading is turned off and the entire drawing is loaded.

✦ **Enabled:** Demand loading is turned on and only the part of the drawing that is required is loaded. This option locks the file so it can't be edited by others by opening it or by using the REFEDIT command.

✦ **Enable with copy:** Demand loading is turned on and only the part of the drawing that is required is loaded. This option also creates a copy of the drawing file, and the copy gets loaded into AutoCAD. The original file is not locked, so others can edit the file by opening it or by using the REFEDIT command. This is the default option.

If you use demand loading, you can take advantage of indexing in your drawing file. Indexing allows AutoCAD to locate specific objects and layers in a drawing that's being referenced. AutoCAD offers two types of indexing: spatial and layer. I talk more about spatial and layer indexing in Chapter 3 of Book VIII.

Binding an xref

An xref can be bound to its parent (or host) drawing. You can also bind select named styles to an xref's parent drawing. To integrate all the geometry and named objects in an xref, right-click the xref that you want to bind in the File References area on the External References palette and select Bind from the shortcut menu. The Bind Xrefs dialog box appears, which allows you to specify one of the two bind types: Bind or Insert.

If you choose Bind for the bind type, the named objects in the xref are bound with the name structure of

```
file name$#$symbol name
```

For example, if you bind an xref with the file name Grid Plan that has a layer called Grid into a drawing, it is bound with the name Grid Plan0Grid. If you choose Insert for the bind type, the same layer name as previously mentioned is just Grid. The named objects are merged cleanly into the existing named objects of the parent drawing when the Insert bind type is used.

When you use the Insert option the resulting named objects are easier to read but this can also be an issue. If a layer named Grid exists in the parent drawing and also in the xref, the xref will take on the properties of the parent's Grid layer. This can cause the drawing to look and potentially plot differently. The same holds true for other named objects, but the problem shows up more with named objects such as text styles and dimension styles. So based on how you look at it, the Insert bind type can be a good thing or bad thing.

You can bind named objects from an xref attached to a drawing, but not any objects in the xref, by using the XBIND command. The XBIND command displays the Xbind dialog box (see Figure 3-5). In the Xbind dialog box, expand the xref in the Xrefs area and expand the node for the supported named objects that you want to bind into the parent drawing. Select the named object and click the Add -> button. The named object is added to the Destinations to Bind area. Click OK to bind the selected named objects to the parent drawing.

Figure 3-5:
Xbind
allows you
to bind
selected
named
objects into
the parent
drawing.

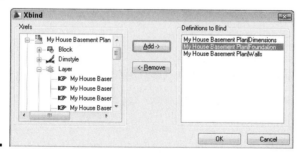

Raster Images

In addition to referencing drawing files, AutoCAD allows you to reference many kinds of raster images. You may want to reference a raster image that holds a company logo, an aerial view of a new subdivision, or a rendered image of a model. Raster images are files that are made up of a series of dots, which are referred to as *pixels*. AutoCAD and AutoCAD LT are vector-based programs, which means they store objects in the form of coordinate values and properties to regenerate the objects when the file is opened, viewed, or plotted. Raster images are referenced into a drawing the same way that you reference a drawing file. Unlike xrefs, raster images can't be bound to a drawing. You use the External References palette to attach, reload, unload, and detach raster images.

AutoCAD LT 2009 allows you to attach raster images with the External References palette or the IMAGEATTACH command.

Attaching a raster image

To attach raster images to a drawing, you use the External References palette or the IMAGEATTACH command. During the attachment process, you need to determine where in the drawing the image should be placed, its scale and rotation, and the path type that you want to use. When an image is scaled, it can appear grainy on-screen; when plotted, the graininess is due to how the image was created and its DPI (dots per inch) property. The greater the DPI, the larger the image can be scaled before it starts to appear grainy.

To start the IMAGEATTACH command and display the Image dialog box, use one of these methods:

✦ On the ribbon, click Blocks & References tab⇨Reference panel⇨Image.

✦ On the menu browser or menu bar, click Insert menu⇨Raster Image Reference.

✦ On the Reference or Insert toolbar, click the Attach Image button.

✦ At the command prompt, type **IMAGEATTACH** or **IAT** and press Enter.

✦ On the External References palette, right-click over the File References area and choose Attach Image from the shortcut menu.

To attach a raster image to your drawing, follow these steps. For more information on some of the options in the Image dialog box, see the "Attaching an xref" section earlier in this chapter.

> *1.* **Start the IMAGEATTACH command by using one of the methods in the preceding list.**
>
> The Select Image File dialog box appears.

2. **Browse to the raster image file that you want to attach and select it. Use the Files of Type drop-down list to filter the displayed files in the dialog box. Click Open.**

The Select Image File dialog box closes, and the Image dialog box (see Figure 3-6) is displayed. The path to and the name of the file you selected appear in the Found In and Saved Path fields, respectively. The Name drop-down list allows you to select a previously attached raster image file, and Browse allows you to specify a different raster image file to reference.

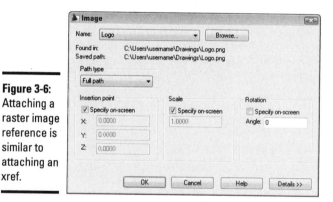

Figure 3-6:
Attaching a raster image reference is similar to attaching an xref.

3. **Click Details to display additional information about the selected image.**

The Image Information area provides feedback on how the image will be scaled when it's inserted. AutoCAD automatically calculates the number of pixels by the current units to determine the size of the image when it's inserted. The current AutoCAD units are determined by the setting in the Insertion Scale area of the Units dialog box. You use the UNITS command to display the Units dialog box.

4. **In the Path Type area, specify the path format that should be maintained when attaching the raster image.**

5. **In the Insertion Point area, specify how and where the image should be inserted.**

6. **In the Scale area, specify how the image should be scaled.**

7. **In the Rotation area, specify how the image should be rotated.**

8. **Click OK.**

The Image dialog box closes and you are returned to the drawing window. The IMAGEATTACH command may still be running depending on whether you selected any of the Specify On-Screen options for the insertion point, scale, or rotation. The following prompts might be displayed:

```
Specify insertion point <0,0>:
Specify scale factor or [Unit] <1>:
Specify rotation angle <0>:
```

Clipping a raster image

Like xrefs, raster images can be clipped to show only part of the image. Only showing what is necessary in the drawing can help to save time when you need to regenerate the drawing during panning or zooming, especially if a large image is attached, because only the necessary section of the image is displayed. The IMAGECLIP command controls the clipping boundary of a raster image. The IMAGECLIP command has the same options as the XCLIP command, with the exceptions of Generate Polyline, Select Polyline, and Invert Clip options.

To start the IMAGECLIP command, do one of the following:

✦ On the ribbon, click Blocks & References⇨Reference panel's title bar⇨Clip Image.

✦ On the menu browser or menu bar, click Modify menu⇨Clip⇨Image.

✦ On the Reference toolbar, click the Clip Image button.

✦ At the command prompt type **IMAGECLIP** or **IC** and press Enter.

✦ Select a raster image and right-click, and then choose Image⇨Clip.

Clip a raster image

The following steps explain how to clip a raster image based on a rectangular boundary:

1. **Start the IMAGECLIP command by using one of the methods in the preceding list.**

2. **At the *Select image to clip:* prompt, select the raster image you want to clip and press Enter.**

3. **Press Enter to accept the default option for creating a new boundary or select one of the other available options.**

4. **Press Enter to accept the default option for creating a rectangular clipping boundary or select the other available option.**

5. **Specify the first corner and then the opposite corner of the rectangular clipping boundary.**

   The points should be outside the area of the image you want left visible.

The boundary displayed before and after you use the IMAGECLIP command can be controlled on the menu browser or menu bar by clicking Modify menu⇨ Object⇨Image⇨Frame (which starts the IMAGEFRAME command). The visibility of all the image frames is toggled on and off. By default the frame is displayed and plotted. You have three options to control how the frame should be displayed: 0, the frame is not displayed and is not plotted, 1, the frame is displayed and is plotted, and 2, the frame is displayed and is not plotted.

You can use the IMAGEFRAME command and a value of 0 to lock images so they can't be selected.

Editing a clipped raster image

You can modify the clipped boundary of a raster image by running the IMAGECLIP command again or by selecting the clip boundary and using grips to modify its size and shape to control what part of the image is displayed. You can use the IMAGECLIP command to replace the clipping boundary that is already assigned to the image, remove the clip boundary, or turn the clip boundary on or off. IMAGEFRAME must be set to a value of 1 or 2 to select the image so that the clipped boundary can be modified.

In AutoCAD only (sorry AutoCAD LT users), you can use the IMAGEEDIT command that comes with the Express Tools to open a raster image in an external image-editing application such as MS Paint or Adobe PhotoShop. The IMAGEEDIT command opens the selected raster image reference in the system default editor unless the IMAGEAPP command is used to specify a different image editor application. You can start the IMAGEEDIT command on the menu browser or menu bar by clicking Express menu⇨File Tools⇨ Edit Image. The IMAGEAPP command can be run only from the command prompt.

Controlling the appearance of a raster image

AutoCAD allows you to tweak an image after it's attached to a drawing. You can alter the appearance of an image by changing its level of brightness, contrast, or fade. You can use the Properties palette or the IMAGEADJUST command (select the image, right-click, and choose Image⇨Adjust). The IMAGEADJUST command displays the Image Adjust dialog box (see Figure 3-7) for controlling the brightness, contrast, or fade levels of the selected image, and as the values are changed, the preview in the dialog box is updated. If you use the Properties palette, the changes are applied dynamically to the image in the drawing window.

**Book VI
Chapter 3**

External References

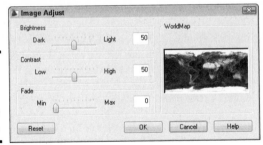

Figure 3-7:
Adjusting the appearance of an image.

If you have a fairly large image, it can slow down the regeneration process of the drawing. You can clip the image, but this is not always an option, depending on the drawing you're working on. The IMAGEQUALITY command (on the menu browser or menu bar, click Modify menu⇨Object⇨Image⇨ Quality) allows you to control the quality of the image that you see on-screen. You can choose from either High or Draft; selecting Draft can help to decrease the amount of time it takes to regenerate the display of the drawing. This setting does not affect plotting because plotting is always done at High quality. If your attached image type supports transparency, you can control whether the image is displayed as transparent so objects beneath it are displayed. The TRANSPARENCY command (select the image, right-click, and choose Image⇨ Transparency) allows you to toggle transparency for an image on or off.

DWF and DWFx Underlays

Design Web Format (DWF and DWFx) files are commonly used for exchanging drawings in a secure electronic format that non-CAD users can use to view, print, and mark up with Autodesk Design Review 2009, which is a free viewer that can be downloaded from Autodesk.com. DWF, DWFx, and drawing files are vector-based files, unlike raster images, which are made up of pixels. When a DWF or DWFx file is attached to a drawing, it is known as an *underlay*.

Because DWF and DWFx files are vector-based files, AutoCAD allows you to snap to the objects that are part of a DWF or DWFx underlay. Unlike an xref, a DWF or DWFx file can't be bound to a drawing file, which helps to maintain the file's security. I talk about how to create and view DWF and DWFx files in Book VIII. In this chapter, when I refer to DWF files, I am talking about both DWF and DWFx unless otherwise noted. You use the External References palette to attach, reload, unload, and detach DWF underlays.

AutoCAD 2009 and AutoCAD LT 2009 support the creation of DWFx files, which is the next evolutionary step of the DWF file format. DWFx is an XPS-compliant format that allows someone with Internet Explorer 7 or Vista the ability to view the file without having to download additional software.

Attaching a DWF underlay

To attach a DWF file to a drawing, you use the External References palette or the DWFATTACH command. When you attach a DWF file, you need to determine where in the drawing the DWF underlay should be placed, its scale and rotation, the path type that should be used, and which one of the sheets in the DWF file is being referenced. Attaching DWF files is limited to 2D DWF files only; if you select a 3D DWF file, AutoCAD informs you that the selected file doesn't contain any sheets that can be attached. Layer information is imported into the drawing when a DWF file is attached as long as the layer information was published to the DWF file.

When a DWF underlay is attached to a drawing, it's placed on the current layer. However, you may be able to control the display of the objects in the DWF underlay based on whether the DWF file was published with the original drawing's layer information. You use the DWGLAYERS command to turn on and off the display of objects on a layer in a DWF underlay. The DWFLAYERS command displays the DWF Layers dialog box (see Figure 3-8), which allows you to turn the display of a layer on or off by clicking the light bulb icon next to the layer name in the dialog box. To display the DWF Layers dialog box, enter DWFLAYERS at the command prompt, or select a DWF underlay, right-click, and choose DWF Layers from the shortcut menu.

Book VI
Chapter 3

External References

Figure 3-8:
The display
of layers in
a DWF
underlay is
controlled
with the
DWF Layers
dialog box.

To start the DWFATTACH command and display the Attach DWF Underlay dialog box, do one of the following:

✦ On the ribbon, click Blocks & References tab⇨Reference panel⇨DWF.

✦ On the menu browser or menu bar, click Insert menu⇨DWF Underlay.

✦ On the Insert toolbar, click the Insert a DWF Underlay button.

✦ At the command prompt, type **DWFATTACH** and press Enter.

✦ On the External References palette, right-click the File References area and choose Attach DWF from the shortcut menu.

To attach a DWF file, use the following steps. (For more information on some of the options in the Attach DWF Underlay dialog box, see the "Attaching an xref" section.)

1. **Start the DWFATTACH command by using of the methods in the preceding list.**

   The Select DWF File dialog box appears.

2. **Browse to and select the DWF file that you want to attach. Click Open.**

   The Select DWF File dialog box closes, and the Attach DWF Underlay dialog box (see Figure 3-9) is displayed. The path to and the name of the file you selected appear in the Found In and Saved Path fields, respectively. The Name drop-down list allows you to select a previously attached DWF file, and Browse allows you to specify a different DWF file to reference.

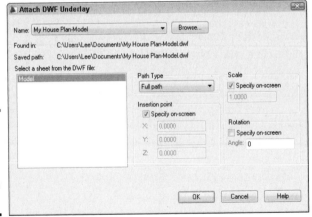

Figure 3-9:
Attaching a DWF file is similar to attaching an xref.

3. **In the Select a Sheet from the DWF File list box, select a sheet.**

   The selected sheet is highlighted and is the one that will be attached.

4. **In the Path Type area, specify the path format that should be maintained when attaching the DWF underlay.**

5. **In the Insertion Point area, specify how and where the DWF underlay should be inserted.**

6. **In the Scale area, specify how the DWF underlay should be scaled.**

7. **In the Rotation area, specify how the DWF underlay should be rotated.**

8. **Click OK.**

The DWF Attach Underlay dialog box closes, and you're returned to the drawing window. The DWFATTACH command may still be running, depending on whether you selected any of the Specify On-Screen options for the insertion point, scale, or rotation. The following prompts might be displayed:

```
Specify insertion point:
Specify scale factor or [Unit] <1.0000>:
Specify rotation angle <0>:
```

Only one sheet from a DWF file can be attached at a time. If you need to attach multiple sheets from a DWF file, you must repeat the preceding steps for each of the sheets that you want to attach.

Book VI
Chapter 3

External References

The DWFOSNAP system variable controls whether object snaps can be used on objects that are part of a DWF underlay. By default, you can use object snaps with DWF underlays. Set the DWFOSNAP system variable to a value of 0 (zero) to disable the use of object snaps with DWF underlays, or 1 to enable the use of object snaps with DWF underlays. When using object snaps to snap to objects in a DWF file, the tooltip for an object snap is prefixed with the text *DWF (approximate):*. The *approximate* reminds you that while DWF files can be used as referenced geometry, the objects in the file lack the precision that might be necessary for some designs. The precision of the objects in the DWF file are set during the plotting or publishing of the source drawing file.

Clipping a DWF underlay

DWF underlays can be clipped just like xrefs to show only part of the referenced sheet. The DWFCLIP command is used to control the clipping boundary of a DWF underlay. The DWFCLIP command has the same options as the XCLIP command, with the exception of the Generate Polyline, Select Polyline, and Invert Clip options.

To start the DWFCLIP command, do one of the following:

✦ On the ribbon, click Blocks & References⇨Reference panel's title bar⇨Clip DWF.

✦ At the command prompt, type **DWFCLIP** and press Enter.

✦ Select a DWF underlay, right-click, and then choose DWF Clip from the shortcut menu.

Clip a DWF underlay

To start the DWFCLIP command and clip a DWF underlay based on a rectangular boundary, follow these steps:

1. **Start the DWFCLIP command by using one of the methods in the preceding list.**

2. **Press Enter to accept the default option of creating a new boundary or select one of the other available options.**

3. **Press Enter to accept the default option of creating a rectangular clipping boundary or select the other available option.**

4. **Specify the first corner and then the opposite corner of the rectangular clipping boundary.**

   The points should be outside the area of the DWF underlay that you want visible.

You can control the boundary that's displayed before and after you use the DWFCLIP command by using the DWFFRAME system variable. The DWF-FRAME system variable controls the display of the frames for all DWF underlays in a drawing. By default the frame is displayed and not plotted. You have three options to control how the frame should be displayed: 0, the frame is not displayed and is not plotted, 1, the frame is displayed and is plotted, and 2, the frame is displayed and is not plotted.

Editing a clipped DWF underlay

You can modify the clipped boundary of a DWF underlay by running the DWFCLIP command again, or by selecting the clip boundary and using grips to modify its size and shape to control what is displayed of the DWF underlay. You can use the DWFCLIP command to replace the clipping boundary that is already assigned to the DWF underlay, remove the clip boundary, or turn the clip boundary on or off.

Controlling the appearance of DWF underlay

AutoCAD allows you to adjust the appearance of the objects of a DWF underlay by changing its level of brightness, contrast, or fade. You can use the Properties palette or the DWFADJUST command. The DWFADJUST command, unlike the IMAGEADJUST command, works only from the command prompt. If you use the Properties palette, the changes are applied dynamically to the DWF underlay right in the drawing window.

DGN Underlays

Design (DGN) files are created with Bentley's MicroStation. DGN files are commonly used when exchanging files with users who work in the civil and infrastructure industries but can be found in AEC industry as well. DGN files such as DWF, DWFx, and drawing files are vector-based files. When a DGN file is attached to a drawing, just like a DWF file, it is known as an *underlay*. Because DGN files are vector-based files, AutoCAD allows you to snap to the objects that are part of a DGN underlay. Unlike xrefs, a DGN file can't be bound to a drawing file. You use the External References palette to attach, reload, unload, and detach DGN underlays.

AutoCAD 2009 and AutoCAD LT 2009 support the ability to import and attach V7 DGN files.

Attaching a DGN underlay

To attach a DGN file to a drawing, you use the External References palette or the DGNATTACH command. When you attach a DGN file, you need to determine where in the drawing the DGN underlay should be placed, its scale and rotation, the path type that should be used, which one of the models in the DGN file is being referenced, and the units that should be used for the conversion. Layer information is imported into the drawing when a DGN file is attached. The layers that come in from a DGN file are not managed with the Layers Properties Manager palette like layers in the parent drawing or xrefs are.

To control the display of the objects in a DGN underlay, you use the DGN-LAYERS command. The DGNLAYERS command displays the DGN Layers dialog box (see Figure 3-10), which allows you to turn the display of a layer on or off by clicking the light bulb icon next to the layer name in the dialog box. To display the DGN Layers dialog box, enter DGNLAYERS at the command prompt, or select a DGN underlay, right-click, and choose DGN Layers from the shortcut menu.

Figure 3-10: The layers for a DGN underlay are kept out of the parent drawing but can be accessed with the DGN Layers dialog box.

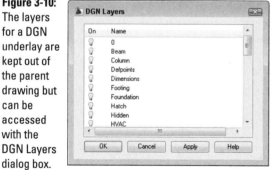

To start the DGNATTACH command and display the Attach DGN Underlay dialog box, do one of the following:

✦ On the ribbon, click Blocks & References tab➪Reference panel➪DGN.

✦ On the menu browser or menu bar, click Insert menu➪DGN Underlay.

✦ On the Insert toolbar, click the Insert a DGN Underlay button.

✦ At the command prompt, type **DGNATTACH** and press Enter.

✦ On the External References palette, right-click over the File References area and choose Attach DGN from the shortcut menu.

To attach a DGN file, use the following steps. (For more information on some of the options in the Attach DGN Underlay dialog box, see the "Attaching an xref" section.)

1. **Start the DGNATTACH command by using one of the methods in the preceding list.**

The Select DGN File dialog box appears.

2. **In the Select DGN File dialog box, browse to and select the DGN file that you want to attach. Click Open.**

The Select DGN File dialog box closes, and the Attach DGN Underlay dialog box (see Figure 3-11) is displayed. The path to and the name of the file you selected appear in the Found In and Saved Path fields. The Name drop-down list allows you to select a previously attached DGN file, and Browse allows you to specify a different DGN file to reference.

Figure 3-11: Attaching a DGN file is similar to attaching other external referenced files.

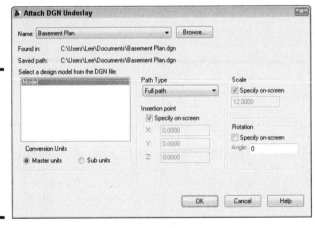

3. **In the Select a Design Model from the DGN File list box, select a model.**

The selected model is highlighted and is the one that will be attached.

4. **In the Conversion Units area, choose Master Units or Sub Units.**

These options control which unit AutoCAD uses for the conversion of the objects in the DGN file to the current drawing.

5. **In the Path Type area, specify the path format that should be maintained when attaching the DGN underlay.**

6. **In the Insertion Point area, specify how and where the DGN underlay should be inserted.**

7. **In the Scale area, specify how the DGN underlay should be scaled.**

8. **In the Rotation area, specify how the DGN underlay should be rotated.**

9. **Click OK.**

   The DGN Attach Underlay dialog box closes, and you're returned to the drawing window. The DGNATTACH command may still be running, depending on whether you selected any of the Specify On-Screen options for the insertion point, scale, or rotation. The following prompts might be displayed:

   ```
   Specify insertion point:
   Specify scale factor or [Unit] <12.0000>:
   Specify rotation angle <0>:
   ```

Book VI
Chapter 3

External References

Only one model from a DGN file can be attached at a time. If you need to attach multiple models from a DGN file, repeat the preceding steps for each of the models you want to attach.

The DGNOSNAP system variable controls whether object snaps can be used on objects that are part of a DGN underlay. By default, you can use object snaps with DGN underlays. Set the DGNOSNAP system variable to a value of 0 (zero) to disable the use of object snaps with DGN underlays, or 1 to enable the use of object snaps with DGN underlays. When using object snaps to snap to objects in a DGN file, the tooltip for an object snap is prefixed with the text *DGN:*.

Clipping a DGN underlay

DGN underlays can be clipped just like xrefs, DWF underlays, and raster images to show only part of the referenced model. The DGNCLIP command is used to control the clipping boundary of a DGN underlay. The DGNCLIP command has the same options as the XCLIP command, with the exceptions of the Generate Polyline, Select Polyline, and Invert Clip options.

To start the DGNCLIP command, do one of the following:

✦ On the ribbon, click Blocks & References➪Reference panel's title bar➪Clip DGN.

✦ At the command prompt, type **DGNCLIP** and press Enter.

✦ Select a DGN underlay, right-click, and then choose DGN Clip from the shortcut menu.

Clip a DGN underlay

To start the DGNCLIP command and clip a DGN underlay based on a rectangular boundary, follow these steps:

1. **Start the DGNCLIP command by using one of the methods in the preceding list.**

2. **Press Enter to accept the default option of creating a new boundary or select one of the other available options.**

3. **Press Enter to accept the default option of creating a rectangular clipping boundary or select the other available option.**

4. **Specify the first corner and then the opposite corner of the rectangular clipping boundary.**

   The points should be outside the area of the DGN underlay that you want visible.

You can control the boundary that's displayed before and after you use the DGNCLIP command by using the DGNFRAME system variable. The DGN-FRAME system variable controls the display of the frames for all DGN underlays in a drawing. By default the frame is displayed and not plotted. You have three options to control how the frame should be displayed: 0, the frame is not displayed and is not plotted, 1, the frame is displayed and is plotted, and 2, the frame is displayed and is not plotted.

Editing a clipped DGN underlay

You can modify the clipped boundary of a DGN underlay by running the DGNCLIP command again, or by selecting the clip boundary and using grips to modify its size and shape to control what's displayed of the DGN underlay. You can use the DGNCLIP command to replace the clipping boundary that is already assigned to the DGN underlay, remove the clip boundary, or turn the clip boundary on or off.

Controlling the appearance of a DGN underlay

AutoCAD allows you to adjust the appearance of the objects of a DGN underlay by changing its level of brightness, contrast, or fade. You can use the Properties palette or the DGNADJUST command. The DGNADJUST command, unlike the IMAGEADJUST and DWFADJUST commands, works only from the command prompt. If you use the Properties palette, the changes are applied dynamically to the DGN underlay right in the drawing window.

Draw Order

Draw order determines how objects are displayed on-screen and how they are plotted. When you draw new objects, they're placed at the top of the draw order and therefore appear above other objects in the drawing. AutoCAD provides several commands that allow you to control the draw order of objects in the drawing. You use the DRAWORDER and TEXT-TOFRONT commands to help control the order in which objects are displayed. For example, you can use the DRAWORDER command to display objects on top of a raster image or text in front of other objects when it is assigned a background mask so that it hides the objects that need to be masked out below the text.

The DRAWORDER command has four options that allow you to bring objects all the way to the front, send them all the way to the back, or bring them up in front or behind selected objects. When working with external referenced files, you may need to control the display of hatched areas as well as other objects to make sure they display correctly. The TEXTTOFRONT command allows you to quickly bring all text or dimensions or both to the front. If you're using fills or background masks with your text and dimensions, you want to make sure that they're all the way at the top of the display order to make sure that all objects below them are properly masked.

Object Linking and Embedding (OLE)

Object linking and embedding — or OLE as it's often referred to — allows you to place information from one Windows-based application into another while retaining the ability to edit the information by using the original application. For example, you can link information from a spreadsheet and display it in AutoCAD. Then if the spreadsheet is updated, the changes are reflected in AutoCAD the next time the drawing file is loaded. You use the INSERTOBJ command to insert and link a document into a drawing. The INSERTOBJ command displays the Insert Object dialog box (see Figure 3-12).

Figure 3-12:
Attaching a file to a drawing other than a drawing, a DWF file, or an image.

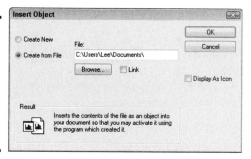

To start the INSERTOBJ command and display the Insert Object dialog box, do one of the following:

✦ On the ribbon, click Blocks & References tab➪Data panel➪OLE Object.

✦ On the menu browser or menu, click Insert menu➪OLE Object.

✦ On the Insert toolbar, click the OLE Object button.

✦ At the command prompt, type **INSERTOBJ** and press Enter.

To start the INSERTOBJ command and link a word processor document, follow these steps:

1. **Start the INSERTOBJ command by using one of the methods in the preceding list.**

   The Insert Object dialog box appears.

2. **Select the Create from File option.**

   Create from File allows you to link to an existing file. Create New enables you to link to a newly created file.

3. **Select the Link check box.**

   This way, you keep a live link between the drawing and the selected file.

4. **Click Browse and then select the word processing document or the file that you want to link to in your drawing. After you select the file, click Open to return to the Insert Object dialog box.**

   This way, you keep a live link between the drawing and the selected file.

5. **Click OK and the document is placed into the drawing.**

   The document is placed in the upper-left corner of the drawing window.

After an OLE object is placed in the drawing, you can modify it by using many of the standard AutoCAD commands. If you want to edit the document, you can either double-click the object or select the OLE object, right-click, and then choose an option from the OLE submenu. OLE objects can't be rotated and are plotted best when using a system printer rather than a plotter.

Managing External References Outside AutoCAD

Managing external references in one drawing is not too difficult, but trying to manage them across 10, 20, or 100 drawings can be a big challenge. To help manage external references, you can use a utility called Reference Manager. From the name, you can tell that it must do something with external references. Reference Manager allows you to modify the paths of external references attached to drawing files that you might create or receive from a contractor. This can make updating the locations of external references much easier than having to open each file one by one and then update the external references' locations. Reference Manager enables you to update the locations of xrefs, DWF and DGN underlays, raster images, plotter configurations, plot styles, shapes, and font files.

Reference Manager is available only with AutoCAD and not with AutoCAD LT.

Follow these steps to access and edit the dependency files of a drawing through Reference Manager:

1. Click Start (Windows button)⇨[All] Programs⇨Autodesk⇨AutoCAD 2009⇨Reference Manager.

The Reference Manager dialog box appears (see Figure 3-13).

2. Click Add Drawings.

The Add Drawings dialog box appears.

3. Browse and select the drawing files in which you want to check or edit the dependencies. Click Open.

The Reference Manager — Add Xrefs dialog box is displayed.

Red slash indicates missing reference file

Pencil indicates reference path was edited

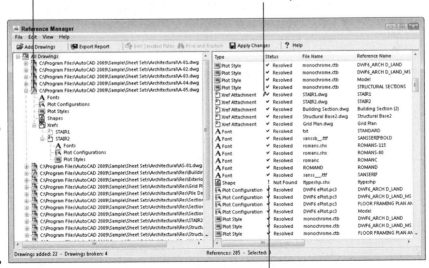

Figure 3-13:
Editing the dependencies of a drawing with Reference Manager.

Red exclamation mark indicates reference was not found

4. **Click Add All Xrefs Automatically Regardless of Nesting Level to load any nested xrefs that might be contained in the xrefs of the selected drawings, or click Add Only the First-Level Xrefs to not check for nested xrefs.**

   The selected files are added to the tree view in Reference Manager.

5. **If a slash appears through the drawing icon in the tree view, the file has a problem. Select the drawing, and all the dependencies for the drawing appear in the list view on the right.**

   A blue check mark means the dependency file was found; a red exclamation point means the file was not found.

6. **Double-click an item that has a status of Not Found, indicated by a red exclamation point, to fix the path to the file.**

   The Edit Selected Paths dialog box is displayed.

7. **Click the ellipsis button to browse for the folder in which the file is located. Select the folder and click OK.**

   The selected folder appears in the New Saved Path text box.

8. **Click OK.**

   The item you double-clicked should now have the status of Resolved with a blue check mark in front of it with a pencil. The pencil shows which dependencies you have edited during the current session of Reference Manager.

9. **Keep editing any dependencies that need to be updated. When you have finished updating the dependencies, click Apply Changes (at the top of Reference Manager).**

   The Summary message box is displayed and provides information about the number of host and reference drawings that have been updated successfully and the number of files that could not be updated. Click OK to close the Summary message box or click Details to figure out why a file could not be updated.

10. **Choose File menu⇨Exit.**

    Reference Manager closes. If you didn't apply the changes, you're prompted to do so. Click Yes to save the changes, No to discard the changes, or Cancel to stay in Reference Manager.

Chapter 4: Organizing Your Drawings

In This Chapter

✔ **Implementing standards**

✔ **Using the Windows Clipboard**

✔ **Using DesignCenter**

✔ **Understanding tool palettes**

AutoCAD enables you to create content once and then reuse it in other drawings. Being able to create reusable content is one thing, but being able to organize and manage all that reusable content is another. AutoCAD offers many ways to manage and organize usable content. You can use the Windows Clipboard to transfer content between two open drawings or to another Windows-based application. It's not always efficient to open a drawing just to access its content, so AutoCAD comes with two interfaces to help you access content from drawings that might be saved locally on your computer or on a network drive. These two interfaces are called DesignCenter and tool palettes.

Why Bother to Organize Drawings?

It takes time to develop accurate drawings, but you can make the process go faster and faster over time. By creating good CAD standards and high-quality reusable content, you can improve your efficiency. I talk about CAD standards in detail in Book VIII, but for now, I address the importance of properly naming and managing reusable content.

Many things in AutoCAD that can be reused, such as a text style, a layer, or even a layout, are given a name. It's a good idea to keep these names meaningful so that you or anyone else looking at the name can decipher its intended purpose. At times this can cause problems; obviously, if you're sharing drawings with other clients, you'll most likely both have a title block in your drawings. It's a good idea to prefix or suffix your blocks with text that denotes scale, units, or even a company identifier to avoid problems with duplicate names. This not only avoids problems when exchanging drawings with other contractors and clients, but also helps you when searching for named objects in your own drawings.

An example of creating a uniquely named block to be used for an A-sized title block by company ABC might be *TitleBlock-A-ABC.* Now this is only a recommendation that I have observed through the years of exchanging drawings with other companies. There's nothing wrong with calling your title block *TB* or *TitleBlock,* but you do run the risk of a naming conflict with just a generic name. No matter how you decide to name objects, it's a good idea to develop a naming convention and make sure everyone in your company follows it. Doing so makes managing CAD drawings much easier.

Using the Windows Clipboard

AutoCAD is a Windows-based application, and like most Windows-based applications, AutoCAD is capable of using the Windows Clipboard to exchange information between two applications. The two applications may be two instances of AutoCAD, or AutoCAD and another Windows-based application such as Microsoft Word. You can copy or cut objects from a drawing and place them on the Windows Clipboard. From there, you can paste them into AutoCAD or another application. You can also copy information from other Windows-based applications and paste that information into an open drawing.

Copying objects from a drawing

 You can copy objects to the Windows Clipboard in a couple of ways. You can do a basic copy of selected objects in the drawing window by using the COPYCLIP command, pressing the standard keyboard shortcut Ctrl+C, or clicking Home tab⇨Utilities panel⇨Copy flyout⇨Copy Clip on the ribbon. When you use COPYCLIP on objects in a drawing, AutoCAD copies the objects to the Windows Clipboard and calculates an insertion point to use when pasting the copied objects from the Clipboard. The insertion point is based on the lower-left corner of the extents of the selected objects, also known as the *bounding box* of the selected objects.

 If you want control over choosing the insertion point of the copied objects, you can use the COPYBASE command, press the keyboard shortcut Ctrl+Shift+C, or click Home tab⇨Utilities panel⇨Copy flyout⇨Copy with Base Point on the ribbon. If you're not concerned with accurate placement, you can copy objects within the same drawing or between two drawings by dragging them on-screen with the left mouse button. If you select the objects without any command running and start dragging the objects, they're moved if you release the mouse button. But if you hold the Ctrl key while dragging the objects, a plus sign appears near the crosshairs, allowing you to copy the objects instead of moving them.

Cutting objects from a drawing

Copying objects in your drawing or between files by using the Windows Clipboard is nice, but at times you may just want to cut (or move) objects. To cut objects from one drawing and place them onto the Windows Clipboard, use the CUTCLIP command, press Ctrl+X, or click Home tab➪Utilities panel➪Cut from the ribbon. When you use CUTCLIP on objects in a drawing, AutoCAD moves the objects to the Windows Clipboard and calculates an insertion point to use when pasting the copied objects from the Clipboard. The insertion point is based on the lower-left corner of the bounding box for the selected objects.

AutoCAD doesn't provide a cut operation that is similar to the COPYBASE command. You can cut objects within the same drawing by dragging them on-screen with the left mouse button. If you select the objects without any command running and start dragging the objects, they're moved when you release the mouse button.

Book VI
Chapter 4

Organizing Your
Drawings

Pasting objects into a drawing

After you place objects on the Windows Clipboard, you can paste them into a drawing or into another Windows-based application. The pasted results vary based on the application into which you are pasting the objects. You can choose from three options to paste between drawings. The first is a standard paste, which doesn't give you much control over the placement of the objects you are pasting. This option of paste is started by using the PASTECLIP command, pressing Ctrl+V, or clicking Home tab➪Utilities panel➪ Paste flyout➪Paste from the ribbon. If you used the COPYBASE command, you already know the insertion point of the objects being pasted back into AutoCAD. If you used COPYCLIP or CUTCLIP, you don't know the insertion point until you begin pasting the objects into the drawing.

The second option for pasting is to paste objects to their original coordinates where they were before they were copied or cut to the Windows Clipboard. This option of paste is started by the PASTEORIG command. This can be useful when copying and pasting title blocks between layouts or drawings.

The final option of pasting content between drawings is the ability to paste the contents of the Windows Clipboard as a block. This option of paste is started by using the PASTEBLOCK command, pressing Ctrl+Shift+V, or clicking Home tab➪Utilities panel➪Paste flyout➪Paste as Block on the ribbon.

If you're pasting objects from other Windows-based applications, you may want to use the PASTESPEC command. Using this command, you can define how objects on the Windows Clipboard are pasted into AutoCAD. For example, if you copy cells in a spreadsheet program to the Windows Clipboard, you can paste the copied cells into AutoCAD as a table object. You can find all the Paste commands on the menu browser or menu bar by clicking the Edit menu, or on the ribbon by clicking Home tab⇨Utilities panel⇨Paste flyout.

AutoCAD DesignCenter

 AutoCAD DesignCenter is an interface that allows you to perform data mining. Data mining is a popular buzz phrase in the marketing world, but you can do it with AutoCAD drawings, as well. *Data mining* allows you to locate information that is of importance to you and reuse it. In marketing, data mining might determine whether a product will sell to a targeted audience; in AutoCAD, you are mining your data for reusable content in the form of drawings, images, layers, blocks, and other named objects.

DesignCenter (see Figure 4-1) was introduced in AutoCAD 2000, and was born out of an AutoCAD LT feature called Content Explorer. It allows you to access content that is stored in a drawing, a hatch pattern, a linetype pattern, and image files, and then reuse the content in any drawing that you have open or add it to a tool palette. You use the ADCENTER command to display DesignCenter.

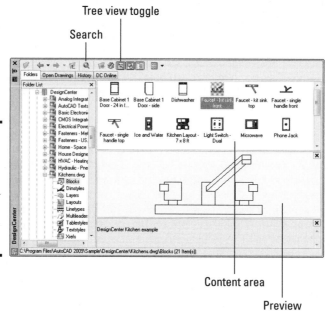

Figure 4-1: DesignCenter allows you to mine your drawing for reusable content.

To start the ADCENTER command and display the DesignCenter palette, do one of the following:

✦ On the ribbon, click View tab⇨Palettes panel⇨DesignCenter.

✦ On the menu browser or menu bar, click Tools menu⇨Palettes⇨DesignCenter.

✦ On the Standard or Standard Annotation toolbar, click the DesignCenter button.

✦ At the command prompt, type **ADCENTER** or **ADC** and press Enter.

✦ Press Ctrl+2.

Book VI
Chapter 4

Locating resources in drawings

By using DesignCenter, you can access content in a number of ways. You can access content that has or has not been opened in AutoCAD. The content can be stored locally on your computer, on a network, or even in an online library of blocks. To locate information by browsing, you use one of the four tabs along the top of the DesignCenter palette:

Organizing Your
Drawings

✦ **Folders:** Browse your local and network drives for drawing or image files.

✦ **Open Drawings:** Access any drawing files currently open.

✦ **History:** Access any drawing files that have been recently opened during the current AutoCAD session.

✦ **DC Online:** Access blocks from an online portal hosted by Autodesk. The online portal has many different 2D and 3D blocks available for use in your drawings, and they're organized into categories to make it easier to find which blocks you might be interested in.

Browsing for content is not always the most efficient way to find something, especially when you don't remember exactly which drawing file something might be located in. Well, you are in luck; DesignCenter has a search feature that allows you to look for drawings that contain specific content. Maybe there is a drawing with a block in it that you want to use in your current drawing; it is possible to search for that block based on a wild character string. Click the Search button on the DesignCenter toolbar to display the Search dialog box (see Figure 4-2).

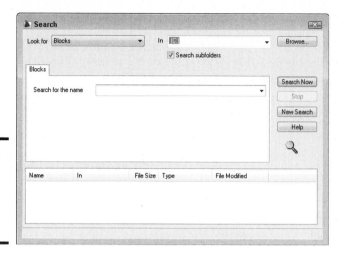

Figure 4-2:
Using the
Search
feature of
Design
Center.

To search for a block, follow these steps:

1. **Start the ADCENTER command by using one of the previously mentioned methods.**

The DesignCenter palette appears.

2. **In the DesignCenter palette, click Search.**

The Search dialog box appears.

3. **In the Look For drop-down list, select Blocks.**

Normally, you select the type of content that you want to search for in the Look For drop-down list. The type of content selected from the Look For drop-down list controls many of the available options in the Search dialog box.

4. **Either select a folder in the In drop-down list to scan for content, or click Browse and browse to the location where you want to start scanning for content.**

If you click Browse, the Browse for Folder dialog box appears. Browse to the folder you want to select in the Browse for Folder dialog box, select the folder, and then click OK. You can also deselect the Search Subfolders option to limit the scanning for content in the folder that you select.

5. **In the Search for the Name text box, enter the block name for which you want search.**

You can use wild characters to help broaden the search if you don't quite remember the name of the block. A pound (#) symbol replaces a single character or an asterisk (*) replaces a range of characters.

6. **Click Search Now.**

   The search results appear at the bottom of the dialog box.

7. **Click Stop to end the search early if you found what you were looking for, or wait until the search has completed.**

8. **Right-click the content you want to place in the drawing or load into the Content Area of DesignCenter.**

   Based on the content for which you were searching, the options vary on the right-click menu. You can choose Add to load the selected content into the current drawing or Load into Content Area to browse to the content in DesignCenter.

9. **Click the Close button (X) in the Search dialog box to close it, or leave the dialog box displayed so you can continue to search for other content later if necessary.**

10. **Click the Close button (X) in DesignCenter to close it, or leave it displayed.**

Adding resources to drawings

After you find the content you want by using one of the four tabs or the Search dialog box, you can add it to a drawing. Position DesignCenter so that you can see the drawing window that you want to drop the content into, and then select the icon that represents the content from the content area (refer to Figure 4-1). Press and hold the left mouse button over the icon and drag it over the drawing window. Release the mouse button to insert the selected block into a drawing or add one of the other types of named objects to a drawing window. AutoCAD ignores duplicate named objects.

To add a block to a drawing, follow these steps:

1. **Start the ADCENTER command by using one of the previously mentioned methods.**

   The DesignCenter palette is displayed.

2. **In the DesignCenter palette, click the Folders tab.**

   The Folders tab and Folders List tree view appear. If they do not, click the Tree View toggle button along the top of the DesignCenter palette.

3. **In the Folders List tree view, browse to the folder that contains the drawing with the block you want to add to your drawing.**

   The Folders List tree view is similar to Windows Explorer.

4. **When you locate the drawing that contains the block you want to place in your drawing, select the drawing.**

The available named objects are displayed in the content area to the right of the Folders List tree view.

5. **In the content area, double-click the Blocks icon.**

Icons for the blocks in the drawing are displayed in the content area.

6. **Right-click the icon for the block that you want to insert in the drawing and select Insert Block.**

The Insert dialog box appears.

7. **In the Insert dialog box, select the options you want and click OK to place the block. Follow any command prompts that are displayed.**

You can also drag and drop the block from the content area into a drawing, but you don't have as much control over the block's placement.

8. **Click the Close button (X) on DesignCenter to close it, or leave it displayed.**

Inserting hatches and loading linetypes

Hatch patterns can be dragged and dropped from DesignCenter. Using the Folders tab, you can browse to a folder that contains hatch pattern (PAT) files. By default the hatch pattern files that come with AutoCAD are in the following folder:

```
C:\Documents and Settings\<user name>\Application
    Data\Autodesk\AutoCAD 2009 (or AutoCAD LT 2009)\R17.2 (or
    R14.0)\enu\Support
```

The *<user name>* varies based on what your Windows login. Select the hatch pattern file from the Folders List tree view, and then drag and drop the pattern from the content area into a closed boundary in your drawing to create a hatch object. You can load linetypes from a linetype pattern (LIN) file in the same way you drag and drop hatch patterns into a drawing.

Using the Tool Palettes Window

 The Tool Palettes window is an interface that allows you to organize reusable content on palettes of tools. These palettes of tools can be used to reference existing content such as blocks, xrefs, or images, and even custom commands. Tool palettes can be organized so that they can be shared across the company with other drafters, making it easy to develop and maintain CAD standards with them. The Tool Palettes window (see Figure 4-3) was introduced in AutoCAD 2004. You use the TOOLPALETTES command to display the Tool Palettes window.

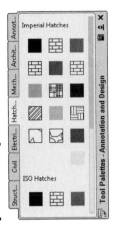

**Book VI
Chapter 4**

**Organizing Your
Drawings**

Figure 4-3:
The Tool
Palettes
window.

To use one of the tools on a tool palette, click the tab or the stack of tabs under the last tab if all can't be displayed, and then click the tool or drag and drop the tool onto the drawing window. Based on the tool you use or how you use it, you'll be prompted for additional information. For example, if you click a hatch tool, you're prompted for the area to hatch. If you drag and drop a hatch tool onto a closed boundary, you're not prompted to pick a point because you do that when you release the mouse button.

To start the TOOLPALETTES command and display the Tool Palettes window, use one of the following methods:

✦ On the ribbon, click View tab⇨Palettes panel⇨Tool Palettes.

✦ On the menu browser or menu bar, click Tools menu⇨Palettes⇨Tool Palettes.

✦ On the Standard or Standard Annotation toolbar, click the Tool Palettes Window button.

✦ At the command prompt, type **TOOLPALETTES** or **TP** and press Enter.

✦ Press Ctrl+3.

Blocks, xrefs, images, tables, and hatches

Tool palettes are designed to allow you to add and organize content on-the-fly from drawings that you are currently working on or even drawings that have already been created. Tool palettes allow you to organize blocks, xrefs, images, tables, hatch patterns, and gradient fills (AutoCAD only). To create a tool out of these objects, you simply open a drawing and drag and drop the content directly from the drawing window onto the Tool Palettes window. Dragging and dropping from a drawing works to create many of these different tools, but you can also drag and drop content such as drawings and images from Windows Explorer or linetypes, blocks, hatch patterns, and images from DesignCenter.

Command and flyouts tools

Commands and flyouts can be added to a tool palette so that you can more easily access the commands that you use regularly. Commands can be customized so they perform a specific combination of commands and command options called a *macro*. A flyout is somewhat limited in the level of customization that can be done with them. Commands can be added to a tool palette by dragging some types of geometry such as lines, arcs, and dimensions from a drawing onto a tool palette, or by dragging commands from the Command List pane in the Customize User Interface (CUI) Editor. To add commands from the CUI Editor, right-click the Tool Palettes window and choose Customize Commands, and then drag and drop commands from the Command List pane onto the Tool Palettes window. For more information on creating tools on tool palettes, choose User's Guide⇨The User Interface⇨The Ribbon, Menus, and Other Tool Locations⇨Other Tool Locations⇨Tool Palettes⇨Customize Tool Palettes on the Contents tab of the online Help system.

Modifying tools on a tool palette

You can modify any of the tools that are placed on a tool palette. The properties you can customize depend on the type of tool. Most tools have a set of general properties that are common to all tools, such as layer, color, and linetype. To modify a tool, select the tab in which the tool you want to modify is on and right-click the tool. From the shortcut menu, choose Properties to display the Tool Properties dialog box (see Figure 4-4). Change the properties as necessary and click OK to apply the changes.

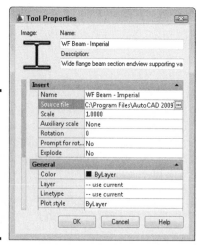

Figure 4-4: The properties of each tool on a tool palette can be tailored to a specific need.

Customizing and organizing tool palettes

You can customize the appearance of tools on a tool palette by right-clicking the tool palette and choosing View Options from the shortcut menu. In the View Options dialog box, you can control whether tools appear as icons only, icons with text, or in a list view with icons displayed to the left of the tools' description. You can also control the size of the icons for tools.

To make tools as accessible as possible, you can organize tools on tool palettes that are represented by tabs on the Tools Palettes window and with tool palette groups. Tool palette groups control which tool palettes are displayed. To switch between tool palette groups, right-click the title bar of the Tool Palettes window and select one of the tool palette groups from the bottom of the shortcut menu.

For more information on controlling the display and organization of tools on tool palettes, choose User's Guide⇨The User Interface⇨The Ribbon, Menus, and Other Tool Locations⇨Other Tool Locations, and click the links for either Change Tool Palette Settings or Organize Tool Palettes on the Contents tab of the online Help system.

Book VII

Publishing Drawings

The 5th Wave   By Rich Tennant

"Well, there's your raster image scanned into your book report. I just can't figure out what that grey fuzzy thing is along the edge."

Contents at a Glance

Chapter 1: Page Setup 493

Preparing for Output with Page Setups 494
Organizing a Drawing with Layouts 500
Looking at a Model through Viewports 506

Chapter 2: Sheet Sets without Regret 515

Overview of a Sheet Set 515
Sheet Set Manager 517
Creating a Sheet Set 517
Managing Drawings with a Sheet Set 522
Publishing, eTransmitting, and Archiving a Sheet Set 541

Chapter 3: Print, Plot, Publish 543

You Say Printing, I Say Plotting, They Say Publishing 543
Output Made Easy 555
Publishing Drawings 561

Chapter 1: Page Setup

In This Chapter

✔ **Creating page setups to aid in outputting your drawings**

✔ **Organizing your drawings with layouts**

✔ **Viewing your model from a viewport**

*T*his minibook walks you through the process of efficiently generating a hard copy of your drawing. After all, the design process should be the difficult part and getting your drawing on paper or as a file for sharing should be straightforward. I wish I could say creating a hard copy of your drawing is as easy as 1-2-3 — but it does take a little more effort than that.

Printing in AutoCAD and AutoCAD LT is referred to as *plotting* or *publishing*. If you're wondering why the term *printing* isn't used, it's because plotting deals with larger sheets of paper and specialized devices called *plotters*. Printing, on the other hand, deals with smaller paper sizes for things such as office documents. Plotting is done one drawing and one layout at a time, so if you have multiple drawings and layouts to plot, you'll likely find yourself using the Publish feature.

Before you plot or publish your drawings, you need to do some setup work. The type and amount of setup that you need to do before you can generate a hard copy of your drawing is determined by whether you are plotting a drawing from the Model tab or a paper space layout. Plotting from the Model tab is the easiest way, but it doesn't allow as much flexibility as plotting from a paper space layout.

Layouts allow you to take advantage of floating viewports to specify different views of your drawing at different scales while keeping the geometry at full scale. When you plot a drawing from the Model tab and want to plot objects at different scales, you need to duplicate and scale the geometry of different parts of the design. This can result in lost time while you ensure that everything is properly updated. One way to help manage drawing views and sets of drawings for plotting is to use sheet sets. Sheet sets allow you to electronically represent a set of drawings in AutoCAD, which allows you to quickly navigate, manage, and distribute a set of drawing files.

Preparing for Output with Page Setups

Sending a drawing to a plotter or to an electronic file for output can be challenging at first because of the number of options that AutoCAD and AutoCAD LT offer. AutoCAD offers a feature called page setups, which control how the Model tab or paper space layouts in a drawing are outputted.

The options that are part of a page setup are a subset of the options in the Plot dialog box, which is covered in Chapter 3 of this minibook. Page setups help to provide consistency in the way your drawings are plotted. You use Page Setup Manager (see Figure 1-1) to create new page setups, import page setups from other drawing files, and assign page setups to layouts within a drawing.

Figure 1-1:
Page Setup
Manager.

Each layout in a drawing can have its own page setup, but to get the most flexibility out of using page setups, you should use one page setup for multiple layouts in the same drawing. Page setups are most commonly created in a drawing template (DWT) file so that they are available when a new drawing is created based on the drawing template or as page setup override when publishing a drawing. For more information on drawing templates, see Chapter 1 of Book VIII.

Options of a page setup

From Page Setup Manager, you can create or modify an existing page setup. To create or modify a page setup, you use the Page Setup dialog box (see Figure 1-2). The Page Setup dialog box is where you make the actual option selections that define the characteristics of a page setup. As I previously mention, a page setup contains a subset of the options found in the Plot dialog box.

Following is a general overview of the types of options that are part of a page setup.

✦ **Printer/Plotter:** Specifies the default device that should be used when plotting or publishing the Model tab or a paper space layout. This allows you to quickly create different page setups that might be used during the checking process and for final output.

✦ **Paper size:** Specifies the default paper size to be used, whether it's a check plot that you print on a 11 x 17 sheet of paper to validate a design with a senior member of your design team to ensure that it includes all the necessary information before being sent out or the final design to be plotted on an ANSI E 34 x 44 large format paper.

✦ **Plot area:** Specifies the default area of the drawing that you want to output. This can be the limits of the drawing, a named view, a windowed area, the current display, the extents of the model when the Model tab is current, or the layout when a Layout tab is current. The options that you can select depend on how your drawing was set up and whether you are outputting from the Model tab or a paper space layout.

✦ **Plot offset:** Specifies the offset value for the origin of the printable area and whether or not the plot should be centered within the printable area.

✦ **Plot scale:** Specifies how the objects in the plot area should be scaled in order for them to be displayed properly on the specified paper size. You can specify an exact scale such as 1/4" = 1'–0" or a custom size that fits the specified area to be plotted to the specified paper size.

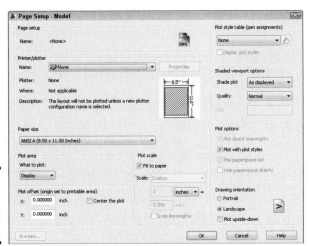

Figure 1-2:
The Page Setup dialog box.

✦ **Plot style table:** Specifies which plot style should be used when outputting the Model tab or paper space layout. A plot style can control the color and lineweights of objects as they are sent to a printer, plotter, or electronic file.

✦ **Shaded viewport options:** Control how viewports defined on a layout should be plotted.

✦ **Plot options:** Control how the final plot appears and whether plot styles and lineweights are used during output.

✦ **Drawing orientation:** Controls the direction in which the drawing should be output — portrait or landscape. You can also specify that the output be generated upside down. Based on the type of device you are using for output, you may need to specify the upside-down option for the output to come out correctly.

Working with page setups

You can add page setups to a drawing in a couple of ways. You can use Page Setup Manager and define a new page setup through the Page Setup dialog box, or you can import them from an existing drawing or drawing template (DWT) file. When you create a page setup or import it into a drawing, you can then assign it to a layout. If the page setup in a drawing is later changed, all the layouts that reference the page setup are updated. To display Page Setup Manager, you use the PAGESETUP command.

To start the PAGESETUP command, use one of the following methods:

✦ On the ribbon, click Output tab⇨Plot panel⇨Page Setup Manager.

✦ On the menu browser or menu bar, click File menu⇨Page Setup Manager.

✦ On the Layouts toolbar, click the Page Setup Manager button.

✦ At the command prompt, type **PAGESETUP** and press Enter.

✦ When the Model and layout tabs are visible, right-click the current tab at the bottom of the drawing window and select Page Setup Manager from the shortcut menu.

Creating a page setup

When you create a page setup, you first determine whether you're plotting from the Model tab or a paper space layout. If you create a page setup for the Model tab, it can be used only with the Model tab. Page setups created with a paper space layout are available only for paper space layouts. Alternatively, you can create a page setup based on the current settings in the Plot dialog box instead of using the Page Setup dialog box.

To create a page setup, follow these steps:

1. **Click the Quick View Layouts button on the status bar, and choose the layout for which you want to create a page setup.**

2. **Start the PAGESETUP command by using one of the methods in the preceding list.**

Page Setup Manager is displayed.

3. **Click New.**

The New Page Setup dialog box appears (see Figure 1-3).

Figure 1-3:
Naming the
new page
setup.

4. **In the New Page Setup Name text box, type a name for the page setup.**

5. **In the Start With list box, select one of the existing page setups or choose <None> to start with default settings only.**

Selecting a page setup from the Start With list box can be helpful if a page setup already exists that is close to the one you want to create.

6. **Click OK.**

The New Page Setup dialog box closes and the Page Setup dialog box appears.

7. **Specify the different options you want to use when plotting or publishing the Model tab or paper space layout.**

8. **Click OK.**

The Page Setup dialog box closes and you return to Page Setup Manager. The page setup that was created should now be listed in the list box in the Page Setups section.

9. **Click Close.**

Page Setup Manager closes and you return to the drawing window.

At the bottom of Page Setup Manager is a check box labeled Display When Creating a New Layout. If the check box is selected, Page Setup Manager is displayed when a paper space layout is initialized the first time or when a new paper space layout is created. The option is also available from the Display tab of the Options dialog box but is labeled Show Page Setup Manager for New Layouts.

Importing a page setup

Importing a page setup is the fastest and most efficient way of adding a page setup to a drawing. To import a page setup from an existing drawing file, follow these steps:

1. **Start the PAGESETUP command by using one of the methods in the previous list.**

2. **In Page Setup Manager, click Import.**

   The Select Page Setup from File dialog box appears.

3. **Browse to and select a drawing, drawing template (DWT), or DXF file that contains the page setup you want to import. Click Open.**

   The Import Page Setups dialog box appears with the available page setups listed (see Figure 1-4).

4. **In the Page Setups list box, select the page setup(s) you want to import. You can select multiple page setups by holding down the Ctrl or Shift keys when selecting a page setup. Click OK.**

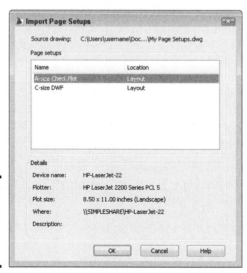

Figure 1-4:
Reusing page setups through importing.

The Import Page Setups dialog box closes and you return to Page Setup Manager. The selected page setups are displayed in the Page Setups list box.

5. **In Page Setup Manager, click Close.**

Assigning a page setup to a layout

After you create or import a page setup into your drawing, you can put it to work. To assign a page setup to the current layout, follow these steps:

1. **Click the Quick View Layouts button on the status bar, and choose the layout for which you want to create a page setup.**

2. **Start the PAGESETUP command by using one of the methods listed previously.**

Page Setup Manager appears.

3. **In the Page Setups list box, select the page setup.**

Layouts are listed first in the list box and have an asterisk (*) before and after their names. Named page setups are listed after the layouts in the list box. If a layout has been assigned a named page setup, the name of the page setup is displayed after the layout's name and placed within parentheses. An example of the naming convention is *Layout1 (A-size Check Plot)*.

4. **Click Set Current.**

The page setup is assigned to the current layout and its name is displayed to the right of the *Current page setup* label just above the Page Setups list box. You can also double-click a page setup to assign it to the Model tab or current layout.

5. **Click Close.**

Editing a page setup

When editing a page setup, you use the Page Setup dialog box and any layouts that reference the page setup are automatically updated with the changes made. The following steps outline how to modify a page setup:

1. **Click the Quick View Layouts button on the status bar, and choose the layout for which you want to create a page setup.**

2. **Start the PAGESETUP command by using one of the methods listed previously.**

3. **In Page Setup Manager, select the page setup you want to modify and then click Modify.**

4. **In the Page Setup dialog box, specify the different options you want to use when plotting or publishing the Model tab or paper space layout.**

5. **Click OK.**

6. **In Page Setup Manager, click Close.**

Organizing a Drawing with Layouts

Layouts are used to help control how a drawing is plotted or published. In AutoCAD R14 and earlier, the Model tab and paper space layouts were simply referred to as *Model Space* and *Paper Space.* This changed with the introduction of layouts with AutoCAD 2000. AutoCAD R14 and earlier releases supported a single Model Space (or Model tab) and a single Paper Space (or paper space layout tab). AutoCAD 2000 made it possible to have one Model tab and multiple paper space layouts.

AutoCAD 2009 and AutoCAD LT 2009 allow you to save all the way back to the AutoCAD R14 file format, which does not support multiple paper space layout tabs. To exchange a drawing that contains multiple layout tabs with a user on AutoCAD R14, you need to set each layout current, one at a time, and save the drawing out once for each layout. You need to do this only if you use more than one paper space layout in your drawing and if the receiver of the drawing files needs to have access to each of the layout tabs.

If you do find that you need to share your drawings with a user who is on AutoCAD R14 and needs access to the information on each layout tab, you can use the new EXPORTLAYOUT command (on the ribbon, click Output tab⇨Send panel⇨Export Layout to Model or right-click a layout tab at the bottom of the drawing window and choose Export Layout to Model. Some other CAD programs that your clients and vendors use might understand only one paper space layout, so you might need to export a layout to a new drawing in these conditions as well.

Think of a layout as a piece of paper and a way to visually organize how parts of your drawing will appear on the sheet of paper. Generally, you should do all your designing and drawing on the Model tab, but there are some exceptions to this rule. At times, you may need to add annotation and dimensions related to part of your drawing that is being displayed through a floating viewport, but otherwise you'll be working mainly on the Model tab.

You use *floating viewports* to display parts of the drawing from the Model tab at a specific scale onto a paper space layout. I cover floating viewports later in this chapter in the "Looking at a Model through Viewports" section. Most commonly, you'll find a title block that has been inserted or referenced on a layout, in addition to one or more floating viewports.

Working with layouts

Layouts, unlike page setups, are not managed through a dialog box. Layouts are managed by clicking the tabs that appear along the bottom of the drawing window or the Quick View Layouts button on the status bar. Everything that you might need for creating or modifying a layout is at the tip of your cursor. The LAYOUT command is used to create and manage paper space layouts.

To start the LAYOUT command, use one of the following methods:

✦ On the menu browser or menu bar, click Insert menu⇨Layout and then one of the available options.

✦ On the Layouts toolbar, click the New Layout or Layout from Template button.

✦ At the command prompt, type **LAYOUT** and press Enter.

✦ On the status bar, click Quick View Layouts⇨Quick View Layouts panel⇨New Layout.

✦ When the Model and paper space layout tabs are visible, right-click a paper space layout tab at the bottom of the drawing window and select one of the different options above the top separator bar of the menu.

Creating a layout by using the Create Layout Wizard

Layouts typically contain title blocks, floating viewports, annotation, and utilize references to page setups. To make the process of creating and setting up a layout as efficient as possible, AutoCAD comes with the Create Layout Wizard (see Figure 1-5), which you launch with the LAYOUTWIZARD command.

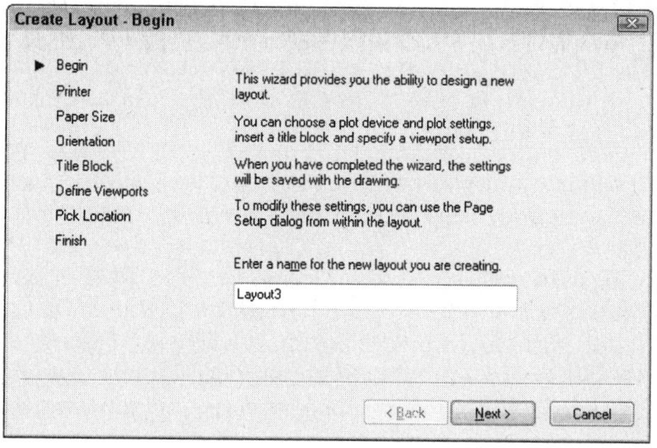

Book VII Chapter 1

Page Setup

Figure 1-5:
The Create Layout Wizard gets you on the fast track to creating a layout.

Create Layout - Begin

▶ Begin
Printer
Paper Size
Orientation
Title Block
Define Viewports
Pick Location
Finish

This wizard provides you the ability to design a new layout.

You can choose a plot device and plot settings, insert a title block and specify a viewport setup.

When you have completed the wizard, the settings will be saved with the drawing.

To modify these settings, you can use the Page Setup dialog from within the layout.

Enter a name for the new layout you are creating.

Layout3

< Back   Next >   Cancel

To use the Create Layout Wizard, follow these steps:

1. **At the command prompt, type** layoutwizard **and press Enter (or on the menu browser or menu bar, choose Insert menu⇨Layout⇨Create Layout Wizard).**

   The Create Layout Wizard appears.

2. **On the Begin page, enter a name in the Enter a Name for the New Layout You Are Creating text box. Click Next.**

   The name of the layout can be a maximum of 255 characters, which is a very long layout name. The layout tab displays roughly 31 characters (at the most).

3. **On the Printer page, select one of the available printers or plotters. Click Next.**

   The printer you specify is used as the default output device for the layout. I cover adding plotters in Chapter 3 of this minibook.

4. **On the Paper Size page, select one of the available paper sizes from the drop-down list and the drawing units. Click Next.**

   The paper size is assigned to the layout and used during output. The paper sizes that you can select from are determined by the printer or plotter that you selected in Step 3. Drawing units are typically in inches or millimeters, but if you choose a printer that generates an image file, you also have the option of pixels. The measurement size of the paper is displayed in the Paper Size in Units section.

5. **On the Orientation page, select either Portrait or Landscape. Click Next.**

   The orientation controls which way the paper is turned in the drawing window and for output.

6. **On the Title Block page, select one of the available drawing files to use as the title block on the layout or select None. If you select a title block, you need to specify how the title block is placed on the layout: block or xref. Click Next.**

   The title blocks that you can choose from are the ones that come with AutoCAD by default. The title blocks that you can select from are determined by the path in which AutoCAD looks for drawing templates. To change the path where AutoCAD looks, choose Tools menu⇨Options on the menu bar or menu browser. Then in the Options dialog box, click the Files tab and expand Template Settings⇨Drawing Template File Location. Select the path below Drawing Template File Location and click Browse. In the Browse for Folder dialog box, specify the new path and click OK.

7. **On the Define Viewports page, select one of the four viewport setups and the scale of the objects in the viewports created. You can also set the spacing between each viewport and the number of viewports created when the Array option is used under Viewport Setup. Click Next.**

   The available options are usually not exactly what you want, but they do allow for a good starting point. After the viewports are created, you can resize and adjust them with grips and the Properties palette later.

8. **On the Pick Location page, click Select Location to specify the area where you want the viewports to be created on the layout. Click Next.**

   You return to the drawing window to define the location for the viewports. After you specify two points, you return to the Create Layout Wizard.

9. **On the Finish page, click Finish.**

   The Create Layout Wizard closes, and the new layout is created based on the options that you specified with the wizard.

Importing a layout

The Create Layout Wizard is nice, but there are some things you will most likely need to do after you use the wizard, such as assign a page setup and define the layouts so they display the desired parts of the drawing from the Model tab. As with page setups, AutoCAD allows you to import layouts from an existing drawing. Importing a layout allows you to spend less time setting up your drawing and more time drafting. To import a layout from another drawing, you use the Template option of the LAYOUT command, or right-click a paper space layout tab or the Quick View Layouts button on the status bar and choose From Template.

To import a layout into a drawing, follow these steps:

1. **On the menu browser, click Insert menu⇨Layout⇨Layout from Template.**

   The Select Template from File dialog box is displayed. This dialog box allows you to browse to a drawing, drawing template (DWT), or DXF file that contains the layout you want to import.

2. **Select the drawing, drawing template (DWT), or DXF file that contains the layout you want to import. Click Open.**

   The Insert Layout(s) dialog box is displayed and lists the available paper space layouts that can be imported (see Figure 1-6).

3. **Select a layout or multiple layouts from the list box. Click OK.**

   The layouts are imported to the drawing and positioned to the right of the last layout tab.

Book VII Chapter 1

Page Setup

Page setups are not automatically imported when importing a layout. If you want to keep the page setup with the layout, you must first import the page setup that the layout references and then import the layout.

Modifying a layout

You can modify layout tabs in a variety of ways. You can remove them from a drawing or change their order. You can use the LAYOUT command for many of these tasks, but you can also use the shortcut menu of a layout tab, the Quick View Layouts button on the status bar, or a layout preview on Quick View Layouts. Most of the following options are available for modifying a layout, regardless of the method you use:

✦ **Delete:** Allows you to remove the selected layout from the drawing. (This option is not accessible when you right-click the Quick View Layouts button on the status bar.)

✦ **Rename:** Allows you to rename a layout by using the in-place editor. (This option is not accessible when you right-click the Quick View Layouts button on the status bar.)

✦ **Move or Copy:** Displays the Move and Copy dialog box so you can control the order in which layouts are displayed and quickly create a copy of an existing layout in the drawing.

✦ **Select All Layouts:** Allows you to select all the layouts in the drawing except for the Model tab.

Navigating layouts

A drawing contains at least one paper space layout at all times and one Model tab, but may contain many more paper space layouts than that. When you get past about four or five layouts, navigating layouts becomes a little more difficult because tabs start becoming hidden from view. AutoCAD offers a couple of ways to navigate through the tabs that represent the paper space layouts in the drawing. The most common way to navigate the layout tabs is to click the tab you want to activate or use the set of four controls located at the bottom of the drawing window (see Figure 1-7) when there are more tabs than there is space for all the paper space layout tabs.

Figure 1-7:
Layout
navigation
controls.

The far left control jumps to the first layout tab, and the far right control jumps to the last layout tab. The two controls located in the middle allow you to step one layout tab at a time to the next or previous tab. You can also use the keyboard combinations Ctrl+Page Up and Ctrl+Page Down to step to the next or previous layout tab one at a time.

You can turn off the display of the layout tabs and still access different layouts efficiently. If you right-click a layout tab, you can hide the Model tab and paper space layout tabs by choosing Hide Layout and Model tabs from the shortcut menu. When the layout tabs are hidden, two new controls are displayed in the status bar area to allow you to access the Model tab and the previous paper space layout in the drawing.

To switch between paper space layouts when the layout tabs along the bottom of the drawing window are hidden, you can click the Quick View Layouts button on the status bar and then the layout you want to set current. You can also use Quick View Layouts when the tabs are displayed.

Appearance of layouts

The appearance of layouts and the layout tab can be controlled through the Display tab of the Options dialog box. To access the Options dialog box, on the menu bar or menu browser click Tools menu⇨Options. The Layout Element section controls many of the visual cues that are present when a layout tab is current (see Figure 1-8). These include the printable area, the overall paper size, and a shadow to give the paper a 3D look.

The background color can be modified as well so you can tell when you're on a layout tab instead of the Model tab, or you can make the background for the Model tab and the layout tabs appear the same. The different color options are available through the Colors button in the Window Elements section of the Display tab in the Options dialog box. You can also control the color of the UCS Icon when a layout tab is active through the UCS Icon dialog box. To display the UCS Icon dialog box, on the menu bar or menu browser click View menu⇨Display⇨UCS Icon⇨Properties.

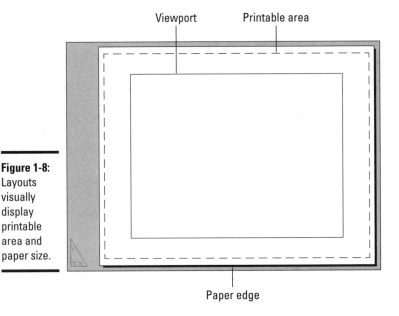

Viewport   Printable area

Paper edge

Figure 1-8:
Layouts
visually
display
printable
area and
paper size.

Looking at a Model through Viewports

Layouts by themselves do not provide all the necessary components for getting a drawing ready for output. When you use the Create Layout Wizard, you are prompted to define the viewports and provide a scale for them, so you know viewports are important on a layout. Viewports allow you to see part or all the objects that are on the Model tab and to have those objects displayed at a specific scale.

AutoCAD offers two types of viewports: model (or tiled) and floating. *Model* (or *tiled*) *viewports* are created only on the Model tab and provide a way to navigate easily between different areas of the drawing; they are not used to output areas of the drawing. *Floating viewports* are created only on a paper space layout and are used to organize a drawing for output. The following sections cover how to create and work with floating viewports on a layout.

Defining a viewport's shape

AutoCAD supports two types of floating viewports: rectangular and irregular (polygonal and closed objects, such as a circle or spline). Rectangular viewports are the more common of the two, but being able to create a viewport from a circle or closed polyline can allow you to conserve space on a layout or jazz one up. You use the VPORTS command to create both rectangular and irregular viewports.

AutoCAD LT 2009 now supports the ability to create irregular-shaped floating viewports.

To start the VPORTS command, use one of the following methods:

✦ On the ribbon, click View tab➪Viewports panel➪New.

✦ On the menu browser or menu bar, click View➪Viewports➪Named Viewports.

✦ On the Viewports or Layouts toolbar, click the Display Viewports Dialog button.

✦ At the command prompt, type **VPORTS** and press Enter.

Creating a rectangular viewport

Rectangular viewports are the most common and easiest types of viewports to create. The Viewports dialog box, shown in Figure 1-9, offers some standard configurations for quickly laying out rectangular viewports. You can specify up to four viewports, each with a different visual style and view. The Viewports dialog box offers some default views for 3D drawings as well, such as Top, Left, and Southwest isometric.

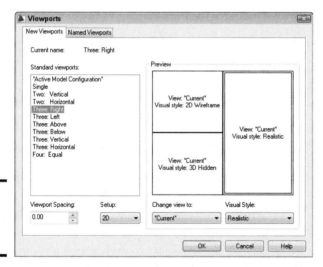

Figure 1-9:
The
Viewports
dialog box.

To add viewports to a layout based on a standard configuration, follow these steps:

1. **Select the paper space layout on which you want to create floating viewports.**

Make sure that no viewports already exist on the layout by erasing any that are there, or be sure to have enough area to add additional ones.

2. **Start the VPORTS command by using one of the methods described previously.**

3. **In the Viewports dialog box, make sure that the New Viewports tab is displayed. In the Standard Viewports list box, select the configuration you want to use.**

The Preview area updates to reflect the viewport configuration you selected.

4. **In the Viewport Spacing text box, enter the amount of space you want between the viewports that are created. This affects only the viewports you are currently creating.**

The size of the spacing should be small because you need to specify a scale of 1 in the Plot dialog box when plotting a paper space layout.

5. **If your drawing is of a 3D model, select 3D in the Setup drop-down list; otherwise, leave it as the default 2D value.**

If you specify 3D, you have some additional views to choose from in the Change View To drop-down list. Otherwise, there is no other difference between specifying 2D or 3D.

6. **In the Preview area, click the different sections of the preview that represent the viewports that will be created.**

When you make selections in the different sections of the Preview, you're setting that representation of a viewport current to adjust its view and visual style.

7. **With the representation of the viewport set current, select a named view in the Change View To drop-down list.**

The selected named view is displayed in the Preview section for the selected viewport.

8. **In the Visual Style drop-down list, select a visual style to assign it to the selected viewport.**

The selected visual style is displayed in the Preview section for the selected viewport.

9. **Repeat Steps 6 through 8 for each of the viewports in the Preview section.**

10. **Click OK.**

The Viewports dialog box closes, and you return to the drawing window. The following prompt is displayed at the command line:

```
Specify first corner or [Fit] <Fit>:
```

11. In the drawing window, specify the first point for the viewports to be created in the printable area on the current layout.

You are specifying a rectangular area where the viewports will be created. The next prompt is displayed at the command line:

```
Specify opposite corner:
```

12. Specify the opposite corner to finish defining the area where you want the viewports to be created.

The viewports are created in the defined area based on the options specified in the Viewports dialog box. You should notice that the objects on the Model tab are displayed in each of the viewports.

Creating an irregular viewport

You create irregular viewports by using the command line version of the VPORTS command, which is –VPORTS (a hyphen in front of the command). The –VPORTS command has some additional options that the dialog box version of the command doesn't have for working with viewports and creating irregular viewports.

The two options that the –VPORTS command offers for creating irregular viewports are Polygonal and Object. The –VPORTS command displays the following prompt at the command line when it is first started:

```
Specify corner of viewport or
[ON/OFF/Fit/Shadeplot/Lock/Object/Polygonal/Restore/LAyer/2/3
   /4] <Fit>:
```

With the –VPORTS command, you can also create a single rectangular-shaped viewport by specifying two points. To create a single rectangular viewport, type **–VPORT** at the command prompt, choose View menu⇨Viewports⇨1 Viewport on the menu bar or menu browser, or choose Single Viewport on the Viewports toolbar. Then specify a base point and then the opposite corner for the rectangular viewport.

To add an irregular viewport to a layout by using the Polygonal option, follow these steps:

1. Select the paper space layout on which you want to create an irregular-shaped floating viewport.

Book VII
Chapter 1

Page Setup

2. **On the ribbon, click View tab⇨Viewports panel⇨Polygonal.**

   The –VPORTS command starts and displays the following prompt at the command line:

   ```
   Specify start point:
   ```

3. **In the drawing window, specify the first point of the polygonal object that will be used to define the viewport.**

   After specifying the first point of the polygonal object, the following prompt appears at the command line:

   ```
   Specify next point or [Arc/Length/Undo]:
   ```

4. **Specify the next point or select one of the available options. This example assumes that you selected the next point.**

   After selecting the next point of the polygonal object, the previous prompt is displayed again, except with a Close option added:

   ```
   Specify next point or [Arc/Close/Length/Undo]:
   ```

5. **Continue specifying points as necessary to define the polygonal object.**

6. **When you have finished specifying points, right-click and select Close, or type** C **at the command prompt and press Enter.**

   The command ends and the objects on the Model tab are displayed in the viewport.

Irregular viewports can be created in a drawing based on closed objects. The objects that can be used to create an irregular viewport are circles, closed polylines, ellipses, closed splines, and regions. To create an irregular viewport, draw the closed object you want to use as the shape of the viewport on a paper space layout; then click View menu⇨Viewports⇨Object on the menu browser or menu bar (or on the ribbon, click View tab⇨Viewports⇨Object). After you start the –VPORTS command, select the closed object to convert to a viewport. The command ends and the objects from the Model tab are displayed in the viewport.

Controlling scale

Paper space layouts are plotted at a scale of 1:1, so to get the objects in the viewports to be plotted and displayed correctly, you specify a scale for each viewport. You do this by using the scale list on the Viewports toolbar, the Standard Scale property in the Properties palette, or the Viewport Scale list on the status bar. The following procedure uses the Properties palette to change the scale for a floating viewport.

1. **On a paper space layout, select the viewport whose scale you want to change.**

The grips for the selected viewport appear.

2. **With the viewport selected, right-click and select Properties from the shortcut menu.**

   The Properties palette appears.

3. **On the Properties palette, select the desired scale for the viewport in the drop-down list for the Standard Scale property.**

   The viewport is updated to display the objects on the Model tab at the specified scale. You can also specify a custom scale by typing the scale value in the Custom Scale text box on the Properties palette. In addition to controlling the scale of objects in the viewport, if you have annotation objects such as blocks, dimensions, or text, you also need to set the annotation scale for the viewport. You set the annotation scale for a viewport by using the Annotation Scale property on the Properties palette, or you can synchronize the annotation scale of a viewport so it's the same as the scale of the viewport by clicking Annotation Synchronize to the right of the Viewport Scale list on the status bar.

You can use the SCALELISTEDIT command to display the Edit Scale List dialog box to control which scales are available for use in one of the scale lists for AutoCAD. The list of scales in the Edit Scale List dialog box controls which scales are available in the scale list on the Viewports toolbar, the Plot and Page Setup dialog boxes, and the Viewport Scale list on the status bar among other places.

Book VII Chapter 1

Page Setup

Controlling the display within a viewport

You can move in and out of viewports on a paper space layout by double-clicking inside or outside a viewport. This places you in model space so you can interact with the objects on the Model tab. By entering the viewport this way, you can control which objects on the Model tab are displayed through the viewport by panning. After you have the objects positioned correctly, you can then lock the viewport so the scale and view of the objects in the viewport are not accidentally changed. To lock the display of a viewport, select the viewport and click the Lock/Unlock Viewport button on the status bar until the image of a padlock appears closed/locked, or right-click the selected viewport and choose Display Locked⇨Yes (choose No to unlock the viewport).

At times you may want to edit objects through a viewport but want to avoid accidentally changing the scale and view of the objects in the viewport. In this case, there's a way to open the viewport so that it fills the entire drawing area. If you double-click on the viewport's border, the viewport is maximized in the drawing window. This allows you to pan and zoom in the viewport even if its display has been locked to prevent any accidental changes to its scale. Figure 1-10 shows a viewport that has been maximized. You can tell when a viewport is maximized by the appearance of a red border made up of slash marks that goes around the inside of the drawing window. Double-clicking outside the red border of a maximized viewport restores the viewport to its original size and scale. You can also click the Maximize and Minimize Viewport controls in the status bar.

At times, you'll want to hide objects on certain layers that might contain objects that you don't want displayed in a particular viewport. In this case, you can specify whether objects are frozen only in the viewport rather than globally across the entire drawing. To freeze layers for a specific viewport, double-click to enter the viewport in which you want to freeze a layer. You'll be able to tell that the focus has been shifted to the viewport when its border is displayed as bold and crosshairs are present within the viewport. On the Layers toolbar, click the Freeze or Thaw in Current Viewport icon (see Figure 1-11) next to the layer that you want to freeze for the viewport. On the ribbon, click Home tab⇨Layers panel⇨Layers drop-down list. You can also use the Layer Properties Manager palette. To exit the viewport, simply double-click outside the viewport's border.

Starting in AutoCAD 2008, you could override the properties for a layer in a viewport by using Layer Properties Manager. When in a viewport, you can override the color, linetype, lineweight, and plot style of the layers for that particular viewport. To do so, display the Layers Properties Manager palette and scroll to the right. The columns starting with *VP* are specific to the current viewport. To undo the layer overrides, select the viewport to remove all the layer overrides for the viewport and choose Remove Viewport Overrides for All Layers from the shortcut menu.

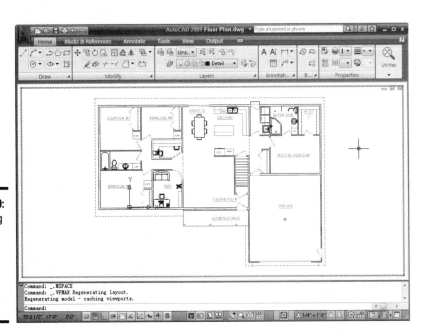

Figure 1-10:
Maximizing a viewport can make editing within it much easier.

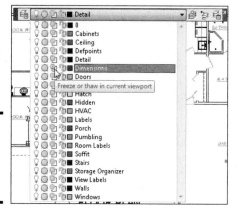

Figure 1-11:
Freezing a layer in the current viewpoint.

Another way to control the display of objects in a viewport is by completely turning off the viewport. The viewport remains in the drawing, but any objects that would normally be displayed through the viewport are not displayed. To control the display of the objects through a viewport, select the viewport, right-click, and choose Display Viewport Objects⇨No. (Choose Yes to display the objects in a viewport.)

In addition to controlling the layer properties and display of the actual objects in a viewport, you can designate how 3D objects are displayed. When a viewport is active, you can designate its visual style by setting a visual style current through Visual Styles Manager; by using the ribbon by clicking Visualize tab⇨Visualize Styles panel⇨Visual Styles drop-down list; or by selecting a viewport, right-clicking, and choosing a visual style or render preset in the Shade Plot submenu. For more on visual styles and rendering, see Chapter 6 of Book V.

Modifying a viewport

You can modify a viewport by using the Properties palette, the MOVE and COPY commands, grips, and many other standard modify commands. Using grip editing is by far one of the most efficient ways to adjust the size, shape, and location of a viewport. Adjusting a viewport by using grips has no effect on the scale or the viewpoint within the viewport. It will, however, affect which objects are displayed through the viewport. The VPCLIP command can also be used to shape the viewport by re-creating its overall shape; the viewpoint and scale of the viewport are not affected.

To start the VPCLIP command, use one of the following methods:

✦ On the ribbon, click View tab⇨Viewports panel⇨Viewport Clip.

✦ On the menu browser or menu bar, click Modify menu⇨Clip⇨Viewport.

✦ On the Viewports toolbar, click the Clip Existing Viewport button.

✦ At the command prompt, type **VPCLIP** and press Enter.

✦ Select a floating viewport, right-click, and choose Viewport Clip from the shortcut menu.

The following steps explain how to clip a floating viewport based on a polygonal boundary:

1. **Start the VPCLIP command by using one of the methods in the preceding list.**

The following prompt appears at the command line:

```
Select viewport to clip:
```

2. **At the prompt, select the floating viewport that you want to clip.**

The following prompt appears at the command line:

```
Select clipping object or [Polygonal] <Polygonal>:
```

3. **Press Enter to accept the default option of clipping a floating viewport based on a polygonal boundary.**

The following prompt appears at the command line:

```
Specify start point:
```

4. **Continue specifying points for the new clipping boundary. When you're finished, type c and press Enter,**

The clipping boundary is closed and the command ends.

You can use the VPCLIP command to create an irregular-shaped viewport by selecting the viewport and then the closed object you want to use as the new clipping boundary.

When you use the COPYCLIP command to copy viewports between layouts, AutoCAD and AutoCAD LT now automatically turn the layout on when you paste a copied viewport. You can still control the display of objects in a viewport on a layout by selecting a viewport, right-clicking, and then choosing Display Viewport Objects⇨Yes.

If you freeze or turn off the layer on which the viewport is drawn, you can hide the border of the viewport, making only the objects in the viewport visible when you plot or publish the drawing.

Chapter 2: Sheet Sets without Regret

In This Chapter

✔ **Understanding sheet sets**

✔ **Creating your first sheet set**

✔ **Managing your drawings with a sheet set**

✔ **Publishing, eTransmitting, and archiving your sheet set**

Sheet sets were introduced in AutoCAD 2005 and are still a relatively new concept in AutoCAD. They're the digital equivalent of an old drafting concept called a *drawing set*. A drawing set contains numerous drawings, and often includes references to details, sections, and elevations within the drawing set, along with a drawing or two that contain an index of all drawings in the set.

AutoCAD LT does not support sheet sets.

Overview of a Sheet Set

Sheet sets take advantage of the existing drawings you have been creating over the years. A sheet set contains sheets, which are references to paper space layouts — sorry, you can't use the Model tab as a sheet. If you use the Model tab for plotting and publishing today, you need to switch to the use of paper space layouts to take advantage of sheet sets. A sheet set and all the references to its sheets are stored in a file with the DST extension and are accessed through Sheet Set Manager (see Figure 2-1). By using references to the drawing files, you can use your own directory structures while taking advantage of the benefits of sheet sets. Some of these benefits are

✦ **Fast file access:** Because a sheet set knows right where a file is located, drawings can be accessed in a short amount of time without the need to browse and open a file.

✦ **Consistent drawing creation:** Sheet sets can be set up to specify the directory structure and location in which new sheets should be created when they are added to the sheet set. You can also specify which drawing template (DWT) file should be used to create new sheets and drawings.

✦ **Quick updates:** Sheet sets allow you to create references to views on sheets (paper space layouts) and manage the names and numbers of views. This allows you to quickly renumber a view and not have to worry about exactly where that view is placed. The next time the drawing is opened, the numbering is updated. This also works very well for project information in a title block that is on a paper space layout.

✦ **Publish drawings:** Creating a drawing set can be time consuming when it's time to package things and get them ready to send to the client. Sheet sets allow you to organize drawings and then quickly publish the entire set of drawings or selected drawings.

✦ **Package drawings:** During a normal project cycle, you'll need to send drawings electronically to others and create revisions of drawings in a drawing set. With sheet sets, you can eTransmit or archive an entire set of drawings.

✦ **Create an index table of sheets:** One of the things that can take time to generate, but is fairly automated with sheet sets, is the creation of an index of all the sheets in a sheet set. Because all the sheets are named and numbered in the sheet set, you can create an index with just a few mouse clicks.

Figure 2-1:
Sheet Set Manager allows you to work with DST files.

Sheet Set Manager

 Sheet Set Manager is the tool in AutoCAD that you'll be using to work with sheet sets. It allows you to do everything you need to do to work efficiently with a sheet set. From inside Sheet Set Manager, you can open sheets (drawings), add and remove sheets, add and remove subsets, change the order of subsets and sheets, work with model views, and much more. Sheet Set Manager is organized into three areas, each represented by a tab: Sheet List, Sheet Views and Model Views.

The Sheet List tab is where you access sheets and subsets in the sheet set. You use the Sheet Views tab to manage any of the named views that have been placed on the sheets that are part of the sheet set from the Model Views tab. The Model Views tab lists the drawings and any of the named views that are stored in them; these drawings are only used for placing views on sheets in the current sheet set. You use the SHEETSET command to display Sheet Set Manager.

To start the SHEETSET command, do one of the following:

✦ On the ribbon, click View tab⇨Palettes panel⇨Sheet Set Manager.

✦ On the menu browser or menu bar, click Tools menu⇨Palettes⇨Sheet Set Manager.

✦ On the Standard or Standard Annotation toolbar, click the Sheet Set Manager button.

✦ Press Ctrl+4.

✦ At the command prompt type **SHEETSET** or **SSM** and press Enter.

Creating a Sheet Set

Sheet sets are commonly created by using the Create Sheet Set Wizard. The Create Sheet Set Wizard allows you to create a new sheet set by using an existing sheet set as a template or by creating one from scratch. You typically create a sheet set from scratch the first time you create one so you can define the common properties that your projects will have, and then use that sheet set as a template for future sheet sets that you create. After you create a sheet set, you can import references to paper space layouts from your existing drawing files.

After you add some drawing layouts to a sheet set, you typically organize those layouts in the sheet set by using subsets. Subsets enable you to organize sheets into folders that can be used to represent actual folder locations on a drive or not. After the subsets have been created, you can designate a drawing template (DWT) file to use for any new sheets that are created in that subset or move existing sheets from other subsets or the root of the sheet set to better organize the sheets with Sheet Set Manager. A drawing template (DWT) file that is used with sheet sets commonly has a title block that contains attributes that are adjusted to take advantage of fields specific to properties of a sheet or sheet set.

The last part of setting up a sheet set involves working with model (named) views. Sheet sets allow you to place named views on a sheet. When you place a named view on a sheet, AutoCAD creates an external reference (xref) to the drawing that contains the named view and a new viewport on the layout that the view is being placed on. The viewport contains the objects in the named view.

I cover creating named views in Chapter 3 of Book II. To access named views from other drawings, they must first be in a location that has been designated through Sheet Set Manager as a resource location for the sheet set. To finish the setup for adding views to a sheet, you need to specify which callouts and label blocks will be used when views are placed on a sheet. To get started, you don't need to use all the features that sheet sets offer at once. Often people start using sheet sets as a way to organize and access drawings to simplify file navigation and plotting.

Starting from scratch

The Create Sheet Set Wizard option to create a new sheet set by using existing drawings from scratch requires the most input. This option provides for a good understanding of what is involved with the initial setup of a sheet set. After you create a sheet set according to your company standards, you can use the other option of creating a sheet set from an existing one. You use the NEWSHEETSET command to start the Create Sheet Set Wizard.

To start the NEWSHEETSET command, do one of the following:

✦ On the menu browser or menu bar, click File menu⇨New Sheet Set.

✦ At the command prompt, type **NEWSHEETSET** and press Enter.

✦ In Sheet Set Manager, click the down arrow on the drop-down list along the top and select New Sheet Set.

To create a new sheet set, follow these steps:

1. **Start the NEWSHEETSET command by using one of the methods in the preceding list.**

The Create Sheet Set Wizard appears. To create a sheet set from Sheet Set Manager you must have at least one drawing open.

2. **Select the Existing Drawings option and click Next.**

The Existing Drawings option allows you to create a sheet set from scratch. If you already have a sheet set created and want to create a new sheet set based on the existing one, select the An Example Sheet Set option.

3. **In the Name of New Sheet Set text box (see Figure 2-2), type a name for the sheet set.**

The name entered is used as the name for the DST file when the wizard is finished. This is also the name of the top-level node displayed in Sheet Set Manager when the sheet set is opened.

Figure 2-2:
The Create
Sheet Set
Wizard —
Sheet Set
Details
page.

4. **In the Description (optional) text box, type a description for the sheet set.**

The description is displayed in Sheet Set Manager and can be referenced in a field and placed as part of the index sheet.

5. **Specify where to create the new sheet set.**

To do so, enter a path in the Store Sheet Set Data File (.dst) Here text box or click the ellipsis (...) button to browse to a folder. If you click the ellipsis button, the Browse for Sheet Set Folder dialog box is displayed. Browse to a location in the dialog box and select the folder that you want to use. Click Open to use the selected folder. By default, the folder used to store sheet sets is in AutoCAD Sheet Sets under Documents or My Documents, depending on the operating system you are running.

The specified location is where the DST file will be created when the Create Sheet Set Wizard is finished. It's a good idea to place sheet sets on a network drive so that others in the office can access them.

6. **Click Sheet Set Properties to specify standard and custom properties for the sheet set.**

The Sheet Set Properties dialog box appears (see Figure 2-3). The dialog box allows you to set a variety of properties that range from the location in which callout blocks are stored to the project name and even custom properties that you can add, such as who drew or checked a drawing. Custom properties are explained later under the "Managing Drawings with a Sheet Set" section.

7. Click OK.

The Sheet Set Properties dialog box closes, and you are returned to the Create Sheet Set Wizard.

8. Click Next.

The wizard advances to the next page.

9. On the Choose Layouts page, click Import Options to control the behavior for importing layouts.

The Import Options dialog box appears (see Figure 2-4). This dialog box controls the naming and folder structure used when importing layouts.

10. Specify the options that you want and then click OK.

Select or deselect the Prefix Sheet Titles with File Name option to control whether the name of the file is added to the layout name to make up the sheet title. The Create Subsets Based on Folder Structure and Ignore Top Level Folder options control how the folder structure on the drive that the layouts are being imported from affect the sheet set's organization structure.

11. On the Choose Layouts page, click Browse.

The Browse for Folder dialog box is displayed.

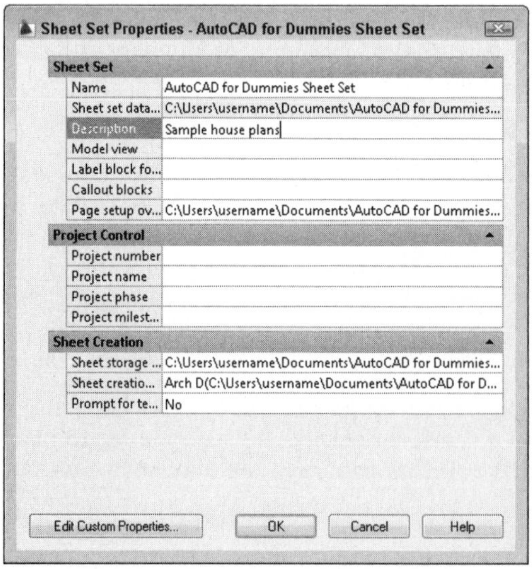

Figure 2-3:
Sheet Set
Properties
dialog box.

Figure 2-4:
Specifying
an import
behavior in
the Import
Options
dialog box.

12. **Select a folder and click OK.**

A list of the drawings in that folder are displayed in a tree view along with the folder structure of the selected folder and the paper space layouts in each drawing (see Figure 2-5). Only drawings that are not part of a sheet set already are displayed and can be imported into a sheet set.

13. **In the tree view, deselect the layouts you don't want to import as references into the sheet set and then click Next.**

The selected layouts are marked for import after the Create Sheet Set Wizard is finished.

14. **On the Confirm page, review the Sheet Set Preview section. Click Back to make any necessary changes in the wizard. Click Finish when everything looks good.**

The Create Sheet Set Wizard closes, and the new sheet set DST file is created with the specified name and in the designated folder. Sheet Set Manager is displayed if it was hidden and the DST file opens.

Figure 2-5:
The tree
view
displays the
folder
structure
and
available
layouts in
drawings for
import.

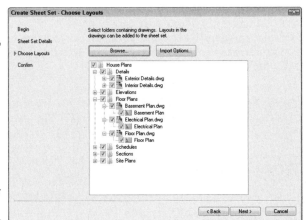

Starting from an existing sheet set

You can create a sheet set by using an existing sheet set as a template. The following steps explain how:

1. **Start the NEWSHEETSET command by using one of the previously described methods.**

The Create Sheet Set Wizard appears.

2. **Select the An Example Sheet Set option and click Next.**

The An Example Sheet Set option allows you to select an existing sheet set to use as a template.

3. **Select the Select a Sheet Set to Use as an Example option and then select one of the available sheet sets from the list, or select Browse to Another Sheet Set to Use as an Example and then click the ellipsis (...) button to specify which DST file you want to start with. Click Next.**

If you choose the Select a Sheet Set to Use as an Example option, the DST files that are listed are located in the Template directory. The location of the DST files can be changed through the Files tab of the Options dialog box by choosing Template Settings⇨Sheet Set Template File Location.

4. **Specify the new sheet set's name, description, and save to location, and change its properties with the Sheet Set Properties dialog box. Any subsets are copied over, but any references to layouts that make up the sheets in the sheet set template are not carried over to the new sheet set. Click Next.**

You get everything that was in the selected sheet set file, minus any sheets. If you want to keep the sheets in the new sheet set, you must make a copy of the original sheet set file by using Windows Explorer.

5. **On the Confirm page, review the Sheet Set Preview section. Click Back to make any necessary changes in the wizard. Click Finish when everything looks good.**

The Create Sheet Set wizard closes and the new sheet set (DST) file is created with the specified name and in the designated folder. Sheet Set Manager is displayed if it was hidden and the DST file opens.

Managing Drawings with a Sheet Set

You can work with drawings through a sheet set in a number of ways, such as navigating to and opening existing drawing files, creating new sheets (drawings), working with title block information, and placing model views. Some companies have taken the approach of first implementing sheet sets as a way to open and publish drawings much faster, and others have changed their entire drafting process to include the use of sheet sets to manage the views and title block information as well as the benefits of opening and publishing drawings much faster.

Opening a sheet set

After closing and restarting AutoCAD, the OPENSHEETSET command allows you to open an existing sheet set (DST) file. Just like the NEWSHEETSET command, the OPENSHEETSET command displays Sheet Set Manager if it's not currently displayed after you select an existing sheet set.

To start the OPENSHEETSET command, do one of the following:

✦ On the menu browser or menu bar, click File menu⇨Open Sheet Set.

✦ At the command prompt, type **OPENSHEETSET** and press Enter.

✦ In Sheet Set Manager, click the down arrow on the drop-down list along the top and select Open Sheet Set.

You can open one of the ten most recently used sheet set (DST) files from the drop-down list in Sheet Set Manager.

To open a sheet set file, follow these steps:

1. **Start the OPENSHEETSET command by using one of the methods in the preceding list.**

The Open Sheet Set dialog box appears. You can use this dialog box to browse and select an existing sheet set (DST) file.

2. **In the Open Sheet Set dialog box, select the sheet set (DST) file you want to open. Click Open.**

The Open Sheet Set dialog box closes and the selected sheet set (DST) file is loaded into Sheet Set Manager. If Sheet Set Manager is not currently displayed, it is displayed after the Open Sheet Set dialog box is closed.

Importing existing drawings as sheets

If you've been using AutoCAD at your company for many years, you most likely have created hundreds, if not thousands, of drawings. This is one of the concerns that Autodesk kept in mind when implementing sheet sets in AutoCAD 2005. Sheet sets are designed to work well with your existing drawing files without having to worry about migrating your files just so they can be used with sheet sets. You can import paper space layouts from drawings when you create a sheet set based on existing drawings by using the Create Sheet Set Wizard. Most of the time, however, you won't know which drawings need to be imported right away, or which drawings might come from a vendor and need to be added to the sheet set later.

Book VII Chapter 2

Sheet Sets without Regret

Sheet Set Manager allows you to import paper space layouts from a drawing into a sheet set file after it has been created. This allows for a lot of flexibility in the workflow of a project. Paper space layouts can be imported to the main root of a sheet set or a subset; it all just depends on how the sheet set is laid out. The following steps explain how to import paper space layouts as sheets and assumes you already have a sheet set open in Sheet Set Manager. To open an existing sheet set, refer to the "Opening a sheet set" section.

1. **In Sheet Set Manager's Sheet List tab, right-click the top-level node that displays the sheet set's name.**

You can also right-click a subset if you want to add layouts to it. I cover subsets in the next section.

2. **On the shortcut menu, click Import Layout as Sheet.**

The Import Layouts as Sheets dialog box appears (see Figure 2-6). The dialog box allows you to browse for drawings that contain paper space layouts that you want to import as sheets.

3. **Click Browse for Drawings.**

The Select Drawing dialog box appears, allowing you to browse for drawing files. You can select more than one drawing by holding down the Ctrl or Shift keys while selecting files.

4. **Click Open.**

The Select Drawing dialog box closes, and you return to the Import Layout as Sheets dialog box. The selected files are scanned for paper space layouts. During the scanning, the layouts are added to the grid in the center of the dialog box and evaluated as to whether they are already referenced by a sheet set.

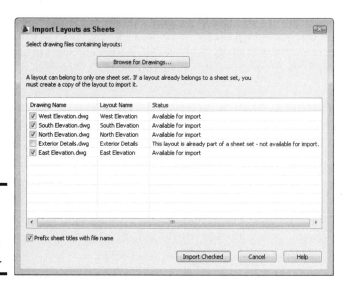

Figure 2-6:
Importing layouts as sheets into a sheet set.

5. **Deselect the layouts you do not want to import as sheets into the sheet set.**

   By default, if a layout is already associated with a sheet set, the layout is deselected, and all other layouts are selected. Only paper space layouts can be imported.

6. **Deselect or select the Prefix Sheet Titles with File Name option.**

   This option controls whether the file name that a layout comes from is added to the sheet's title. This can be helpful if you do not normally give your layout tabs a specific name in each drawing. The sheet's title can be changed later.

7. **Click Import Checked.**

   The dialog box closes and the checked layouts are added to the sheet set as sheets.

Organizing with subsets

Subsets are used to organize sheets in a sheet set. A subset may represent a folder on a local or network drive, but it doesn't have to. Subsets can be created at the root level of a sheet set or within another subset. Typically, a subset is used to group similar drawings (such as by floor or discipline) so that you can quickly find the sheets you're looking for. The following steps explain how to create a subset. The steps assume that you have a sheet set open in Sheet Set Manager. To open a sheet set, refer to the "Opening a sheet set" section.

1. **In Sheet Set Manager's Sheet List tab, right-click the top-level node that displays the sheet set's name or a subset.**

2. **On the shortcut menu, click New Subset.**

   The Subset Properties dialog box appears (see Figure 2-7). You can use this dialog box to specify the name of the subset, whether the folder is created relative to its parent, where new sheets that are added to the subset are created, and which drawing template (DWT) file to use to create new sheets under the subset.

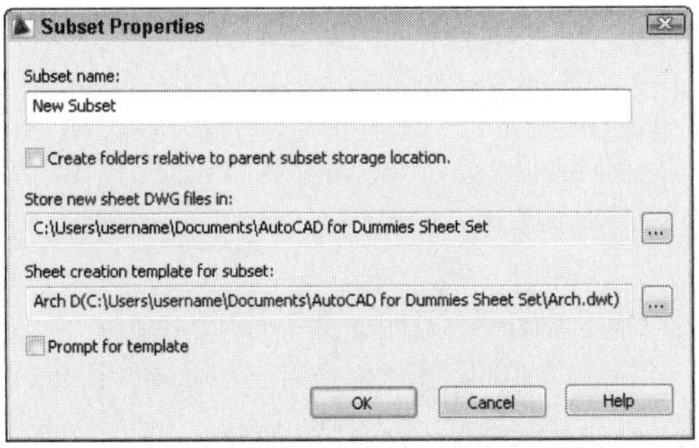

Figure 2-7: Specifying properties for a subset.

3. **In the Subset Name text box, specify the name of the subset.**

   The name is used in Sheet Set Manager and for the folder in which new sheets will be created.

4. **Click the ellipsis (...) button to the right of Store New Sheet DWG Files In.**

   The Browse for Folder dialog box appears.

5. **Browse to and select the folder that represents the subset. Click Open.**

   The selected folder will be used to store any new drawings that are created when you create new sheets under the subset.

6. **If you want the folder to be created relative to its parent in the tree on the Sheet List tab, select the Create Folders Relative to Parent Subset Storage Location.**

   A new folder is created as necessary, based on the options you specify.

7. **Click the ellipsis button to the right of Sheet Creation Template for Subset.**

   The Select Layout as Sheet Template dialog box appears.

8. **Browse to and select the drawing template that should be used when a new sheet is created under the subset. Select the layout to use for new sheets in the Select a Layout to Create New Sheets list and click OK.**

   If the Prompt for Template option is checked, the user of the sheet set will be prompted to specify a drawing template when a new sheet is created under the subset.

9. **Click OK.**

   The Subset Properties dialog box closes, and the new subset is created.

You can control the order in which sheets and subsets appear on the Sheet List tab by dragging them up and down. Sheets can also be added to a subset by dragging them onto a subset or into a specific location within a subset.

Setting up a sheet set and subset for adding new sheets

Sheets can be created at both the sheet set and the subset level. To make this process as streamlined as possible, you must do some minor setup for each of these areas of a sheet set. Three properties need to be set, and they are the same between the sheet set and subset. The only difference in the process is how you access the properties.

Setting up drawing template settings for a sheet set

The following steps explain how to change the properties used for a new sheet that is added to the root level of a sheet set. I assume you already have a sheet set open in Sheet Set Manager. To open a sheet set, refer to the "Opening a sheet set" section.

1. **In Sheet Set Manager's Sheet List tab, right-click the top-level node that displays the sheet set's name.**

2. **On the shortcut menu, click Properties.**

The Sheet Set Properties dialog box is displayed.

3. **In the Sheet Creation area, click the Sheet Storage Location field to display an ellipsis (...) button.**

4. **Click the ellipsis button to browse to and select the location where new sheets will be added when created. Click Open.**

The Browse for Folder dialog box is displayed, allowing you to browse and select the folder where any new sheets will be saved. After clicking the Open button you are returned to the Sheet Set Properties dialog box.

5. **Click the Sheet Creation Template field to display an ellipsis button.**

6. **Click the ellipsis button to browse to and select the drawing template (DWT) file that you want to use when a new sheet is added to the sheet set.**

The Select Layout as Sheet Template dialog box appears (see Figure 2-8).

7. **In the Drawing Template File Name text box, enter the path and file name for a drawing template file. Or click the ellipsis button to browse for and select a drawing template (DWT) file.**

If the ellipsis button is clicked, the Select Drawing dialog box is displayed. Browse to and select the drawing, drawing template, or drawing standards file that contains the layout you want to use as the template for new sheets. Click Open to close the Select Drawing dialog box and return to the Select Layout as Sheet Template dialog box.

Figure 2-8:
Using a layout in a drawing as a template for new sheets.

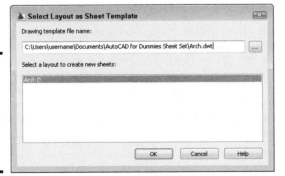

8. **In the Select a Layout to Create New Sheets list box, select the layout you want to use as the sheet template and then click OK.**

The Select Layout as Sheet Template dialog box closes, and the specified drawing file and selected layout are applied to the Sheet Creation Template property in the Sheet Set Properties dialog box.

9. **In the Sheet Creation area, specify Yes or No in the Prompt for Template property.**

The Prompt for Template property controls whether the template specified in the sheet creation template is used when a new sheet is created. You can use the specified sheet creation template or one of your own choosing.

10. **Click OK.**

The Sheet Set Properties dialog box closes and the changes to the properties are applied to the sheet set.

Setting up drawing template settings for a subset

Setting up a drawing template to use when a new sheet is created under the subset is similar to setting up a sheet set. Refer to the preceding topic for information on setting up the properties related to defining how a new sheet is added to a sheet set. The following steps provide a quick walkthrough of how to access the properties of a subset (not a full in-depth walkthrough of each property) and assume that you have a sheet set open in Sheet Set Manager. To open a sheet set, refer to the "Opening a sheet set" section.

1. **In Sheet Set Manager's Sheet List tab, right-click the subset for which you want to adjust the properties and choose Properties.**

The Subset Properties dialog box appears.

2. **Specify the subset's name, the location where the sheets will be created, the drawing template that will be used when adding new sheets to the subset, and whether the user will be prompted to specify a drawing template when a new sheet is added to the subset.**

The properties in the Subset Properties dialog box, except for the Subset Name field, are the same as those in the Sheet Creation area of the Sheet Set Properties dialog box. See the "Setting up drawing template settings for a sheet set" section for more information on these properties.

3. **Click OK.**

The Subset Properties dialog box closes and the changes to the properties are saved.

Adding a new sheet

You can add a new sheet to a sheet set or a subset. How the new sheet is defined is based on the properties that have been set up for the sheet set or subset. When a new sheet is created, a new drawing file is also created. The new drawing then has its layout referenced into the sheet set file at the location that the new sheet was created. After you define the properties for the sheet set or subset, a new sheet is rather easy to create.

The following steps explain how to add a new sheet to either the root level of a sheet set or to a subset, and assumes that you already have a sheet set open in Sheet Set Manager. To open a sheet set, refer to the "Opening a sheet set" section.

1. **In Sheet Set Manager's Sheet List tab, right-click the sheet set or subset in which you want to add a new sheet.**

2. **On the shortcut menu, click New Sheet.**

The New Sheet dialog box appears (see Figure 2-9). The dialog box allows you to specify a number, a title, and a file name for the new sheet, and open the new sheet after it is created.

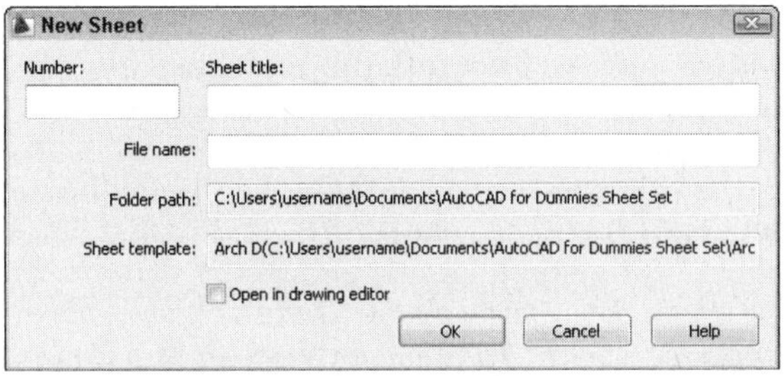

Figure 2-9:
Adding a new sheet to a sheet set or subset.

3. **In the Number text box, enter a drawing number for the sheet.**

The number can be displayed in a title block through the use of a field or as part of the index sheet table, and is shown in the tree view on the Sheet List tab.

4. **In the Sheet Title text box, type a title for the sheet.**

The title can be displayed in a title block through the use of a field or as part of the index sheet table, and is shown in the tree view on the Sheet List tab.

5. **In the File Name text box, type a file name for the sheet.**

AutoCAD uses the file name you enter to save the new sheet to the specified location in the Folder Path text box.

6. Click OK.

The New Sheet dialog box closes and the new sheet is added to the sheet set or the subset. Optionally, select the Open in Drawing Editor option to open the new sheet after it's created.

New in AutoCAD 2009, after you add a new sheet you now have the option to open it right away by selecting the Open in Drawing Editor option in the New Sheet dialog box.

Opening a sheet

To open a sheet from a sheet set, you double-click the sheet. The drawing that the sheet references is opened, along with the specific layout within the drawing that is associated with the sheet. If you want, you can also right-click a sheet and choose Open or Open Read-only from the shortcut menu.

Removing, renaming, and renumbering a sheet

At times you may find yourself needing to remove, rename, or renumber a sheet based on whether it is being moved in a sheet set or no longer needed. Removing a sheet from a sheet set allows you to get rid of it when you no longer need it. To remove a sheet from a sheet set, right-click the sheet and choose Remove Sheet from the shortcut menu. When asked to confirm the removal of the sheet, click OK. AutoCAD removes the sheet only from the sheet set; it does not remove from disk the actual drawing file that is linked to the sheet.

You can change the title and number of a sheet through the Rename & Renumber Sheet dialog box (see Figure 2-10). This dialog box allows you to change the number of the sheet, its title and layout name in the drawing file, and even the file name of the drawing file that the layout is contained in. To rename and renumber a sheet, right-click the sheet and choose Rename & Renumber from the shortcut menu. Change the number and title in the dialog box, and, if you want, the layout and file name of the drawing as well. You can navigate to the next or previous sheet in the subset and rename or renumber it without leaving the dialog box.

AutoCAD 2009 allows you to rename the layout and drawing that is associated with a sheet in a sheet set. From the Rename & Renumber Sheet dialog box, you can rename a sheet's layout to match the sheet title and number, and you can rename the drawing file that the sheet is contained in so that it matches the sheet's title and number.

Although you can use AutoCAD or Windows Explorer to rename drawing files, it's best to use Sheet Set Manager to rename drawings linked to a sheet in a sheet set to avoid missing drawing files.

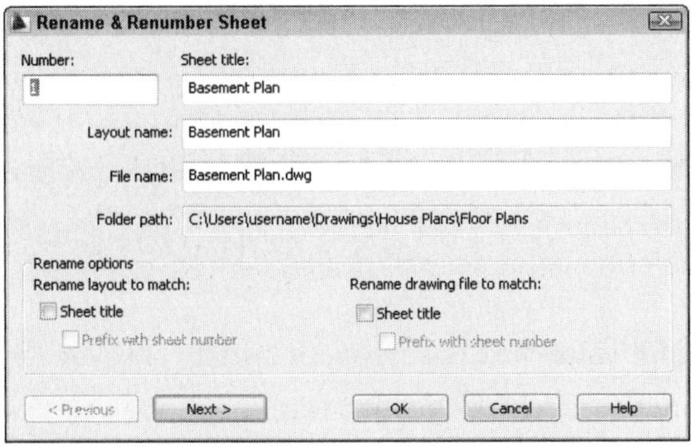

Figure 2-10: Renaming and renumbering a sheet.

Sheet set and sheet properties

Sheet sets and individual sheets use two types of properties, standard and custom. Standard properties are available for you to use without doing any additional setup. Standard properties can be accessed by right-clicking the top-level node of the sheet set or the sheet and selecting Properties. Based on which one you right-click, different properties are available. Some of these properties can be referenced in a text or attribute object through fields.

Custom properties require a little more work because you need to define the property before you can use it. Custom properties allow you to incorporate the use of sheet sets into your current drafting process much more easily because you can define properties that you may be accustomed to using during your project management cycle for client, drafter, or project information. Although sheet sets and sheets come with predefined properties for you to use, they do not cover everything that you might want to store with a sheet set or sheet. Custom properties, like standard properties, can be displayed in a title block through fields.

The following steps explain how to define a custom property for a sheet and then change its value. I assume that you already have a sheet set open in Sheet Set Manager. To open a sheet set, refer to the "Opening a sheet set" section.

1. **In Sheet Set Manager's Sheet List tab, right-click the top-level node that displays the sheet set's name and choose Properties.**

   The Sheet Set Properties dialog box appears.

2. **Click Edit Custom Properties.**

   The Custom Properties dialog box appears (see Figure 2-11). The dialog box allows you to add and modify custom properties that you can have at the sheet or sheet set level. These custom properties allow you to populate information down to title blocks in your sheets so that the information can be edited from a central location without opening each sheet individually.

**Book VII
Chapter 2**

**Sheet Sets
without Regret**

3. Click Add.

The Add Custom Property dialog box appears (see Figure 2-12). This is where you define a new sheet set or sheet property.

4. In the Name text box, type a name for the custom property.

The name of the property can be pretty much anything you want to use. The property created is accessible in the Sheet Set Properties, Sheet Properties, and Field dialog boxes.

5. In the Default Value text box, type an initial value for the property.

This value is the default value for the property.

6. In the Owner area, select the Sheet Set option.

The owner type controls where the property will be accessible from, even though both types of custom properties are created through the Sheet Set Properties dialog box.

7. Add a sheet custom property by repeating Steps 3 through 6, but in Step 6 select the Sheet option.

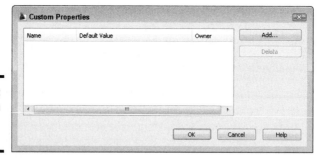

Figure 2-11:
The Custom Properties dialog box.

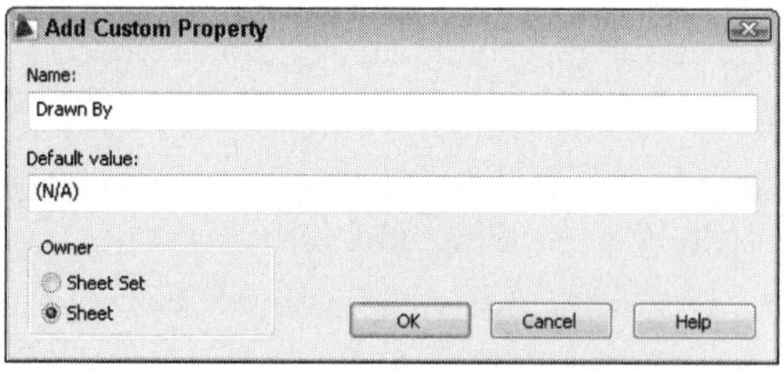

Figure 2-12:
Adding a custom property.

8. **Click OK.**

The Add Custom Property dialog box closes and you are returned to the Custom Properties dialog box. The new custom property should now be listed. After the custom property is created, you can change only its default value. If you want to change its name or owner, you need to delete the custom property and then re-create it. Be careful about deleting custom properties; if the custom property is used in a field, it will become unresolved because it no longer exists. Double-click the default value for the custom property to edit the value.

9. **In the Custom Properties dialog box, click OK.**

The Custom Properties dialog box closes, and you are returned to the Sheet Set Properties dialog box. If you added a custom property that had its owner set to Sheet Set, the properties are displayed in the Sheet Set Custom Properties section (see Figure 2-13). Also notice that custom properties designated as an owner of Sheet are displayed in the Sheet Custom Properties section. This allows you to change the default value of a sheet's custom property that is applied when a new sheet is created.

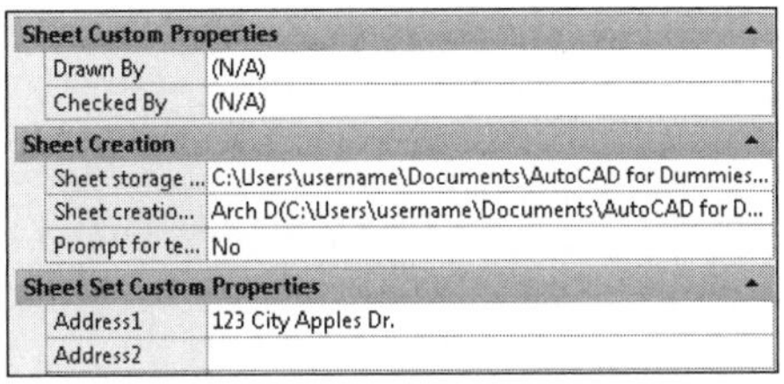

Figure 2-13:
All custom properties are accessible from the Sheet Set Properties dialog box.

Sheet Custom Properties	
Drawn By	(N/A)
Checked By	(N/A)
Sheet Creation	
Sheet storage ...	C:\Users\username\Documents\AutoCAD for Dummies...
Sheet creatio...	Arch D(C:\Users\username\Documents\AutoCAD for D...
Prompt for te...	No
Sheet Set Custom Properties	
Address1	123 City Apples Dr.
Address2	

10. **In the Sheet Set Properties dialog box, click OK.**

The Sheet Set Properties dialog box closes and you are returned to Sheet Set Manager.

11. **In Sheet Set Manager, right-click the sheet whose custom properties you want to change and choose Properties.**

The Sheet Properties dialog box appears (see Figure 2-14).

12. **In the Sheet Custom Properties section, change the value of the custom sheet property .**

Click in the text box next to the custom property and make the change to its value.

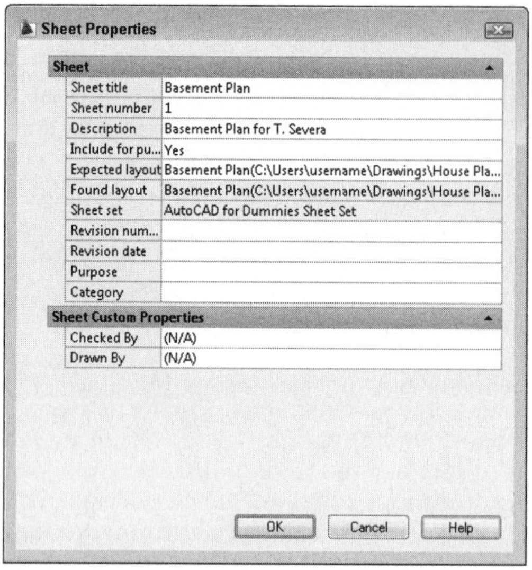

Figure 2-14:
Sheet
properties
are
changed
through the
Sheet
Properties
dialog box.

13. **Click OK.**

The Sheet Properties dialog box closes and you return to Sheet Set
Manager. The sheet set and sheet properties and their values are displayed in the Preview/Details pane at the bottom of Sheet Set Manager
when an item in the tree view of the Sheet List tab is selected. If the
Preview/Details pane is not displayed, right-click an empty area of the tree
view and choose Preview/Details Pane. If the Details area is not displayed,
click the Details button just below the tree view on the Sheet List tab.

Setting up callouts and label blocks

You use callout and label blocks with model space views that are placed on a
sheet from the Model Views tab. Label blocks are automatically placed under
a model space view when placed onto a sheet. They commonly hold the
number and title for a view, and the scale of the viewport that is created to
show the view. Views that are placed on the sheets are numbered and titled
through the Rename & Renumber View dialog box from the Sheet Views tab.
Placing views on a sheet is discussed in the "Adding model views to a sheet"
section.

Callout blocks, unlike label blocks, are not automatically placed in a drawing.
A callout block typically has the view number and the sheet number on
which the view is placed. The callout points to a particular side of a building
plan, indicating where the elevation or view is located in the sheet set.

When a callout block is added to a sheet, AutoCAD creates a hyperlink back to the sheet on which the view is placed. This allows you to move quickly to the sheet with the view on it by holding down the Ctrl key while double-clicking the callout block.

Callout and label blocks use fields to reference information contained in the sheet set. These fields are defined through the SheetSetPlaceholder field name in the SheetSet category in the Fields dialog box. To find more about fields, refer to Book III. For information on creating blocks, refer to Book VI.

Setting up label blocks

The following steps explain how to define label blocks for placing with model space views. I assume that you have a sheet set open in Sheet Set Manager. To open a sheet set, refer to the "Opening a sheet set" section.

1. **In Sheet Set Manager's Sheet List tab, right-click the top-level node that displays the sheet set's name and choose Properties.**

   The Sheet Set Properties dialog box is displayed.

2. **In the Sheet Set area, click the Label Block for Views text box to display an ellipsis (...) button.**

3. **Click the ellipsis button to specify a block or drawing file.**

   The Select Block dialog box appears (see Figure 2-15). You can use this dialog box to browse for a drawing file and then use the drawing file as the label block, or select a block from the drawing as a label block.

4. **Click the ellipsis button to the right of the Enter the Drawing File Name text box.**

   The Select Drawing dialog box appears, allowing you to select a drawing or drawing template (DWT) file that contains the block you want to use as a label block.

**Book VII
Chapter 2**

Sheet Sets without Regret

Figure 2-15:
Select Block dialog box allows you to select a block contained in a drawing.

5. **Browse to and select the drawing or drawing template file that contains the label block you want to use when placing model space views. Click Open.**

   The Select Drawing dialog box closes and the selected file is added to the Select Block dialog box.

6. **In the Select Block dialog box, select the Select the Drawing File as a Block option or the Choose Blocks in the Drawing File option.**

   The selected option determines which block is used for a label block.

7. **If you select Choose Blocks in the Drawing File, select a block from the list box.**

   The selected block is used as the label block.

8. **Click OK.**

   The Select Block dialog box closes, and the block name and path are assigned to the Label Block for Views property in the Sheet Set Properties dialog box.

9. **In the Sheet Set Properties dialog box, click OK.**

   The Sheet Set Properties dialog box closes, and the changes are saved.

Setting up callout blocks

Setting up callout blocks is similar to setting up a label block, except you can associate multiple blocks from a drawing for use as callout blocks. The following steps explain how to define which callout blocks are available for placing in a drawing with a model space view on a sheet, and assumes that you have a sheet set open in Sheet Set Manager. To open a sheet set, refer to the "Opening a sheet set" section.

1. **In Sheet Set Manager's Sheet List tab, right-click the top-level node that displays the sheet set's name and choose Properties.**

   The Sheet Set Properties dialog box appears.

2. **In the Sheet Set area, click the Callout Blocks text box to display an ellipsis (...) button.**

3. **Click the ellipsis button to specify a block or drawing file.**

   The List of Blocks dialog box (see Figure 2-16) appears.

4. **Click Add.**

   The Select Block dialog box appears, allowing you to browse for a drawing file, and use the drawing file as the callout block or select a block(s) from the drawing as a callout block.

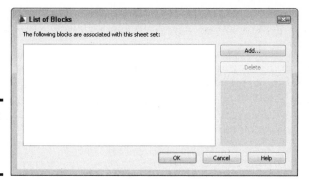

Figure 2-16:
The List of
Blocks
dialog box.

5. **Click the ellipsis button to the right of the Enter the Drawing File Name text box.**

   The Select Drawing dialog box appears.

6. **Select the drawing or drawing template file that contains the label block you want to use when placing model space views. Click Open.**

   You return to the Select Block dialog box.

7. **Select the Select the Drawing File as a Block option or the Choose Blocks in the Drawing File option.**

8. **If you select Choose Blocks in the Drawing File, select a block from the list box.**

9. **Click OK.**

   The Select Block dialog box closes, and you return to the List of Blocks dialog box. The selected file or block(s) or both are added to the list box.

10. **Click OK.**

    The List of Blocks dialog box closes, and you return to the Sheet Set Properties dialog box, where the callout blocks are added to the Callout Blocks property.

11. **Click OK.**

    The Sheet Set Properties dialog box closes, and the changes are saved.

Adding resource drawings

Sheet sets allow you to take advantage of model space views that you have defined in drawings that might or might not be part of the sheet set. The drawings with model views might be details or other parts of a drawing that might be commonly shared with one or more projects. The location of these drawings needs to be made available to Sheet Set Manager for you to place the model views onto a sheet. Resource drawings are defined through the

Book VII
Chapter 2

Sheet Sets
without Regret

Model Views tab of Sheet Set Manager. The locations added for resource drawings most commonly contain details or elevations but can also be for plans.

The following steps explain how to define a drawing resource location for a sheet set. I assume that you already have a sheet set open in Sheet Set Manager. To open a sheet set, refer to the "Opening a sheet set" section.

1. **In Sheet Set Manager's Model Views tab, click the Add New Location button (along the top).**

The Browse for Folder dialog box appears.

2. **Specify the folder that contains the drawings with the model views that you want to place on a sheet. Click Open.**

AutoCAD loads all the drawings from the folder you select into the Locations section on the Model Views tab of Sheet Set Manager (see Figure 2-17).

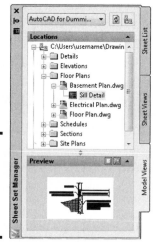

Figure 2-17:
Resource drawings available to the sheet set.

Adding model views to a sheet

After you have set up the callout and label blocks and the resource drawings for the sheet set, you're ready to place model space views on a sheet. Model space views must first be created and saved in a drawing that is in the location where your resource drawings are stored. A model view can be assigned a category and a layer state. The layer state affects how layers appear in the viewport that's created when the model view is added to a sheet. The category is used to organize views on Sheet Set Manager's Sheet Views tab, and in ShowMotion, which allows you to navigate a drawing by accessing named views from the status bar area. For information on model views and ShowMotion, see Chapter 3 of Book II.

Model views that are placed on a sheet don't introduce any new concepts in AutoCAD, but they do use a combination of existing features. Model views use named views to define what is to be displayed, xrefs to get the geometry into the Model space of the drawing that the sheet is part of, viewports to display the xref'd drawing, and blocks and attributes to help link the information from a sheet set to the attributes in the callout and label blocks that are placed on the sheet.

The following procedure explains how to place a model view on a sheet and adjust the number and title for the view that is placed. The procedure assumes that you have defined a resource location for drawings that contains the model space views you want to place on a sheet, specified a label block to use for the sheet set, set up the properties for creating a new sheet, and have a sheet set open. If you need help with any of these tasks, refer to previous sections in this chapter.

1. **On Sheet Set Manager's Sheet List tab, create a new sheet or open an existing one. The model space views will be placed on the sheet, so make sure that the sheet is open before you continue.**

2. **On the Model Views tab, click the plus sign next to one of the drawings defined by the resource location under the Locations pane.**

   The node for the drawing is expanded and any views contained in the drawing are displayed as nodes below it.

3. **Using the left mouse button, select one of the model views below the drawing; continue to hold down the mouse button and drag the view over the drawing window.**

   As you drag the view, the name of the view is dragged with the cursor. You can also right-click a model view and choose Place on Sheet.

4. **Release the mouse button over the drawing window to start the referencing process.**

   A preview of the view is displayed for dragging in the drawing window along with the label block that is configured for the sheet set. The label block is located below the lower-left corner of the viewport.

5. **Right-click the drawing window to specify a specific scale for the view.**

   AutoCAD guesses at a scale based on the size of the drawing and the view that is being referenced. By right-clicking, you can choose the scale you want to use from the shortcut menu.

6. **Select a scale from the shortcut menu to use for the view.**

   The preview image that is being dragged is updated to reflect the new scale.

7. **Pick a point in the drawing window to place the model view, and create the viewport and insert the label block.**

The viewport is created based on the specified scale, and the label block is inserted below the viewport.

8. **On the Sheet Views tab, locate the view that was added to the tree based on the sheet name or category of the view placed. Right-click the view and select Rename & Renumber.**

   The Rename & Renumber View dialog box appears (see Figure 2-18).

Figure 2-18:
Renaming
and
renumbering
a view.

9. **In the Rename & Renumber View dialog box, enter a number in the Number text box for the view. A title should already exist, because it is the name of the model space view.**

   The number can be any text you want, but usually it's a number with maybe a letter. Click the Previous or Next buttons to continue renaming views without leaving the dialog box.

10. **Click OK.**

   The Rename & Renumber View dialog box closes, and you return to Sheet Set Manager.

11. **At the command prompt, type** regen **and press Enter.**

   Fields are not updated until an action in the drawing causes a regen or a save. The field in the label block will be updated with the number and title changes that you made in the Rename & Renumber View dialog box.

12. **On the Sheet List tab, open a sheet that needs to have callout blocks added to it to reference the sheet with the model view on it. Zoom to the location where the callout block needs to be inserted.**

   The sheet opens in its open drawing window.

13. **On the Sheet Views tab, locate the view in which you need to place callout blocks. Right-click the view and select Place Callout Block, and then select the block you want to place.**

   A preview of the callout block appears in the drawing window and is ready to be placed.

The first time you place a callout block for the view, the option Select Blocks may appear on the shortcut menu only. If Select Blocks is on the shortcut menu, click it to display the View Category dialog box so you can set up the callout blocks that you can place for a view. In the Select the Callout Blocks to Be Used in This Category list box, place a check mark next to each block you want to use as a callout block. Click OK

14. **Pick a point in the drawing window to place the callout block.**

The callout block is inserted into the drawing and any fields should be resolved.

Publishing, eTransmitting, and Archiving a Sheet Set

After you create all the sheets for your sheet set and add any views that you need on a sheet, you can package the set and send it off to the client. An entire sheet set or selected sheets can be published by using the page setup that is assigned to each layout or a page setup override, along with the ability to publish the sheets to a multisheet DWF or DWFx file. To work with the publish options for a sheet set, right-click the top-level node of the sheet set and choose an option from the Publish submenu. I explain publishing in Chapter 3 of this minibook.

eTransmitting and archiving a sheet set are similar. When you *eTransmit* a sheet set, you create a package of all the drawings and support files (including xrefs) that are used with that sheet set to send to a client or customer electronically. When you *archive* a sheet set, you are essentially doing an eTransmit, but the package is not sent to a client or customer. You can eTransmit a subset within a sheet set, but you can't archive a subset. You can archive only the entire sheet set.

You can start the eTransmit process by right-clicking the sheet set or a subset and choosing eTransmit, or by using the ETRANSMIT command outside Sheet Set Manager when the sheet set is open. Doing so opens the Create Transmittal dialog box.

To create an archive of a sheet set, right-click the sheet set node and click Archive, or use the ARCHIVE command when the sheet set is open in Sheet Set Manager. Doing so opens the Archive a Sheet Set dialog box.

For information on using the eTransmit and archive features of sheet sets, refer to AutoCAD's online Help system.

**Book VII
Chapter 2**

**Sheet Sets
without Regret**

Chapter 3: Print, Plot, Publish

In This Chapter

✔ **Configuring printers and plotters**

✔ **Defining and using plot styles**

✔ **Plotting from the Model tab and paper space**

✔ **Publishing drawings**

*E*ven with the growth of the Internet and online project collaboration sites, many people still want or need drawings to be delivered in hard-copy format — in other words, printed. Many years ago, the idea of a paper-less society was born with the introduction of the Internet. Despite what some predicted, however, our dependency on paper has not dwindled that much, so you still need to hang onto those printers and plotters for the time being.

Throughout this book, I've covered many of the necessary techniques to set up your drawings and prepare them for output. Page setups and layouts play an important role in getting your drawings onto a sheet of paper, but to get to the finish line, you need to do a bit more work yet. This chapter looks at configuring a printer or plotter to output your drawings and also covers plot styles, which can be used to affect how the linework of your drawing looks when it's outputted.

You Say Printing, I Say Plotting, They Say Publishing

Printing, *plotting*, and *publishing* are all terms that I cover in this chapter. For the most part, they all produce the same result: a hard copy or an electronic file for sharing from your drawing files. The process of getting to the end result varies, based on which path you decide to take. In AutoCAD, printing usually involves small drawings that can be output to a laser or inkjet printer. Output is usually done on an 8½ × 11 sheet of paper, but might also be 11 × 17, based on your printer's capabilities. Most AutoCAD users think of printing as something that word processing and spreadsheet programs do, whereas plotting is what AutoCAD does.

Plotting is a common way of outputting a drawing from AutoCAD to a hard copy because drawing files are usually printed on very large sheets of paper. Plotting requires specialized hardware that holds rolls of paper in different widths for printing drawings that are often greater in size than 8½ × 11 or 11 × 17. Some older plotters required you to manually load sheets of paper. Based on the plotter you have available, it might also be able to print 8½ × 11 and 11 × 17 sheets. When a drawing is printed or plotted, only the Model tab or a paper space layout can be sent to a device at a single time. To get around this limitation, you can use the publishing feature in AutoCAD.

Publishing is used to output more than just the Model tab or one paper space layout at a time. Publishing allows you to set up multiple drawings and layouts contained in the files for outputting to a device. This can make sending out a drawing set easier because a list of drawings and layouts can be saved for future use. You can publish all the sheets in a sheet set directly from Sheet Set Manager. For more information on sheet sets and Sheet Set Manager, see Chapter 2 of this minibook.

Working with drivers

To use printers and plotters with software, you often have to install additional software called *print drivers*. Print drivers come from the hardware manufacturer and provide a way for software applications such as AutoCAD to communicate with them. So when you or someone from your IT department installs a printer through Windows, you are setting up what AutoCAD refers to as a *system printer*. System printers are the printers that AutoCAD and other Windows-based applications have access to. For most applications this is enough, but AutoCAD is not just any ordinary program.

AutoCAD allows manufacturers to develop a form of print drivers that can enhance the abilities of their printers or plotters in a way that can't be done through a standard print driver. AutoCAD refers to these drivers as *nonsystem drivers,* which means that the driver can't be installed as part of the Windows operating system. Most companies that develop plotters, such as Hewlett-Packard (HP), Xerox, and Océ, develop custom drivers that AutoCAD can use. These drivers are often much more efficient and flexible in communicating with the printer or plotter the driver is designed for. Some of the improvements in nonsystem drivers allow you to control which paper sizes are available, as well as additional features such as line merge and AutoSpool.

It's much easier to set up and use system drivers than it is nonsystem drivers. The ease of setup and use of system drivers is balanced out by the better control that nonsystem drivers offer. Because printing and plotting in AutoCAD is so different from other Windows-based applications, the Help system offers some great information on the topic. For additional information on print drivers, launch the online Help for AutoCAD; on the Contents tab, expand Driver and Peripheral Guide and then choose Use Plotters and Printers.

Configuring a printer or plotter

Configuring a device for AutoCAD usually requires a little more work than installing a system printer. At times, you might even find that configuring a system printer as a nonsystem printer might have some advantages. The first thing you want to do before configuring a new device is to determine whether it may have already been configured for you. (CAD managers and IT personnel often set up printers and plotters to ensure that there is consistency to the output for all drafters.) After you have determined which devices you have available, you can set up a new one if you need to.

Determining which printers and plotters are available

The first step on the road to plotting is making sure that AutoCAD can access the device to which you want to output. The following steps explain how to see which system and nonsystem printers are available:

1. **Right-click the command window or drawing area and choose Options.**

2. **In the Options dialog box, click the Plot and Publish tab.**

The Plot and Publish tab (see Figure 3-1) is set current.

System printers

**Book VII
Chapter 3**

Print, Plot, Publish

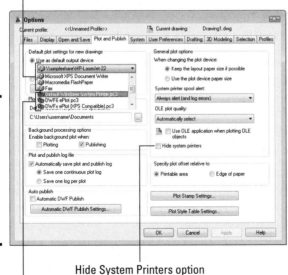

Figure 3-1:
Many of the plotting and publish options in AutoCAD are in the Options dialog box.

Hide System Printers option

Nonsystem printers

3. **In the Default Plot Settings for New Drawings area, click the down arrow on the Use as Default Output Device drop-down list.**

Both system and nonsystem printers are displayed in the drop-down list, unless the Hide System Printers option has been selected in the General Plot Options section.

- System printers are indicated by an icon that shows a small laser printer with a sheet of paper on top next to its configured name in Windows.

- Nonsystem printers are indicated by an icon that shows a plotter with a sheet of paper coming out in front next to its configured name in AutoCAD.

Nonsystem printers configured for AutoCAD are displayed in the list with the PC3 file extension, which stands for AutoCAD Plotter Configuration and the third generation of the file format. The PC3 files were first used with AutoCAD 2000 and are still used with AutoCAD 2009 and AutoCAD LT 2009.

4. **Click somewhere other than the Use as Default Output Device drop-down list to close the drop-down list.**

AutoCAD has access to all the system printers and some select nonsystem printers out of the box. The nonsystem printers that are available by default allow you to produce output to electronic files, such as DWF, DWFx, and PDF files, and some that create commonly used raster image files used with the Publish to Web feature. Now that you have an idea of which printers and plotters are available to you from AutoCAD, you should know if you are missing one that your office uses on a daily basis for production drawings.

5. **Click Cancel to close the Options dialog box.**

Setting up a nonsystem printer

 AutoCAD provides a wizard to help you set up nonsystem printers. You can access the wizard from within AutoCAD or through the Windows Control Panel. No matter which method you use, the Add Plotter Wizard is displayed. You use the PLOTTERMANAGER command to display a window that allows you to access the wizard and any previously defined nonsystem printers.

To start Plotter Manager, do one of the following:

✦ On the ribbon, click Output tab⇨Plot panel⇨Plotter Manager.

✦ On the menu browser or menu bar, click File menu⇨Plotter Manager.

✦ At the command prompt, type **PLOTTERMANAGER** and press Enter.

✦ In the Options dialog box, click the Plot and Publish tab, and then in the Default Plot Settings for New Drawings area, click Add or Configure Plotters.

The following steps explain how to launch the Add Plotter Wizard and create a nonsystem printer:

1. **Open Plotter Manager by using one of the methods in the preceding list.**

The Plotters window is displayed.

2. **Locate the Add-A-Plotter Wizard shortcut and double-click it.**

The Add Plotter Wizard is launched.

3. **Read through the information on the Introduction page, and click Next.**

The next page of the wizard is displayed and is really the starting point of configuring a new nonsystem printer (see Figure 3-2).

Figure 3-2:
The Add
Plotter
Wizard is
used to
configure a
nonsystem
printer.

**Book VII
Chapter 3**

Print, Plot, Publish

4. **Select one of the three types of plotters to set up. For this example, select My Computer. Click Next.**

The page allows you to choose from three different types of plotters:

• **My Computer:** The plotting is handled locally by your computer through a port, through a plot to a file, or by using a specified AutoSpool utility (an application that controls where the plot file is sent).

• **Network Plotter Server:** The plotting is done through a folder in a network location where the plotter checks for plot files.

- **System Printer:** The plotting is done through a system printer. By configuring a nonsystem printer for a system printer, you allow AutoCAD to take advantage of additional features that can change the way the plot information is handled before it's sent to the system printer.

Note: Clicking Next advances the wizard to the next page, which is different depending on which of the three options you selected. In this example, I use the My Computer option because it covers the most steps in the wizard.

5. **On the Plotter Model page, select a manufacturer from the list on the left and then one of the available models from the list on the right. For this example, select Autodesk ePlot (DWF) from the Manufacturers list and DWF eView (optimized for viewing) from the Models list. Click Next.**

Based on the selected manufacturer, you might have a list of models for a physical device or a virtual device. A *physical device* is a plotter that you can see and touch, whereas a *virtual device* allows you to take the output from AutoCAD and convert it into a specific file format.

6. **If you have a PCP or PC2 file that you want to use, do the following. Otherwise, click Next to continue.**

   a. **Click the Import File button.**

   PCP files were the first plotter configuration files that AutoCAD used and were created with AutoCAD R13 and earlier releases. PC2 files were the second generation of the plotter configuration file type and were created with AutoCAD R14.

   b. **In the Import dialog box, browse to and select a PCP or PC2 file that was exported out of an earlier release.**

   c. **Click Import.**

   d. **In the Imported Data Information dialog box, click OK.**

   You might see a warning message about paper sizes not matching between the device you are configuring and the device contained in the PCP or PC2 file. Click OK to the warning message. The Imported Data Information message should be displayed after the warning message (if one was displayed). The Imported Data Information message displays the settings that have been imported for the plotter that you are configuring. Click OK to close the Imported Data Information dialog box, and you return to the Add Plotter Wizard.

   e. **Click Next.**

7. In the Add Plotter Wizard on the Ports page, select the type of port to be used for the plotter, and then select a port from the list based on the port option you selected. Click Next.

You can choose from three types of ports:

- **Plot to Port:** Allows for output to be sent to a location such as LPT1 or a UNC path. This option depends on whether you selected a physical or virtual plotting device.

- **Plot to File:** Specifies that the output will be created as an electronic file that can then be viewed or sent to a graphics or print shop for printing.

- **AutoSpool:** Specifies that the output should be sent to an application that determines how to route the output file. The program used for AutoSpool is specified on the Files tab of the Options dialog box in the Print File, Spooler, Prolog Section Names, Print Spool Executable node. An AutoSpool program can be used to log plots or even redirect output based on paper size.

8. On the Plotter Name page, enter a name in the Plotter Name text box. Click Next.

The name you enter is displayed in the lists that allow you to specify an output device in AutoCAD and is also used for the name of the PC3 file that is created when the wizard is finished.

9. On the Finish page, click Edit Plotter Configuration or Calibrate Plotter to further configure the new device. Click Finish.

Based on the device you are configuring, the Calibrate Plotter button might be disabled. The Calibrate Plotter button allows you to verify drawing measurements that the device can handle. The Edit Plotter Configuration button launches the Plotter Configuration Editor dialog box (see Figure 3-3) and allows you to specify custom paper sizes and other device specific settings. Make any necessary changes in the Plotter Configuration Editor dialog box, and click OK to save changes and close the dialog box. To find more about the options in the Plotter Configuration Editor dialog box, click the Help button to open the online Help system to the page in help specific to this dialog box.

In the Plotters window, the new device is added and ready for use in AutoCAD.

10. Click the X in the Plotters window to close it.

Book VII
Chapter 3

Print, Plot, Publish

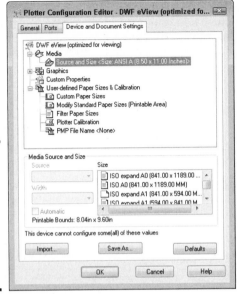

Figure 3-3:
The Plotter
Configura-
tion Editor
enables you
to tweak
custom
settings of
the plotter.

Editing a nonsystem printer configuration

At times, you may want to edit a nonsystem printer configuration to add or remove available paper sizes, along with options such as line merge. The following procedure explains how to modify a plotter configuration (PC3) file for a nonsystem printer:

1. **Open Plotter Manager by using one of the previously listed methods.**

2. **In the Plotters window, double-click the plotter configuration (PC3) file you want to edit.**

The Plotter Configuration Editor dialog box is displayed.

3. **In the Plotter Configuration Editor dialog box, make the necessary changes.**

4. **Click Save & Close.**

The changes are saved to the PC3 file.

5. **Click the X on the Plotters window to close it.**

Putting style in your plots

AutoCAD uses *plot styles* to control the output of objects in a drawing. Plot styles can be used to control the lineweights and even the colors in which objects are plotted. Most printers and plotters in offices today are capable of outputting in grayscale, whereas some may even support color. Even though AutoCAD drawings are displayed and created in color, you can use plot styles to control whether that is the same with the final output. Plot styles can be used to map colors to grayscale colors or even to a different color altogether.

AutoCAD supports two plot styles: *color dependent* and *named*. Color-dependent plot styles are the most commonly used of the two and represent how plotting was handled before the introduction of plot styles in AutoCAD 2000. Color-dependent plot styles allow you to map specific AutoCAD colors to different lineweights and even to different colors. Although AutoCAD supports true colors, which allows you to choose from about 16.7 million colors, color-dependent plot styles utilize only the basic 255 colors of AutoCAD. So AutoCAD maps true colors to the nearest AutoCAD Color Index (ACI) color. When you create a new drawing, the drawing template determines the type of plot style used when plotting.

You can switch from color-dependent or named plot styles in a drawing by using the CONVERTPSTYLES command.

Named plot styles, the newest of the two plotting methods, allow you to create a name and assign that name a specific lineweight and color. This allows you to display multiple colors on-screen but use one plot style for multiple layers and colors. You can apply a named plot style to a layer as well as to individual objects in a drawing. You can't override the plot style assigned to a layer when using color-dependent plot styles unless you change the color of the layer. Named plot styles, unlike color-dependent plot styles, have some limitations. Named plot styles are not supported well when it comes to objects such as tables and dimensions that can display multiple colors and have multiple different levels of objects.

For example, a table can have a different color for the grid and text but can be assigned only one plot style. In this case, the object is plotted by using one named plot style; whereas if you use color-dependent plot styles, each color can be plotted by using a different lineweight. Plot styles are saved in files outside AutoCAD with the CTB (AutoCAD Color-Dependent Plot Style Table) and STB (AutoCAD Plot Style Table—Named) file extensions. CTB stands for color-dependent plot style table, and STB stands for named plot style table.

You use the Add Plot Style Table Wizard to create new plot styles. Like the Add Plotter Wizard, the Add Plot Style Table Wizard can be launched from AutoCAD or the Windows Control Panel. The STYLESMANAGER command is used to display the Plot Styles window, which allows you to access the Add Plot Style Table Wizard and any previously defined plot styles.

**Book VII
Chapter 3**

Print, Plot, Publish

To start the STYLESMANAGER command, do one of the following:

+ On the ribbon, click Output tab⇨Plot panel⇨Plot Style Manager.

+ On the menu browser or menu bar, click File menu⇨Plot Style Manager.

+ At the command prompt, type **STYLESMANAGER** and press Enter.

+ In the Options dialog box, click the Plot and Publish tab, and then click Plot Style Table Settings. In the Plot Style Table Settings dialog box, click Add or Edit Plot Style Tables.

Setting up a plot style

The following steps use the Add Plot Style Table Wizard to create a color-dependent plot style:

1. **Open Plot Style Manager by using one of the previously listed methods.**

   A window titled Plot Styles is displayed.

2. **Locate the Add-A-Plot Style Table Wizard shortcut and double-click it.**

   The Add Plot Style Table Wizard is launched.

3. **In the Add Plot Style Table Wizard, read through the information and then click Next.**

   The next page of the wizard is displayed and is really the starting point for configuring a plot style table (see Figure 3-4).

4. **Select one of the four methods for configuring a plot style. For this procedure, select Start from Scratch. Click Next.**

   The four methods for configuring a plot style are

   • **Start from Scratch:** Use this option if you're not upgrading from a release prior to AutoCAD 2000, or if you don't want to base the new plot style on an existing style.

   • **Use an Existing Plot Style Table:** If you have an existing plot style that's close to the one you want to configure, use the existing one as a template for the new plot style.

   • **Use My R14 Plotter Configuration (CFG):** Pen tables, as they once were called in AutoCAD R14, were stored in a configuration (CFG) file. If you have one of these files around, you can import the pen information into the wizard for the new plot style.

   • **Use a PCP or PC2 File:** AutoCAD R14 and earlier releases allowed you to export your plot device configuration and pen table to a single configuration file that could be shared with other computers. The pen table contained in these files can be imported into the wizard for the new plot style.

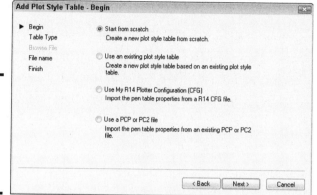

Figure 3-4:
You use the
Add Plot
Style Table
Wizard to
create a
plot style.

Clicking Next advances the wizard to the next page, which is different based on which of the four options you selected. This set of steps uses the Start from Scratch option.

5. **On the Pick Plot Style Table page, select the Color-Dependent Plot Style Table option or the Named Plot Style Table option. For this example, click Color-Dependent Plot Style Table. Click Next.**

   Select the Color-Dependent or Named Plot Style Table option, based on the type your drawings use.

6. **In the File Name text box, enter a name. Click Next.**

   The name you enter is the one that's displayed in the list of plot styles in AutoCAD and is also used for the name of the CTB or STB file that's created when the wizard is finished.

7. **Click Plot Style Table Editor to configure the lineweights, colors, and other settings for the new plot style.**

   The Plot Style Table Editor dialog box (see Figure 3-5) is displayed and allows you to define how the linework will look when it's plotted.

8. **Select the color (or named plot style) in the Plot Styles list box on the Form View tab. Then modify the properties based on how you want the linework assigned to the plot style to appear when plotted.**

   Based on the plot style you are creating, you may want to assign a lineweight or linetype property that will override the values assigned to the objects in a drawing when it's plotted.

9. **Click Save & Close.**

   The changes to the plot style are saved, and the new plot style is added to the Plot Style window and is ready to use in AutoCAD.

Book VII
Chapter 3

Print, Plot, Publish

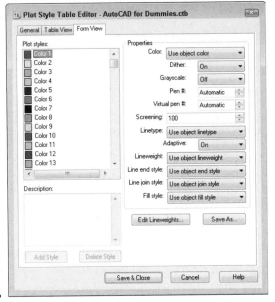

Figure 3-5:
The Plot
Style Table
Editor
enables you
to tweak
settings for
the plot
style table.

10. **In the Add Plot Style Table Wizard, click Finish.**

The Add Plot Style Table Wizard closes.

11. **Click the X in the Plot Styles window to close it.**

Editing a plot style

As your CAD standards change, you may need to make changes to the colors that you use for layers or the lineweights used during output. To edit a plot style file:

1. **Open the Plot Style Manager by using one of the previously listed methods.**

2. **In the Plot Styles window, double-click the plot style (CTB or STB) file you want to edit.**

The Plot Style Table Editor dialog box is displayed.

3. **Make the necessary changes and then click Save & Close.**

The changes are saved to the CTB or STB file.

4. **Click the X in the Plot Styles window to close it.**

Output Made Easy

Plotting is not as easy as creating a line, for instance, and this is mainly due to the number of options that are available. Over the years, plotting has been streamlined (after you define your plot configurations and plot styles), but you still need to know a number of things before you can plot. This section helps get you on the fast track to understanding plotting step by step. Depending on whether you're plotting from the Model tab or a paper space layout tab, the general process is the same but some options are slightly different.

To plot out the Model tab or a paper space layout tab, you use the PLOT command. (You don't use the PRINT command, but those folks at Autodesk did create a command alias so you can type **PRINT** at the command prompt to get to the PLOT command.) To start the PLOT command, use one of the following methods:

✦ On the ribbon, click Output tab⇨Plot panel⇨Plot.

✦ On the menu browser or menu bar, click File menu⇨Plot.

✦ On the Standard or Standard Annotation toolbar, click the Plot button.

✦ Press Ctrl+P.

✦ At the command prompt, type **PLOT** and press Enter.

✦ On the status bar, click the Quick View Layouts button, and then click the Plot icon when it is displayed as the mouse hovers over one of the previews for a paper space layout.

✦ Right-click the Model tab or paper space layout tab, and choose Plot.

Plotting the Model tab

The following procedure takes you through the basics of plotting from the Model tab of a drawing:

1. **Click the Model tab at the bottom of the drawing window or click the Model button in the status bar area.**

2. **Start the PLOT command by using one of the previously listed methods.**

   The Plot dialog box (see Figure 3-6) is displayed.

3. **If a named page setup is contained in your drawing, select it from the Name drop-down list under the Page Setup heading and skip ahead to Step 10. If you don't have a named page setup, continue on with the next step.**

   A page setup saves you the time of having to specify the name of the printer/plotter, paper size, what to plot, scale, and other settings. Page setups were covered in Chapter 1 of this minibook.

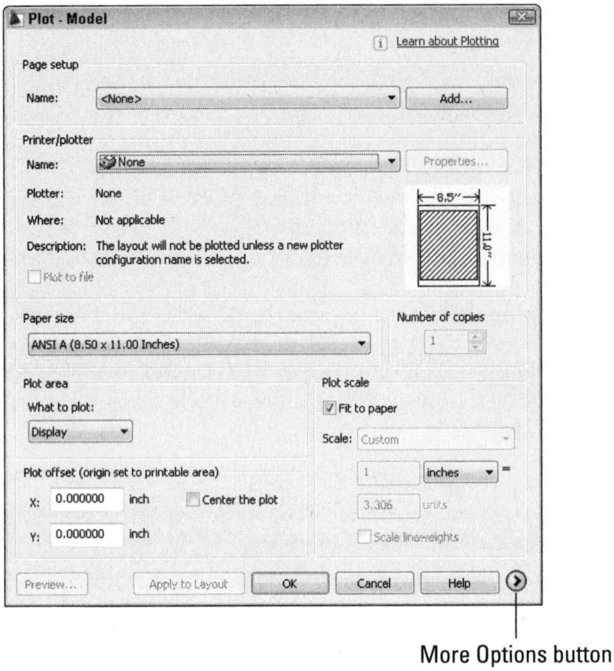

Figure 3-6:
The Plot dialog box is the gateway to outputting your drawing.

More Options button

4. **In the Printer/Plotter area, select a printer from the Name drop-down list.**

   The drop-down list contains both the system and nonsystem printers, unless the Hide System Printers option is selected on the Plot and Publish tab of the Options dialog box.

5. **In the Paper Size area, select the paper size on which your drawing will best fit for the area that will be plotted and the designated scale.**

   The drop-down list contains all the available paper sizes that the device can output to. If you're using a PC3 file, you can add or remove paper sizes from the list through the Plotter Configuration Editor dialog box. For more information on editing a plotter configuration, see the "Editing a nonsystem printer configuration" section in this chapter.

6. **In the Number of Copies area, enter the number of copies you want to produce.**

   This option is disabled if the selected device outputs to a file.

7. **In the Plot Area heading, select what you want to plot in the drawing — often, you select Extents when plotting from the Model tab.**

   The drop-down list contains a number of options to select from. These options are

- **Display:** Outputs the objects that are currently displayed in the drawing window.

- **View:** Allows you to plot the objects defined by a named view that is saved in the drawing.

- **Window:** Allows you to specify a rectangular area in the drawing that should be output by picking two points in the drawing. What is displayed inside the selected area is what is outputted.

- **Limits:** If you've properly set up the limits for your drawing, you can use this option to specify the objects that are displayed within this area.

- **Extents:** Calculates the extents of the drawing and uses them to print all the objects contained in the drawing.

8. In the Plot Offset area, either specify an X and a Y offset from the edge of the printable area or select the Center the Plot check box.

The option that you selected in the Plot Area determines whether the Center the Plot check box is enabled.

9. In the Plot Scale area, either specify the print area to be fit on the specified paper size by selecting Fit to Paper, or deselect Fit to Paper and specify a scale (by selecting a standard scale from the drop-down list or entering a number in the text boxes for a custom scale).

During production, you specify a specific scale when plotting, but you might choose Fit to Paper for a check plot or if you're doing conceptual designs and aren't concerned about a specific scale. For more information on scaling your drawing, see the "Scaling your drawing" section later in this chapter.

10. Click Preview and verify that everything you want to plot will fit. Then right-click and choose Exit to quit the Preview and return to the Plot dialog box.

If you choose a specific plot scale and the scale doesn't match the current annotation scale, the Plot Scale Confirm dialog box is displayed. Click Continue to continue to the preview of the drawing or Cancel to return to the Plot dialog box and change the current plot scale. When the preview is displayed, you can verify that the drawing fits on the specified paper size and that it is not too small. If it is too small or the wrong area of the drawing is displayed, return to the Plot dialog box and make the necessary changes.

11. Click OK.

If the Plot Scale Confirm dialog box is displayed, click Continue or Cancel as necessary. The drawing is sent to the specified printer or plotter device, using the options that you selected.

**Book VII
Chapter 3**

Print, Plot, Publish

You've created a basic plot in 11 steps. As I mention, however, other settings can affect your plot, and those are covered in the "More plotting options" section later in this chapter.

You can click the Apply to Layout button at the bottom of the Plot dialog box to save the option changes that you just made. When you return to the Plot dialog box the next time, the options are already set for you based on the previous plot that you created.

After the plotting process has finished, you might see a small notification balloon (see Figure 3-7) displayed in the lower-right corner of AutoCAD. This balloon informs you when plotting has been completed successfully or if an error was encountered. This notification is extremely handy if background plotting is enabled, when you plot to a DWF or DWFx file, or when you're using the PUBLISH command. Both background plotting and the PUBLISH command are explained later in this chapter.

Figure 3-7:
The plot
notification
balloon.

If you plot to a DWF or DWFx file, you can right-click the Plot/Publish notification balloon and choose View DWF File to open the last created DWF or DWFx file in Autodesk Design Review. I cover viewing DWF and DWFx files in Chapter 4 of Book VIII.

Plotting a paper space layout

In the preceding section, I discuss plotting a drawing from the Model tab. Plotting a layout really is not much different, and if you have properly set up your layouts in your drawing, plotting a drawing from a layout tab is actually easier than plotting from the Model tab. The reason is that you don't have to worry about drawing scales because that has been defined for each of the viewports on the layout. If you used a page setup for your layouts, your device and paper sizes should already be defined as well. Otherwise, you pretty much need to configure the name of the printer/plotter and paper size, and set the plot scale to 1:1 and the layout to what you are plotting. The following steps outline how to plot a paper space layout:

1. **Set one of the paper space layout tabs current.**

To do so, click the tab at the bottom of the drawing window, or click the Quick View Layouts button on the status bar area and then one of the paper space layouts.

2. **Start the PLOT command by using one of the previously listed methods.**

   The Plot dialog box is displayed.

3. **If necessary, specify the printer/plotter, paper size, and number of copies.**

4. **In the Plot Area section, select what you want to plot in the drawing — often, you select Layout when plotting a paper space layout tab.**

   The drop-down list contains a number of options that you can select. The only difference is that Layout is available only for plotting paper space layouts and the Limits option is only available for plotting from the Model tab. With the Layout option, all the objects on the layout that fall within the specific printable area of the specified paper size are printed.

5. **In the Plot Offset area, specify an X and a Y offset from the edge of the printable area.**

6. **In the Plot Scale area, specify a scale in the drop-down list. In almost all cases, you should specify a scale of 1:1.**

   A scale of 1:1 is selected because the scale of the model geometry is handled by each of the floating viewports on the layout.

7. **Click Preview and verify that everything you want to plot will fit. After you have finished verifying your drawing, right-click and choose Exit.**

   You return to the Plot dialog box

8. **Click OK.**

Scaling your drawing

When you output your drawings, you must specify a specific scale for your drawing. This means you that don't use the Fit to Paper check box in the Plot dialog box much. If you are plotting from the Model tab, you specify a drawing scale. The drawing scale is usually always determined upfront before you begin drawing, and in Book I, Chapter 6 I explain how to calculate this value. If you are plotting from a paper space layout, you use a scale of 1 to 1 (1:1) because the scaling of the geometry is handled by the floating viewports on the layout.

More plotting options

The Plot dialog box has a button with an arrow on it located in the lower-right corner (refer to Figure 3-6). This is a toggle that expands the Plot dialog box and reveals additional settings that are not required to output a drawing but do affect the appearance of the output. Following is a list of the additional options that are revealed when you click the More Options button:

✦ **Plot Style Table (Pen Assignments):** Allows you to specify a plot style that can be used to control the color and lineweights of the drawing during output. You can use the Edit button to the right of the drop-down list to edit the selected plot style. I cover plot styles in the "Putting style in your plots" section earlier in this chapter.

✦ **Shaded Viewport:** Controls how shaded and rendered views are output. The Shade Plot drop-down list allows you to specify how views that don't have a specific visual style assigned to them are displayed. The Quality drop-down list and the DPI text box control the resolution in which shaded and rendered views are outputted.

✦ **Plot:** Controls a wide range of settings:

  • **Plot in Background:** Determines whether control of AutoCAD is released after a plot is sent and the process of the plot is finished in the background so you can get back to work sooner. If the option is deselected, you have to wait until the plot has completed processing and is sent to the printer or plotter before you can do anything else. Enabling background plotting is slower, so if you need a plot right away, don't use background plotting.

    You can control background plotting through the Plot and Publish tab of the Options dialog box in the Background Processing Options area. There's an option for Plotting and one for Publishing (by default, Publishing is the only one selected). I discuss how to publish drawings in the next section.

  • **Plot Object Lineweights:** Controls whether object lineweights assigned to layers and objects are used instead of the assigned plot style.

  • **Plot with Plot Styles:** Controls whether plot styles are used when plotting.

  • **Plot Paperspace Last:** Controls whether paper space geometry is plotted before model space geometry.

  • **Hide Paperspace Objects:** Controls whether AutoCAD automatically performs the HIDE command on the paper space layout.

  • **Plot Stamp On:** Adds a plot stamp along the edge of the drawing when it's outputted. The plot stamp is configured by using the PLOT-STAMP command or by clicking the Plot Stamp Settings button when the Plot Stamp On option is selected.

  • **Save Changes to Layout:** Specifies whether changes to the plotting settings for the layout are saved when you click OK. This option automatically saves the changes made to the plot options so you don't have to remember to click the Apply to Layout button before clicking OK.

✦ **Drawing Orientation:** Controls whether the drawing is plotted in the portrait or landscape direction. You can also specify whether the drawing is plotted upside down by selecting the Plot Upside-Down option.

Publishing Drawings

Using the PLOT command to output your drawings is easy if you have only a few drawings or layouts for which you need to create hard copies, but it can be a large task if you have many drawings and layouts to plot. The PUBLISH command allows you to batch a number of drawings together to output them all based on their defined page setups or override that page setup with one of your choice. The other feature that the PUBLISH command supports is creating single-sheet or multisheet DWF or DWFx files and controlling the order in which drawings are output.

To start the PUBLISH command, use one of the following methods:

✦ On the ribbon, click Output tab⇨Publish panel⇨Publish.

✦ On the menu browser or menu bar, click File menu⇨Publish.

✦ On the Standard or Standard Annotation toolbar, click the Publish button.

✦ At the command prompt, type **PUBLISH** and press Enter.

✦ On the status bar, click the Quick View Layouts button, and then click the Publish icon when it is displayed as the mouse hovers over one of the previews for a paper space layout.

✦ Hold down the Ctrl key and select each paper space layout tab you want to publish, right-click, and choose Publish Selected Layouts.

The following steps take you through the basics of using the Publish dialog box:

1. **Start the PUBLISH command by using one of the methods in the preceding list.**

The Publish dialog box (see Figure 3-8) is displayed. If no layout tabs were selected, all the layouts from the drawings you have open are pulled into the dialog box by default.

2. **Click the Add Sheets button along the top of the dialog box to add layouts from other drawings not currently open in AutoCAD.**

The Select Drawings dialog box is displayed.

Book VII
Chapter 3

Print, Plot, Publish

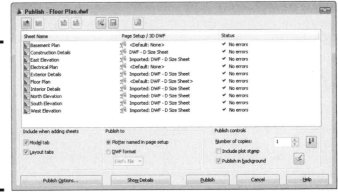

Figure 3-8:
The Publish
dialog box
makes
printing
multiple
layouts and
drawings
a breeze.

3. **Browse to and select the drawings whose layouts you want to add to the Publish dialog box. Click Open.**

   The Select Drawings dialog box closes and all the layouts in the selected drawings are imported into the list box.

4. **If you do not want a layout that has been imported, select the layout from the list, right-click, and choose Remove.**

5. **In the Publish To area, make a selection:**

   • Select Plotter Named in Page Setup to plot the layout based on the last page setup used to output the layout.

   • Select DWF format and either DWF file or DWFx file to plot to a DWF file. Click Publish Options to control the behavior of plotting to a DWF file.

6. **Click Publish to start the publishing process.**

   The Save Sheet List dialog box is displayed.

7. **Click Yes to save the list of sheets to a Drawing Set Description (DSD) file.**

   The DSD file can be reopened later in the Publish dialog box to republish all the selected layouts in the sheet list again.

   The Processing Background Plot dialog box (see Figure 3-9) is displayed when background plotting is enabled for the PLOT or PUBLISH command. By default, AutoCAD displays the same notification balloon when the PUBLISH command finishes as when the PLOT command finishes.

You can set the AUTOPUBLISH system variable to 1 to have AutoCAD automatically create a DWF file each time a drawing is saved or closed. Setting AUTOPUBLISH to 0 disables the automatic creation of DWF files when saving or closing a drawing.

Figure 3-9:
The
background
plotting
message.

Plot - Processing Background Job

Your printing or publishing job is processing in
the background.

Double-click the print queue icon in the lower, right-hand
corner for more details.

☐ Do not show me this message again   OK

You can use the PUBLISHALLSHEETS system variable to control if only the Model tab and/or layouts in the current drawing are added to the Publish dialog box or if the Model tab and layouts from all open drawings is added. A value of 0 loads only the layouts from the current drawing into the Publish dialog box, and a value of 1 loads all the layouts from all open drawings.

The PUBLISHCOLLATE system variable controls whether a sheet set when published is handled as multiple single-plot jobs or a single-plot job. A value of 0 causes each sheet to be plotted as separate plot jobs, and a value of 1 plots all sheets as a single-plot job.

AutoCAD 2009 and AutoCAD LT 2009 introduce a new system variable named PUBLISHHATCH. The PUBLISHHATCH system variable controls how hatch objects are published to DWF or DWFx files. If a value of 0 is used, hatch objects are published as separate objects; a value of 1 causes hatch objects to be plotted as single objects. This does not affect how DWF and DWFx files are viewed but does affect how hatch objects are imported into Autodesk Impression.

Book VIII

Collaboration

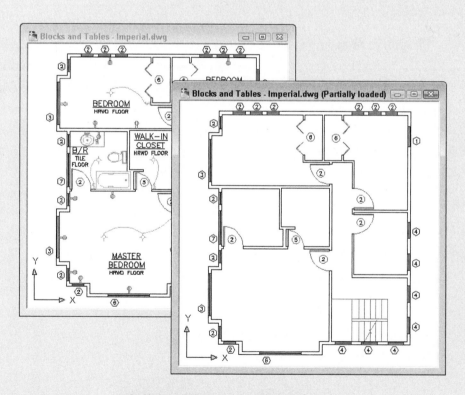

Collaborating made collaborative.

Contents at a Glance

Chapter 1: CAD Management: The Necessary Evil 567

Getting a Handle on the Basics of CAD Management 568
Managing the Drafting Environment...570
Creating a Good Foundation 571

Chapter 2: CAD Standards 579

CAD Standards Overview..579
Using AutoCAD's CAD Standards Tools..581

Chapter 3: Working with Drawing Files 597

It's All in the Name: File-Naming Conventions..597
Part of a Drawing Can Be a Good Thing: Working with Partial Open 598
Controlling What Happens during a Save 601
Protecting Your Drawings 604

Chapter 4: Sharing Electronic Files .617

Sharing Drawings with Non-AutoCAD-based Products 617
Taking Drawings to the Internet...618
Emulating Paper Digitally..628
Working with DWF and DWFx Files 631

Chapter 1: CAD Management: The Necessary Evil

In This Chapter

✔ **Understanding the basics of CAD management**

✔ **Managing the drafting environment**

✔ **Creating a good foundation with drawing templates**

*A*utoCAD 2009 & AutoCAD LT 2009 All-in-One Desk Reference For *Dummies* is designed to help both AutoCAD and AutoCAD LT users improve the quality of the designs that they publish and to effectively share them with others. As you progress through this book, you discover how to manage the drafting environment and CAD standards for your company and some of the different ways to effectively work with drawing files.

CAD standards is a topic that isn't discussed enough in the office, and yet they play an important role in sharing drawing files. CAD standards ensure that the drawings you create look similar to the drawings that everyone else in the office creates. All the drawings should have the same look and feel when they're presented to a potential client or the shop floor. If your work doesn't have a uniform look, the client might get the impression that your company doesn't have enough experience to handle the project or is simply disorganized, which can stop talks cold at the table.

After you've finished creating your set of drawings for a project, it's usually time to share them with others, whether a client or someone in manufacturing. During this stage of a project, you might find that printing hard copies and mailing them to the client or off-site team members can take a lot of time. If you need a timely response to a question or a change, you'll most likely need to share files electronically. The type of file sharing you use depends on your target audience and the phase of the project. You might use a Web site to present and transfer files and images or use an Internet project hosting site such as Buzzsaw. In the end, you have to ensure that you can efficiently collaborate with your client and members of your design team.

Getting a Handle on the Basics of CAD Management

CAD management refers to managing the day-to-day operations involved with drafting; typically this includes processes related to and unrelated to AutoCAD that must be followed to complete a project. CAD management is not necessarily the sole responsibility of one individual in a company or functional area, but often it is one individual who is assigned the official duties of being the designated *CAD manager*. A CAD manager may or may not be a supervisor — in the sense that we often think of a manager — at the company.

If you work in a mid- to large-size company, you might have a full-time CAD manager; in a smaller company, the CAD manager is more likely to be a senior level drafter that pulls double duty. Some small companies even pool their resources and hire an outside consultant to do their CAD management tasks.

CAD management commonly covers the following areas:

✦ **Budgeting:** Estimating the amount of money needed for a specific period of time for CAD-related expenses. This might be software upgrade costs (such as subscription fees), hardware purchases, office supplies (such as paper for the plotter), training costs, and even consulting fees.

✦ **CAD standards enforcement:** Making sure that all drafters are following the company's defined CAD standards — this is a responsibility that many don't like about CAD management. Ensuring that CAD standards are followed, however, helps ensure that a high level of quality is maintained for drawings that are sent out.

✦ **Managing the drafting environment:** Maintaining and managing support files through a centralized location to make sure that all drafters are using the same set of files when working with drawing files. This helps to reduce potential errors and the extra cost of keeping the files in sync if they're all running locally on each user's own computer. CAD managers might do this themselves or bring in a consultant.

✦ **Conducting and coordinating training:** Rolling out new procedures or even providing upgrade training for a new release. Training for upgrades might be outsourced, but the coordination of this training is usually handled by the individual responsible for CAD management in the office. Training might be specific to what your company does or general software training. If an outside company conducts your training, make sure that the training is related to any company and departmental policies.

✦ **Resource management:** Overseeing the resource pool of CAD drafters to ensure that current and future projects are completed in a timely manner.

A project involves much more than just one drafter creating drawing files with AutoCAD; instead, a whole team with specialized skills is usually at work on a project. This team might include individuals who are responsible for overseeing the project, drafters, estimators, manufactures and builders, and the client. This is the same approach that should be taken with CAD management and standards. One individual might have leadership responsibility but everyone should be involved to a degree. Having everyone involved at some level helps to ensure that the standards are widely accepted and are uniform across the company.

Due to the growing complexity of projects these days, more people from different areas of the company are getting involved, so having representation from across the company in defining CAD standards is a good idea. CAD standards shouldn't just stay in the drafting department: The output from drawing files might be used for marketing material, in print or on the Internet, and will surely end up in front of your clients as well. Clients end up reviewing drawings during many phases of a project, and, from these drawings, they build a perception of your company's skill level. For these reasons, many people need to get involved with CAD standards.

Some of the most interesting ideas for improving CAD standards and using the information maintained in a drawing file can come from different groups in a company coming together. That doesn't mean that everyone in the company should have a direct vote in what is part of the CAD standards, but getting feedback from individuals in the company who deal with the information that is generated from a drawing file is a good idea. Often CAD standards are thought of in terms of drawings only, but they encompass everything related to how the CAD information is used.

Here are some items that are part of nontypical CAD standards that should be looked at as a company:

✦ **Title blocks:** Information added to a title block can be used downstream to populate a project management system, if one exists.

✦ **Content of a drawing:** How a drawing is created can affect how its information can be used downstream for things such as renderings and animations that might be done by an internal or external art department.

✦ **Annotation, such as notes and dimensions:** Some notes on a drawing might be there for legal reasons; it's good to have a company view on these types of notes because the information might already be covered in a bid packet or specification document.

✦ **AutoCAD support file locations:** Companies want to make sure that file access is optimal for all users throughout the company. This ensures an efficient working environment and also ensures that everything is properly backed up in case of a catastrophe.

✦ **File exchange practices (use of e-mail or FTP sites):** Policies in place for the use of e-mail — such as the total allowable size of all files coming in or going out during normal business hours — might delay the sending of information for a project. It's wise to communicate with internal and external departments to see what can be sent out efficiently without conflicting with company e-mail policy. Your company may have an FTP site that can be used to exchange large files with people.

✦ **Drawing name convention and storage locations:** Naming conventions are important so that individuals in the company can find a drawing file in a timely manner. This could affect how the files might be archived and the file rights that individuals may need to access them. Storing these types of files in a centralized location on a network drive that is accessible to everyone is good practice.

✦ **Training, seminars, and learning material:** Sending employees to training or purchasing training materials for them is often hard to justify financially because at times the true return of investment (ROI) is unclear. You must determine as a company how training is conducted when a new release of AutoCAD comes out or a new individual is hired.

Managing the Drafting Environment

AutoCAD is a complex drafting program with many settings and support files that it relies on. Proper management of the AutoCAD environment is not something that just happens overnight. Given the sophisticated drafting environment in AutoCAD, a small group of appointed individuals at your company should be in charge of making updates to the support files that are used by the different drafters in your company. Having a small group in charge of updates is especially critical in preventing unauthorized changes that could affect new or existing drawings in a negative way when the files are shared with a group of drafters. So what is included in the drafting environment?

When I mention the *drafting environment,* I'm not talking about background colors or the size of the crosshairs — those things don't affect the final output of a drawing file. Instead, I'm referring to template files and where they are located, along with the locations where AutoCAD looks for support files such as blocks, fonts, and customization. When you install AutoCAD, it often looks locally for things such as menu customization, hatch patterns, blocks, fonts, drawing template files, and anything else that is ordinarily shipped with the product. Because AutoCAD doesn't force specific locations for files, it allows you the flexibility to determine how you want to manage all support files. The default out-of-the-box locations for support files are locally on the computer, but this is not the best way to manage support files.

Commonly shared files should be stored in a networked location so they can be accessed by all drafters. The reason for using a shared network location is to make it easy to maintain and update the files. If a CAD standard changes and all the drafters have a copy of the company support files on their local drive, each computer would need to be updated one by one instead of just updating the files on a network. Instead of letting users have their own copies of the support files, you place a copy of the files that you want to share and then redirect AutoCAD to look on the network.

 All the support paths that AutoCAD uses to locate support files are on the Files tab of the Options dialog box. This means that you can have your drawing template files, plot style files, font files, linetype definition files, and blocks on a network location so you don't have to worry about any users using outdated files when changes are made. This also gives you control over who can make changes to these files, as opposed to whether they are stored locally on each computer. The other advantage of having support files on the network is that they don't get lost or forgotten during an upgrade to a newer release.

Creating a Good Foundation

This book is designed to put you on the right path from the start and to help you develop good drafting habits when creating objects such as layers, text styles, and blocks. A solid foundation in anything you do, whether it's CAD management or constructing a building, is vital. In AutoCAD, the foundation that I'm talking about is a drawing template. I cover how to create a new drawing using one of the drawing templates that comes with AutoCAD in Book I, Chapter 4, but it's best to use your own drawing templates.

When creating new drawings, you'll find that you use the same layers, line-types, title blocks, and specific styles again and again. As you know, a layer can be added by using Layer Properties Manager, but adding layers manually to each new drawing file can be time consuming and can introduce errors. This is where the concept of drawing template files comes into play. These files have the DWT file extension and are located by default here:

```
<drive>:\Users\<user
    name>\AppData\Local\Autodesk\<product>\<release>\
    <language>\Template
```

or here for Windows XP users:

```
<drive>:\Documents and Settings\<user name>\Local Settings\
    Application Data\Autodesk\<product>\<release>\<language>\
    Template
```

If the concept of templates sounds familiar, it's because applications that are part of Microsoft Office utilize templates to store formatting and styles that can be reused when creating a new document.

A drawing template is not much different than the drawing files you create in AutoCAD. The only difference is that you can provide a description for the template that appears when you use the StartUp dialog box. And when you use a drawing template to create a new drawing, AutoCAD creates a new unnamed drawing with those styles and features and the default name *Drawing1*. The numeral at the end of the default name is incremented for each new drawing that is created while the session of AutoCAD is open.

You use a drawing template file to ensure that the styles and formatting are ready to go when you need to create a drawing and that styles and formatting are consistent among drawings. The most common items included in a drawing template file are

✦ **Blocks** (Book VI, Chapter 2)

✦ **Dimension styles** (Book III, Chapter 2)

✦ **Layers** (Book I, Chapter 6)

✦ **Layouts** (Book VII, Chapter 1)

✦ **Linetypes** (Book I, Chapter 6)

✦ **Materials** (Book V, Chapter 6)

✦ **Multileader styles** (Book III, Chapter 2)

✦ **Multiline styles** (Book II, Chapter 1)

✦ **Page setups** (Book VII, Chapter 1)

✦ **Render presets** (Book V, Chapter 6)

✦ **Table styles** (Book III, Chapter 1)

✦ **Text styles** (Book III, Chapter 1)

✦ **UCSs, or User Coordinate System** (Book V, Chapter 3)

✦ **Viewports** (Book VII, Chapter 1)

✦ **Views** (Book II, Chapter 3)

✦ **Visual styles** (Book V, Chapter 3)

✦ **Drawing objects in model and paper space** (Book I, Chapter 6)

✦ **Drawing limits and some drafting settings** (Book I, Chapters 6 and 7)

✦ **System variables** (Book I, Chapter 3)

AutoCAD LT does not support the creation or editing of materials used for rendering 3D objects, multiline styles used to create multiline objects, render presets for rendering, and visual styles used to stylize 3D objects without rendering.

Creating a drawing template file

The following steps explain how to create a drawing template file:

1. **Create any reusable content in a drawing that you want to have available when you use the drawing template to create a new drawing.**

2. **On the menu browser, click File⇨Save As.**

The Save Drawing As dialog box is displayed.

3. **In the Files of Type drop-down list, select AutoCAD Drawing Template (*.DWT).**

AutoCAD automatically navigates to the location of the Template folder. I explain how to change the location where AutoCAD looks for drawing templates under the "Specifying the location of drawing template files" section later in this chapter.

4. **Browse to a different location or use the location specified by AutoCAD for the drawing template file.**

5. **In the File Name box for the drawing template, type a file name.**

You may want to add some information to the file name to help identify what the template is used for. For example, you might give your template the name *E-Size Floor Plan* if you're doing architectural drawings or *B-size Part* if you're doing mechanical drawings.

6. **Click Save.**

The Template Description dialog box (see Figure 1-1) is displayed and allows you to specify a description, the type of measurement to use, and how new layers are handled.

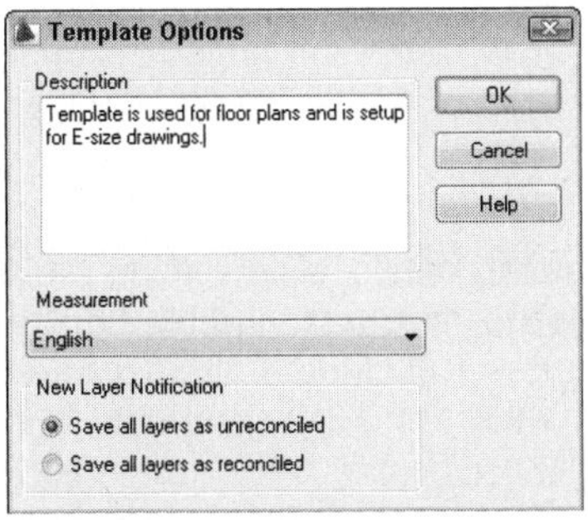

Figure 1-1:
The Template Description dialog box.

Template Options

Description
Template is used for floor plans and is setup for E-size drawings.

OK
Cancel
Help

Measurement
English

New Layer Notification
◉ Save all layers as unreconciled
○ Save all layers as reconciled

7. In the Measurement drop-down list, specify the type of measurement. Optionally enter a description for the template in the Description box and set how new layers should be handled.

The Measurement option controls which linetype and hatch pattern files are used, along with controlling some settings for inserting blocks into a drawing. The description is displayed in the Create New Drawing and Startup dialog boxes. The New Layer Notification option controls whether or not new layers are reconciled when the drawing is saved. For more on reconciling layers, see AutoCAD's online Help system.

8. Click OK.

The Template Description dialog box closes and the drawing template is saved to the specified location.

The measurement option in the Template Description dialog box controls a system variable called MEASUREMENT. This variable can be changed at any time by typing **MEASUREMENT** at the command prompt and entering the new value. Use a value of 0 to specify English (Imperial), or 1 to specify Metric.

You can also use the LAYEREVALCTL system variable to enable or disable the reconciling of new layers when saving the drawing. A value of 0 disables the notification of new layers, and a value of 1 enables the notification system

Using a drawing template file

After you create a drawing template file, you must understand how to use it to create a new drawing. Following are some of the common ways to use a drawing template to create a new drawing:

✦ **NEW command:** Start the NEW command and select the drawing template that you want to use.

✦ **QNEW command:** The QNEW command is similar to the NEW command, with one key difference. You can specify a default drawing template file that will be used to create a new drawing when the command is used or each time AutoCAD starts. If no default template file is specified, the QNEW command behaves like the NEW command. See the "Specifying a drawing template file for use with QNEW" section to find out how to set the drawing template to use with the QNEW command.

✦ **Startup and Create New Drawing dialog boxes:** Both the Startup and Create New Drawing dialog boxes are controlled by the STARTUP system variable. When STARTUP is set to 1, these dialog boxes are displayed when AutoCAD first starts or when the NEW command is started. By default STARTUP is set to a value of 0. See Book I, Chapter 4 to find out about the Startup and Create New Drawing dialog boxes.

✦ **Double-click a drawing template file:** From Windows Explorer, you can double-click a drawing template file to create a new drawing. If AutoCAD is not running, it starts, and the new drawing is created.

Specifying a drawing template file for use with QNEW

Often, you find yourself using a specific drawing template repeatedly. The QNEW command was created for just this situation. But out of the box, QNEW works just like the NEW command because AutoCAD doesn't know about the drawing template that you may want to use. To make the QNEW command achieve its full potential, you need to specify the drawing template to use. This saves you some time because you don't have to browse and select the drawing template you commonly use for most of the new drawings you create.

The following steps explain how to specify the drawing template to use with the QNEW command:

1. **Right-click the command line window and choose Options.**

The Options dialog box is displayed.

2. **Click the Files tab.**

The Files tab is used to specify things such as support folders for AutoCAD to find hatch pattern files, blocks or plotter device information.

3. **Click the plus sign next to Template Settings to expand it.**

The settings related to this group are displayed with additional nodes (see Figure 1-2).

AutoCAD users see a total of four different template path options, whereas AutoCAD LT users see only two. The options Drawing Template File Location and Default Template File Name for QNEW apply to both AutoCAD and AutoCAD LT.

Book VIII Chapter 1

CAD Management: The Necessary Evil

Figure 1-2:
The settings related to template settings.

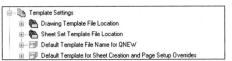

4. **Click the plus sign next to Default Template File Name for QNEW.**

If no template has been specified, you should see the value None, which indicates that QNEW is working just like NEW.

5. **In the Default Template File Name for QNEW node, select None or the current value and then click Browse.**

The Select a File dialog box is displayed and allows you to select a drawing template file.

6. **Specify the drawing template that you want to use when the QNEW command is used.**

The selected drawing template file should be highlighted and the name placed in the File Name box.

7. **Click Open.**

The Select a File dialog box closes and the value is added under the Default Template File Name for QNEW node.

8. **In the Options dialog box, click Apply or OK.**

Clicking Apply saves the changes made and keeps the dialog box displayed, whereas clicking OK saves the changes and closes the Options dialog box.

Specifying the location of drawing template files

If you create templates for a number of users in your office, you want to be sure they can access them. Place the drawing templates that you create in a centralized location and then redirect AutoCAD to them. To specify where AutoCAD looks for drawing template files, you change a setting in the Options dialog box.

The following procedure explains how to specify a new location for AutoCAD to look for drawing template files when the NEW command is started (or at AutoCAD startup if the Startup dialog box is displayed):

1. **Right-click the command line window and choose Options.**

The Options dialog box is displayed.

2. **Click the Files tab.**

3. **Click the plus sign next to Template Settings to expand it.**

The settings related to this group are displayed with additional nodes.

4. **Click the plus sign next to Drawing Template File Location.**

5. **Select the value under Drawing Template File Location and click Browse.**

   The Browse for Folder dialog box is displayed and allows you to select a new location where AutoCAD looks for drawing template files.

6. **In the Browse for Folder dialog box, specify the location AutoCAD should look for drawing template files.**

   The location can be on a local or network drive. Most commonly, if you're maintaining drawing template files for a group of users, you specify a location on the network.

7. **Click OK.**

   The Browse for Folder dialog box closes and the value is added under the Drawing Template File Location node.

8. **In the Options dialog box, click Apply or OK.**

   Clicking Apply saves the changes and keeps the dialog box displayed, whereas clicking OK saves the changes and closes the Options dialog box.

Chapter 2: CAD Standards

In This Chapter

✔ **Understanding CAD standards**

✔ **Checking drawings for CAD standards**

✔ **Translating layer standards**

✔ **Checking standards in batches**

*A*utoCAD is a robust and complex drafting tool, so not all users discover or thoroughly understand every feature of the product; one such frequently overlooked feature is the built-in CAD standards tool. This chapter helps to shine some light on the topic of CAD standards and the built-in tools that AutoCAD offers to help make the managing of CAD standards easier. Don't get discouraged: Developing a good set of CAD standards and getting them implemented takes some time.

CAD standards can be handled in lots of ways, as you may already know from your experiences of working at different companies or working with a client's set of drawings. Many companies create their own set of CAD standards; others adopt an industry standard like those defined by an organization such as the American Institute of Architects (AIA), National CAD Standards, or Construction Standards Institute (CSI). No matter how your CAD standards came about, they must be followed to avoid potential problems. If your company doesn't have such standards, maybe this is your time to shine by helping to establish them.

CAD Standards Overview

Book VIII, Chapter 1 is a primer of what is involved in establishing CAD standards. Drawing template files are one of the cornerstones of CAD standards because they help to promote the use of a company's standards. However, drawing templates alone won't get the job done. Creating and maintaining CAD standards is something of an art form when you consider everything you need to understand and appreciate to get drawings to look the way you want them to.

CAD standards affect both creating and editing geometry. You want to use CAD standards to make sure that all your drawings have a consistent look when they are plotted.

As you draw and use established CAD standards, they help to create logical variations in a drawing — such as different lineweights, linetypes, or even text styles — that emphasize parts of the design. CAD standards cover a range of drafting processes from creation to presentation. In most mid- to large-size companies, CAD standards are determined by a CAD manager; in smaller companies, a senior-level drafter often takes on the responsibility. No matter who defines the CAD standards, they must be defined and understood by all drafters.

Following is an overview of some of the important things you should keep in mind when establishing or modifying a set of CAD standards:

✦ **Remember plotting:** One of the key things to keep in mind when establishing CAD standards is how your drawings will look when they are plotted. Drawing properties that can affect a drawing when it is plotted are linetype scale, text size, dimension scale, and lineweights, among others.

✦ **Don't make constant changes:** I don't recommend making changes to your CAD standards on a daily or even weekly basis; otherwise, you really are defeating the purpose of standards. And, as obvious as it sounds, remember to keep track of the changes you make. Changes might cause problems for third-party applications or even possibly your own internal customization. Tracking changes not only details when changes were made but also offers a way to communicate the standards to other drafters in the office when problems arise. Having an implementation date as to when the standards were updated ensures that everyone stays on the same page.

✦ **Keep it simple:** One thing that can save you time is to create customization that incorporates your established CAD standards. If dimensions should be on a specific layer, consider customizing the user interface so that the dimension commands set a specific layer current before the command start. You don't have to be a power user to set up this type of customization, and it can cut down on errors and save time.

✦ **Make it straightforward:** CAD standards should not be in the form of complex manuals that require the use of a secret decoder ring to understand them. CAD standards should make sense not only to your internal drafters but also to those with whom you share files. If you use cryptic or abbreviated names for layers and styles, a new person may have a hard time stepping in and becoming efficient right away. The length of file names and the amount of memory were limited in the olden (DOS) days before giga this and tera that, but now you can be more descriptive with the names you use for named objects such as layer names and text styles.

Following is a list of the most common named objects and items you should consider incorporating into your CAD standards:

✦ **Blocks** (Book VI, Chapter 1)

✦ **Dimension styles** (Book III, Chapter 2)

✦ **Drawing template (DWT) files** (Book VIII, Chapter 1)

✦ **Layers** (Book I, Chapter 6)

✦ **Layouts** (Book VII, Chapter 1)

✦ **Linetypes** (Book I, Chapter 6)

✦ **Multileader styles** (Book III, Chapter 2)

✦ **Page setups** (Book VII, Chapter 1)

✦ **Sheet set template (DST) files** (Book VII, Chapter 2)

✦ **Table styles** (Book III, Chapter 1)

✦ **Text styles** (Book III, Chapter 1)

✦ **Tool palettes** (Book VI, Chapter 4)

✦ **Viewports** (Book VII, Chapter 1)

✦ **Views** (Book II, Chapter 3)

The remainder of this chapter focuses on the CAD standards tools found in AutoCAD, not AutoCAD LT.

Using AutoCAD's CAD Standards Tools

AutoCAD provides several different tools that help keep drawings in sync with defined CAD standards. These tools are

✦ **Standards Manager:** Configures and checks for CAD standard violations.

✦ **Layer Translator:** Configures layer mappings and aligns layers in a drawing to match those defined by your CAD standards.

✦ **Batch Standards Checker:** Checks a set of drawings against a defined set of CAD standards.

The CAD standards tools provided with AutoCAD help with only a small subset of the items that are part of a good set of CAD standards. Blocks, layouts, page setups, and table styles, for example, are not part of the CAD standards tools that come with AutoCAD.

Drawing standards (DWS) files

A drawing standards (DWS) file is, for the most part, the same as a drawing or drawing template file, except for its file extension and the type of content that might be saved in it. Here are the most common items found in a drawing standards file:

✦ **Dimension styles** (Book III, Chapter 2)

✦ **Layers** (Book I, Chapter 6)

✦ **Linetypes** (Book I, Chapter 6)

✦ **Text styles** (Book III, Chapter 1)

The reason for the limited content of drawing standards files is that these are the types of objects supported with the built-in CAD standards tools.

The following steps save the current drawing as a drawing standards file:

1. **Create a new drawing based on a drawing template or from scratch. Add any layers, linetypes, dimension styles, or text styles that you want in the drawing standards file.**

2. **On the menu browser, choose File⇨Save As.**

The Save Drawing As dialog box is displayed.

3. **In the Files of Type drop-down list, select AutoCAD Drawing Standards (*.DWS).**

4. **Browse to a different location or use the location specified by AutoCAD for saving your drawing standards file.**

It's a good idea to store drawing standards files in a network location so they can be used by others in the office. If the files are stored locally and someone else opens the file, he or she may not be able to use the CAD standards tools because AutoCAD can't find the drawing standards file.

5. **Enter a file name for the drawing standards file.**

You may want to name the drawing standards file based on a project name or the type of drawing with which the drawing standards file will be used. For example, you might give the drawing standards file the name *Elevations* for your elevation drawings, or name the drawing standards file *Project 123* based on the name of a project.

6. **Click Save.**

The drawing standards file is saved with the specified name and location.

Managing standards

AutoCAD provides a set of tools that allows you to associate a drawing standards file with a drawing and then check that drawing against the associated drawing standards files. This set of tools is known as Standards Manager and is broken up into two parts: The first configures drawing standards files and associates drawing standards files to a drawing, and the second checks for violations in the drawing and then fixes them.

When configuring a drawing to use a drawing standards file, you're specifying which file should be used to check CAD standards against and which plug-ins should be used (essentially, a plug-in is a set of rules used to determine whether the drawing has problems). During the checking of the drawing file, you can fix any problems the plug-in finds.

Configuring standards

A drawing standards file can be associated with a drawing by using the STANDARDS command. You can start this command in a number of ways:

- ✦ On the ribbon, click Tools tab⇨Standards panel⇨Configure.
- ✦ On the menu browser or menu bar, click Tools menu⇨CAD Standards⇨Configure.
- ✦ On the CAD Standards toolbar, click the Configure button.
- ✦ At the command prompt type **STANDARDS** or **STA** and press Enter.

The following steps explain how to configure a drawing to use a drawing standards file and specify which standards plug-ins to use:

1. **On the ribbon, click Tools tab⇨Standards panel⇨Configure.**

The Configure Standards dialog box (see Figure 2-1) is displayed.

2. **Click the Standards tab.**

On the Standards tab, you associate the drawing standards files to be used for the current drawing. If more than one drawing standards file is specified, the order of the files is important. For example, if more than one of the associated drawing standards files has the same name for a layer, the first one encountered from the top of the list is used for validating the standard.

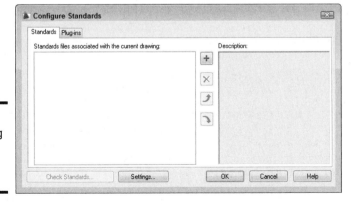

Figure 2-1:
Configuring standards for a drawing.

3. **Click the + (plus sign) button located in the middle of the dialog box.**

   The Select Standards File dialog box is displayed. In this dialog box, you can select which drawing standards files you want to associate with the drawing. Although more than one drawing standards file can be associated with a drawing, you can select only one at a time in the Select Standards File dialog box.

4. **Browse to and select the drawing standards file you want to associate with the drawing.**

5. **Click Open.**

   The drawing standards file is added to the list box on the left and some of the file's properties are displayed in the list box on the right.

6. **Add any additional drawing standards files that you need.**

   When more than one drawing standards file is associated with a drawing, the Move Up and Move Down buttons are enabled, allowing you to change the order in which the files are used to check for standards violations.

7. **Click the Plug-Ins tab.**

   On the Plug-Ins tab (see Figure 2-2), you can select which plug-ins you want to use for checking the drawing for violations against the associated drawing standards files. AutoCAD comes with a total of four plug-ins — this number hasn't changed since the feature was introduced.

8. **Select the plug-ins that you want to use when checking for standards violations in the current drawing.**

   A check mark next to the plug-in means it will be used when checking standards.

Figure 2-2:
Selecting
plug-ins for
checking
standards.

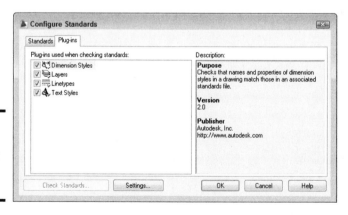

9. **Click the Settings button at the bottom of the Configure Standards dialog box.**

The CAD Standards Settings (see Figure 2-3) dialog box is displayed.

10. **Make your selections.**

In this dialog box, you can control the display of the notification icon that appears in the status bar when CAD standards are configured and specify how errors are handled during the process of checking for standards violations.

11. **Click OK.**

The drawing standards files are associated with the current drawing and the dialog box is closed. By default, a book icon (see Figure 2-4) appears in the status bar, denoting that at least one drawing standards file is associated with the drawing.

You can right-click some of the notification icons in the status bar trays to access specific settings for that feature. For example, if you right-click the book icon used for CAD standards, you can access some of the options for configuring and checking standards.

Figure 2-3:
Fine-tuning the behavior of the CAD standards tools.

Figure 2-4:
Icon in the status bar denotes the use of CAD standards.

Checking standards

After you associate a drawing standards file with a drawing, you can begin to check for standards violations. You use the CHECKSTANDARDS command to check CAD standards for a drawing. You can start this command in a number of ways:

✦ On the ribbon, click Tools tab⇨Standards panel⇨Check.

✦ On the menu browser or menu bar, click Tools menu⇨CAD Standards⇨Check.

✦ On the CAD Standards toolbar, click the Check button.

✦ At the command prompt, type **CHECKSTANDARDS** or **CHK** and press Enter.

Follow these steps to check a drawing for violations against its associated drawing standards files and the selected plug-ins:

1. **On the ribbon, click Tools tab⇨Standards panel⇨Check.**

The Check Standards dialog box (see Figure 2-5) is displayed. If no standards file has been associated with the drawing file yet, the Associate Standards (see Figure 2-6) message box is displayed. If the message box is displayed, click OK to go to the Configure Standards dialog box.

2. **In the Check Standards dialog box, review the standards violations found in the Problem area.**

The Problem area lets you know exactly what violation was detected during the checking process.

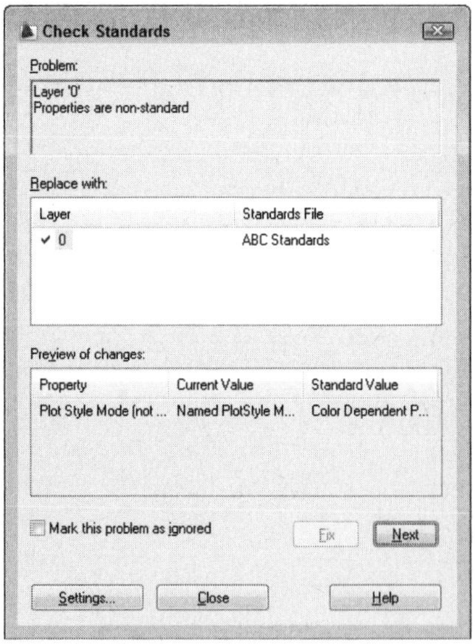

Figure 2-5: A violation has been detected.

Figure 2-6:
No standards file has been associated with this drawing yet.

3. **In the Replace With area, select one of the available fixes.**

   The Replace With area allows you to designate which one of the named objects in the associated drawing standards files should be used to fix the problem. When the drawing is compared to the drawing standards files, AutoCAD attempts to locate a recommended fix, which is designated with a blue check mark next to. After an item is selected from the Replace With area, the Preview of Changes area displays an overview of the changes that will be made.

4. **Click Fix to correct the standards violation. If you want to skip a violation, click Next and no fix will be made. If you also want to skip the violation the next time the drawing is checked for standards violations, select Mark This Problem as Ignored.**

   Clicking Fix updates the properties of the named object in the drawing to match the drawing standards file after you are through checking for standards violations.

5. **After all violations have been evaluated, the Check Complete message box is displayed. Click Close to return to the Check Standards dialog box.**

   The Check Complete message box (see Figure 2-7) displays a summary of the corrections made or not made.

6. **Click Close.**

   The Check Standards dialog box closes and the corrections made are reflected in the drawing.

Figure 2-7:
All violations have been evaluated.

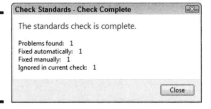

As you work in a drawing with associated drawing standards files, a notification balloon is displayed when a standards violation occurs (see Figure 2-8). The book icon in the status bar tray also changes to a book with an exclamation point in a yellow triangle. Click the Run Check Standards link in the balloon to display the Check Standards dialog box to fix the violations.

Figure 2-8:
Balloons
aren't just
for parties.

Translating layers

The Configure and Check Standards tools help automate the process of keeping similarly named layers and styles in sync. But what happens if you get a set of drawings from a client or customer and need to make their drawings conform to your layers? You don't want to have to go through each drawing one by one and map each layer or group of layers to the layer used in your CAD standards.

This is where Layer Translator comes into play. Layer Translator allows you to map a single layer or a group of layers to a single layer based on your established CAD standards. After the translation map for layers is set up, you can save the layer map to a drawing, drawing standards, or drawing template file for use later on additional drawings.

The Layer Translator is accessed through the LAYTRANS command. You can start this command in several ways:

✦ On the ribbon, click Tools tab➪Standards panel➪Layer Translator.

✦ On the menu browser or menu bar, click Tools menu➪CAD Standards➪Layer Translator.

✦ On the CAD Standards toolbar, click the Layer Translator button.

✦ Type At the command prompt, type **LAYTRANS** and press Enter.

Follow these steps to create a layer translation map and translate the layers in a drawing:

1. **On the ribbon, click Tools tab➪Standards panel➪Layer Translator.**

The Layer Translator dialog box (see Figure 2-9) is displayed.

2. **In the Translate To area, click New.**

   The New Layer dialog box (see Figure 2-10) is displayed.

   In the New Layer dialog box, you're creating a new layer from scratch to be used in the layer translation process. At minimum, you must specify a name.

3. **Modify the properties as necessary for the new layer and click OK.**

   The new layer is added to the list in the Translate To area.

4. **In the Layer Translator dialog box's Translate To area, click Load.**

   The Select Drawing File dialog box is displayed, so you can select a drawing, drawing standards, or drawing template file to load layers from for use in the Translate To list.

Figure 2-9:
Translating from one layer to another.

Figure 2-10:
Create a new layer to map to.

5. **Browse to and select an existing file that contains the layers you want to use in the layer translation and then click Open.**

   The layers in the selected file are added to the list in the Translate To area.

6. **Click Map Same, which is between the Translate From and Translate To areas.**

   Any layers that have the same name between the two lists are mapped. This helps speed up the process when creating the translations for a drawing with a larger number of layers.

7. **In the Translate From area, select the layer or layers for which you want to create a layer translation map.**

   The selected layer or layers become highlighted. You can press and hold down the Ctrl key to select multiple layers or the Shift key to select a range of files.

   Layers that appear with a white icon next to them in the Translate From area do not have any objects on them. These layers can be purged from the list and the drawing by right-clicking them in the list and choosing Purge Layers.

   Use the Selection Filter field to quickly select a number of layer names that are similar in name. You can use wild-card characters to help create a complex criterion if needed. For example, you can enter **TXT*** and click Select to highlight all the layers that begin with the letters TXT.

8. **In the Translate To area, select the layer that you want to map to the selected layer or layers in the Translate From area.**

   Layers in both the Translate From and Translate To areas should now be highlighted.

9. **Click Map to create the layer translation.**

   The layer translation is added to the Layer Translation Mappings area near the bottom of the dialog box. Each layer that has a translation is removed from the Translate From list to let you know which ones have not been mapped yet.

10. **Click the Settings button.**

   The Settings dialog box (see Figure 2-11) is displayed. The default settings are the best to help maintain good quality CAD standards. The last option in the Settings dialog box is nice if you're not sure what is on a layer; when a layer is selected in the Translate From list, only those layers are displayed in the drawing while the Layer Translator dialog box is displayed.

Figure 2-11:
Taking full
control of
the
translation.

11. **In the Settings dialog box, select the desired options and click OK.**

The changes to the settings are saved and the Settings dialog box is closed.

12. **In the Layer Translator dialog box, click Save.**

The Save Layer Mappings dialog box is displayed, allowing you to save
the layer translations that you have created for reuse.

13. **In the Save Layer Mappings dialog box, browse to the location where
you want to export the layer translations to, specify a name for the
file, and then click Save.**

Use the Files of Type drop-down list to create either a drawing or drawing standards file.

14. **In the Layer Translator dialog box, click Translate.**

The Layer Translator dialog box closes and the layers are updated based
on the specified layer translations.

Batch checking drawings

Both standards tools discussed up to this point must be set up on an individual
drawing. This isn't an efficient process if you have hundreds of drawings for a
single project. Wouldn't it be nice if a utility could check a large number of drawings at once so you wouldn't have to go through each drawing one by one?

You're in luck! An external utility called Batch Standards Checker allows you
to take a number of drawings and check them for standards violations. Batch
Standards Checker is similar to the Configure Standards dialog box in how
some of the tabs work. One downside to Batch Standards Checker is that it
doesn't fix any problems it finds; it only checks for violations, but it's still
much faster than checking each file individually.

**Book VIII
Chapter 2**

CAD Standards

The following steps use Batch Standards Checker to check drawing files for any standards violations:

1. **Click Start button⇨[All] Programs⇨Autodesk⇨AutoCAD 2009⇨Batch Standards Checker.**

The Batch Standards Checker (see Figure 2-12) application is displayed.

2. **Click the Drawings tab.**

The Drawings tab allows you to specify which drawing and drawing template files you want to check for standards violations.

3. **Click the + (plus sign) button to add drawing or drawing template files to the list for processing.**

The Batch Standards Checker – File Open Dialog box is displayed so you can select multiple drawing and drawing template files.

4. **Browse for and select the files that you want to check for standards violations and then click Open.**

The selected files are added to the Drawings to Check list. You can view some of the properties of the files in the Description area on the right side of the dialog box. You can change the order in which the files are processed or remove them from the list by using the buttons in the middle of the dialog box.

5. **(Optional) Select the Check External References of Listed Drawings option.**

When the check box is selected, each external reference in a drawing is also checked for standards violations.

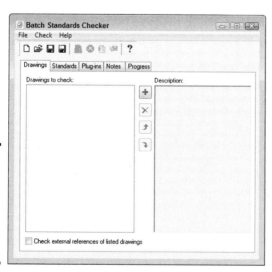

Figure 2-12:
Checking standards for more than one drawing at a time.

6. **Click the Standards tab.**

The Standards tab (see Figure 2-13) allows you to specify which drawing standards files should be used to check for standards violations.

7. **Select one of the two options to control which drawing standards files to use when checking the selected drawing files.**

The top option, Check Each Drawing Using Its Associated Standards Files, is useful if each drawing on the Drawings tab has at least one associated drawing standards file. If not, use the Check All Drawings Using the Following Standards Files option.

a. **If you select Check All Drawings Using the Following Standards Files, click the + (plus sign) button to add a drawing standards file to the list for processing.**

The Batch Standards Checker – File Open Dialog box is displayed.

b. **Browse to and select the drawing standards files you want to use and then click Open.**

The selected files are added to the Standards Used for Checking All Drawings list. You can view some of the properties of the files in the Description area on the right side of the dialog box. You can change the order in which the files are processed or remove them from the list by using the buttons in the middle of the dialog box.

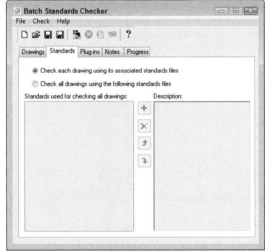

Figure 2-13:
The Standards tab is similar to the Configure Standards dialog box.

8. **Click the Plug-Ins tab.**

The Plug-Ins tab (see Figure 2-14) appears.

9. **Select or deselect the plug-ins that you want to use for checking standards against the specified drawing files.**

The same plug-ins are available here that are available in the Configure Standards dialog box that's displayed with the STANDARDS command.

10. **Click the Notes tab.**

The Notes tab allows you to provide a description of the drawings that are being checked. The notes are saved with the standards check file, which contains the selected drawings, the method of standards checking you selected, and the plug-ins specified. This allows you to refer to any comments about the batched drawings at a later date in case you have to reprocess the same drawing files.

11. **In the Enter Notes to Be Included in the Report text box, type a note.**

12. **On the toolbar, click Save.**

The Batch Standards Checker – File Save Dialog box is displayed.

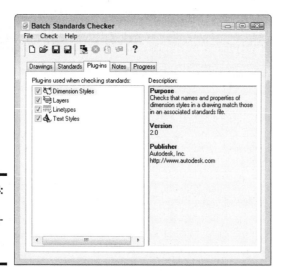

Figure 2-14:
Controlling which plug-ins are used.

13. **Browse to a location and enter a name for the Standards Check (CHX) file and then click Save.**

The Standards Check file is created in the specified location with the provided name. The Standards Check file contains information about which drawings are to be processed, the drawing standards files to use, and the other options you have specified up to this point.

14. **On the toolbar, click Start Check.**

The Progress tab is displayed and shows the current progress of the files being checked.

15. **When the process is finished, the Standards Audit Report is displayed.**

The Standards Audit Report (see Figure 2-15) is displayed in your Internet browser. You can view the different results by clicking the controls located on the left side of the report. The information is stored in the Standards Check file that you saved earlier and can be viewed later by opening the file and choosing View Report from the Check menu.

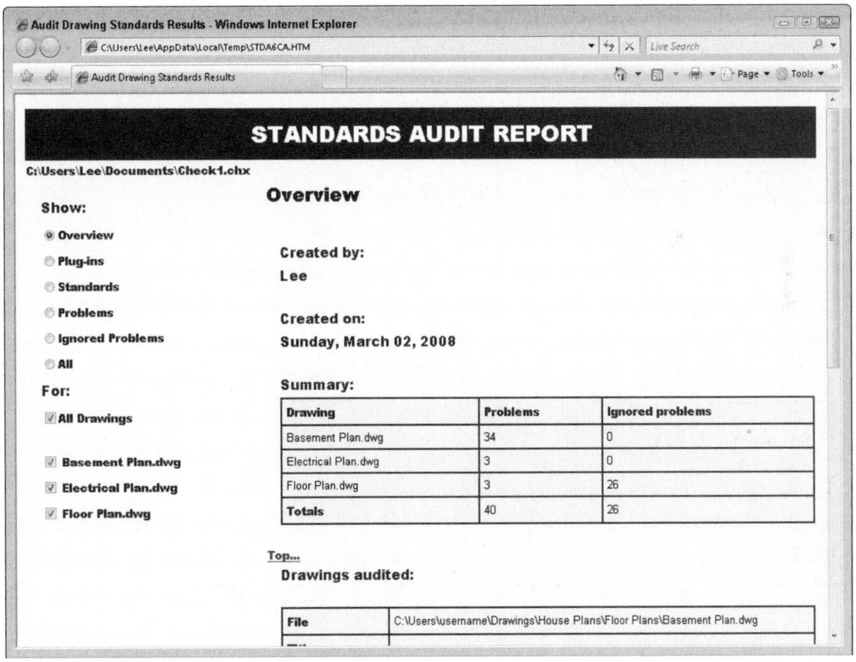

Figure 2-15: The Standards Audit Report reveals all the problems with your standards (well, okay, maybe not *all* problems).

Chapter 3: Working with Drawing Files

In This Chapter

✔ Naming files

✔ Partially loading a drawing

✔ Controlling what happens during a save operation

✔ Password-protecting and digitally signing drawings

As you may have noticed, drawing files (.dwg) are the main byproduct of using AutoCAD. They are much more important than the hard copies or the electronic files generated when plotting. Hard copies of drawings are designed for presenting a concept or design, but they can't be modified like the drawing file can be. For this reason, you need to take care of your drawing files by storing them in safe locations. You also must ensure that you back them up and use a logical naming convention so you can easily find the files later.

Many users of AutoCAD don't fully realize the amount of control they have over their drawing files. This chapter explains some of the concepts that you might not know about for working with drawing files. The concepts I cover here range from file-naming conventions, to password-protecting or digitally signing drawing files when you share them, to controlling how objects and layers are indexed to make loading a drawing as an external reference more efficient.

It's All in the Name: File-Naming Conventions

Using a naming convention is critical to being able to easily find any document, whether it was created with Microsoft Word or AutoCAD. A series of drawing files named Drawing1, Drawing2, and so on won't be helpful to you in the future. Instead, you should come up with a meaningful naming convention that tells you at a glance what project a drawing file pertains to. The key to creating a good naming convention is to make it meaningful and easy to understand. If it's overly complicated, users may wander from the convention and do their own thing, making it harder to find files later.

If you're in the architectural field, you may want to include such things as the project number, building number, drawing type, and drawing size in your file name conventions. An example of such a file name might be

A12345-01-P-D.DWG. This type of convention ensures that files related to the same part of the building and project are grouped together. Of course, good file organization also helps to make your projects run more efficiently.

AutoCAD comes with a feature called sheet sets. Many users ignore this feature because they don't fully understand it. Sheet sets are great for helping you organize drawings not just by file but also through a structure that might or might not match the folder structure on a local or network drive. (I cover sheet sets in Book VII, Chapter 2.) Sheet sets provide not only a way to organize drawings but also some structure for naming drawings.

AutoCAD 2006 and later releases extend the Windows search feature, which you can use to find text strings in a drawing file. This can help you find drawing files that might not have been placed in the correct project folder.

Part of a Drawing Can Be a Good Thing: Working with Partial Open

Part of a drawing is a good thing? You may be thinking that I might not be getting enough sleep and therefore have lost my mind. You could be right, but hear me out before you jump to any conclusions; I'm referring to a feature called Partial Open, which has been part of the product for the past few releases. This feature allows you to open part of a drawing file into AutoCAD, based on a view and selected layers.

AutoCAD LT does not support the Partial Open feature.

Partially opening a drawing file can be a great way to save time versus opening a large drawing that contains a lot of annotation, hatches, and dimensions. Instead of waiting for the annotation and geometry to load at the beginning of the editing process, you can choose not to load that information until you need to see it. If you happen to need any information in part of the drawing that has not been loaded, you can specify the area of the drawing that you want those objects to be displayed in. The key to being able to take full advantage of this feature is a good set of layer standards and the use of named views. Figure 3-1 shows the same drawing file two ways: The drawing on the left was opened by using Open, and the one on the right was opened by using Partial Open.

A drawing file can be partially opened by using the OPEN or PARTIALOPEN command. You can start these commands in one of the following ways:

✦ At the command prompt, type **PARTIALOPEN** and press Enter.

✦ Start the OPEN command. In the Select File dialog box, click the drop-down arrow to the right of the Open button, and choose Partial Open or Partial Open Read-Only.

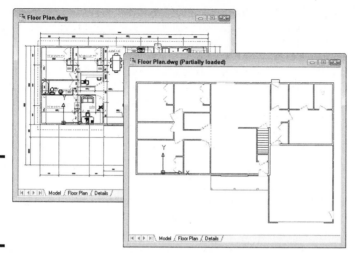

Figure 3-1:
Using Open versus Partial Open.

The following procedure explains how to use the Partial Open feature to load geometry based on a selected view and layers, and how to control the loading of xrefs when a drawing is being partially opened:

1. **On the Quick Access toolbar, click Open.**

The Select File dialog box appears.

2. **Browse to and select the drawing file you want to partially open. Click the drop-down arrow next to Open and choose Partial Open.**

The Partial Open dialog box (see Figure 3-2) is displayed.

3. **In the View Geometry to Load area, select a named view.**

By default, two named views are available in every drawing file. These are *Extents*, which represents the drawing's extents (the largest area required to display all objects in a drawing), and *Last*, which represents the view the drawing was saved with.

4. **(Optional) In the Index Status area, select the Use Spatial Index check box.**

Spatial indexing allows for information to be located in a drawing much faster, although it does increase the file size. See "Indexing the contents of a drawing" later in this chapter for more information. This option is available only if either spatial or layer indexing was enabled when the file was last saved.

5. **In the Layer Geometry to Load area, select the layers that contain the geometry you want to load.**

**Book VIII
Chapter 3**

**Working with
Drawing Files**

You don't need to specify any layers, but if you don't specify at least one, AutoCAD prompts you with a message box (see Figure 3-3). Click No to select some layers before continuing.

6. If the file you are loading contains xrefs, you can select the Unload All Xrefs on Open option in the lower-left corner.

Selecting this check box unloads all the xrefs attached to the drawing before it is loaded. The xrefs are not displayed until they're reloaded through the External References palette. This is a great feature if you want to quickly load a drawing that contains a lot of xrefs and then view only the ones that you're interested in.

7. Click Open to finish the partial open process.

The drawing is partially opened. You can tell when you're working in a partially opened drawing in two ways: The first is that the Partial Load option is available on the File menu, and the second is that the text *(Partially Loaded)* appears after the drawing name in the title bar (see Figure 3-4).

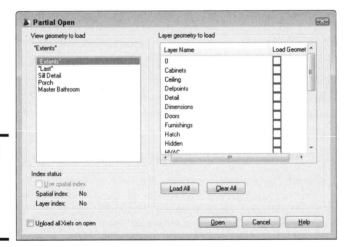

Figure 3-2:
Selecting what you want to partially open.

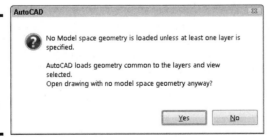

Figure 3-3:
AutoCAD's friendly reminder that you forgot to do something.

8. **If you need to load additional layers, you can use the Partial Load option on the File menu.**

   This displays the Partial Load dialog box (see Figure 3-5), which is similar to the Partial Open dialog box.

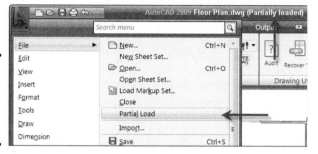

Figure 3-4:
The signs of a partially opened drawing file.

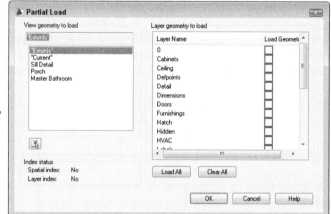

Figure 3-5:
Loading more layers in a partially opened drawing file.

Controlling What Happens during a Save

AutoCAD is a powerful application that contains many features designed for specialized uses. Some of these features are not always easy to find or understand because they're not in the standard workflow. Some of these items are the ability to control the default format in which drawing files are saved in, password protection, digital signatures, and utilizing indexing for your drawings.

**Book VIII
Chapter 3**

**Working with
Drawing Files**

Getting a handle on drawing file formats

What is a drawing file format and why is it important? A *drawing format* is the structure of how AutoCAD stores information in a drawing file. A format change occurs when major changes are made to the application to support new object types and features. AutoCAD has been on a regular schedule of making a format change about every three releases. By giving you a number of older drawing file formats to save to, AutoCAD makes it easier for you to share your drawing files with customers who might be using an older release than you are. I cover the different drawing file formats and which releases they belong to in Book I, Chapter 2.

If you need to exchange drawings with users who still use AutoCAD R12 or R13, you can save your drawings to an R12 DXF file format. By saving to the R12 DXF file format, some object types are converted to simpler types of objects that earlier releases understand. Multiline text, for example, is converted to a block that contains single-line text, and dimensions are no longer associative.

If your company is in the process of upgrading to a newer version, saving drawings back to a previous file format during the rollout period is often a good idea so that everyone can access drawings created with the newer release. This is important because AutoCAD files might not be backward compatible to the release you are upgrading from. For this reason, Autodesk introduced a feature to allow you to specify the default file format when the SAVE, QSAVE, or SAVEAS command is used. You can find this option in the Options dialog box.

The following steps explain how to set the default file format for saving:

1. **Right-click the command line window and choose Options.**

   The Options dialog box is displayed.

2. **Click the Open and Save tab.**

   The Open and Save tab is used to specify options related to saving and opening files.

3. **In the File Save area, click the drop-down arrow on the drop-down list below Save As and make a selection.**

   The drop-down list contains the different DWG, DWT, and DXF file formats that you can specify as the default file format for saves.

4. **Click Apply or OK.**

   Clicking Apply saves the changes and keeps the Options dialog box open, whereas clicking OK saves the changes and closes the Options dialog box.

Indexing the contents of a drawing

Indexing a drawing is not quite the same as filing someone's name in a Rolodex or indexing a book, but the results are similar. The reason you want to index a drawing is so AutoCAD can find objects easier and faster. AutoCAD offers two types of indexing: layer indexing and spatial indexing.

Both types of indexing improve the performance of demand loading a drawing. *Demand loading* is the process used with loading external references (xrefs) and when partially opening a drawing. When demand loading is used, AutoCAD loads only the data from the drawing that is required to properly display the drawing file — objects are loaded as they are required from the drawing. *Layer indexing* improves the loading of objects on layers that are on and thawed. Objects on a layer that is frozen or off are not read in with the drawing file. Those layers are read in only when specifically requested.

Spatial indexing is used to organize objects in 3D space and improves the loading performance of a referenced file that has been clipped. Clipping a referenced file allows you to define which part of a referenced file is displayed in the drawing by defining the area to be displayed by using a rectangular or polygonal boundary. (Clipping referenced files is covered more in Book VI, Chapter 3.) Both layer and spatial indexing are helpful only if the file is being used as an xref or is being partially opened. If indexing is enabled, saving the drawing file takes slightly longer. Indexing is available in four options:

✦ **None:** Indexing is disabled.

✦ **Layer:** Only layer indexing is enabled.

✦ **Spatial:** Only spatial indexing is enabled.

✦ **Layer & Spatial:** Layer and spatial indexing are enabled.

The following steps explain how to set the indexing type when saving a drawing file:

1. **On the menu browser, choose File menu⇨Save As.**

The Save Drawing As dialog box is displayed.

2. **Choose Tools⇨Options.**

The Saveas Options dialog box (see Figure 3-6) is displayed. It contains some different options for both DWG and DXF file formats.

3. **In the Index Type drop-down list, click the down arrow.**

The drop-down list displays the various indexing options you can use.

4. **Select an option in the drop-down list.**

5. **Click OK.**

   The Saveas Options dialog box closes and you return to the Save Drawing As dialog box.

6. **Specify the file name and location for the drawing you're saving and then click Save.**

   The Save Drawing As dialog box closes and the drawing is saved with the indexing type specified.

In AutoCAD LT, you must use the INDEXCTL system variable to specify the type of indexing that should be used when saving a drawing. A value of 0 indicates indexing is disabled, 1 indicates only layer indexing is enabled, 2 indicates only spatial indexing is enabled, and 3 indicates both layer and spatial indexing are enabled. You can use the INDEXCTL system variable with AutoCAD as well. To set the indexing to use with INDEXCTL, enter the variable name and value at the command prompt and then save the drawing file.

Figure 3-6:
Drawing file options.

Protecting Your Drawings

You work hard to create the perfect design, so you have every right to make sure that it's kept safe. AutoCAD offers two options to make sure that your design doesn't get altered without your permission: password protection and digital signatures. Password protection locks the file and doesn't allow anyone to view it without first entering a password. Digital signatures aren't as secure as password-protected files, but they do offer a level of protection by indicating whether the file was altered after it was signed. This can be critical when you need to have a client sign off on a design.

AutoCAD LT does not support the ability to password-protect drawing files.

Password-protecting

Password-protecting a drawing file in AutoCAD is similar to password-protecting a file in other applications: You provide a password or phrase and specify the type of encryption you want to use. Although password protection offers benefits, it also has a downside.

If you use password protection, you must record the password in a safe place so that you don't forget it; otherwise, you won't be able to open the file. No amount of magic can unlock the file after the password has been lost, so you may want to make a backup copy of the drawing file without the password before you save it with one.

I also recommend that you talk to your CAD manager or a senior-level drafter before you start using password protection on drawing files. After all, the drawing file does belong to the company or client and not to you.

Assigning a password to a drawing file

The following steps explain how to password-protect a drawing file:

1. **On the menu browser, click File menu⇨Save As.**

   The Save Drawing As dialog box is displayed.

2. **Choose Tools⇨Security Options.**

   The Security Options dialog box, which contains the options for working with passwords and digital signatures (see Figure 3-7), is displayed.

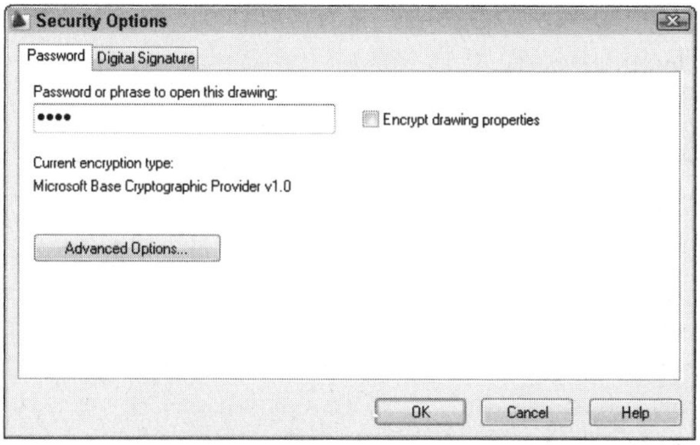

Figure 3-7:
Securing the contents of a drawing with a password.

Book VIII Chapter 3

Working with Drawing Files

3. **In the Password or Phrase to Open This Drawing box, type the password or phrase.**

   The value that you enter is masked in the box as you enter it.

4. **(Optional) Select the Encrypt Drawing Properties option.**

   Drawing properties provide information through Windows Explorer about a drawing file, such as author, title, and custom properties. Figure

3-8 shows what the Properties dialog box looks like in Windows Explorer when it is not encrypted through the use of password protection (on the left) and when it is encrypted (on the right). The left image shows that three additional tabs (Summary, Statistics, and Custom) are displayed when the drawing file is not password-protected.

5. (Optional) In the Security Options dialog box, click Advanced Options.

The Advanced Options dialog box (see Figure 3-9) is displayed. Select the encryption provider that you want to use and the key length. The key length determines the overall length of the encryption key. The higher the value, the greater the level of security your drawing will have. Based on your operating system and what country you're in, your encryption options may vary. I recommend using the greatest key length possible for the encryption provider you select — in most cases, the value is 128. After all, you want to be sure that your data is protected. When you finish, click OK to accept the changes.

6. In the Security Options dialog box, click OK.

The Confirm Password dialog box (see Figure 3-10) is displayed. It warns you of the dangers of forgetting or losing your password, which I mention earlier in this chapter.

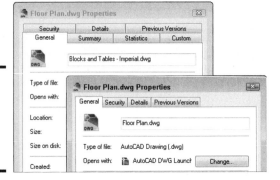

Figure 3-8: Encrypting properties helps to hide some content.

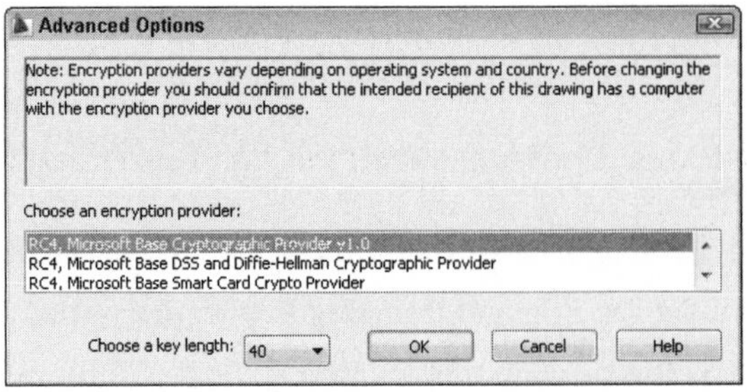

Figure 3-9: Choosing an encryption type.

Figure 3-10:
Confirming
your
password
is a good
thing.

7. **Reenter the password in the Reenter Password to Open This Drawing text field and then click OK.**

   If the passwords match, both the Confirm Password and Security Options dialog boxes close, and you return to the Save Drawing As dialog box.

8. **Finish specifying the file name and location for the drawing you're saving and click Save.**

   The Save Drawing As dialog box closes and the drawing is saved with the specified password.

If you remove the value from the Password or Phrase to Open This Drawing box (refer to Step 3), the password protection from the drawing file is removed.

Working with a password-protected drawing

Password protection goes beyond just needing to enter a password to open a drawing file. Password protection affects any operation that reads the contents of the drawing file into another drawing, such as opening the drawing file, referencing the drawing file externally, or inserting the drawing file into another drawing.

Follow these steps to open a drawing that has been saved with a password:

1. **On the Quick Access toolbar, click Open.**

   The Select File dialog box is displayed.

2. **Browse to and select the drawing file you want to open.**

3. **Click Open.**

   The Select File dialog box closes and the Password dialog box is displayed (see Figure 3-11).

4. In the Password dialog box, enter the password and click OK.

If you entered the correct password, the drawing file should finish loading. If not, an error message is displayed asking you to retry or to cancel the operation. The password is cached in memory, so if you close the drawing and reopen it without restarting AutoCAD, you won't need to reenter the password.

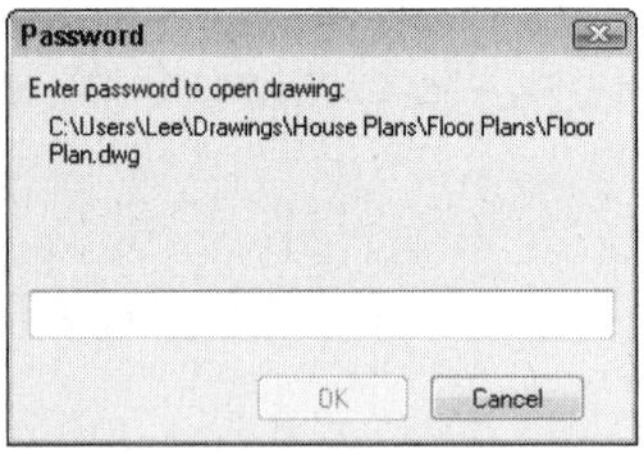

Figure 3-11:
Password,
please.

Digital signatures

Unlike password protection, digital signatures don't keep anyone from viewing the contents of a file. Instead, they notify the person viewing the file whether a change has been made after it was signed. Digital signatures require a little more work to use the first time because you must first obtain a digital ID.

You have to obtain a digital ID from a company such as VeriSign (www.verisign.com) or IdenTrust (www.digsigtrust.com). After you obtain a digital ID, you can start signing drawing files. Digital IDs can be used with other applications besides AutoCAD; some programs such as Outlook also support digital IDs for signing e-mails. Some companies offer trial periods for testing the use of a digital ID and then require a small annual fee to keep the digital ID valid beyond the trial period.

Obtaining a digital signature from VeriSign

Autodesk has wired AutoCAD to take you to VeriSign's Web site to obtain a digital signature for signing drawing files, so I thought I would follow Autodesk's recommendation. The following steps are an overview of how to obtain a digital signature from VeriSign, but feel free to use a different vendor if you want. The steps will vary from vendor to vendor. If you don't have a digital ID yet, the Valid Digital ID Not Available dialog box is displayed (see Figure 3-12).

Removing the security option for password-protecting a drawing file

Some companies worry that employees might abuse the capability to password-protect drawing files. This is one reason why Autodesk allows the CAD manager or Information Technology (IT) department to remove the feature during installation. The option can be disabled when Custom is selected on the Select the Installation Type screen during the installation process. If Typical was selected during installation, you can remove the password-protect feature through

the Programs and Features option on Windows Vista or the Add and Remove Programs on Windows XP in the Windows Control Panel. The figure shows the Drawing Encryption option that controls whether the password protection feature is available. Disabling this feature only prevents people from password-protecting a drawing file and has no affect on their ability to receive and open drawings that are password-protected by others.

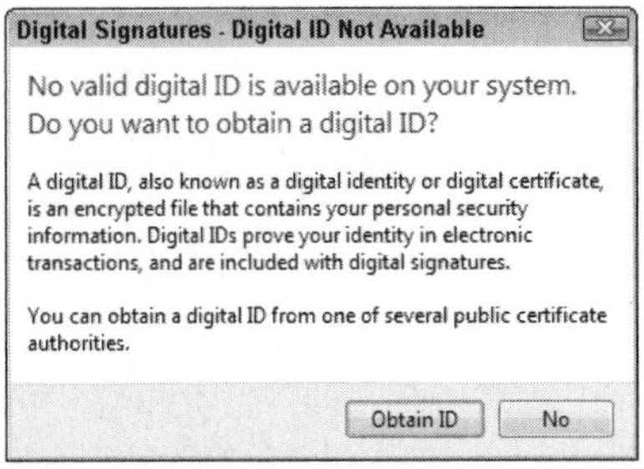

Digital Signatures - Digital ID Not Available

No valid digital ID is available on your system.
Do you want to obtain a digital ID?

A digital ID, also known as a digital identity or digital certificate,
is an encrypted file that contains your personal security
information. Digital IDs prove your identity in electronic
transactions, and are included with digital signatures.

You can obtain a digital ID from one of several public certificate
authorities.

Obtain ID   No

Figure 3-12:
No digital ID
found on the
computer.

Follow these steps to obtain a digital ID from VeriSign:

1. **On the menu browser, choose File menu⇨Save As.**

The Save Drawing As dialog box is displayed.

2. **Choose Tools⇨Security Options.**

The Security Options dialog box is displayed and contains different
options for working with passwords and digital signatures.

3. **Click the Digital Signature tab.**

The Valid Digital ID Not Available dialog box is displayed.

4. **Click Obtain ID.**

The Products & Services page of VeriSign's Web site is displayed (see
Figure 3-13). The Products & Services page can be confusing — none of
the options seem to call out and say "Pick me if you're using AutoCAD!"

5. **In the Security Services section, click the Managed PKI Services link.**

The Managed PKI Services page is displayed with even more options.

6. **In the Managed PKI Services Include section, click the PKI
Applications link.**

The PKI Applications page is displayed with more options.

7. **Click the Digital IDs for Secure Email link. (Confused yet? You're not
the only one!)**

The Digital IDs for Secure Email page is displayed.

8. **Click Buy Now. (Don't worry, you get the chance to take a digital ID
for a test-drive before you buy one.)**

The Digital IDs for Secure Email — Digital ID Enrollment page is
displayed.

9. **Click Buy Now again. (This time the program lets you know that you
have an option for a 60-day trial.)**

The Choose Your Browser page is displayed.

Figure 3-13:
Oh, so many
products
and
services to
choose
from.

10. **Click Microsoft or Netscape.**

The Enrollment page is displayed.

11. **Enter all the required information and click Accept.**

After you submit the information, you receive an e-mail explaining how
to obtain the new digital signature. Follow the information in the e-mail
to complete the process.

Digitally signing a drawing file

The following steps explain how to digitally sign a drawing file. I assume that
you've already obtained a digital signature from a vendor of your choice or
from VeriSign, as explained in the preceding steps.

1. **On the menu browser, click File menu⇨Save As.**

The Save Drawing As dialog box is displayed.

2. **Choose Tools⇨Security Options.**

The Security Options dialog box is displayed and contains different
options for working with passwords and digital signatures.

**Book VIII
Chapter 3**

**Working with
Drawing Files**

3. **Click the Digital Signature tab.**

The Digital Signature tab (see Figure 3-14) displays the different digital signatures found on the computer and some options.

4. **Select the Attach Digital Signature After Saving Drawing option.**

After you select this option, other controls on the tab become enabled.

5. **In the Select a Digital ID (Certificate) area, select a digital ID.**

The first digital ID in the list is selected by default; if you have more than one digital ID, you need to specify which one you want to use.

6. **In the Get Time Stamp From drop-down list, you can specify a time stamp, which I recommend doing.**

The time stamp helps to validate the digital signature.

7. **(Optional) In the Comment area, you can add comments for the individual who will be opening or viewing the file.**

For example, you may want to add a comment about whether the file has been approved for manufacturing.

8. **Click OK.**

The Security Options dialog box closes and you return to the Save Drawing As dialog box.

9. **Finish specifying the file name and location for the drawing you're saving and then click Save.**

The Save Drawing As dialog box closes and the drawing is saved with a digital signature. You know that the drawing has been signed when the Validate Digital Signatures icon (see Figure 3-15) appears in the status bar.

Figure 3-14:
No ink is required for using digital signatures.

Figure 3-15:
Success!
The drawing
has been
digitally
signed.

Opening a digitally signed drawing file

Digitally signed drawings serve a different purpose than a drawing you might be creating or editing. This is why they are displayed in a slightly different way in Windows Explorer. The icon for a digitally signed drawing file includes two red and yellow marks (okay, I know you can only see them in black and white in this book) in the center or upper-right corner (see Figure 3-16).

Figure 3-16:
The
markings on
the bottom
icon
indicate that
the drawing
file has
been
digitally
signed.

The following steps explain how to open a drawing that has been saved with a digital signature:

1. **On the Quick Access toolbar, click Open.**

The Select File dialog box is displayed.

2. **Browse to and select the file you want to open.**

The selected file should be highlighted in the dialog box and its name displayed in the File Name box.

3. **Click Open.**

The Select File dialog box closes and the Digital Signature Contents dialog box is displayed (see Figure 3-17).

**Book VIII
Chapter 3**

**Working with
Drawing Files**

4. **Review the information to make sure that everything is correct, and then click Close.**

The Validate Digital Signatures icon is displayed in the status bar. If the digital signature is invalid, you see a warning notification at the top of the Digital Signature Contents dialog box (see Figure 3-18).

You can control the display of the Digital Signature Contents dialog box with the SIGWARN system variable. Enter SIGWARN at the command prompt to change its current value. A value of 0 suppresses the display of the dialog box unless the digital signature is invalid. A value of 1 displays the dialog box. (This is the default behavior.)

Figure 3-17:
Digital
signature
information.

Figure 3-18:
When digital
signatures
go bad.

Digitally signing a batch of drawings

If you have a large set of drawing files that need to be digitally signed all at once, Autodesk offers an external utility to do so. This utility is properly named Attach Digital Signatures. It's pretty basic and easy to understand. The following steps explain how to access and digitally sign multiple drawing files at one time:

1. **Click Start menu⇨[All] Programs⇨Autodesk⇨AutoCAD 2009⇨Attach Digital Signatures.**

The Attach Digital Signatures dialog box (see Figure 3-19) is displayed.

2. **Click the Add Files button.**

The Select File dialog box is displayed.

3. **Browse to and select the drawing files that you want to digitally sign.**

4. **Click Open.**

The Select File dialog box closes and you return to the Attach Digital Signatures dialog box. The names of the selected files are added to the list box in the Files to Be Signed area.

5. **Specify the digital ID, time stamp, and comments as desired.**

6. **Click the Sign Files button.**

The process of signing the files begins. When it is completed, you are given a summary of the number of files that were signed.

7. **In the Signing Complete message box, click OK.**

8. **In the Attach Digital Signatures dialog box, click Close.**

The Attach Digital Signatures dialog box closes.

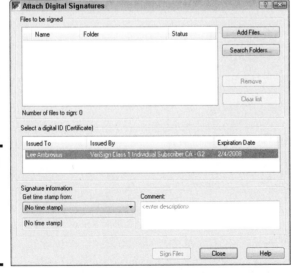

Figure 3-19: Attaching digital signatures to multiple drawing files.

Chapter 4: Sharing Electronic Files

In This Chapter

✔ Sharing drawings with non-AutoCAD products

✔ Moving drawings to the Internet

✔ Emulating paper digitally

✔ Working with Design Web Format (DWF and DWFx) files

Drawing files are one of the byproducts of AutoCAD. When you work with AutoCAD you have two choices: to keep a design digital or create a physical hard copy of the drawing. The electronic drawing is much more important than the hard copy of a drawing that can be produced with the PLOT or PUBLISH commands. To efficiently deliver a set of drawings to a client or someone else, drawings should remain digital. This doesn't mean that a hard copy of the drawing file isn't important; it's just that it's a slower way to deliver and communicate changes.

This chapter focuses on delivering a representation of a drawing file in a digital format that can't be modified — well, the original drawing isn't affected anyway. Sharing drawing files can be challenging; others want your drawing files, but they may not be able to view or use them with their software application of choice. AutoCAD offers a few solutions to help you share drawing files with people who don't own a CAD program or people who do own a CAD program but use something other than AutoCAD.

AutoCAD also offers a variety of options for accessing FTP sites, project management sites developed by Autodesk to work with their products such as Buzzsaw and Streamline, and publishing drawing files to Web sites.

Sharing Drawings with Non-AutoCAD-based Products

When you work with CAD, you often need to share your drawing files with others. However, not everyone's CAD application is the same. For this reason, CAD applications must be able to communicate in other file formats. AutoCAD provides various output file formats so that it can more easily exchange drawing files with other programs. You may be familiar with some of these file formats, but not others.

You use four primary commands to export to a different file type: SAVEAS, EXPORT, PLOT, 3DDWF and PUBLISH. Other commands, such as BMPOUT, PNGOUT, JPGOUT, and TIFOUT, are available for exporting objects in a drawing to a raster image file. Here is a list of the file formats that you can export out of AutoCAD.

✦ **DXF:** Drawing Interchange Format

✦ **WMF:** Microsoft Windows Metafile

✦ **ACIS:** ACIS solid object file

✦ **STL:** Solid object stereolithography file

✦ **EPS:** Encapsulated Postscript file

✦ **DXX:** Attribute extract DXF file

✦ **BMP:** Windows Bitmap file

✦ **JPG:** JPEG graphic file

✦ **PNG.** Portable Network Graphics file

✦ **TIF:** Tag Image File Format

✦ **3D DWF:** 3D Autodesk Design Web Format

✦ **3D DWFx:** 3D Autodesk Design Web Format

✦ **DWF:** Design Web Format

✦ **DWFx:** Design Web Format (XPS Compliant)

✦ **DGN (V7):** MicroStation V7 Design file

✦ **DGN (V8):** MicroStation V8 Design file

✦ **PDF:** Adobe Acrobat Portable Document File

✦ **PLT:** AutoCAD Plot file

AutoCAD LT does not support the ACIS, STL, EPS, DXX, 3D DWF, or 3D DWFx file formats.

AutoCAD and AutoCAD LT now support the ability to export MicroStation V7 Design files and DWFx Design Web Format files that are XPS compliant. 3D DWFx files can be created only with AutoCAD.

Taking Drawings to the Internet

AutoCAD can and does play a role in being able to connect to the Internet to access drawings that have been posted for you to reference, or to be able to push content to a Web site. All of AutoCAD's primary file access commands are capable of utilizing FTP — *File Transfer Protocol*. This allows you to access and place files on a remote server that could be just around the block or halfway around the world. For the most part, the use of FTP is transparent to you because it's integrated into AutoCAD.

Along with using FTP, Autodesk offers two project collaboration sites that users of their products can sign up to use for a fee. The project collaboration sites are similar to FTP sites and how they are integrated into AutoCAD and other Autodesk products, but they offer much more than just a place to park drawing files. These sites allow for history tracking when files change, embedded file viewers, permissions-based access, and a built-in notification system, to just name a few of the features that the sites offer.

Project collaboration sites are great, but sometimes they are based on the type of information you need to share across the Internet. Autodesk does offer publishing tools that can take a set of drawing files and publish them to Web-friendly formats, such as DWFx, DWF, JPG, and PNG. This feature is basic in its abilities, but if you are not familiar with Web page design, it's great for putting together a nice little interface for your clients use to access drawings and information.

Using an FTP site

Working with an FTP site from AutoCAD is similar to accessing an FTP site through Internet Explorer. Both require the location, a user name, and a password. The only difference is that you can open and save to the FTP site right from AutoCAD instead of downloading the files first and then re-uploading them later.

Virtually every file navigation dialog box inside AutoCAD can access an FTP site. One of the nice features of using FTP with AutoCAD is that you can configure an FTP site as a reusable location. So if you happen to be working on a project over a period of time, you won't have to worry about forgetting the address, user name, or password. Instead, you just need to set up the FTP site once and it is there until you remove it.

The following steps explain how to configure and use an FTP location from inside AutoCAD:

1. **On the Quick Access toolbar, click Open.**

   The Select File dialog box appears.

2. **Choose Tools⇨Add/Modify FTP Locations.**

   The Add/Modify FTP Locations dialog box appears (see Figure 4-1).

3. **In the Name of FTP Site box, enter a name for the location.**

Even though the box is called Name of FTP Site, you enter the URL (uniform resource location) for the FTP location. A sample URL is ftp.websitename.com/drawings.

4. **In the Log On As area, select the logon type.**

If you specify User, you must enter the user name that has been set up for you to access the FTP site. If no user name was set up and the site is open to the general public, you can use Anonymous.

5. **In the Password box, type the password associated with the user name, if one exists.**

As the password is entered, it is automatically masked (the keys pressed do not appear on-screen).

6. **Click the Add button.**

An entry for the FTP location is added to the list box at the bottom of the dialog box. You can later select the FTP location from the list box and click Modify or Remove to make changes to it.

7. **Click OK.**

The Add/Modify FTP Location dialog box closes and you return to the Select File dialog box.

8. **In the shortcuts pane on the left side, click FTP.**

The Select File dialog box updates and displays an FTP Locations item that contains the FTP locations that have been defined.

9. **Browse to the file you want to open just as if it was on your local or network drive, and click Open.**

The Select File dialog box closes and the drawing is opened. Do not forget that you can access the FTP location from most file navigation dialog boxes in AutoCAD.

Autodesk i-drop

Autodesk i-drop is a technology that allows for content to be dragged and dropped from a Web page into AutoCAD. There are two parts to i-drop. One part is used on a Web page to indicate where the content is stored and which part of the Web page should be clicked to access the content. The second part is built into AutoCAD and picks up when content from an i-drop–enabled Web page is dropped into the drawing window. The AutoCAD side downloads the content to the local drive. The downloaded content usually contains a drawing file that is to

be inserted as a block but can also contain things such as company spec guides or marketing material. The figure shows an image of the DC Online tab of DesignCenter; this tab utilizes i-drop technology.

To use an i-drop–enabled image such as the ones found in DesignCenter, you place the cursor over the image. If the image supports i-drop, an eyedropper icon appears. Click and hold down the mouse button over the image, and then drag and drop the content over the drawing window.

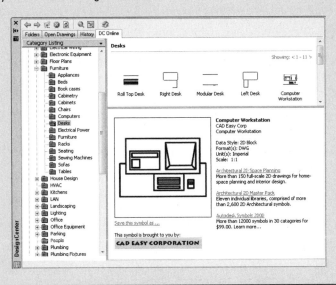

Publishing drawings to the Web

 One of the great things about AutoCAD is its robust set of features that does not just focus on drafting-based features but contains tools for presenting design concepts across the Internet. One of these presentation tools helps to deliver drawing files to the Web through a wizard. This wizard allows you to specify some basic Web template designs, the visual output for the drawing files specified, and different layouts in drawing files. Autodesk calls this feature Publish to Web.

The Publish to Web feature is not meant to be one-size-fits-all; it is designed for people unfamiliar with HTML and Web page design. If you're familiar with HTML and creating Web pages, you may find that the implementation is limiting. However, if you don't know how to create Web pages, you may find Publish to Web purely magical. The feature offers some nice capabilities for dragging and dropping drawing files from a Web page with the use of i-drop, along with the ability to quickly modify a Web page. See the sidebar, "Autodesk i-drop," for information on i-drop.

Drawing files can be published to Web pages by using the PUBLISHTOWEB command. You can start this command in a number of ways:

✦ On the ribbon, click Output tab⇨Publish panel⇨Publish to Web.

✦ On the menu browser or menu bar, click File menu⇨Publish to Web.

✦ At the command prompt type **PUBLISHTOWEB** or **PTW** and press Enter.

Follow these steps to create a simple Publish to Web project:

1. **Save the current drawing before continuing.**

   The Publish to Web feature can't be used on drawings that aren't first saved.

2. **On the ribbon, click Output tab⇨Publish panel⇨Publish to Web.**

   The Publish to Web dialog box appears (see Figure 4-2).

3. **Select Create New Web Page and click Next.**

   The option is pretty self-explanatory. If you select Edit Existing Web Page, you're prompted to select an existing file with the PTW extension that was previously created with the Publish to Web Wizard. After you specify the file, you can edit the page's title and description.

4. **On the Create Web Page page, enter the name of the Web page you're creating, the location where you want the file created, and a description to display with the Web page. Click Next.**

   You can use the Create Web Page page to specify basic configuration information (see Figure 4-3).

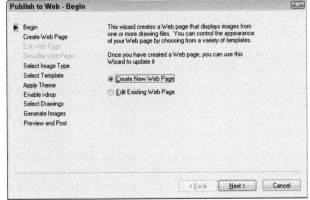

Figure 4-2:
Publishing
content with
Publish to
Web for
viewing on
the Internet.

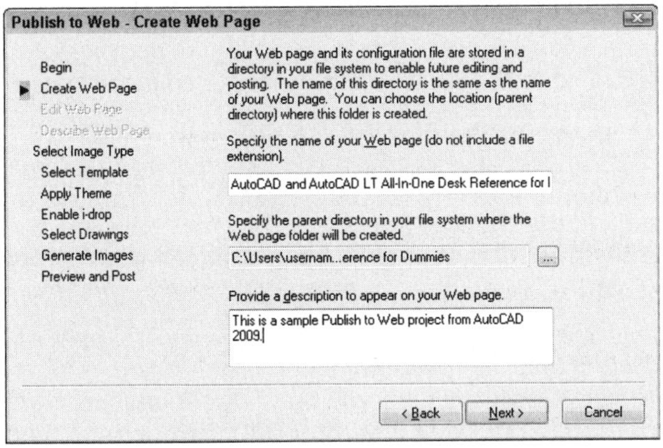

Figure 4-3:
Configuring
the Publish
to Web file.

5. On the Select Image Type page, specify the type of image to create and its size. Click Next.

The Select Image Type page is used to specify the output format for the drawing layouts when they are published. You can choose from four image types: DWFx, DWF, JPEG, and PNG. The image size is available when you specify JPEG and PNG. You can choose from four sizes: Small, Medium, Large, and Extra Large.

6. On the Select Template page, select the template for the desired layout in the Templates list box. Click Next.

The Select Template page is used to specify the basic layout of the images and text on the Web page when the final output is published (see Figure 4-4). You can choose from four templates: Array of Thumbnails, Array plus Summary, List of Drawings, and List plus Summary.

7. On the Apply Theme page, specify the color theme for the Web page by selecting it in the drop-down list. Click Next.

The Apply Theme page is used to add some color to the Web page. If you know HTML, you can change the colors later beyond the seven themes that AutoCAD provides.

8. **On the Enable i-drop page, specify whether i-drop should be enabled on the Web page. Click Next.**

The Enable i-drop page is used to enable i-drop for the thumbnails generated during the publish process. This allows users of the Web page to drag and drop associated drawing files from the Web page into the drawing window.

9. **On the Select Drawings page, specify the layouts from the current drawing file or select a different file. Each layout can have its own label and description. Click Add after you have specified a layout and its label and description.**

The Select Drawings page is used to specify the layouts you want to add to the final published Web page (see Figure 4-5). You work with one drawing at a time and add each layout that you want to the drawing set to be processed. Each layout added to the Web page is displayed in the Image list.

10. **Click Next when you finish adding different layouts.**

There's no limit to the number of layouts that can be specified.

11. **On the Generate Images page, specify which files should be regenerated: only those files that have been changed or all drawing files. Click Next.**

The Generate Images page gives you some control over how long the republishing of a Web page will take. Based on the number of layouts and the size of drawing files, you may want to regenerate the output only for changed drawing files. AutoCAD starts processing the images for output.

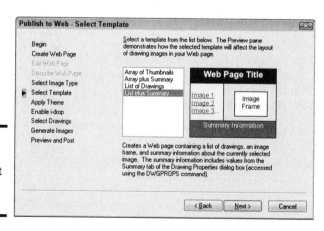

Figure 4-4: Organizing the content of the Web page.

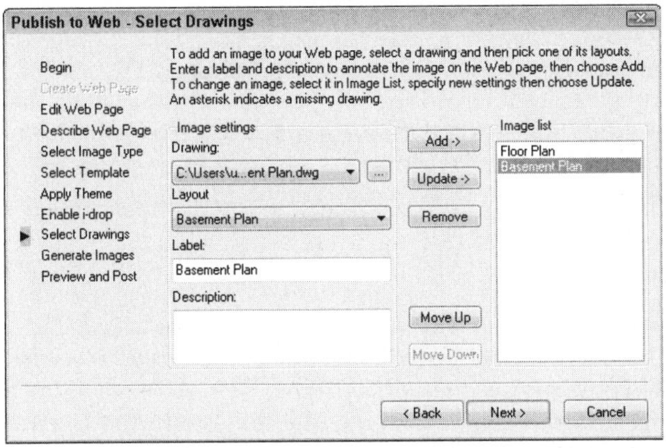

Figure 4-5:
Specifying
drawings
that should
be part of
the Web
page.

12. **On the Preview and Post page, you can preview the results that have been published to the output directory or post them directly to a specific location. Click Preview to preview the Web page.**

The Preview and Post page lets you view what work the feature has done (see Figure 4-6) and allows you to step back and make any necessary changes. Click Post Now to save the Web page to a specific location after the page looks the way you want it to look.

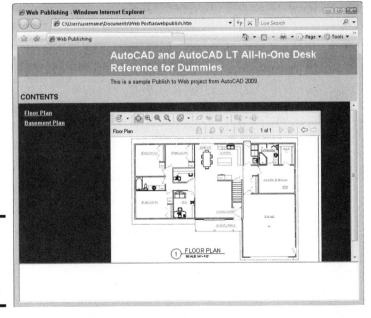

Figure 4-6:
The results
of
publishing
to the Web.

Using Web-based project sites

As the Internet becomes more content enriched and users become more accustomed to using it, software companies are expanding its possibilities for business use. Some software companies, such as Autodesk, are building project-based collaboration sites that allow their customers to share and post drawing files for members of project teams to access.

Autodesk Buzzsaw is a project collaboration site designed around the AEC community (see Figure 4-7). There's even a quick way to access Autodesk Buzzsaw from the file navigation dialog boxes in AutoCAD for opening or saving a drawing file. The project site allows you to define who is part of a project and what type of rights they have. The site is used for placing not just drawing files but any kind of file that might be used to complete a project. The site works similarly to that of a standard file browser application except it has built-in revision tracking and allows you to view files. You can get a free 30-day trial of Autodesk Buzzsaw by visiting www.autodesk.com/buzzsaw/.

Autodesk Buzzsaw has a sister (or brother) site called Autodesk Streamline that's targeted at manufacturers rather than the AEC community. You can use Autodesk Buzzsaw for any type of project, but Autodesk Streamline is optimized to work with the supply chain and suppliers. You can get a free 30-day trial of Autodesk Streamline by visiting www.autodesk.com/streamline/.

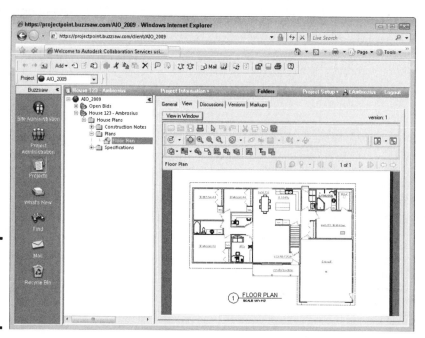

Figure 4-7:
The Autodesk Buzzsaw project site.

The following steps demonstrate how to create a shortcut to a project on Autodesk Buzzsaw and then open a drawing from the site. To complete the steps, a project site has to be created first on Autodesk Buzzsaw.

1. **On the Quick Access toolbar, click Open.**

The Select File dialog box appears.

2. **In the Places list on the left side, click Buzzsaw.**

The Site list box in the center of the dialog box displays a listing of the project site shortcuts that have already been created. You can use one of these shortcuts if the project site you want to access is listed.

3. **In the list, double-click Add a Buzzsaw Location Shortcut.**

The Log In to Buzzsaw Site dialog box appears (see Figure 4-8).

4. **In the Buzzsaw Site box, enter the URL to the project site. Then in the Buzzsaw User Name and Password boxes, enter your assigned user name and password.**

The login information can be retained by selecting the Save Login Name and Password check box.

5. **Click OK.**

The Create a Buzzsaw Location Shortcut dialog box appears (see Figure 4-9).

6. **Under the project site that you entered in Step 4, specify a folder that you want to use for the shortcut. Also enter a name for the shortcut as you want it to appear in the Site list box after it is created. Click OK.**

If you're not sure of the path to the project folder, click the Browse button and a dialog box with a tree view appears so that you can select a folder (see Figure 4-10). After you click OK in the Create a Buzzsaw Location Shortcut dialog box, you return to the Select File dialog box.

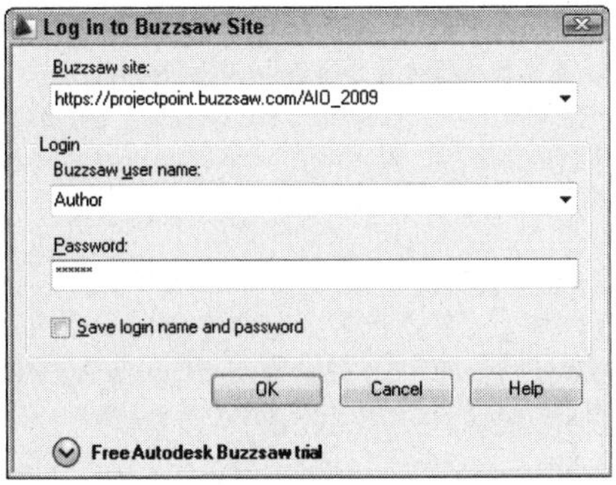

Figure 4-8: Logging into the Autodesk Buzzsaw project site.

7. In the Select File dialog box, open the new shortcut to the Buzzsaw project and select the file you want to open. Click Open.

The Select File dialog box closes, and the selected file opens in the drawing window.

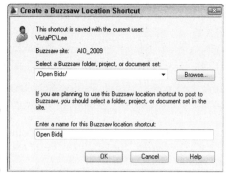

Figure 4-9:
Finalizing
the shortcut.

Figure 4-10:
Selecting a
folder from
Buzzsaw.

Emulating Paper Digitally

The concept of our society using less and less paper when the Internet was born was a great vision, but it's almost a decade since the Internet went mainstream and the shift has yet to happen. The design industry is making the shift to relying more on electronic file sharing than producing hard copies, but a fair amount of paper is still being used.

Paper drawing sets have the following costs:

✦ **Paper:** Paper doesn't simply grow on trees; well, in a way it does, but it costs money to print drawing files on any size of paper.

✦ **Delivery:** Someone has to deliver your printed drawing files to your client, and that usually leads to paying a delivery service. This cost can quickly grow based on the number of drawing sets sent, how much they weigh, and how quickly they need to be delivered.

✦ **Time:** You have to wait for the set of drawings to be delivered by a delivery service to your client's doorstep, and then you have to wait for the drawings to be marked up and returned.

✦ **Hardware maintenance:** The more you plot out to hard copy, the more frequently your plotters and printers will need to be serviced. This can cause downtime and increase the cost of ownership to keep the hardware going.

Going completely electronic isn't the answer either, but based on the phase and size of the project, you may find that speed of delivery and lower costs are nicely associated with using electronic files. Two common electronic file formats are often used to share drawing files: Design Web Format (DWF and DWFx) and Portable Document Format (PDF).

AutoCAD and AutoCAD LT now support the creation of 2D and 3D DWFx files. DWFx is a new version of DWF that is designed for use with Microsoft's XPS Viewer, which comes with Windows Vista and can be installed on a computer running Windows XP. So users of Windows Vista do not require a special viewer to view DWFx files. The DWFx files that can be viewed with the XPS Viewer are limited to 2D geometry only. AutoCAD LT can produce only 2D DWFx files.

Design Web Format (DWF and DWFx)

DWF and DWFx are Autodesk's solutions to a paperless representation of a drawing file or a set of drawing files in a file format that is secure and small enough to be easily e-mailed. A DWF or DWFx file doesn't include all the object properties that are in a drawing file — just enough information to display the drawing accurately on-screen. DWF and DWFx files, like DWG files, are vector-based files rather than raster files. This allows for them to be loaded faster and allows you to manipulate certain aspects of the file as if you were viewing the original drawing file.

DWF and DWFx files have grown in popularity over recent years with more AutoCAD users using them with their clients. Autodesk has been increasing the efficiency and features that DWF and DWFx support in recent releases. DWF files started with support for only 2D objects in a single-sheet file, but now the DWF file format supports 2D and 3D objects, metadata, realtime shading and viewing, and multisheet support.

Most of the products that Autodesk develops for the design community can produce DWF and DWFx files with commands such as PLOT and PUBLISH or

**Book VIII
Chapter 4**

Sharing Electronic Files

a system printer such as the Autodesk DWF Writer, which can be used to print a Word document to a DWF file or any other document that can be printed.

A few releases back, Autodesk had two DWF file viewers: Autodesk DWF Viewer, which was free, and Autodesk DWF Composer, which cost around $100 to $200. Autodesk now offers a single viewer that replaces both Autodesk DWF Viewer and Autodesk DWF Composer. The newest DWF viewer, Autodesk Design Review, is free. It allows you to view, mark up, and print DWF and DWFx files. If a client is running Windows Vista, you can exchange 2D DWFx files with them, and they can use the preinstalled XPS Viewer to view the file with limited methods of navigation.

Portable Document File (PDF)

PDF is Adobe's solution to a paperless representation of a drawing file or any other document that can be printed. A number of PDF drivers are on the market, so when I refer to PDF, I'm referring to it as a file format. Some of the drivers don't take advantage of all the features equally. If you want to take full advantage of the file format, use an application such as Acrobat Professional from Adobe. A PDF file can be viewed by using a free viewer from Adobe called Adobe Acrobat Reader.

Unlike DWF or DWFx, PDF is a much more widely used file format because it has been around longer and is more commonly used for nonengineering-type file formats, such as Word documents and spreadsheets. Over recent years, PDF has gone through some transformations to help improve the type of data that can be stored in the files, so it is much more useful to the design community. PDF files offer security options in the form of password protection and digital signatures.

The ability to produce a PDF file from AutoCAD out of the box has been on the wish list for many years now. AutoCAD 2009 comes with its own plotting device to output to a PDF file format. This driver is called DWG to PDF.pc3 and is available through the PLOT or PUBLISH command.

Head-to-head comparison

DWF, DWFx, and PDF files have their places in the design community; it just depends on your needs and who you are working with. The file format that you choose to use comes down to what the client wants in most cases. Following is a comparison between the three file formats.

+ **Sharing:** DWF or DWFx files are much smaller than PDF files, which is partly because of the optimization of the viewer engine. DWF or DWFx was originally designed for design data and PDF was designed for Word documents. However, most clients likely have Adobe Acrobat Reader on their computer versus Autodesk Design Review used to view DWF and DWFx files.

✦ **Efficiency:** DWF, DWFx, and PDF files can be created in AutoCAD without the need to download and install additional software.

✦ **Viewing:** Both Autodesk Design Review and Adobe Acrobat Reader support panning and zooming of a file, but Autodesk supports a much wider range of resolutions. This allows you to zoom in on a small area of a DWF or DWFx file and have it still look crisp and clear. All three file formats support 3D objects, but DWF and DWFx display 3D geometry better. If you want to create a 3D PDF, though, you need to purchase an additional program from Adobe.

✦ **Printing:** All three file formats can be printed by using both standard and large paper formats.

✦ **Markups:** Autodesk Design Review and Adobe Acrobat Reader support marking up files, but the process is smoother between DWF or DWFx and AutoCAD because of the integrated tools. If you need to do markups, Autodesk Design Review costs less (because it is free) than Adobe Acrobat (not to be confused with Adobe Acrobat Reader, which is free).

✦ **Speed:** It takes less time to create a DWF or DWFx file from a drawing file when compared to a PDF file. This is due to the way the files are generated.

✦ **Compatibility:** Each version of AutoCAD, starting with AutoCAD 2000, has shipped with the ability to create DWF files. AutoCAD 2007 was the first to support PDF, and AutoCAD 2009 is the first to support DWFx. So if you have other releases of AutoCAD in your office, you may need to obtain a PDF print driver from Adobe or a third-party provider or set up a separate computer for just plotting to PDF and DWFx files. Some third-party utilities and even Adobe Acrobat might not always support the latest version of AutoCAD, so it's nice to have a PDF driver that ships with AutoCAD.

✦ **Security:** DWF, DWFx, and PDF files support password protection, but PDF goes beyond that with support for digital signatures.

Working with DWF and DWFx Files

Creating a DWF or DWFx file by using the PLOT or PUBLISH command is straightforward, but what happens after the file has been created? After you create the file, you can share it, and based on those you are sharing it with, they will need a viewer. Autodesk offers a DWF viewer called Autodesk Design Review that allows you to view and print a DWF or DWFx file as well as merge DWF files, mark up files, and perform measurements from point to point. You can download Autodesk Design Review from Autodesk's Web site by going to www.autodesk.com/designreview/.

Creating a DWF or DWFx file

Autodesk provides a number of ways for you to create a DWF or DWFx file, whether you're using AutoCAD or one of the many Autodesk products. From inside AutoCAD, you can use the PLOT and PUBLISH commands to create a DWF or DWFx file. The following steps create a DWF file with the PLOT command:

1. **On the ribbon, click Output tab⇨Plot panel⇨Plot.**

The Plot dialog box is displayed.

2. **In the Printer/Plotter drop-down list, choose DWF6 ePlot.pc3.**

The DWF6 ePlot.pc3 plot device becomes active. Use the DWFx ePlot (XPS Compatible).pc3 plot device to create a DWFx file.

3. **Click the Properties button just to the right of the Printer/Plotter drop-down list.**

The Plotter Configuration Editor — DWF6 ePlot.pc3 dialog box appears. From here, you can access various properties for the device.

4. **In the tree view, select Custom Properties. In the Access Custom Dialog area, click Custom Properties.**

The DWF6 ePlot Properties dialog box appears (see Figure 4-11). In this dialog box, you can specify various options related to creating a DWF file. Properties range from embedding fonts to whether layer names and on/off states are saved with the DWF or DWFx file.

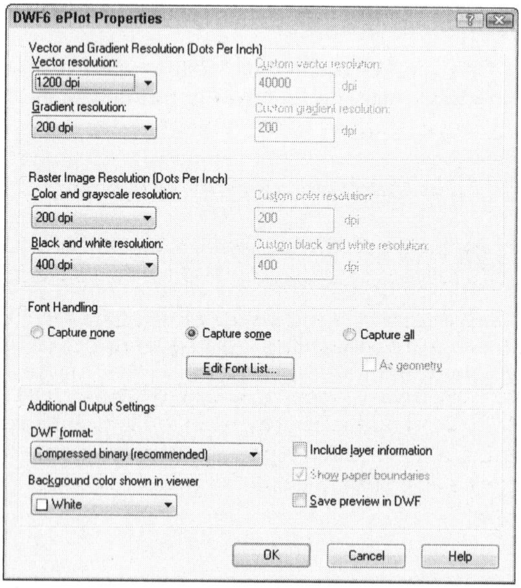

Figure 4-11: Unlocking the properties of the DWF6 ePlot device.

5. **Specify the options as necessary. Click OK twice to return to the Plot dialog box.**

   The changes are saved, and the DWF ePlot Properties and Plotter Configuration Editor — DWF6 ePlot.pc3 dialog boxes are closed.

6. **In the Plot dialog box, specify the necessary options for the plot and then click OK.**

   The Browse for Plot File dialog box appears, allowing you to specify the name of the DWF file that will be created and the location where you want to create it.

7. **Enter the name for the file and where you want to save it, and then click Save.**

   The DWF file is created in the specified location with the name that you entered. After the plot is created, a notification balloon appears to inform you that the Plot and Publish job has completed (see Figure 4-12). You can right-click over the Plot/Publish icon and select View DWF File to view the DWF file.

Figure 4-12:
Plot
notification
balloon.

Viewing a DWF or DWFx file

Autodesk Design Review is not designed for engineers or individuals who already know AutoCAD, but for someone who is familiar with browsing the Internet and creating word processing documents.

DWF and DWFx files can be viewed in a variety of ways. Here are a few:

✦ **Embedded in a document:** DWF and DWfx files can be embedded in a Microsoft Word document or even a PowerPoint presentation file.

✦ **Viewed from a browser:** DWF and DWFx files can be placed online on a Web page to allow for direct viewing and interaction.

✦ **Standalone file viewing:** Autodesk Design Review supports the ability to open a file directly from a local, network, or remote file location. The file is not embedded in a document or part of a Web page. You can launch the viewer to view a DWF or DWFx file by double-clicking the file in Windows Explorer.

The following steps use Autodesk Design Review to open a DWF or DWFx file:

1. **Choose Start (Windows button)⇨[All] Programs⇨Autodesk⇨Autodesk Design Review.**

Autodesk Design Review is launched and by default displays the Getting Started page.

2. **On the menu bar, choose File⇨Open.**

The Open File dialog box appears.

3. **Browse to and select the DWF or DWFx file you want to open. Click Open.**

The selected file opens in Autodesk Design Review. After the file opens, you can pan and zoom around in the file and view the drawing properties published with the file.

Electronically marking up a DWF or DWFx file

You can use DWF and DWFx files with Autodesk Design Review to communicate changes, or *revisions,* to a drafter. Autodesk Design Review contains a number of markup and commenting tools that range from creating a simple line to much more complex tools that allow for the creation of revision clouds around areas in the file. As markup and commenting objects are added, Autodesk Design Review records who added them and when they were added to the DWF or DWFx file.

After the markups and comments have been added to the DWF or DWFx file by using Autodesk Design Review, you can send them back to a drafter to make the necessary changes or plot them off with the viewer. If the DWF or DWFx file with markups is sent back to a drafter who has access to the original drawing file, the markups can be imported into AutoCAD and overlaid over the objects in the drawing by using Markup Set Manager.

Even though you can attach DWF and DWFx files in AutoCAD, the markups are not imported and managed this way. AutoCAD uses the Markup Set Manager palette. You launch the Markup Set Manager palette by using the MARKUP command. You can start the MARKUP command in one of the following ways:

✦ On the menu browser or menu bar, click Tools menu⇨Palettes⇨Markup Set Manager.

✦ On the Standards toolbar, click Markup Set Manager .

✦ Press Ctrl+7.

✦ At the command prompt, type **MARKUP** or **MSM** and press Enter.

To find out more about how to mark up a DWF or DWFx file in Autodesk Design Review, launch Autodesk Design Review and from the menu bar choose Help menu⇨Help.

Book IX

Customizing AutoCAD

The 5th Wave

By Rich Tennant

"Somebody order a birthday cake in the shape of an aluminum VTEK engine block?"

Contents at a Glance

Chapter 1: The Basics of Customizing AutoCAD 639

Why Customize AutoCAD?...639
Customizing the AutoCAD Startup Process.............................641
Changing Options and Working with User Profiles...................647
Creating and Managing Command Aliases...............................652

Chapter 2: Customizing the Interface 657

Influencing Your Status (Bar) 657
Training Your Toolbars, Panels, and Dockable Windows to Stay 662
Controlling the Appearance of AutoCAD and the Drawing Window 664
Organizing Your Space...668

Chapter 3: Customizing the Tools 675

How Customizing the User Interface Has Changed 675
Getting to Know the Customize User Interface Editor 676
Customizing Toolbars, Pull-Down and Shortcut Menus,
   and the Ribbon 684
Creating a New Shortcut Key..696
Customizing Double-Click Actions..697
Customizing the Quick Properties Panel and Rollover Tooltips...........698
Migrating and Transferring Customization...............................700
Working with Partial and Enterprise Customization Files 702

Chapter 4: Delving Deeper into Customization 705

Working from a Script...705
Getting Familiar with Shapes..709
Working with Express Tools 710

Chapter 5: Recording Your Actions 717

Actions and Action Recorder 717
Recording and Managing Action Macros 718
Editing Actions and Recorded Values.....................................723
Just Press Play..724

Chapter 1: The Basics of Customizing AutoCAD

In This Chapter

✔ **Understanding the benefits of customizing AutoCAD**

✔ **Customizing the AutoCAD startup process**

✔ **Changing options and using user profiles**

✔ **Creating and managing command aliases**

*B*ook IX is designed to help both AutoCAD and AutoCAD LT users improve their workflow through customization. The majority of the customization options in Book IX are available in both AutoCAD and AutoCAD LT. Although AutoCAD LT supports a majority of the same customization options that AutoCAD does, there are exceptions. In this chapter, I mention these exceptions as they arise.

Have you ever wanted to find out how to start AutoCAD with a specific user profile or add your own custom command aliases? Maybe you already understand some of the available customization options but want to find out more about others. Whatever the reason, customization can help to improve drawing accuracy and efficiency. Customization is not necessarily easy, but you don't have to be a programmer to take advantage of these features either.

Why Customize AutoCAD?

AutoCAD is one of the most popular computer-aided drafting programs on the market today, but if you take a good look at the program, you'll probably find that you've barely scratched the surface of what it can do. AutoCAD is designed to be flexible and adaptive to the way you work. And if you don't like the layout of the program, you can always change the way it looks.

Not only can you customize the user interface, or UI, but you can also make changes to reduce repetitive tasks and ensure that CAD standards are followed. The level of customization that AutoCAD offers is much more dynamic than many other programs. Customizing AutoCAD is often confused with topics such as AutoLISP and VBA. While AutoLISP and VBA can be used to customize AutoCAD, they fall into the category of programming and are covered in Bonus

Chapters 2 through 5 at www.wiley.com/go/autocad2009aio. You can customize AutoCAD without resorting to any programming.

AutoCAD offers a large variety of customization options — so many, in fact, that you'll probably not use all of them. The options range from creating new ways to start commands to defining how AutoCAD starts. Customization can be used also to define the appearance of line work in a drawing with custom linetypes or custom patterns for hatched areas. Following is an overview of the different customization options available in AutoCAD:

✦ **Drawing templates:** You might not have thought of drawing templates as a form of customization, but they can contain user created objects such as a title block and any drafting settings that might be needed for a new drawing. For more information on drawing templates, see Book I, Chapter 4 and Book VIII, Chapter 1.

✦ **Blocks:** Blocks are a form of customization because you are creating reusable content that can be used in as many drawings as you want. This is one of the most natural forms of customization because you are extending the capabilities of AutoCAD without really knowing that you're customizing it. For more information on blocks, see Book VI, Chapters 1 and 2.

✦ **Linetypes:** Linetypes are used to control the appearance of line work in a drawing file when it's viewed and plotted. AutoCAD comes with a variety of default linetypes, but you may need to create your own for a project to represent, for example, a cable line or a flow direction. For more information on customizing linetypes, see Chapter 4 of this minibook. I talk about using linetypes in Book I, Chapter 6.

✦ **Shapes:** Shapes are one of the earliest forms of creating groups of reusable geometry, predating even blocks. Shapes are still useful when you want to create a complex linetype that can't be represented with dashes, dots, and gaps. For more information on shapes, see Chapter 4 of this minibook.

AutoCAD LT does not support the creation of custom Shape files because it does not support the COMPILE command.

✦ **Hatch patterns:** Hatch patterns control the appearance of filled or hatched areas. AutoCAD ships with a number of default patterns, but you may want to create hatch patterns to represent construction materials such as wood or other patterns not available by default. For more information on hatch patterns, see Chapter 4 of this minibook.

✦ **Tool palettes:** Tool palettes have been around since AutoCAD 2004, and they provide ways to organize and access reusable content such as blocks, hatches, and command tools. Tool palettes allow for multiple levels of organization, so you can access the right tool or content quickly based on the task you're performing. For more information on customizing tool palettes, see Book VI, Chapter 4.

+ **User profiles:** User profiles control the appearance of AutoCAD, drafting settings, and where AutoCAD should look to find core and user-customized files. For more information on user profiles, see "Changing Options and Working with User Profiles" later in this chapter.

+ **User interface:** The user interface refers to the visual aspect of AutoCAD's controls, such as toolbars, ribbon panels, and pull-down menus. Many components of the user interface can be customized by using the Customize User Interface (CUI) editor. For more information on customizing the user interface, see Chapter 3 of this minibook.

+ **Diesel:** Diesel is a macro language that can be used to customize the status bar area of AutoCAD and to control parts of the user interface, such as pull-down menu items. For more information on using Diesel, see Chapter 2 of this minibook.

+ **Command aliases:** Command aliases are used to allow faster access to commands from the command line. Many common commands in AutoCAD are associated with a command alias. An example of a command alias is L for the LINE command. For more information on command aliases, see "Creating and Managing Command Aliases" later in this chapter.

+ **Scripts:** Script files are structured files that allow you to automate standard commands and options. Because these files are based on commands and options that you already use, they are fairly easy to create to reduce repetitive tasks. For more information on script files, see Chapter 4 of this minibook.

+ **Command line switches:** Command line switches allow you to control the startup behavior of AutoCAD. For more information on command line switches, see "Using command line switches" later in this chapter.

+ **Action macros:** Action macros are the newest option AutoCAD offers for customizing and reducing repetitive tasks. With Action Recorder, you can record many of the commands that you're already familiar with and then play back the recorded sequence of commands. For more information on action macro files and Action Recorder, see Chapter 5 of this minibook.

Customizing the AutoCAD Startup Process

AutoCAD offers a number of options to control how it starts. Some of these options can be controlled through the desktop shortcut (or icon), whereas others are controlled through specially named files.

Startup options

Several startup options are available to you. Some require a basic knowledge of programming. AutoCAD LT does not support any of the programming options that AutoCAD does, so it is limited to the startup options that do not involve a programming language. Following is an overview of the startup options in AutoCAD:

✦ **Command line switches:** Command line switches are parameters that can be defined with a shortcut file that is used to start AutoCAD. Command line switches can perform a variety of tasks, from starting with a specific drawing template to specifying the default workspace. For more information on command line switches, see "Using command line switches" later in this chapter.

✦ **Acad.dvb:** Acad.dvb is a VBA project that is automatically loaded at startup. For more information on the Acad.dvb file, see Bonus Chapter 3 on the Web (www.wiley.com/go/autocad2009aio).

✦ **Acad.lsp, Acaddoc.lsp, Acad2009.lsp, Acaddoc2009.lsp:** These AutoLISP files are automatically loaded at the startup of AutoCAD. Neither Acad.lsp nor Acaddoc.lsp ships with the program but instead must be created by you. For more information on the files Acad.lsp, Acaddoc.lsp, Acad2009.lsp, and Acaddoc2009.lsp, see Bonus Chapter 3 at www.wiley.com/go/autocad2009aio.

✦ **Acad.mnl:** Acad.mnl is an AutoLISP file that is associated with the Acad.cui customization file and is loaded when the customization file is loaded. For more information on the Acad.mnl file, see Chapter 3 in this minibook.

✦ **Acad.rx:** Acad.rx is a plain text file that defines which ObjectARX or ObjectDBX files should be loaded at startup. For more information on the Acad.rx file, see Bonus Chapter 3 on the Web (www.wiley.com/go/autocad2009aio).

✦ **Appload — Startup Suite:** The Startup Suite is a feature of the Application Load dialog box to load custom programs developed with AutoLISP, VBA, and ObjectARX. For more information on using the Startup Suite, see Bonus Chapter 3 on the Web (www.wiley.com/go/autocad2009aio).

✦ **LISP Files node:** The LISP Files node in the Customize User Interface (CUI) Editor can be used to load files when the CUI file is loaded. For more information on adding AutoLISP files to the LISP Files node of a CUI file, see Chapter 3 in this minibook.

Of the startup options that were just mentioned, AutoCAD LT supports only the use of command line switches. All the other options are related to programming, which AutoCAD LT does not support.

Using command line switches

Command line switches control the behavior of AutoCAD when it is started from a desktop shortcut or the Start menu. You can customize the desktop shortcut so that a specific drawing template is used to create the default drawing displayed when AutoCAD is started. You can use command line switches also to control which user profile is used when AutoCAD starts. This enables you to have multiple profiles for AutoCAD on the computer and use different desktop shortcuts to switch between them. When using command line switches, make sure that you use " " (double quote marks) around the name of a drawing or drawing template file, a workspace, or a path that contains a space. If you don't use " " around a name or path that contains a space, AutoCAD will assume it is another command line switch or argument.

Table 1-1 lists the different command line switches that are available for AutoCAD.

Table 1-1	Command Line Switches
Switch and Syntax	Description
No switches "...\acad.exe" "drawing1" drawing2 drawing*n*"	If a list of drawings with spaces between each one is provided, AutoCAD opens each file passed to it that can be found.
/b "...\acad.exe" ["drawing"] /b "script"	The /b switch indicates to AutoCAD that it should run the specified script file after it has been started and the default or specified drawing has been opened. For more on using script files, see Chapter 4 in this minibook.
/c "...\acad.exe" /c "configuration file"	Allows you to specify the location of the acad2009.cfg (acadlt2009.cfg) file.
/ld "...\acad.exe" /ld "objectarx/objectdbx_file"	Allows you to load an ObjectARX or ObjectDBX file at startup. For more information on Object ARX and ObjectDBX files, see Bonus Chapter 2 on the Web (www.wiley.com/go/autocad2009aio).
/nohardware "...\acad.exe" /nohardware	Disables hardware acceleration if it was enabled prior to AutoCAD closing the last time it was used.
/nologo "...\acad.exe" /nologo	Suppresses the AutoCAD splash screen at startup./nossm
"...\acad.exe" /nossm	Suppresses Sheet Set Manager when AutoCAD starts, if it was open the last time AutoCAD was closed. For more on Sheet Set Manager, see Book VII, Chapter 2.

continued

Table 1-1 *(continued)*

Switch and Syntax	Description
/p "…\acad.exe" /p "profile_name"	Controls which AutoCAD user profile is used at startup. In addition to being able to specify a profile name, you can also specify the file name of an exported profile that has the ARG extension. When an ARG file is specified, the file is imported and is set current. For more on user profiles, see "Changing Options and Working with User Profiles" later in this chapter.
/pl "…\acad.exe" /p "publish_drawing_set_descriptions"	Allows you to publish a saved drawing set descriptions in the background that is saved with the PUBLISH command. For more information on publishing, see Book VII, Chapter 3.
/r "…\acad.exe" /r	Restores the system-pointer device settings and creates a backup of the current configuration file.
/s "…\acad.exe" /s "path"	Allows you to specify additional support paths that might not be defined on the Files tab of the Options dialog box. For more on support paths and options, see "Changing Options and Working with User Profiles" later in this chapter.
/set "…\acad.exe" /set "sheetset_file"	Allows you to specify a Sheet Set file that should be loaded at startup. For more on Sheet Set Manager, see Book VII, Chapter 2.
/t "…\acad.exe" /t "drawing_template"	Allows you to specify the drawing template that should be used to create the default drawing that is created when AutoCAD starts. For more on drawing templates, see Book I, Chapter 4.
/v "…\acad.exe" "drawing.DWG"/v "kitchen"	Allows you to specify a specific view in the drawing that is being opened. For more information on views, see Book II, Chapter 3.
/w "…\acad.exe" /w "workspace"	Allows you to specify a workspace that should be loaded upon startup. The workspace must exist in one of the loaded customization (CUI) files. For more on workspaces and CUI files, see Chapter 2 of this minibook.

The command line switches /ld, /nohardware, /nossm, /p, /pl, /r, /s, and /set are not supported in AutoCAD LT.

Creating a new desktop shortcut

Follow these steps to create a new desktop shortcut:

1. **Right-click the Windows Start button and click Explore.**

   Windows Explorer is launched.

2. **Navigate to the AutoCAD install folder.**

   By default, AutoCAD 2009 is installed in the folder C:\Program Files\AutoCAD 2009 (or AutoCAD LT 2009 for AutoCAD LT users). The contents of the AutoCAD 2009 (or AutoCAD LT 2009) folder are displayed in the pane on the right side of Windows Explorer.

3. **Locate the acad.exe (or acadlt.exe) file, right-click the file name, and choose Copy.**

   The information about the executable file is copied to the Windows Clipboard.

4. **Minimize all open applications until you see the Windows desktop.**

5. **Right-click an empty area of the desktop and choose Paste Shortcut from the shortcut menu.**

   A new desktop shortcut is created titled Shortcut to acad.exe (or Shortcut to acadlt.exe).

You can right-click an empty area of the Windows taskbar and click Show the Desktop instead of minimizing all application windows one at a time. If you have a keyboard with a flying Windows key, you can also press and hold down the key while pressing the M key to minimize all application windows.

Modifying a desktop shortcut

Follow this procedure to modify the AutoCAD desktop shortcut and add a command line switch:

1. **Right-click the AutoCAD (or AutoCAD LT) desktop shortcut and choose Properties.**

   The Properties dialog box (see Figure 1-1) for the desktop shortcut is displayed.

2. **Click the General tab. In the Name text box next to the icon, enter a new name for the desktop shortcut (see Figure 1-2).**

3. **Click the Shortcut tab. Locate the Target text field just above the middle of the Shortcut Properties dialog box.**

   The Target text field controls the string that's executed when the short-cut is double-clicked with the pointing device.

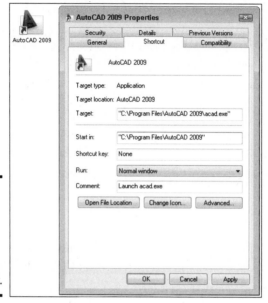

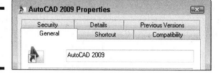

4. **Position the cursor to the right of the text in the Target text field and click.**

The cursor should be located to the right of the text C:\Program Files\AutoCAD 2009\acad.exe (or AutoCAD LT 2009\acadlt.exe).

5. **Enter a space and then add the command line switches you want to use (see Figure 1-3).**

For example, you might enter **/nologo /t "Tutorial-iArch"**. The /nologo switch suppresses the splash screen and the /t switch with the specified drawing template is used to create the default Drawing1.dwg file.

If a value that is used with a command line switch has a space, you must place it between double quotation marks (" and "). This applies to values such as file paths and profile names.

6. **Click OK to save the changes and exit the shortcut Properties dialog box.**

7. Double-click the desktop shortcut to start AutoCAD.

You should notice that no splash screen is displayed when AutoCAD starts and the default drawing Drawing1.dwg now has a title block based on the one defined in the drawing template Tutorial-iArch.DWT.

Figure 1-3:
Setting the target and command line switches for the shortcut.

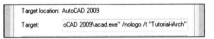

Target location: AutoCAD 2009

Target: oCAD 2009\acad.exe" /nologo /t "Tutorial-iArch"

Changing Options and Working with User Profiles

The Options dialog box (Figure 1-4) is the central hub for controlling many of the behavioral attributes of AutoCAD. From the Options dialog box, you can control drafting settings for grips, selection methods, and the appearance of AutoSnap markers when using running object snaps. The Options dialog box also contains settings that control the appearance of AutoCAD and where it looks to find its support files.

Figure 1-5 shows the Options dialog box in AutoCAD LT.

Figure 1-4:
AutoCAD's Options dialog box.

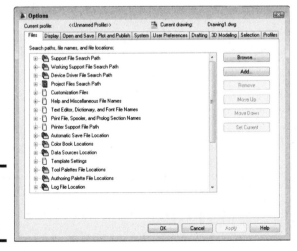

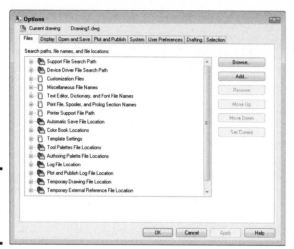

Figure 1-5:
AutoCAD
LT's Options
dialog box.

Launching the Options dialog box

To launch the Options dialog box, use one of these methods:

✦ On the menu browser or menu bar, click Tools menu⇨Options.

✦ Type **OPTIONS** or **OP** at the command prompt and press Enter.

✦ Right-click the command line window and select Options from the short-cut menu. You can also right-click an empty area of the drawing window and choose Options from the shortcut menu.

Overview of AutoCAD options

The Options dialog box has way too many options for me to list each one individually. Instead, here is an overview of the types of options found on each tab in the dialog box:

✦ **Files:** The folders that the program uses to search for support, menu, user-defined, and other files.

✦ **Display:** Options that control how a drawing is viewed, along with settings that control the appearance of the program's application window.

✦ **Open and Save:** Options that control the processes of opening and saving files.

✦ **Plot and Publish:** Options for outputting a drawing or a set of drawings to hard copy or electronic formats.

✦ **System:** Options that control the pointing device and some other general options that control the behavior of the program.

+ **User Preferences:** Options that are unique to users and the way they work with certain features in the program.

+ **Drafting:** Options that affect how things, such as points, are selected in a drawing and how you are prompted for input.

+ **3D Modeling:** Options that affect the creation of 3D objects and navigating a 3D model.

+ **Selection:** Options that affect how objects are selected and the behavior of grip editing.

+ **Profiles:** Options to create and manage user profiles.

The Options dialog boxes for AutoCAD and AutoCAD LT have numerous differences. The two biggest differences are that AutoCAD LT does not support user profiles or 3D modeling, so it does not have the 3D Modeling and Profiles tabs.

Some options are stored in the drawing, whereas others are not saved at all or are stored in the Windows Registry. The options that can be set through the Options dialog box and are stored in the drawing are denoted with the small drawing file icon to the left of the option.

Working with user profiles

A user profile stores options that are defined in the Options dialog box by a given name. This allows you to access a specific configuration of options for task-based procedures or to share them with others in your company. User profiles are stored in the Windows Registry.

Creating a user profile

Follow this procedure to create a new user profile in AutoCAD:

1. **Launch the Options dialog box by using one of the previously described methods.**

The Options dialog box is displayed.

2. **Click the Profiles tab.**

The options for working with profiles are displayed. In the upper-left corner, you can find out which profile is current (see Figure 1-6).

Figure 1-6:
Identifying
the current
user profile.

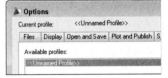

3. Click the Add to List button.

The Add Profile dialog box (see Figure 1-7) is displayed.

4. In the Profile Name text box, enter a name. In the Description text box, enter a description.

The name is what appears in the Available Profiles list and what can be used with the /p command line switch to load a profile at startup. For more information on command line switches, see the "Using command line switches" section earlier in this chapter.

5. Click Apply & Close to add the profile to the list.

The Add Profile dialog box closes, the new user profile is added to the Available Profiles list, and you return to the Options dialog box.

6. Click OK to exit the Options dialog box.

Figure 1-7:
User profiles are added with the Add Profile dialog box.

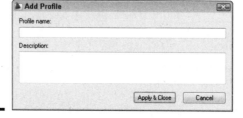

Setting a user profile current

Follow this procedure to set a user profile current:

1. Launch the Options dialog box by using one of the previously described methods.

2. Click the Profiles tab.

3. In the Available Profiles list, select the user profile that you want to set current and then click Set Current.

The user profile is set current and the options are applied to AutoCAD.

4. Click OK to exit the Options dialog box.

Exporting and importing a user profile

Profiles can be exported from AutoCAD, which enables you to back them up in case you need to reinstall AutoCAD or to share them with other AutoCAD users in your company. Follow these steps to export a user profile and then import it back into AutoCAD:

1. **Launch the Options dialog box by using one of the previously described methods.**

2. **In the options dialog box, click the Profiles tab.**

3. **In the Available Profiles list, select the user profile that you want to export and then click Export.**

The Export Profile dialog box is displayed. This dialog box is a standard Windows file navigation dialog box.

4. **In the Export Profile dialog box, browse to and select the folder that you want to export the user profile to, and enter a name for the file in the File Name text box.**

By default, AutoCAD uses the name of the current drawing file for the name of the file that the user profile is being exported to.

5. **Click Save.**

The user profile is exported using the specified file name and folder, and you return to the Options dialog box. The user profile file has the ARG file extension.

6. **In the Options dialog box, click Import.**

The Import Profile dialog box is displayed. This dialog box is a Windows standard file navigation dialog box.

7. **Browse to the folder that contains the exported user profile file that you want to import and select the file.**

8. **Click Open.**

The Import Profile dialog box (see Figure 1-8) is displayed; this dialog box is different from the previous Import Profile dialog box.

Figure 1-8:
Profiles can be exported from AutoCAD and imported back in with the Import Profile dialog box.

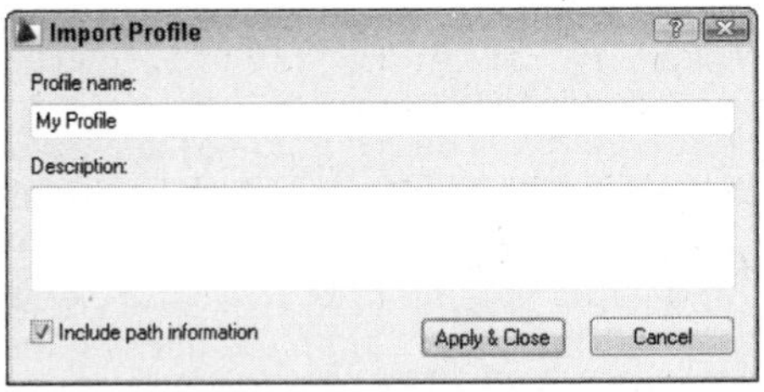

9. **You can use the default name and description or make any necessary changes before importing the profile.**

You also have the option of including the paths stored in the user profile file or use the paths from the current profile. To use the paths from the user profile file that is being imported, click Include Path Information.

10. **Click Apply & Close to complete the importing of the user profile.**

A new user profile based on the imported user profile file is added to the Available Profiles list; if a profile with the same name as the one specified in the Name text box of the Import Profile dialog box already existed, the options of the existing profile are updated.

11. **Click OK to exit the Options dialog box.**

Creating and Managing Command Aliases

Command aliases provide a quick way for you to access a command from the command prompt without being forced to type the entire command name. Command aliases are stored in the Acad.pgp (or Aclt.pgp) file, which is a plain text file stored by default under C:\Documents and Settings*<user name>*\Application Data\Autodesk\AutoCAD 2009\R17.2\enu\Support (or C:\Documents and Settings*<user name>*\Application Data\Autodesk\ AutoCAD LT 2009\R14\enu\Support). You often hear these files referred to as the program's PGP (Program Parameters) files. An example of a command alias is L, which is used to start the LINE command.

Editing the PGP file

Because a PGP file is a plain text file, it can be edited by using a text editor such as Notepad. Two different formats of aliases can be created: external commands and command aliases. External commands allow you to start applications such as Notepad outside AutoCAD, and command aliases allow you to start commands found inside AutoCAD such as the LINE command. Typically, you use command aliases more often than external commands.

The PGP file allows you to define your own command aliases or modify the ones that come with AutoCAD. Adding any new command aliases to the bottom of the PGP file is the best practice: If you do, AutoCAD can identify which ones you have added when you upgrade to a future release of AutoCAD. One thing to note is that if two command aliases define the same alias, the latter one defined in the file is the one that AutoCAD recognizes when it is entered at the command prompt.

Here's a sample of the PGP file:

```
J,          *JOIN
L,          *LINE
LA,         *LAYER
```

The syntax for a command alias is as follows:

```
Alias, *AutoCAD Command Name
```

You should keep the alias to as few characters as possible because the whole idea of an alias is to save you keystrokes. Between the alias and command name, you must use a comma to separate the two arguments, and the command name must be prefixed with * (an asterisk).

AutoCAD LT doesn't support external commands in the PGP file.

Opening the PGP file

To open the PGP file for the program, use one of the following methods:

✦ On the menu browser or menu bar, click Tools menu➪Customize➪Edit Program Parameters (acad.pgp) or (aclt.pgp).

✦ Start Notepad, browse to the location of the PGP file, and open it.

Adding a new command alias

Follow these procedures to create a new command alias:

1. **Open the PGP file by using one of the previously described methods.**

2. **Scroll to the bottom of the file to the User Defined Command Aliases section.**

This is where you should add your own command aliases. Command aliases placed below this section can be migrated forward by using the Migrate Custom Settings dialog box when you upgrade to a new release of AutoCAD.

AutoCAD uses the last alias it finds in the file; this way, your custom command alias can be migrated to a new release if you decide to upgrade in the future.

3. **On a new line, enter the alias you want and the AutoCAD command that should be executed when the alias is typed at the command prompt.**

A command alias uses the syntax Alias,*Command.

Don't make changes to any of the command aliases that come with AutoCAD; instead, create a new command alias with the same alias name and add it to the User Defined Command Aliases section. If you make changes to the command aliases that come with AutoCAD, the command aliases will not be migrated to a future release when you install an upgrade to the program in the future.

The new command alias is now defined in the PGP file.

4. **On the menu bar in Notepad, choose File⇨Save.**

   The new command alias is saved to the PGP file.

5. **Switch back to AutoCAD, and type** REINIT **at the command prompt and press Enter.**

   The Re-initialization dialog box (see Figure 1-9) is displayed.

Figure 1-9:
Clear!!!!
Use the Re-initialization dialog box to reload the PGP file.

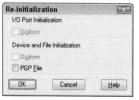

6. **Select the PGP File option and then click OK.**

   The changes to the PGP file are available for use right away; you don't need to close and restart AutoCAD.

Working with the AutoCAD Alias Editor

You may have heard about a collection of tools called Express Tools, which extend the base functionality of AutoCAD in a variety of useful ways. One of the tools in the collection is called the AutoCAD Alias Editor (see Figure 1-10).

This utility allows you to create both external commands and command aliases by using a dialog box interface instead of a text editor like Notepad. It also provides you with a list of all the available commands and system variables in the program. For more information on Express Tools, see Chapter 4 in this minibook.

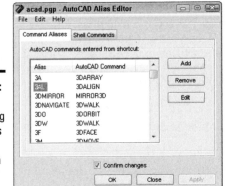

Figure 1-10:
The Alias
Editor dialog
box assigns
a new
identity to a
command.

To launch the AutoCAD Alias Editor dialog box, do one of the following:

✦ On the menu browser or menu bar, click Express
menu⇨Tools⇨Command Alias Editor.

✦ On the command line, type **ALIASEDIT** and press Enter.

Express Tools are not supported for AutoCAD LT because they are a collection of custom programs written with AutoLISP, VBA, and ObjectARX, which AutoCAD LT does not support.

Chapter 2: Customizing the Interface

In This Chapter

✔ Defining what is displayed on the status bar

✔ Training your toolbars, panels, and dockable windows to stay

✔ Controlling the appearance of AutoCAD

✔ Tuning the display of objects in a drawing

✔ Organizing your space

AutoCAD allows you to personalize the overall appearance of the application window and display settings that can affect performance. Many users personalize their AutoCAD session to reflect the way they like to work or the way they want things displayed on-screen. AutoCAD provides you with a lot of control over the appearance of colors and font sizes throughout the application window. The appearance settings include changing the background color of the drawing window and the color of the crosshairs, and controlling the font style and size of text in the command line window.

Not only does AutoCAD offer a variety of options to control the appearance of specific elements found in the application, but it also provides options to control where and if certain user interface elements are displayed. Some of the features that you can control are the buttons on the status bar and the icons in the AutoCAD tray. This chapter explains how to control the appearance of AutoCAD and how to control the display and placement of user interface items such as toolbars and pull-down menus.

Influencing Your Status (Bar)

AutoCAD takes full advantage of every space on its application window. Auto CAD has two status bars, one located at the bottom of the application window and another at the bottom of the drawing window. Both status bars offer a variety of tools that allow for quick access to drafting settings and even notifications about changes taking place in the software and the current drawing.

Some of the tools allow you to toggle a drafting setting on or off; others access a dialog box related to a drafting tool so you can control the behavior of the tool; still others can be used to start a command or change switch scales. For more information on each control on the status bar, see Book I, Chapter 3.

AutoCAD allows you to control the display of various user interface elements, and the status bar is no different. You can control the display of each of the different controls found on the application and drawing window status bars. The application status bar displays the controls and icons available to all open drawings; the drawing window status bar displays the controls and icons specific to the current drawing. When the drawing window status bar is turned off, all the controls and icons are displayed in the application status bar.

You control the display of the drawing status bar and which controls are displayed on the application status bar by clicking the Status Bar Menu button. There are two Status Bar Menu buttons; one is specific to the application and the other is specific to a drawing window. The Status Bar Menu buttons appear as a small downward-pointing black arrow in the lower-right corner of the application or drawing window (see Figure 2-1).

When one of the Status Bar Menu buttons is clicked, a pop-up menu is displayed that contains options to control the display of the different controls on the status bar. Select the item whose display you want to toggle. A check mark next to an item signifies that that item is currently displayed on the status bar. Figure 2-2 shows the pop-up menu that is displayed when the Application Status Bar Menu button is clicked.

Displaying the drawing status bar

The drawing status bar allows you to keep the application status bar clean and simple looking. There is no significant reason to use it or not, other than a personal preference. As mentioned, if the drawing status bar is not displayed, all the controls that would be displayed on the drawing status bar are displayed on the application status bar.

Follow these steps to turn the drawing status bar on and off:

1. **Click the Application Status Bar Menu button (refer to Figure 2-1).**

A pop-up menu with options to control the different tools on the application status bar is displayed.

2. **Select Drawing Status Bar.**

If the Drawing Status Bar option was not selected, the drawing status bar is displayed. Otherwise, the drawing status bar display is turned off.

Figure 2-1:
Ordering
some status
controls
with the
status bar
menus.

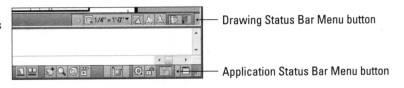

— Drawing Status Bar Menu button

— Application Status Bar Menu button

Figure 2-2:
Application
status bar
menu.
What's on
today's
menu?

Toggling the display of a control on the status bars

If there are things on the status bar that you just don't use, you might want to turn them off. For example, if you don't use the Cursor Coordinate Values display because you use dynamic input, you might want to turn it off.

Follow these steps to toggle the display of a control on the status bar:

1. **Click the button for the application or drawing status bar (refer to Figure 2-1).**

A pop-up menu with options to control the different tools on the status bar is displayed.

2. **Select an item other than Tray Settings.**

The display of the selected item is toggled on or off, and the position of the remaining controls on the status bar is updated.

Tray icons, located in the lower-right corner of the application or drawing status bar, allow you to quickly access certain features. For more information on each of the icons that you may encounter in the application or drawing tray, see Book I, Chapter 3.

You can customize the display of the icons in the tray along with other settings that affect the notification system used in AutoCAD for the services represented by the icons. Here is an overview of the tray settings:

✦ **Display icons for services:** Controls whether icons for services that are running in AutoCAD are displayed in the icon tray on the status bar.

✦ **Display notifications from services:** Controls whether the services display a notification balloon when something they are monitoring changes.

✦ **Display time:** Controls the maximum length of time (in seconds) that a notification balloon should be displayed before it's automatically closed. The time range is from 1 to 10 seconds.

✦ **Display until closed:** Controls whether a notification balloon for a service is displayed until it's dismissed.

Follow these steps to change a tray setting:

1. **Click the Application Status Bar Menu button (refer to Figure 2-1).**

A pop-up menu with options to control the different tools on the application status bar is displayed.

2. **On the menu, select Tray Settings.**

The Tray Settings dialog box (see Figure 2-3) is displayed.

3. **Change the options to the desired settings and click OK.**

The Tray Settings dialog box closes and the notification system and status bars are updated based on the selected options.

Figure 2-3:
Customize
the
notification
system.

Powering the status bar with DIESEL

DIESEL (Direct Interpretively Evaluated String Expression Language) is a macro language that allows you to control the behavior of menu macros and display text on the application status bar. This can be a great way to display information about drafting settings that is not normally displayed on the application status bar, such as linetype scale or the current elevation for drawing new objects. The MODEMACRO system variable is used to display a DIESEL macro on the application status bar. The result of the macro is displayed on the far left side of the application status bar (see Figure 2-4).

Figure 2-4:
Fueling
AutoCAD's
application
status bar
with DIESEL.

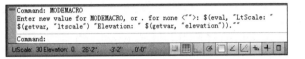

```
Command: MODEMACRO
Enter new value for MODEMACRO, or . for none <"">: $(eval, "LtScale: "
$(getvar, "ltscale") "Elevation: " $(getvar, "elevation"))."
Command:
```

```
LtScale: 30 Elevation: 0.  26'-2",    -3'-2"   ,0'-0"
```

The DIESEL expression used to generate the results shown in Figure 2-4 is

```
$(eval, "LtScale: " $(getvar, "ltscale") " Elevation: "
    $(getvar, "elevation"))
```

Because DIESEL is a macro language, you can use a number of functions with it. DIESEL offers functions for manipulating strings, performing mathematics, and getting system variable values. Some of the more common functions available in DIESEL are

+ **Eval:** Passes the DIESEL expression to the evaluator and returns a value

+ **Upper:** Converts the string to all uppercase letters

+ **If:** Returns one of two values based on whether the conditional expression is true or false

+ **Getvar:** Returns the current value of the specified system variable

+ **+:** Returns the sum of all the provided numbers

+ **–:** Returns the results of subtracting all the provided numbers from each other

For more information on other DIESEL functions, refer to the Catalog of DIESEL Functions topic in the AutoCAD Help system.

Follow these steps to display the results of a DIESEL expression on the status bar:

1. **At the command prompt, type MODEMACRO.**

AutoCAD displays the command prompt:

```
Enter new value for MODEMACRO, or . for none <"">:
```

2. **Enter the DIESEL expression that you want evaluated and displayed on the application status bar, or enter just a period (.) to end the evaluation of the current DIESEL expression and reset the value back to no DIESEL expression (""). Then press Enter to start the evaluation.**

AutoCAD updates the application status bar with the results of the DIESEL expression or returns an error message (see Figure 2-5) in its place. The figure shows that the + function can't be evaluated by displaying $(+, ??) on the application status bar. The error occurred because a string (A) can't be added to a number (2).

Figure 2-5:
Oops, the + function is not evaluating correctly.

Training Your Toolbars, Panels, and Dockable Windows to Stay

Have you ever tried to click a toolbar, panel, or dockable window (palette) only to accidentally move it? This can cause all sorts of cascading effects: Toolbars and panels can end up being shuffled or, even worse, the toolbar, panels, or dockable window might even disappear from the screen. Most of us like everything to stay put.

This is where the user interface (UI) lock option comes into play. With the UI lock option, you can make toolbars, panels, and dockable windows that are floating or docked stay put on-screen. When the option is turned on, you can't accidentally move them from their current position. This is especially useful if you're using a dual monitor setup, where you might have the toolbars, panels, and dockable windows on a separate monitor.

Locking toolbars, panels, and dockable windows

To lock toolbars, panels, and dockable windows, use one of these methods:

✦ On the menu browser or menu bar, click Window menu⇨Lock Location and select one of the available options.

✦ Click the Toolbar/Window Positions icon on the application status bar and then click one of the available options from the shortcut menu.

✦ At the command prompt, type **LOCKUI** and specify a value based on the sum of the bitcodes for the UI elements you want locked or unlocked.

Table 2-1 lists the bitcodes for the LOCKUI system variable.

Table 2-1	LOCKUI Bitcodes
Value	*Description*
0	Toolbars, panels, and dockable windows are not locked.
1	Docked toolbars and panels are locked.
2	Docked dockable windows are locked.
4	Floating toolbars and panels are locked.
8	Floating dockable windows are locked.

Because the value of the LOCKUI system variable is the sum of all the bit-codes, to lock both docked toolbars and dockable windows, you use a value of 3. A value of 1 controls the locking toolbars and panels and a value of 2 controls the locking of the dockable windows (1 + 2).

Locking and unlocking toolbars, panels, and dockable windows

Follow these steps to lock and unlock toolbars, panels, and dockable windows in the AutoCAD user interface:

1. **On the menu browser or menu bar, click Window menu⇨Lock Location⇨Docked Toolbars.**

The grip handles on the left side of the toolbar (see Figure 2-6) are removed and the toolbar can't be undocked or relocated. A check mark appears next to Docked Toolbars.

Figure 2-6:
Image shows the handle (or grip) on a toolbar before (left) and after (right) locking docked toolbars.

Before UI locked   After UI locked

2. **On the menu browser or menu bar, again click Window menu⇨Lock Location⇨Docked Toolbars.**

The grip handles on the left side of the toolbar are visible again. The toolbar can be undocked and relocated once again. The check mark next to Docked Toolbars disappears.

Controlling the Appearance of AutoCAD and the Drawing Window

AutoCAD allows you to customize not only the display of controls on the status bars but also the color scheme used throughout the application. The color scheme can range from the background color of the drawing window to the color of the crosshairs.

The display settings for AutoCAD can be found in the Options dialog box; on the menu browser or menu bar, choose Tools menu⇨Options. In the Options dialog box that appears, click the Display tab. Make the desired changes to the display options and click OK. In the next sections, I cover many of the options found on the Display tab (see Figure 2-7) that affect the appearance of AutoCAD.

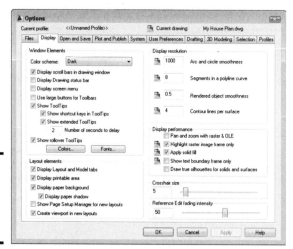

Figure 2-7: The Display tab of the Options dialog box.

Window elements

The options for AutoCAD's window elements are in the Options dialog box on the Display tab under Window Elements. The Window Elements section holds settings for controlling the color scheme of AutoCAD, the display of the screen menu, and whether toolbar buttons are displayed as normal or large buttons, among other settings.

Here is an overview of the options in the Window Elements section:

✦ **Color Scheme:** Controls the internal color scheme used for various user interface elements that are part of the AutoCAD application window. The user interface elements that are affected are toolbars, palettes, the ribbon bar, status bars and the menu browser frame.

✦ **Display Scroll Bars in Drawing Window:** Toggles the display of the vertical and horizontal scroll bars in a drawing window.

✦ **Display Drawing Status Bar:** Toggles the display of the drawing status bar in a drawing window.

✦ **Display Screen Menu:** Toggles the display of the legacy screen menu (sidebar menu).

✦ **Use Large Buttons for Toolbars:** Toggles whether toolbars should be displayed with icons that are 16 × 16 or 32 × 32 pixels.

✦ **Show ToolTips:** Toggles the display of tooltips when the cursor is hovering over a toolbar button.

✦ **Show Shortcut Keys in ToolTips:** Toggles the display of shortcut keys associated with a command as part of the tooltip when the cursor is hovering over a toolbar button.

✦ **Show Extended ToolTips:** Toggles the display of extended tooltips, which are displayed when the cursor continues to hover over a menu item on the menu browser or a button on a toolbar or ribbon panel.

✦ **Number of Second Delay:** Specifies the delay (in seconds) before the extended tooltip is displayed. If set to 0, the extended tooltip is displayed with no delay.

✦ **Show Rollover ToolTips:** Toggles the display of rollover tooltips, which are displayed when the crosshairs continue to hover over an object in the drawing window. The rollover tooltip displays the values of a specified set of properties for the object over which the crosshairs is hovering.

✦ **Colors:** Opens the Drawing Window Color dialog box (see Figure 2-8) and allows you to change the color for the defined interface elements of the different application contexts.

✦ **Fonts:** Opens the Command Line Window Font dialog box (see Figure 2-9) so you can specify the attributes of the font that should be used for text in the command line window and AutoCAD text window.

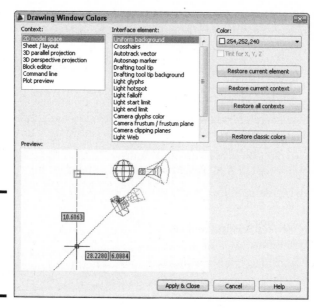

Figure 2-8:
The Drawing Window Colors dialog box.

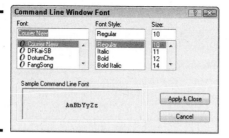

Figure 2-9:
The Command Line Window Font dialog box.

Layout elements

The options for AutoCAD's layout elements are in the Options dialog box on the Display tab. The Layout Elements section holds settings for controlling the appearance of Layout tabs other than the Model tab, the visibility of both Model and Layout tabs at the bottom of the drawing window, and other settings.

Here is an overview of the options in the Layout Elements section:

✦ **Display Layout and Model tabs:** Controls the display of the Model and Layout tabs at the bottom of the drawing window.

✦ **Display Printable Area:** Controls the display of the printable area. The printable area when enabled is represented by the area within the dashed line on a Layout tab.

✦ **Display Paper Background:** Controls the display of the area that represents the size of the paper. The paper background is determined by the selected paper size and the specified plot scale.

✦ **Display Paper Shadow:** Controls the display of a shadow around the bottom and right edges of the paper background to give the effect that you are working on a piece of actual paper.

✦ **Show Page Setup Manager for New Layouts:** Controls the display of Paper Setup Manager when a new layout is added to a drawing. The dialog box is displayed only if the layout has not been initialized yet.

✦ **Create Viewport in New Layouts:** Controls whether or not a single viewport is created when switching to a layout that has not been initialized yet.

Size of the crosshairs

The option for controlling the size of the crosshairs is in the Options dialog box on the Display tab in the Crosshair Size section. You can specify the size of the crosshairs as a percentage of the total screen size. The default percentage of the drawing window is 5, but the range is from 1 to 100.

Using a value of 100 can make it easy to visually align dimensions or text objects. Of course, when it comes to accurately creating objects in a drawing, you shouldn't rely on the eyeball, or close-enough, technique. When you need to accurately create objects, be sure to use objects snaps and other drawing aids. After all, the accuracy of the drawings you create can be critical.

Other settings

In addition to the display-related settings on the Display tab of the Options dialog box, other settings in the Options dialog box affect the appearance of many other features that you've already encountered in AutoCAD. Some of these settings control the color and size of grips as well as the tooltips used for dynamic input. The following is a list of additional places where you can look to alter the appearance of AutoCAD and some of its tools and user interface elements:

✦ **Drafting tab of the Options dialog box:** The Drafting tab allows you to control the appearance of the aperture size on the crosshairs, the AutoSnap marker size and color (which is used with object snaps), drafting tooltips settings for dynamic input, and the settings for light and camera glyphs.

AutoCAD LT does not have light and camera glyph settings on the Drafting tab of the Options dialog box.

✦ **3D Modeling tab of the Options dialog box:** The 3D Modeling tab allows you to control the appearance of the 3D crosshairs and when the View Cube or UCS icon is displayed. For more information on the ViewCube and working in 3D, see Book V.

The 3D Modeling tab of the Options dialog box is not in AutoCAD LT because it doesn't support working with 3D models other than being able to view them.

✦ **UCS Icon dialog box:** The UCS Icon dialog box allows you to control the style, size, and color of the UCS icon. For more information on customizing the UCS icon and using the UCS icon, see Book V, Chapter 2.

Organizing Your Space

AutoCAD uses a feature called *workspaces* to allow you to control the layout of user interface elements. Workspaces control user interface elements such as toolbars, pull-down menus, and dockable windows. Workspaces are saved with a user-defined name in a customization (CUI) file. A majority of workspace customization is handled through the Customize User Interface (CUI) Editor, but you can also do some customization of the workspace directly from the application window of AutoCAD with the help of the WORKSPACE command.

The WORKSPACE command allows you to set a workspace current, save, edit, rename or delete a workspace, change the settings under which a workspace is updated, and control the order in which workspaces are displayed in the user interface. For more information on how to use the CUI Editor with workspaces, see the section, "Using the Customize User Interface Editor," later in this chapter.

Using the Workspaces toolbar

The Workspaces toolbar (see Figure 2-10) offers some level of control over workspaces but not the full control that the Customize User Interface (CUI) Editor does.

Figure 2-10:
Workspaces
toolbar.

Workspace Settings

My Workspace

From the Workspaces toolbar, you can do the following:

✦ **Set a Workspace Current:** From the drop-down list, you can select one of the defined workspaces and set it current.

✦ **Save a Workspace:** From the drop-down list, you can select the Save Current As option to save the current display settings for toolbars, ribbon panels, and dockable windows. The Save Workspace dialog box (see Figure 2-11) is displayed, allowing you to save the changes to overwrite an existing workspace or create a new one.

✦ **Workspace Settings:** The button to the right of the drop-down list on the Workspaces toolbar displays the Workspace Settings dialog box (see Figure 2-12). The Workspace Settings dialog box allows you to specify which workspace is set current when the My Workspace button is clicked on the Workspaces toolbar. The dialog box also allows you to change the order in which workspaces appear in the drop-down list of the Workspaces toolbar and the Workspaces submenu on the Tools menu located on the menu browser or menu bar, and control whether changes to the current workspace are saved automatically before switching workspaces.

✦ **My Workspace:** Sets the workspace specified in the Workspace Settings dialog box current.

Figure 2-11:
Save
Workspace
dialog box.

Figure 2-12:
Workspace
Settings
dialog box.

All the tools that are on the Workspaces toolbar, except for the My Workspace tool, are on the menu browser and menu. Simply choose Tools menu⇨Workspaces.

Creating a new workspace

Follow these steps to create a new workspace by using the Workspaces toolbar:

1. **If the Workspaces toolbar is not displayed, right-click the Quick Access toolbar and choose Toolbars⇨AutoCAD (or AutoCAD LT if you're using AutoCAD LT)⇨Workspaces.**

2. **Move some of the toolbars and dockable windows around on-screen.**

By moving some of the toolbars and dockable windows, you should be able to tell whether the changes have been saved to the new workspace.

3. **On the Workspaces toolbar, select Save Current As from the Workspaces drop-down list.**

The Save Workspace dialog box is displayed.

4. **In the Name text box, enter a name for the new workspace. Click Save.**

The new workspace is saved to the main customization file and added to the drop-down list on the Workspaces toolbar. An entry for the new workspace is also added under Tools menu⇨Workspaces on the menu browser and menu bar.

5. **Switch between different saved workspaces from the drop-down list to see how they are different.**

Saving changes to an existing workspace

To update an existing workspace, follow the same steps that were in the preceding section, "Creating a new workspace." However, instead of entering a name in the Name text box in Step 4, select an existing workspace in the drop-down list. Then click the Save button to update the workspace.

Using the Customize User Interface Editor

The Customize User Interface (CUI) Editor, unlike the Workspaces toolbar, offers a full range of control over workspaces. The one thing that you can't define by using the CUI Editor is which workspace is displayed when the My Workspace button on the Workspaces toolbar is clicked.

From the CUI Editor, you can do the following:

✦ **Create a workspace:** The Customizations In pane allows you to create a new workspace.

✦ **Manage workspaces:** The Customizations In pane allows you to rename, delete, and set a workspace current, among other options.

✦ **Transfer workspaces:** The Transfer tab allows you to transfer workspaces between two different CUI files.

✦ **Display and order menus:** The Workspace Contents pane allows you to specify which menus from the loaded CUI files are displayed on the menu browser or menu bar of AutoCAD and the order in which they appear.

✦ **Display and position toolbars:** The Workspace Contents pane allows you to specify the location of a toolbar and which ones should be visible when the workspace is set current.

✦ **Display and position dockable windows:** The Workspace Contents pane allows you to specify the location of a dockable window and which ones should be visible when the workspace is set current, along with some other properties specific to a dockable window.

✦ **Display and position ribbon panels:** The Workspace Contents pane allows you to specify which ribbon panels are displayed and the order in which they appear on the ribbon bar.

✦ **Access commands on the Quick Access toolbar:** The Workspace Contents pane allows you to specify the commands displayed on the Quick Access toolbar, along with the order in which they appear.

✦ **Specify other user interface options:** The Properties pane allows you to specify additional user interface settings to control the display of scroll bars, the status bar, and the Model and Layout tabs, among other settings.

Creating a new workspace

Follow these steps to create a new workspace by using the CUI Editor:

1. **On the menu browser or menu bar, click Tools menu⇨Customize⇨ Interface.**

The Customize User Interface (CUI) Editor is displayed.

2. **Click the Customize tab.**

3. **In the Customizations In pane, right-click the Workspaces node and choose New⇨Workspace.**

The Workspaces node expands and a new workspace named *Workspace1* is added.

4. **Enter a new name for the workspace in the in-place editor, or change the default name in the Name field in the Properties pane.**

The workspace is renamed.

5. **In the Workspace Contents pane, click Customize Workspace.**

The workspace is now opened for editing.

6. **In the Customizations In pane, expand the Toolbars, Menus, and Ribbon Tabs nodes. Choose the toolbars, menus, and ribbon tabs you want displayed when the workspace is set current.**

As you select toolbars, menus, and ribbon tabs from the Customizations In pane, they are added to the corresponding nodes in the Workspace Contents pane.

7. **In the Workspace Contents pane, click Done.**

The changes are saved to the workspace.

8. **Click OK.**

The changes are saved to the main CUI file.

Changing the order of pull-down menus

Follow these steps to reorder the menus that are part of a workspace:

1. **On the menu browser or menu bar, click Tools menu⇨Customize⇨ Interface.**

The Customize User Interface (CUI) Editor is displayed.

2. **Click the Customize tab.**

3. **In the Customizations In pane, click the plus sign next to the Workspaces node to expand it.**

The Workspaces node expands, revealing the workspaces in the main CUI file.

4. **Select the workspace in which you want to change the menu order.**

The Workspace Contents pane is displayed, allowing you to make changes to the properties of the associated toolbars, menus, and ribbon tabs.

5. **In the Workspace Contents pane, click the plus sign next to the Menus node.**

The associated menus are displayed under the Menu node.

6. **Select the menu you want to reposition. Keep holding down the mouse button and drag the menu to its new position. Then release the mouse button.**

A horizontal indicator is displayed between the menus to show where the menu being dragged will be placed when the mouse button is released.

If you move the CUI Editor so that you can see the menu bar along the top of AutoCAD, you can click Apply to see the menus change position without exiting the CUI Editor first. If the menu bar is currently not displayed, set the Menu Bar property in the Properties pane to On. See the next section to change the properties associated to a workspace.

7. Click OK.

The updated position of the menus is saved to the main CUI file.

Other workspace properties

Follow these steps to adjust some of the other properties for the workspace:

1. On the menu browser or menu bar, click Tools menu⟹Customize⟹ Interface.

The Customize User Interface (CUI) Editor is displayed.

2. Click the Customize tab.

3. In the Customizations In pane, click the plus sign next to the Workspaces node to expand it.

The Workspaces node expands, revealing the workspaces in the main CUI file.

4. Select the workspace for which you want to change properties.

The Properties pane is displayed, allowing you to access the properties for the workspace.

5. Change the properties for the workspace as desired.

The Properties pane contains many properties that control some of the different user interface elements in AutoCAD.

If you select one of the rows in the Properties pane for the workspace, a brief description appears in the lower portion of the pane for the selected row.

6. Click OK.

The property changes are saved to the main CUI file.

Maximizing the drawing space

AutoCAD displays tools such as toolbars, menus, the ribbon bar, and status bars throughout the user interface so you can quickly access different drafting tools as you need them. At times, you may not need these tools and may instead want more space to work with. AutoCAD offers a tool that suppresses the display of some of the user interface elements so you have more drawing real estate; this tool is called Clean Screen.

Clean Screen does exactly what the name suggests: It gives you a clean screen to work with. It maximizes AutoCAD, turns off all the toolbars, ribbon panels, and dockable windows (palettes), and even hides the caption bar along the top of AutoCAD. The menu bar is still available along with the command line window if they're displayed before Clean Screen is enabled.

To use the Clean Screen tool, do one of the following:

✦ On the menu browser or menu bar, click View menu⇨Clean Screen.

✦ Click the Clean Screen icon, which is located on the rightmost side of the application status bar.

✦ Press Ctrl+0 (zero).

✦ At the command prompt, type **CLEANSCREENON** and press Enter. Typing **CLEANSCREENOFF** and pressing Enter returns AutoCAD to its previous state.

Chapter 3: Customizing the Tools

In This Chapter

✓ **Getting to know the Customize User Interface (CUI) Editor**

✓ **Creating commands in the CUI Editor**

✓ **Customizing toolbars, menus, shortcut keys, and the ribbon**

✓ **Customizing double-click actions**

✓ **Controlling the display of properties for the Quick Properties panel and rollover tooltips**

✓ **Migrating and transferring customization**

✓ **Working with partial and enterprise customization files**

*A*utoCAD customization goes beyond just being able to change the appearance of the application window or controlling the regeneration process of a drawing. AutoCAD allows you to create your own toolbars, menus, shortcut keys, and ribbon tabs and panels, among other user interface elements. This flexibility allows you to further integrate AutoCAD into your workflow and to manage CAD standards.

To customize the user interface, you use the Customize User Interface (CUI) Editor. The CUI Editor is a graphical editor that reads and writes to customization files that have a CUI file extension. The CUI Editor and CUI file format were introduced in AutoCAD 2006.

How Customizing the User Interface Has Changed

Users have been able to customize the user interface dating all the way back to AutoCAD R12 and even earlier releases. Since then, many additions have been made to the user interface, including toolbars and shortcut keys, but one thing has always remained consistent: Customization was done by editing an ASCII text file with a text editor outside AutoCAD. That all changed with AutoCAD 2006 and the CUI file format.

If you are relatively new to AutoCAD, you might not know much about previous releases of the program. Those of you who have done some menu customization with AutoCAD 2005 and earlier releases might be familiar with the MNU, MNS, MNC, and MNR file types. The CUI file format replaced the MNU, MNS, and MNC file formats, but the MNR file type is still used even to this date. A description of each file type that I just mentioned follows:

✦ **MNU:** A Menu Template file was used to build MNS files and contained comments and the structure that defined the elements in the user interface. This file needed to be updated manually and was an ASCII text file.

✦ **MNS:** A Menu Source file was based on an MNU file and usually contained fewer comments than the MNU file from which it was created, but also contained the defined structure plus some additional elements that might have been added by using the Customize dialog box in AutoCAD. The file was an ASCII text file.

✦ **MNC:** A Compiled Menu file was a binary version of an MNS file and was the file that was loaded into AutoCAD to speed up the loading of the user interface elements before the introduction of the CUI file.

✦ **CUI:** A Customization file that is an XML-based file that replaced the use of the MNU, MNS, and MNC files for customizing the user interface of AutoCAD.

✦ **MNR:** A Menu Resource file contains all the images used for the commands in the complied MNU/MNS file or CUI file, and is a binary file.

Getting to Know the Customize User Interface Editor

The Customize User Interface (CUI) Editor (see Figure 3-1) is a graphically based editor that allows you to customize many of the user interface elements, such as toolbars, menus, and the ribbon. It is also designed to allow you to migrate and transfer existing menu customizations into the latest release of AutoCAD. In the next few sections, I cover the different panes of the CUI Editor, launching the CUI Editor, and some of the basics involved with customizing the AutoCAD user interface.

The CUI Editor has three main panes: Customizations In pane, Command List pane, and Dynamic pane. The Dynamic pane covers the entire right side of the Customize tab of the CUI Editor and is the most active pane — it displays information and properties for the selected item in the Customizations In or Command List pane.

Figure 3-1:
The
Customize
User
Interface
(CUI) Editor.

The Customizations In pane

In the Customizations In pane (see Figure 3-2), you access the user interface elements of any of the loaded customization files in the CUI Editor. Two different base customization files can be loaded: *main* and *enterprise customization* files. The main and enterprise customization files can load additional files known as *partial customization* files. Enterprise and partial customization files make managing and sharing customization with multiple users easier. Each of the loaded customization files can contain any number and type of user interface elements, such as toolbars, menus, shortcut keys, and ribbon panels and tabs. The main and enterprise customization files that should be loaded are specified under the Customization Files node of the Files tab in the Options dialog box. For more information on partial and enterprise customization files, see the section "Working with Partial and Enterprise Customization Files" later in this chapter.

At the top of the Customizations In pane, you can open a customization file, load a partial customization file, and save the changes to all the current customization files. The tree view under the Customizations In pane is where you create new user interface elements such as toolbars and menus. The tree view allows you to add commands to a user interface element and control the order in which they appear after the CUI Editor is closed.

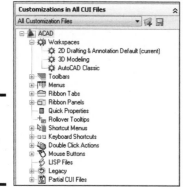

Figure 3-2:
The Customizations In pane.

The Command List pane

The Command List pane (see Figure 3-3) is where you find all the commands contained in the loaded CUI files. This is one of the best changes in menu customization since AutoCAD 2005 and earlier. In releases of AutoCAD prior to 2005, if you wanted to use the same command for a toolbar button, a menu item, and a shortcut key, you had to duplicate the command macro three times. If you needed to make a change to the macro, you had to change it three separate times. With the introduction of the CUI file and the CUI Editor, commands are maintained in a centralized location and are referenced by the user interface element that they are placed on and are not copies of the command.

Figure 3-3:
The Command List pane.

The Command List pane is also where you go when you want to add a reference of a command to a user interface element, such as a toolbar. To add a command to a toolbar, you drag it from the Command List pane and drop it onto the correct node under the Toolbars node. Just above the Command list in the Command List pane is a drop-down list that contains a set of categories that can be used to filter the commands displayed in the Command List pane. You can also use the Search Command List box and the Filter the Commands button to filter the Command list based on a specific keyword.

The Dynamic pane

The Dynamic pane runs vertically down the entire right side of the CUI Editor and reacts to what you select in the Customizations In and Command List panes. The Dynamic pane can display a number of different panes based on what is selected on the left side of the CUI Editor. Here is an overview of each of the different panes that can be displayed in the Dynamic pane:

✦ **Button Image:** The Button Image pane (see Figure 3-4) allows you to access and select one of the preloaded images for a button or create a new image. The Button Image pane is active when a command is selected below one of the nodes in the Customizations In pane or in the Command List pane.

✦ **Information:** The Information pane provides an overview of each top-level node in the Customizations In pane. The Information pane is available only when a top-level node in the Customizations In pane is selected or when one of the nodes under Keyboard Shortcuts or Legacy is selected.

✦ **Panel Preview:** The Panel Preview pane allows you to get an idea of what a panel looks like while you are adding, removing or modifying commands and controls on a ribbon panel before you close the CUI Editor. The Panel Preview pane is available only when a ribbon panel is selected under the Ribbon Panels node of the Customizations In pane.

✦ **Properties:** The Properties pane (see Figure 3-5) allows you to adjust the properties of a selected item in the CUI Editor. The properties that can be edited change based on the item selected.

Figure 3-4:
The Button
Image pane.

Figure 3-5:
The
Properties
pane.

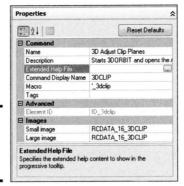

✦ **Quick Properties:** The Quick Properties pane allows you to control which object types and their properties are available when you use the Quick Properties panel or rollover tooltips. You can control the display of general properties and object-specific properties. The properties that are available to display are the same ones that are displayed on the Properties palette.

The Quick Properties pane is new in AutoCAD 2009 and is used for customizing the properties of the Quick Properties panel and rollover tooltips.

✦ **Shortcuts:** The Shortcuts pane provides you with an overview of all the shortcut and temporary override keys that have been defined and also allows you to print a copy of the keys or to copy the list of keys to the Windows Clipboard.

✦ **Toolbar Preview:** The Toolbar Preview pane allows you to get an idea of what a toolbar looks like while you are adding, removing, or modifying commands and controls on a toolbar before you close the CUI Editor. The Toolbar Preview pane is available only when a toolbar is selected under the Toolbars node of the Customizations In pane.

✦ **Workspace Contents:** The Workspace Contents pane allows you to customize which commands are displayed on the Quick Access toolbar, and which toolbars, menus, ribbon tabs, and dockable windows should be displayed when the workspace is set current. The pane is also used to control the order of menus on the menu browser and menu bar, and the order in which ribbon tabs appear on the ribbon.

Launching the CUI Editor

To launch the CUI Editor, use one of these methods:

✦ On the ribbon, click Tools tab⇨Customization panel⇨User Interface.

✦ On the menu browser or menu bar, click Tools menu⇨Customize⇨Interface.

✦ At the command line, type **CUI** and press Enter.

✦ Right-click a toolbar or ribbon panel, and then click Customize from the shortcut menu that appears.

Commands in the CUI Editor

Commands in the CUI Editor are not the same as an AutoCAD command such as LINE. A command in the CUI Editor can be made up of AutoCAD commands, command options, and AutoLISP expressions. After you create a command, you can use it with most of the user interface elements supported in the CUI Editor.

Understanding a command macro

At the core of a command in the CUI Editor is its macro property. The macro is what is carried out when the command is selected from a toolbar or ribbon button, menu item, or one of the other user interface elements that is referencing the command. Macros can contain special characters that are normally not allowed at the command line.

Table 3-1 lists the most frequently used special characters that can be part of a macro.

Table 3-1	Special Characters for a Macro
Special Character	*Description*
; or [blank space]	Acts like the user pressed the Enter key
\	Pauses for user input
_	Translates the command or option so it can be used in an international version of AutoCAD
*	Repeats the command until Esc is pressed
^C	Acts like the Esc key was pressed a single time
\\	Allows for the use of the backslash in a macro
.	Forces AutoCAD to use the standard AutoCAD command even if the command was undefined or redefined as something else

An example of a macro is

```
^C^C^C._line;\\\_c
```

This macro starts the LINE command, allows the user to select a total of three points, and then closes the object, as follows:

+ `^C^C^C` issues three cancels to exit any running command.

+ `._line` starts the LINE command.

+ `;` issues an Enter to start the LINE command.

+ `\\\` asks the user for three different input values. In this case, the input should be in the form of coordinate input values.

+ `_c` uses the Close option of the LINE command to draw a line between the first and last points.

When you want to make sure that no other command is running when your macro begins, use three ^C sequences to make sure that the current command that might be active has ended. The DIM command requires two ^C sequences to exit the command, while the –LAYER command can require up to three at the lowest level of the Color option.

Creating a new command

Follow these steps to create a new command in the CUI Editor:

1. On the ribbon, click Tools tab➪Customization panel➪User Interface.

The CUI Editor is displayed.

2. In the Command List pane, click Create a New Command.

A new command named *Command1* is added to the list box by default, and the Button Image and Properties panes are displayed. If the name already exists, the new command is named *Command2* and so on.

3. In the Properties pane, change the command's Name, Macro, and Element ID.

The Name allows you to identify the command in the list under the Command List pane; the Macro defines what happens when the command is selected from the user interface; and the Element ID uniquely identifies the command through automation or when migrating the command between releases. For information on these and other properties, take a look at the description provided at the bottom of the Properties pane.

4. Click Apply save the changes and stay in the CUI Editor, or click OK to save the changes and exit the CUI Editor.

The changes are saved to the file.

The Tags and Extended Help File properties are new in AutoCAD 2009. The Tags property allows you to group commands and locate commands when performing a search for a command with the Search box on the menu browser. The Extended Help File property allows you to add additional help to a command's tooltip that can contain illustrations and rich formatted text.

Assigning an image to a command

Assigning a small and large image to a command is optional. However, if you plan on using the command on a toolbar, menu, or ribbon panel, you may want to add images to the command so that it matches many of the commands that come with AutoCAD. Follow these steps to assign an image to a command:

1. **On the ribbon, click Tools tab⇨Customization panel⇨User Interface.**

The CUI Editor is displayed.

2. **Select a command in the list.**

The command is highlighted and its properties are displayed in the Properties pane.

3. **In the Button Image pane, select either the Large, Small, or Both option. Then click one of the images in the list.**

Based on the size option that you select, the value is populated in the Small or Large (or both) Image properties for the command. Optionally, you can also edit an existing image to create a new image for your command by using the Edit button. If you have an image that you created in a separate program or one that exists from a previous release, you can select the Small or Large Image fields in the Properties pane and then click the ellipsis (. . .) button that is displayed (see Figure 3-6).

4. **Click Apply to save the changes and stay in the CUI Editor, or click OK to save the changes and exit the CUI Editor.**

AutoCAD provides a special location for you to store custom icons for commands. The location that AutoCAD designates by default is

```
C:\Documents and Settings\<user name>\Application
     Data\Autodesk\AutoCAD 2009\R17.2\enu\Support\Icons
```

You can store your custom icons in this location or in one of AutoCAD's support paths. You can change the location for the custom icons by clicking Customization Files⇨Custom Icon Location on the Files tab of the Options dialog box.

Figure 3-6:
Browsing
for a custom
image.

Assigning a help string to a command

Assigning a help string to a command is optional. However, a help string can give the users of the custom command a brief description of the command before they select it. Help strings appear in the status bar when the cursor hovers over a menu item on a pull-down or shortcut menu, or in a tooltip for a menu item on the menu browser or a button on a toolbar or ribbon panel.

Even though user interface elements such as toolbars and menus have a description property, the value entered is never displayed in the user interface like it is for commands and therefore can be used for entering comments about the toolbar or menu, such as revision information. Follow these steps to assign a help string to a command:

1. **On the ribbon, click Tools tab⇨Customization panel⇨User Interface.**

The CUI Editor is displayed.

2. **Select a command in the list.**

The command is highlighted and its properties are displayed in the Properties pane.

3. **In the Properties pane, enter the help string value in the Description box.**

4. **Click Apply to save the changes and stay in the CUI Editor, or click OK to save the changes and exit the CUI Editor.**

In addition to using the Description box to provide a help string or tooltip for a command, you can assign an extended help item stored in an XAML file that can contain additional information about the command and might display an image to visually illustrate what the command does. Extended help is displayed when the cursor hovers over a command on the menu browser, toolbar, or ribbon panel for a designated time interval. To find out more about creating and assigning extended help, open AutoCAD's Help by pressing F1 and then click Contents tab⇨Customization Guide⇨Customize the User Interface⇨Customize Commands⇨Create Tooltips and Extended Help for Commands.

Extended help is displayed when the Show Extended ToolTip and Show ToolTips options on the Display tab of the Options dialog box are selected. In the Number of Seconds to Delay box on the Display tab of the Options dialog box, you can set the time interval that the cursor must hover over a command. Setting a time interval of 0 seconds causes the extended help to be displayed when the tooltip is displayed.

Customizing Toolbars, Pull-Down and Shortcut Menus, and the Ribbon

Because AutoCAD is a Windows-based application, it utilizes toolbars, menus, shortcut menus, and the ribbon as part of its user interface. These are by far the most widely used UI elements in AutoCAD because they provide access to a majority of the drafting and editing commands that AutoCAD has to offer.

Quick Access toolbar

The Quick Access toolbar is displayed in the upper-left corner of AutoCAD, just to the right of the Menu Browser button. You can use the CUI Editor to customize the Quick Access toolbar by adding, removing, and repositioning commands. The commands that are displayed on the Quick Access toolbar are based on the current workspace, so to customize the Quick Access toolbar you must first select the workspace you want to edit by selecting a workspace under the Workspaces node in the Customizations In pane.

After a workspace is selected, the Workspace Contents pane is displayed in the Dynamic pane. Expand the Quick Access Toolbar node and perform the following:

- ✦ **Add a command:** Select a command in the Command List pane. Hold down the left or right mouse button, drag the selected command to the Quick Access Toolbar node, and release the mouse button when the cursor is over the Quick Access Toolbar node or the splitter bar is displayed where you want the command displayed.

- ✦ **Remove a command:** Right-click a command under the Quick Access Toolbar node, and choose Remove from Workspace.

- ✦ **Reposition a command:** Select a command under the Quick Access toolbar and hold down the left or right mouse button. Then drag the command up or down and release the mouse button when the splitter bar is displayed where you want the command to be displayed on the Quick Access toolbar.

The Quick Access toolbar is a new user interface element that has been added to AutoCAD 2009 and allows you to access a set of commands no matter which toolbar or ribbon tabs are displayed.

Toolbars

Toolbars are small windows that can be docked along the edges of the application window or undocked *(floating)*. They allow you to quickly access commands and options through buttons, drop-down lists, and flyouts. A *flyout* is a way to access the commands contained on another toolbar through a single button. They help keep the user interface looking clean without the need to display the entire toolbar.

Creating a new toolbar

Follow these steps to create a new toolbar and assign a command from the Command List pane:

1. **On the ribbon, click Tools tab⇨Customization panel⇨User Interface.**

The CUI Editor is displayed.

2. **In the Customizations In pane, right-click the Toolbars node and choose New Toolbar.**

A new toolbar with the default name *Toolbar1* is created under the Toolbars node.

3. **In the Properties pane, change the name and alias of the toolbar by using the Name and Alias boxes.**

The name allows you to identify the toolbar in the CUI Editor. The alias uniquely identifies the toolbar through automation when migrating the toolbar between releases, or when using the toolbar as a flyout. You can also control how the toolbar is initially displayed through the properties in the Appearance section.

4. **In the Command List pane, select the command that you want to add to the toolbar. Hold down the mouse button and drag the command to the new toolbar under the Toolbars node of the Customizations In pane. Release the mouse button when the cursor is over the toolbar (see Figure 3-7).**

A reference to the command is added under the toolbar.

To select more than one command at a time to assign to a toolbar, hold down the Shift or Ctrl key while selecting commands.

5. **Click Apply to save the changes and stay in the CUI Editor, or click OK to save the changes and exit the CUI Editor.**

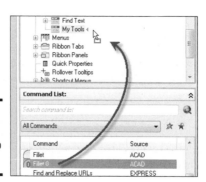

Figure 3-7:
Adding a command to a toolbar.

When adding a new user interface element such as a toolbar or menu, make sure to add a command to it before clicking Apply. Otherwise, the user interface element will not be saved to the file.

Creating a new flyout

Follow these steps to create a flyout on a toolbar:

1. **On the ribbon, click Tools tab⇨Customization panel⇨User Interface.**

   The CUI Editor is displayed.

2. **Create a new toolbar and change its name and alias by using the Name and Aliases boxes in the Properties pane.**

   A new toolbar is created under the Toolbars node, and the Name and Alias properties are updated based on the provided values.

3. **Click and drag the new toolbar above or below one of the commands on the toolbar on which you want to create the flyout.**

   A new reference to the toolbar is created on the toolbar (see Figure 3-8).

4. **Add commands to the new toolbar or flyout.**

   The new commands are displayed under the toolbar and flyout.

5. **Click Apply to save the changes and stay in the CUI Editor, or click OK to save the changes and exit the CUI Editor.**

Figure 3-8:
Adding a
flyout to a
toolbar.

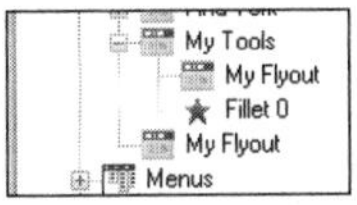

You can also right-click a toolbar and choose New Flyout to create a new toolbar and add the flyout reference to a toolbar. This method does introduce at least one additional step: When you rename the toolbar, the name of the flyout does not change automatically to match the toolbar's name, so you have to rename both the flyout and the toolbar.

Commands and flyouts can be repositioned on a toolbar. Select the command or flyout. Hold down the mouse button, drag up or down, and release the mouse button when the splitter bar is displayed where you want the command or flyout to be displayed.

Menus

Menus take up much less space than toolbars and contain a much wider selection of commands when compared to toolbars. Menus are not as efficient as toolbars because they require additional clicks to access a command, but they do offer much greater organization. Pull-down menus support submenus, which are like flyouts on a toolbar in that they both organize groups of similar commands. Submenus are different than flyouts because they are part of the menu and do not rely on another menu for their content. Menus can be displayed on the menu browser and the menu bar.

Creating a new menu

Follow this procedure to create a new menu:

1. **On the ribbon, click Tools tab⇨Customization panel⇨User Interface.**

The CUI Editor is displayed.

2. **In the Customizations In pane, right-click the Menus node and choose New Menu.**

A new menu with the default name *Menu1* is created under the Menus node.

3. **In the Properties pane, change the name and alias of the menu by using the Name and Aliases boxes.**

The name allows you to identify the menu and is the value displayed as the caption of the menu when it's displayed on the menu browser or menu bar. The alias uniquely identifies the menu through automation or when migrating the menu between releases.

4. **In the Command List pane, add any of the commands that you want to be displayed on the menu.**

5. **Click Apply to save the changes and stay in the CUI Editor, or click OK to save the changes and exit the CUI Editor.**

Creating a new submenu

Follow these steps to create a submenu on a menu:

1. **On the ribbon, click Tools tab⇨Customization panel⇨User Interface.**

The CUI Editor is displayed.

2. **In the Customizations In pane, click the plus sign next to the Menus node.**

The menus are displayed under the Menus node.

3. **Right-click the menu to which you want to add a submenu and choose New Sub-menu.**

A new submenu is added under the menu.

4. **In the Properties pane, change the name of the submenu in the Name box.**

The name of the submenu is displayed under the menu.

5. **In the Command List pane, add any of the commands that you want to be displayed on the submenu.**

6. **Click Apply to save the changes and stay in the CUI Editor, or click OK to save the changes and exit the CUI Editor.**

Commands and submenus can be repositioned on a menu or submenu. Select the command or submenu and hold down the mouse button. Then drag up or down and release the mouse button when the splitter bar is displayed where you want the command or submenu to be displayed.

Using special characters with a menu item's name

Menu item names can contain special characters to control some of the display behavior for the item. Table 3-2 lists some of the special characters that can be used in combination with a menu item's name.

Table 3-2	Special Characters for a Menu Item Name
Special Character	*Description*
&	Displays an underscore under the character that follows the ampersand, allowing users to access the menu item from the menu bar by pressing the Alt key plus the underlined character
&&	Displays an ampersand
~	Disables the menu item, making it not selectable
!c or !.	Puts a check mark in front of the menu item
\t (or tab character)	Forces the text to the right side of the menu item; this is often used to display the command alias for a command on a menu

Here's an example of using a special character for a menu item:

```
Save &As...
```

The A is the access key from the keyboard. To access the Save As command, press Alt+F to open the File menu from the menu bar when it is displayed and then press Alt+A. Pressing Alt+F displays the menu browser with the Files menu selected if the menu bar is not visible.

Shortcut menus

Shortcut menus — also known as right-click or context sensitive menus — are used to display additional options specific to the selected object(s) or the active command or the current state of AutoCAD. Shortcut menus are displayed by pressing the right mouse button over the drawing window and are based on the current value of the SHORTCUTMENU system variable. By default, the SHORTCUTMENU system variable is set to a value of 11, which indicates to AutoCAD that it should display shortcut menus when options are available for the active command, when no command is active and objects are selected, or when no command is active and no objects are selected.

Shortcut menus are created much like menus for the menu browser and menu bar with one main exception: their aliases. Most shortcut menus are set up to work specifically with a specific command or object(s). To designate a shortcut menu to be used with a command, you use the alias syntax of COMMAND_*commandname*. An example of an alias used to assign additional options to the LINE command's right-click menu is COMMAND_LINE. The alias is assigned to the Aliases property of the shortcut menu in the Properties pane of the Dynamic pane.

Shortcut menus can be associated to a specific object type, and when a single object of the designated object type is selected in the drawing window and the right mouse button is pressed, additional options are displayed on the shortcut menu. To designate a shortcut menu to be used when an object of a certain type is selected, you use the alias syntax of OBJECT_*objectname*. Just like the alias for a command-based shortcut menu, the alias is assigned to the Aliases property of the shortcut menu. AutoCAD comes with many shortcut menus. One example is the Hatch Object Menu, which uses the alias OBJECT_HATCH to display the Hatch Edit option on the shortcut menu when a hatch object is selected in the drawing before you press the right mouse button.

To identify the object name for an object, you can use the LIST command on the object. The LIST command displays the object name in the AutoCAD text window. This example shows the results of the LIST command in the AutoCAD text window after a line was selected:

```
        LINE        Layer: "0"
                    Space: Model space
          Handle = 93
    from point, X=  14.5169  Y=   7.9505  Z=   0.0000
      to point, X=  27.3742  Y=  15.9583  Z=   0.0000
Length =  15.1471,   Angle in XY Plane =     32
   Delta X =  12.8573, Delta Y =    8.0077, Delta Z =   0.0000
```

The object name is listed as part of the first line of text of the returned values, in this case, LINE. An example of an alias used to assign additional options to the Edit shortcut menu when a line object is selected is OBJECT_LINE. If you want to display a shortcut menu when one or more object of a specific object type is selected, you use the alias syntax of OBJECTS_*objectname*.

In some instances, the object name is not used, and that is because the LIST command returns the same object name for different conditions that an object might have. An example of an object having multiple different conditions is an insert object (or block).

Table 3-3 lists the names to be used for blocks and external reference (xref) objects.

Table 3-3	Special Object Names Used for Blocks and xrefs
Object Name	*Description*
BLOCKREF	Block without attributes
ATTBLOCKREF	Block with attributes
DYNBLOCKREF	Dynamic block without attributes
ATTDYNBLOCKREF	Dynamic block with attributes
XREF	External reference

Follow these steps to create a shortcut menu:

1. **On the ribbon, click Tools tab➪Customization panel➪User Interface.**

The CUI Editor is displayed.

2. **In the Customizations In pane, right-click the Shortcut Menus node and choose New Shortcut Menu.**

A new shortcut menu with the default name *ShortcutMenu1* is created under the Shortcut Menus node.

3. **In the Properties pane, change the name of the shortcut menu in the Name box.**

The Name is used to locate the shortcut menu.

4. **In the Properties pane, change the shortcut menu's alias. To do this, click in the Aliases field and then click the ellipsis (. . .) button on the right side of the field.**

The Aliases dialog box is displayed (see Figure 3-9).

Figure 3-9:
The Aliases
dialog box.

5. **In the Aliases dialog box, position the cursor behind the last alias in the list box and click. Press Enter to start a new line.**

   A new line is started for the new alias.

6. **Enter the new alias for the shortcut menu.**

   Aliases are used to uniquely identify a shortcut menu or when migrating the shortcut menu between releases. Aliases determine the associated operation: edit or command.

7. **Click OK to save the changes made and exit the Aliases dialog box.**

   The aliases in the Aliases dialog box are added to the Aliases property.

8. **In the Command List pane, add any commands that you want to have available when the shortcut menu is displayed.**

9. **Click Apply to save the changes and stay in the CUI Editor, or click OK to save the changes and exit the CUI Editor.**

The Ribbon

The ribbon is an evolution of the Dashboard that was introduced in AutoCAD 2007 and also behaves like the ribbon in Microsoft Office 2007. With the CUI Editor, you can customize the panels and tabs that appear on the ribbon. Ribbon panels are used to organize the display of commands and controls, and ribbon tabs are used to group and control the display of ribbon panels on the ribbon. You control the display of ribbon tabs through workspaces. To find out more about the ribbon, see Book I, Chapter 3.

The ribbon in AutoCAD 2009 replaces the Dashboard.

Ribbon panels

You create and modify ribbon panels by selecting the Ribbon Panels node in the Customizations In pane. After you expand the Ribbon Panels node, you expand the ribbon panel you want to modify. Ribbon panels are customized similar to toolbars, except you use rows to organize commands and controls horizontally on a ribbon panel and you can also use subpanels to further group commands and controls.

As you add commands and controls to a ribbon panel, you can control the size and how the command or control is displayed. Along with commands and controls, you can also add flyouts, which are similar to submenus on a menu because they do not reference a toolbar like a flyout on a toolbar does. Ribbon panels are divided into two areas, the area that is displayed by default and the expanded area. The two areas are separated by a <PANEL SEPARATOR> item. Figure 3-10 shows how the different elements of a ribbon panel are shown in the CUI Editor.

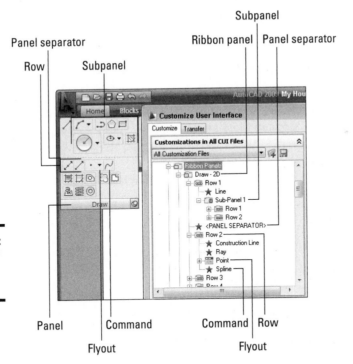

Figure 3-10: Anatomy of a ribbon panel.

Follow these steps to create a ribbon panel and organize commands by using rows and subpanels:

1. **On the ribbon, click Tools tab⇨Customization panel⇨User Interface.**

The CUI Editor is displayed.

2. **In the Customizations In pane, right-click the Ribbon Panels node and choose New Panel.**

A new ribbon panel with the default name *Panel1* is created under the Ribbon Panels node. The ribbon panel is created with one default row and a panel separator.

3. **In the Properties pane, change the name and display title of the ribbon panel in the Name and Display Title boxes.**

The name is used to locate the ribbon panel. The display text is the text string displayed in the title bar of the ribbon panel.

4. **In the Properties pane, change the ribbon panel's alias.**

To do this, click in the Aliases field and enter a unique value for the ribbon panel.

5. **Add rows and subpanels to organize the commands, controls, or fly-outs that you want to add to the ribbon panel.**

To do so, right-click a ribbon panel in the Customizations In pane and choose New Row or New Sub-panel.

6. **In the Command List pane, add any commands to the rows of the ribbon panel that you want to have available when the ribbon panel is displayed on a ribbon tab.**

7. **For the rows you want to always display on the ribbon panel, drag them above the <PANEL SEPARATOR> item. For rows you want to display only when the ribbon panel is expanded, drag them below the <PANEL SEPARATOR> item.**

8. **Click Apply to save the changes and stay in the CUI Editor, or click OK to save the changes and exit the CUI Editor.**

You can create ribbon panels by using existing toolbars. To create a ribbon panel from a toolbar, expand the Toolbars node in the Customizations In pane. Right-click a toolbar under the Toolbars node and choose Copy to Ribbon Panels. A new ribbon panel is created under the Ribbon Panels node.

Ribbon tabs

Ribbon tabs are used to organize and display ribbon panels on the ribbon. You create and modify ribbon tabs by expanding the Ribbon Tabs node in the Customizations In pane. To create a ribbon tab, right-click the Ribbon Tabs node and choose New Tab. Ribbon panels are added to a ribbon tab by dragging a ribbon panel from under the Ribbon Panels node to the ribbon tab node on which you want the ribbon panel to be displayed. Ribbon panels are removed from a ribbon tab by right-clicking the reference to the ribbon panel under the ribbon tab and choosing Remove.

After you create a ribbon tab, you control its visibility on the ribbon through a workspace. Select a workspace and then use the Workspace Contents pane to add or remove ribbon tabs from the ribbon, and control the order in which ribbon panels appear on a ribbon tab and the order ribbon tabs appear on the ribbon.

Follow these steps to create a ribbon tab, add ribbon panels to the tab, and control the display of ribbon tabs on the ribbon:

1. **On the ribbon, click Tools tab⇨Customization panel⇨User Interface.**

   The CUI Editor is displayed.

2. **In the Customizations In pane, right-click the Ribbon Tabs node and choose New Tab.**

   A new ribbon tab with the default name *New Tab* is created under the Ribbon Tabs node.

3. **In the Properties pane, change the name of the ribbon tab in the Name box.**

   The name is used to locate the ribbon tab and is also the text string displayed on the tab when it's on the ribbon.

4. **In the Customizations In pane, select the ribbon panels to add to the ribbon tab. Hold down the left mouse button and drag and drop the selected ribbon panels on the node for the ribbon tab.**

   References to the selected panels are added to the ribbon tab.

5. **Expand the Workspaces node, and select the workspace you want to use to control the display of the ribbon tabs on the ribbon and the order in which the ribbon panels and tabs appear on the ribbon.**

6. **In the Workspace Contents pane, click Customize Workspace.**

7. **In the Customizations In pane, expand the Ribbon Tabs node and select the ribbon tabs that you want to display on the ribbon.**

8. In the Workspace Contents pane, expand the Ribbon Tabs node and drag the ribbon tabs in the order you want them to appear on the ribbon.

9. In the Workspace Contents pane, expand a ribbon tab under the Ribbon Tabs node, and drag the ribbon panels into the order you want them displayed on the ribbon tab.

10. In the Workspace Contents pane, click Done.

11. Click Apply to save the changes and stay in the CUI Editor, or click OK to save the changes and exit the CUI Editor.

Separator bars

Separator bars are used to organize and group commands on a toolbar, menu, shortcut menu, or ribbon panel. Separator bars can be inserted by right-clicking a toolbar, menu, shortcut menu, or ribbon panel and choosing Insert Separator or Add Separator, based on the node you right-click. A separator bar is displayed as a horizontal or vertical line in the user interface and as a short dash in the CUI Editor.

Creating a New Shortcut Key

Shortcut keys allow you to access commands by using a keyboard combination that includes at least one modifier key (a noncharacter key such as Ctrl or Alt) and another key on the keyboard. Shortcut keys must use the Ctrl modifier key, but the Ctrl key can also be combined with the Shift or Alt key.

Follow this procedure to create a shortcut key:

1. On the ribbon, click Tools tab⇨Customization panel⇨User Interface.

The CUI Editor is displayed.

2. In the Customizations In pane, click the plus sign next to the Keyboard Shortcuts node.

The Keyboard Shortcuts node is expanded and displays two additional nodes: Shortcut Keys and Temporary Overrides.

3. In the Command List pane, select the command for which you want to create a shortcut key. Hold down the mouse button and drag the command up to the Shortcut Keys node of the Customizations In pane. Release the mouse button when the cursor is over the node.

A new shortcut key is created based on the command dropped onto the node.

4. **In the Properties pane, select the Key(s) field and click the ellipsis (. . .) button that appears on the right side of the field.**

   The Shortcut Keys dialog box is displayed (see Figure 3-11).

5. **In the Shortcut Keys dialog box, click in the Press New Shortcut Key box.**

6. **Press and hold down the Ctrl key while pressing one of the other modifier keys or a key from the keyboard.**

   The key combination appears in the field. If the combination is already assigned to a command, the other assignment is listed below the Press New Shortcut Key text field.

Figure 3-11:
The
Shortcut
Keys dialog
box.

7. **Click OK to assign the key combination and exit the Shortcut Keys dialog box.**

   The Shortcut Keys dialog box is closed and the key combination is placed in the Key(s) property field.

8. **Click Apply to save the changes and stay in the CUI Editor, or click OK to save the changes and exit the CUI Editor.**

Customizing Double-Click Actions

Double-click actions control what happens when you double-click an object in the drawing window. Double-clicking objects in the drawing window allows you to quickly access an editing command that is set up by object name like shortcut menus are. Double-click actions require the use of an object name to identify which command should be run when a user double-clicks the object in the drawing window.

The object name is the value listed by the LIST command or for special object names used for blocks and xref objects. For information on the special object names used for blocks and xrefs, see the section "Shortcut menus" and Table 3-3 presented previously in this chapter.

Follow these steps to create a double-click action:

1. **On the ribbon, click Tools tab⇨Customization panel⇨User Interface.**

The CUI Editor is displayed.

2. **In the Customizations In pane, right-click the Double-Click Actions node and choose New Double-Click Action.**

A new double-click action with the default name *DoubleClick1* is created under the Double-Click Actions node.

3. **In the Properties pane, change the name of the double-click action in the Name box.**

The name is used to locate the double-click action.

4. **In the Object Name property field, enter the object name with which the double-click action should be associated.**

The object name identifies which double-click action should be used when an object is double-clicked in the drawing window.

5. **In the Command List pane, select the command that you want to associate with the double-click action. Hold down the mouse button and drag the command up to the new double-click action in the Customizations In pane. Release the mouse button when the cursor is over the node.**

The command is now associated with the double-click action and the specified object name.

6. **Click Apply to save the changes and stay in the CUI Editor, or click OK to save the changes and exit the CUI Editor.**

Customizing the Quick Properties Panel and Rollover Tooltips

You can customize the properties displayed on the Quick Properties panel and rollover tooltips by using the CUI Editor. To customize the properties for the Quick Properties panel or the rollover tooltips, you select either the Quick Properties or the Rollover Tooltips node in the Customizations In pane. The Quick Properties pane is displayed in the Dynamic pane. In the Quick Properties pane (see Figure 3-12), you can choose which objects interact with the Quick Properties panel or participate in rollover tooltips. For more on the Quick Properties panel, see Book II, Chapter 2; for more on rollover tooltips, see Book I, Chapter 3.

The Quick Properties panel and rollover tooltips are new features in AutoCAD 2009.

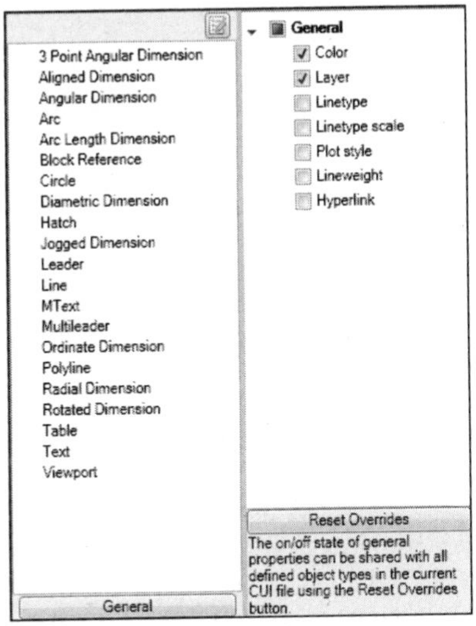

Figure 3-12:
Specifying object types and their properties with the Quick Properties pane of the CUI Editor.

To control which object types are used with the Quick Properties panel or rollover tooltips, click Edit Object Type List located at the top of the Object List pane in the Quick Properties pane. In the Edit Object Type List dialog box (see Figure 3-13), select the object types for which you want to display properties or remove the check mark next to those for which you don't want to display properties. Click OK to return to the CUI Editor and the Quick Properties pane.

After you select the object types you want to interact with, you specify the properties to display for an object by selecting an object type in the Object List pane and then select the properties to display for the object in the Properties pane. The Properties pane displays the properties for the selected object. Along with the properties specific to an object type, you can also define the general properties for all objects by clicking General located at the bottom of the object list and then selecting the general properties that you want enabled for all object types. After the general properties are selected, click Reset Overrides at the bottom of the Properties pane.

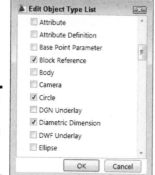

Figure 3-13:
Plethora of object types to choose from.

Migrating and Transferring Customization

Upgrading to a new release of AutoCAD has always been a time-consuming problem with all the customizations and settings that need to be updated. Since AutoCAD 2005, AutoCAD has offered the Migrate Custom Settings utility, which allows you to easily migrate a majority of your custom settings to a new release.

The utility migrates only settings, profiles, and customizations located in specific support files, and supports limited migration for menu customization contained in the CUI files that come with AutoCAD, such as acad.cui in AutoCAD and acadlt.cui in AutoCAD LT. To be able to migrate all customizations between two CUI files, you use the Transfer tab in the CUI Editor. The Transfer tab allows you to migrate custom toolbars, menus, ribbon panels, and other user interface elements between CUI files.

Transferring customizations with AutoCAD 2005 and prior versions was a manual process: You opened two menu files with a text editor, and then copied and pasted sections between the two files. The problem is that the approach of copying and pasting between two files can result in missing information or a file structure problem. The CUI Editor resolves this problem by allowing you to graphically migrate user interface elements by dragging and dropping them between two CUI files right in the Editor.

Follow these steps to transfer customizations from one customization file to another and to migrate customizations from a legacy MNU or MNS file format:

1. **On the ribbon, click Tools tab⇨Customization panel⇨User Interface.**

   The CUI Editor is displayed.

2. **Click the Transfer tab.**

   A second Customizations In pane is displayed on the right side of the CUI Editor (see Figure 3-14).

3. **In the Customizations In pane on the right side, click Open Customization File.**

   The Open dialog box is displayed, allowing you to select a customization file (CUI) or a menu file (MNU/MNS).

4. **Select the type of file you want to open by choosing one of the options in the Files of Type drop-down list and browsing for the file you want to open.**

   The selected file's name appears in the File Name box.

5. **Click Open.**

   The selected file is opened and displayed in the Customizations In pane. If you selected a MNU/MNS file, a CUI file is generated automatically.

6. **Expand the nodes of the two files and then drag and drop the user interface elements from the pane on the right to the one on the left.**

   The user interface elements are added to the file, along with any commands associated with the elements.

   The Legacy node contains tablet, image tile, and screen menu customization. If you've customized any of these sections in previous releases, don't forget to transfer these user interface elements too.

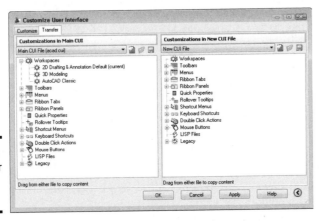

Figure 3-14:
The Transfer
tab of the
CUI Editor.

7. **Switch back to the Customize tab and make any necessary changes to the transferred user interface elements.**

   You may need to add additional commands or even update workspaces to include or exclude toolbars and menus.

8. **Click Apply to save the changes and stay in the CUI Editor, or click OK to save the changes and exit the CUI Editor.**

Working with Partial and Enterprise Customization Files

Partial and enterprise customization files are ways to organize and share customization among multiple users. Whether you work in a large or small company, you can use an enterprise customization file to share standard company tools with all the members of your drafting team. You might add commands to an enterprise customization file that ensure that layer and annotation standards are followed and allow access to company title blocks.

A partial customization file can contain a subset of customization when compared to the main customization file. The customization in the partial customization file is usually personal or task-based customization. You might use different partial customization files for different disciplines within your company, such as civil or architectural.

Loading an enterprise customization file

Follow these steps to load an enterprise customization file:

1. **Right-click the drawing window and choose Options.**

   The Options dialog box is displayed.

2. **On the Files tab click the plus sign next to the Customization Files node.**

   The Customization Files node expands and shows some additional nodes: Main Customization Files, Enterprise Customization File, and Custom Icon Location.

3. **Click the plus sign next to the Enterprise Customization File node.**

   The Enterprise Customization File node expands and shows the current value; by default, the value is a period (.).

4. **Select the current value and click Browse.**

   The Select a File dialog box is displayed.

5. **Browse to the location of the customization (CUI) file that you want to use for the enterprise customization file. Select the file and click Open.**

   The location of the selected file is added under the Enterprise Customization File node.

6. **Click Apply to save the change and stay in Options dialog box, or click OK to save the change and exit the Options dialog box.**

   The change is saved to the current AutoCAD profile.

Loading a partial customization file

Follow the steps to load a partial customization file:

1. **On the ribbon, click Tools tab⇨Customization panel⇨User Interface.**

   The CUI Editor is displayed.

2. **Click the Customize tab to make it current, and click Load Partial Customization File under the Customizations In pane.**

   The Open dialog box is displayed.

3. **Browse to the location of the customization (CUI) file that you want to load as a partial customization file. Select the file and click Open.**

   The selected file is loaded as a partial customization file and is added to the Partial CUI Files node.

4. **In the Warning box that appears, click OK.**

   The Warning box notifies you that any workspaces in the partial customization file won't be available for use. The partial customization file is displayed in the Customizations In pane.

5. **In the drop-down list at the top of the Customizations In pane, select All Customization Files to see all the loaded customization files.**

   The tree view in the Customizations In pane returns to its default display state.

6. **Click Apply to save the changes and stay in the CUI Editor, or click OK to save the changes and exit the CUI Editor.**

Chapter 4: Delving Deeper into Customization

In This Chapter

✔ Working with scripts

✔ Introducing shapes

✔ Getting to know Express Tools

Many aspects of customizing AutoCAD are left untapped by most users. Much of this is due to the many ways AutoCAD can be customized beyond just the user interface and appearance of the application window. AutoCAD allows you to automate repetitive tasks with standard AutoCAD commands and command options by creating script files. AutoCAD also comes with a set of utilities known as *Express Tools* that allow you to complete tasks in AutoCAD more efficiently.

Working from a Script

No, AutoCAD will not help you land a role in Hollywood, but AutoCAD scripts can help you be more efficient at your job. Have you ever received a set of drawings from a client that didn't use the same drafting settings or conform to the CAD standards that you use? Or maybe you've had to manually update older drawings to match your company's new CAD standards? Script files can be used for these tasks and much more.

What's in a script?

A *script* is used to automate functionality in AutoCAD by using standard AutoCAD commands, options, and AutoLISP expressions. (AutoLISP expressions are not supported by AutoCAD LT, however.)

For more information on AutoLISP, see Bonus Chapter 4 on the Web, which you can download from www.wiley.com/go/autocad2009aio.

You create a script by using a text editor such as Notepad. After you create the script, you save it to a plain text file with the SCR file extension, which lets AutoCAD know that the contents of the file is a script. The structure of a script is similar to the way AutoCAD commands and options are entered at the command line. Here is an example of a script file that does some basic drawing setup and demonstrates how to use comments in a script file:

```
; Created 12/08/07 by Lee Ambrosius
LTSCALE 24
BLIPMODE 0
LIMITS 0,0 24,17
ZOOM EXTENTS
```

The opening line is a comment that is ignored during the execution of the script. Comments don't get executed, but they can contain important information that comes in handy when updates are needed to the script file, for example. Comment lines begin with a semicolon; AutoCAD ignores everything to the right of a semicolon.

The second line, LTSCALE 24, sets the linetype scale system variable to a value of 24. The space between LTSCALE and the value 24 is just like pressing the Enter key while entering values at the command prompt. AutoCAD automatically issues an Enter for each new line as the script is being evaluated.

The next line, BLIPMODE 0, turns blip markers off. The line after that, LIMITS 0,0 24,17, sets the lower-left and upper-right drawing limits. The last line, ZOOM EXTENTS, makes sure that the drawing is zoomed to its limits. At the end of the script file, make sure that there is a single blank line to let AutoCAD know when the script file ends.

Alternatively, commands and options can be on separate lines or on the same line. Neither method is right or wrong. The following example shows the same script but with commands and options on separate lines.

```
; Created 12/08/07 by Lee Ambrosius
LTSCALE
24
BLIPMODE
0
LIMITS
0,0
24,17
ZOOM
EXTENTS
```

Using script files to automate repetitive tasks has both disadvantages and advantages. Here are some of the disadvantages, just to get the negative out of the way first:

✦ There is no way to pause for user input during a command. However, if you really need to pause for input, you can use AutoLISP.

✦ Dialog boxes can't be called during the execution of the script. To work around this, you need to know a few more commands. For example, you use the –LAYER command rather than the LAYER command.

✦ Only a single script can be running in AutoCAD at a single time. You can't call another script while a script is running.

✦ AutoCAD doesn't ship with any sample scripts, which can make it difficult to get started creating your own scripts.

Here are some of the advantages:

✦ The syntax is basic and can be created by anyone who can use commands in AutoCAD.

✦ Scripting is great for automating basic and repetitive tasks.

✦ Scripts require minimal maintenance from release to release.

✦ Scripts can be used transparently with AutoCAD commands.

✦ AutoLISP expressions can be used in a script (if you're not using AutoCAD LT and know how to use AutoLISP). Using AutoLISP with your scripts allows you to build much more complex and robust scripts.

Here are some commands specifically used for working with script files:

✦ **RSCRIPT:** Repeats the last run script file.

✦ **RESUME:** Continues a script that has been paused (but not paused for input) by pressing the Escape or Backspace key during the execution of a script. Pausing a script allows you to return to AutoCAD to perform a set of tasks and then return to running the script again later.

✦ **DELAY:** Pauses a script for the specified duration, which is expressed in milliseconds. One thousand milliseconds is equal to 1 second, and the maximum delay is a value of 32,767, which is equal to just a little longer than 32 seconds. You might use a delay to display slides from a slide library by using the VSLIDE command. For more information on slides and the VSLIDE command, see AutoCAD's online Help system.

✦ **SCRIPT:** Loads and runs a script file through a standard Windows file navigation dialog box.

✦ **–SCRIPT:** Loads and runs a script file from the command prompt.

Creating a script file

Because script files are plain text files, you can create and edit them with an application such as Notepad. Follow these steps to create a new script file by using Notepad:

1. **Choose Start⇨[All] Programs⇨Accessories⇨Notepad.**

Notepad is launched and a blank document is created.

2. **On the menu bar in Notepad, choose File⇨Save As.**

The Save As dialog box is displayed.

3. **In the File Name text box, enter a name for the script file and make sure that you add .SCR to the end of the file name.**

4. **Browse to the location where you want to save the script file and click Save.**

The script file is created with the specified name and location.

5. **In Notepad, enter the AutoCAD commands and options that you want to execute when the script file is run.**

Don't forget that each command and option must be followed by a space, unless it is the last command or option on the line. The text area of Notepad should contain the commands and options that you want to use in the script file.

6. **On the menu bar in Notepad, choose File⇨Save.**

The contents of the Notepad document are saved to the script file.

Loading and running a script file

Use one of these methods to load and run a script file:

✦ On the ribbon, click Tools tab⇨Applications panel⇨Run Script.

✦ On the menu browser or menu bar, click Tools menu⇨Run Script.

✦ At the command prompt, type **SCRIPT** or **SCR** and press Enter.

These steps describe how to load and run a script file.

1. **Start the SCRIPT command by using any of the methods just listed.**

The Select Script File dialog box is displayed.

2. **Browse to the location where the script file is stored and select it.**

3. **Click Open.**

The selected script file is executed in AutoCAD.

To load and run a script in an open drawing file, drag and drop the script file from Windows Explorer onto the drawing window.

Running a script file at startup

You can load and run a script file by using one of the command line switches with a desktop shortcut. The /b command line switch allows you to load and run a script at startup. This can be a great way to make sure that session-specific drafting settings are configured when AutoCAD is first launched. Following is an example target path using the /b switch with a script file:

```
"C:\Program Files\AutoCAD 2009\acad.exe" /b Startup
```

This example starts AutoCAD with a script file named Startup. The script file in this example must exist in the support search paths of AutoCAD. You can also specify the absolute path for the script file as well so that the script file does not need to be in one of AutoCAD's support paths. See Chapter 1 in this minibook for more information about command line switches.

Getting Familiar with Shapes

Shape files were the only way to create a blocklike object in early releases of AutoCAD. Shapes are not as commonly used now that AutoCAD has a true block object, but they are still used with complex linetypes and are very efficient. A shape is defined through a series of lines, arcs, and circles, but these elements are defined through a series of codes.

A shape is comprised of three components: a shape number, definition bytes, and the shape name. The syntax of a shape as it appears in a shape file is

```
*shapenumber, definitionbytes, shapename
```

An example of a shape that looks like an equilateral triangle is

```
*139,5,TRIGEQ
1,013,01D,018,0
```

To find out more about creating shape files, refer to the "Create Shape Definition Files" topic in the AutoCAD online Help files.

AutoCAD LT does not support the creation of shape files because it lacks the COMPILE command. The COMPILE command is used to generate a compiled shape file (SHX) from a shape file (SHP).

Express Tools comes with a utility that allows you to make a shape out of geometry in a drawing. This utility is great when trying to find out how to create your own shapes. The utility can be found on the menu browser or menu bar under Express menu⇨Tools⇨Make Shape. AutoCAD LT does not support Express Tools.

Working with Express Tools

Express Tools is a collection of tools that are not part of the core AutoCAD program. These tools are provided as-is without any type of support from Autodesk. Many of the tools provide enhanced functionality beyond what is in the core program or provide unique functionality to assist in certain tasks.

Slowly, over the past several releases, many of the commonly used Express Tools have been making their way into the core program, which is great for users of AutoCAD LT. This section provides only a brief overview of the commonly used tools that are still part of Express Tools. To find out more about each of these tools, see the online Help file for Express Tools. (On the menu browser or menu bar click Express menu⇨Help.)

Express Tools is not available for AutoCAD LT, but feel free to read on to find out about some of the tools that you may be missing out on.

Installing Express Tools

Express Tools is installed during the installation of AutoCAD. To install Express Tools with AutoCAD, on the Review — Configure — Install page of the AutoCAD 2009 Installation Wizard select AutoCAD 2009 from the Select a Product to Configure drop-down list and then click Configure. Then select the license type that you want to use on the Select the License Type page, and click Next. On the Select the Installation Type page (see Figure 4-1), click the Express Tools check box under Install Optional Tools — it should be selected by default. Finish selecting the settings on the Select the Installation Type page, and click Next. Complete the configuration and installation of AutoCAD by clicking Configuration Complete and then clicking Install.

If you installed AutoCAD without installing Express Tools, you can use the Control Panel in Windows to make changes to the installation by using Uninstall or Change a Program. Choose Start⇨Control Panel⇨Programs: Uninstall a Program (or Programs and Features if Classic View is active). If you're using Windows 2000 or Windows XP, you can change AutoCAD's installation by using Add or Remove Programs. Choose Start⇨Control Panel⇨Add or Remove Programs.

After Express Tools has been installed, the Express menu should appear on AutoCAD's menu browser or menu bar. If the Express menu is not displayed, type **EXPRESSMENU** or **EXPRESSTOOLS** on the command line to display the Express Menu.

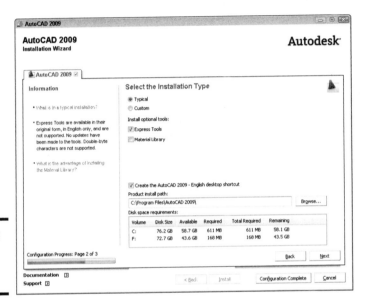

Figure 4-1:
Installing
Express
Tools.

Block tools

The Block tools give you capabilities ranging from exploding a block and having the attributes converted to text objects to converting a block to an external reference (xref).

+ **List Xref/Block Properties:** Gets information about a nested object in a block or an xref.

+ **Copy Nested Objects:** Makes a copy of objects in a block without exploding the block first.

+ **Explode Attributes to Text:** Explodes a block, but instead of attribute definitions being created after the explosion, you are left with text objects with the value that was in the attribute before the block was exploded.

+ **Convert Shape to Block:** Generates a block based on a shape definition.

✦ **Export Attribute Information:** Exports attribute and block name information to a tab-delimited text file. This allows you to work with the information in a spreadsheet program.

✦ **Import Attribute Information:** Imports previously exported attribute and block name information back into AutoCAD to sync the values.

✦ **Convert Block to Xref:** Replaces a block with a specified xref.

✦ **Replace Block with Another Block:** Replaces a block with a specified block.

Text tools

The Text tools give you capabilities ranging from creating text along an arc to changing the case of several selected text objects at one time:

✦ **Text Fit:** Stretches or shrinks a text object by selecting a new point or an end point

✦ **Text Mask:** Places a mask object behind a text or mtext object with an offset value

✦ **Unmask Text:** Removes a mask object from behind a text or mtext object

✦ **Explode Text:** Explodes a text or mtext object into geometry that can be assigned a thickness or an elevation

✦ **Convert Text to Mtext:** Selects text objects and creates a single mtext object with the values from the selected text objects in the order the text objects were selected

✦ **Arc-Aligned Text:** Creates a text object that follows an arc's curve

✦ **Rotate Text:** Changes the orientation of text, mtext, or an attribute

✦ **Enclose Text with Object:** Places a circle, slot, or rectangle around a text or mtext object

✦ **Automatic Text Numbering:** Creates a numbered list

✦ **Change Text Case:** Changes the case of selected text and mtext objects

Layout tools

The Layout tools offer capabilities ranging from listing a viewport's scale to synchronizing viewports:

✦ **Align Space:** Adjusts a viewport based on points selected in model space and paper space

✦ **Synchronize Viewports:** Updates a viewport's zoom factor based on a specified viewport

+ **List Viewport Scale:** Obtains a viewport's current scale factor

+ **Merge Layout:** Merges the objects in a layout into another layout or creates a new layout based on the layouts being merged

Dimension tools

The Dimension tools range from leader tools to tools that enable you to import and export dimension styles out of a drawing:

+ **Leader Tools:** Attaches and detaches leader lines to multiline text, tolerance, or block reference objects

+ **Dimstyle Export:** Exports a specified dimension style out of a drawing to a text file

+ **Dimstyle Import:** Imports a previously exported dimension style into a drawing

Selection tools

The Selection tools allow you to create a selection set of objects based on layer and object type, and create a selection set based on objects that touch a selected object.

Modify tools

The Modify tools give you capabilities ranging from performing multiple editing operations in a row to controlling the display order by color:

+ **Multiple Object Stretch:** Performs more than one crossing polygon before doing a stretch

+ **Move/Copy/Rotate:** Performs move, copy, and rotate operations in a row on objects created during the command

+ **DrawOrder by Color:** Controls the draw order of objects in a drawing by their assigned color or by the color of the layer they are on

+ **Delete Duplicate Objects:** Removes any objects that are stacked on top of other objects and are the same, and combines line and arc segments that overlap with objects of the same type

+ **Flatten Objects:** Allows you to convert 3D objects into 2D objects

Draw tools

The Draw tools range from inserting a break-line symbol to a feature known as Super Hatch, which allows you to use an image, a block, an external reference (xref), or a wipeout object as a hatch pattern.

File tools

The File tools help with the management of drawing and backup files. The utilities perform functions ranging from moving backups to a specified location to saving all open drawings in AutoCAD:

✦ **Move Backup Files:** Specifies where BAK files should be placed after each save.

✦ **Save All Drawings:** Saves all open drawings without needing to switch to each one and saving each individually.

✦ **Quick Exit:** Exits all open drawings; you are prompted only for the ones that need to be saved. AutoCAD closes automatically after the command is finished.

✦ **Revert to Original:** Closes and reopens the current drawing.

Web tools

The Web tools allow you to work with URLs (also known as hyperlinks) that are attached to objects in a drawing. You can have all the URLs in the drawing listed in a dialog box so they can be edited, change the URL attached to an object or objects, and do a find and replace on a URL in the drawing.

Tools

The Express Tools also contains miscellaneous tools that range from allowing you to edit the PGP file to creating custom linetypes:

✦ **Command Alias Editor:** Creates new and modifies existing command aliases in a PGP file

✦ **System Variable Editor:** Views and modifies the values of system variables through a dialog box rather than at the command line

✦ **Make Linetype:** Generates a linetype based on the geometry in a drawing

✦ **Make Shape:** Generates a shape based on the geometry in a drawing

Command line only tools

Some Express Tools are not found in the Express Tools pull-down menu. These commands are available only from the command line. Some of these commands are mentioned in the following list. In parentheses after the name of the command is the command name that has to be typed at the command line to run it:

✦ **Block Count (BCOUNT):** Gets a quick count of the number of times a block is inserted into a drawing.

✦ **Edit Time (EDITTIME):** Keeps track of the amount of time that you are spending in a drawing file. You can specify a timeout period so if nothing happens in AutoCAD, the timer tracking is suspended after a specified interval.

✦ **List AutoLISP Commands (LSP):** Gets information about loaded AutoLISP routines.

✦ **Create Selection Set (SSX):** Creates a selection set based on some filtering options that you can select by using the "previous" selection option.

✦ **Toggle Frames (TFRAMES):** Toggles the frames used for raster images and wipeouts on or off.

Chapter 5: Recording Your Actions

In This Chapter

✓ Understanding actions and Action Recorder

✓ Recording actions and managing action macro files

✓ Playing back action macro files

✓ Enhancing action macros with user interaction

*A*lready in this minibook, you've discovered how to customize AutoCAD through creating command aliases and desktop shortcuts, customizing the user interface with the Customize User Interface (CUI) Editor, writing scripts, and much more. Action macros are yet another form of customizing AutoCAD, and they're fairly easy to create when you understand the workflow. If you liked the idea of creating scripts to automate repetitive tasks in Chapter 4 of this minibook, you will no doubt feel that action macro files will be an even better choice for you. Instead of using a text editor to type the commands and command options you want to use as you do for a script file, you use AutoCAD to run through the series of commands that you want to be able to use over and over again. While doing so, AutoCAD uses its Action Recorder to take notes as to which commands and command options you're using and how you're providing input for the commands.

Action Recorder is a new feature in AutoCAD 2009 that allows you to automate repetitive tasks. Like most of the different customization options available in AutoCAD, AutoCAD LT users can't use this feature. So if you're using AutoCAD LT 2009, you can read through the chapter to find out what you're missing out on, but there's nothing for you otherwise.

In this chapter, I take you through recording and managing action macro files, playing them back and eventually enhancing an action macro file so it requests user input during playback. If you haven't come to grips with the ribbon yet, you want to make sure that you do so and soon, as Action Recorder lives on the ribbon in the form of a panel on the Tools tab.

Actions and Action Recorder

Anything that you do in AutoCAD, from creating or modifying objects to even plotting a drawing, is considered an *action*. I know you might be confused slightly because dynamic blocks also support actions, but if you think about it for a moment it all makes sense. Actions in a dynamic block modify objects within the block they're defined in, and because modifying an object is an action, it makes sense that they're called actions as well, right?

Even though the two types of interaction might share the term *action,* the result is not the same. When I talk about actions in this chapter, I'm talking about the input that AutoCAD collects when Action Recorder is in the recording state. While Action Recorder is in the recording state, most commands and command options used along with the input specified are collected in the form of an action macro. Actions are the smallest element of an action macro, which represents a command or interaction with a user interface, such as a palette or a ribbon panel. Other input collected by Action Recorder is related to the command options or input provided during the use of a command or interaction with a user interface element, such as a property on the Properties palette.

Recording and Managing Action Macros

As mentioned, you use Action Recorder to record actions. Recorded actions can then be saved to an action macro file that has a file extension of ACTM, which allows you to play back those actions at a later time. When you save an action macro file, it's saved to a default location on your local drive. Any action macro files located in the default folder used to store recorded action macros can be played back through Action Recorder.

Recording actions

You access Action Recorder from the ribbon (see Figure 5-1) on the Action Recorder panel — conveniently named, I might add — on the Tools tab. From the Action Recorder panel you can record, edit, and play back action macros. After you start recording an action macro, most actions that you perform in AutoCAD are added to the Action Tree in the form of an action node or a value node.

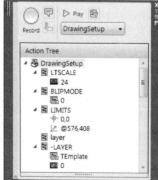

Figure 5-1:
Action
Recorder —
AutoCAD's
version of a
DVR.

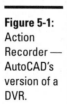

After you finish telling AutoCAD which actions should be in the action macro, you click the Save button on the Action Recorder panel. This displays the Action Macro dialog box (see Figure 5-2), which allows you to save the recorded actions to an action macro file with the ACTM file extension. You can also enter a description for the file, which is displayed in a tooltip when the cursor hovers over the action macro's node at the top of the Action Tree. Along with naming an action macro and giving it a description, you can decide whether the view prior to the start of an action macro is restored when playback of the action macro is complete and when the action macro requests user input.

The Check for Inconsistencies when Playback Begins option has Action Recorder check the current state of the drawing environment against the settings that were in use when the action macro was recorded. Identifying if there are differences in the settings lets you know whether there might be potential problems with successfully playing back the action macro.

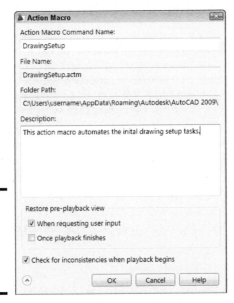

Figure 5-2:
Saving an action macro for playback later.

The following steps explain how to create an action macro that performs some basic drawing setup functions. The action macro will change the linetype scale to 24, turn off blipmode, change the drawing limits, create a nonplottable layer, draw a rectangle, and then zoom to the extents of the drawing. It is almost identical to the example script that was shown in Chapter 1 of this minibook:

1. **If the ribbon is not already displayed, type** RIBBON **at the command prompt and press Enter.**

2. **On the ribbon, click Tools tab⇨Action Recorder panel⇨Record.**

   Action Recorder panel expands, revealing the Action Tree, and a red dot appears near the crosshairs to indicate that AutoCAD is ready to record commands and input.

3. **At the command prompt, type** LTSCALE **and press Enter.**

   The LTSCALE system variable is started.

4. **When prompted for a new scale, type** 24 **and press Enter.**

5. **At the command prompt, type** BLIPMODE **and press Enter.**

   The BLIPMODE system variable is started.

6. **When prompted for the new value, type** 0 **and press Enter.**

7. **On the menu browser or menu bar, click Format menu⇨Drawing Limits.**

8. **When prompted for the lower-left corner of the drawing limits, type** 0,0 **and press Enter.**

   Although you would normally just press Enter to accept the default value, this can lead to issues when recording a macro. Just because the default value is 0,0 for the lower-left corner of the drawing limits when the action macro is recorded, don't expect that it will be that when the action macro is played back. So always enter the value you want to use and then press Enter.

9. **When prompted for the upper-right corner, type** 576,408 **and press Enter.**

10. **On the ribbon, click Home tab⇨Layers panel⇨Layer Properties.**

    The Layer Properties Manager palette is displayed.

11. **Click the New Layer button.**

12. **In the in-place editor, type** Border **and then click the white color swatch in the Color column.**

    The Select Color dialog box is displayed

13. **Choose the color 6 (magenta) color swatch and click OK.**

14. **In the Plottable column, click the plotter icon so it has a slash through it.**

15. **Right-click the Border layer and choose Set Current.**

16. **Click the X in the title bar for the Layer Properties Manager palette.**

    A new layer named Border is created with the color magenta and made nonplottable. After the layer is made, it is set as the current layer.

17. On the ribbon, click Home tab⇨Draw panel⇨Draw panel's title bar⇨Rectangle.

The RECTANGLE command starts.

18. When prompted for the first corner, type 0,0 **and press Enter.**

19. When prompted for the opposite corner, type 576,408 **and press Enter.**

A rectangle the same size as the drawing limits is drawn.

20. At the command prompt, type ZOOM **and press Enter.**

The ZOOM command starts.

21. When prompted for a zoom option, type E **and press Enter.**

The drawing is zoomed to its extents.

To stop recording and save the action macro, follow these steps:

1. On the ribbon, click Tools tab⇨Action Recorder panel⇨Stop.

The Action Macro dialog box is displayed.

2. In the Action Macro Command Name text box, enter a name (for example, DrawingSetup).

The Action Macro Command Name is used for the name of the action macro file and the command that can be used to start the action macro.

3. (Optional.) In the Description text box, enter a description.

For example, you might enter **This action macro automates initial drawing setup tasks.**

4. Click OK.

The action macro is saved to the name you entered in the Action Macro Command Name text box and the folder displayed in the Folder Path text box. The macro is also added to the Action Macro list on the Action Macro panel.

Although Action Recorder can capture the display of a dialog box, it doesn't record any of the values entered. When creating action macros, just like when creating scripts, avoid the use of commands that display dialog boxes and in some cases palettes. The palettes that *are* supported are Properties and Layer Properties Manager, and both DesignCenter and the Tool Palettes window offer limited support for actions that can be recorded.

For more information on recording action macros, see AutoCAD's online Help system. On the Contents tab, navigate to User's Guide⇨The User Interface⇨Action Macros. There are topics on recording action macros, examples of action macros, and tips for using Action Recorder.

Managing and editing action macro files

Action Recorder not only allows you to create an action macro file and then play it back later, but also allows you to manage the action macro files that you've already created. From Action Recorder, you can manage action macro files in the following ways:

✦ **Delete:** Allows you to delete the action macro file. The action macro file is not actually deleted but moved to the Recycle Bin.

✦ **Rename:** Displays the Action Macro dialog box and allows you to change the name or any of the other properties of the action macro.

✦ **Copy:** Creates a copy of the action macro and displays the Action Macro dialog box. The copy of the action macro file is not created until you click OK.

✦ **Insert User Message:** Displays the Insert User Message box, which allows you to specify a text string that should be displayed when the action macro is played back. The user message can be inserted at any location in the action macro by selecting an action or value node before right-clicking in the Action Tree. The user message is displayed during playback.

✦ **All Points Are Relative:** Converts any absolute coordinates in the action macro to be relative to the previous point selected in the drawing. By default the first user coordinate value in an action macro is defined as absolute.

✦ **Properties:** Displays the Action Macro dialog box and allows you to change any properties of the action macro.

To manage an action macro file, select the action macro file from the Action Macros drop-down list and then expand the Action Recorder panel by clicking its title bar. Right-click the action macro's node in the Action Tree and choose one of the options available for managing the action macro file.

Managing the location of action macro files

AutoCAD uses two settings to manage action macro files. The most important location is where Action Recorder places any action macros that you record. The second location is where it should look for any additional action macros that can be played back. By default, Action Recorder saves recorded action macro files to the Actions folder, which can be found in one of the following locations based on the operating system you're using:

✦ **Windows XP:** *<drive>*:\Documents and Settings*<username>*\
Application Data\Autodesk\AutoCAD 2009\R17.2\enu\Support\Actions

✦ **Windows Vista:**
<drive>:\Users*<username>*\AppData\Autodesk\AutoCAD
2009\R17.2\enu\Support\Actions

You use the Options dialog box to change the default location used to store recorded action macro files and where AutoCAD can find other action macros for playback. In the Options dialog box, click the Files tab and expand the Action Recorder Settings node to reveal the file locations used for recording and playing back action macro files. Expand the Actions Recording File Location node to see the current location used for storing recorded action macro files. Select the path and click Browse to specify a different location that newly recorded action macro files should be saved to. When you click Browse, the Browse to Folder dialog box is displayed, allowing you to select a different location. Click OK to use the selected path.

Expand the Additional Actions Reading File Locations node to see the additional locations that Action Recorder looks for action macro files, and then click Add to add a new location to the node. To update an existing location, select the path and click Browse. You use the Browse to Folder dialog box to add or update a location. If you plan on sharing the action macros you record, it's best to place the ACTM files in a network location and then add the location to the Additional Actions Reading File Locations node.

Editing Actions and Recorded Values

After an action macro has been recorded and saved, you can edit the recorded actions or values to achieve the desired results and insert requests for user input. You can edit a recorded action and value by right-clicking one of the nodes that represents a recorded action or value in the Action tree. You can edit a recorded action and value in the following ways:

✦ **Insert User Message:** Displays the Insert User Message box, which allows you to specify a text string that should be displayed when the action macro is played back. The user message can be inserted at any location in the action macro by first selecting an action or value node before right-clicking in the Action Tree. The user message is displayed during playback.

+ **Request User Input:** Allows you to have the user provide a value in response to a value node when the action macro is played back. The user has the option to provide input or use the value that was recorded with the action macro.

+ **Edit:** Allows you to edit the current value of a value node.

+ **Relative to Previous:** Allows you to toggle a coordinate value that was provided as an absolute value to be relative to the previous coordinate value recorded in the action macro. All coordinate values are captured as absolute, but all coordinates other than the first are played back as relative to the previous point by default.

+ **Delete:** Allows you to delete a recorded action. Only actions can be deleted; you can't delete a value node that is used by an action.

+ **Use Pick First Set:** Uses the objects selected prior to the playback of the action macro. The PICKFIRST system variable must be set to 1; otherwise, the objects selected are deselected prior to the playback of the action macro and you are prompted to select objects during playback instead.

+ **Macro-Created Object Selection:** Selects any objects that are created during the playback of the action macro.

+ **Re-specify New Selection Set:** You are prompted to select a new selection set of objects during playback.

For more information on editing and working with different types of actions and value nodes, see AutoCAD's online Help system and use the Index tab to look up Action Macros, Node Icons.

Just Press Play

After you record an action macro file, set up the recorded value nodes as desired, and add any necessary user messages, you're ready to play back the action macro in a new or existing drawing. To play back a recorded action macro, you select the action macro that you want to play back from the Action Macros drop-down list and then click Play.

If a recorded value has been changed to request user input during playback, you'll be presented with the ability to provide user input in the form of a value that you enter at the command prompt, specify a point in the drawing window, or select objects. You can also play back the action macro based on its recorded value, or abort playback if you're prompted for user input during playback.

Along with being presented with a request for user input, you might also be presented with a user message that informs you of what the action macro might do or what settings are required to successfully play back the action macro. Click Yes to continue playing back the action macro or No to abort the playback.

When AutoCAD finds an action macro in one of the specified locations under the Action Recorder Settings node on the Files tab of the Options dialog box, AutoCAD automatically sets up a command with the same name as the action macro, as long as a command with the same name is not already defined. Just like any other command in AutoCAD, you can type its name at the command line to start it. So entering the name of an action macro at the command prompt plays back that action macro.

Index

Symbols

@ symbol, 131, 133, 134, 162
/b command line switch, 643
/c command line switch, 643
-INSERT command, 424
-LAYER command, 707
/ld command line switch, 643
/nologo command line switch, 643
/nossm command line switch, 643
/p command line switch, 644
-PAN command, 217
/pl command line switch, 644
/r command line switch, 644
/s command line switch, 644
-SCRIPT command, 707
/set command line switch, 644
/t command line switch, 644
/v command line switch, 644
-VPORTS command, 509–510
/w command line switch, 644

Numerics

2-point circle, 89
2D Drafting & Annotation workspace, 15
2D drawing
  3D models, creating from, 381, 385–389
  AutoCAD compared to AutoCAD LT, 325
  coordinate system, 127
  DWFx file format, 629
  exchanging AutoCAD and AutoCAD LT, 342
  new, creating, 16–19
2D solid, 160, 178
3-point arc, 165
3-point circle, 89
3D model. *See also* rendering in 3D
  arrays, 392
  AutoCAD abilities, 32
  AutoCAD compared to AutoCAD LT, 323, 324, 325–326, 327, 342–343, 349, 355, 373, 375
  coordinate system, 127, 351–356
  creating solids, 393–398
  DWF attachment limitations, 467
  DWFx file format, 629
  editing solids, 399–402
  helixes, 384–385
  introduction, 349
  modifying, 390–392
  navigation in, 226, 373–378
  polylines, 384, 393
  regions, 381–384
  spatial indexing, 603
  templates, 73
  types, 350–351
  viewport display of objects, 513
  views, 369–380
  VIZ 2008, 336
3D Modeling tab, Options dialog box, 668
3D models from 2D drawing, 381, 385–390
3DALIGN command, 391–392
3DARRAY command, 392
3DCORBIT command, 374
3DDISTANCE command, 376
3DFLY command, 376
3DFORBIT command, 374
3DMIRROR command, 392
3DMOVE command, 390
3DORBIT command, 374
3DPAN command, 376
3DPOLY command, 384
3DROTATE command, 391
3DSWIVEL command, 376
3DWALK command, 376
3DZOOM command, 376

A

absolute coordinates, 129–131, 352
acad.dvb, 642
accuracy compared to precision, 125–126
action in AutoCAD, definition, 717
action macro (ACTM) file format, 719, 722–723
Action Macro dialog box, 719
action macros, 328, 641, 717–725
Action Recorder, 328, 641, 717–725
actions, dynamic blocks, 433–434, 436, 437

ACTM (action macro) file format, 719, 722–723
ADCENTER command, 482–486
Add object selection mode, 188
Add Plot Style Table Wizard, 551–554
Add Plotter Wizard, 546–550
Add Profile dialog box, 650
Advanced Render Settings palette, 48, 412
Advanced Setup Wizard, 70–71
Aerial View option, 216
AIA (American Institute of Architects) (Web site), 82, 83, 579
alias, command, 86, 334, 641, 652–655, 690–692
Alias Editor, 654–655
ALIGN command, 391
alignment
  3D model, 391–392
  text, 238, 240–242, 249–250, 259, 712
Alignment parameter, dynamic blocks, 440
All option, ZOOM command, 220
ALL selection mode, 188
Allow/Disallow Dynamic UCS mode, 52
Allow Docking option, 48
American Institute of Architects (AIA) (Web site), 82, 83, 579
anchoring palettes, 48
angles, setting up, 71–72
angular units, 98, 99
animation, 344, 413
ANITPATH command, 413
ANNOREST command, 319

annotation. *See also* dimensions; hatch pattern; text
  AutoCAD compared to AutoCAD LT, 325, 343–344
  dimensions, drafting, 28–29
  introduction, 27–30
  scaling of, 313–320
  standards for, 569
  tool access options, 159
Annotation Object Scale dialog box, 317–318
annotative scaling, hatch patterns, 303, 308–309, 316
Annotative style, text, 245, 246, 248
Application Load dialog box, 642
application status bar, 51–56, 658, 660
arc, 24, 158, 164–165, 177–178, 712
arc-aligned text, 712
ARC command, 158, 164–165
architectural units, 98, 99, 101–102
ARCHIVE command, 541
archiving, sheets/sheet sets, 541
array, 193, 204–205, 439
Array action, dynamic blocks, 439
ARRAY command, 193, 204–205
associative property, hatch patterns, 186, 303
Attach DGN Underlay dialog box, 472–473
Attach Digital Signatures utility, 614–615

attachment type of xref, 451, 452
ATTDEF command, 158, 428, 436
ATTDIA system variable, 431
ATTEXT command, 432
ATTREQ system variable, 431
Attribute Definition dialog box, 428–430, 436
Attribute Editor, 431
attributes. *See also* block
  adding to blocks, 428
  annotative scaling of, 316
  AutoCAD LT's limitations, 325, 432
  default value for, 429
  definition, 238, 417, 428–430, 436
  editing, 431
  exporting/importing information, 712
  extracting, 432
  inserting, 430–431
  introduction, 427–428
  synchronizing to blocks, 432
  tool access options, 158
ATTSYNC command, 432, 439
auto-list option, 256
AutoCAD. *See also* AutoCAD LT
  advantages of, 1, 31–32
  communication methods, 56–58
  customizing, 34–35, 341, 639–640
  definition, 1
  dynamic blocks in earlier versions, 448
  editions, 1

feature set overview, 34–35

files and formats, 32, 617–618

Help system, 60–63

installation and deployment, 341, 710

interface overview, 41–56

introduction, 1–9, 13–16

online resources, 63

real-world units compared to, 98–99

running commands, 58–60

starting, 14, 37–40

as vector-based program, 462

version considerations, 32, 75, 76, 79, 335, 500, 631

viewers for, 335, 338, 466, 630

AutoCAD 2008 3D Modeling Workbook For Dummies, 349

AutoCAD Block (Web site), 337

AutoCAD Certification (Web site), 361

AutoCAD Color Index (ACI), 122, 551

AutoCAD LT
  3D limitations, 323, 324, 325–326, 327, 342–343, 349, 355, 373, 375
  Action Recorder, lack of, 717
  attribute limitations, 325, 432
  AutoCAD, comparing with, 33–34, 325, 328–330, 343–344
  AutoCAD, working together with, 339–345

boundaries and limitations of, 323–329

cameras, lack of, 371

color systems, 122

command line switch limitations, 644

Content Explorer, 482

custom shape limitation, 640

customizing, 341

DLINE command, 171

document protection limitations, 604

dynamic UCS, lack of, 368

Express Tools, lack of, 328, 655

extending, 331–338

external command alias limitation, 653

file format limitations, 618

gradient fill restrictions, 310

groups of objects, 192

Hatch dialog box, 304

indexing of drawing content in, 604

installation and deployment, 341

layer properties, 121

light and camera limitations, 667

new features, 35

options differences, 649

Partial Open feature, lack of, 598

REFEDIT command, lack of, 425

shade modes, 379, 380

shape file limitation, 709

sheet sets, lack of, 515

ShowMotion option, lack of, 232

starting, 14, 641–642

SteeringWheel feature, 228

template limitations, 575

thickness property, 385

versions, 33

ViewCube, lack of, 370

viewport features, 507

xref limitations, 455, 458, 465, 477

AutoCAD OEM, 323. *See also* AutoCAD LT

AutoCAPS feature, 257

Autodesk, 1, 323, 336, 337–338

Autodesk Buzzsaw (Web site), 626–628

Autodesk Design Review, 466, 630, 631–635

Autodesk discussion groups (Web site), 63

Autodesk DWF Composer, 630

Autodesk DWF Viewer, 630

Autodesk DWF Writer, 630

Autodesk i-drop, 621, 624

Autodesk Impression (Web site), 336

Autodesk Streamline (Web site), 626

Autodesk Symbols 2000 (Web site), 336

Autodesk VIZ 2008 (Web site), 336

AutoLISP, 642, 705, 707, 715

automatic crossing selection box, 187

automatic window selection box, 187

AUTOPUBLISH system variable, 562

AutoVue (Web site), 338

B

/b command line switch, 643
background
  displaying with Layout Elements, 666
  plotting in, 560
  rendering process, 410–411
BACKGROUND command, 410
Background dialog box, 410
background mask, text, 257–258
backup, file, 66, 83–84, 617–618
Backwards option for text, 248
BACTION command, 436
BACTIONTOOL command, 442–443
BASE command, 427
base point, 198, 308, 418, 420, 440
Base Point parameter, dynamic blocks, 440
Batch Standards Checker, 581, 591–595
BATTMAN command, 432
BCOUNT command, 715
BCYCLEORDER command, 446
BEDIT command, 425, 431, 433, 437–438
Bentley's MicroStation, 470
binding xrefs, 460–461
block. *See also* attributes; dynamic block
  annotative, 421
  in AutoCAD LT, 325, 332, 342

Autodesk collection, 336
  callout, 534, 536–537, 540–541
  clipping, 459
  creating, 315, 418–421
  customizing, 640
  definition, 417
  editing, 425
  exploding, 421, 711
  Express Tools for, 711–712
  external references, relationship to, 449–450, 712
  inserting, 422–424, 426, 430–431, 446–447, 715
  introduction, 417–418
  label, 534–536, 540
  LIGHTSINBLOCKS system variable, 407
  list of, 536–537
  managing, 424–427
  naming, 418, 419, 424–425
  redefining, 425
  scaling, 421, 439
  selecting, 418, 420, 535–536
  static, 433, 448
  in tables, 263
  third-party products (Web sites), 337–338
  title block, 428, 502, 569
  tool access options, 158
  units for, 421
  visibility states, 436, 443–446
Block Authoring palettes, 435, 436, 437, 440–443
BLOCK command, 158, 418
Block Definition dialog box, 315, 418–421
block definition table, 422
Block Editor feature, 425, 433–439

block reference, definition, 422
BLOCKEDITLOCK system variable, 437
BMAKE command, 431
board drafting, 1
body options, solids, 400
boundary, creating, 158, 308–309
BOUNDARY command, 158
Boundary Definition Error, 306
bounding box, 253, 480
BOX command, 393, 395
box shape, 393, 395
BPARAMETER command, 435, 440–441
Brava! Viewer (Web site), 338
BREAK command, 194, 207
BREAK@ (break at point) command, 208
breaks, object, 194, 207, 208
budgeting in CAD management, 568
bulleted lists, text, 255–256
Button Image pane, CUI Editor, 679, 683
Buzzsaw (Web site), 327, 626–628
BVHIDE command, 436
By Layer, 112, 120, 121, 196, 213

C

/c command line switch, 643
CAD (Computer Aided Drafting/Design). *See also* collaboration
  history, 31
  introduction, 1–9

CAD standards
annotation, 569
AutoCAD compared to AutoCAD LT, 327–328, 344–345
AutoCAD tools introduction, 581
batch checking drawings, 591–595
block definition, 421
CAD management role, 568
CAD Web site, 83
collaboration issues, 567, 569
drawing setup, 123
DWS file format, 75, 77, 344–345, 581–583
file exchange practices, 569
file locations, 569, 570–571
importance in organizing reusable content, 479
introduction, 16
layer translation, 588–591
linetype, 122–123
management of, 567, 582–588
naming and storage for drawings, 569
overview, 579–581
title blocks, 569
training, 569
CAD Standards Notification tray icon, 55
CADdepot (Web site), 337
CADOPOLIS.COM (Web site), 337
CADToolsOnline.com (Web site), 338
CADViewer (Web site), 338
callout blocks, 534, 536–537, 540–541
CAMERA command, 371

Camera Preview dialog box, 372
CAMERAGLYPH system variable, 372
cameras, 344, 371–372
Cartesian coordinate system, 126–128
case of text, 712
Cell Styles area, 261
Center, Diameter option, circle, 89
Center, Radius option, circle, 89, 163
Center justification option, 241
Center option, ZOOM command, 220
CFG (configuration) file format, 552
chamfer, 179, 194, 210, 401
CHAMFER command, 194, 210, 401
CHANGE command, 317
Change Space option, title bar, 194
Change to Current Layer option, 120
Check option, solid bodies, 400
Check Standards dialog box, 586–587
CHECKSTANDARDS command, 586
CHSPACE command, 194, 211
circle, 23, 88–90, 158, 163–164
CIRCLE command, 23, 89, 158, 163–164
Circumscribed option, POLYGON command, 180
Classic view, 44

Clean option, solid bodies, 400
Clean Screen, 49, 56, 674
CLEANSCREENOFF command, 49, 674
CLEANSCREENON command, 49, 674
Clipboard as organizing tool, 480–482
clipping
AutoCAD compared to AutoCAD LT, 342
DGN underlay, 473–474
DWF underlay, 469–470
external references, 458–459
raster images, 464
viewport, 513–514
clipping frame, 342
Clockwise check box, 102
clouds, revision, 160
collaboration. *See also* sharing electronic files
AutoCAD abilities, 32
AutoCAD compared to AutoCAD LT, 327, 345
digital signatures, 608–615
drafting environment, 568, 570–571
external file consider-ations, 68
introduction, 567–570
password-protecting drawings, 604–608
saving drawings for, 602
standards setting for, 567, 569
templates, 571–577
color
AutoCAD Color Index, 122, 551
edges of solids, 399
faces, 400

color *(continued)*
  gradient fills, 159, 303, 310–311, 325, 343
  layer property, 19, 111, 113–114
  layout tabs, 505
  as object property, 121
  object snaps, 667
  plot styles, 551
  Window Elements, 665, 666
Color Books system, 122
color-dependent plot style, 72, 551
columns, multiline text, 256
command aliases, 86, 334, 641, 652–655
command line/prompt. *See also individual commands*
  aliases, 86, 334
  canceling commands, 59
  CUI Editor, 680–684
  drawing primitive objects, 87–88, 161–164
  entering coordinates at, 129, 131, 133, 134–135
  Express Tools for, 715
  grip-edit, 214
  Help access through, 61
  introduction, 51, 56–57
  repeating commands, 58, 165
  running commands, 58–60
  tool palette commands, creating, 488
  tooltips, 61
  transparent commands, 59–60
  window, 51, 57
command line switches, 334, 641, 642–647
Command List pane, CUI Editor, 678

Command Reference feature, 161
communication in drafting process, 340
compass feature for 3D views, 371
COMPILE command, 709
Compiled Menu (MNC) file format, 676
compiled shape (SHX) file format, 66, 245, 709
complex solids, 401
Computer Aided Drafting/ Design (CAD). *See also* collaboration
  history, 31
  introduction, 1–9
cone, 394, 396
CONE command, 394, 396
configuration (CFG) file format, 552
Configure Standards dialog box, 583–585
Constrained Orbit option, 374
construction line (xline), 160, 166–168, 169
Construction Specifications Institute (CSI) (Web site), 82, 83, 579
Content Explorer, 482
context-sensitive (shortcut) menus, 38–40, 45, 59, 60–61, 690–692
Continuous Orbit option, 374
CONVERTPSTYLES command, 551
coordinate systems
  2D drawing, 127
  3D model, 127, 351–356, 371
  absolute, 129–131, 352

cylindrical, 352–353
direct distance entering, 126, 135–136, 352
dynamic input, relationship to, 130, 132, 134, 137–141
entering coordinates, 129–135
introduction, 20–21, 126–128
polar, 352–354
relative, 131–135, 352–354
spherical, 353–354
status bar display, 51, 52
user (UCS), 128–129, 356
world (WCS), 128–129
COPY command, 25, 194, 198–199
COPYBASE command, 480
COPYCLIP command, 194, 198, 480, 514
copying
  to Clipboard, 480
  edges of solids, 399
  editing commands list, 194
  faces, 400
  MATCHPROP command, 195, 211, 311
  nested objects, 711
  objects to layers, 120
COPYMODE system variable, 200
COPYTOLAYER command, 120
CPolygon selection mode, 188
Create Layout Wizard, 501–503
Create New Drawing dialog box, 69, 574
Create Sheet Set Wizard, 517, 518–522

Create Viewport in New Layouts option, Layout Elements, 666

crosshairs, controlling size, 667

Crossing window selection mode, 188

CSI (Construction Specifications Institute) (Web site), 82, 83, 579

CTB (plot style table) file format, 67, 551

Ctrl key, 696

cubes, 393, 395

CUI (Custom User Interface) file format, 675, 676. *See also* Customize User Interface (CUI) Editor

current layer, settings for, 119, 120

current workspace, setting, 669

Custom User Interface (CUI) file format, 675–676. *See also* Customize User Interface (CUI) Editor

Customizations In pane, CUI Editor, 677–678

Customize User Interface (CUI) Editor
AutoCAD LT, 333
Command List pane, 678
commands in, 488, 680–684
Customizations In pane, 677–678
double-click actions, 697–698
Dynamic pane, 679–680
enterprise customization files, 677, 702–703
introduction, 675–677

launching, 680
menu customizing, 688–689
migrating customizations, 700–702
overview, 641
partial customization files, 677, 702, 703
Quick Properties, 213, 698–700
ribbon customizing, 692–695
rollover tooltips, 698–699
separator bars, 696
shortcut keys, 696–697
shortcut menus, 690–692
toolbar, 680, 684–688
workspaces, 668, 670–671

customizing
Action Recorder, 328, 641, 717–725
blocks, 640
command aliases, 652–655
DesignCenter. *See* DesignCenter
display settings, 664–668
dockable windows, 662–663
Express Tools. *See* Express Tools
hatch patterns, 310, 332, 640
introduction, 639–641
linetypes, 332, 640
overview of options, 34–35, 341, 647–649
panels, 662–663
programming method, 639–640
script files as tools for, 705–709
shapes, 640, 709–710
sheets/sheet set properties, 531–534

startup process, 641–647, 709
status bars, 641, 657–662
templates, 123, 572, 640
tool palettes, 488–489, 640, 685–686
toolbars, 662–664, 671, 680, 684–688
user interface. *See* Customize User Interface (CUI) Editor
user profiles, 641, 649–652
workspaces, 668–674

CUTCLIP command, 194, 481

cutting objects with Clipboard, 481

cylinder, 394, 397

CYLINDER command, 394, 397

cylindrical coordinates, 352–353

D

Dashboard. *See* ribbon

data exchange, AutoCAD compared to AutoCAD LT, 327

Data Extraction Wizard, 432

Data Link Manager, 263–264

Data Link tray icon, 55

data mining, 482

database, AutoCAD object storage in, 32

DATAEXTRACTION command, 262

DATALINK command, 263–264

DATALINKUPDATE command, 264

DBConnect Manager palette, 48, 328

DC Online, 483

decimal degrees units, 98, 99

decimal units, 98, 99

DEFAULTLIGHTINGTYPE system variable, 404

DEFPOINTS layer, 109

deg/min/sec units, 98, 102

DELAY command, 707

Delete option, faces, 399

DELOBJ system variable, 381

demand loading of xrefs, 460, 603

Design Review, 466, 630, 631–635

Design Web Format (DWF/ DWFx) file format

marking up for revision, 634–635

PDF file format, compared to, 630–631

publishing in, 561

sharing electronic files, 629–630, 631–635

as underlays for xrefs, 67, 466–470

viewing options, 558, 633–634

DesignCenter

adding resources to drawings, 485–486

in AutoCAD LT, 332

DC Online, 483

dynamic blocks, 446

hatch patterns, 307, 486

inserting stored blocks, 426

introduction, 482–483

linetypes, 486

palette, 48

ready-to-use blocks, 336

resource drawing locations, 483–485

desktop icons, modifying, 334

desktop shortcut, creating, 645–647

DGN (Microstation design) file format, 67, 470–474, 618

DGNADJUST command, 474

DGNATTACH command, 471–473

DGNCLIP command, 473–474

DGNFRAME system variable, 474

DGNLAYERS command, 471

DGNOSNAP system variable, 473

dialog boxes

Action Recorder limitations, 721

modal compared to modeless, 58

overview, 58

tooltips, 61

DIESEL (Direct Interpretively Evaluated String Expression Language), 333, 641, 660–662

digital ID, 608, 610–611

Digital Signature Contents dialog box, 614

digital signatures, 608–615

Dimension menu, 44

dimensioning, manual compared to AutoCAD tools, 125

dimensions

angular, 98, 99

AutoCAD compared to AutoCAD LT, 325

commands list, 284–286

creating, 270–271, 283–293

default units, 67

editing, 293–296

geometric tolerances, 301–302

introduction, 267–269

leaders, 296–301

linear, 28–29, 98, 99, 101–102

order of, 103

radius, 88

real-world units compared to AutoCAD, 98–99

scaling to, 107

styles, 271–283, 315

tools, 713

types, 269–270

units setup, 97–102

values definition, 238

DIMLINEAR command, 28–29

DIMSCALE system variable, 28, 320

direct distance entering, coordinates, 126, 135–136, 352

Display Drawing Status Bar option, Window Elements, 665

Display Layout and Model tabs option, Layout Elements, 666

Display Paper Background option, Layout Elements, 666

Display Paper Shadow option, Layout Elements, 666

Display Printable Area option, Layout Elements, 666

Display Screen Menu option, Window Elements, 665

Display Scroll Bars in Drawing Window option, Window Elements, 665
display settings. *See also* panning; views; zooming
  backgrounds for layouts, 666
  coordinate systems in status bar, 51, 52
  customizing, 664–668
  Grid Display mode, 52
  Layout Elements, 665–666
  lights, 344
  toolbars, 193
  viewports, 511–513
  Window Elements, 664–665
Display tab, Options dialog box, 505–506
DISTANTLIGHT command, 406
Distributed justification option, 242
distribution of drawings, AutoCAD abilities, 32
DLINE command, 158, 171, 325
docking of window elements, 48, 662–663, 671
donut, 158, 180
DONUT command, 158, 180
dot (point)
  2-point circle, 89
  3-point arc, 165
  3-point circle, 89
  base/insertion, 198, 308, 418, 420, 440
  breaking at, 208
  inserting, 161–162, 165–166

placing/formatting, 88, 165–166
styles, 165–166
tool access options, 159
double-click actions, customizing, 697–698
double line, tool access options, 158
DPI (dots per inch) for raster images, 462
drafting, manual, 31
drafting modes on status bar, 52
Drafting Settings dialog box, 16–17, 137–141
Drafting tab, Options dialog box, 667–668
dragging and dropping files into drawing window, 79–80
Draw menu, 44
draw order, 194, 211, 475
Draw panel, 3–4, 157, 158–160, 164
Draw tools, Express Tools, 713
drawing area, 49, 71, 495. *See also* model space; paper space
drawing (DWG) file format
  attaching as xref, 452–454
  attaching to each other, 67
  AutoCAD versions, 33
  as basic AutoCAD drawing file, 65–66
  naming, 597–598
  saving options, 75
drawing interchange format (DXF) file format, 75, 77
Drawing orientation option, Page Setup, 496
drawing set, definition, 515
Drawing Set Description (DSD) file format, 562

drawing standards (DWS) file format, 75, 77, 344–345, 581–583
drawing template (DWT) file format, 72, 77, 494. *See also* templates
drawings
  3D. *See* 3D model
  annotation. *See* annotation
  AutoCAD compared to AutoCAD LT, 325
  Clipboard as organizing tool, 480–482
  coordinate system, 127
  DesignCenter, 482–486
  display options. *See* views
  exchanging AutoCAD and AutoCAD LT, 341–342
  external references (xrefs). *See* external references (xrefs)
  indexing of content, 460, 604
  layers. *See* layers
  layouts. *See* layouts
  limits, 17–18, 102–104, 106–107
  model space. *See* model space
  modifying objects, 25–26
  multiple, 80–81
  naming conventions, 597–598
  new, creating, 16–25, 68–73
  object properties, 120–123
  opening existing, 76–78
  organization overview, 479–480
  orientation, 496, 561
  paper space. *See* paper space

drawings *(continued)*
Partial Open feature, 598–601
protecting, 604–615
publishing, 516, 561–563
recent list, 78
saving, 16, 73–80, 601–604, 602
scale settings, 104–107
setup, 16–19
sheet sets. *See* sheets/sheet sets
standards setup, 123
startup overview, 68–73
status bar, 56, 658–659
templates. *See* templates
title bar, 41
tool overview, 157–161
Tool Palettes window, 486–489
units of measurement, 97–102
views. *See* views
Web-based, 619, 622–625
DRAWORDER command, 194, 211, 475
DSD (Drawing Set Description) file format, 562
DST (sheet set) file format, 345, 515, 523
DSVIEWER command, 216
DTEXT command, 27–28, 238, 240
DUCS (dynamic UCS), 326, 368
duplicating objects, 25
DWF Composer, 630
DWF/DWFx (Design Web Format) file format
marking up for revision, 634–635
PDF file format, compared to, 630–631

publishing in, 561
sharing electronic files, 629–630, 631–635
as underlays for xrefs, 67, 466–470
viewing options, 558, 633–634
DWF Viewer, 630
DWF Writer, 630
DWF6 ePlot device, 632–633
DWFADJUST command, 470
DWFATTACH command, 467–469
DWFCLIP command, 469–470
DWFFRAME system variable, 470
DWFLAYERS command, 467
DWFOSNAP system variable, 469
DWG (drawing) file format
attaching as xref, 452–454
attaching to each other, 67
AutoCAD versions, 33
as basic AutoCAD drawing file, 65–66
naming, 597–598
saving options, 75
DWG TrueView (Web site), 33, 335
DWS (drawing standards) file format, 75, 77, 344–345, 581–583
DWT (drawing template) file format, 72, 77, 494. *See also* templates
DXF (drawing interchange format) file format, 75, 77
dynamic block
adding parameters and actions, 439–446
creating, 434–439
definition, 433

in earlier AutoCAD versions, 448
inserting, 446–447
introduction, 433–434
modifying, 447
dynamic input
3D modeling, 352
coordinate system, relationship to, 130, 132, 134, 137–141
introduction, 51
status bar access, 52
workings of, 57, 58
Dynamic option, ZOOM command, 219
Dynamic pane, CUI Editor, 679–680
dynamic UCS (DUCS), 326, 368

E

EATTEDIT command, 431
EATTEXT command, 432
Edge Effects panel, 379–380
Edge option, POLYGON command, 180
edges, solid, 399
Edit Attributes dialog box, 431
Edit Block Definition dialog box, 437–438
editing
attributes, 431
blocks, 425
commands list, 194
dimensions, 293–296
external references (xrefs), 455–457
fill pattern, 311
with grips, 93, 213–214
hatch patterns, 195, 211, 311
multiline text, 258, 259

page setup, 499–500
plot style, 554
polylines, 195, 211
scaling objects, 196, 511
single-line text, 258, 259
solids, 399–402
text, 258–259
EDITTIME command, 715
ELEV command, 356
elevation, setting in 3D, 355–356
ellipse, 158, 176–178
ELLIPSE/Arc command, 177–178
ELLIPSE command, 158, 176
encryption of drawings, 605–606
Endpoint object snap mode, 24
engineering units, 98
enterprise customization files, 677, 702–703
ERASE command, 94, 194, 197
Esc key, uses of, 59
ETRANSMIT command, 541
eTransmit feature, 68, 327, 541
Excel, Microsoft, linking to spreadsheet, 263–264
EXPLODE command, 194, 208, 270, 383, 421
exploding
  blocks, 421, 711
  dimensions, 270
  polylines, 208
  regions, 383
  text, 712
  tool access options, 194
  workings of command, 208
Explorer, Windows, accessing files from, 40, 79

exporting
  attribute information, 712
  AutoCAD compared to AutoCAD LT, 327
  block definition, 426–427
  DXF file format, 75
  to non-AutoCAD file formats, 617–618
  TABLEEXPORT command, 263, 264
  user profile, 650–652
EXPORTLAYOUT command, 500
Express Tools
  accessing toolbar for, 81
  Alias Editor, 654
  AutoCAD LT's lack of, 328, 655
  block tools, 711–712
  command line/prompt, 715
  dimension tools, 713
  Draw tools, 713
  File tools, 714
  images, opening outside of AutoCAD, 465
  installation option, 44
  installing, 710–711
  introduction, 710
  layout tools, 712–713
  Modify tools, 713
  selection tools, 713
  shape tool, 710
  text tools, 712
  Web tools, 714
EXPRESSMENU command, 711
EXPRESSTOOLS command, 711
EXTEND command, 194, 208
Extended Help File property, CUI commands, 682

extended tooltips, 61–62
Extents option, ZOOM command, 220, 222
external files, 66–67. *See also* external references (xrefs)
External Reference Notification tray icon, 55
external references (xrefs). *See also* block
  attaching, 452–454
  AutoCAD compared to AutoCAD LT, 325, 342
  binding, 460–461
  block conversion to, 712
  blocks, compared to, 449–450
  clipping, 458–459
  definition, 67, 418, 449
  DGN underlays, 470–474
  draw order, 475
  DWF/DWFX underlays, 466–470
  editing, 455–457
  increasing performance, 460–461
  introduction, 449
  managing across drawings, 476–478
  model views, 539
  notification of, 454–455
  OLE, 418, 475–476
  Partial Open feature, 600
  raster image references, 462–466
  sheet sets, relationship to, 518
  tools for, 450–452
  unloading, 460
EXTERNALREFERENCES command, 450–451

External References palette, 48, 450
EXTRUDE command, 385–386
extruded objects, 385–386, 399

F

face, 350–351, 399–400, 410
Fence selection mode, 188
fields, 238, 257, 325, 343–344
file formats. *See also* DWF/DWFx (Design Web Format) file format; DWG (drawing) file format
  ACTM, 719, 722–723
  AutoCAD LT limitations, 618, 709
  CFG, 552
  CTB, 67
  CUI, 675, 676
  default setting, 602
  DGN, 67, 470–474
  DSD, 562
  DST, 345, 515, 523
  DWS, 75, 77, 344–345, 581–583
  DWT, 72, 77, 494
  DXF, 75, 77
  exporting AutoCAD to different, 617–618
  KML/KMZ, 408
  LIN, 67
  MNC, 676
  MNR, 676
  MNS, 676
  MNU, 676
  overview, 65–68
  PAT, 67
  PC3, 546

  PDF, 629, 630
  PGP, 652
  saving to earlier, 602
  SCR, 706
  SHP, 709
  SHX, 66, 245, 709
  STB, 67, 551
  TTF, 66
File menu, 43
File References area, External References palette, 450
File tools, Express Tools, 714
files. *See also* external references (xrefs); file formats; sharing electronic files
  action macro location, 722–723
  backing up, 66, 83–84, 617–618
  CAD standards, 569, 570–571
  closing, 81–82
  dragging and dropping into drawing window, 79–80
  enterprise customization, 677, 702–703
  external, 66–67
  image, 67, 449, 462–466
  managing, 82–83
  multiple-drawing environment, 80–81
  naming, 82–83, 569, 597–598
  new drawing start options, 68–73
  partial customization, 677, 702, 703
  Partial Open feature, 598–601

  saving, 73–80
  script, 331–332, 641, 643, 705–709
  searching, 77–78
  storing, 83
  types, 75
  underlay, 67, 466–474
  Windows Explorer, accessing from, 40, 79
fill pattern. *See also* hatch pattern
  adding, 304–307
  editing, 311
  gradient, 159, 303, 310–311, 325, 343
  solid, 303, 309–310
fillet, 179, 194, 210, 401
FILLET command, 194, 210, 401
filters, point/dot/xy, 151–153, 354
Find and Replace dialog box, 264
finding
  drawings, 483–484, 598
  files, 77–78
  text, 264
Fit justification option, 241
Fit tolerance, spline, 175
FLATSHOT command, 388
Flip action, dynamic blocks, 440
Flip parameter, dynamic blocks, 440
floating toolbars, 685
floating viewports, 320, 500, 506–508
flyouts
  creating, 687
  definition, 685
  introduction, 5
  location and function of, 220–221

submenus, compared to, 688

tool palette, creating on, 488

folders, managing, 83, 483

FONTALT system variable, 245

FONTMAP system variable, 245

fonts, 66, 239, 244–245, 665, 666

Fonts option, Window Elements, 665, 666

Format menu, 44

formatting

fonts, 66, 239, 244–245, 665, 666

justification, 238, 240–242, 249–250, 259

multiline text, 252–253, 254–255

fractional units, 98

Frame option, WIPEOUT command, 183

Free Orbit option, 374

FREESPOT command, 405

FREEWEB command, 405

Freeze/Thaw in New Viewport layer mode, 113

Freeze/Thaw layer mode, 112

freezing

layers, 112–113, 120, 512–513, 514, 603

viewports, 113, 512–513, 514

From a Data Link option, starting table, 262, 264

From Object Data in the Drawing option, starting table, 262

FTP (File Transfer Protocol), 619–621

Full Navigation wheel, 376

G

gap tolerances, 307

generic lights, 404

Geographic Location dialog box, 407, 408

geometric tolerances, dimensions, 301–302

glyph

camera, 371, 372

light, 407

Google Earth, 408

GRADIENT command, 159

gradient fills, 159, 303, 310–311, 325, 343

grads units, 98

graphic images, 67, 449, 462–466

grayscale, converting from color to, 551

grid. *See also* snap

setting, 16–17, 126, 141–143

size limits, 17–18, 103

Grid Display mode on status bar, 52

grips

3D model modification with, 390–391

camera glyph, 372

dynamic block, 434, 447

editing objects with, 93, 213–214

solid, 399, 400–401

viewport, 513

GROUP command, 192–193, 194

groups, object, 192–193, 194, 325

H

Hatch and Gradient dialog box, 304–309

HATCH command, 159, 305

Hatch dialog box, 304

hatch pattern

adding, 304–307

annotative scaling of, 303, 308–309, 316

associative property, 186, 303

AutoCAD compared to AutoCAD LT, 343–344

boundary options, 308–309

customizing, 310, 332, 640

editing, 195, 211, 311

gradient fills, 159, 303, 310–311, 325, 343

inserting into drawings, 486

introduction, 303–304

island detection, 308–309

origin (base point), 308

palette, 305–306, 307

PAT files, 67, 100

predefined, 309

publishing, 563

scale/spacing, 107, 316

settings, 307–309

tool access options, 159, 307

types, 309–310

user-defined, 309–310

Hatch Pattern Palette dialog box, 305–306

HATCHEDIT command, 195, 211, 311

hatching (PAT) file format, 67, 100

height of text, setting, 243–244, 248, 250–251, 313

helix, 384–385

HELIX command, 384–385

help string, assigning to CUI command, 683–684

Help system, 60–63, 161

HIDE command, 350, 351, 380

historical drawings, searching, 483

Home tab, ribbon
  Draw panel, 164
  function of, 360
  Layers panel, 113, 119
  Modify panel, 210
  Solid Editing panel, 399

Home view of 3D model, 377, 378

HPGAPTOL system variable, 307

Hyperlink option, block definition, 421

1

i-drop, 621, 624

icons
  adding to CUI commands, 679, 682–683
  desktop, modifying, 334
  status bar tray, 55–56, 454–455, 659–660
  UCS, 505, 668
  Workspace Switching, 4354

IdenTrust (Web site), 608

Image Adjust dialog box, 465–466

Image dialog box, 463

IMAGEADJUST command, 465–466

IMAGEAPP command, 465

IMAGEATTACH command, 462–463

IMAGECLIP command, 464–465

IMAGEEDIT command, 465

IMAGEFRAME command, 465

IMAGEQUALITY command, 466

images, graphic, 67, 449, 462–466

imperial compared to metric units of measure, 67, 97–98, 100, 123

implied windowing selection method, 186

importing
  attribute information, 712
  AutoCAD compared to AutoCAD LT, 327
  drawings as sheets, 523–525
  DXF format, 75
  KML/KMZ files, 408
  layouts, 503–504, 523–525
  page setups, 498–499
  user profile, 650–652

Impression (Web site), 336

Imprint option, solid bodies, 400

In option, ZOOM command, 220

in-place text editor, definition, 252

INDEXCTL system variable, 604

indexing
  drawing contents, 460, 603–604
  layer, 603
  sheet list, 516
  spatial, 603

infinite lines (RAY command), 158, 168–169

InfoCenter (formerly Info Palette), 62

Information pane, CUI Editor, 679

INSBASE system variable, 427

Inscribed option, POLYGON command, 180

Insert bind type, 461

INSERT command, 422, 446

Insert dialog box, 422

Insert menu, 44

Insert Object dialog box, 475–476

insertion cycling order, dynamic blocks, 446–447

insertion point, 198, 308, 418, 420

INSERTOBJ command, 475–476

installation, AutoCAD, modifying, 710

interface, overview, 41–56. *See also* Customize User Interface (CUI) Editor

Internet. *See also* Web sites
  DC online, 483
  online resources for AutoCAD, 63
  Publish to Web feature, 327, 622–625
  Web-based collaboration sites, 619, 626–628
  Web-based drawings, 619, 622–625
  Web tools, Express Tools, 714

INTERSECT command, 383, 401

irregular viewports, 506, 509–510
island detection, hatch pattern boundary, 308–309
ISO 128 linetypes, 123
ISO/DIS 12011 specification, 123
Isolate Layer to Current Viewport option, 120
isometric views, 369

J

JIS linetypes, 123
JOIN command, 195, 208
justification
  multiline shape, 172
  text, 238, 240–242, 249–250, 259
Justified justification option, 242
JUSTIFYTEXT command, 259

K

keyboard entry
  advantages as input device, 51
  Ctrl key, 696
  Esc key, uses of, 59
  grouping of objects shortcut, 192
  palette shortcuts, 47–48
  saving shortcuts, 74
  selection shortcuts, 189
  Shift key navigation for 3D, 375
  shortcut keys, customizing, 696–697
  showing shortcut keys in tooltips, 665

switching among drawings, 81
view toggles, 48–49
KML/KMZ files for geographic location, importing, 408

L

label blocks, 534–536, 540
Last object selection mode, 188
LAYCUR command, 120
LAYDEL command, 120
layer, current, 120
LAYER command, 707
Layer Control drop-down list, 118
Layer Delete option, 120
Layer Freeze option, 120
Layer Isolate option, 120
Layer Lock option, 120
Layer Match option, 119
Layer Merge option, 120
Layer Off option, 120
Layer palette, 47
Layer Properties Manager, 109–118, 512
layer state, 538
Layer States Manager, 119
Layer Translator, 581, 588–591
Layer Unisolate option, 120
Layer Unlock option, 120
Layer Walk option, 119
layer 0, 109, 421
layers
  By Layer, 112, 120, 121, 196, 213
  copying objects to, 120
  creating, 18–19, 109–110
  current, 120
  DEFPOINTS, 109

description property, 111
drawing settings, 108–120
DWFLAYERS command, 467
freezing/thawing, 112–113, 120, 512–513, 514, 603
indexing, 603
layer state, 119, 538
LAYERVALCTL system variable, 574
material assignment by, 409
modes, 112, 117–118
modifying settings, 113
named views, 231–232
naming, 109
overview, 108–109
palette for, 47
Partial Open feature, 598, 599, 601
plot styles, 111, 551
properties of, 18–19, 110–111, 121
translation to CAD standards, 588–591
in viewports, 111, 120, 512
Layers panel, 113, 119
LAYERSTATE command, 119
LAYERVALCTL system variable, 574
LAYFRZ command, 120
LAYISO command, 120
LAYLCK command, 120
LAYMCH command, 119
LAYMCUR command, 119
LAYMRG command, 120
LAYOFF command, 120
LAYON command, 120
Layout button, 50
LAYOUT command, 501, 504
Layout Elements options, 666–667

layout space. *See also* layouts; viewports
  introduction, 49–50
  lineweight in, 116
  model space, compared to, 107–108, 242–244, 500
  plotting from, 493, 496
  sheet sets in, 515
  text size in, 244
layouts. *See also* viewports
  advantages for plotting, 493
  appearance controls, 505–506
  creating, 501–503
  Express Tools, 712–713
  importing, 503–504, 523–525
  introduction, 500
  modifying, 504
  multiple, 500
  navigating, 504–505
  page setup, 494, 499, 504
  plotting from, 105, 108, 500–506, 558–559, 560
  templates, 503
  title block, 502
  views, 53, 232, 501, 504, 505
LAYOUTWIZARD command, 501–503
LAYTHW command, 120
LAYTRANS command, 588
LAYULK command, 120
LAYUNISO command, 120
LAYVPI command, 120
LAYWALK command, 119
/ld command line switch, 643
leader text, definition, 237
leaders, 296–301, 315, 320
legacy blocks, definition, 433

LENGTHEN command, 195, 207
lettered list option, 256
license management, software, 328–329
LIGHT command, 406–407
LIGHTGLYPHDISPLAY system variable, 407
lighting, display of
  AutoCAD compared to AutoCAD LT, 344
  default for 3D models, 404, 406
  rendering, 403–408
LIGHTINGUNITS system variable, 404
LIGHTLIST command, 407
Lights in Model palette, 407
Lights palette, 48
Lights panel, 404
LIGHTSINBLOCKS system variable, 407
limits, drawing, 17–18, 102–104, 106–107
LIMITS command, 103–104
Limits option, plotting, 103
LIN (linetype) file format, 67, 100
line. *See also* linetype; lineweight; polylines
  construction line (xline), 160, 166–168, 169
  creating, 22–23, 85–88, 161–162
  definition, 85
  dimension, 28–29
  double, 158
  joining, 208
  lengthening, 207
MLINE command, 171–173, 325
  parallel, 171–173
  polylines, compared to, 180–181

RAY command, 158, 168–169
temporary line segment, 87
tool access options, 159
LINE command, 22, 86–88, 159, 161–162, 180–181
Linear parameter, dynamic blocks, 439
linear units, 28–29, 98, 99, 101–102
linetype
  customizing, 332, 640
  inserting into drawings, 486
  layer property, 111, 114–116
  LIN files, 67, 100
  as object property, 121
  overview, 122–123
  scaling, 107
linetype (LIN) file format, 67, 100
lineweight
  display options, 52, 117
  layer property, 111, 116–117
  as object property, 121
  plot styles, 551, 560
linking information to drawings, 418. *See also* external references (xrefs)
LISP files node, 642
LIST command, 383
List of Blocks dialog box, 536–537
lists, text, 255–256
Live Section, 343
Lock/Unlock layer mode, 113
Lock/Unlock Viewport button, 54, 511

locking
  layers, 113, 120
  panels, window, 662–663
  toolbars, 662–664
  viewports, 54, 511
LOCKUI system variable,
    662–663
LOFT command, 386
Lookup action, dynamic
    blocks, 440
Lookup parameter,
    dynamic blocks, 440
loop shapes, definition, 381
LSP command, 715
LWT button, 117

M

macros
  action, 328, 641, 717–725
  CUI command, 681–682
  DIESEL, 333, 641, 660–662
main customization file, 677
Make Object's Layer
    Current option, 119
Manage Xrefs status bar
    tray icon, 454–455
MARKUP command, 634
Markup Set Manager
    palette, 48, 634
masking objects (wipeout),
    160, 182–183, 712
MASSPROP command, 382,
    383–384
MATCHPROP command,
    195, 211, 311
MATERIALASSIGN
    command, 410
MATERIALATTACH
    command, 121, 409
materials, 48, 121, 409–410
MATERIALS command, 409
Materials palette, 48, 409

MBUTTONPAN system
    variable, 226
MEASUREINIT system
    variable, 101
MEASUREMENT system
    variable, 100, 309, 574
menu bar, overview, 5–6,
    42–43
menu browser, 2–3, 15,
    42–43
Menu Resource (MNR) file
    format, 676
Menu Source (MNS) file
    format, 676
Menu Template (MNU) file
    format, 676
menus
  context-sensitive
    (shortcut), 38–40, 45,
    59, 60–61, 690–692
  customizing, 688–689
  display option, 665
  Navigation Modes,
    374–375
  Object Snap, 22
  overview, 43–44
  Status Bar Menu, 658
  submenus, 688–689
  workspace, 671, 672–673
metric compared to
    imperial units of
    measure, 67, 97–98,
    100, 123
Microsoft XPS Viewer, 629
Microspot DWG Viewer
    (Web site), 338
Microstation design (DGN)
    file format, 67, 470–474,
    618
MicroStation DGN files, 67,
    470–474, 618
Middle justification
    option, 241

Midpoint object snap
    mode, 22–23
Migrate Custom Settings
    utility, 700
migrating and transferring
    customizations,
    700–702
minimize/maximize
    button, 53
MIRROR command, 195,
    200–201
mirroring, 26, 195, 200–201,
    392
MLEADERSCALE system
    variable, 320
MLEDIT command, 171
MLINE command, 171–173,
    325
MNC (Compiled Menu) file
    format, 676
MNR (Menu Resource) file
    format, 676
MNS (Menu Source) file
    format, 676
MNU (Menu Template) file
    format, 676
modal dialog box, 58
model space (Model tab)
  introduction, 49–50
  layout display options,
    666
  lineweight in, 116
  paper space, compared
    to, 107–108, 242–244,
    500
  plotting from, 105, 493,
    496, 555–558
  sheets/sheet set views in,
    538–541
  text placement, 242–244
  tool access options, 53
  viewports, relationship to,
    506, 511

model views, 232, 517, 537–539

modeless dialog box, 58. *See also* palettes

MODEMACRO system variable, 660

Modify compared to Edit menu, 43

Modify panel, 210

Modify toolbar, 193

Modify tools, Express Tools, 713

mouse, navigating with, 50, 221, 222, 227, 375

Move action, dynamic blocks, 439

MOVE command, 195, 197–198

Move option, faces, 399

MREDO command, 195

MSLTSCALE system variable, 320

MTEXT command, 238

MTEXTED system variable, 259

MTEXTJIGSTRING system variable, 254

MTEXTTOOLBAR system variable, 253

multileader styles, 315

multiline object
AutoCAD compared to AutoCAD LT, 342
DLINE command, 158, 171, 325
introduction, 86
MLINE command, 171–173, 325
scaling, 172–173
tool access options, 159

multiline text (mtext)
annotative scaling of, 316
background masks, 257–258

columns, 256

creating, 253–256

definition, 237

editing, 258, 259

formatting, 252–253, 254–255

introduction, 239–240

lists, 255–256

overview, 252–253

text tools for, 712

Multiline Text panel, 252–253

multiple-drawing environment, 80–81

My Workspace, 669, 670

N

named plot styles, 72, 551

named views
background settings, 410
cameras, compared with, 371
creating, 228–231
model views, 539
Partial Open feature, 598
plotting, 229
sheet sets, relationship to, 518
sheet views, 518

naming
action macros, 725
blocks, 418, 419, 424–425
drawings, 569, 597–598
files, 82–83, 569, 597–598
layers, 109
resuable content, 479–480
sheet views, 518
sheets/sheet sets, 530–531, 535, 540
xrefs, 452, 461

National CAD Standards (Web site), 83, 579

navigation, AutoCAD. *See* panning; zooming

Navigation Modes menu, 374–375

NAVSMOTION command, 215, 216, 233

NAVSWHEEL command, 215, 216, 226–227, 377

NAVSWHEELMODE system variable, 226

nested objects, copying, 711

Network Deployment Wizard, 328–329

network location for drafting tools, 570–571

NEW command, 46, 68, 574

New Features Workshop, 14

NEWSHEETSET command, 518, 522

NEWSHOT command, 216

NEWVIEW command, 217

/nologo command line switch, 643

Non-Uniform Rational B-Splines (NURBS), 174

nonsystem print drivers, 544, 545–547

/nossm command line switch, 643

notification system, 660

noun/verb selection mode, 93, 185, 189, 190–191, 197

Number of Seconds Delay option, Window Elements, 665

numbered lists, text, 255–256

numbering of text, 712

O

object enablers in AutoCAD LT, 334–335
Object Linking and Embedding (OLE), 418, 475–476
Object option, irregular viewport, 509
Object option, ZOOM command, 220
object snap (OSNAP). *See also* snap
  3D modeling, 354–355
  color customizing, 667
  DGN underlays, 473
  DWF underlays, 469
  elevation, 356
  modes, 22–24
  overview, 126, 147–151
  xlines, relationship to, 167
Object Snap menu, 22
Object Snap mode on status bar, 52
Object Snap Tracking mode, 52, 126, 153–154, 355
ObjectARX, 642, 643
ObjectDBX, 642, 643
objects. *See also* selecting objects
  annotative, 319
  arc, 24, 158, 164–165, 177–178
  array, 193, 204–205, 439
  block. *See* block
  breaks in, 194, 207, 208
  circle, 23, 88–90, 158, 163–164
  cone, 394, 396
  copying, 120, 198–199, 711
  cube, 393, 395
  cutting, 481

cylinder, 394, 397
donut, 158, 180
draw order, 194, 211, 475
drawing primitive, 87–88, 161–164
ellipse, 158, 176–178
erasing/deleting, 197
extruded, 385–386, 399
grip-editing, 93, 213–214
groups, 192–193, 194, 325
hatch pattern. *See* hatch pattern
inserting, 475–476
joining, 195, 208
lengthening, 195, 207
line. *See* line
list of, 383
masking, 182–183, 712
material assignment to, 409
mirroring, 26, 195, 200–201, 392
modifying, 25–26, 93–96
moving, 195, 197–198
multiline. *See* multiline object
offsets, 201–203
pasting, 195, 199, 481
point. *See* point
polyline. *See* polylines
properties, 110, 120–123, 211–213, 382, 383–384
pyramid, 394, 398
ray, 159, 168–169
rectangle, 20–21, 159, 179
region, relationship to, 382
rotating, 206, 391, 399, 440
scaling, 317–318
source, 200
sphere, 397
stretching, 196, 206, 439
table. *See* table

torus, 394, 398
trimming, 196, 208–209
viewports, display in, 511–513
wedge, 394, 396
OBJECTSCALE command, 317
Oblique angle option for text, 249
offset, 195, 201–203, 399, 495
OFFSET command, 195, 201–203
OLE (object linking and embedding), 418, 475–476
On/Off layer mode, 112
OOPS command, 95, 195
OPEN command, 46, 76, 598–599
Open Drawing dialog box, 40
open drawings, searching, 483
OPENSHEETSET command, 523
OPTIONS command, 648
Options dialog box, 647–648
orbiting, 3D model, 373–378
orientation, drawing, 496, 561
origin, coordinate system, 127
Ortho mode, 21, 52, 126, 143–144, 355
orthographic views, 369
OSNAP (object snap). *See also* snap
  3D modeling, 354–355
  color customizing, 667
  DGN underlays, 473
  DWF underlays, 469

OSNAP (object snap)
(continued)
  elevation, 356
  modes, 22–24
  overview, 126, 147–151
  xlines, relationship to, 167
OSOPTIONS system
    variable, 309
Out option, ZOOM
    command, 220
Output tab, ribbon, 360
overlapping objects,
    selecting, 189
overlay type of xref, 451

P

/p command line switch,
    644
page setup
  assigning to layout,
    494, 499
  creating, 496–498
  editing, 499–500
  importing, 498–499
  introduction, 494
  layouts, relationship to,
    494, 499, 504
  options, 494–496
  showing for new layouts,
    666
Page Setup dialog box,
    495–496
Page Setup Manager,
    494–500
PAGESETUP command,
    496–499
palettes
  Action Recorder-
    supported, 721
  Advanced Render
    Settings, 48, 412
  anchoring, 48
  in AutoCAD LT, 324, 333

Block Authoring, 435, 436,
    437, 440–443
  commands, creating, 488
  customizing, 488–489, 640,
    685–686
  DBConnect Manager,
    48, 328
  DesignCenter, 48
  External References,
    48, 450
  hatch pattern, 305–306,
    307
  InfoCenter, 62
  keyboard shortcuts, 47–48
  Layer, 47
  Lights, 48
  Lights in Model, 407
  Markup Set Manager,
    48, 634
  Materials, 48, 409
  as modeless dialog boxes,
    58
  overview, 46–48
  Properties. *See* Properties
    palette
  QuickCalc, 48
  Ribbon, 47
  Sheet Set Manager, 48
  Sun Properties, 407, 408
  title bar, 42
  Tool Palettes window, 48,
    446, 486–489
  tools, creating for, 487–488
  Visual Styles, 48, 379
Pan button, 53
PAN command, 91, 215, 217,
    224–225
Panel Preview pane, CUI
    Editor, 679
panels
  accessing, 42
  Action Recorder, 719–720
  customizing, 671, 692–695

Draw, 3–4, 157, 158–160,
    164
  Edge Effects, 379–380
  Layers, 113, 119
  Lights, 404
  locking, 662–663
  Modify, 210
  Multiline Text, 252–253
  Panel Preview pane, 679
  Quick Properties, 52,
    212–213, 680, 698–700
  Solid Editing, 399
  toolbars, creating from,
    694
  Visual Styles, 379–380
panning
  3D navigation with, 375
  introduction, 91
  tools for accessing, 217
  transparency, 224–225
  in viewport, 511
  with wheel mouse, 227
  workings of, 215
Paper button, 53
paper compared to
    electronic sharing of
    files, 628–629
Paper size option, Page
    Setup, 495
paper space. *See also*
    layouts; viewports
  introduction, 49–50
  lineweight in, 116
  model space, compared
    to, 107–108, 242–244,
    500
  plotting from, 493, 496
  sheet sets in, 515
  text size in, 244
paragraph (multiline) text
  annotative scaling of, 316
  background masks,
    257–258
  columns, 256

creating, 253–256
definition, 237
editing, 258, 259
formatting, 252–253, 254–255
introduction, 239–240
lists, 255–256
overview, 252–253
text tools for, 712
parallel lines (multiline object)
  AutoCAD compared to AutoCAD LT, 342
  DLINE command, 158, 171, 325
  introduction, 86
  MLINE command, 171–173, 325
  scaling, 172–173
  tool access options, 159
parallel view, 373, 374
parameter set, definition, 437, 443
parameters
  dynamic blocks, 433–434, 435, 437, 439, 440–441, 443–446
  PGP file format, 652
partial customization files, 677, 702, 703
Partial Open feature for drawings, 598–601
PARTIALOPEN command, 598–599
password-protection of drawings, 327, 604–608, 609
PASTEBLOCK command, 481
PASTECLIP command, 195, 199
PASTEORIG command, 481
PASTESPEC command, 481–482

pasting objects, 195, 199, 481–482
PAT (hatching) file format, 67, 100
path information for xrefs, 451–452
pattern, hatch
  adding, 304–307
  annotative scaling of, 303, 308–309, 316
  associative property, 186, 303
  AutoCAD compared to AutoCAD LT, 343–344
  boundary options, 308–309
  customizing, 310, 332, 640
  editing, 195, 211, 311
  gradient fills, 159, 303, 310–311, 325, 343
  inserting into drawings, 486
  introduction, 303–304
  island detection, 308–309
  origin (base point), 308
  palette, 305–306, 307
  PAT files, 67, 100
  predefined, 309
  publishing, 563
  scale/spacing, 107, 316
  settings, 307–309
  tool access options, 159, 307
  types, 309–310
  user-defined, 309–310
PC3 (plotting) file format, 546
PDF (Portable Document Format) file format, 629, 630
PEDIT command, 195, 211
pen assignments, 560
pen tables, 552

Performance Tuner tray icon, 55
PERSPECTIVE command, 373
perspective view, 373, 374, 378
PGP (Program Parameters) file format, 652
photometric lighting, 404, 406
pickbox, 50, 187
pixels, definition, 462
/pl command line switch, 644
Places list, Save Drawing As dialog box, 75
PLINE command, 180–182. *See also* polylines
Plot area option, Page Setup, 495
PLOT command, 46, 105, 319, 555, 559, 632
Plot dialog box, 494, 556–558, 559–561
Plot/NoPlot layer mode, 113
plot notification balloon, 558
Plot Notification tray icon, 55
Plot offset option, Page Setup, 495
Plot options, Page Setup, 496
Plot scale option, Page Setup, 495
plot stamp, 560
plot style
  adding, 550–554
  color-dependent, 72, 551
  CTB file format, 67, 551
  editing, 554
  layers, 111, 551
  lineweight, 551, 560
  named, 72, 551

plot style *(continued)*
  as object property, 121
  page setup, 496
  pen assignments, 560
  STB file format, 67, 551
  template choices, 72
Plot Style Table Editor, 554
plot style table (CTB) file
    format, 67, 551
plot style table (STB) file
    format, 67, 551
Plot style table option, Page
    Setup, 496
plots/plotting. *See also*
    paper space
  annotative objects, 319
  configuring devices,
    545–550
  DWF6 ePlot device,
    632–633
  emulating paper with
    electronic files, 628–631
  introduction, 29–30, 46,
    493–494
  layouts, 105, 108, 493,
    500–506, 558–559, 560
  limits on drawing, 103
  from Model tab, 105, 493,
    496, 555–558
  named views, 229
  options, 559–561
  page setups, 494–500, 666
  to PDF format, 630
  Plot/NoPlot layer mode,
    113
  print drivers, 544, 545–547
  printing, relationship to,
    543–544
  publishing, relationship
    to, 543–544
  scaling for, 105, 495, 559
  sheets. *See* sheets/sheet
    sets

standards for, 580
styles. *See* plot style
viewports. *See* viewports
Plotter Configuration
    Editor, 549–550
PLOTTERMANAGER
    command, 546–547
plotting (PC3) file format,
    546
plug-ins, drawing
    standards, 584
point
  2-point circle, 89
  3-point arc, 165
  3-point circle, 89
  base/insertion, 198, 308,
    418, 420, 440
  breaking at, 208
  inserting, 161–162,
    165–166
  placing/formatting, 88,
    165–166
  styles, 165–166
  tool access options, 159
POINT command, 159
point/dot/xy filters,
    151–153, 354
point light type, 404–405
Point parameter, dynamic
    blocks, 439
pointer, mouse, 50, 221,
    222, 227, 375
POINTLIGHT command, 405
polar arrays, 204, 205
polar coordinate system,
    352–354
Polar parameter, dynamic
    blocks, 439
Polar Stretch action,
    dynamic blocks, 439
polar tracking, 52, 126,
    144–147
Polar Tracking mode on
    status bar, 52

polygon, 159, 179–180
POLYGON command, 159
Polygonal option, irregular
    viewport, 509–510
polylines
  3D models, 384, 393
  chamfers, 179, 194, 401
  creating, 180–182
  donut, 180
  editing, 195, 211
  exploding, 208
  fillets, 179, 194, 210, 401
  lines, compared to,
    180–181
  overview, 21
  polygon, 179–180
  rectangle, 20–21, 179
  revision clouds, 160
  spline curve, 160, 174–175,
    196, 211
  tool access options, 159
  trace, compared to, 169
polysolid, 393, 394–395
POLYSOLID command,
    393, 395
Portable Document Format
    (PDF) file format,
    629, 630
Postscript PFB fonts, 245
precision compared to
    accuracy, 125–126
predefined hatch pattern,
    309
preset view, 232, 369–370
press and drag selection
    method, 186
previewing
  camera views, 372
  CUI Editor changes,
    679, 680
  drawings, 81
  text, 249
  thumbnail images, 378

Previous object selection mode, 188

Previous option, ZOOM command, 218, 220

primitive objects, definition, 85, 157, 393. *See also* objects

PRINT command, 555

print drivers, installing, 544, 545–547

printable area, 666

Printer/Plotter option, Page Setup, 495

printing, relationship to plotting, 543–544. *See also* plots/plotting

profiles, user, 328, 641, 643, 644, 649–652

Program Parameters (PGP) file format, 652

program title bar, 41

programming. *See also* macros

  AutoCAD compared to AutoCAD LT, 328

  AutoLISP, 642, 705, 707, 715

  as customizing method, 639–640

  DIESEL, 333, 641, 660–662

  script files, 641, 643, 705–709

  startup options, 642

  VBA language, 642

PROPERTIES command, 196, 211–212

Properties palette

  annotative scaling, 316–317

  camera settings, 371

  dynamic blocks, 424, 446

  introduction, 47

  lighting options, 406–407

  location and function of, 211–212

Properties pane, CUI Editor, 679

protection, drawing

  digital signatures, 608–615

  introduction, 604

  password-protection, 604–608, 609

  proxy graphic, 334–335

PUBLISH command, 561–563, 632

Publish to Web feature, 327, 622–625

PUBLISHALLSHEETS system variable, 563

PUBLISHCOLLATE system variable, 563

PUBLISHHATCH system variable, 563

publishing. *See also* plots/plotting

  command line switch, 644

  drawings, 561–563

  introduction, 493

  plotting, relationship to, 543–544

  sheet set function in, 516

  to Web, 327, 622–625

PUBLISHTOWEB command, 622

pull-down menus, 43–44, 671, 672–673, 688–689

PURGE command, 425–426

pyramid, 394, 398

PYRAMID command, 394, 398

Q

QDIM command, 325

QNEW command, 69, 574, 575–576

QSAVE command, 76

Quick Access toolbar, 15, 43, 46, 671, 685

Quick Properties panel, 52, 212–213, 680, 698–700

Quick Setup Wizard, 70–71

Quick View Drawings button, 53, 80–81

Quick View Layouts button, 53, 501, 504, 505

QuickCalc palette, 48

quotes in command line switch arguments, 643

R

/r command line switch, 644

radians units, 98

radius dimensions, 88

raster images, 67, 449, 462–466

ray, 159, 168–169

RAY command, 159, 168–169

Re-initialization dialog box, 654

Realistic visual style, AutoCAD LT's lack of, 344

realtime pan and zoom, 91–93, 217, 218, 221–226

Recent Documents option, 78

recording macros, 328, 641, 717–725

RECTANG command, 159, 179

rectangle, 20–21, 159, 179

rectangular array, 204–205

rectangular viewport, 506, 507–509

REDO command, 96, 196

REDRAW command, 217, 234

REDRAWALL command, 217

REFEDIT command, 425, 433, 455–456

Reference Edit dialog box, 456–457

Reference Manager, 328, 476–478

REGEN/REGENALL/REGENA UTO commands, 217, 234, 436

region

  additional information on, 383

  creating, 382

  introduction, 381–382

  modifying, 382–383

  tool access options, 160

REGION command, 160, 382

relative coordinates, 131–135, 352–354

Remove object selection mode, 188

Rename & Renumber Sheet dialog box, 530–531, 540

RENAME command, 424–425

RENDER command, 411

Render Window dialog box, 411, 412

RENDERCROP command, 411

rendering in 3D

  AutoCAD compared to AutoCAD LT, 326

  backdrop, 410–411

  introduction, 403

  lighting, 403–408

  materials, 409–410

  presets, 411–412

  process of, 411–413

repeating of commands, 58, 165

RESETBLOCK command, 447

resizing (scaling) objects

  annotative, 313–320

  attributes, 316

  AutoCAD abilities, 32

  blocks, 421, 439

  dimensions, 107

  drawing settings, 104–107

  editing, 196, 511

  hatch patterns, 107, 303, 308–309, 316

  introduction, 91

  linetype, 107

  objects, 172–173, 196, 206, 317–318

  for plots, 105, 495, 559

  text, 107, 243–244, 259, 316

  viewports, 54, 105, 107, 319–320, 510–511

  zoom options, 220

resource drawings, 483–485, 537–538

resource management, CAD, 568–569

RESUME command, 707

reusable content. *See* block; external references (xrefs)

reuse of drawings, 32

REVCLOUD command, 160

revision clouds, 160

REVOLVE command, 387

Rewind tool, SteeringWheel feature, 227, 377

ribbon. *See also* tabs

  2D workspace, 15

  Action Recorder panel, 719–720

  customizing, 671, 692–696

  introduction, 3–5

  panel introduction, 42

Ribbon palette, 47

right-click (shortcut)

  menus, 38–40, 45, 59, 60–61, 690–692

Right justification option, 242

rollover tooltips, 62, 698–699

ROTATE command, 196, 206

Rotate option, faces, 399

rotating

  objects, 206, 391, 399, 440

  text, 251, 712

Rotation action, dynamic blocks, 440

Rotation parameter, dynamic blocks, 440

RSCRIPT command, 707

RTPAN command, 91–93

RTZOOM command, 91–93

ruler for multiline text box, 253

S

/s command line switch, 644

Save Drawing As dialog box, 74, 75

SAVE/SAVEAS command, 46, 66, 74

Scale action, dynamic blocks, 439

SCALE command, 91, 196, 206

scale factor, 105–107, 244

Scale option, ZOOM command, 220

scale/scaling

  annotative, 313–320

  attributes, 316

  AutoCAD abilities, 32

  blocks, 421, 439

  dimensions, 107

drawing settings, 104–107
editing, 196, 511
hatch patterns, 107, 303, 308–309, 316
introduction, 91
linetype, 107
objects, 172–173, 196, 206, 317–318
for plots, 105, 495, 559
text, 107, 243–244, 259, 316
viewports, 54, 105, 107, 319–320, 510–511
zoom options, 220
SCALELISTEDIT command, 511
SCALETEXT command, 259
scene, 3D model as (rendering)
AutoCAD compared to AutoCAD LT, 326
backdrop, 410–411
introduction, 403
lighting, 403–408
materials, 409–410
presets, 411–412
process of, 411–413
schedules, drawing, 418
scientific units, 98
SCR (script) file format, 706
SCRIPT command, 707, 708
script files, 331–332, 641, 643, 705–709
script (SCR) file format, 706
scroll bars, panning with, 225
SDI (Single Document Interface) system variable, 81
searching
drawings, 483–484, 598
files, 77–78
text, 264

SECTIONPLANE command, 388–389
security, drawing
digital signatures, 608–615
introduction, 604
password-protection, 604–608, 609
Select Block dialog box, 535–536
Select File dialog box, 77
Select Template dialog box, 69, 70
selecting objects
basic methods, 187–193
blocks, 418, 420, 535–536
copying with Clipboard, 480
defining selection modes, 93
for erasing, 95
Express Tools, 713
with grips, 93, 213–214
groups, 192–193
noun/verb mode, 93, 185, 189, 190–191, 197
options (Selection tab), 185–186
by type, 189
verb/noun selection mode, 93, 189, 190–191, 198
selection sets, 185–186
Separate solids option, solid bodies, 400
separator bars, adding, 696
/set command line switch, 644
SETBYLAYER command, 196, 213
SHADE command, 380
shade modes, 379
shaded viewport, 496, 560
Shaded viewport options, Page Setup, 496

SHADEMODE command, 380
shadows, rendering in 3D, 404, 405–406
Shape Manager, 400
shape (SHP) file format, 709
Shape (SHX) (vector font) files, 66, 245, 709
shapes. *See also* objects
box, 393, 395
converting to blocks, 711
custom, 640, 709–710
loop, 381
SHP file format, 709
SHX files, 66, 245, 709
viewport shape setting, 506–510
sharing electronic files. *See also* collaboration
DWF/DWFx files, 629–630, 631–635
emulating paper, 628–631
exporting to non-AutoCAD file formats, 617–618
FTP tool for, 619–621
introduction, 617
publishing onto Web, 619, 622–625
Web-based collaboration sites, 619, 626–628
Sheet Properties dialog box, 531–534
sheet set (DST) file format, 345, 515, 523
Sheet Set Manager, 515, 516, 517, 643
Sheet Set Manager palette, 48
Sheet Set Properties dialog box, 519–521
sheet view, 232
Sheet Views tab, 517

sheets/sheet sets
  archiving, 541
  AutoCAD LT's lack of, 345
  callout blocks, 534,
    536–537, 540–541
  command line switch, 644
  creating, 517–522
  definition, 493
  as drawing organization
    tool, 598
  DST file format, 345, 515,
    523
  eTransmit, 541
  importing drawings as
    sheets, 523–525
  introduction, 515–516
  label blocks, 534–536
  model space views,
    538–541
  new sheet, adding, 529
  opening, 523
  opening single sheet, 530
  properties, 530–534
  publishing, 541, 563
  removing, 530
  renaming, 530–531, 540
  renumbering, 530–531
  resource drawings,
    adding, 537–538
  subsets, 525–526, 528
  suppression of Sheet Set
    Manager, 643
  template settings for,
    526–528
SHEETSET command, 517
SheetSetPlaceholder field
  name, 535
Shell option, solid
  bodies, 400
Shift key
  3D navigation with, 375
  fillet/chamfer intersection
    lines, 210

Shift to Add selection
  method, 185–186
shortcut keys, customizing,
  696–697
shortcut menus, 38–40, 45,
  59, 60–61, 690–692
SHORTCUTMENU system
  variable, 690
Shortcuts pane, CUI Editor,
  680
Show Extended ToolTips
  option, Window
  Elements, 665
Show/Hide Lineweight
  mode on status bar,
  52, 117
Show Page Setup Manager
  for New Layouts
  option, Layout
  Elements, 666
Show Rollover ToolTips
  option, Window
  Elements, 665
Show Shortcut Keys in
  ToolTips option,
  Window Elements, 665
Show ToolTips option,
  Window Elements, 665
ShowMotion option, 53,
  216, 232–233, 344
SHP (shape) file format, 709
SHX (compiled shape) file
  format, 66, 245, 709
SIGWARN system variable,
  614
single-line text
  creating, 249–251
  definition, 237
  editing, 258, 259
  introduction, 239, 240
  justification options,
    241–242

sizing (scaling) objects
  annotative, 313–320
  attributes, 316
  AutoCAD abilities, 32
  blocks, 421, 439
  dimensions, 107
  drawing settings, 104–107
  editing, 196, 511
  hatch patterns, 107, 303,
    308–309, 316
  introduction, 91
  linetype, 107
  objects, 172–173, 196, 206,
    317–318
  for plots, 105, 495, 559
  text, 107, 243–244,
    259, 316
  viewports, 54, 105, 107,
    319–320, 510–511
  zoom options, 220
SKETCH command, 160,
  170–171
SKPOLY system variable,
  171
SLICE command, 402
slices of solids, 402
slideouts, introduction,
  3, 4–5
snap. *See also* object snap
  (OSNAP)
  basic settings, 16–17, 126,
    141–143
  polar, 147
Snap mode on status
  bar, 52
SOLDRAW command, 389
SOLID command, 160, 178
Solid Editing panel, 399
solid fills, 303, 309–310. *See
  also* gradient fills
SOLIDEDIT command, 399,
  401, 410

solids. *See also* 3D model
2D, 160, 178
creating primitive, 160, 178, 393–398
editing primitive, 399–402
overview, 351
polysolid, 393, 394–395
SOLPROF command, 389, 390
SOLVIEW command, 389
source objects, definition, 200
spatial indexing, 603
SPELL command, 264–265
sphere, 394, 397
SPHERE command, 394, 397
spherical coordinates, 353–354
SPLINE command, 160, 174–175
spline curve, 160, 174–175, 196, 211
spline-fit polyline, 174
SPLINEDIT command, 196, 211
SPOTLIGHT command, 405
STAMP command, 560
standard properties, sheets/sheet sets, 531
Standard style
table, 260–261
text, 245–247
standards
annotation, 569
AutoCAD compared to AutoCAD LT, 327–328, 344–345
AutoCAD tools introduction, 581
batch checking drawings, 591–595
block definition, 421
CAD management role, 568
CAD Web site, 83

collaboration issues, 567, 569
drawing setup, 123
DWS file format, 75, 77, 344–345, 581–583
file exchange practices, 569
file locations, 569, 570–571
importance in organizing reusable content, 479
introduction, 16
layer translation, 588–591
linetype, 122–123
management of, 567, 582–588
naming and storage for drawings, 569
overview, 579–581
title blocks, 569
training, 569
Standards Audit Report, 595
STANDARDS command, 583
Standards Manager, 581, 582–588
Start Center End arc, 164–165
Start from Empty Table option, 262
Start In folder, setting up, 39–40
Start menu, Windows, adding shortcuts to, 38–39
Startup dialog box, 69, 574
startup process, 37–38, 641–647, 709
Startup Suite, 642
STARTUP system variable, 69, 70, 574
static blocks, 433, 448
status bar
application, 51–56, 658, 660
customizing, 641, 657–662

DIESEL feature, 333
display options, 665
overview, 51–56
tray icons, 54–56, 454–455, 659–660
Status Bar Menu buttons, 658
STB (plot style table) file format, 67, 551
SteeringWheels feature, 53, 216, 226–228, 376–377
Streamline (Web site), 626
Stretch action, dynamic blocks, 439
STRETCH command, 196, 206
stretching objects, 196, 206, 439
STYLE command, 238
styles. *See also* plot style
definition of text, 238
dimension, 271–283, 315
multileader, 315
point, 165–166
table, 260, 261
text, 244–249, 250, 254–255, 315
Visual Styles, 48, 379–380
STYLESMANAGER command, 551
submenus, customizing, 688–689
subsets, 517–518, 525–526, 528
SUBTRACT command, 383, 401
Sun & Sky Background dialog box, 410, 411
Sun Properties palette, 407, 408
sunlight, adding to rendering, 407–408
surface model, 350–351
surveyor units, 98, 99
SWEEP command, 387

Symbols 2000 (Web site), 336
symmetrical object (mirroring), 26, 195, 200–201, 392
system-pointer device settings, 644
system printer, 544, 545–546
system variables
ATTDIA, 431
ATTREQ, 431
AUTOPUBLISH, 562
BLOCKEDITLOCK, 437
CAMERAGLYPH, 372
COPYMODE, 200
DEFAULTLIGHTINGTYPE, 404
DELOBJ, 381
DGNFRAME, 474
DGNOSNAP, 473
DIMSCALE, 320
DWFFRAME, 470
DWFOSNAP, 469
FONTALT, 245
FONTMAP, 245
HPGAPTOL, 307
INDEXCTL, 604
INSBASE, 427
LAYERVALCTL, 574
LIGHTGLYPHDISPLAY, 407
LIGHTINGUNITS, 404
LIGHTSINBLOCKS, 407
LOCKUI, 662–663
MBUTTONPAN, 226
MEASUREINIT, 101
MEASUREMENT, 100, 309, 574
MLEADERSCALE, 320
MODEMACRO, 660
MSLTSCALE, 320
MTEXTED, 259
MTEXTJIGSTRING, 254
MTEXTTOOLBAR, 253

NAVSWHEELMODE, 226
OSOPTIONS, 309
overview, 60
PUBLISHALLSHEETS, 563
PUBLISHCOLLATE, 563
PUBLISHHATCH, 563
SDI (Single Document Interface), 81
SHORTCUTMENU, 690
SIGWARN, 614
SKPOLY, 171
STARTUP, 69, 70, 574
THICKNESS, 385
XCLIPFRAME, 459
XFADECTL, 457
XREFNOTIFY, 455
ZOOMFACTOR, 222

T

/t command line switch, 644
table
block definition, 422
block in, 263
definition, 238
exporting, 263, 264
pen, 552
plot style, 67, 496, 551–554
Standard style, 260–261
startup options, 262, 264
styles, 260, 261
text, 259–264
tool access options, 160
TABLE command, 160, 261–262, 264
TABLEEXPORT command, 263, 264
tabs. *See also* Home tab; model space
Block Editor, 435–436
layout, 505, 666
Options dialog box, 505–506, 667–668

ribbon, 42, 360, 695–696
Sheet List, 517
Sheet Views, 517
Transfer tab, CUI Editor, 700–702
tag, attribute, 429
Tags property, CUI commands, 682
Tan, Tan, Radius option, circle, 89
Tan, Tan, Tan option, circle, 89
Taper option, faces, 400
TARGETPOINT command, 405
Template Description dialog box, 573
templates
command line switch, 644
creating customized, 123, 572, 640
default location of, 571
drafting environment control with, 570–571
drawing setup, 72–73
DWT file format, 72, 77, 494
importing layouts from, 503
items included in, 572
layouts, 503
menu, 676
new drawing from, 15–16, 69, 574–576
page setups in, 494
for Publish to Web features, 623
saving text styles in, 246
selecting, 69, 70
sheet sets, 515, 517–518, 526–528
standard, 72–73
as standard-compliance tools, 579

starting from scratch, compared to, 70
storage location, changing, 576–577
subsets, 528
temporary line segment, 87
text
  alignment, 238, 240–242, 249–250, 259, 712
  annotation. *See* annotation
  ATTEXT command, 432
  attributes. *See* attributes
  background mask, 257–258
  creating single-line, 249–251
  definition, 238
  DTEXT command, 27–28, 238, 240
  EATTEXT command, 432
  editing, 258–259
  exploding, 712
  Express Tools, 712
  finding, 264
  fonts, 66, 239, 244–245, 665, 666
  height setting, 243–244, 248, 250–251, 313
  introduction, 237–240
  justification, 238, 240–242, 249–250, 259
  leader, 237
  lists, 255–256
  model compared to paper space for, 242–244
  multiline text. *See* multiline text
  rotating, 251, 712
  scaling, 107, 243–244, 259, 316
  searching, 264
  single-line text. *See* single-line text

spell checker, 264–265
styles, 244–249, 250, 254–255, 315
tables, 259–264
templates, 246
text boxes overview, 27
tool access options, 159
TEXT command, 160, 238, 240
Text Formatting toolbar, 253
Text Style dialog box, 247
TEXTTOFRONT command, 475
TFRAMES command, 715
Thaw All Layers option, 120
THICKNESS system variable, 385
3-point arc, 165
3-point circles, 89
3D model. *See also* rendering in 3D
arrays, 392
AutoCAD abilities, 32
AutoCAD compared to AutoCAD LT, 323, 324, 325–326, 327, 342–343, 349, 355, 373, 375
coordinate system, 127, 351–356
creating solids, 393–398
DWF attachment limitations, 467
DWFx file format, 629
editing solids, 399–402
helixes, 384–385
introduction, 349
modifying, 390–392
navigation in, 226, 373–378
polylines, 384, 393
regions, 381–384
spatial indexing, 603
templates, 73

types, 350–351
viewport display of objects, 513
views, 369–380
VIZ 2008, 336
3D Modeling tab, Options dialog box, 668
3D models from 2D drawing, 381, 385–390
3DALIGN command, 391–392
3DARRAY command, 392
3DCORBIT command, 374
3DDISTANCE command, 376
3DFLY command, 376
3DFORBIT command, 374
3DMIRROR command, 392
3DMOVE command, 390
3DORBIT command, 374
3DPAN command, 376
3DPOLY command, 384
3DROTATE command, 391
3DSWIVEL command, 376
3DWALK command, 376
3DZOOM command, 376
Thumbnail Preview Settings dialog box, 378
tiled viewports, 506
title bar, 41–42, 193, 194
title block, 428, 502, 569
tool palettes
  Action Recorder-supported, 721
  Advanced Render Settings, 48, 412
  anchoring, 48
tool palettes *(continued)*
  in AutoCAD LT, 324, 333
  Block Authoring, 435, 436, 437, 440–443
  commands, creating, 488
  customizing, 488–489, 640, 685–686

DBConnect Manager, 48, 328
DesignCenter, 48
External References, 48, 450
hatch pattern, 305–306, 307
InfoCenter, 62
keyboard shortcuts, 47–48
Layer, 47
Lights, 48
Lights in Model, 407
Markup Set Manager, 48, 634
Materials, 48, 409
as modeless dialog boxes, 58
overview, 46–48
Properties. *See* Properties palette
QuickCalc, 48
Ribbon, 47
Sheet Set Manager, 48
Sun Properties, 407, 408
title bar, 42
Tool Palettes window, 48, 446, 486–489
tools, creating for, 487–488
Visual Styles, 48, 379
Tool Palettes window, 48, 446, 486–489
Toolbar Preview pane, CUI Editor, 680
Toolbar/Window Lock button, 54
toolbars
accessing, 42
adding commands to, 678
creating, 686–687
customizing, 662–664, 671, 680, 683–688
display settings, 193
floating, 685
large buttons for, 665

locking, 662–664
Modify, 193
opening, 81
overview, 5, 44–45
panels, creating from, 694
Quick Access, 15, 43, 46, 671, 685
ribbon panels, creating from, 694
Text Formatting, 253
Workspaces, 668–670
TOOLPALETTES command, 486–487
Tools menu, 44
tooltips, 58, 61–62, 665, 698–699
torus, 394, 398
TORUS command, 394, 398
Tour Building navigation wheel, 376
TRACE command, 160, 169–170
training, drafter, 340, 568
Transfer tab, CUI Editor, 700–702
TRANSPARENCY command, 466
transparent zoom and pan, 224
tray icons, status bar, 54–56, 454–455, 659–660
TRIM command, 196, 208–209
tripod feature for 3D views, 371
True Color system, 122
TrueType font (TTF) file format, 66, 245
Trusted Autodesk DWG tray icon, 55
TTF (TrueType font) file format, 66, 245
Turn All Layers On option, 120

2-point circle, 89
2D Drafting & Annotation workspace, 15
2D drawing
3D models, creating from, 381, 385–389
AutoCAD compared to AutoCAD LT, 325
coordinate system, 127
DWFx file format, 629
exchanging AutoCAD and AutoCAD LT, 342
new, creating, 16–19
2D solid, 160, 178

U

UCS Icon dialog box, 505, 668
UCS (user coordinate system), 128–129, 356
underlay files, 67, 466–470, 470–474
UNDO command, 46, 95, 196
unerasing option, 95
UNION command, 383, 401
units
angular, 98, 99
architectural, 98, 99, 101–102
AutoCAD compared to real-world, 98–99
block, 421
decimal, 98, 99
decimal degrees, 98, 99
defaults, 67
deg/min/sec units, 98, 102
drawing setup, 97–102
formats, 98
fractional, 98
grads, 98

imperial compared to metric, 67, 97–98, 100, 123

linear, 28–29, 98, 99, 101–102

radians, 98

real-world compared to AutoCAD, 98–99

scientific, 98

setting up, 71, 97–102

surveyor, 98, 99

templates based on, 73

unlocking

layers, 113, 120

panels, window, 662–663

toolbars, 662–664

viewports, 54, 511

Unreconciled New Layers tray icon, 55

uppercase text as default, 257

Upside down option for text, 248

Use Big Font option, 247

Use Large Buttons for Toolbars option, Window Elements, 665

user coordinate system (UCS), 128–129, 356

user-defined hatch patterns, 309–310

user interface (UI), overview, 41–56. *See also* Customize User Interface (CUI) Editor

user lights for 3D models, 404–406

user profiles, 328, 641, 643, 644, 649–652

utilities, Autodesk, 335

V

/v command line switch, 644

Validate Digital Signatures tray icon, 56

validation of 3D solids, 400

VBA programming language, 642

vector-based program, AutoCAD as, 462

verb/noun selection mode, 93, 189, 190–191, 198

Verisign (Web site), 608, 610–611

Vertical option for text, 248

VIEW command, 215, 218, 370

View Manager dialog box, 229, 232, 371, 410

View menu, 44

View Object navigation wheel, 376

View tab, ribbon, 360

ViewCube feature, 370, 377–378

viewers for AutoCAD files, 335, 338, 466, 630

Viewpoint Presets dialog box, 369, 370

Viewport Scale button, 54

viewports

advantages for plotting, 493

clipping, 513–514

defining shape, 506–510

definition, 108

display of objects in, 511–513

Express Tools, 712–713

floating, 320, 500, 506–508

freeze/thaw controls, 113, 512–513, 514

grips, 513

irregular, 506, 509–510

layers, 111, 120, 512

Layout Elements options, 666

locking/unlocking, 54, 511

model space, relationship to, 506, 511

model views, 539

modifying, 513–514

navigation button, 53

Page setup options, 496

rectangular, 506, 507–509

scaling, 54, 105, 107, 319–320, 510–511

shaded, 496, 560

solid commands, 389

tiled, 506

VPCLIP command, 513–514

Viewports dialog box, 507–509

VIEWRES command, 218

views. *See also* display settings; named views

3D modeling, 369–380

AutoCAD compared to AutoCAD LT, 326, 344

background settings, 410

categories, 232

Classic, 44

command line switch, 644

introduction, 215–219

isometric, 369

keyboard toggles, 48–49

layer associations, 231–232

views *(continued)*

layouts, 53, 232, 501, 504, 505

model, 232, 517, 537–539, 539

motion feature, 232–233

orthographic, 369

panning. *See* panning
parallel, 373, 374
perspective, 378, 373374
preset, 232, 369–370
redraw, 234
regenerate, 234
sheets/sheet sets, 232,
    516, 538–541
SteeringWheels feature,
    226–228
zooming. *See* zooming
Visibility parameter,
    dynamic blocks, 440,
    443–446
visibility states, blocks, 436,
    443–446
Visibility States dialog box,
    443–446
visual styles, 48, 378–380,
    513
Visual Styles palette,
    48, 379
Visual Styles panel, 379–380
visualization, 3D drawing,
    AutoCAD compared to
    AutoCAD LT, 326, 344
Visualize tab, ribbon, 360
VISUALSTYLES command,
    379
VIZ 2008 (Web site), 336
VPCLIP command, 513–514
VPOINT command, 371
VPORTS command, 506–509

W

/w command line switch,
    644
walkthrough of 3D model,
    413
WBLOCK command,
    426–427
WCS (world coordinate
    system), 128–129

Web
    collaboration sites on,
        619, 626–628
    Publish to Web feature,
        327, 622–625
    publishing drawings on,
        619, 622–625
Web-based book content, 8
Web sites
    American Institute of
        Architects, 82, 83, 579
    AutoCAD Block, 337
    AutoCAD Certification,
        361
    Autodesk discussion
        groups, 63
    AutoVue, 338
    Brava! Viewer, 338
    Buzzsaw, 327
    CADdepot, 337
    CADOPOLIS.COM, 337
    CADToolsOnline.com, 338
    CADViewer, 338
    Construction
        Specifications Institute,
        82, 83, 579
    DWG TrueView, 33
    IdenTrust, 608
    Impression, 336
    Microspot DWG Viewer,
        338
    National CAD
        Standards, 83
    object enablers, Autodesk,
        334
    Streamline, 626
    Symbols 2000, 336
    Verisign, 608
    VIZ 2008, 336
Web tools, Express Tools,
    714
WEBLIGHT command,
    405–406
wedge, 394, 396

WEDGE command, 394, 396
wheel mouse, navigating
    with, 221, 222, 225
Width Factor option for
    text, 248
Window Elements,
    customizing, 664–665
Window option, ZOOM
    command, 219
Window selection mode,
    188
Windows, Microsoft,
    starting AutoCAD in,
    37–38
Windows Clipboard as
    organizing tool,
    480–482
windows (dockable),
    customizing
    workspace, 662–663,
    671
Windows Registry, 649
Windows Vista, adding
    shortcuts to Start
    menu, 39
wipeout (masking objects),
    160, 182–183, 712
wireframe model, 350
WIPEOUT command, 160,
    182–183
wizards
    Add Plot Style Table,
        551–554
    Add Plotter, 546–550
    Advanced Setup, 70–71
    Create Layout, 501–503
    Create Sheet Set, 517,
        518–522
    Data Extraction, 432
    Network Deployment,
        328–329
    Quick Setup, 70–71

workspace
2D Drafting & Annotation, 15
command line switch, 644
customizing, 668–674, 680
ribbon tab visibility,
695–696
saving toolbars in, 46
switching, 43, 54
WORKSPACE command, 668
Workspace Contents pane,
CUI Editor, 680
Workspace Switching
button, 43, 54
world coordinate system
(WCS), 128–129
WPolygon selection mode,
188
Write Block dialog box,
426–427

X

x axis, 127
XCLIP command, 325,
458–459
XCLIPFRAME system
variable, 459
XATTACH command, 452
XBIND command, 461
Xbind dialog box, 461
XFADECTL system variable,
457
XLINE command, 160,
166–168

xline (construction line),
160, 166–168, 169
XOPEN command, 455, 457
XPLODE command,
196, 208
XREFNOTIFY system
variable, 455
xrefs (external references).
See also block
attaching, 452–454
AutoCAD compared to
AutoCAD LT, 325, 342
binding, 460–461
block conversion to, 712
blocks, compared to,
449–450
clipping, 458–459
definition, 67, 418, 449
DGN underlays, 470–474
draw order, 475
DWF/DWFX underlays,
466–470
editing, 455–457
increasing performance,
460–461
introduction, 449
managing across
drawings, 476–478
model views, 539
notification of, 454–455
OLE, 418, 475–476
Partial Open feature, 600
raster image references,
462–466

sheet sets, relationship
to, 518
tools for, 450–452
unloading, 460
XY parameter, dynamic
blocks, 440
xy plane, 127
xy point filter, 151–153, 354
xz point filter, 354

Y

y axis, 127

Z

z axis, 127, 165, 351–356
Zoom button, 53
ZOOM command, 91–93,
103, 215, 218, 219
ZOOMFACTOR system
variable, 222
zooming
3D navigation with, 375
basic navigation, 91–93
command options, 219
drawing limits,
relationship to, 103
tool access options, 215
viewport, 511
views management with,
215
with wheel mouse, 227
zy point filter, 354

Notes

~~JSINESS, CAREERS & PERSONAL FINANCE~~ BUSINESS, CAREERS & PERSONAL FINANCE

Fundraising
FOR DUMMIES

0-7645-9847-3

Investing
FOR DUMMIES

0-7645-2431-3

Also available:
- Business Plans Kit For Dummies
  0-7645-9794-9
- Economics For Dummies
  0-7645-5726-2
- Grant Writing For Dummies
  0-7645-8416-2
- Home Buying For Dummies
  0-7645-5331-3
- Managing For Dummies
  0-7645-1771-6
- Marketing For Dummies
  0-7645-5600-2

- Personal Finance For Dummies
  0-7645-2590-5*
- Resumes For Dummies
  0-7645-5471-9
- Selling For Dummies
  0-7645-5363-1
- Six Sigma For Dummies
  0-7645-6798-5
- Small Business Kit For Dummies
  0-7645-5984-2
- Starting an eBay Business For Dummies
  0-7645-6924-4
- Your Dream Career For Dummies
  0-7645-9795-7

~~OME & BUSINESS COMPUTER BASICS~~ HOME & BUSINESS COMPUTER BASICS

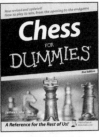

Laptops
FOR DUMMIES

0-470-05432-8

Windows Vista
FOR DUMMIES

0-471-75421-8

Also available:
- Cleaning Windows Vista For Dummies
  0-471-78293-9
- Excel 2007 For Dummies
  0-470-03737-7
- Mac OS X Tiger For Dummies
  0-7645-7675-5
- MacBook For Dummies
  0-470-04859-X
- Macs For Dummies
  0-470-04849-2
- Office 2007 For Dummies
  0-470-00923-3

- Outlook 2007 For Dummies
  0-470-03830-6
- PCs For Dummies
  0-7645-8958-X
- Salesforce.com For Dummies
  0-470-04893-X
- Upgrading & Fixing Laptops For Dummies
  0-7645-8959-8
- Word 2007 For Dummies
  0-470-03658-3
- Quicken 2007 For Dummies
  0-470-04600-7

~~OOD, HOME, GARDEN, HOBBIES, MUSIC & PETS~~ FOOD, HOME, GARDEN, HOBBIES, MUSIC & PETS

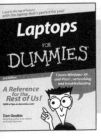

Chess
FOR DUMMIES

0-7645-8404-9

Guitar
FOR DUMMIES

0-7645-9904-6

Also available:
- Candy Making For Dummies
  0-7645-9734-5
- Card Games For Dummies
  0-7645-9910-0
- Crocheting For Dummies
  0-7645-4151-X
- Dog Training For Dummies
  0-7645-8418-9
- Healthy Carb Cookbook For Dummies
  0-7645-8476-6
- Home Maintenance For Dummies
  0-7645-5215-5

- Horses For Dummies
  0-7645-9797-3
- Jewelry Making & Beading For Dummies
  0-7645-2571-9
- Orchids For Dummies
  0-7645-6759-4
- Puppies For Dummies
  0-7645-5255-4
- Rock Guitar For Dummies
  0-7645-5356-9
- Sewing For Dummies
  0-7645-6847-7
- Singing For Dummies
  0-7645-2475-5

~~NTERNET & DIGITAL MEDIA~~ INTERNET & DIGITAL MEDIA

eBay
FOR DUMMIES

0-470-04529-9

iPod & iTunes
FOR DUMMIES

0-470-04894-8

Also available:
- Blogging For Dummies
  0-471-77084-1
- Digital Photography For Dummies
  0-7645-9802-3
- Digital Photography All-in-One Desk Reference For Dummies
  0-470-03743-1
- Digital SLR Cameras and Photography For Dummies
  0-7645-9803-1
- eBay Business All-in-One Desk Reference For Dummies
  0-7645-8438-3
- HDTV For Dummies
  0-470-09673-X

- Home Entertainment PCs For Dummies
  0-470-05523-5
- MySpace For Dummies
  0-470-09529-6
- Search Engine Optimization For Dummies
  0-471-97998-8
- Skype For Dummies
  0-470-04891-3
- The Internet For Dummies
  0-7645-8996-2
- Wiring Your Digital Home For Dummies
  0-471-91830-X

*Separate Canadian edition also available
Separate U.K. edition also available

vailable wherever books are sold. For more information or to order direct: U.S. customers visit www.dummies.com or call 1-877-762-2974.
.K. customers visit www.wileyeurope.com or call 0800 243407. Canadian customers visit www.wiley.ca or call 1-800-567-4797.

SPORTS, FITNESS, PARENTING, RELIGION & SPIRITUALITY

0-471-76871-5

0-7645-7841-3

Also available:
- Catholicism For Dummies
  0-7645-5391-7
- Exercise Balls For Dummies
  0-7645-5623-1
- Fitness For Dummies
  0-7645-7851-0
- Football For Dummies
  0-7645-3936-1
- Judaism For Dummies
  0-7645-5299-6
- Potty Training For Dummies
  0-7645-5417-4
- Buddhism For Dummies
  0-7645-5359-3

- Pregnancy For Dummies
  0-7645-4483-7 †
- Ten Minute Tone-Ups For Dummies
  0-7645-7207-5
- NASCAR For Dummies
  0-7645-7681-X
- Religion For Dummies
  0-7645-5264-3
- Soccer For Dummies
  0-7645-5229-5
- Women in the Bible For Dummies
  0-7645-8475-8

TRAVEL

0-7645-7749-2

0-7645-6945-7

Also available:
- Alaska For Dummies
  0-7645-7746-8
- Cruise Vacations For Dummies
  0-7645-6941-4
- England For Dummies
  0-7645-4276-1
- Europe For Dummies
  0-7645-7529-5
- Germany For Dummies
  0-7645-7823-5
- Hawaii For Dummies
  0-7645-7402-7

- Italy For Dummies
  0-7645-7386-1
- Las Vegas For Dummies
  0-7645-7382-9
- London For Dummies
  0-7645-4277-X
- Paris For Dummies
  0-7645-7630-5
- RV Vacations For Dummies
  0-7645-4442-X
- Walt Disney World & Orlando
  For Dummies
  0-7645-9660-8

GRAPHICS, DESIGN & WEB DEVELOPMENT

0-7645-8815-X

0-7645-9571-7

Also available:
- 3D Game Animation For Dummies
  0-7645-8789-7
- AutoCAD 2006 For Dummies
  0-7645-8925-3
- Building a Web Site For Dummies
  0-7645-7144-3
- Creating Web Pages For Dummies
  0-470-08030-2
- Creating Web Pages All-in-One Desk
  Reference For Dummies
  0-7645-4345-8
- Dreamweaver 8 For Dummies
  0-7645-9649-7

- InDesign CS2 For Dummies
  0-7645-9572-5
- Macromedia Flash 8 For Dummies
  0-7645-9691-8
- Photoshop CS2 and Digital
  Photography For Dummies
  0-7645-9580-6
- Photoshop Elements 4 For Dummies
  0-471-77483-9
- Syndicating Web Sites with RSS Feeds
  For Dummies
  0-7645-8848-6
- Yahoo! SiteBuilder For Dummies
  0-7645-9800-7

NETWORKING, SECURITY, PROGRAMMING & DATABASES

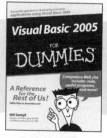

0-7645-7728-X

0-471-74940-0

Also available:
- Access 2007 For Dummies
  0-470-04612-0
- ASP.NET 2 For Dummies
  0-7645-7907-X
- C# 2005 For Dummies
  0-7645-9704-3
- Hacking For Dummies
  0-470-05235-X
- Hacking Wireless Networks
  For Dummies
  0-7645-9730-2
- Java For Dummies
  0-470-08716-1

- Microsoft SQL Server 2005 For Dummie
  0-7645-7755-7
- Networking All-in-One Desk Reference
  For Dummies
  0-7645-9939-9
- Preventing Identity Theft For Dummies
  0-7645-7336-5
- Telecom For Dummies
  0-471-77085-X
- Visual Studio 2005 All-in-One Desk
  Reference For Dummies
  0-7645-9775-2
- XML For Dummies
  0-7645-8845-1

...ALTH & SELF-HELP

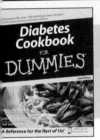

0-7645-8450-2

0-7645-4149-8

Also available:

- Bipolar Disorder For Dummies
  0-7645-8451-0
- Chemotherapy and Radiation
  For Dummies
  0-7645-7832-4
- Controlling Cholesterol For Dummies
  0-7645-5440-9
- Diabetes For Dummies
  0-7645-6820-5* †
- Divorce For Dummies
  0-7645-8417-0 †

- Fibromyalgia For Dummies
  0-7645-5441-7
- Low-Calorie Dieting For Dummies
  0-7645-9905-4
- Meditation For Dummies
  0-471-77774-9
- Osteoporosis For Dummies
  0-7645-7621-6
- Overcoming Anxiety For Dummies
  0-7645-5447-6
- Reiki For Dummies
  0-7645-9907-0
- Stress Management For Dummies
  0-7645-5144-2

...UCATION, HISTORY, REFERENCE & TEST PREPARATION

0-7645-8381-6

0-7645-9554-7

Also available:

- The ACT For Dummies
  0-7645-9652-7
- Algebra For Dummies
  0-7645-5325-9
- Algebra Workbook For Dummies
  0-7645-8467-7
- Astronomy For Dummies
  0-7645-8465-0
- Calculus For Dummies
  0-7645-2498-4
- Chemistry For Dummies
  0-7645-5430-1
- Forensics For Dummies
  0-7645-5580-4

- Freemasons For Dummies
  0-7645-9796-5
- French For Dummies
  0-7645-5193-0
- Geometry For Dummies
  0-7645-5324-0
- Organic Chemistry I For Dummies
  0-7645-6902-3
- The SAT I For Dummies
  0-7645-7193-1
- Spanish For Dummies
  0-7645-5194-9
- Statistics For Dummies
  0-7645-5423-9

Get smart @ dummies.com®

- **Find a full list of Dummies titles**
- **Look into loads of FREE on-site articles**
- **Sign up for FREE eTips e-mailed to you weekly**
- **See what other products carry the Dummies name**
- **Shop directly from the Dummies bookstore**
- **Enter to win new prizes every month!**

Separate Canadian edition also available
Separate U.K. edition also available

...ailable wherever books are sold. For more information or to order direct: U.S. customers visit www.dummies.com or call 1-877-762-2974.
...K. customers visit www.wileyeurope.com or call 0800 243407. Canadian customers visit www.wiley.ca or call 1-800-567-4797.